A Companion to Shakespeare's Works

Volume IV

Blackwell Companions to Literature and Culture

This series offers comprehensive, newly written surveys of key periods and movements and certain major authors, in English literary culture and history. Extensive volumes provide new perspectives and positions on contexts and on canonical and post-canonical texts, orientating the beginning student in new fields of study and providing the experienced undergraduate and new graduate with current and new directions, as pioneered and developed by leading scholars in the field.

A Companion to Shakespeare's Works

A COMPANION TO

SHAKESPEARE'S WORKS

VOLUME IV

THE POEMS,
PROBLEM COMEDIES,
LATE PLAYS

EDITED BY **RICHARD DUTTON**
AND JEAN E. HOWARD

Blackwell
Publishing

Editorial material and organization copyright © 2003 by
Blackwell Publishing Ltd

350 Main Street, Malden, MA 02148-5018, USA
108 Cowley Road, Oxford OX4 1JF, UK
550 Swanston Street, Carlton South, Melbourne, Victoria 3053, Australia
Kurfürstendamm 57, 10707 Berlin, Germany

First published 2003 by Blackwell Publishing Ltd

Library of Congress Cataloging-in-Publication Data has been applied for.

ISBN 0-631-22635-4 (hardback)

ISBN 1-405-10730-8 (four-volume set)

A catalogue record for this title is available from the British Library.

Set in 11 on 13pt Garamond 3
by SNP Best-set Typesetter Ltd, Hong Kong
Printed and bound in the United Kingdom
by MPG Books Ltd, Bodmin, Cornwall

For further information on
Blackwell Publishing, visit our website:
http://www.blackwellpublishing.com

Contents

Notes on Contributors

David M. Bergeron is Conger-Gabel Teaching Professor of English (2001–4) at the University of Kansas. He has published extensively on Shakespeare, Renaissance drama, and the Stuart royal family. His most recent books include *King James and Letters of Homoerotic Desire* (1999) and *Practicing Renaissance Scholarship: Plays and Pageants, Patrons and Politics* (2000).

Bruce Boehrer is a Professor of English Renaissance Literature at Florida State University and founding editor of the *Journal for Early Modern Cultural Studies*. His latest book, *Shakespeare Among the Animals*, was published in 2002.

Dympna Callaghan is William P. Tolley Professor in the Humanities at Syracuse University. Her books include *Women and Gender in Renaissance Tragedy, Shakespeare Without Women,* and the edited collection, *A Feminist Companion to Shakespeare.*

Linda Charnes is Associate Professor of English and Cultural Studies at Indiana University, Bloomington. She is the author of *Notorious Identity: Materializing the Subject in Shakespeare* (1993) and the forthcoming *Hamlet's Heirs: Essays on Inheriting Shakespeare.*

Karen Cunningham is Visiting Associate Professor of English at the University of California, Los Angeles, where she teaches Renaissance drama, Milton, and Renaissance law and literature. She is the author of *Imaginary Betrayals: Subjectivity and the Discourses of Treason in Early Modern England* (2002).

Susan Frye is Professor of English with appointment in Women's Studies at the University of Wyoming. She is the author of *Elizabeth I: The Competition for Representation* (1997) and co-editor with Karen Robertson of *Maids and Mistresses, Cousins and Queens: Women's Alliances in Early Modern England* (1999). She has published on Spenser, Shakespeare, and women writers and is currently completing a book on the material relations between early modern women's work and women's writing.

John Gillies is Professor of Literature at the University of Essex and has studied and worked in Australia and England at various times in his career. His interests include the poetics of space in Renaissance literature, theatre, and culture; also Shakespearean performance issues and performance history. He explores uses of multimedia as an analytic tool in performance studies. He is the author of *Shakespeare and the Geography of Difference* in addition to various articles and book chapters.

Suzanne Gossett is Professor of English at Loyola University, Chicago, and is currently editing *Pericles* for Arden Three and *Eastwood Ho!* for the Cambridge Jonson. Her other editions include Jonson's *Bartholomew Fair*, Middleton's *A Fair Quarrel* and, with Josephine Roberts and Janel Mueller, Lady Mary Wroth's *Urania, Book Two*. She has written extensively about early modern drama, most recently in the chapter on "Dramatic Achievements" in *The Cambridge Companion to English Literature 1500–1600*, edited by Arthur F. Kinney.

Diana E. Henderson is Associate Professor of Literature at MIT. She is the author of *Passion Made Public: Elizabethan Lyric, Gender, and Performance* (1995) and numerous articles including essays on early modern drama, poetry, and domestic culture, Shakespeare on film, James Joyce, and Virginia Woolf. Recent work includes "Shakespeare: The Theme Park" in *Shakespeare After Mass Media*, edited by Richard Burt (2002), "Love Poetry" in Blackwell's *A Companion to English Renaissance Literature and Culture*, edited by Michael Hattaway (2002), "The Disappearing Queen: Looking for Isabel in *Henry V*" in *Shakespeare and his Contemporaries in Performance*, edited by Edward Esche (2000) and "King and No King: 'The Exequy' as an Antebellum Poem" in *The Wit to Know: Essays on English Renaissance Literature for Edward Tayler*, edited by Eugene D. Hill and William Kerrigan (2000). Her current book manuscript is entitled *Uneasy Collaborations: Transforming Shakespeare across Time and Media*.

Theodora A. Jankowski is the author of *Women in Power in the Early Modern Drama* (1992) and *Pure Resistance: Queer Virginity in the Early Modern English Drama* (2000). She has written numerous articles on Shakespeare, John Lyly, Thomas Heywood, John Webster, Margaret Cavendish, and Andrew Marvell. She is currently working on a project which argues for the use of "class" as a legitimate modality of analysis within early modern English literary texts and also explores the development, in Thomas Heywood's plays, of a "middle-class" identity that is clearly set in contrast to gentry identity.

John Jowett is Reader in Shakespeare Studies at the Shakespeare Institute, University of Birmingham. He edited plays for the *Oxford Shakespeare Complete Works* (1986), and is currently an Associate General Editor of the forthcoming Oxford edition of *Thomas Middleton's Collected Works*. Publications include *Shakespeare Reshaped 1606–1623* (1993) with Gary Taylor, and the Oxford edition of *Richard III* (2000).

Coppélia Kahn is Professor of English at Brown University, and is the author of *Man's Estate: Masculine Identity in Shakespeare* (1981) and *Roman Shakespeare: Warriors, Wounds, and Women* (1997). She has also written articles on Shakespeare, early modern drama, and gender theory. Her current work deals with the racialized construction of Shakespeare in the early twentieth century.

Russ McDonald teaches at the University of North Carolina at Greensboro. He is the author of *The Bedford Companion to Shakespeare*, has edited four plays in the *New Pelican Shakespeare* series, is at work on a critical study of Shakespeare's late style, and is preparing a collection for Blackwell called *Shakespeare Criticism, 1945–2000*.

Barbara A. Mowat is the Director of Academic Programs at the Folger Shakespeare Library, Senior Editor of the *Shakespeare Quarterly*, and Chair of the Folger Institute. She is co-editor, with Paul Werstine, of the *New Folger Library Shakespeare* and the author of *The Dramaturgy of Shakespeare's Romances* and of essays on Shakespeare's plays and on the editing of his plays.

Marion O'Connor teaches at the University of Kent at Canterbury. She has published widely on dramatic revivals and theatrical reconstructions.

Richard Rambuss is Professor of English at Emory University. He is the author of *Spenser's Secret Career* and *Closet Devotions*. His numerous essays in journals and edited volumes range from Renaissance literature to various topics in cultural studies and gender studies.

Julie Sanders is Reader in English at Keele University. She is the author of *Ben Jonson's Theatrical Republics* (1998) and *Novel Shakespeare: Twentieth-Century Women Writers and Appropriation* (2002). She is currently editing *The New Inn* for *The Cambridge Edition of the Works of Ben Jonson*.

Bruce R. Smith is Professor of English at Georgetown University. He is the author of *Homosexual Desire in Shakespeare's England: A Cultural Poetics* (1991), *The Acoustic World of Early Modern England* (1999), and *Shakespeare and Masculinity* (2000).

Barbara Howard Traister is Professor of English at Lehigh University. She is the author of *The Notorious Astrological Physician of London: Works and Days of Simon Forman* and *Heavenly Necromancers: The Magician in English Renaissance Drama*.

Valerie Traub is Professor of English and Women's Studies at the University of Michigan. She is the author of *Desire and Anxiety: Circulation of Sexuality in Shakespearean Drama* and *The Renaissance of Lesbianism in Early Modern England*.

Daniel Vitkus is an Assistant Professor in the Department of English at Florida State University. He specializes in Shakespeare, Renaissance drama, and the culture of early modern England and is especially interested in cross-cultural encounters. He has edited *Three Turk Plays from Early Modern England* (2000) and *Piracy, Slavery and Redemption: Barbary Captivity Narratives from Early Modern England* (2001) and has recently completed *Turning Turk: English Theater and the Multicultural Mediterranean, 1570–1630*.

Valerie Wayne is Professor of English at the University of Hawaii. She has edited *The Matter of Difference: Materialist Feminist Criticism of Shakespeare* (1991), Edmund Tilney's *The Flower of Friendship: A Renaissance Dialogue Contesting Marriage* (1992), and Thomas Middleton's *A Trick to Catch the Old One* in *The Collected Works of Thomas Middleton* (forthcoming), for which she also served as an Associate General Editor. She is preparing an edition of *Cymbeline* for the Arden Shakespeare, Third Series.

Paul Yachnin is Tomlinson Professor of Shakespeare studies at McGill University. His first book is *Stage-Wrights: Shakespeare, Jonson, Middleton, and the Making of Theatrical Value* (1997); his second, co-authored with Anthony Dawson, is *The Culture of Playgoing in Shakespeare England: A Collaborative Debate* (2001). He is an editor of the forthcoming Oxford edition of *The Works of Thomas Middleton*, and editor of *Richard II*, also for Oxford. His book-in-progress is *Shakespeare and the Dimension of Literature*, which will argue that literature's political consequentiality is an effect of the long term rather than the short term.

Introduction

The four *Companions to Shakespeare's Works* (*Tragedies*; *Histories*; *Comedies*; *Poems, Problem Comedies, Late Plays*) were compiled as a single entity designed to offer a uniquely comprehensive snapshot of current Shakespeare criticism. Complementing David Scott Kastan's *Companion to Shakespeare* (1999), which focused on Shakespeare as an author in his historical context, these volumes by contrast focus on Shakespeare's works, both the plays and major poems, and aim to showcase some of the most interesting critical research currently being conducted in Shakespeare studies.

To that end the editors commissioned scholars from many quarters of the world – Australia, Canada, France, New Zealand, the United Kingdom, and the United States – to write new essays that, collectively, address virtually the whole of Shakespeare's dramatic and poetic canon. The decision to organize the volumes along generic lines (rather than, say, thematically or chronologically) was made for a mixture of intellectual and pragmatic reasons. It is still quite common, for example, to teach or to write about Shakespeare's works as tragedies, histories, comedies, late plays, sonnets, or narrative poems. And there is much evidence to suggest that a similar language of poetic and dramatic "kinds" or genres was widely current in Elizabethan and Jacobean England. George Puttenham and Philip Sidney – to mention just two sixteenth-century English writers interested in poetics – both assume the importance of genre as a way of understanding differences among texts; and the division of Shakespeare's plays in the First Folio of 1623 into comedies, histories, and tragedies offers some warrant for thinking that these generic rubrics would have had meaning for Shakespeare's readers and certainly for those members of his acting company who helped to assemble the volume. Of course, exactly *what* those rubrics meant in Shakespeare's day is partly what requires critical investigation. For example, we do not currently think of *Cymbeline* as a tragedy, though it is listed as such in the First Folio, nor do we find the First Folio employing terms such as "problem plays," "romances," and "tragicomedies" which subsequent critics have used to designate groups of plays. Consequently, a number of essays in these volumes self-consciously examine the meanings and lineages of the terms used to separate one genre from another and to compare the way Shakespeare and his contemporaries reworked the generic templates that were their common heritage and mutually constituted creation.

Pragmatically, we as editors also needed a way to divide the material we saw as necessary for a Companion to Shakespeare's Works that aimed to provide an overview of the exciting scholarly work being done in Shakespeare studies at the beginning of the twenty-first century. Conveniently, certain categories of his works are equally substantial in terms of volume. Shakespeare wrote about as many tragedies as histories, and again about as many "festive" or "romantic" comedies, so it was possible to assign each of these groupings a volume of its own. This left a decidedly less unified fourth volume to handle not only the non-dramatic verse, but also those much-contested categories of "problem comedies" and "late plays." In the First Folio, a number of plays included in this volume were listed among the comedies: namely, *The Tempest*, *Measure for Measure*, *All's Well That Ends Well*, and *The Winter's Tale*. *Troilus and Cressida* was not listed in the prefatory catalog, though it appears between the histories and tragedies in the actual volume and is described (contrary to the earlier quarto) as a tragedy. *Cymbeline* is listed as a tragedy, *Henry VIII* appears as the last of the history plays. *Two Noble Kinsmen* and *Pericles* do not appear at all. This volume obviously offers less generic unity than the other three, but it provides special opportunities to think again about the utility and theoretical coherence of the terms by which both Shakespeare's contemporaries and generations of subsequent critics have attempted to understand the conventionalized means through which his texts can meaningfully be distinguished and grouped.

When it came to the design of each volume, the editors assigned an essay on each play (or on the narrative poems and sonnets) and about the same number of somewhat longer essays designed to take up larger critical problems relevant to the genre or to a particular grouping of plays. For example, we commissioned essays on the plays in performance (both on stage and in films), on the imagined geography of different kinds of plays, on Shakespeare's relationship to his contemporaries working in a particular genre, and on categorizations such as tragedy, history, or tragicomedy. We also invited essays on specific topics of current interest such as the influence of Ovid on Shakespeare's early narrative poems, Shakespeare's practice as a collaborative writer, his representations of popular rebellion, the homoerotic dimensions of his comedies, or the effects of censorship on his work. As a result, while there will be a free-standing essay on *Macbeth* in the tragedy volume, one will also find in the same volume a discussion of some aspect of the play in Richard McCoy's essay on "Shakespearean Tragedy and Religious Identity," in Katherine Rowe's "Minds in Company: Shakespearean Tragic Emotions," in Graham Holderness's "Text and Tragedy," and in other pieces as well. For those who engage fully with the richness and variety of the essays available within each volume, we hope that the whole will consequently amount to much more than the sum of its parts.

Within this structure we invited our contributors – specifically chosen to reflect a generational mix of established and younger critics – to write as scholars addressing fellow scholars. That is, we sought interventions in current critical debates and examples of people's ongoing research rather than overviews of or introductions to a topic. We invited contributors to write for their peers and graduate students, rather than tailoring essays primarily to undergraduates. Beyond that, we invited a diversity of approaches; our aim was to showcase the best of current work rather than to advocate for any particular critical or theoretical perspective. If these volumes are in any sense a representative trawl of contemporary critical practice, they suggest that it would be premature to assume we have reached a post-theoretical era. Many lines of theoretical practice converge in these essays: historicist, certainly, but also Derridean, Marxist, performance-oriented, feminist, queer, and textual/editorial. Race, class, gender, bodies, and emotions, now carefully historicized, have not lost their power as organizing rubrics for original critical investigations; attention to religion, especially the Catholic contexts for Shakespeare's inventions, has perhaps never been more pronounced; political theory, including investigations of republicanism, continues to yield impressive insights into the plays. At the same time, there is a marked turn to new forms of empiricist inquiry, including, in particular, attention to early readers' responses to Shakespeare's texts and a newly vigorous interest in how Shakespeare's plays relate to the work of his fellow dramatists. Each essay opens to a larger world of scholarship on the questions addressed, and through the list of references and further reading included at the end of each chapter, the contributors invite readers to pursue their own inquiries on these topics. We believe that the quite remarkable range of essays included in these volumes will be valuable to anyone involved in teaching, writing, and thinking about Shakespeare at the beginning of the new century.

1

Shakespeare's Sonnets and the History of Sexuality: A Reception History

Bruce R. Smith

Most readers of Shakespeare's sonnets today first encounter the poems in the form of a paperback book. Even a moderately well stocked bookstore is likely to offer a choice. Some of these editions are staid academic affairs. Others, however, package the sonnets as ageless testimonials to the power of love. A particularly striking example is *Shakespeare in Love: The Love Poetry of William Shakespeare*, published by Hyperion Press in 1998. The title says it all. The book was published as a tie-in to Marc Norman and Tom Stoppard's film of the same name, also released in 1998. There on the cover is Joseph Fiennes passionately kissing Gwyneth Paltrow. Other photographs from the film illuminate scenes and speeches from selected plays, along with the texts of sixteen of the 154 sonnets first published as Shakespeare's in 1609. These sixteen sonnets, presented to the unwary buyer as *"the* love poems of William Shakespeare," have been carefully chosen and cunningly ordered. The first two selections, sonnets 104 ("To me, fair friend, you never can be old") and 106 ("When in the chronicles of wasted time / I see descriptions of fairest wights"), give to the whole affair an antique patina. Next comes that poem of ten thousand weddings, sonnet 116 ("Let me not to the marriage of true minds / Admit impediments"). Two sonnets explicitly referring to a woman, 130 ("My mistress' eyes are nothing like the sun") and 138 ("When my love swears that she is made of truth, / I do believe her"), then establish a thoroughly hetero-sexual, if not altogether conventional, context for the eleven sonnets that follow (18, 23, 24, 29, 40, 46, 49, 57, 71, 86, 98), even though all eleven of these poems in the 1609 Quarto form part of a sequence that seems to be addressed to a fair young man. All told, the paperback anthology of *Shakespeare in Love* participates in the same het-erosexualization of the historical William Shakespeare that Norman and Stoppard's film contrives (Keevak 2001: 115–23).

Contrast that with the earliest recorded reference to Shakespeare's sonnets. Francis Meres included in his book of commonplaces, *Palladis Tamia, Wit's Treasury* (1598), a catalog of England's greatest writers, matching each of them with a famous ancient writer. "The soul of Ovid," Meres declares, "lives in mellifluous and honey-tongued

Shakespeare, witness his *Venus and Adonis*, his *Lucrece*, and his sugared sonnets among his private friends" (Meres 1938: fols. 280v–281).[1] It was a high compliment. For Renaissance writers and readers, Ovid was the greatest love poet of all time: witness his how-to manual (*Ars Amatoria*), his love lyrics (*Amores*), and his encyclopedia of violent transformations wrought by love (*Metamorphoses*). The love Ovid wrote about was not, however, the sort that led to the marriage of true minds. Shakespeare's narrative poems *Venus and Adonis* and *The Rape of Lucrece* share with Ovid's *Metamorphoses* a fascination with the violence of desire. Venus's predatory lust for Adonis ends in the young man's being gored by a wild boar. Tarquin's brutal violation of the chastity of his friend's wife ends in her sheathing a knife in her breast. Of the 154 sonnets included in *Shake-speare's Sonnets Never Before Imprinted* (1609), fully half express disillusionment or cynicism. The first editions of both of Shakespeare's narrative poems bear dedications to Henry Wriothesley, Earl of Southampton. The "private friends" mentioned by Meres as the first readers of Shakespeare's sonnets may have included the other young men who counted Southampton as friend and patron. The nature of the books dedicated to Southampton, as well as the testimony of at least one eyewitness, suggest that the earl was, in Katherine Duncan-Jones's words, "viewed as receptive to same-sex amours" (Duncan-Jones 2001: 79). With this group of readers Joseph Fiennes and Gwyneth Paltrow sort very oddly indeed. The distance from Southampton House on The Strand in the 1590s to *Shakespeare in Love* at the local cineplex in the 1990s points up the need for a reception history of Shakespeare's sonnets.

Meres's allusion to Ovid likewise suggests the need for a history of sexuality. In describing the various configurations of erotic desire in Ovid's poems we are apt to say that the poems imply a certain sexuality, or perhaps a certain range of sexualities. Sexual acts between man and boy, sexual acts between woman and woman, sexual acts between woman and beast, sexual acts between father and daughter all find places in Ovid's *Metamorphoses*. With what authority, however, can we speak of "sexuality" in connection with Ovid's poems? Or Shakespeare's? "Sexuality," after all, is a relatively recent word. It was coined about 1800 as a strictly biological term, as a name for reproductive activity that involves male and female apparatus. In fact, the earliest recorded application of the word in English refers specifically to the reproductive processes of plants (*OED* "sexuality" 1). It was not until the later nineteenth century that the word came to mean manifestations of a sexual "instinct" and not until the early twentieth century, with the publication of Sigmund Freud's works, that the subjective experience of sexual desire was added to the ensemble of meanings (Smith 2000b: 318–19). (Curiously, both of these later meanings are absent from the *OED*, even in its revised 1989 edition.) "Sexuality" and "sexual" are not in Shakespeare's vocabulary. The word "sex" occurs in Shakespeare's plays twenty-one times but only in the anatomical sense of female as distinguished from male. "You have simply misused our sex in your love prate," Celia chides Rosalind after she has said unflattering things about women to Orlando (*As You Like It* 4.1.185 in Shakespeare 1988).[2]

To describe stirrings of feeling in the genitals the word that Shakespeare and his readers would have used instead was "passion." Sonnet 20, for example, addresses the speaker's beloved as "the master mistress of my passion" (20.2). The word "passion" in this context carries a quite specific physiological meaning. According to the ancient Greek physician Galen and his early modern disciples, light rays communicating the shape and colors of another person's body enter the crystaline sphere of the eyes, where the sensation is converted into an aerated fluid called *spiritus*. *Spiritus* conveys the sensation to the brain, where imagination receives the sensation and, via *spiritus*, sends it to the heart. The heart then determines whether to pursue the object being presented or to eschew it (Wright 1988: 123). Whichever the choice, the body's four basic fluids undergo a rapid change. If the heart decides to pursue the object, quantities of choler, phlegm, and black bile are converted into blood. The person doing the seeing experiences this rush of blood as passion. What a person told himself or herself was happening when a good-looking person excited feelings of desire was thus different in the 1590s from how the same experience would be explained today. What causes a person to feel desire for genital contact with another body? A sudden flux of blood, or release of the infantile id? The very question proves the validity of Michel Foucault's claim that sexuality is not a natural given. Sexuality has a history: "It is the name that can be given to a historical construct: not a furtive reality that is difficult to grasp, but a great surface network in which the stimulation of bodies, the intensification of pleasures, the incitement to discourse, the formation of special knowledges, the strengthening of controls and resistances, are linked to one another, in accordance with a few major strategies of knowledge and power" (Foucault 1980: 105–6).

In the course of his multi-volume *History of Sexuality*, left unfinished at his death, Foucault suggests several points when major paradigm shifts occurred, but for the purposes of Shakespeare's sonnets the crucial change came about in the eighteenth century. It was during the Enlightenment that sexuality was isolated as an object of rational inquiry. What had been an ethical concern in Shakespeare's time ("Two loves I have, of comfort and despair, / Which like two spirits do suggest me still," declares sonnet 144) became in Diderot's time a medical concept (Foucault 1980: 23–4). In the course of the nineteenth century the medical concept became a psychological concept. It is Freud who is responsible for the modern conviction that sexuality is a core component of self-identity. We have, then, two histories to consider in these pages: the history of how Shakespeare's sonnets have been read and interpreted and the history of how men and women have experienced and articulated feelings of bodily desire. We can trace these interrelated histories in four broad periods, each defined by a major event in the publishing history of Shakespeare's sonnets: 1590–1639, 1640–1779, 1780–1888, and 1889 to the present.

The Man of Two Loves: 1590–1639

Each word in Meres's reference to Shakespeare's "sugared sonnets among his private friends" is worthy of scrutiny. Of the six words, "sugared" may be the oddest. In the days before coffee and tea had reached England, what was most likely to be "sugared" was wine. Biron in *Love's Labor's Lost* mentions three varieties, "metheglin, wort, and malmsey," in one of his verbal games with the Princess (5.2.233). In *1 Henry IV* Poins adds a fourth when he hails Falstaff as "Sir John Sack and Sugar" (1.2.112–13). But the adjective is still puzzling. By the 1590s "sonnets" were a well-established verse form, perfectly devised for expressing both sides of being in love, the pleasures and the pains, thanks to the *volta* or "turn" that typically divides the fourteen lines into two parts. Shakespeare's sonnets, taken as a whole, are rather longer on the pains than the pleasures. Metheglin, wort, malmsey, and sack might be appropriate ways of describing Michael Drayton's sonnets or Edmund Spenser's or Sir Philip Sidney's but hardly the piquant, often bitter poems that make up most of the 1609 Quarto of *Shake-speare's Sonnets*. Combined with the reference to "mellifluous [literally, "honey-flowing"] and honey-tongued Shakespeare," Meres's taste metaphor may have less to do with the poems' content than with the feel of Shakespeare's words in the mouth. In his own time Shakespeare was known, not as a creator of great characters, but as a writer of great lines, and lots of them.

"Sugared" may also refer to the way the sonnets were circulated, "among his private friends." In 1598, when Meres was writing, Shakespeare's collected sonnets were eleven years away from publication in print. Before then, they seem to have been passed around in manuscript, probably in single copies or in small groups rather than as a whole 154-poem sequence. The word "among" suggests the way manuscript circulation in the sixteenth and early seventeenth centuries served to establish and maintain communities of readers who shared a certain place of residence, institutional affiliation, profession, religion, or political purpose (Love 1993; Marotti 1995). The word "his" confirms Shakespeare's already recognized status as an author unmistakable for anyone else; the words "private" and "friends," the close-knit, even secretive character of the readers who passed his sonnets from one to another. This sharing of poems, Meres implies, was like sharing a cup of sweetened wine, perhaps like kissing on the lips. Ben Jonson catches the scenario in a famous lyric: "Drink to me only with thine eyes, / And I will pledge with mine; / Or leave a kiss but in the cup, / And I'll not look for wine" (Jonson 1985: 293). Reading Shakespeare's sonnets in manuscript, Meres seems to imply, was in itself an act of passion.

Be that as it may, reading Shakespeare's sonnets in manuscript was an act of identity-formation, both for individuals and for the social group to which they belonged. To judge from surviving manuscripts, erotic desire figured prominently in that process of identity-formation. No manuscripts of the sonnets from Shakespeare's own time have survived, but a single sheet of paper, datable to 1625–40 and bound up a century or so later in Bodleian Library MS Rawlinson Poetic 152, gives us some idea of how Shakespeare's sonnets may have circulated as individual poems in the 1590s.[3] On the six-by-six-inch sheet, five poems – all of them about the pains and the pleasures of love – have been written out in a neat italic hand. Vertical and horizontal creases in the paper suggest how it might once have been folded for passing from hand to hand. In the sequence of poems two stanzas from John Dowland's song "Rest awhile, you

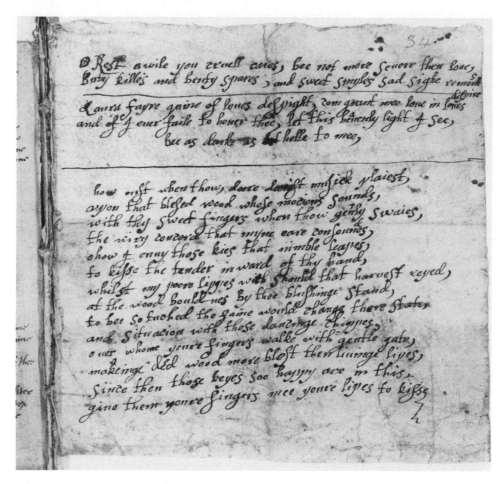

Sonnet 2 in Manuscript Circulation, Bodleian MS Rawlinson Poetic 152, fol. 345 (1625–40)

cruel cares" precede a version of the Shakespeare sonnet that figures as number 128 in the 1609 Quarto ("How oft, when thou my music music play'st"), which is in turn followed by two more love poems, "This is love and worth commanding, / Still beginning, never ending" and "I bend my wits and beat my brain / To keep my grief from outward show" (MS Rawlinson Poetic 152, fols. 34–34v). Neither Dowland nor Shakespeare is credited with the first two poems, even though the source in each case was almost certainly a printed book that prominently displayed the author's name on the title page: *Songs or Ayres . . . Composed by John Dowland* (1597) and *Shake-speare's Sonnets* (1609). Instead, the writer has appropriated the poems: he has given them his own voice, imbued them with his own passion. (It is not impossible, of course, that the sheet was written out by a woman, especially considering that italic hand was commonly taught to women.) Shakespeare's sonnet takes its place in a veritable litany of ever mounting desire. The first Dowland stanza asks for smiles; the second wants more: "Come grant me love in love's despair." Shakespeare's sonnet continues the progression toward physical closeness: the speaker uses a phallic pun ("saucy jacks") to fantasize about kissing first "the tender inward" of the lady's hands and then her lips. The third poem carries the erotic fantasy even further: "twining arms, exchanging kisses, / Each partaking other's blisses, / Laughing, weeping, still together / Bliss in one is mirth in either." If the third poem represents consummation, the final poem finds no release from the writer's desires: "I force my will, my senses I constrain / To imprison in my heart my secret woe, / But musing thoughts, deep sighs, or tears that flow / Discover what my heart hides all in vain." The transcription of sonnet 2 demonstrates graphically how Shakespeare's sonnets, for the poems' earliest readers, were not part of a sequence that came equipped with its own narrative implications. Copied out by hand, each poem became the writer's poem and the reader's poem; the passions of the poem became the writer's passion and the reader's passion.

That became even more true when certain sonnets were copied, along with diverse other poems, into blank books like the "tables" mentioned in sonnet 122 ("Thy gift, thy tables, are within my brain / Full charactered with lasting memory"). Aside from the single sheet in MS Rawlinson Poetic 152, all nineteen other survivals of Shakespeare's sonnets in early seventeenth-century manuscripts occur in this form. Many of these books belonged to single individuals, even if the poems came from a common repertory; others show marks of joint compilation. The earliest is a miscellany of poems put together by George Morley (1597–1684) while he was a student at Christ Church, Oxford, between 1615 and 1621, just a few years after Shakespeare's death in 1616. Morley went on to become Bishop of Winchester, and his manuscript resides today in the library of Westminster Abbey. The poem that Morley copied is a version of the sonnet that appears as number 2 in the 1609 Quarto, "When forty winters shall besiege thy brow." No fewer than 31 variations in Morley's version from the 116 words in the Quarto text suggest to Gary Taylor that Morley may have been copying from a manuscript of an earlier version of the poem than the 1609 Quarto presents, especially since the variations betray parallels with scripts that Shakespeare was writing in the 1590s (Taylor 1985). Morley does not provide an attribution. Like the writer of the single sheet in MS Rawlinson Poetic 152, he seems to be less interested in who originally wrote the poem than in his own uses for it.

What Morley has done is to imagine the sonnet as a seduction device very much of a piece with the other poems he has copied: he entitles it "To one that would die a maid." Now, "maid" in early modern English could refer to a virgin of either sex, male as well as female, but the other poems in Morley's collection suggest that it was a female recipient he had in mind. Morley's version of sonnet 2, Taylor has demonstrated, is likely the exemplar for four other surviving manuscript copies of sonnet 2, all of which repeat the title "To one that would die a maid" (Taylor 1985: 217). One other manuscript, from the 1630s, heads the poem "A lover to his mistress" (Beal 1980: 452–4). The title suggests that the copyists thought of sonnet 2 more as an ingenious argument for getting someone into bed than as a persuasion to marry and beget children. The "you" of the poem is assumed to be a woman, not the fair young

man implied by the first nineteen sonnets in the 1609 Quarto. Among the poems collected in Morley's manuscript is Donne's elegy "On his mistress going to bed" (Westminster Abbey MS 41, fols. l4v–15). The tone of the entire collection can be gathered
from the poem that immediately precedes Shakespeare's sonnet, an epigram on an old
woman who has worn her teeth away with talking too much, and the poem that
follows it, a memorial tribute to a fart inadvertently let out by a speaker in parliament (fols. 49–49v).

Another group of manuscript copies of sonnet 2 comes closer to the context created
in the 1609 Quarto. In four of the surviving table-books the poem bears the title "*Spes
Altera*," "Another Hope," which implies that the collectors took the sonnet's third
quatrain quite seriously: "O how much better were thy beauty's use / If thou couldst
say, 'This pretty child of mine / Saves my account and makes my old excuse,' / Making
his beauty by succession thine" (2.9–12 as transcribed in Taylor 1985: 212). The title
"*Spes Altera*," as Taylor points out, comes from the last book of Virgil's *Aeneid*, where
Aeneas's son Ascanius is praised as "*magnae spes altera Romae*" (12.168), "great Rome's
other hope," just before the decisive battle in which Aeneas defeats Turnus, wins the
hand of Lavinia, and secures the lands that become the site of Rome. In political terms
this scenario resembles the context provided for sonnet 2 in the 1609 Quarto, where
it appears second in a sequence of poems advising a noble young man to marry and
beget heirs. In sexual terms the emphasis falls, not on the genital pleasure of a single
night, but on a vision of fecundity that spans time and space. In this respect, "*Spes
Altera*" is not unlike the moment of sexual consummation that Edmund Spenser imagines for himself and his bride in the *Epithalamion* he wrote for his own wedding day.
First Spenser invokes Juno, goddess of marriage, then

> glad Genius, in whose gentle hand
> The bridal bower and genial [i.e., generative] bed remain
> Without blemish or stain,
> And the sweet pleasures of their loves' delight
> With secret aid does succor and supply
> Till they bring forth the fruitful progeny.
> (lines 398–403 in Spenser 1989: 678)

Similar images color the marriage-night blessing that Puck pronounces at the end of
A Midsummer Night's Dream. The curtains and hangings on early modern bedsteads,
richly embroidered with plants and animals, suggest that Spenser's and Shakespeare's
contemporaries, some of them at any rate, liked to imagine themselves in just such
settings of procreative plenitude when they had sex (Smith 1996: 95–121).

Yet another sexual scenario is set in place by the first book in which any of
Shakespeare's sonnets appeared in print, *The Passionate Pilgrim*, published by William
Jaggard in either 1598 or 1599. Only fragments of that first edition survive; the title
page is not among them. A second edition followed in 1599 and a third in 1612,
both proclaiming the entire book to be "*by W. Shakespeare*." Despite that claim,
only five of the twenty verses in the first and second editions can be attributed to

Shakespeare on the basis of other evidence: the two poems that lead off the collection, "When my love swears she is made of truth, / I do believe her" (the poem that became sonnet 138 in the 1609 Quarto) and "Two loves I have, of comfort and despair" (144 in the 1609 Quarto), versions of two sonnets that are incorporated into the dialogue of *Love's Labour's Lost* ("Did not the heavenly rhetoric of thine eye / . . . / Persuade my heart to this false perjury?" [4.3.57–70] and "If love make me forsworn, how shall I swear to love?" [4.2.106–19]), and a song that likewise figures in that play ("On a day – alack the day – / Love whose month is ever May / Spied a blossom passing fair / Playing in the wanton air" [4.3.99–118]). The other fifteen selections include, without any attributions, Christopher Marlowe's lyric "[Come] live with me and be my love," followed by Sir Walter Raleigh's reply, as well as poems by Richard Barnfield and Bartholomew Griffin. All in all, *The Passionate Pilgrim* reads like a sheaf of leaves taken from a manuscript table-book.

More than Shakespeare's sonnets, it is Marlowe's poem, printed here for the first time, that establishes the tone of the whole affair: "Live with me and be my love, / And we will all the pleasures prove / That hills and valleys, dales and fields, / And all the craggy mountains yield" (Shakespeare 1939: sig. D5). The implicit setting for all twenty poems is the pastoral dream world that Shakespeare and his contemporaries knew as a *locus amoenus* (literally, a "delightful place"), a landscape of flowers and fields where the season is always May and the only occupations are being in love and writing poems about being in love. In this context, "When my love swears she is made of truth" is drained of all the acerbic cynicism it has in the 1609 Quarto. In the final couplet of *The Passionate Pilgrim* version the speaker simply abandons himself to voluptuous pleasure: "Therefore I'll lie with love, and love with me, / Since that our faults in love thus smothered be" (sig. A3). Compare that with the wincing pun on "lie" in the 1609 version: "Therefore I lie with her, and she with me, / And in our faults by lies we flattered be" (138.13–14 in Shakespeare 1977).[4] If there is a story line to *The Passionate Pilgrim* it is provided by four sonnets, dispersed through the first half of the collection, that recount Venus' attempted seduction of Adonis. The tremendous popularity of Shakespeare's narrative poem on the same subject, first published five years earlier and already reprinted four times, made it plausible for readers in 1598 to imagine that he had written these four sonnets, too. A smirking sensuality pervades the four Venus and Adonis sonnets: to warn Adonis of the thigh-wounds he might receive from hunting the boar, "She showed hers, he saw more wounds than one" (Shakespeare 1939: sig. B3). Amid the bowers of bliss erected in *The Passionate Pilgrim* the sonnet "Two loves I have, of comfort and despair" becomes no more than a conventional lament about unsatisfied desire, or perhaps a boast that the sonneteer enjoys not one love but two.

By 1609, when Thomas Thorpe published *Shake-speare's Sonnets Never Before Imprinted*, quite a few of the poems had, therefore, a sexual history already – and a remarkably varied one, at that. The addition of a substantial number of other sonnets in the 1609 volume and their arrangement into a 154-poem sequence reconfigured the place of the sonnets in the history of sexuality once again. Shakespeare's personal connection with the 1609 publishing venture is a controversial issue (Duncan-Jones 1983). Whoever may be responsible for the arrangement of the poems, the 1609 Quarto does suggest several groupings. Sometimes the connections are imagistic, as in the many pairs of sonnets that ask to be read as a diptych. In sonnet 27, for example, the speaker first specifies an occasion – "Weary with toil, I haste me to my bed" (27.1) – and then describes how he cannot rest from the cares of the day, how his thoughts "intend a zealous pilgrimage to thee" (278.6). The beloved's "shadow" appears to him "like a jewel hung in ghastly night" (27.11). Sonnet 28 follows as a natural conclusion – "How can I then return in happy plight / That am debarred the benefit of rest" (28.1–2) – and repeats the images of night, starlight, journey, and oppression. Other groupings are thematic. Sonnets 1–19, all seemingly addressed to the same young man, are concerned with securing immortality, either through the begetting of children or, later in the group, through the verses that the poet writes. Sonnet 20 introduces erotic desire by addressing the recipient as "the master mistress of my passion" (20.2), praising his woman-like beauties (20.1, 5), celebrating his manly constancy (20.3–6) and skin coloring (20.7–8), and making punning sport with his penis (20.11–14). Still other groupings seem situational. Sonnets 33–42 contain dark allusions to some offence that the beloved has committed, possibly by stealing the poet's mistress ("That thou hast her, it is not all my grief" [42.1]). A rival poet is implied in sonnets 78–86. Finally there is the question of whom the poet addresses or whom he is thinking about from poem to poem. Sonnets 1–19 and 20–1 clearly imply a male recipient. Sonnet 126 ("O thou, my lovely boy, who in thy pow'r / Dost hold time's fickle glass, his sickle hour"), with its male addressee, is followed by a poem that abruptly introduces a dark-hued woman as the subject of most of the ensuing poems: "In the old age black was not counted fair" (127.1). Read in isolation, many of the sonnets seem ambiguous with respect to the subject's gender (Dubrow 2000: 113–34).

What do they imply when read in sequence? Thorpe mystifies the question by providing a dedication that looks on the page like an epigram engraved on stone. It reads like a riddle. Who is "M[aste]r W. H.," identified by Thorpe as "the only begetter" of the sonnets? Who, for that matter, is "the well-wishing adventurer" who is "setting forth"? Syntactically he has to be Thomas Thorpe, who is setting forth the poems in print, but many readers of the collected sonnets have felt themselves to be cast in the role of adventurer or explorer amid the sonnets' cryptic allusions. By connecting Master W. H. with "that eternity promised by our ever-living poet," Thorpe's dedication prepares the reader to assume that the ensuing sonnets, the first nineteen of them at least, are addressed to Master W. H. Nothing explicitly challenges that assumption until sonnet 127. Do the poems, then, fall into a group addressed to the man right fair and a group addressed to the woman colored ill? At the least we can say that all the sonnets explicitly addressed to a male subject occur before sonnet 126, while all those explicitly addressed to a female subject occur after 127. Whether that distinction applies to *every* poem before 126 and after 127 is harder to tell. Certainly sonnet 20 is not the only sonnet in the first group to speak of the man right fair in erotic terms. Sonnet 106 ("When in the chronicle of wasted time / I see descriptions of the fairest wights") takes Petrarchan poetry's conventional blazon of a lady's hand, foot, lip, eye, and brow and applies it to "ev'n such a beauty as you *master* now" (106.8, emphasis added). The sentiment voiced in the couplet of sonnet 106 – "For we which now behold these present days, / Have eyes to wonder, but lack tongues to praise" (106.13–14) – is typical of the way the poems addressed to the fair young man preserve the idealism of the Petrarchan sonnet tradition, even as the gender of the subject changes from female to male. Contrast with the sexual cynicism bruited in many of the poems addressed to the woman colored ill could hardly be sharper.

What sonnets 20 and 106 do *not* register is anxiety over erotic appreciation of the fair young man's beauty. Aristotle's valuation of bonds between male and male over all other human ties, marriage included, was maintained in early modern ethics. Such bonds, after all, cemented the political power of patriarchy. The fact that male–male bonds could be celebrated in erotic images, in the very terms that might be read as signs of sodomy, constitutes one of the central ironies of early modern culture (Bray 1994: 40–61). In their own time, Margreta de Grazia (2000) has argued, the real "scandal" of Shakespeare's sonnets was to be found in the poems addressed to the woman colored ill, not in the poems addressed to the man right fair. All the distinctions on which the edifice of early modern society was founded – not just sexual difference but social rank, age, reputation, marital status, moral probity, even physical availability – are undermined by sonnets 127–52: "It is Shakespeare's gynerastic longings for a black mistress that are perverse and menacing, precisely because they threaten to raze the very distinctions his poems to the fair boy strain to preserve" (p. 106). Sonnet 144 confirms such a reading: "Two loves I have of comfort and despair / Which like two spirits do suggest me still; / The better angel is a man right fair, / The worser spirit a woman colored ill" (144.1–4).

The circulation of Shakespeare's sonnets in manuscript from the 1590s through the 1630s, the printing of two of them in *The Passionate Pilgrim* in 1598–9, and the appearance of a collected edition in 1609 point up a fundamental fluidity, not only in what the poems could mean to different readers, but in what those readers' passions made them desire in other people. Our need to have an authorized fixed text and our need to typecast people according to "sexual orientation" are both revealed to be anachronistic back-projections.

The Cavalier Poet: 1640–1779

The most telling evidence of how people read the 1609 Quarto of Shakespeare's sonnets is to be found in manuscript table-books of the 1620s and 1630s, in which poems from the printed edition passed back into the manuscript culture from which they had originally emerged. Aside from sonnet 2, which seems to have circulated independently of the Quarto, the surviving manuscripts include single instances of sonnets 8, 32, 71, 116, 128, and 138. The only sonnet to be copied more than once, number 106, shows the same personal appropriation that we have noticed already with respect to sonnet 2. The two collectors who copied out "When in the chronicle of waste time, / I see descriptions of the fairest wights" in MS Pierpoint Morgan MA 1057 and Rosenbach MS 1083/16 seem not to have noticed the gender of the verb in the phrase "Even such a beauty as you master now"; both of them entitle the poem "On his mistress" (Beal 1980: 452–4). At least two readers of the 1609 Quarto, however, seem to have picked up on the homoeroticism of many of the first 126 sonnets. A copy of the Quarto in the Rosenbach Library in Philadelphia bears the comment after sonnet 154, "What a heap of wretched infidel stuff," with the word "infidel" capitalized and tricked out in fresh ink (Shakespeare 1998b: 69). "Infidel" may refer to Shakespeare's apostasy before the court of love; it may also have specific reference to Moors, who were infamous as sodomites (Hutcheson 2001). A more appreciative response to the sonnets' erotic ambidexterity is registered in Sir John Suckling's play *Brennoralt* (written ca. 1640), in which lines adapted from sonnets 33, 99, 104, and 140 are given to a woman who lives her life disguised as a man (Shakespeare 1998b: 73–4).

In 1640, the very year that Suckling was writing his play, there appeared a revised edition of the sonnets that smoothed over any awkward questions about erotic feelings being addressed to a man. In his preface to *Poems Written by Wil. Shake-speare, Gent.* the editor, John Benson, claims to be giving the reader "some excellent and sweetly composed poems, of Master William Shakespeare, which in themselves appear of the same purity, the author himself then living avouched" (Shakespeare 1640: sig.*2). Now, "purity" may refer to the style Benson attributes to the sonnets – later in the preface he calls them "serene, clear, and elegantly plain" (sig.*2v) – or perhaps to the accuracy of the texts he has edited. To "avouch" purity, however, seems to be making some kind of moral claim. By rearranging the order of the poems from the 1609 Quarto Benson destroys any sense of a narrative that involves a man right fair and a woman colored ill. Generic titles invite the reader to regard the book as the kind of random miscellany that more up-to-date poets like Thomas Carew were publishing in the 1640s (Baker 1998). Thus "Two loves I have" becomes "A Temptation"; "When my love swears she is made of truth" becomes "False belief." Thematically related sonnets get grouped into threes that are printed as new 42-line poems (albeit with the three concluding couplets of each sonnet indented). The sonnets numbered 1, 2, and 3 in the 1609 Quarto, for example, become "Love's cruelty." Interspersed with the 1609 are poems from the 1612 edition of *The Passionate Pilgrim*, including the amorous sonnets on Venus and Adonis. Through it all, a conventional male-to-female eroticism is insinuated.

Whether Benson set out to censor the homoeroticism in the 1609 Quarto or whether he was simply trying to turn Shakespeare into a "cavalier" poet like Carew is open to question (de Grazia 2000). Serene, clear, and elegantly plain, cavalier poetry typically strikes a politer, more public tone than Shakespeare's anguished, idiosyncratic sonnets (Baker 1998). On three occasions, but just three, Benson supplies titles that specify a female addressee for poems that the 1609 Quarto groups among those addressed to the fair young man; on three other occasions Benson alters the texts of the poems themselves so that "he" becomes "she." At the same time, however, Benson retains intact sonnet 20 ("A woman's face") and gives it a title, "The Exchange," that calls witty attention to Nature's substitution of penis for vagina in lines 9–12. In context, the poem could be read as spoken by Venus, since it is preceded, first by one of the Venus and Adonis sonnets from *The Passionate Pilgrim*, then by one of the Petrarchan sonnets from *Love's Labour's Lost*, "If love make me forsworn." It is followed by a particularly passionate amalgam of three sonnets, "The disconsolation," made up of "Weary with toil, I haste me to my bed," "How can I then return in happy plight," and "When in disgrace with Fortune and men's eyes."

At least one early reader of the 1640 edition was not distracted by Benson's coy title for sonnet 20. In a copy of the book in the Folger Shakespeare Library the reader has provided, as he does for many of the poems, an alternative title: "The m[ist]ress masculine" (Shakespeare 1640: sig. B4). Does this imply that the reader has taken the poem's "master mistress" to be a manly woman? Perhaps. On the other hand, the reader may be echoing Thersites in *Troilus and Cressida* when the straight-talking satirist taunts Patroclus as "Achilles' male varlet," his "masculine whore" (5.1.14, 16). By 1640 the phrase *masculus amor*, "masculine love," had emerged as a code word for male–male eroticism (Cady 1992: 9–40). Benson may have attempted to forestall such sodomitical readings by grouping under the title "The benefits of friendship" three sonnets from the young man group: "When to the sessions of sweet silent thought / I summon up remembrance of things past," "Thy bosom is endearéd with all hearts," and "If thou survive my well-contented day." Worth noting is the fact it was precisely during these years, during the 1630s and 1640s, that increasing prudery about female homoeroticism began to be registered in English translations of Ovid's heroical epistle from Sappho to Phaon. The implication is that writers and readers were newly aware of sexual behavior that had passed without comment fifty years before (Andreadis 2001: 30–7). The very phrase *masculus amor* means that, in the 1620s and 1630s, something new was being recognized that now required a name. Was that something the very thing that Benson wished *not* to name?

Benson's edition had staying power. It formed the basis for every reprinting of Shakespeare's sonnets for 126 years. An edition of *Venus and Adonis*, *The Rape of Lucrece*, and Shakespeare's "miscellany poems" printed in 1709 retains Benson's texts and titles, even as it breaks up the amalgamated poems into their three-sonnet constituent parts (Shakespeare 1709: title page). Bernard Lintott's edition of about two years later returns to the 1609 Quarto text but bills the entire sequence as "One hundred and fifty sonnets, all of them in praise of his mistress" (Shakespeare 1998b: 43). Lintott's title page – *A Collection of Poems in Two Volumes . . . Being All the Miscellanies of Mr. William Shakespeare, Which Were Published by Himself in the Year 1609* – stresses the diffuseness of the poems and does not encourage readers to look for any sort of plot, much less one that involves a male beloved. It was just in the years that these editions were being printed that the sex of the bodies one desired was beginning to be taken as an index of one's own gender identity. Randolph Trumbach has pointed out how the rake-figure in comedies of the 1660s, 1670s, 1680s, and 1690s, with his mistress on one arm and his boy-lover on the other, came to be bifurcated: the rake who prefers men and the rake who prefers women (Trumbach 1990: 105–24). In the sixteenth and early seventeenth centuries erotic desire itself was felt to be effeminating, regardless of the sex of the bodies a man might desire. Hearing of Mercutio's murder, Romeo exclaims, "O sweet Juliet, / Thy beauty hath made me effeminate / And in my temper softened valour's steel" (3.1.113–15). By the early eighteenth century it was only men who desired other men who were identified as effeminate (Bray 1982: 81–114; Trumbach 1989: 129–40; 1998: 49–65). In such a culture, to declare "Two loves I have" was to invite criminal charges. The isolation of the man who desires other men made him an easier target not only for satire but for legal prosecution. The eighteenth century witnessed a huge increase in prosecutions for sodomy (Crompton 1985: 12–62).

The National Bard: 1780–1888

Authenticity was the watchword that guided Edmund Malone, the first great Shakespeare scholar, in editing Shakespeare's sonnets in 1780. Malone's edition appeared as a supplement to Samuel Johnson and George Steevens's edition of Shakespeare's plays, published two years earlier. Where editors and publishers since the seventeenth century had been content to reprint the most recent edition of Shakespeare's texts, Johnson, Steevens, and Malone returned to the earliest texts. Malone in particular brought to the project an historian's sense of the cultural distance that separated late-eighteenth-century readers from the texts they were reading (de Grazia 1991). When it came to the sonnets, Malone's quest for authenticity ran into problems. The public and conventional cast that Benson and his successors had given to the sonnets disappeared when Malone took the 1609 Quarto as his copy text. Above all, there was the problem of the first 126 sonnets. It is to Malone that readers ever since have owed the conviction that sonnets 1–126 all concern a man and sonnets 127–54 a woman. Steevens, for his part, made no attempt to hide his repugnance at the first group. For Malone's 1780 edition Steevens supplied this note on sonnet 20: "It is impossible to read this fulsome panegyric, addressed to a male object, without an equal mixture of disgust and indignation" (Vickers 1981: 288). To leave no question about what he was talking about, he cited the term "male varlet" from *Troilus and Cressida*.

Malone, in the first edition, seems to have agreed. When Steevens complained, in a note to sonnet 127, that the sonnet form in general was not to his taste, Malone conceded that Shakespeare's sonnets do seem to have two "great defects": "a want of variety, and the majority of them not being directed to a female, to whom alone such ardent expressions of esteem could with propriety be addressed" (Vickers 1981: 294). For the edition of 1783 Malone went further: he tried to explain away these "ardent expressions of esteem" by appealing to history. In reply to Steevens's note on sonnet 20 Malone wrote, "Some part of this indignation might perhaps have been abated if

it had been considered that such addresses to men, however indelicate, were customary in our author's time, and neither imported criminality, nor were esteemed indecorous" (Vickers 1981: 551). And to prove the point he cites Shakespeare's use of the
word "lover" in contexts that are clearly not sexual. In a note on sonnet 32 Malone
repeats his assertion about historical difference and goes on to note that Shakespeare's
age "seems to have been very indelicate and gross in many other particulars besides
this, but certainly did not think themselves so" (Vickers 1981: 552). That, basically,
has been the dodge adopted ever since by critics who feel uneasy about the first 126
sonnets. Steevens remained unconvinced. In his 1793 edition of Shakespeare's plays
Steevens spoke for many eighteenth-century readers in dismissing the sonnets, along
with *Venus and Adonis* and *The Rape of Lucrece*, as essentially unreadable works: "We
have not reprinted the sonnets etc. of Shakespeare, because the strongest act of Parliament that could be framed, would fail to compel readers into their service; noth-
withstanding these miscellaneous poems have derived every possible advantage from
the literature and judgement of their only intelligent editor, Mr. Malone" (quoted in
Shakespeare 1998b: 75).

With respect to sexuality, Malone's notes on the sonnets display two rather contradictory aims: on the one hand to extirpate suspicions of sodomy by thoroughly historicizing the poems and, on the other, to get at the authentic Shakespeare by reading
the poems autobiographically. Thus Malone can seize on lines from one of the sonnets
addressed to the young man – "So shall I live, supposing thou art true, / Like a
deceived husband" (93.1–2) – and put them forward as proof that the historical
William Shakespeare knew sexual jealousy from the inside: "he appears to me to have
written more immediately *from the heart* on the subject of jealousy than on any other;
and it is therefore not improbable that he might have felt it" (Vickers 1981: 291,
emphasis original). When Malone amplified this opinion in the 1783 edition, he
insisted that jealousy "is a passion which it is said 'most men who have ever loved
have in some degree experienced'" (Vickers 1981: 554). Malone is caught here between
his desire that Shakespeare be understood in historically informed terms and his desire
that Shakespeare be regarded as just such a man as Malone and his eighteenth-century
contemporaries would have him be. Key to both concerns is Shakespeare's imputed
sexuality. No better evidence than Malone's notes could be found of Foucault's contention that sexuality emerged as a distinct domain of knowledge in the late eighteenth century. In speculating about Shakespeare's sexuality Steevens and Malone are
not just talking about certain physical actions that a man might make with his body;
they are talking about a whole way of *being* as a person. They desperately want Shakespeare to share their middle-class values. Among the Shakespearean forgeries that
William Henry Ireland concocted in the 1790s was a love-letter from "Willy" to his
wife "dearest Anna," enclosing a lock of his hair. "I pray you," the letter goes, "perfume
this my poor lock with thy balmy kisses, for then indeed shall kings themselves bow
and pay homage to it" (Folger MS W.b.496, fol. 93). Michael Keevak has suggested
that Ireland's forgery was a response to imputations of sodomy in Malone's notes to
the sonnets (Keevak 2001: 23–40). Shakespeare's ethical probity was important in the

eighteenth century because it was precisely then that Shakespeare was being constructed as "the national poet" of Great Britain (Dobson 1992).

Malone's desire to read Shakespeare's sonnets autobiographically touched off two centuries of speculation about who Master W. H. might have been (William Herbert, Earl of Pembroke? Wriothesley, Henry? William [Shakespeare] Himself?), not to mention the dark lady (Anne Hathaway? Mary Fitton? Emilia Lanyer?) (Schoenbaum 1991: 314–30, 376–7). It also anticipates an early nineteenth-century shift in what readers ever since have understood poetry to *be*. Well into the eighteenth century poets could still aspire to speak in the public voice that Milton had assumed or, in matters of the heart, with the smooth urbanity that John Benson tried to impose on Shakespeare's sonnets. With the Romantic revolution in style and sensibility came the conviction that the very reason for poetry's existence is to express the writer's private, subjective experience. Shakespeare's sonnets, with their insistent "I," seemed, to Romantic readers, to be just poems. By one count, forms of the first-person singular pronoun – "I," "me," "my," "mine" – constitute the single most frequently recurring word group in Shakespeare's sonnets: 1,062 instances in all (Spevack 1968, 2: 1255–87). Writers of Wordsworth's generation grew up with the eighteenth-century's contempt for the sonnet as an artificial, un-English verse form. By 1827, however, Wordsworth had changed his mind, at least with respect to Shakespeare. In a sonnet called "Scorn not the sonnet" Wordsworth gave Shakespeare's sonnets the highest praise a Romantic poet could give: "With this key / Shakespeare unlocked his heart" (Wordsworth 1981, 2: 635). What nineteenth-century readers found in Shakespeare's heart, especially if they read the sonnets in sequence, did not match their own notions of sexual propriety.

For Wordsworth, the cynical sonnets to the dark lady were the problem; for Coleridge, it was the poems to the young man (Stallybrass 2000: 75–88). In 1803 Coleridge made private notes about the thoughts he had on reading Shakespeare's sonnets, in particular the thoughts he had on reading sonnet 20. He imagines his infant son Hartley reading the poem many years later. He realizes that Hartley will need some knowledge of Greek history and "the Greek lovers." Coleridge instances "that Theban band of brothers over whom Philip, their victor, stood weeping." "This pure love," Coleridge writes to himself, "Shakespeare appears to have felt – to have been in no way ashamed of it – or even to have suspected that others could have suspected it." And yet, surely, Shakespeare would have realized that "so strong a love would have been more completely a thing of permanence and reality, and have been more blessed by nature and taken under her more especial protection, if this object of his love had been at the same time a possible object of desire – for nature is not soul only" (quoted in Stallybrass 2000: 81–2). Coleridge recognizes sonnet 20 as a poem of homoerotic desire but denies the possibility that such a love could ever really exist.

Thirty years later he came back to the issue in *Table Talk*. Sonnet 20, he decided, was "a purposed blind." The sonnets "could only have come from a man deeply in love, and in love with a woman" (quoted in Stallybrass 2000: 82–3). Reasons for such denial were viscerally immediate: prosecutions for sodomy in England reached an all-time high in the early nineteenth century (Crompton 1985: 12–62). Peter Stallybrass has summarized the dilemma: "Steevens and Malone between them had constructed and passed down an impossible legacy: a legacy from Malone of the *Sonnets* as crucial documents of the interior life of the national bard; a legacy from Steevens of that interior life as one that would destroy the life of the nation" (Stallybrass 2000: 84). Coleridge speaks for many later nineteenth-century readers of the sonnets in knowing what the poems are about and yet willfully *not* knowing what they are about. Henry Hallam, the ardent friend of Tennyson and the subject of "In Memoriam," lamented the "circumstances" of the sonnets' production and concluded, "It is impossible not to wish that Shakespeare had never written them" (quoted in Stallybrass 2000: 83).

Hostage in the Culture Wars: 1889–present

For many readers in the eighteenth and nineteenth centuries, probably for most readers in fact, the sexuality implied by Shakespeare's sonnets was not an issue for the simple reason that those readers encountered the poems as scattered items in anthologies and not as a 154-poem sequence. That remains true for most readers today, the readers of *Shakespeare in Love* included. Alexander Chalmers, who collected the works of major British poets in the early nineteenth century and published them in multi-volumed sets, speaks for received opinion about Shakespeare's non-dramatic poems when he almost apologizes for printing all 154 sonnets. Chalmers quotes Steevens's judgment about Shakespeare's non-dramatic poems needing more than an act of parliament to make them popular. "Severe as this may appear," Chalmers concludes, "it only amounts to the general conclusion which modern critics have formed. Still it cannot be denied that there are many scattered beauties among the sonnets" (Chalmers 1810: 15). Looking for "scattered beauties" permitted editors to avoid questions of sexuality altogether.

A major example is the selection of Shakespeare's sonnets printed in Francis Turner Palgrave's *The Golden Treasury of the Best Songs and Lyrical Poems in the English Language*, first published in 1861. Put together with advice from Tennyson, Britain's Poet Laureate from 1850 to 1892, the anthology was frequently reprinted and extended throughout the nineteenth and twentieth centuries. In 2001 the sixth edition was still in print. Palgrave's principles of selection and arrangement for the original edition are specified in the preface. Individual poems have been chosen simply because they constitute "the Best" (Palgrave 1890: vii, capitalization original); within the chronological limits of the anthology's four books, the poems have been arranged "in gradations of feeling or subject." Poems by different authors are interspersed with each other. The result, Palgrave trusts, will be "a certain unity, 'as episodes,' in the noble language of Shelley, 'to that great Poem which all poets, like the co-operating thoughts of one great mind, have built up since the beginning of the world'" (ibid: ix, capitalization original). Within Book One, which covers the years 1525 to 1616,

Palgrave notes a progression from the "simplicity" of the earlier poems, through "pastoral fancies and Italian conceits," to "the passionate reality of Shakespeare" (ibid: 417).

With respect to sexuality, Shelley's one great mind turns out to have thoroughly predictable and anodyne thoughts. In the 1890 edition of Palgrave's *Golden Treasury* Book One contains 80 poems, 34 of which are by Shakespeare, a little more than 40 percent of the whole. Palgrave's notion of what constitutes "the Best" can be suggested by a tally of poems by other poets: William Drummond of Hawthornden seven, Thomas Campion six, Sir Philip Sidney five, Ben Jonson zero, John Donne zero. The predominance of Campion, the writer of lute-songs, is telling: fully 14 of the 34 Shakespearean selections are songs from the plays. Of the 20 sonnets that are printed, only 2 come from the group numbered 126 to 154 in the 1609 Quarto. Lifted out of their context in the Quarto, neither sonnet 146 ("Poor soul, center of my sinful earth") nor 148 ("O me! what eyes hath love put in my head, / Which have no correspondence with true sight!") gives any idea of the tortured relationship between the speaker and the dark lady. Neither poem makes any explicit reference to the lady, her darkness, or her sexual treachery.

What of the fair young man? He, too, is absent. Although 18 sonnets from the group 1–126 are included in *The Golden Treasury*, not a single one refers explicitly to the young man. The context in which the reader is expected to view the sonnets is created by the first six poems in Book One. Thomas Nashe's rollicking lyric "Spring" leads off the collection; then comes a poem by Drummond that has been given the title "A Summons to Love." The first two Shakespeare sonnets, the Quarto's number 64 ("When I have seen by Time's fell hand defaced / The rich proud costs of outworn buried age") and 65 ("Since brass, nor stone, nor boundless sea, / But sad mortality o'ersways their power"), are grouped together under the title "Time and Love." The poems that follow, Marlowe's "Come live with me and be my love" and the anonymous song lyric "Fain would I change that note / To which fond love has charmed me," maintain the amorous cast of the episode but keep it utterly non-specific. Throughout *The Golden Treasury* generic titles reminiscent of Benson's edition of 1640 maintain this public character. For example, Shakespeare's sonnets 18 ("Shall I compare thee to a summer's day?") and 106 ("When in the chronicle of wasted time / I see descriptions of the fairest wights") are printed successively under the same repeated title: "To his love." The effect is to invite the reader to project his or her own sexuality onto the poems. And that sexuality is plainly assumed to be the sexuality of middle-class Britons of the mid-to-late nineteenth century. "The passionate reality of Shakespeare" turns out to be the quotidian reality of the Victorian reader. The moral cast of the whole affair is suggested by Book One's final episode, which is concerned with death. The last three Shakespeare sonnets in Palgrave's sequence are numbers 71 ("No longer mourn for me when I am dead"), 146 ("Poor soul, center of my sinful earth"), and 66 ("Tir'd with all these, for restful death I cry"). Through it all Palgrave displays an absolute unwillingness to see homoeroticism, even when it is staring him in the face in sonnet 106's celebration of "such a beauty as you master now."

Oscar Wilde changed all that. Alan Sinfield has argued that it was Wilde's arraignment for gross indecency with Lord Alfred Douglas in 1895 that solidified the notion of "the male homosexual" that still has wide currency (Sinfield 1994: 1–24). Before the trial many of Wilde's associates could accept his effeminate manner and his aesthetic interests without ever entertaining the idea that he had pursued sexual relations with other men. After the trial it was hard not to make that connection. We can see that process of identity-formation in Wilde's story "The Portrait of Mr. W. H.," printed in *Blackwood's Magazine* in 1889 and enlarged (though not republished) four years later. Although a piece of fiction, the story amounts to a scholarly case that Master W. H. was a boy actor named Willie Hughes. All the competing theories of Mr. W. H's identity from the eighteenth century and after are considered. The reluctance of commentators since Malone to push the question of Shakespeare's sexuality too far is registered even by the character in the story who concocts the theory, Cyril Graham. The first-person narrator of the story hears about Cyril's theory second hand, from Cyril's friend Erskine. "The problem he pointed out," Erskine tells the narrator,

> was this: Who was that young man of Shakespeare's day who, without being of noble birth or even of noble nature, was addressed by him in terms of such passionate adoration that we can but wonder at the strange worship, and are almost afraid to turn the key that unlocks the mystery of the poet's heart? Who was he whose physical beauty was such that it became the very corner-stone of Shakespeare's art; the very source of Shakespeare's inspiration; the very incarnation of Shakespeare's dreams? (Wilde 1994: 56)

Cyril goes so far as to pay an artist to forge a portrait of Willie Hughes. Pictured with his right hand resting on an open copy of the sonnets, the boy presents an intriguingly ambiguous appearance with respect to gender:

> He seemed about seventeen years of age, and was of quite extraordinary personal beauty, though evidently somewhat effeminate. Indeed, had it not been for the dress and the closely cropped hair, one would have said that the face, with its dreamy wistful eyes, and its delicate scarlet lips, was the face of a girl. (Ibid: 50)

The telling word here is the "though" that follows "beauty." The reason for Cyril's dedication to the theory is patent: he is just such a person himself. The uncle who raised him thought him effeminate, and at Eton Cyril turned out to be good at riding and fencing but despised football. "The two things that really gave him pleasure were poetry and acting" (p. 52). When the forgery is exposed, Cyril commits suicide. Erskine, in a letter to the narrator, frames his own death as martyrdom to the cause of Willie Hughes. The narrator's attitude to the theory, and to putting one's life on the line in the theory's defense, is presented with exquisite irony: first he dismisses it, then he embraces it, finally he holds it at an ambivalent distance. As well he might. The deaths of Cyril and Erskine imply that the fantasy of homosexual love could not be tolerated in Victorian society. "I believe there is something fatal about the idea," Erskine confesses to the narrator (p. 62).

Ambivalence is something Wilde himself was not able to maintain when he was brought to trial in 1895. Wilde's public exposure gave a voice and a body to "the male homosexual" that Freud was soon to theorize in *Three Essays on the Theory of Sexuality* (1905) and later writings. That voice and that body Wilde shared with Cyril Graham. Wilde's appearance, according to one of his friends, was anything but vigorous: "fleshly indulgence and laziness, I said to myself, were written all over him . . . He shook hands in a limp way I disliked; his hands were flabby, greasy; his skin looked bilious and dirty" (quoted in Sinfield 1994: 2). In locating sexual identity in the first 126 sonnets Wilde put the dark lady of sonnets 127–54 in a decidedly pre-carious position. Read in terms of Freud's binary sexual typology, the dark lady sonnets present an identity crisis. If sonnets 1–126 are homosexual poems, and sonnets 127–54 are heterosexual poems, then what about the two together? They can only constitute a pathological middle identity as "bisexual" poems. It is precisely the first seventeen sonnets' advice about marrying that makes the narrator of "The Portrait of Mr. W. H." at first doubt Cyril Graham's theory. He finally decides, however, that what Shakespeare had in mind was a "marriage" between Mr. W. H. and Shakespeare's muse. Actual women have no place in Cyril's scheme. For the both/and of the sonnets in their own day the Freudian theory of sexuality substituted either/or.

Until very recently Freudian theory and middle-class propriety have governed dis-cussions of the sexuality implied by Shakespeare's sonnets. When W. H. Auden dis-missed the possibility of homosexuality in his preface to the 1964 Signet Classics edition, he did so in terms supplied by Sigmund Freud fifty years before. Respond-ing to the eagerness of "the homosexual reader" "to secure our Top-Bard as the patron saint of the Homintern," Auden says of the sonnets that "men and women whose sexual tastes are perfectly normal, but who enjoy and understand poetry, have always been able to read them as expressions of what they understand by the word *love*, without finding the masculine pronoun an obstacle" (Auden 1973: 99–100). "Normal," a medical term, is the operative word here. Auden finds in the sonnets a "Vision of Eros" (capitals original) that transcends the labels "heterosexual" and "homosexual," a vision that "cannot survive an actual sexual relationship" (p. 101). When Auden made that statement, it was still three years until the British parlia-ment would decriminalize consensual sexual relations between adult men and two years more until the Stonewall Riot would set an agenda for gay liberation in America. Nonetheless, Auden was denying the nature of his own private life, not to mention the personal convictions about the sonnets that he shared with friends, as Joseph Pequigney reveals in *Such Is My Love: A Study of Shakespeare's Sonnets* (1985), the first systematic riposte to prevailing evasions of the sexuality question. The reluctant acceptance that Pequigney's book met with can be witnessed in Robert M. Adams's judgment in *The New York Review of Books*: "This is certainly a book that had to be written, that will make impossible any return to the old vague euphemisms, but that, after reading, one will be glad to keep distant in one's memory, if one wants to enjoy the sonnets themselves" (Adams 1986). If scholars and general readers have been more reluctant to acknowledge homoeroticism in Shakespeare's sonnets than in his plays, the reason might be found in the sonnets' insistent "I." Too many readers have too much invested in Shakespeare's speaking "I" to consider that the sexuality of that "I" may not be the same as their own. Too much is at stake, as well, for Western civilization. If Shakespeare is to remain the lynchpin in the canon, he certainly can't be gay. Or even bisexual. Or so the unspoken argument goes.

Since the middle of the twentieth century, however, the drift of academic criticism of Shakespeare's sonnets has been away from the autobiographical preoccupations of Malone and his successors. Each of the critical methodologies that have been adopted since the 1940s gives a different sort of attention to sexuality. New criticism, with its disciplined focus on the text itself, attempts to dodge the question of sexuality entirely. "William Shakespeare was almost certainly homosexual, bisexual, or heterosexual," Stephen Booth quips. "The sonnets provide no evidence on the matter" (Shakespeare 1977: 548). Helen Vendler's extensive commentary on the sonnets is premised on the assumption that the sonnets are "lyrics" and hence bear only a tangential relationship to social and psychological concerns. "Contemporary emphasis on the participation of literature in a social matrix," she contends, "balks at acknowledging how lyric, though it may *refer* to the social, remains the genre that directs its *mimesis* toward the performance of the mind in *solitary* speech" (Vendler 1997: 1–2, emphasis original). The "true 'actors' in lyric" are not dramatic persons but words (p. 3). Sonnet 144 in Vendler's reading becomes a poem about a breakdown in the distinction between the words "angel" and "fiend," reflected in the shifting places, left and right, those two words (and their synonyms) occupy in succeeding lines of the sonnet (605–6). By refusing to examine questions of sexuality, New Critics tend, by default, to assume a normative heterosexuality. Vendler will accept that the "controlling motive" of the first 126 sonnets is "sexual infatuation," but she insists that the speaker's infatuation with the young man "is so entirely an infatuation of the eye – which makes a fetish of the beloved's countenance rather than of his entire body – that gazing is this infatuation's chief (and perhaps best and only) form of intercourse" (p. 15).

New historicism, by contrast, has made sexuality a central issue. The emphasis in new historicist studies like Margreta de Grazia's "The Scandal of Shakespeare's Sonnets" and Valerie Traub's "Sex without Issue: Sodomy, Reproduction, and Signification in Shakespeare's Sonnets" falls, not on speculation about Shakespeare's emotional life or on love as a thematic concern, but on the social work that the sonnets were doing with respect to sexuality for the poems' original readers (de Grazia 2000: 89–112; Traub 2000: 431–54). Foucault's insistence that sexuality is a cultural construct invites a reading of Shakespeare's sonnets as part of a social process whereby erotic feelings and certain bodily acts are coordinated toward politically useful ends. Thus in de Grazia's analysis it is unruly desires expressed in the dark lady sonnets, not affection for the man right fair, that threatened the social order of early modern England. Sonnet 144 epitomizes the situation by casting the man right fair as "the better angel" and the woman colored ill as "the worser spirit" (144.4).

Deconstructionist readings seize on the fact that the various kinds of social work that the sonnets were performing in 1609 may not have been mutually compatible. Difference-marking is the place where such contradictions are most likely to appear. In my own essay "I, You, He, She, and We: On the Sexual Politics of Shakespeare's Sonnets" I attempt to deconstruct the seeming fixity of all these pronouns, with particular attention to the way "he" is implicated in "she," just as "she" is implicated in "he." Sonnet 144 may try to keep the two separate, but sonnets 106 ("When in the chronicle of wasted time / I see descriptions of the fairest wights") and 133 ("Beshrew that heart that makes my heart to groan / For that deep wound it gives my friend and me") demonstrate how much "he" depends on "she" for its very existence – and how much "I" depends on both (Smith 2000a: 411–29). In sonnet 144 "I" is constituted totally in terms of "he" and "she."

Sexual desire assumes existential importance in Jacques Lacan's psychoanalytical theory. For Freud, identity-formation is a function of sexual development; for Lacan, it is a function of language. Entering into the symbolic order of language, Lacan argues, entails an estrangement from the illusion of wholeness with the world that all human beings know as infants. That lost sense of wholeness becomes, for Lacan, the fundamental object of human desire, not only desire for the interiority of another person's body but desire for the escape that fictions seem to offer from one's own language-boundedness. In a sophisticated and subtle application of Lacan's theory, Joel Fineman has found in Shakespeare's sonnets a tension between the visual and the verbal that constitutes, Fineman believes, the very source of modern subjectivity. In Fineman's reading, sonnet 144 figures as a paradigm of this tension. The poet's image of "one angel in another's hell" (144.12) conflates the man right fair and the lady colored ill, so that both figures undermine the poet's ideals and the adequacy of his language. The dark lady becomes "the material conclusion of an originally immaterial imagination, the loathsome heterosexual object of an ideally homosexual desire" (Fineman 1986: 58). Correspondence is severed between the poet's vision and the words he has to express that vision.

If surviving manuscripts of Shakespeare's sonnets, successive editions, and critical interpretations have anything in common, it is the fact that sexuality is a culturally contingent concept. Hence, readings of Shakespeare's sonnets since the 1590s inescapably reflect the concerns and the concepts of the people who have been doing the reading across those four centuries and more. As documents in the history of sexuality Shakespeare's sonnets belong to the 1690s, the 1790s, the 1890s, the 1990s, and the 2090s as much as they belong to the 1590s.

NOTES

1 Unless otherwise noted, spelling and orthography in this and other original texts have been modernized.
2 All quotations from Shakespeare's plays are taken from *Complete Works*, ed. Stanley Wells and Gary Taylor (Oxford: Clarendon Press, 1988) and hereafter are cited in the text.

3   A census of surviving manuscripts containing sonnets by Shakespeare is provided in Beal (1980), 1, 2: 452–4.

4   Quotations from the 1609 Quarto of Shakespeare's sonnets are taken from *Shakespeare's Sonnets*, ed. Stephen Booth (1977) and hereafter are cited in the text.

REFERENCES AND FURTHER READING

Adams, R. M. (1986). Review of Joseph Pequigney, *Such Is My Love: A Study of Shakespeare's Sonnets. New York Review of Books*, 33, 50.

Andreadis, H. (2001). *Sappho in Early Modern England: Female Same-Sex Literary Erotics 1550–1714.* Chicago, IL: University of Chicago Press.

Auden, W. H. (1973). *Forewords and Afterwards.* New York: Random House.

Baker, D. (1998). Cavalier Shakespeare: The 1640 *Poems* of John Benson. *Studies in Philology*, 95, 2, 152–73.

Beal, P. (1980). *Index of English Literary Manuscripts*, Vol. 1 (1450–1625), Part 2. London: Mansell.

Bodleian Library, Oxford University. MS Rawlinson Poetic 152.

Bray, A. (1982). *Homosexuality in Renaissance England.* London: Gay Men's Press.

——(1994). Homosexuality and the Signs of Male Friendship in Elizabethan England. In J. Goldberg (ed.) *Queering the Renaissance.* Durham, NC: Duke University Press.

Cady, J. (1992). "Masculine Love," Renaissance Writing, and the "New Invention" of Homosexuality. In C. J. Summers (ed.) *Homosexuality in Renaissance and Enlightenment England: Literary Representations in Historical Context.* New York: Harrington Park Press.

Chalmers, A. (ed.) (1810). *The Works of the English Poets*, Volume 5. London: Printed for J. Johnson et al.

Crompton, L. (1985). *Byron and Greek Love: Homophobia in 19th-Century England.* Berkeley: University of California Press.

de Grazia, M. (1991). *Shakespeare Verbatim: The Reproduction of Authenticity and the 1790 Apparatus.* Oxford: Clarendon Press.

——(2000). The Scandal of Shakespeare's Sonnets. In J. Schiffer (ed.) *Shakespeare's Sonnets: Critical Essays.* London: Routledge.

Dobson, M. (1992). *The Making of the National Poet.* Oxford: Clarendon Press.

Dubrow, H. (2000). "Incertainties Now Crown Themselves Assur'd": The Politics of Plotting Shakespeare's Sonnets. In J. Schiffer (ed.) *Shakespeare's Sonnets: Critical Essays.* London: Routledge.

Duncan-Jones, K. (1983). Was the 1609 *Shake-speares Sonnets* Really Unauthorized? *Review of English Studies*, 34, 151–71.

——(2001). *Ungentle Shakespeare: Scenes from His Life.* London: Thompson.

Fineman, J. (1986). *Shakespeare's Perjured Eye: The Invention of Poetic Subjectivity in the Sonnets.* Berkeley: University of California Press.

Folger Shakespeare Library, Washington. MS W.b.496.

Foucault, M. (1980). *The History of Sexuality*, Volume 1: *An Introduction*, trans. R. Hurley. New York: Random House.

Hutcheson, G. S. (2001). The Sodomite Moor: Queerness in the Narrative of *Reconquista*. In G. Burger and S. F. Kruger (eds.) *Queering the Middle Ages.* Minneapolis: University of Minnesota Press.

Jonson, B. (1985). *Ben Jonson*, ed. I. Donaldson. Oxford: Oxford University Press.

Keevak, M. (2001). *Sexual Shakespeare: Forgery, Authorship, Portraiture.* Detroit, MI: Wayne State University Press.

Love, H. (1993). *Scribal Publication in Seventeenth-Century England.* Oxford: Clarendon Press.

Marotti, A. (1995). *Manuscript, Print, and the English Renaissance Lyric.* Ithaca, NY: Cornell University Press.

Meres, F. (1938). *Palladis Tamia, Wit's Treasury* (1598), ed. D. C. Allen. New York: Scholars' Facsimiles and Reprints.

Palgrave, F. T. (1890). *The Golden Treasury of the Best Songs and Lyrical Poems in the English Language*. London: Macmillan.

Pequigney, J. (1985). *Such Is My Love: A Study of Shakespeare's Sonnets*. Chicago, IL: University of Chicago Press.

Schoenbaum, S. (1991). *Shakespeare's Lives*. Oxford: Clarendon Press.

Shakespeare, W. (attributed) (1939). *The Passionate Pilgrim*, ed. J. Q. Adams. New York: Scribners.

Shakespeare, W. (1640). *Poems Written by Wil. Shake-speare, Gent*, ed. T. Benson. London: Thomas Cotes.

——(1709). *Works*, Volume 7, ed. C. Gildon. London: E. Curll.

——(1977). *Shakespeare's Sonnets*, ed. S. Booth. New Haven, CT: Yale University Press.

——(1988). *Complete Works*, ed. S. Wells and G. Taylor. Oxford: Clarendon Press.

——(1998a). *Shakespeare in Love: The Love Poetry of William Shakespeare*. New York: Hyperion Press.

——(1998b). *Shakespeare's Sonnets*, ed. K. Duncan-Jones. The Arden Shakespeare. London: Thomas Nelson.

Sinfield, A. (1994). *The Wilde Century*. London: Cassell.

Smith, B. R. (1996). L[o]cating the Sexual Subject. In T. Hawkes (ed.) *Alternative Shakespeares*, Vol. 2. London: Routledge.

——(2000a). I, You, He, She, and We: On the Sexual Politics of Shakespeare's Sonnets. In J. Schiffer (ed.) *Shakespeare's Sonnets: Critical Essays*. London: Routledge.

——(2000b). Premodern Sexualities. *Publications of the Modern Languages Association*, 115, 3, 318–29.

Spenser, E. (1989). *The Yale Edition of the Shorter Poems of Edmund Spenser*, ed. W. A. Oram et al. New Haven, CT: Yale University Press.

Spevack, M. (1968). *A Complete and Systematic Concordance to the Works of Shakespeare*. Hildesheim: Olms.

Stallybrass, P. (2000). Editing as Cultural Formation: The Sexing of Shakespeare's Sonnets. In J. Schiffer (ed.) *Shakespeare's Sonnets: Critical Essays*. London: Routledge.

Taylor, G. (1985). Some Manuscripts of Shakespeare's Sonnets. *Bulletin of the John Rylands University Library of Manchester*, 68, 210–46.

Traub, V. (2000). Sex without Issue: Sodomy, Reproduction, and Signification in Shakespeare's Sonnets. In J. Schiffer (ed.) *Shakespeare's Sonnets: Critical Essays*. London: Routledge.

Trumbach, R. (1989). The Birth of the Queen: Sodomy and the Emergence of Gender Equality in Modern Culture, 1660–1750. In M. B. Duberman, M. Vicinus, and G. Chauncey, Jr. (eds.) *Hidden from History: Reclaiming the Gay and Lesbian Past*. New York: New American Library.

——(1990). Sodomy Transformed: Aristocratic Libertinage, Public Reputation and the Gender Revolution of the 18th Century. In M. S. Kimmel (ed.) *Love Letters between a Certain Late Nobleman and the Famous Mr. Wilson*. New York: Harrington Park Press.

——(1998). *Heterosexuality and the Third Gender in Enlightenment London*. Chicago, IL: University of Chicago Press.

Vendler, H. (1997). *The Art of Shakespeare's Sonnets*. Cambridge, MA: Harvard University Press.

Vickers, B. (ed.) (1981). *Shakespeare: The Critical Heritage*, Volume 6: 1774–1801. London: Routledge and Kegan Paul.

Westminster Abbey, MS Dean and Chapter 41.

Wilde, O. (1994). *Complete Short Fiction*, ed. I. Small. London: Penguin Books.

Wordsworth, W. (1981). *The Poems*, 2 vols., ed. J. O. Hayden. New Haven, CT: Yale University Press.

Wright, T. (1988). *The Passions of the Mind in General*, ed. W. Webster Newbold. New York: Garland.

2

The Book of Changes in a Time of Change: Ovid's *Metamorphoses* in Post-Reformation England and *Venus and Adonis*

Dympna Callaghan

William Shakespeare was born a year prior to the publication of Arthur Golding's *The XV Bookes of P. Ouidius Naso, entytuled Metamorphosis . . .* (1565). Shaped by an unprecedented manifestation of English Christianity in their irrevocable difference from all that preceded them, Shakespeare's generation went on from an early introduction to Latin authors in the grammar schools to more profound encounters with classical paganism. In this essay I want to look at what I will call the secular-aesthetic in the 1590s. By this I mean the advent of a new articulation of the aesthetic that came about through an absorption and iteration of the Roman poet Ovid that was to be found neither in the decades that preceded it nor in those that were to follow in poetry characterized by a divorce both from didacticism and from immediately political purposes. Marked primarily by its distinctive tone – ebullient, racy, urbane and yet by turns somber and even tragic – the new secular-aesthetic is far closer to Ovid's subtle modulations of voice in the Latin original than its precursors. The species of Ovidianism that flowers in the 1590s belongs, conceptually speaking, not only in its substance, but also vitally in its expression and its constantly shifting generic expectations, to the period's anticipation and, ultimately, its inauguration of a definitively secular modernity.

In a firmly Protestant culture, Ovid, and paganism more generally, still had a vexed relation with orthodox religion. While to modern readers nothing seems further from religious controversy than racy Ovidian verse, in early modern terms it is in fact charged with the ideological force of post-Reformation polemic.[1] Far from belonging to a realm beyond religious schism, then, there are many ways in which Ovidianism in general parallels, shadows, and at times even overlaps with the era's fundamentally religious concerns. More specifically, the component images and ideas of the period's most completely Ovidian poems might themselves be said in some sense *to be* religious. This is because Ovidian myth in the English Renaissance serves precisely as *mystères littéraires*, that is, the transfer of specifically religious rites into the realm of the secular aesthetic created by a series of shifts and displacements in social but especially religious practice. The secular-aesthetic of 1590s Ovidianism demonstrates how the pagan past permits in the present a new and specifically literary orientation towards religious discourse, ideology, and practice. This is what C. S. Lewis described as "an extension of religion, a rival of religion, and escape from religion" (quoted in Evans 1955: 11). The turn to classical literature, then, constituted neither an epistemological break with religion, nor even a kind of recreational departure from religious polemic, but rather bears unmistakably religious features. Erotic Ovidian English Renaissance poems do not demonstrate the survival of an earlier popular piety, whether pagan or Catholic, so much as its rearrangement and transmutation into new and ultimately secular forms.

The most notable if short-lived of these forms is the epyllion, the genre of the little epic, the erotic narrative poem, popular at the zenith of English Renaissance in the 1590s. Since Ovid's *Metamorphoses* is itself structured as a series of epyllia, it is perhaps not surprising that the epyllion as a genre stands out on the verse landscape of the English Renaissance as its most singularly Ovidian moment. As a genre, neither inherently tragic nor comic and with no English precedent, in the epyllion English poets crafted the perfect vehicle for the new Ovidianism that epitomizes the secular-aesthetic (see Bate 1993: 118–214). There is a blend of ironic distance, passionate engagement, sparkling wit, "delicate travesty," and sober reflection (Rand 1925: 46). These rhetorical strategies are modeled after the *Metamorphoses* itself: "Now it seems comedy, now elegy, now pastoral. Now it becomes a hymn, now tragedy" (ibid: 67–8). The acme of this Ovidian tone and style is to be found in the finest epyllia of the era, Shakespeare's *Venus and Adonis* and Marlowe's *Hero and Leander*, but while the latter takes its plot primarily from the Alexandrian Greek poet Museus, Shakespeare's poem is Ovidian in all of its dimensions. Totally unlike its predecessors because it is devoid of any moral purpose, this new, more aesthetic and pagan conception of Ovid represents a breach with orthodox allegorical Christian interpretation of classical authors (Keach 1977: 33; Bush 1957: 72). Although the epyllion as a genre did not survive the turn of the century, its resolute rejection of didacticism combined with the embrace of artifice, ornament, and frank eroticism, served to define as never before the contours of a dangerously secular and irreducibly (aesthetic) literary culture.

The first part of this essay seeks to establish exactly what kind of moral and aesthetic problem Ovid posed for the iconoclastic and more fastidious religious climate of post-Reformation English culture.[2] The second part shows, albeit by means of very selective examples rather than the comprehensive treatment my topic truly requires, how what seems utterly secular to us is wrought out of the discarded, appropriated, and reframed elements of earlier pagan and Catholic cultures.

I

In assessing how "the new paganism and the new secularism which accompanied the rediscovery of ancient works of literature and art" (Campbell 1959: vii) came about we would do well to begin with Ovid himself. It is not too far fetched to say that the culture of the English Renaissance began when he was born Publius Ovidius Naso in 45 BC. Ovid celebrated sex, married three times, and wrote the world's first, and surely the most eloquent, handbook on how to engage in sexual (especially adulterous) liaisons. Ovid's own society found him at least as troubling as post-Reformation England. The Emperor Augustus exiled Ovid from Rome in 8 BC to the desolate and cold region of Tomis where he died in AD 17 or 18. Ovid's "offense" was undoubtedly to write the *Ars Amatoria* (*The Art of Love*), and possibly, though less certainly, a romantic liaison with Julia, the emperor's granddaughter (believed in the Renaissance to be the emperor's daughter), an affair famously represented on the English stage in Ben Jonson's *Poetaster* (see Boas 1947: 2; Thibault 1964: 20–32). Ovid's verse narratives, whose protagonists not infrequently engage in bizarre acts of sexual perversion and turn into animals or trees and plants, were themselves metamorphosed into an often dour form of Christian didacticism. The urbane poet himself was turned into "a ruddy country gentleman with tremendous gusto, a sharp eye on the life around him, an ear for racy speech, and a gift for energetic doggerel" (Nims, quoted in Braden 1978: 2). Probably because the *Metamorphoses* posed an implicit challenge to Christian notions such as resurrection and redemption, translations of Ovid offer moralizing allegorical, didactic, and bizarre interpretations. Certainly, by the time of Golding's translation in the 1560s, his moralizing represents more than a culturally residual approach to Ovid, namely moral allegory such as that evident in the French *Ovide moralisé* or the Latin *Metamorphosis Ovidiana moraliter . . . explanata* (see Smith 1972: 67). Golding may be also adopting a pious persona in the face of Protestant factionalism, especially in its "hotter" or more Puritan elements:

> I would not wish the simple sort offended for too bee,
> When in this booke the heathen names of feynèd Godds they see.
> Which causèd them the name of Godds o[w]n creatures too bestowe.
> For nature beeing once corrupt and knowledge blynded quyght
> By *Adams* fall, those little seedes and sparkes of heavenly lyght
> That did as yit remayne in man, endevering foorth to burst
> And wanting grace and powre too growe too that they were at furst,
> Too superstition did decline: and drave the fearefull mynd,
> Strange woorshippes of the living God in creatures for too fynd.
> (Golding Preface 1–10)

Ovid was Golding's last printed translation of pagan imaginative literature (Braden 1978: 12),[3] and the fact that he translated seven works of Calvin, the first exactly

contemporary with Ovid, is something of a puzzle, even though it also explains
Golding's anxiety to offer Christian rationales and explanations of the mythological
original (ibid: 8). However, Gordon Braden suggests "it is more useful to take the
situation as a way of defining a certain historical moment, both in Golding's own life
and in the course of English culture . . . Certainly, ca. 1567 Elizabethan society
showed only early signs of its later [Protestant] cleavage, and one could hold together
honorably possibilities that in time would insist on a choice" (ibid: 9).

No one could accuse Golding of undue fidelity to the original, and his prefatorial
remarks smack of defensiveness, but not without cause. For while Protestantism was
indeed established in England as the state religion, its precise direction had not yet
been determined, made plain by the fact that the Thirty-Nine Articles of the Church
of England defining Anglicanism as the state religion did not become law until 1571,
six years after the English *Metamorphoses* was published. Nor was Golding at the end
of this line of moral allegorical interpretation, which continued on into the seventeenth century with George Sandys's translation in *Ovids Metamorphosis Englished,
Mythologiz'd, and Represented in Figures*, published in 1632.

Yet, for all that he might have troubled Christian sensibilities, Ovid was ubiquitous.[4] What Golding signally represents is that most Ovid in the English Renaissance
is so profoundly — there is no other word for it — un-Ovidian, so gutted of its voluptuous pagan and libidinal impulses and energies as to be alien to its origins. In this,
Golding resembles poets like Drayton, whose *England's Heroicall Epistles* (1597) were
taken from Ovid's *Heroides*, and Spenser, who was heavily indebted to Ovid for the
plots and themes of *The Faerie Queene*. Yet the determined ideological projects (Protestant nationalism) of both these poets disqualify them from truly Ovidian status. There
was, however, no doubt about the status of Shakespeare's verse as quintessentially
Ovidian. Francis Meres's catalog of English writers in *Palladis Tamia* (1598) famously
claimed "the sweet witty soul of Ovid lives in mellifluous and hony-tonged Shakespeare." Despite, then, the strenuous endeavors of Protestant translators of the *Metamorphoses* to make Ovid into a pre-Christian moralist, he remained in Latin a challenge
if not a threat to Christian mores. Unlike Virgil, famously translated by Henry
Howard, Earl of Surrey into English blank verse, which had the respectability of epic
poetry, in the right circumstances, Ovid, from the radical Protestant perspective at
least, could be dangerous. None of this is meant to imply that Ovid was unavailable
to medieval readers. In fact, the trajectory of English Renaissance Ovidianism runs
from Chaucer's debt to Ovid in *The Legend of Good Women* and Gower's *Confessio
Amantis*, both of which rework the Pyramus and Thisbe story in Book IV of the *Metamorphoses*. But perhaps because of the socially disruptive potential of his verse, even in
the wake of an exponential increase in English translations in the sixteenth century,
the *Ars Amatoria*, Ovid's cheekily avuncular advice on how to find sex in the city of
Rome, was not translated until the next century as Thomas Heywood's *Love's Schoole:
PVBLII OVIDII NASONIS DE ARTE AMANDI Or The Art of Love* (1625). Earlier
translations, however, may have survived into the Elizabethan era: William Caxton's
Ovyd, Hys Booke of Methamorphose (1483) and Wynkyn de Worde's *The flores of Ovide de*

arte amandi with theyr englysshe afore them (1513). However, the former may never have been printed, and the latter in all likelihood was no more than a schoolbook selection of aphorisms, or purple passages commonly referred to as "flowers," which probably had the erotic narrative juice emphatically pressed out of them (Donno 1963: 3; Boas 1947: 3).

Indeed, as "the consummate model of polished versification and rhetorical ornament" Ovid remained popular as a tool for the teaching of Latin style even though in the sixteenth century concern was expressed among those whose religious and moral sensibilities were offended by the content of the poems (Keach 1977: 24).[5] For example, Thomas Elyot believed a schoolboy should read Ovid for the Latin, but that the more scurrilous content should be expurgated:

> I would set next unto him two books of Ovid, the one called the *Metamorphoses*, which is as much to say as changing of men onto other figure or form, the other is entitled *De fastis*, where the ceremonies of the gentiles and specially the Romans be expressed — both right necessary for the understanding of other poets. But because there is little other learning in them concerning either virtuous manners or policy, I suppose it were better that, as fables and ceremonies happen to come in a lesson, it were declared abundantly by the master, than in the said two books a long time should be spent and almost lost, which might be better emplowyed on such authors that do minister both eloquence, civil policy and exhortation to virtue. (Elyot, *The Governor*, in Martindale 1985: 83)

Notably, the other work by Ovid that Elyot simultaneously recommends and warns against is the *Fasti*, the verse calendar of the religious feast days of the pagan year, which has an inherently and specifically religious theme. Other writers were more circumspect, like William Webb, who argued that the young should not be exposed to pagan writers like Ovid and Martial: "If they be prohibited from the tender and unconstant wits of children and young mindes, I thinke it is not without good reason" (quoted in Fraser 1970: 177). John Stockwood, who preached against reading erotic poems and "a great part of Ovid" at St. Paul's Cross on May 10, 1579, concurred with Webb:

> And albeeit I confes that there is in some teachers such a hatred of filthines, that they overpasse such most foule places in the authors: yet who is so ignorant, he knoweth not that the nature of man is to strive most untoo that which it is most fobidden: & that boyes are most desirous too understande that place which they shal perceive their master to have overslipped, herein resembling not unfitly the nature of swine, which delite rather too wallow in the stincking mire, the[n] to ly in the sweet & pleasant grass . . . [Let] *Tibullus, Catullus, Propertius, Gallus, Martialis*, a greate parte of *Ovid*, togethir with al other filthy Poets & comedies be sent again to Rome fro[m] whence they first came. (Baldwin 1944, I: 109–10)

Since learning Latin could be dangerous in itself, some Elizabethans boasted of their ignorance as a sign of Protestant piety. Such anti-intellectualism was upbraided by Thomas Nashe: "They contemne Arts as unprofitable, contenting themselves with a little Countrey Grammer knowledge, god wrote, thanking God with that abscendarie Priest in Lincolnshire, that he never knewe what Romish popish Latine meant" (McKerrow 1958: 25). Yet even the writing of educated advocates of the reformed religion points out the dangers of literacy and especially Latinity. For example, Thomas Salter claims that Rome's glory rested precisely on its exclusion of allegedly harmful intellectual influences:

> I should peradventure be suspected of some for such a one as did the same to the derogation, slander, and reproofe of learnyng, which thing I utterly denie, and yet I can alledge infinite examples to prove my proportion [proposition], as first, Roome the chiefe Citie and seate of the worldy empire, and victorious over all Nationes, I can approve and bryng in authoritie, that it hath been six hundred yeres and more without the knowledge of Letters, and also that from thence all Philosophers by publicke proclamations were exiled, as coruptors of good and vertuous life: Contrariwise, when the studie of Philosophie and Eloquence flourished therein, it loste libertie, and finallie fell to the servitude and obedience of one man. (Salter 1579: n.p.)

While Salter is anxious to avoid the charge that he advocates ignorance, he is also keen to point out that tyranny may be the inevitable consequence of literacy. Salter names Ovid in particular as a danger to the Christian maiden:

> But my intent is not, neither was it ever, to attribute suche evill as springeth from the mallice of wicked men, and their corupte nature, to the sacred studie of learnyng, to which I have given up my mynde so much as in me laye all my life tyme. But my purpose is to prove that in a vertuous Virgine, and modest Maiden, such use is more daungerous and hurtfull, then necessarie or praise woorthie . . . who can deny, that, seying of herself she is able to reade and understande the Christian Poetes, too wete, Prudentio, Prospero, Iuuenco, Pawlino, Nazianzeno, and such like, that she will not also reade the Lascivious bookes of Ovide. (Ibid)

Admittedly, Salter is anxious about all pagan verse, including Virgil and Homer, and especially so because of "the filthie love (if I maie terme it love) of the Goddes themselves, and of their wicked adulteries and abhominable fornications." Interestingly, there is some evidence (both fictional and actual) that Salter was correct in his assessment of women's reading habits. In Thomas Middleton's *A Mad World My Masters* (1608) a violently jealous husband, Harebrain, confiscates his wife's "wanton pamphlets" and tries, without much success, to substitute them with a Jesuit tract, *The First Book of the Christian Exercise Pertaining to Resolution*, which he thinks more the appropriate reading matter for women:

> *Harebrain.* I have conveyed away all her wanton pamphlets, as *Hero and Leander*, *Venus and Adonis*; oh, two luscious mary-bone pies for a young married wife. Here, there, prithee take the *Resolution* and read to her a little.

Courtesan. She's set up her resolution already, sir.

Harebrain. True, true, and this will confirm it the more. There's a chapter of hell, 'tis good to read this cold weather. Terrify her, terrify her; go, read to her the horrible punishments for itching wantonness . . . (1.2.44–52)

Harebrain's recommendation of Catholic literature implies that it is not just Protestant piety that is an enemy to the Ovidianism which is thought to tickle the ears of women in early modern London. On the other hand, in 1619, Lady Anne Clifford records that her cousin is reading Parsons's *Resolutions by Religion* (1603) *and* Ovid's *Metamorphoses* (Williamson 1922: 139; see Collins 1940: 151–4), which suggests that these works are not seen by every reader as mutually exclusive. For all that, characters on stage who rail against Marlowe and Shakespeare's epyllia were no doubt parodies of real life figures, like Philip Stubbes who railed against "prophane Scheduls, sacriligious Libels and Hethnicall pamplets of toyes and bableries, (the Authors whereof may challenge no small reward at the hands of the devil for inventing the same) to corrupt mens mindes, pervert good wits, allure to Bawdry, induce to whoredome, suppresse vertue and erect vice" (Stubbes 1583: 139–40). While the diatribes against pagan poetry seem comic to us, as they clearly did to Middleton, it is important not to underestimate either their frequency or intensity and to understand the uneasy coexistence (Anne Clifford's cousin not withstanding) of classical paganism with Christianity.

The "war against poetry" did not, of course, originate with the English Renaissance. Plato famously exiles poets from the Republic, Augustus banished Ovid, and though he was executed in 1498, the Florentine ascetic Savonarola was a vital precursor of Reformation antipathy to art:

There is a false race of pretended poets, who can do naught but run after the Greeks and Romans, repeating their ideas, copying their style and their metre; and even invoking the same deities, almost as though we were not men as much as they, with reason and religion of our own. Now this is not only false poetry, but likewise a most hateful snare to our youth. (Quoted in Campbell 1959: 11)

Savonarola, like many later English detractors of poetry, feared that it corrupted the young (and indeed the primary audience for erotic epyllia seems to have been young men) and was especially wary of its effects among schoolboys. His concerns are not dissimilar to those of Stephen Gosson in *The Schoole of Abuse* (1579), who sets out to chart the course of "amarous [*sic*] Poets" whose "whole practice"

eyther with fables to shew theyr abuses, or with plaine tearmes to unfold theyr mischiefe, discover theyr shame, discredit themselves, and disperse their poyson through all the worlde. *Virgill* sweates in describing his Gnat: *Ovid* bestireth him to paintout his flea: the one shewes his art in the lust of *Dido*, the other his cunning in the inceste of *Myrrha*, and that trumpet of Baudrie, the Craft of love.

> I must confesse that Poets are the whetstones of wit, not withstanding that wit is
> dearly bought: where hony and gall are mixed, it will be hard to sever the one from the
> other. (Gosson 1598: 2)

For Gosson, pagan poetry is poison "which draws the mind from virtue, and con-
foundeth wit" (p. 4). Of Ovid's works Gosson singles out the *Ars Amatoria* and Book
X of the *Metamorphoses*, Shakespeare's source for *Venus and Adonis*, specifically the story
of Adonis' mother Myrrah, who gave birth to him after copulating with her own
father. "Many good sentences are spoken . . . and written by Poets, as ornamentes to
beautifye their woorkes, and sette theyr trumperie too sale without suspect" (Gosson
1598: 2–3). On these grounds, he commends Augustus' wisdom in banishing Ovid
from Rome (p. 5).

While these diatribes are all too familiar, there is a new emphasis in Shakespeare's
time on the inutility of verse over and above its lubricity (see Fraser 1970: 4). "Honest
plain matter" is far superior to "Poeticall additions or faigned Allegories" according
to George Wither, whose own didactic doggerel cannot be accused of being obscured
by rhetorical tropes (Fraser 1970: 17). There is an urge toward *nuda veritas*, the naked,
unadorned truth, and a belief that such a commodity exists and is only willfully evaded
or obscured by figurative representation (see Fraser 1970: 180). Poetry, the moralizers claim, obfuscates divine and scriptural truth by means of visual images which
diametrically opposed the post-Reformation iconoclastic impulse. As Ben Jonson put
it, poetry has "correspondence to no uses & purpose" (ibid: 9). For Gosson, this was
not always so, and he is nostalgic for a time when poetry had a wholesome social
function:

> The right use of auncient Poetrie was too have the notable explytes of woorthy
> Captaines, the holesome councels of good fathers, and vertuous lives of predecessors set
> down in numbers, and song to the Instrument at solemne feastes, that the sound of one
> might draw the hearers from kissing the cupp too often, the sense of the other put them
> in minde of things past, and chaulk out the way to do the like . . .
>   To this end are instruments used in battaile, not to tickle the eare, but too teach
> every souldier when to strike and when to strap, when to flye, and when to follow.
> (Gosson 1598: 7)

Poetry, then, should have a specific use, of the order of battle music, and its aesthetic
aspects, its capacity to arouse the senses, and even to titillate, "tickle the eare," are to
be completely subordinate to such uses. Only the purposeful, moral, and ameliorative
effects of poetry are legitimate, according to Gosson. He gives us, however, a glimpse
into why the frivolous world of epyllia as a diminutive (diminished) and feminine
form of epic presents such a threat to the masculine grandeur of epic, and the sweep
of monumental, Protestant history.

It was precisely this concern with teaching English history that led the Privy
Council to issue an order to the queen's ecclesiastical commissioners against the teaching of Ovid on April 21, 1582:

A letter to the Commissyoners for Causes Ecclesiasticall in London that whereas there
hathe bene of late a booke written in Latyn verse by one Christofer Ockland, intituled
Anglororum prelia, . . . forasmuche as his travell therein with the qualitie of the verse
hathe receyved good comendacion, and that the subjecte or matter of the said booke as
his is worthie to be read of all men, and especially in the common schooles, where divers
heathen poetes are ordinarily read and taught, from the which the youthe of the Realme
receyve rather infectyon in manners and educatyon then advauncement in vertue, in
place of which poetes their Lordships thincke fitte this booke were read and taught in
grammer schooles . . . for the benefitte of the youthe and the removing of such lascivy-
ous poetes as are commonly read and taught in the said grammer schooles, requiring
them uppon the receipt hereof to write their letters unto all the Busshoppes through
the Realme to geve commaundement that in all the gramer and free schooles within
their severall Dyoces the said bookes *de Anglorum proeliis* and peaceable government
of her Majestie maye be, in place is some of the heathen poetes nowe read among
them, as Ovide *de arte amandi*, *de tristibus*, or suche lyke . . . (Baldwin 1944, I: 112;
Wilkinson 1955: 429)

Crucially, the attacks on poetry are not marginal to Protestant epistemology, but
are rather key to its dynamic.[6] While it is impossible to explain such changes as causal
effects of other cultural shifts, it remains the case, nonetheless, that the period's apprehension of pagan aesthetics in general and Ovid in particular, is inextricably related
to the engine of religious transformation ignited by Henry VIII's break from Rome.[7]

Lamenting "the multitude of bookes, full of all synne and abominations" that "have
nowe fulled the world," Edward Dering wishes "O that there were among us some
zealous Ephesians, that bookes of so great vanity might be burned up" (Dering 1572:
A iv). Similarly, one "F. S." complains that "filthy and unchast Pamphlets, (whereof
the World is too full) are fitter to be burned as corrupters of youth" (quoted in Fraser
1970: 178). In this climate of opinion the time was right for an English version of
Savonarola's Bonfire of the Vanities, which in 1497 incinerated volumes of Latin and
Italian poets and valuable printed parchments and illuminated manuscripts. Only a
year after Meres had made what is, at least from the literary point of view, the laudatory comparison between Shakespeare and Ovid, Christopher Marlowe's translation
of Ovid's *Amores* was consigned to the flames on episcopal order on June 4, 1599 at
the Stationers' Hall along with a number of other "prophane . . . sacriligious . . . and
Heathenicall" works, precisely along the order of those that Stubbes had complained
of over ten years before.[8]

II

I have been arguing that in early modern England there was a culture of change,
and that it was one in which, in the midst of religious turmoil, the category of the
secular-aesthetic, that is, a fully urban and urbane poetry with a significant degree
of autonomy from court and church, was coming into being. However, I also want to

put pressure on what exactly secularization means in the specific historical context of post-Reformation England. For "secular" verse was not beyond the boundaries of religious polemic, but as we have seen, very much embroiled within the religious conflicts of the period. In this context the process of secularization involves often pragmatic displacement and continuity of old ideas rather than their complete reversal or erasure.

Paradoxically, from Douglas Bush onwards, criticism has demonstrated a tendency to regard epyllia, no matter how technically accomplished, as "void verses, empty rhymes." That is, it has viewed these poems from exactly the standpoint of Protestant aesthetics, a trend that has only recently been modified by an interest in the Ovidianism from the perspective of gender studies and a serious interest in "erotic gallimaufries" (Brown 1998; Stanivukovic 2001; Enterline 2000). Clark Hulse offers the following description of epyllia: "By and large the poems of the minor epic genre have no great ethical import and little redeeming social value. They are by turns artificial, frivolous, arcane" (Hulse 1981: 3). Another critic claims nothing can "deepen the significance of the poem, which appeals only to the sense" (Wilkinson, in Kolin 1997: 419). Critics have too often accepted the moralistic view of the poetry expounded in the period by its detractors, or at best have claimed, erroneously in my view, that the poems are courtly and Italianate (Bush 1997: 97), on which grounds much fault has been found with the homely rural and allegedly unsophisticated aspects of Shakespeare's poem. "Shakespeare still had some heavy provincial Warwickshire loam sticking to his boots" as M. C. Bradbrook says of *Venus and Adonis* (Bradbrook 1951: 62). Indeed, the poem is *not* courtly. Rather, it is part of a secular amorous literature located not in the court with its reverence for Petrarchan rhetoric (evident, for example, in writers such as Sir Philip Sidney), but among the wits and poets of urban London, many of whom hailed from the provinces.[9]

The epyllion as a form and the 1590s as a decade see a shift, albeit one which was to prove temporary, from rendition of myth as didactic allegory with "a moral thereunto," as Thomas Howell had put it in his version of the Narcissus story, to poetry which embraced Ovidianism with unapologetic enthusiasm. Yet this embrace often entailed a profound exploration of images that reveled in ornament and decoration for their own sakes, but without first denuding them of meanings Protestant iconoclasm was so anxious to erase. In *Hero and Leander*, for instance, Marlowe expands into thirty lines one epithet in his primary source, Musaeus' description of the temple of Venus. The rich description is indebted to Ovid's palace of the Sun at the beginning of *Metamorphoses* Book II: "*Regia Solis erat sublimibus alta columnis / clara micante auro flammasque imitante pyropo*": "The Princely Pallace of the Sunne stood gorgeous to beholde / On stately Pillars builded high of yellow burnisht golde" (II.1–2) (Wilkinson 1955: 409). But it is also invariably reminiscent of pre-Reformation Catholic ornament:

> The wals were of discolored Jasper stone,
> Wherein was Proteus carved, and o'rehead,
> A livelie vine of greene sea agget spread;
> Where by one hand, light headed Bacchus hoong,

And with the other, wine from grapes out wroong.
Of Christall shining faire, the pavement was,
The towne of Sestos, cal'd it Venus glasse,
Where you might see the gods in sundrie shapes,
Committing headdie ryots, incest, rapes.
Hero and Leander (131–44)

This constitutes exactly the type of "excess" in decoration which Golding had taken pains to moderate in his translation of Ovidian temples into "churches" (Lyne 2001: 65–6). Marlowe's are, of course, distinctly pagan images but the materials out of which they are crafted resemble all too closely the materials in which allegedly idolatrous ornaments were wrought. Precisely such objects were condemned by John Jewell in *The Second Tome of Homilies* (1563): "The glorious gylte images and ydolles, all shynynge and glyttering with metall and stone, and covered with precious vestures" (sigs. Dd4). This is not to suggest that epyllia are allegories of Reformation thinking, merely that they appropriate its materials. The last line quoted above is a more poetic and subtly parodic version of Stephen Gosson's assertion that "Apollo was a buggerer, and Schoolemaister of perjurie; Mars a murderer, Mercury a theefe." One might as well, Gosson claimed, "dwell in the earth, for heaven is full of whores" (quoted in Fraser 1970: 73).

Marlowe, as a professed atheist who demonstrates a neo-pagan reading of Ovid, shares with the ancient poet a sophisticated distance from belief, since, as modern commentators concur, Ovid did not "believe in" at least in any literal, or perhaps more accurately "culturally Christian" way, the existence of the gods and goddesses whose exploits he describes (Keach 1977: 5; Segal 1969: 372–80; Frankel 1945: 17–18). Nor is it clear, however, that most early moderns necessarily "believed in" Christianity much more deeply than Marlowe. (I must point out that "belief in" is a hopelessly inadequate and ahistorical abbreviation for the relations that variously obtain between subjectivity and spirituality and doctrines and institutions.) As Norman Jones points out:

> For men and women living through the Reformation, the question was more often "What do I do now?" than "What do I believe now?" They were not consulted about their theological opinions by the people who imposed Reformation upon them, but they had to adapt to the changes in order to continue the business of living. English people did not have the option of ignoring the Reformation. It touched them in too many different ways. (Jones 2002: 2)

That is, as one of the necessary consequences of the Reformation, religion came to be for the majority of people as much or more a matter of practice than belief. This served to build in precisely the kind of ironic distance that Ovid had from the images of the deities he produced, or at the very least, the opportunity to try on that perspective in relation to pagan deities.

While the analogy between pagan and popish religion is a relatively straightforward one, there is a deeper level engaged by the way the epyllion plays with images and surfaces. Epyllia are indeed, then, "artificial, frivolous, arcane," but this does not amount to superficiality or lack of intellectual depth. Rather, these purely literary, ornamental qualities comport with the hieratic view of poetry available from the encounter with an Ovid freed from the necessity of reconciliation with Christian values. Writing in 1589, Thomas Nashe, for example, condemns the intellectual energy that has been wasted in reading Ovid as moral allegory by "Gentlemen well studied in Philosophie" who "trotted over all the Meteors bredde in the highest Region of the ayre" to reconcile 1 Corinthians 3 with "Ovids fiction of Phaetons firing of the world" (Donno 1970: 5). Instead, Nashe argues for the following:

> I account Poetrie, as of a more hidden & divine kind of Philosophy, enwrapped in blinde Fables and darke stories, wherein the principles of more excellent Arts and morrall precepts of manners . . . [and that] the fables of Poets must of necessitie be fraught with wisedome and knowledge. (McKerrow 1958, I: 25–6)

Similarly, it is this quasi-mystical view of poetry that Marlowe espouses in his acknowledgment of his precursor: "Amorous Leander, beautifull and yoong, / (Whose tragedie divine Musaeus soong)." Musaeus sang the *tragedy* of the two lovers; but as Nashe points out in *Lenten Stuffe* (1599), it was "a diviner Muse than he, Kit Marlow who sang their *comedy*." This connection with mystery and the divine is neither merely the result of the erroneous Renaissance belief that the fifth-century Alexandrian poet Musaeus was the student of Orpheus, nor the accidental rhetoric of panegyric. There was, after all, classical precedent for the absorption of popular religious rites into the realm of the aesthetic, namely the Eleusian mysteries, which entailed among other things a spiritual cult of the senses. These were rites of popular initiation, which purged participants from fear of death and admitted them to the company of the blessed. They were bound forever after by a vow of silence, which, given that we know little of these ceremonies, must have been quite effective (Wind 1958: 1). However, as Edgar Wind has explained: "since the sacred rites were administered to a multitude without regard to individual merit, philosophers [were] inclined to look upon them with a certain disdain" (ibid). Eventually, as a result, the *mystères cultuels* were replaced by "a figurative use of the terms and images which were borrowed from the popular rites but transferred to the intellectual disciplines of philosophical debate and meditation" (p. 3).

Conventional wisdom has it, then, that the epyllion is troubling *because* it is light and frivolous, insignificant. Nashe's interpretation of the value of poetry certainly suggests that there are potentially other "hidden & divine," though crucially *not allegorical*, meanings within the apparent superficiality of verse. These "hidden and divine" meanings are what Leonard Barkan has termed the mystical aspects of the metamorphosis, "the mystery of the divine embedded in the real" (Barkan 1986: 18). While the image of metamorphosis is freighted with the magical, the mysterious, and the divine, it is simultaneously unmoored from any programmatic moral content by "the sustained complex simultaneity of irony, humor, verbal wit, grotesqueness, and erotic pathos" of Ovidian verse (Keach 1977: 24; see Barkan 1986: 17).

It is in its comic pathos in particular that English poetry becomes most definitively Ovidian. William Keach has observed that erotic pathos "provides a better standard for judging the extent of genuine Ovidianism in Elizabethan epyllia than does the presence of irony, comedy, and verbal wit" (Keach 1977: 24). All Elizabethan epyllia – not just *Hero and Leander* and *Venus and Adonis* – contain reflections of the humorous, ironic, satirical, aspects of Ovid's poetry. But "what really sets [Marlowe and Shakespeare's] epyllia apart is the level of erotic pathos" (Keach 1977: 24). It is in this that these poems absorb earlier religious and iconographic impulses in the making of a new secular-aesthetic via an erotic pathos that depends upon the inversion of typical gender roles, and especially an emphasis on female power. While this phenomenon deserves a much fuller treatment than I have space to give it here, I want to examine some of its operations in the representation of Venus at the ending of *Venus and Adonis*.

The poem emphasizes female power especially in the form of sexual initiative. These are aspects of pagan goddess cults and Marian piety, both already revitalized in occluded form in the figure of Elizabeth I. Yet for most of the poem Venus manifests as a figure of comic femininity: Venus *vulgaris*, Venus *genetrix* – the reproductive and quasi-maternal wooer who urges Adonis to the joys of reproduction. Fearing Adonis dead, she is like a "milch doe whose swelling dugs do ache" (ll. 875–6), sympathetic and maternal yet still carnal and animal. Such images bridge the chasm between Venus in her dolor and the more obviously comic aspects of her characterization.

On the death of Adonis, of course, Venus becomes wholly maternal, and Shakespeare offers a powerful meditation on the image of the sorrowing, lachrymose Venus; the moment when Venus becomes the *Mater Dolorosa* whose epitome and prototype were to be found in the sorrowing Mother of Christ.

> Here overcome, as one full of despair,
> She vail'd her eyelids, who like sluices stopp'd
> The crystal tide that from her two cheeks fair
> In the sweet channel of her bososm dropp'd;
> But through the flood-gates breaks the silver rain,
> And with his strong course opens them again.

> O how her eyes and tears did lend and borrow!
> Her eye seen in the tears, tears in her eye:
> Both crystals where they view'd each other's sorrow,
> Sorrow that friendly sighs sought still to dry;
> But like a stormy day, now wind, now rain,
> Sighs dry her cheeks, tears make them wet again. (955–66)

> Whereat her tears begin to turn their tide,
> Being prison'd in her eye like pearls in glass;

> Yet sometimes falls an orient drop beside,
> Which her cheek melts, as scorning it should pass
>   To wash the fould face of the sluttish ground,
>   Who is but drunken when she seemed drown'd. (979–84)

The three stanzas devoted to her tears alone would invariably have evoked for a Renaissance audience the image of Our Lady of Pity. This was an image that before the destruction of icons in the Reformation was contained in every parish church, and even long afterwards it may have remained well-nigh ubiquitous in many parts of the country. As late as 1644, William Dowsing records destroying pictures and statues, including many images of the Virgin Mary, in St. Peter's Church in Sudbury, Suffolk: "We brake down . . . about an hundred in all . . . and diverse Angels" (Watt 1991: 173). Continental images of the mourning Virgin Mary, most famously Michelangelo's *Pietà*, still survive, but so do a number of English images, such as that at Long Melford in Suffolk.

> A fair image of our Blessed Lady having the afflicted body of her dear Son, as he was taken down off the Cross lying along on her lap, the tears as it were running pitifully upon her beautiful cheeks, as it seemed bedewing the said sweet body of her Son, and therefore named the Image of Our Lady of Pity. (Quoted in Duffy 1992: 260)

This is an immensely powerful image in which the Blessed Mother cradles the body of her dead, adult son.

Many English people would remember, or have transmitted to them via the oral tradition, some version of the sorrows of Mary, such as those contained in the pre-Tridentine Sarum missal, *Missa Compassionis sive Lamentationis beatae Mariae Virginis*:

> *Quis est homo qui non fleret*
>   *Matrem Christi si videret*
>   *In tanto supplico?*

> [Who is there who would not weep, were he to see the Mother of
> Christ, in so great anguish?]

As Eamon Duffy observes, "That question was dramatized in the vernacular in a thousand forms":

> I said I could not wepe I was so harde hartid:
> Shee answered me with wordys shortly that smarted,
> "Lo! Nature shall move thee though muse be converted,
> Thyne owne fadder thys nyght is deed!" – lo thus she
>   thwarted –
>   "So my son is bobbid
>   & of his lif is robbid."
>   forsooth than I sobbid,
>   veryifying the words she seid to me
>   who cannot weep may lern at mee. (Duffy 1992: 260)

The feast of Our Lady of Pity, or Our Lady of Sorrows, was celebrated on September 15, commemorating the thirteenth Station of the Cross in which the Body of Christ is taken down from the cross. Commemoration of this image was widespread. After the terrible losses sustained in Shrewsbury in 1403, when Hotspur and his Cheshire troops were defeated by Henry IV, for example, Sir Roger Hussey had a chantry chapel built depicting the Blessed Virgin in mourning.

What would have made this image even more memorable is the *Stabat Mater dolorosa* (literally, the standing sorrowful mother), one of the greatest Latin hymns, based upon the prophecy of Simeon that a sword would pierce the heart of Christ's mother, Mary (Luke 2: 35). The hymn originated in the thirteenth century during the peak of Franciscan devotion to the crucified Christ and is attributed to Jacopone da Todi (1230–1306):

> At the cross her station keeping, stood the
> mournful mother weeping, close to Jesus to the last.
>
> Stabat Mater dolorosa iuxta crucem lacrimosa dum pendebat Filius
> Cuius animam gementem contristatem et dolentem pertransivit gladius.

In terms of the structure of Shakespeare's epyllion, it is interesting to note that there is a mirror image to this hymn, *Stabat Mater speciosa*, which echoes the joy of the Blessed Virgin Mary at the birth of Jesus. There were also images of the Virgin of Humility suckling the child Jesus that resonate with Shakespeare's Venus as anguished milk doe.

I am not suggesting that in emphasizing its pre-Reformation resonances we recapture *Venus and Adonis* in precisely the kind of Christian moral allegory applied to Ovid that Shakespeare managed to escape. Rather, my point is that the Christian components of these images become detached and separated from morality with the advent of the secular-aesthetic. To Christianize pagan images is to freight them with a moral message they simply do not have and to excise the amorality of which they are unquestionably possessed. For example, the thirteenth-century poet Chrétien Legouais offers a theological allegory of the story of Apollo and Daphne in which Daphne becomes the Virgin Mary and Apollo the love of God. So when Apollo crowns himself with the laurel into which he has transformed the fleeing Daphne, God is, according to Legouais, symbolically enacting the birth from the woman he had made his mother (Rand 1925: 135–6). Further, Venus' sorrow also remains pagan, partly resembling the disturbing and grotesque anthropomorphism of Io, who is transformed into a heifer in the *Metamorphoses*. Io's is in fact not a complete metamorphosis but the coexistence of two conflicting human and animal identities (see Keach 1977: 9):

> et conata quieri mugitus edidit ore
> pertimuitque sonos propriaque exterrita voce est.
> venit et ad ripas, ubi ludere saepe solebat,
> Inachidas: rictus novaque ut conspexit in unda
> Cornua, pertimuit seque exsternata refugit. (I: 637–41)

and when she did assay
To make complaint, she lowed out, which did her so affray,
That oft she started at the noyse, and would have runne away.
Unto hir father Inachs bankes she also did resorte,
Where many a tyme and oft before she had been want to sporte.
Now when she looked in the streame and sawe hir horned hed,
She was agast and from hir selfe would all in haste have fled. (Golding 1565,
I: 789–95)

The horned head here connotes not only bestial transformation, but also the virgin goddess Diana crowned by the crescent moon, in other words the vulnerable power of self-contained female sexuality. The sorrowing Venus does not represent simply a secularization of literature, but rather a poetic reengagement with the nature of the sacred that belongs to the realm of the aesthetic.

George Sandys's *Ovids Metamorphosis Englished* was probably as moralizing as Golding's had been nearly ninety years earlier (see Rubin 1995: 1–18). The unparalleled literary moment of the secular-aesthetic had passed, at least for now. By the seventeenth century there was a new skepticism about myth which developed into satire. As Keach observes: "In the late 1590s the Elizabethan delight in languid eroticism and extravagant artificiality gave way to an increasingly satirical and parodic approach to Ovidian fable – John Marston's *The Metamorphosis of Pigmalions Image* (1598) and Francis Beaumont's *Salmacus and Hermaphroditus* (1602) are indicators of the new direction in which Ovidian poetry was tending" (Keach 1977: 119). There developed also, inspired by the new piety, a travesty of mythology itself (Wilkinson 1955: 406).

Whatever the intellectual probing of the schism of Reformation, it is clear that the imaginative reach of the period's poetry came from its engagement with the classics and particularly with Ovid. The encounter with Ovid was also the encounter with a particular genre of creative imagination, an encounter with myth. While at least in its fantasy of perfected religion Protestantism was all but denuded of ornament, icon, and imagery, Shakespeare's Ovidianism contained a Catholic aesthetic, if you will, with its Christian elements extracted. In this light, *Venus and Adonis* is a profane poem. For us that means blasphemous and ungodly, but in the Renaissance the profane was closer to its Latin meaning, *profanus*, impious, unconsecrated, quotidian – precisely the realm of the secular-aesthetic.

NOTES

1   On the complexities of post-Reformation religious practice and culture, see Duffy (1992), Collinson (1982), Lake (1999), Haigh (1996), Jones (2002), and Cressy (1989), which together pretty much cover the spectrum of historians' opinions on this topic.

2   Russell Fraser (1970) remarks: "The iconoclastic and more fastidious religion which rises with the Renaissance and which is not, on my reading, exclusively Protestant, does not prepare the way for a new social order, but is another exemplification of the same spirit which brings this order to birth" (p. 177).

3 For an important recent collection on Ovid in England, see Taylor (2000: esp. 1–10, 15–30).
4 The widespread fascination with Ovid included Thomas Howell's *The Fable of Ovid tretting of Narcissus, translated out of Latin into English meter, with a moral thereunto, very pleasaunte to rede* (1560), Thomas Peend's *The Pleasant fable of Hermaphroditus and Salmacis* from Book IV of the *Metamorphoses* (1565), William Hubbard's *The Tragicall and lamentable historie of Ceyx, Kynge of Trachine and Alcoine his wife* (1569) (Book XI), and Thomas Underdown's *Invective against Ibis* (1569). See Boas (1947: 4).
5 For a fully theorized and compelling account of the relation between Ovid and rhetoric, see Enterline (2000).
6 On attacks on poetry, see Donno (1970: 82–98) and Fraser (1970).
7 On the connection between religious change and lyric poetry, see Targoff (2001: 6, 57).
8 Arber (1875: 677). See also Moulton (1998: 77–90), Boose (1994: 185–200). The latter essay refutes earlier notions that the burnings of 1599 were essentially an attempt to curb satire. It is important, too, that though this 1599 incineration is broadly analogous to Savonarola's bonfire, the English burning was not a public event.
9 The period's utilization of Ovid is not then primarily an issue of the role of Ovidian myth as a plot or motif in Elizabethan poetry, or even of Ovid as an acceptable cover for explicit eroticism. Boika Sokolova (2000) makes the case that the vogue for erotic writing began with Aretino in early sixteenth-century Italian literature (pp. 392–401). In contrast, William Keach argues: "The alternative to an orthodox 'Elizabethan Ovid,' an Ovid made safe for the Christian reader, is not necessarily a frivolous, indulgently decorative, decadently 'Italianate Ovid'" (Keach 1977: 35).

REFERENCES AND FURTHER READING

Arber, E. (ed.) (1875). *A Transcript of the Registers of the Company of Stationers of London, 1554–1640*, vol. 3. London.

Baldwin, T. W. (1944). *William Shakespere's Small Latine & Lesse Greeke*, 2 vols. Urbana: University of Illinois Press.

Barkan, L. (1986). *The Gods Made Flesh: Metamorphosis and the Pursuit of Paganism*. New Haven, CT: Yale University Press.

Bate, J. (1993). *Shakespeare and Ovid*. Oxford: Clarendon Press.

Beaumont, F. (1602). *Salmacus and Hermaphroditus*. London.

Boas, F. S. (1947). *Ovid and the Elizabethans*. London: English Association.

Boose, L. (1994). The 1599 Bishop's Ban, Elizabethan Pornography, and the Sexualization of the Jacobean Stage. In R. Burt and J. Archer (eds.) *Enclosure Acts: Sexuality, Property, and Culture in Early Modern England*. Ithaca, NY: Cornell University Press.

Bradbrook, M. C. (1951). *Shakespeare and the Elizabethan Poets*. Cambridge: Cambridge University Press.

Braden, G. (1978). *The Classics and English Renaissance Poetry*. New Haven, CT: Yale University Press.

Brown, G. (1998). Breaking the Canon: Marlowe's Challenge to the Literary Status Quo in *Hero and Leander*. In P. W. White (ed.) *Marlowe, History, and Sexuality: New Critical Essays on Christopher Marlowe*. New York: AMS Press.

Bush, D. (1957). *Mythology and the Renaissance Tradition in English Poetry*. New York: Pageant.

——(1997). Venus and Adonis and Mythology. In P. C. Kolin (ed.) *Venus and Adonis: Critical Essays*. New York: Garland.

Campbell, L. B. (1959). *Divine Poetry and Drama in Sixteenth-Century England*. Cambridge: Cambridge University Press.

Collins, J. B. (1940). *Christian Mysticism in the Elizabethan Age*. Baltimore, MD: Johns Hopkins University Press.

Collinson, P. (1982). *The Religion of Protestants: The Church in English Society, 1559–1625*. Oxford: Clarendon Press.

Cressy, D. (1989). *Bonfires and Bells: National Memory and the Protestant Calendar in Elizabethan and Stuart England*. Berkeley: University of California Press.

Dering, E. (1572). *A Brief and Necessary Instruction*. London.

Donno, E. S. (1963). *Elizabethan Minor Epics*. New York: Columbia University Press.

——(1970). The Epyllion. In C. Ricks (ed.) *English Poetry and Prose 1540–1674*. London: Barrie and Jenkins.

Drayton, M. (1597). *England's Heroicall Epistles*. London.

Duffy, E. (1992). *The Stripping of the Altars: Traditional Religion in England 1400–1580*. New Haven, CT: Yale University Press.

Enterline, L. (2000). *The Rhetoric of the Body from Ovid to Shakespeare*. Cambridge: Cambridge University Press.

Evans, M. (1955). *English Poetry in the Sixteenth Century*. London: Hutchinson University Library.

Frankel, H. (1945). *Ovid: A Poet Between Worlds*. Berkeley: University of California Press.

Fraser, R. (1970). *The War Against Poetry*. Princeton, NJ: Princeton University Press.

Golding, A. (1565). *The XV Books of P. Ovidius Naso, entytled Metamorphosis*. London.

Gosson, S. (1598). *The Schoole of Abuse*. London.

Haigh, C. (ed.) (1996). *The English Reformation Revised*. Cambridge: Cambridge University Press.

Hulse, C. (1981). *Metamorphic Verse: The Elizabethan Minor Epic*. Princeton, NJ: Princeton University Press.

Jewell, J. (1563). *The Second Tome of Homilies*. London.

Jones, N. (2002). *The English Reformation: Religion and Cultural Adaptation*. Oxford: Blackwell.

Keach, W. (1977). *Elizabethan Erotic Narratives*. New Brunswick, NJ: Rutgers University Press.

Kolin, P. C. (ed.) (1997). *Venus and Adonis: Critical Essays*. New York: Garland.

Lake, P. (1999). Religious Identities in Shakespeare's England. In D. S. Kastan (ed.) *A Companion to Shakespeare*. Oxford: Blackwell.

Lyne, R. (2001) [1567–1632]. *Ovid's Changing Worlds: Metamorphoses*. Oxford: Oxford University Press.

McKerrow, R. B. (ed.) (1958). *The Works of Thomas Nashe*, 5 vols. Oxford: Blackwell.

Marston, J. (1598). *The Metamorphosis of Pigmalions Image*. London.

Martindale J. (ed.) (1985). *English Humanism, Wyatt to Cowley*. Dover, NH: Croom Helm.

Meres, F. (1598). *Palladis Tamia*. London.

Middleton, T. (1608). *A Mad World My Masters*. London.

Moulton, I. F. (1998). "Printed Abroad and Uncastrated": Marlowe's *Elegies* with Davies' *Epigrams*. In P. F. White (ed.) *Marlowe, History, and Sexuality: New Critical Essays on Christopher Marlowe*. New York: AMS Press.

Rand, E. K. (1925). *Ovid and His Influence*. Boston, MA: Marshall Jones.

Ricks, C. (ed.) (1970). *English Poetry and Prose 1540–1674*. London: Barrie and Jenkins.

Rubin, D. (1995). *Ovid's Metamorphoses Englished: George Sandys as Translator and Mythographer*. New York: Garland.

Salter, T. (1579). *The Mirrhor of Modestie*. London.

Segal, C. (1969). *Landscape in Ovid's Metamorphoses: A Study in the Transformation of a Literary Symbol*. Wiesbaden: Hermes.

Smith, H. (1972) [1952]. *Elizabethan Poetry: A Study in Conventions, Meaning, and Expression*. Cambridge: Cambridge University Press; reprinted Cambridge, MA: Harvard University Press.

Sokolova, B. (2000). Erotic Poems. In M. Hattaway (ed.) *A Companion to English Renaissance Literature and Culture*. Oxford: Blackwell.

Spenser, E. (1590). *The Faerie Queene*. London.

Stanivukovic, G. (ed.) (2001). *Ovid and the Renaissance Body*. Toronto: University of Toronto Press.

Stubbes, P. (1583). *The Anatomie of Abuses*. London.

Targoff, R. (2001). *Common Prayer: The Language of Public Devotion in Early Modern England*. Chicago, IL: University of Chicago Press.

Taylor, A. B. (ed.) (2000). *Shakespeare's Ovid: The Metamorphoses in the Plays and Poems*. Cambridge: Cambridge University Press.

Thibault, J. C. (1964). *The Mystery of Ovid's Exile*. Berkeley: University of California Press.

Watt, T. (1991). *Cheap Print and Popular Piety 1550–1640*. Cambridge: Cambridge University Press.

Wilkinson, L. P. (1955). *Ovid Recalled*. Cambridge: Cambridge University Press.

Williamson, G. C. (1922). *Lady Anne Clifford Countess of Dorset, Pembroke & Montgomery 1590–1676: Her Life, Letters and Work*. Kendal: Titus Wilson and Son.

Wind, E. (1958). *Pagan Mysteries in the Renaissance*. London: Faber and Faber.

3
Shakespeare's Problem Plays and the Drama of His Time: *Troilus and Cressida*, *All's Well That Ends Well*, *Measure for Measure*
Paul Yachnin

The category of "the problem plays" derives from F. S. Boas's 1896 study, *Shakspere and his Predecessors*, which characterized *Troilus and Cressida*, *All's Well That Ends Well*, *Measure for Measure*, as well as *Hamlet*, as "dramas so singular in theme and temper [that they] cannot be strictly called comedies or tragedies" (p. 345). Boas borrowed "a convenient phrase from the theatre of today [i.e., the late nineteenth-century Ibsenist drama] and class[ed] them together as Shakspere's problem-plays' (ibid). "All these dramas," he said, "introduce us into highly artificial societies, whose civilization is ripe unto rottenness" (ibid). His sense of the shape of Shakespeare's career was indebted to Victorian biographical criticism, which imagined an embittered and despondent turn-of-the-century Shakespeare, and for that reason much about his argument has been rightly discarded. Yet the category has stuck, at least for *Troilus*, *All's Well*, and *Measure*; and, in spite of numerous objections, it makes sense to consider these three as a group (see Jamieson 1972: 1–2). They are alike in that they place so much pressure on their traditional genres that they explode genre and the usual kinds of response from the inside. *All's Well* and *Measure* end with marriages reaffirmed or impending, so they look like comedies, but they are bereft of celebration and their endings resolve none of the tensions that are aroused by the dramatic action. *Troilus* is the Bilbao Guggenheim of Renaissance plays: it should be a tragedy about the destruction of young love by war and the earth-shattering murder of Hector, but it is in fact a *tour de force* of form-making that looks like nothing on earth.

The artistic exuberance of these plays makes it unlikely that they are the product of a *fin de siècle* malaise. I want, however, to suggest that they do have a connection with Shakespeare's life – not his spiritual life, but his life as a professional in relation to the changing identity of the theatre. My basic claim in this essay is that Shakespeare's position *vis-à-vis* the entertainment market and the system of rank prompted him to become the most inventive dramatist of the period, the one who engaged most fruitfully with literary and dramatic traditions. My specific argument is that the "problem" of the problem plays is only that they are his most radical experiments (indeed, they are in some ways his most representative works), and that they can be understood best against the background of the competitive field of dramatic writing in the decade approximately from 1595 to 1605.

To begin, let us consider two soliloquies from the first scene of *All's Well*, which will serve to introduce us to the conditions of production of the drama and also to Shakespeare's innovations in dramatic form and genre, language, characterization, and ideological perspective. The speeches are remarkable because they place a non-aristocratic, female character in the privileged position of a Prince Hal or Hamlet (protagonists who share their thoughts with the audience near the outset of the action), and because they produce a strong impression of that lower-rank character's inward life. They also develop an orchestration of literary and social languages, which points to the theatre's lively spirit of adaptation and revision. Finally, the speeches can help us locate Shakespeare in relation to the two principal features of the field of dramatic writing: the system of rank (which was the backbone of the social formation) and the entertainment market, whose leading producer was the theatre itself.

The soliloquies occur following a scene of leave-taking (an autumnal beginning for a romantic comedy), darkened by the death of fathers, the king's disease, the loss of freedom, and the separation of mother and son. Lafew has come to bear Bertram away on his journey to Paris:

> *Countess.* In delivering my son from me, I bury a second husband.
> *Bertram.* And I in going, madam, weep o'er my father's death anew; but I must attend his Majesty's command, to whom I am now in ward, evermore in subjection. (1.1.1–5)[1]

Helena also weeps as she receives her mistress's commendations and Bertram's good-bye. After almost eighty lines of crabbed, ill-at-ease exchange, Helena's soliloquy comes as a bit of a surprise; after all, her tears have been taken by the others as badges of daughterly grief:

> . . . I think not on my father,
> And these great tears grace his remembrance more
> Than those I shed for him. What was he like?
> I have forgot him. My imagination
> Carries no favor in't but Bertram's.
> I am undone, there is no living, none,
> If Bertram be away. 'Twere all one
> That I should love a bright particular star
> And think to wed it, he is so above me.
> In his bright radiance and collateral light
> Must I be comforted, not is his sphere.
> Th' ambition in my love thus plagues itself:
> The hind that would be mated by the lion
> Must die for love. 'Twas pretty, though a plague,
> To see him every hour, to sit and draw

> His arched brows, his hawking eye, his curls,
> In our heart's table – heart too capable
> Of every line and trick of his sweet favor.
> But now he's gone, and my idolatrous fancy
> Must sanctify his reliques. (1.1.79–98)

In contrast to the conversation of the others, her language is energetic and lucid, but the content of her speech is as vexed as the Countess's mourning or Lafew's lack of hope for the King. By her account, she is Astrophil to Bertram's Stella, she is the strangely violated artist-lover of Shakespeare's sonnet 24 ("Mine eye hath play'd the painter and hath stell'd / Thy beauty's form in the table of my heart; / My body is the frame wherein 'tis held": lines 1–3), and she is also a bereft Hamlet who weeps for Ophelia rather than for his father (she even has the Prince's "tables" of memory). She is an advocate and transgressor of patriarchal "degree" and an idol-worshipper painfully aware of her own blasphemy (like a Catholic with a nagging Protestant conscience). Her version of herself, especially in contrast with the figure she cuts in the scene that leads up to the soliloquy, startles us into an awareness of her inner life, but we can also see how that inner life, especially her hopeless longing, has been inculcated by the atmosphere of Rossillion and by the principle of rank, which separates people according to the supposed quality of their "blood," and which in fact has both aroused and stymied her love.

Helena's adoration of Bertram also stirs up within her a contrary awareness of his limitations. She emphasizes his outward beauty (to the near exclusion of his other qualities), her vocabulary of praise is marked by words like "line" and "trick" that imply triviality or even deceit, and there is even a suggestion that the impression of his worth owes more to her idolatrous fancy than to his actual qualities. Helena's skepticism cannot overturn her passion, of course, because it is a product of that passion. Such resentful devotion is of a piece with real-life lower-rank attitudes toward the court. Someone like Ben Jonson, the stepson of a laborer, was critical of courtly pretense but nevertheless pursued court connections with alacrity. John Donne, a member of the gentry by birth, was not very much different. In "Satyre IV" he likens Whitehall to Dante's Inferno, but does not hesitate to join those flocking into "the Presence" (Donne 1967: 31–2). The important point is that the system of rank, with the nobility, court, and monarch at its apex, was dominant in society and far more influential than the nascent system of class, which means that aristocratic values and culture stood at the top of a ladder of aspiration rather than in opposition to the fully formed values and culture of some other, opposing class (Hexter 1961: 96–9, 112–16). When Helena says that she loves "a bright particular star" that shines in a sphere above hers, or when she confesses that she is like a hind on a suicide mission of love for a lion, she is placing herself on the unchallengeable ladder of the system of rank.

Yet, stranded as she is near the bottom rung of what J. H. Hexter calls "the hierarchical organic conception of society" (p. 114), she almost immediately discovers a way to begin to scale it. Something seems to have alleviated her immobility. In her second soliloquy she calls it nature, which in an instant transforms what she saw as a natural hierarchy into an artifact of fortune: "The mightiest space in fortune nature brings / To join like likes, and kiss like native things" (1.1.232–3). She is filled with confidence in the remedies that she feels lie in herself – she names it "merit" which she feels is a guarantee of success and which she thinks has heavenly license if not quite divine backing: "The fated sky / Gives us free scope, only doth backward pull / Our slow designs when we ourselves are dull" (1.1.217–19). Throughout, Shakespeare develops the impression of her inward life, nowhere more than in the closing couplet, where her intents, while "fix'd" in her own mind, remain far from transparent in ours: "The King's disease – my project may deceive me, / My intents are fix'd, and will not leave me" (1.1.228–9).

In Ben Jonson's *Volpone* (1606) Sir Politic Would-Be also has "projects" – secret schemes that are supposed to come to fruition in the world of money and power (4.1.46–7 and note). To understand Helena in Jonson's terms is to begin to see that her movement from adoration to action is caused, not so much by nature or merit or heaven's allowance, as by a realization that she indeed has something to trade for Bertram's hand. She comes to this understanding during the dialogue with Parolles that intervenes between her two soliloquies. It is he who redirects the discussion of virginity from the military metaphors introduced by Helena ("Man is enemy to virginity; how may we barricado it against him?": 1.1.112–13) toward the language of the market in consumer goods:

'Tis [i.e., virginity is] a commodity will lose the gloss with lying: the longer kept, the less worth. Off with't while 'tis vendible; answer the time of request. Virginity, like an old courtier, wears her cap out of fashion, richly suited, but unsuitable – just like the brooch and the toothpick, which wear not now. (1.1.153–8)

Helena's entry into the ethos of the market, however inflated by words like "project" or mystified by talk of "something in't / More than my father's skill" (1.3.242–3), can well represent the emergence of what I have called elsewhere "the populuxe theatre" (Dawson and Yachnin 2001: 38–65). Shakespeare and his company, the leading producers of populuxe drama, offered for sale relatively inexpensive, popular versions of deluxe cultural goods. They were able to take hold of the often skeptical adoration that the lower orders felt for the higher, and were able to turn that emotional knot to artistic, commercial, and social account. In doing so, it is important to note, they were neither able nor desirous to relieve the emotional vexations born of the social hierarchy: clearly, it was in their own interests to maintain the worth of what they were selling to the public, and indeed *their* project was aided by a society that continued to admire the upper ranks, with all their failings, as a group set apart from the ordinary run of men and women. Participation in the entertainment market did not allow the players to buy their way out of the system of rank; rather, it helped them to make good within it. Shakespeare, for one, officially became a gentleman because of the profitability of the stage.

He and his fellow sharers were able to insert themselves into the system of rank and to capitalize on the desirability of the language, conduct, dress, literature, and pastimes of the nobility. They were able both to parade their court connections before their paying audiences and to give the cultural consumers of early modern London an experience of ersatz courtly entertainment. For a relatively low price, the spectators could play at being their social betters: they could be entertained by the Lord Chamberlain's or (after 1603) the King's own company of players, and they could take their ease in a magnificent public playhouse, whose supporting columns were made, tellingly, of wood painted to look like marble (see Gurr 1970: 89; Ronayne 1997). Among other delights, and while they did not seek to undo the charisma of the nobility, Shakespeare's players offered dramatic representations of the psychological dynamic attendant upon the system of rank, giving playgoers opportunities to think about as well as to play out their own "idolatrous fancies."

Populuxe counted as a dimension of the appeal of all the acting companies, but the Chamberlain's/King's players developed it most fully. Shakespeare and his fellows were incited to do so by the competitive position-taking of the Admiral's Servants, who staked out a populist style and developed a repertoire of what have been called "citizen" plays, and also by the revived children's companies who traded in more authentically deluxe goods at the upmarket indoor venues in Paul's and the Blackfriars. As Andrew Gurr explains, the two adult companies featured very similar repertories up to around 1595, after which they began to go in separate directions (Gurr 1996: 152–8). That the Chamberlain's Servants were trying to enter an upmarket niche is indicated by the repertory they were developing, by the departure of the knock-about comic Will Kemp, and especially by Burbage's attempt in 1596 to move the company's operations from the Theatre in Shoreditch to the "private" playhouse in Blackfriars:

> The success of Shakespeare's company at the Globe must not be allowed to obscure the fact . . . that it came second to the Blackfriars in James Burbage's planning. Since the Blackfriars swallowed up his available funds he could not have been planning in 1596 to provide both an indoor City playhouse and a suburban amphitheatre for his players. He considered that the future of the adult playing companies lay in the City's hall play-house exclusively. The Globe was a retreat in the face of the unexpected opposition by Burbage's patron and the nobility in the west of the City, a reluctant renewal of the old style of playhouse originally erected thirty-two years before. (Ibid: 26)

It is a fine irony that the failure of Shakespeare's company to set up in the Blackfriars in 1596 facilitated the renewal of the children's companies a few years later and thus contributed to the Chamberlain's Servants' need to find their place in the entertainment market somewhere between Henslowe's company and the "aery of children, little eyases, that . . . are now the fashion, and . . . berattle the common stages" (*Hamlet*, 2.2.339–42).

In very broad terms, these sites of cultural production developed competing representations of the system of rank and the centrality of the court. They also tended to feature different dramatic and verbal styles. Henslowe's company, supplied with plays by writers like Chettle, Dekker, and Heywood, kept alive a post-Armada patriotism and a tradition of political organicism, promulgating an anti-courtly view of the nation as a natural hierarchical community with a monarch always ready to declare common cause with the lower orders. Dekker's *The Shoemaker's Holiday* (1599), about which we will hear more, ends with the king of England, the madcap lord mayor Simon Eyre, and a host of jolly shoemakers celebrating the surreptitious wedding of a young nobleman and the daughter of the former mayor of London. The opening speech of Heywood's *The Four Prentices of London* (?1600) suggests something about the typical language of the repertory, with its balanced iambic line, long, syntactically regular sentences, straightforward vocabulary, conventional emblematic imagery, and clear designation of addressee (the speaker is the "old Earl of Boloigne"):

> Daughter, thou seest how Fortune turns her wheel.
> We that but late were mounted up aloft,
> Lulled in the skirt of that inconstant Dame,
> Are now thrown headlong by her ruthless hand,
> To kiss the earth whereon our feet should stand.
> What censuring eye, that sees me thus deject,
> Would take this shape to be that famous Duke,
> Which hath made Boloigne through the world renowned,
> And all our race with fame and honour crowned?

The writers for the boys' companies (men like Jonson, Marston, Chapman, and Middleton) tended to cultivate a pugnacious anti-courtly tone (theirs was also an anti-courtly ideal of social hierarchy). The "private theatre" dramatists developed a version of the sociocultural field whose high center was urban, gentlemanly – but not courtly – cultural production and reception. They imagined an English community where the Children of Paul's or the Chapel Children (at Blackfriars), their audiences, and their poets, constituted the artistic and moral heart of the nation. A Paul's play like *The Puritan Widow* (published 1606; probably by Middleton) empowers the dramatists and players to punish the immorality of the members of the civic establishment. "Why, sergeant," one character says, "'tis natural in us, you know, to hate scholars, natural. Besides, they will publish our imperfections, knaveries, and conveyances upon scaffolds and stages" (3.3.9–12).

The language of Middleton and his fellow satiric dramatists is ostentatiously inventive in vocabulary, abrupt in its shifts among addressees, syntactically fragmented, given to non-English and parodic usages, and "philosophical." The following exchange is from the first scene of Marston's *What You Will* (1601) (the speakers are Quadratus and the servant Phylus; note how Heywood's Dame Fortune reappears here without her wheel):

Phylus. O! O! I beseech you sir, reclaim his wits,
My master's mad, stark mad, alas for love.
Quadratus. For love? nay, and he be not mad for hate,
'Tis amiable fortune; I tell thee, youth,
Right rare and geason [i.e., rare, scarce]; strange? mad for love,

O show me him. I'll give him reasons straight.
So forcible, so all invincible,
That it shall drag love out: run mad for love?
What mortally exists, on which our hearts
Should be enamoured with such passion?
For love? Come Phylus, come; I'll change his fate,
Instead of love, I'll make him mad for hate.
But troth, say what strains his madness of?
Phylus. Phantastical.
Quadratus. Immure him, sconce him, barracado him in't,
Phantastical mad, thrice blessed heart;
Why hark good Phylus (O that thy narrow sense
Could but contain me now), all that exists
Takes valuation from opinion:
A giddy minion now; pish, thy taste is dull,
And canst not relish me.

It is important to emphasize that the companies were attempting to define their position in the entertainment marketplace *vis-à-vis* the system of rank (rather than trying to reform society) because some recent criticism has mistaken the ideological perspective of these differing repertories. Such criticism argues either that Henslowe's theatre was more democratic in sentiment than Shakespeare's (Helgerson 1992: 193–245), or that playwrights like Marston and Middleton were oppositional and progressive whereas Shakespeare was conservative (Tricomi 1989: 13–24; Taylor 1994). It tends to misconstrue idealizations of community under a monarch or contempt for courtiers as politically progressive. It must be said, however, that plays like *Shoemaker's Holiday* or *Puritan Widow* are far from democratic, and also that anti-courtliness had been a staple attitude of aristocratic culture for generations. Donne's ambivalence was typical, but even insiders shared a certain reserve about the court: one of Elizabeth's peers said of himself "[t]hat he was none of the *Reptilia*, intimating that he could not creep on the ground, and that the Court was not his element" (quoted in Zagorin 1970: 43). These sentiments from among the gentry suggest that literary critiques of the court were, ironically enough, of a piece with the system of rank.

Because Shakespeare's was the leading company in the capital, because Henslowe on one side and the boys' companies on the other had staked out their own niches in the market, and also because position-taking in the field of cultural production has its own momentum, the Chamberlain's/King's players developed populuxe as their standard fare. Since populuxe retails versions of elite culture to socially inclusive audiences, its ideological perspective, as we have begun to see with Helena, will be complex – including both laudatory and critical representations of courtliness and monarchy. That Shakespeare's work was keyed to the ascendancy of the court does not mean that he and his players were the apes of the nobility, producing merely cheap versions of high-class goods that served somehow to keep his playgoers in thrall to the social hierarchy.

In terms of its language, form, and ideological content, his drama was far more complex than that. Even in an early play like *The Taming of the Shrew* (1593?), Shakespeare places a lowbrow, popular tale of shrew-taming in a critical relationship with a highbrow romantic comedy of disguise out of Ariosto: in the end, the characters in the taming plot suggest the superficiality and literariness of the characters in the *Supposes* plot. At the level of language also, Shakespeare's drama is complex. Helena's claim that she has a "heart too capable / Of every line and trick of his sweet favor" registers a certain skepticism about the object of worship, not only by the use of the words "line" and "trick," but also by emphasizing her own inward capacity against Bertram's attractive outward appearance. The phrase "his sweet favour" heightens this contrast, since a "favour" is a face and also a trivial object (for instance, a ring or handkerchief) exchanged in upper-rank rituals of courtship. More broadly, Shakespeare likes to play courtly language against plain speech. To some degree, that is the theme of *King Lear* (1605), which ends with Edgar's admonition to "speak what we feel" (5.3.325). In *Twelfth Night* (1600) the stuffiness of the first, courtly scene gives way to the fresh air and urgency of the survivor Viola (her social rank, while not specified, is certainly below Orsino's: see Malcolmson 1991): the shift is audible in the movement from Orsino's couplet ("Away before me to sweet beds of flow'rs, / Love-thoughts lie rich when canopied with bow'rs": 1.1.39–40) to Viola's line, "What country, friends, is this?" (1.2.1).

Critics who argue that Heywood or Middleton are politically progressive *vis-à-vis* Shakespeare need to take into account the sheer ideological complexity of his plays at the level of language, character, and form. After all, the poor gentlewoman Helena dominates a plot of gender-reversed romantic pursuit in a play that also features her complex inward mental life, as well as speeches from the king of France against both court culture and the notion of the superiority of aristocratic blood. Most important overall is the fact that the playwrights did not use dramatic literature to enter into public debates on matters of governance, but rather included such matters in a contest for theatrical success, a project that included developing dramatic styles that appealed to cultural consumers and that also contributed to the self-definition of the playing companies and audiences. Among much else, the problem plays were involved in a project of institutional identity formation at a particularly lively juncture in the history of the theatre.

In what follows, I consider the problem plays in chronological order and discuss each of them in relation to a particular feature: *Troilus*'s language and genre, *All's Well*'s techniques of inward characterization, and *Measure*'s complex political perspective. (All three plays could of course be discussed in relation to all three features.) As a group, these plays suggest how Shakespeare was developing his own brand of dramatic composition in the face of changing and competitive styles. I should say in passing that my claim is that the field of cultural production provided a strong background for Shakespeare's innovations in the problem plays, not that it determined them: for one thing, these plays elaborate features that can be found in his earlier drama; for another, he influenced the cultural field, especially over the long term, far more than he was influenced by it.

The epistle attached to the 1609 Quarto edition of *Troilus and Cressida* tells us seven times that what we are holding is a comedy – it is "passing full of the palm comical." The title page, however, calls it a history. When the play was published in the 1623 Folio it was designated a tragedy. In the nineteenth century the German poet Heinrich Heine suggested that we must leave it to the future to understand the play: "We can acknowledge its great excellence only in general terms; for a detailed judgement we should need the help of that new aesthetics which has not yet been written" (quoted in Dawson, forthcoming).

It might, however, be worth considering what the past can tell us. The last five years of the sixteenth century did not see precisely the formulation of a new aesthetics, but it did witness the emergence of a new style of playwriting, against which a great deal about *Troilus* becomes clearer. The new vogue in playmaking got its start with Henslowe's company's performance of Chapman's hit, *An Humourous Day Mirth* (1597), and then gravitated toward the children's companies by way of the Chamberlain's Men, for whom Jonson wrote his humors comedies, *Every Man In His Humour* (1598) and *Every Man Out of His Humour* (1599) (see Wiggins 2000: 53–78). Important is the fact that the satiric playwrights undertook a shift away from the strong narrative basis of the traditional dramatic genres. Perhaps prompted by the ideal of courtly otium, their rejection of narrative-based drama resulted in plays that presented a series of loosely organized vignettes where the follies of social types and social languages were put on display. Marston's *What You Will* consists of a series of such scenes loosely bound together by a Plautine plot. *Every Man In* similarly features a succession of scenes whose linking armature is the desire of Lorenzo Junior and Prospero to display and observe a "mess" of humorous fools. In *Poetaster* (1599) Jonson mocked his own method in this disparagement of his ideal poet Horace:

> Alas sir, Horace! He is a mere sponge, nothing but humours and observation; he goes up and down sucking from every society, and when he comes home squeezes himself dry again. (4.3.104–7)

Dramatists like Jonson represented their style as *à la mode* and therefore as higher in status than old-fashioned, narrative-based comedies, tragedies, and histories. Shakespeare himself plays this game in *A Midsummer Night's Dream* (1594) when he gives an old-style tragedy (and the alliterative verse that graces it) to the hard-handed men of Athens, whose antics make the courtiers laugh (Shakespeare gives their laughter a finely measured excess of condescension). In spite of his satire of the Mechanicals, however, he remained more or less wedded to narrative as the basis of dramatic construction.

We can see *Troilus* as a response to the new styles in that it makes use of Jonsonian "humours and observation," the fashion of satirical ranting, and the kind of dramatic design based on the display of social types rather than on narrative. Thersites outrails railing satire, not only because his prose is so vigorous, but also because he assails the central warrior heroes of the Western tradition.

The language of the play provides much that is answerable to Thersites' gall. This includes the Prologue with its inkhorn terms ("From isles of Greece / The princes orgillous, their high blood chafed . . .": lines 1–2), Agamemnon's windy speech in 1.2, and Troilus' soliloquy of appetitive rapture (3.2.18–29). A particularly telling instance is Ulysses' testimonial to Troilus' character:

> . . . a true knight.
> Not yet mature, yet matchless, firm of word,
> Speaking in deeds, and deedless in his tongue,
> Not soon provok'd, not being provok'd soon calm'd;
> His heart and hand both open and both free,
>
> . . .
>
> They call him Troilus, and on him erect
> A second hope, as fairly built as Hector. (4.5.96–109)

This sounds like a moving tribute, especially from an enemy, but at the end of the speech Ulysses reveals that the words of praise are not his but rather only a redaction of a conversation that he had with Aeneas, which does not exactly belie the tribute, but which certainly puts its truth in question and imposes retrospectively a parodic inflection on the manly cut of the speech.

The effect of retrospective parody in Ulysses' speech resembles Shakespeare's handling of scenic design in a number of instances – where Hector wins the argument about Helen only to reveal that he was only playing at conciliar debate (2.2.207–13) or where Troilus' unwillingness to tarry with Cressida (4.2.1–18), once he has satisfied his desire, suggests the shakiness of his words of love. Akin to this retrospective undoing of authentic speech is the play's suspension of narrative progress, the strangely becalmed atmosphere of phony war that settles upon the great and urgent story of Troy. The first scene suggests that the war is ongoing (even if Troilus is not in the mood for fighting), but later Aeneas tells us that Hector is bored – he "in this dull and long-continued truce / Is resty grown" (1.3.262–3). The result is only another deferral of actual conflict – a boyish chivalric challenge that itself devolves into a lazy afternoon and evening of eating and drinking and talking. It is no wonder that Thersites' view holds such sway. Where Falstaff's catechism on honor (*1 Henry 4*, 5.1.129–41) is limited in its force by the compelling rhythm of battle, or where Jaques's "sullen fits" (*As You Like It*, 2.1.67) are contradicted by the radiant courtship of Rosalind and Orlando, Thersites' mockery chimes with the endless consultation, speech-making, backroom strategizing, and gossip that take the place of meaningful utterance and action.

Shakespeare's adoption of the style of dramatic construction that was developed by Chapman and the others serves to enhance the authority of Thersites' satirical observations on the war, but of course his is not allowed to stand as the definitive view. This is the case not because his reduction of aspiration and love to forms of military and sexual violence cannot account for the story of Troilus and Cressida. In fact it can, especially in view of the prominence of Troilus' sexual desire and his failure to mention marriage – an omission that robs the lovers' story of the ethical and affective momentum of a comedy like *As You Like It* or a tragedy like *Romeo and Juliet* (1594). What finally holds Thersites in check, and what makes the drama different in kind from the satirical comedies, is the way the play delivers (after a four-act hiatus) on the Prologue's promise of tragic action. The emergence of tragic narrative in the last act changes the overall quality of the play, producing a generic amalgam with connections to both elite and popular styles and also splicing together elements of satire and tragedy, including conflicting modes of expression, pacing, blocking, and audience response.

The Prologue tells us of "princes orgillous, their high blood chaf'd," and this chafing, which leads on to tragedy, takes place finally in two scenes of observation, 4.5 and 5.2. Achilles angers Hector by his mocking regard; Hector is chafed (see 4.5.260), and his language, which has been affable, heats up with repeated short phrases and internal rhyme: "I'll not kill thee there, nor there, nor there, / But by the forge that stithied Mars his helm, / I'll kill thee every where, yea, o'er and o'er" (4.5.254–6). What follows (after a scene of Thersitean railing and the Greek generals getting lost in their own camp!) is a second, elaborated observation scene where an amazed and angry Troilus watches Cressida with Diomed (and is watched by Thersites). The scene resembles the arrangement of characters and use of asides characteristic of Jonsonian comedy, but the issue belongs to another genre, as we move from this ensemble scene of unseen looking-on and unheard commentary to another group scene, this one almost choric, where Hector's family foretells his death and implores him to stay out of the fight, which he cannot do because his "honor holds the weather of [his] fate" (5.3.26). The use of groupings *vis-à-vis* a focal figure or couple modulates from looking to speaking to killing, as we move from Troilus and the others' observation of Cressida and Diomed to Hector's family members' tragic chorus to the Myrmidons' swarming murder of Hector (the first act of violence seen in the play). The pattern of intensifying contact between a figure and a group, with its climax in the murder of Hector and conclusion in Troilus' speech of grief and revenge, calls for a heightened emotional response alien to satire, where the characters tend to interact at a greater emotional and physical distance.

If that were all, *Troilus* would be even stranger than it is – a tragic tail wagging a satiric dog. But the final movement cannot escape Thersites' blighting presence, and indeed Achilles' treachery is an outrageous parody of Homer. Moreover Pandarus enters after what sounds like the end of a tragedy ("Strike a free march. To Troy with comfort go; / Hope of revenge shall hide our inward woe": 5.10.30–1) in order to deliver a kind of epilogue, in which he parodies tragic emotion by asking the spectators (who are said to be half-blind with syphilis) to pity him – "Your eyes, half out, weep out at Pandar's fall" (5.10.48). The overall effect of these competing modes is extraordinary: a full account would require, I suggest, not a new aesthetics, but rather a complete history of the play's embeddedness in the early modern field of cultural production. The present discussion of Shakespeare's involvement in the field is of necessity only a sketch, to which I will now try to add a couple of other defining features.

After his work on *Troilus*, Shakespeare came back to narrative-based construction with *All's Well That Ends Well*. There was perhaps a year between the two plays, and since *Troilus* might not have been a hit at the Globe (see Dawson, forthcoming: xx), it is possible that the return to narrative was motivated in part by audience preference. Of course, Shakespeare was developing his dramatic art according to his own lights too. I suggest in this section that *All's Well* continues his experiments with form, this time not (as in *Troilus*) by the suspension of narrative, but rather (as in *Hamlet*) with the displacing of story by character as the center of interest. I argue that Shakespeare's art of characterization is his most important innovation *vis-à-vis* the market and the system of rank and the feature of his art of greatest significance over the long term.

Even though *All's Well* includes a playful defensiveness about its own reliance on narrative (Snyder 1992: 28–32), its folk-tale related story indicates a growing distance between Shakespeare's repertory and that of the children's companies. It will therefore be instructive to compare *All's Well* with the Henslowe comedy *A Shoemaker's Holiday*, especially since the two share a number of features. The comparison will also help to fill out the picture of what Jean Howard has called Shakespeare's company's "middle way . . . a mixed and evolving repertory . . . hardly catering exclusively to a sophisticated audience of city wits or courtiers" (Howard 1999: 139).

Both plays are interested in the relationship between romantic love and the system of rank. In both, a woman of the lower ranks marries a man of the nobility; in both, the monarch is accessible to those far below him and supports the cross-rank marriage; in both, foreign war impinges on the course of romance. Both plays end with the affirmation of the marriage under the approving eyes of the king in a way that challenges the system of rank but leaves intact the principle of monarchical rule.

However, the differences between the two plays are more important than the similarities. In Dekker, Lacy (the nephew of the earl of Lincoln) avoids service in France in order to court the daughter of the mayor of London; in Shakespeare, Bertram flees France for the Italian wars so as to avoid consummating his enforced marriage. The marriage of Lacy and Rose is happy, whereas the coupling of Helena and Bertram is not. Dekker's play is set in London, Shakespeare's in France and Italy; Dekker's is based on Thomas Deloney's *The Gentle Craft* (a native English celebration of working people), Shakespeare's on a translation of Boccaccio. Dekker shows us that the lower orders have their prejudices against the higher, including (at least on the part of mayor Oatley) an unwillingness to mix citizen and aristocratic blood. The shoemakers are brimming with pride in their craft, its history, and its heroes; and when Simon Eyre (the representative figure of shoemaker self-esteem) rises in the world, he ascends within an urban hierarchy and does not attempt to escape into the sphere of the gentry. The campaign in France is the occasion of grave social injustice. The poor journeyman Ralph is compelled to go to war (where he loses the use of his legs and very

nearly loses his wife Jane to the designs of a rich city merchant) while the aristocrat
Lacy stays behind in disguise, pursuing his courtship of Rose. Lacy even has the audacity to upbraid Jane for protesting against her husband's military service:

> Woman, be patient. God, no doubt, will send
> Thy husband safe again: but he must go.
> His country's quarrel says it shall be so. (sc.1, 186–8)

Shoemaker's Holiday was not completely outside the popular trade in deluxe goods
– not outside the populuxe booktrade at any rate, since the play was rushed into print
in a Quarto edition whose title page advertised a royal performance on New Year's
Day 1600 (Dekker 1979: "Introduction," 54). Nevertheless, Dekker's play, with its
interest in poverty and injustice and its artisanal, civic, and national pride, throws
into high relief the populuxe cultivation of elite cultural forms in *All's Well*.[2] Not
that Shakespeare's play is without a critical dimension. I have already suggested how
its complex language registers a degree of skepticism about the higher ranks. In addition, while the wars are not (as in Dekker) the occasion of social injustice, they are
represented mostly as a bloody but trivial affair where young French noblemen enjoy
what finally seems like nothing more than recreation. Of a piece with this critique of
the aristocratic contest for distinction is the scene in which Diana measures Bertram's
paltry aristocratic honor against her own honor as a gentlewoman (4.2). Finally,
although Shakespeare seems less interested than is Dekker in the problem of poverty,
both Parolles and Lavatch are shown to be concerned with the need to earn a living.
    To be sure, the political perspective of Shakespeare's representation of society is
complex, as is Dekker's also (his is no naive advertisement for the virtues of trade: see
Kastan 1987; Seaver 1995); but there is nevertheless a strong distinction to be drawn
between Dekker's robust representation of the life of a working household and
Shakespeare's focus, however troubled, on the nobility and the court. In Dekker the
king is a *deus ex machina*, in Shakespeare he is a formative presence; Dekker's protagonists are shoemakers (that excludes Lacy though he works as a shoemaker) whereas
the admirable characters in Shakespeare include aristocrats like Lafew, the countess of
Rossillion, and the king (the protagonist Helena is outside this group even though
she marries into the nobility). Moreover, *Shoemaker's Holiday* develops a civic ethos of
hard work, thrift, collective festivity, and loyalty to the crown that has no equivalent
in *All's Well*. The plays must even have looked and sounded very different. Given the
preponderance of courtly characters and scenes in Shakespeare's play, the costuming
at the Globe would have been more gorgeous than the workaday wardrobe at the Rose.
Finally, the predominant musical element in *All's Well* is the repeated "Flourish
cornets" or "Flourish" for the king or the duke of Florence. *Shoemaker's Holiday* features a much busier soundscape that includes "[a] long flourish or two" (sc. 21sd) for
the king's second entrance, a drum, a tabor and pipe, a hunting horn, much group
shouting and singing, and the pancake bell that summons the apprentices to the
Shrove Tuesday feast (sc. 18.192sd).[3]

Clearly, the emphasis of the King's servants' repertory is on elite style and the appeal of the aristocracy. Gary Taylor (1994) is surely right when he points out Shakespeare's apparent obsession with royalty (pp. 308–10); indeed, I want to extend that insight by suggesting that Shakespeare's art of characterization was of a piece with the development of a populuxe art that marketed deluxe goods – in this case deluxe forms of personhood – to popular audiences. The upshot of my argument, however, will be that Shakespeare's popular versions of elite culture have turned out to be in the long run more effective vehicles for the expression of democratic sentiments than have Dekker's scenes of collective action and festivity.

This has much to do with dramatic style. Dekker's strength lies in lively, socially detailed ensemble scenes and in straightforwardly emotional two-handers. His approach to the soliloquy is perfunctory: at the beginning of sc. 3 Lacy takes twenty-four lines to tell us his plans and to rouse his own spirits; his brief uses of third- and second-person address to himself ("It is no shame for Rowland Lacy then / To clothe his cunning with the Gentle Craft": lines 3–4) suggest the bare fact of his self-awareness but no psychological complexity. The contrast with Helena's first soliloquy, with its evocation of a complex, socially situated inward life, is striking.

In her important study, *Inwardness and Theater in the English Renaissance*, Katharine Maus (1995) has described a number of cultural counterparts of inward characterization on the Renaissance stage, especially inwardness in the spheres of religion and law. One of the models of inward personhood that she does not consider is what Ophelia calls "the observ'd of all observers" (3.1.154) – the nobles, princes, and monarchs who took up far more physical and social space than did people of the lower ranks, and whose moods and thoughts impinged on others far more than others' thoughts impinged on them. I suggest that Shakespearean inward characterization is of a piece with his development of populuxe, and that one unrecognized dimension of his art of characterization is the relationship between inwardness and the necessary invisibility of the bloodline of the aristocratic subject – the inwardness of the aristocrat's claim to be the descendant of a noble race.

Consider the parallel between Hamlet's assertion that he has "that within which passes show" (1.2.85) and Orlando's claim that the spirit of his father, which he thinks is within him, begins to mutiny at his condition of servitude (*As You Like It*, 1.1.22–4). For these characters (and we can add Prince Hal too), inwardness arises because of the introspection they undertake in order to authenticate both their spiritual bond with their fathers and their legitimacy as their fathers' sons. Orlando and especially Hamlet and Hal are avatars of inwardness because they are given to bouts of self-inspection in their keen investigation of their own bloodlines; we might say that they provide the template by which Shakespeare conjures inwardness in other characters, including foreigners to the system of rank such as Shylock and Othello and female characters of the lesser gentry like Viola, Cressida, Isabella, and Helena.

Helena's kinship with Hamlet is marked by the first line of her soliloquy, which suggests how the prince's inwardness is being adjusted to suit a character of lower rank. Lafew's parting words are "You must hold the credit of your father" (1.1.78).

Her response, once the others have left the stage, is, "O, were that all! I think not on my father" (1.1.79). Where Prince Hamlet sees his father in his mind's eye, the image of Gerard de Narbon has been expunged from his daughter's memory by the deep impression of an adored aristocrat: "What was he like? / I have forgot him. My imagination / Carries no favor in't but Bertram's" (1.1.81–3). That Bertram has replaced her father as the object of remembrance, reverence, and desire is appropriate to her rank and sex, since her family line is less important than that of the ruling family of Denmark and since name and "blood" are thought to pass primarily from father to son.

The impression of both Hamlet and Helena's inwardness is produced mainly by the sheer force of their desire to be at one with their beloved; their inwardness is psychologically and socially interesting because of the vexatiousness of their longing. In part this has to do with their doubts about the good qualities of the beloved. Hamlet's case is subtle: his doubts are registered by the great amplitude of his praise, especially when set against his father's punishment in the afterlife. In *All's Well* the matter is clear-cut, since everyone (including his mother) agrees that Bertram is unworthy of Helena.

Hamlet and Helena's desire for union with their beloved is also undercut by their own feelings of unworthiness. In both cases, that sense of inadequacy is keyed to social categories that have got very deeply into their minds. Hamlet thinks of himself in terms of nobility, manliness, and filial duty; he fears that he is a "muddy-mettled rascal" and therefore not "the son of a dear father murdered" (2.2.567, 583). Helena defines herself in terms of an exfoliating idea of the system of rank. She is below Bertram's sphere, a hind in love with a lion, an idolator, one of "the poorer born" (1.1.182), "poor, but honest" (1.3.195), "Indian-like, / religious in [her] error" (1.3.204–5), "a timorous thief" (2.5.81), a "caitiff" (3.2.114), and worthy only for her "reserved honesty" (3.5.62).

Shakespeare dissolves the languages of social difference (cosmological by way of Petrarchan poetry, zoological, theological, colonialist, legal, feudal, and ethical) into the inward struggles of an individual who intends to transgress the very system of rank that informs her sense of who she is and that indeed has aroused her transgressive desire in the first place. The effect of this is to give Helena a degree of ownership of the social categories that shape her subjectivity and desire and to provide playgoers with a potential mirror of their own involvement in the system of rank. Moreover, Helena's awareness of herself (which does not at all free her from the system of values) also helps her character hold the center of the stage and eclipse the importance of the narrative and thematic dimensions of the play as other possible focuses of interest. As is the case with *Hamlet* also, the real meaning of the action depends upon how it is seen by the central character: we tend to be less interested in the fact that Helena ends up with Bertram than with the question of why she wanted him to begin with.

That a poor gentlewoman shares with a prince the same pattern of remembrance of and desire to be at one with a beloved and the same arousal of an inward life dense with social meaning suggests something about the political direction of Shakespearean characterization. Important in the long run is how his plays transvalued courtly culture, making the idea of the dignity of aristocratic personhood available to modernity, a dimension of populuxe that helps explain Shakespeare's long-term appeal in the emerging democracies of the West with their constitutional, legal, and ethical emphasis on the "sovereignty" of the individual. We might say that Dekker's Simon Eyre, with his tag line, "Prince am I not, yet am I nobly born, as being the sole son of a shoemaker" (sc. 7, 49–50) or "Prince am I none, yet bear a princely mind" (sc. 17, 21–2), is involved in the same long process of democratization as is Helena, except that Dekker proceeds by a comic challenge to the system of rank where Shakespeare does his part by mining the hierarchy from within.

The local context of Shakespeare's art of inward characterization has to do with the claim, advanced by Jonson and others, that narrative-based drama was old-fashioned and "base." The Prologue of *Every Man In* (written for the 1616 Folio) jeers at Shakespeare's violation of the unities and his pandering to the popular taste for Marlovian bombast, stage-fights, special effects, and generation-spanning narrative:

> To make a child, now swaddled, proceed
> Man, and then shoot up in one beard and weed
> Past threescore years; or with three rusty swords,
> And help of some few foot-and-half-foot words,
> Fight over York and Lancaster's long jars,
> And in the tiring-house bring wounds to scars.
> He rather prays you will be pleased to see,
> One such today as other plays should be,
> With neither Chorus wafts you o'er the seas,
> Not creaking throne comes down, the boys to please. (Appendix 1, pp. 244–5)

Depth characterization served, I suggest, as a brilliant response to Jonson's portrayal of Shakespeare's drama as a wildly accelerated (and noisy) charge toward the end of the story. Again, this is not to say that Shakespeare developed his style of characterization only in response to immediate market pressures. Indeed, the lineaments of inwardness are evident approximately seven years before Helena in the character who says "My tongue will tell the anger of my heart, / Or else my heart concealing it will break" (*Taming of the Shrew*, 4.3.77–8). Rather, the playwright and the actors must have scoured their resources for what they could do that was better and more broadly appealing than either the Children's upmarket fare or Henslowe's populist drama.

The retailing of versions of aristocratic inward personhood was a good fit with the strengths of their in-house playwright and a natural extension of the company's position in the entertainment market. The artistic effect of this development is that the dramatic action of plays like *Hamlet* and *All's Well* tends to decelerate near the gravitational field of the major characters. Soliloquies are a part of this, especially because they provide the characters with an opportunity to entice the audience into sharing their view of the world and their struggles within that world.[4] There are also a number of techniques that serve to keep the inward life of major characters at center stage. One is the creation of a disparity between what characters say they will do and what they do, which is repeatedly the case with Helena; another is the placement of the character at the center of controversy; a third is the concealment or obscuring of verbal meaning. An ordinary instance is when Helena says about Parolles, "One that goes with him. I love him for his sake, / And yet I know him a notorious fool" (1.1.99–100) where her pronoun references are unclear (and a bit unsettling given her complex feelings for Bertram). A more striking example is where her words simply trail off, leaving us (and Parolles) with an impression of her unspoken thoughts:

> Now shall he –
> I know not what he shall – God send him well!
> The court's a learning place, and he is one – (1.1.175–7)

Shakespeare also uses blocking and pacing. He marks Helena's long hesitation to come on stage for her first meeting with the king (see 2.1.93–4), a moment that actually retards the action and draws our attention firmly to Helena's thoughts and feelings even in the presence of the king and his court.

In general, and in spite of the fact that he tends to build his plays on the foundation of strong narratives, Shakespeare's becomes a drama of character rather than a drama of action. This is what Leonard Digges recounts in his commendatory verses prefixed to *Poems: written by Wil. Shake-speare* (1640), where he praises the popular success and wonderful lifelikeness of Shakespeare's characters and, in this passage, contrasts those qualities with the bookishness of Jonson's drama (as if it did not even have characters):

> So have I seen, when *Caesar* would appear,
> And on the stage at half-sword parley were
> Brutus and Cassius: O how the audience
> Were ravished, and with what wonder they went thence;
> When some new day they would not brook a line
> Of tedious (though well-laboured) *Catiline*. (Quoted in Shakespeare 1974: 1846)

It is particularly interesting to compare Digges's view with Jonson's mockery of what he sees as Shakespeare's reliance on sweeping narrative, actorly athleticism, and special effects.[5] Jonson seems to be attempting to assimilate his fellow playwright's theatre of character (after all, Brutus and Cassius are talking not fighting) to the more spectacular, less sophisticated fare available at Henslowe's playhouse. Digges's poem, however, suggests that Jonson is misrepresenting the success of Shakespeare's appropriation of the dynamic of aristocratic inwardness (one that includes "blood," memory, and filial desire) as an answer to the challenge from more elite forms of commercial theatre, including Jonson's own.

The first thing to say about the ideological perspective of *Measure for Measure* is that the early modern English theatre had no politics but institutional politics. As

Michael Bristol has said, "those who invented the theater had specific interests of their own, most notably an interest in economic survival" (Bristol 1996: 40). It is important to emphasize the playing companies' economic interests (not to mention their artistic and social aspirations) in order to remove the play from the imaginary political field in which Shakespeare can be pictured giving the king advice on matters of rule or presenting royalist (or anti-royalist) arguments to the public. The lax regulation of the drama, the leniency of the authorities when the players did seem to be interfering in matters of state, and the remarkable paucity of mention of the drama in the surviving letters, diaries, and non-dramatic publications of the period all suggest that the theatre did not normally appear on the radar screens of the ruling elite and that the players were not participants in the operations of power (Barroll 1991: 23–69; Yachnin 1997: 1–24).

In this view, the play emerges not as a royalist work, but rather as a drama that bears itself (in part) with a kind of kingly dignity and an attitude of preoccupation with affairs of law and social regulation as if on a visit from Whitehall to Southwark. This is not as outlandish as it sounds. Plays of the first half of the 1590s were doing something similar – the frame plot of *The Taming of the Shrew* imagines that the London playhouse, the Theatre, is a lord's "great house" in the country, and the courtly ambiance of *A Midsummer Night's Dream* has suggested to many scholars that it must have been written for an aristocratic wedding (see Williams 1997: 1–37). Equally, it should not be seen as anti-royalist. That is the case not merely because it was performed at court, but also because it was entertainment first of all (which does not mean that it was without political content, including an element of critique). Moreover, its critical dimension is not a product (as the strong argument of Annabel Patterson would suggest) of the supposedly popular nature of Shakespeare's theatre; rather, the critique of law and government is stimulated by, even imported from the Children's satires of the court and legal system, which themselves were occasioned by the presence of many Inns of Court students in the audience.

That the stage had only institutional politics does not mean that the drama was without political consequences, but it does suggest that it will not be possible to understand those consequences without taking into account the real situation of the players and writers. Also important is the fact that *Measure* can seem indecisive or bifurcated when it is located in the sphere of political discourse, whereas it makes coherent sense within the competitive field of dramatic writing. Elsewhere, I have argued that *Measure* represents Shakespeare's attempt to come to terms with changes within the genre of comedy, especially with Middleton and Jonson's biting satire of the Elizabethan ideal of comedy as an instrument of socially reformative mirth (Yachnin 1997: 65–92). That argument sees *Measure* as a rethinking of the genre. The play allows Jonson and Middleton's view that theatrical mirth is self-serving and that England is past saving as a mirthful community; nevertheless, Shakespeare preserves the ideal of comedy's power for good by shifting the focus from the reformation of the commonwealth to the conversion of the individual. The play also projects the problem of the stage's position between the court and marketplace onto the monarchy itself, in that the instrumentality of the players' profitable trade in royal favor spreads into almost every corner of life in Vienna, extending all the way up to Vincentio – a doer of good works for his subjects but also "the Duke of dark corners" (4.3.157) – the master strategist who ends up with both an enhanced reputation and the much prized Isabella.

Where my previous argument considered *Measure* in relation to comedy as a genre over a long span (from *Dream* (1594) to Jonson's *Bartholomew Fair* (1614)), it is also possible to approach it as one of a tight chronological grouping of plays connected by subject rather than by genre. A comparison with the Paul's satire, Middleton's *The Phoenix* (1604) and the Henslowe history play, the first part of Heywood's *If You Know Not Me, You Know Nobody, Or The Troubles of Queen Elizabeth* (1605), can provide a supplement and corrective to the work of scholars like Leonard Tennenhouse and others, who have situated *Measure* vis-à-vis the monarchy and have characterized it as an early text of Jacobean absolutism, one that served to demonstrate that "only the true monarch is the best form of political power" (Tennenhouse 1982: 143). A comparison with Middleton and Heywood suggests a different conclusion.

Measure is often grouped with *Phoenix* and Marston's *The Malcontent* (1604) as "disguised ruler plays," a subgenre thought to be reflective of an incident in the new king's exercise of power (Bernthal 1992: 247–53). The three that I am considering here could be called "plays of accession," a category that speaks to the anxious uncertainty widespread in 1603 when the queen died without an heir. Middleton and Heywood's accession plays differ from each other as typical examples of the Children's and Henslowe's repertories. Middleton's is a satire of observation within a loosely knit narrative framework that features a young prince in disguise who witnesses corruption at all levels of society, who thwarts the courtier Proditor's attempted assassination of his father the duke, and who is rewarded by his father's decision to yield the throne to his discerning son; Heywood's is almost all narrative, leading spectators step by step from the accession of Queen Mary, to her marriage to Philip of Spain, to her death and the accession of her persecuted sister, the princess Elizabeth. The affective dimension of the plays differs in that Prince Phoenix's penetration and high-mindedness are admirable, whereas Elizabeth's virtue, faith, courage, and beauty are loveable. The plays are intended to appeal to differently disposed audiences.

In one important respect, however, the plays differ very little. Both represent an ideal of monarchy where the relationship between the ruler and the ruled is unmediated by a courtly entourage. In Middleton, the old duke's court is a nest of vipers: with the help of Fidelio, the prince is able to clean it out. In Heywood, there are some well-meaning courtiers, but they are prevented from protecting the princess against her envious older sister by religious and political factionalism. In contrast, Elizabeth counts all the commoners as friends, and once queen, her last speech in the play expresses her love of country and her Christian faith before the citizens and mayor of London, by whom she is given an English Bible. The ideal of government in both plays is absolutist. Political stability requires a single all-powerful ruler because the court is rife with ambitious nobles and factional struggle. Heywood's populist version sees Providence as the agent of Elizabeth's accession. Perhaps the nostalgic portrait of the dead queen also expresses popular xenophobic resentment of the new Scottish king. In contrast, Middleton is more up to date: the old, unseeing duke has ruled for forty-five years (the length of Elizabeth's reign), and his son (clearly a stand-in for James) achieves the throne by dint of virtuous cunning rather than by the hand of Providence.

Middleton and Heywood imagine different but similar versions of absolute rule. But where Middleton's prince can count on his own wits and Heywood's princess is protected by God, *Measure*'s Duke Vincentio depends on individuals such as the Provost, Friar Thomas, and Friar Peter, who are able to aid his project because of their official positions in the state and church. In fact, it is fortunate that he has their help, since neither his intelligence nor divine Providence seems able to overcome the unpredictability of events or the intractability of a number of characters. At the end, Angelo might liken the duke's discernment to "pow'r divine" (5.1.370), but we know that Vincentio's enhanced knowledge of his dukedom and his stunning reappearance have been the work of an ensemble.

Vincentio, of course, only play-acts his (re)accession, as if he wanted to renew his affinity with his subjects (he is also able to foist the clean-up of crime upon Angelo). Indeed his power is never in question. It is striking that there is neither court nor courtiers in Vienna (excepting the motley group named in 4.5), and it is also remarkable that it never occurs to Angelo, even in his wickedest moments, to seek to usurp the throne. Given the unquestioned stability of rule in Vienna (a feature that might have had something to do with the performance at court in the wake of the extended closure of the Globe),[6] and given that the central issue is the administration of justice rather than the consolidation of power, *Measure* is able to imagine a governmental structure that effectively shares power with the ruler. Of course, Vienna is not a constitutional monarchy with a broad distribution of power, but nevertheless it possesses a bureaucracy stable enough to function in the long absence of the duke – and with no apparent threat of a palace coup. Finally, while this bureaucracy includes corrupt or incompetent officials like Angelo and Elbow, it also features Escalus, an administrator who can deliver justice even through the impenetrability of Elbow's "evidence," the virtuous and efficient Provost, and a sufficient number of officers of the court to fill the jail with wrongdoers (see 4.3; note that Shakespeare has imported the inmates from the competing subgenre of city comedy!).

Since Shakespeare and his fellows moved easily between Whitehall and the Globe and traded on the cachet of their court connections before their popular audiences, it is not surprising to find in his plays a habitually complex representation of the powerful. The competition after around 1600 between the Chamberlain's/King's Servants and the Children's companies for the most lucrative customers pushed Shakespeare's treatment of the political world to the top of its form. *Measure*'s amalgamation of the Machiavellism (in the best sense of the term) represented by Middleton's fashionable play and the providentialism of a populist dramatic history like Heywood's *If You Know Not Me* can frustrate readers who expect to find a coherent political message rather than a dense orchestration of Shakespeare's competitors' plots, themes, and political points of view. We might say that the situation of the King's Servants in the field of cultural production encouraged Shakespeare's creative thinking about the con-stitution of the state by requiring from him a high level of formal inventiveness. In *Measure*, I suggest, this inventiveness allowed him to think beyond the absolutism of Jacobean rule. Again, however, it is important to recognize how the play is building upon previous work; indeed, the king in *All's Well* sets the terms of *Measure's* extended treatment of government as a system when he remarks dolefully, "I fill a place, I know 't" (1.2.69).

It is true that *Troilus and Cressida*, *All's Well That Ends Well*, and *Measure for Measure* are, to a degree, pessimistic in their view of the world, and this might reflect (as someone like Boas thought) a spiritual crisis in Shakespeare's life. On the other hand, characters such as Hector, and especially Helena and Isabella, embody strength, moral seriousness, and a capacity for growth. Beyond that, the plays are buzzing with inven-tiveness. Their formal and verbal brilliance, treatment of character, and orchestration of ideology indicate an artist whose imagination was being challenged and stretched by the competitive writing of other artists. To understand the work of Jonson, Dekker, Chapman, Middleton, Heywood, and the other playwrights who competed within the early modern field of cultural production is, I suggest, to begin to solve the problem of the "problem plays."

NOTES

1 All Shakespeare quotations are from the Riverside edition.
2 I have discussed *All's Well's* involvement in the elite trade in news in Dawson and Yachnin (2001: 197–204).
3 For a brilliant discussion of the pancake bell and of the cultural meanings of the Shakespearean sound-scape, see Folkerth (2002: 12–14).
4 It is telling that the *de facto* emblem of Shakespeare's drama is the prince holding the skull – an image that embodies an ideal of solitary contemplation even though Hamlet is not actually alone in the scene.
5 For the different kinds of staging at hall and amphitheatre playhouses, see Gurr (1994).
6 For a plausible suggestion that Shakespeare wrote *Measure* with a royal audience in mind, see Astington (1999: 133–4).

REFERENCES AND FURTHER READING

Astington, J. H. (1999). The Globe, The Court and *Measure for Measure*. *Shakespeare Survey*, 52, 133–42.
Barroll, J. L. (1991). *Politics, Plague, and Shakespeare's Theater: The Stuart Years*. Ithaca, NY: Cornell University Press.
Bernthal, C. A. (1992). Staging Justice: James I and the Trial Scenes of *Measure for Measure*. *Studies in English Literature*, 32, 247–69.

Boas, F. S. (1896). *Shakspere and his Predecessors.* London: John Murray.

Bristol, M. D. (1996). *Big-Time Shakespeare.* London: Routledge.

Chapman, G. (1914). *An Humourous Day's Mirth.* In T. M. Parrott (ed.) *The Plays and Poems of George Chapman: The Comedies.* London: George Routledge and Sons.

Dawson, A. B. (forthcoming). Introduction. *Troilus and Cressida.* Cambridge: Cambridge University Press.

Dawson, A. B. and Yachnin, P. (2001). *The Culture of Playgoing in Shakespeare's England: A Collaborative Debate.* Cambridge: Cambridge University Press.

Dekker, T. (1979). *The Shoemaker's Holiday.* In R. L. Smallwood and S. Wells (eds.) Revels Plays. Manchester: Manchester University Press; Baltimore, MD: Johns Hopkins University Press.

Donne, J. (1967). *The Complete Poetry of John Donne,* ed. J. T. Shawcross. Garden City, NY: Anchor Books.

Farley-Hills, D. (1990). *Shakespeare and the Rival Playwrights, 1600–1606.* London: Routledge.

Folkerth, W. (2002). *The Sound of Shakespeare.* New York: Routledge.

Gurr, A. (1970). *The Shakespearean Stage, 1574–1642.* Cambridge: Cambridge University Press.

——(1994). Playing in Amphitheatres and Playing in Hall Theatres. In A. L. Magnusson and C. E. McGee (eds.) *The Elizabethan Theatre,* 13. Toronto: P. D. Meany, 47–62.

——(1996). *Playgoing in Shakespeare's London,* 2nd edn. Cambridge: Cambridge University Press.

Helgerson, R. (1992). *Forms of Nationhood: The Elizabethan Writing of England.* Chicago, IL: University of Chicago Press.

Hexter, J. H. (1961). The Myth of the Middle Class in Tudor England. In *Reappraisals in History.* London: Longmans, 71–116.

Heywood, T. (1851). *If You Know Not Me, You Know Nobody, Or The Troubles of Queen Elizabeth, Parts 1 and 2,* ed. J. Payne Collier. London: Shakespeare Society.

Howard, J. E. (1999). Other Englands: The View from the Non-Shakespearean History Play. In H. Ostovich et al. (eds.) *Other Voices, Other Views: Expanding the Canon in English Renaissance Studies.* Newark: University of Delaware Press; London: Associated Universities Presses, 133–53.

Jamieson, M. (1972). The Problem Plays, 1920–1970: A Retrospect. *Shakespeare Survey,* 25, 1–10.

Jonson, B. (1983). *Volpone,* ed. R. B. Parker. Revels Plays. Manchester: Manchester University Press.

——(1995). *Poetaster,* ed. T. Cain. Revels Plays. Manchester: Manchester University Press.

——(2000). *Every Man in his Humour,* ed. R. S. Miola. Revels Plays. Manchester: Manchester University Press.

Kamps, I. (1995). Ruling Fantasies and the Fantasies of Rule: *The Phoenix* and *Measure for Measure. Studies in Philology,* 92, 248–73.

Kastan, D. S. (1987). Workshop and/as Playhouse: Comedy and Commerce in *The Shoemaker's Holiday. Studies in Philology,* 84, 324–37.

Kernan, A. (1959). *The Cankered Muse: Satire of the English Renaissance.* New Haven, CT: Yale University Press.

Lawrence, W. W. (1931). *Shakespeare's Problem Comedies.* New York: Macmillan.

McCandless, D. (1997). *Gender and Performance in Shakespeare's Problem Plays.* Bloomington: Indiana University Press.

McLuskie, K. E. (1994). *Dekker and Heywood: Professional Dramatists.* London: St. Martin's Press.

Malcolmson, C. (1991). "What you will": Social Mobility and Gender in *Twelfth Night.* In V. Wayne (ed.) *The Matter of Difference: Materialist Feminist Criticism of Shakespeare.* Ithaca, NY: Cornell University Press, 29–57.

Marston, J. (1938). *What You Will.* In H. H. Wood (ed.) *The Plays of John Marston,* 3 vols. Edinburgh: Oliver and Boyd, 227–95.

Maus, K. E. (1995). *Inwardness and Theater in the English Renaissance.* Chicago, IL: University of Chicago Press.

Middleton, T. (forthcoming). *The Phoenix.* In L. Danson and I. Kamps (eds.) *The Complete Works of Thomas Middleton.* General ed. G. Taylor. Oxford: Clarendon Press.

——(forthcoming). *The Puritan Widow*. In D. B. Hamilton (ed.). *The Complete Works of Thomas Middleton*. General ed. G. Taylor. Oxford: Clarendon Press.

Orgel, S. (1979). Shakespeare and the Kinds of Drama. *Critical Inquiry*, 6, 107–23.

Patterson, A. (1989). *Shakespeare and the Popular Voice*. Oxford: Blackwell.

Ronayne, J. (1997). *Totus Mundus Agit Histrionem*: The Interior Decorative Scheme of the Bankside Globe. In J. R. Mulryne and M. Shewring (eds.) *Shakespeare's Globe Rebuilt*. Cambridge: Cambridge University Press, 121–46.

Seaver, P. S. (1995). Thomas Dekker's *The Shoemaker's Holiday*: The Artisanal World. In D. L. Smith et al. (eds.) *The Theatrical City: Culture, Theatre and Politics in London, 1576–1649*. Cambridge: Cambridge University Press, 87–100.

Shakespeare, W. (1974). *The Riverside Shakespeare*. Textual ed. G. B. Evans. Boston, MA: Houghton Mifflin.

Shapiro, J. (1991). *Rival Playwrights: Marlowe, Jonson, Shakespeare*. New York: Columbia University Press.

Snyder, S. (1992). "The King's Not Here": Displacement and Deferral in *All's Well That Ends Well*. *Shakespeare Quarterly*, 43, 20–32.

Taylor, G. (1994). Forms of Opposition: Shakespeare and Middleton. *English Literary Renaissance*, 24, 2 (spring), 283–314.

Tennenhouse, L. (1982). Representing Power: *Measure for Measure* in its Time. *Genre*, 15, 1–2, 139–56.

Tricomi, A. H. (1989). *Anticourt Drama in England 1603–1642*. Charlottesville: University of Virginia Press.

Wheeler, R. P. (1981). *Shakespeare's Development and the Problem Comedies: Turn and Counter-Turn*. Berkeley: University of California Press.

Wiggins, M. (2000). *Shakespeare and the Drama of his Time*. Oxford: Oxford University Press.

Williams, G. J. (1997). *Our Moonlight Revels: A Midsummer Night's Dream in the Theatre*. Iowa City: University of Iowa Press.

Yachnin, P. (1997). *Stage-Wrights: Shakespeare, Jonson, Middleton, and the Making of Theatrical Value*. Philadelphia: University of Pennsylvania Press.

Zagorin, P. (1970). *The Court and the Country: The Beginning of the English Revolution*. New York: Atheneum.

4

The Privy and Its Double: Scatology and Satire in Shakespeare's Theatre

Bruce Boehrer

> This century no longer understands fecal poetry.
> Antonin Artaud

The Abyss of Kah-Kah

To begin with doubles: Shakespeare's excremental rhetoric finds counterparts throughout the Western dramatic tradition. When Thersites calls Ajax a "thing of no bowels" (*Troilus and Cressida*, 2.1.49); when he describes Ajax as "go[ing] up and down the field, asking for himself" (3.3.244–5); or when he counters the saccharine rhetoric of his superiors with the disgusted exclamation, "Sweet draught! 'Sweet,' quoth 'a? Sweet sink, sweet sewer" (5.1.75–6), he participates in a ubiquitous idiom of abuse, with antecedents as early as Aristophanes' *The Peace* (421 BC) and descendants as recent as the popular television sitcom *South Park* (1997). The sheer persistence of such subject-matter has led to some arrestingly broad pronouncements on the role of the excremental imagination in culture and in human development. Among these, the most prominent continues to be Freud's theory of anality, which posits fascination with the excremental processes as a universalizing, transhistorical principle of identity-formation.[1] Yet individual manifestations of the scatological impulse, from *The Peace* to *South Park*, prove to be highly context-specific and particular in their articulation. One cannot make much sense of *The Peace* without some awareness of its relation to Athenian history and cultural practice;[2] likewise, *South Park* means little if abstracted from the American culture wars of the 1990s.

Shakespeare's *Troilus and Cressida*, too, obeys a particular set of historical imperatives, imperatives that help to differentiate Shakespeare's scatology from that of predecessors like *The Peace* and successors like *South Park*. The excremental discourse of Shakespeare and his theatrical contemporaries frequently comes to bear upon early modern notions of gentility, notions that presuppose an ambivalent relation to the base-matter (and base matter) of scatology itself. This ambivalence, in turn, extends itself into a distinctive preoccupation with doubling devices, devices that mirror the scatological division of the world into clean and unclean, gentle and base, self and other. As a result, within three markedly scatological plays like Shakespeare's *Troilus and Cressida* (1601–2), Jonson's *The Alchemist* (1610), and Middleton's *A Game at Chess* (1624), we may detect a persistent concern with formal pairing and opposition, a concern elaborated in terms of the anus and its products. For purposes of collective study, these plays make a usefully diverse lot; they span the first quarter of the seventeenth century, they represent the work of the period's three most successful dramatists, and they range in subject-matter from classical history to city intrigue to court politics. Yet at the same time, they present us with a spectacle of uniformity. All produced by the King's Men, these plays remain consistently fixated upon issues of gentility and baseness; they employ patterns of scatological reference to explore these issues; and they develop their scatology in ways that render it endemic both to the execrated other and to the gentle subjectivity that the plays valorize. While three such examples do not confirm an invariable rule, they certainly help to establish a trend, suggesting the general relevance of Renaissance scatology to issues of social rank and social interaction that are themselves specific to the early modern imaginary.

So I am interested here in the role whereby Renaissance drama elaborates social binaries: the familiar oppositions (gentle to base, learned to rude, urbane to rustic, etc.) that populate early English moral and social discourse. More particularly, I am interested in how those oppositions invent themselves within the Shakespearean theatre through their association with bodily waste, which may itself be viewed as a binary counterpart to the body that creates it. Etymologically, the familiar European *caca* – shit – reduplicates the ancient Egyptian *kah* – soul – thus rendering explicit in language the binary troping of the body and its products: "The body doubles the soul; shit doubles the body" (Pops 1982: 51). No twentieth-century theorist of the theatre understood this fact better than Antonin Artaud, for whom

> The breath of the bones has a center and this center is the abyss of Kah-Kah, Kah the corporeal breath of shit, which is the opium of eternal survival. (Artaud 1976: 453)

Artaud's eccentric mysticism advances itself through the doubling of sacred and profane, soul-stuff and excrement. In like fashion, Sir John Harington notes in his *Metamorphosis of Ajax* (1596) that "a good stool might move as great a devotion in some man, as a bad sermon" (p. 92). For both the twentieth-century theorist and the sixteenth-century knight, there obtains a close and edifying relation between the defiled and the elite. In Artaud's case, this relation lies at the heart not only of spiritual, but also of dramatic experience.

To this extent, Artaud's work may be viewed as an attempt to de-bourgeoisify the early twentieth-century theatre: to render it less cerebral, less literary, less refined, less circumscribed, more visceral. Not only does Artaud display a fascination with the scatological rivaling that of Shakespeare's Thersites; his work is "in part a reaction against [an] aesthetic of propriety" characteristic of much nineteenth- and twentieth-century drama, but historically alien to the Shakespearean stage (Taylor 2001: 24). Indeed, when considered apart from this aesthetic, the Elizabethan and Jacobean drama presents us – as it did Artaud – with a collection of theatrical masterpieces whose status as such has been largely confirmed by their abstraction from the original circumstances of their performance. Moreover, those original circumstances often seemed deliberately calculated to defy the ethos of sedate refinement to which Artaud was opposed. Indeed, the printed texts of the early modern drama exploit language and situations which could scarcely be accommodated to a bourgeois notion of the theatre, and which, when prominent enough, could render a play virtually unperformable in that theatre.

It was arguably in response to this state of affairs that Shakespeare scholars of the late nineteenth and early twentieth centuries developed the generic designation of the "problem play," a critical category whose specific purpose was to make sense of plays characterized by "a spirit of gloom, disillusion, and morbidity that exceeds dramatic propriety" (Tillyard 1971: 2).[3] Hence, when first introduced by F. S. Boas (1896), the phrase "problem play" was deliberately calculated to evoke questions of theatrical decorum. For one thing, the phrase had recently been "applied to the drama of Ibsen and Shaw" (Howard 1999: 306), work that assailed the theatrical proprieties of its own historical moment. For another, Boas clearly meant for the term to convey a pejorative generic and moral sense of the plays to which he applied it, plays that "cannot be strictly called comedies or tragedies," that depict a "civilization . . . ripe unto rottenness" (p. 345), and whose characters leave everything they touch "polluted with slime" (p. 383). For Boas, in other words, questions of dramatic propriety and moral propriety are linked; later commentators like Ernest Schanzer (1987) render this linkage still more explicit by defining the genre of the problem play through its tendency to make us "doubt . . . our moral bearings" (p. 5). For Artaud, on the other hand, the problem would lie not in the form or content of these plays themselves, but in the standard of "dramatic propriety" to which they were subjected.

Recent scholars have urged us not to consider Shakespeare's problem plays as a self-contained category or biographical aberration, but rather to place them "in a relational grid in which [Shakespeare's] are not the only texts in the conversation" (Howard 1999: 308). If we do so – placing *Troilus and Cressida* alongside *The Alchemist* and *A Game at Chess*, for instance – the "gloom, disillusion, and morbidity" of Shakespeare's works may emerge as one aspect of a broader preoccupation in Jacobean satiric drama with "social problems" (ibid: 306), problems which devolve upon the individual's own sense of identity and the conceptual oppositions that make it possible. In this respect, Shakespeare's language is indeed double, concerned with the making and unmaking of group allegiances, and his scatology needs to be understood as a manifestation of this doubleness. Taken thus, the problem plays appear less as theatrical anomalies than as part of an ongoing dramatic conversation on the nature of social superiority and privilege, and on the interrelation of the attributes that define these qualities.

The Matter of Troy

When he makes his first appearance in *Troilus and Cressida*, the scurrilous railer Thersites is already deep in argument with the illiterate Ajax, whose wit he insults and who thrashes him repeatedly as payback. Entering to this pandemonium, Achilles seeks to calm both parties in the following exchange:

> *Achilles.* Why, how now, Ajax, wherefore do ye thus?
> How now, Thersites, what's the matter, man?
> *Thersites.* You see him there? Do you?
> *Achilles.* Ay, what's the matter?
> *Thersites.* Nay, look upon him.
> *Achilles.* So I do. What's the matter?
> *Thersites.* Nay, but regard him well.
> *Achilles.* Well? why, I do so.
> *Thersites.* But yet you look not well upon him, for whosomever you take him to be, he is Ajax. (2.1.55–64)

The final joke here, as most editors point out, draws upon the phonic similarity of Ajax's name, in its Elizabethan pronunciation, to the Renaissance euphemism for the privy: "a jakes." Additionally, there is some physical humor to be gained from the vacuous Achilles' scrutiny of the still-more-vacuous Ajax; Thersites has staged a *tableau vivant* of Ignorance contemplating Ignorance in ignorance. But critics seldom note the further charge of Achilles' thrice-repeated question, "What's the matter?", which lies at the heart of the passage's satire.

As it appears in this scene, Achilles' question functions as a framing device, for it doubles the language with which Thersites and Ajax had made their entrance fifty lines earlier:

> *Thersites.* Agamemnon, how if he had biles – full, all over, generally?
> *Ajax.* Thersites!
> *Thersites.* And those biles did run – say so – did not the general run, then? Were not that a botchy core?
> *Ajax.* Dog!
> *Thersites.* Then would come some matter from him; I see none now. (2.1.2–9)

As for this earlier passage, Patricia Parker (1987) has remarked of it that "The 'head and general,' supposed to be a source of ordered and reasoned argument, the generation of 'matter' for discourse as well as the hierarchical embodiment of order itself," is hypothetically translated into "the source of 'matter' in an infected body politic" (p. 89). For Thersites, Agamemnon's imagined pus is more real – more material – than his actual wisdom; likewise, as Achilles peers at Ajax, Thersites discerns within the latter character a buried cloacal matter that usurps his nominal identity.

Thus Thersites' words to Achilles structurally parallel his previous words to Ajax, both of which in turn develop a further parallel between competing sorts of discursive and somatic matter. These parallels, in turn, generate a tertiary parallel by juxtaposing the two principal patterns of satirical imagery in Shakespeare's play, the alimentary and the medical. Commentators have long agreed that "images of appetite" and of "disease" are endemic to the language of *Troilus and Cressida* (Bevington 1998: 82–4); more peculiarly, however, these images often seem linked, as in the scene in question. Here the material by-products of morbidity and of digestion function as a kind of bottom-line for the characters' rhetoric, which begins in pus and ends in excrement, the pus and excrement in question being identified with Greek leadership and heroism, respectively, while being also implicitly constituted as complementary substances.

The doublings endemic to such a gesture are impressive, and they become doubly so – as it were – when one discerns their like within the broader structure of Shakespeare's play. For *Troilus* is a profoundly binary artifact. All of its scenes are set in one of two general places, Troy or the Greek camp outside of Troy, and the play's *dramatis personae*, Greek and Trojan, sort themselves out in similar pairs, either complementary or contrasting or both: Achilles and Hector, Diomedes and Troilus, Menelaus and Paris, Helen and Cressida, Thersites and Pandarus, etc. Moreover, this binarism can be traced even in the play's relation to its sources, for *Troilus* provides a notorious counter-narrative to that of Hector's death in Book 22 of the *Iliad*, while likewise rendering Cressida's character more sympathetically than does the general narrative tradition descending from Chaucer, Lydgate, and Henryson.[4] It is as if Shakespeare had read Artaud's (1958) remark that "Every real effigy has a shadow which is its double" (p. 12), and pondering these words, had sought to instantiate them in the structure of his play.

But if *Troilus and Cressida* is a play of shadows, the shadows in question possess unnerving solidity, aching and excreting and suppurating in ways that the characters of the *Iliad*, for all their explicit bloodshed, seldom manage. Thersites offers the best case in point. Making only a single appearance in the *Iliad* (2.211–69), his Homeric character is summoned up only to be conclusively expelled by Odysseus. Yet in Shakespeare's work Thersites develops into a grating, insistent presence whose every second thought is the sewer. He simply will not go away, and his cockroach-like durability undermines the heroic status of the very Greek cause to which Homer's text sacrifices him. Thersites' preoccupation with physicality has elicited considerable scholarly attention,[5] most recently from David Hillman (1997), who sees it anticipating the Nietzschean view of physiology as "inherently anti-idealizing, undercutting metaphysics and transcendent aspirations of any kind" (p. 297). Yet the physicality of *Troilus* arguably has less to do with Nietzsche – for whom the body at least affords a salutary corrective to the idealizing tendencies of Platonic and Hegelian philosophy – than with Artaud – whose "prose and poetry depict a world clogged with matter (shit, blood, sperm), a defiled world" in the keeping of "demonic powers" (Sontag 1988: xlvii). This, I think, is the world of Shakespeare's play: a strangely embodied shadow of the classical heroic ideal.

If this play of shadows and binaries in *Troilus and Cressida* offers a crowning irony, it may well lie in the audience to which the work is self-consciously addressed. First of all, at this late date one cannot know whether that audience originally consisted of spectators or of readers, or, if the former, of public or private theatregoers; the two surviving states of the 1609 Quarto offer contradictory testimony.[6] Moreover, *Troilus and Cressida* extends Shakespeare's signature metadramatic preoccupations in a way that aggressively implicates the play's readers/spectators in the action they witness. Whether in the play's Epilogue, where Pandarus addresses the audience as fellow members of a confraternity of pimps and whores (thereby also emphasizing the proximity of the Globe Theatre to the Bankside brothels); or in the disclosure of Cressida's infidelity, in act 5, scene 2, where a theatre audience must watch Thersites watching Ulysses watching Troilus watching Diomedes and Cressida watching each other; or elsewhere, the play insistently involves its audience in the spectacle it enacts, foregrounding "the complicity of the audience and reader" (Charnes 1993: 100) in the narrative they consume.[7] Yet this complicity does less to unite the audience than to divide it from itself, for *Troilus and Cressida* is by no means a self-consciously popular play; if anything, it is self-consciously *un*popular. Whatever else it does, the preface to the second state of the 1609 Quarto makes this much clear. "Neuer clapper-clawd with the palmes of the vulgar" nor "sullied, with the smoaky breath of the multitude," *Troilus and Cressida* emerges from this prefatory epistle as a comedy comparable to those of Plautus and Terence, designed for an audience of "witte" and "Iudgement." Yet what resemblance could such an audience bear to the "Brethren and sisters of the hold-door trade" (5.11.51) whom Pandarus addresses in his Epilogue? Constituting itself as double, *Troilus* builds itself a doubled public as well.

A principal focus of the play's social discrimination seems to be the intellect, which constitutes, within the play's world, a category of merit inconsistent with the characters' mutual apportionment of rank and dignity. Pitting machiavels and railers against illiterate and "beef witted" lords (2.1.13), *Troilus and Cressida* thus enacts onstage an education-based division of its *dramatis personae* that corresponds roughly to the general distinction between university and public-theatre audiences. (This point may reinforce the opinion of recent editors that *Troilus* was initially composed for university performance.)[8] The play's vulgarity is central to this separation of sheep from goats. To return to Ajax's "matter," for instance: Thersites' ridicule of his witless tormenter works simultaneously to exploit the most simpleminded of privy-jokes and to convey the satirist's distaste for simplemindedness itself. The spectator who laughs at the final line of the exchange – "Whosomever you take him to be, he is Ajax" – needs to laugh twice: once at the coarse Shakespearean quibble and then again at the fatuity of laughing at the coarse Shakespearean quibble, this second laugh being, needless to say, altogether dryer and less amused than its predecessor. Moreover, the quality of the spectator's laughter determines his/her particular relation to the onstage spectacle. To chuckle at the coarseness is to align oneself with those characters onstage (Achilles, for instance, and Patroclus, and to a degree Ajax himself) who suffer Thersites as an allowed fool – "my cheese, my digestion," as Achilles patronizingly calls him (2.3.41). And to align oneself thus is to recapitulate the dynamic staged for us by Thersites, as Achilles stupidly gazes at Ajax without recognizing himself in what he sees. In this case, the spectator offstage thus doubles the spectator onstage; yet if, on the other hand, one laughs the dry laugh of the satirist rather than the coarse laugh of the fool, one recreates instead the stage-position of Thersites himself, the impotent and disgusted misanthrope whose one accomplishment is to entertain himself with the fundamental worthlessness of his compatriots. This is small consolation.

To think of the play's laughter as occupying different and competing registers is inevitably to summon the ghost of Bakhtin, whose notion of all-inclusive carniva-lesque laughter contrasts so pointedly with the thin and cruel humor of the Enlight-enment satirist.[9] For Bakhtin, the laughter of carnival is universal and liberating, signifying "the defeat of divine and human power, of authoritarian commandments and prohibitions, of death and punishments after death" (90–1). That of the Enlight-enment, on the other hand, "is narrow and specific," limited to "private and social vices" (Bakhtin 1984: 67), and Thersites' humor, scarcely triumphant or victorious, focused morbidly on the misdeeds of individuals and the society they have created, conforms nicely to this latter model. Still, *Troilus and Cressida* stages many of the motifs most dear to the Bakhtinian notion of carnival: not only the all-inclusive laugh-ter of the groundling, but also the trope of the world upside-down, the preoccupa-tion with comestibles and sex, the interest in soiling and staining and scatology. But the tone of Shakespeare's work could not be further from Bakhtinian carnival's atti-tude of liberating jollity and tolerance. If *Troilus* plays itself out in a defiled, Artaudian world, it derives no sustenance from the carnivalesque notion that we're all in the same mess together. On the contrary, the play seems to say, only fools would take comfort in such a thought.

Dapper Uncloseted

Unlike *Troilus and Cressida*, Jonson's *Alchemist* is set in a single place: a house in Black-friars during plague-time, occupied in its owner's absence by his rascally butler Jeremy/Face and two confederates, Subtle and Dol Common, who together run a series of confidence-schemes on the local citizenry. The play's plot, in turn, is organized as a series of visits by the citizens in question, who resort to Face, Subtle, and Dol for a variety of self-aggrandizing reasons. Of these various gulls, the first to come and the last to leave is one Dapper, a "fine yong quodling" of a law-clerk (1.1.189) whose initial desire is to obtain a familiar spirit, in the form of a fly, to help him win large stakes at gambling. At play's end, Face, Subtle, and Dol have enlarged his aspirations by convincing him that he is "allyed to the queene of *Faerie*" (1.2.126): a fortunate child about to discover his long-concealed relation to this fabulously wealthy, single, aging monarch. Between the play's beginning and its ending, however, the audience sees very little of Dapper; he only appears onstage three times (1.2, 3.5, 5.3–4), and even these appearances serve primarily to establish his conspicuous absence from most of the onstage action. Indeed, he spends almost the entire second half of the play locked in a privy.

To this extent Dapper both frames and doubles the rest of his play's action. He initiates the parade of dupes which lends structure to Jonson's plot; he is the last dupe to leave before the confidence-game is exposed; and in the meantime he remains prominently out of sight, his absence providing an invisible counterpoint to the impostures transacted onstage. It has long been noted that Face, Subtle, and Dol's acts of impersonation contrast sharply with the reality of their lives: "When Subtle is compared to a priest, the comparison itself shows how much he disappoints the ideal. When Dol calls herself Queen of Faeries, we see how far she really is from the Faery Queen" (Partridge 1958: 157). But what then of Dapper, who sees nothing of the sort, and whom we ourselves scarcely see at all? He lives out the fraud that is exposed for us onstage, and in doing so he draws less attention to its falsity than to its unnerving verisimilitudes. Consigned to the outhouse to await an audience with the Queen of Faerie, he performs a ritual of purification that by its very nature illustrates the interdependence of the exalted and the abject; moreover, this ritual evokes some unexpected historical associations as well. In her role as Queen of Faerie, Dol cannot help but suggest the majesty of the Faery Queen, recapitulating the eccentricity and fondness for younger men to which Queen Elizabeth herself had been subject in her later years: "Her *Grace* is a lone woman, / And very rich, and if she take a phant'sye, / she will doe strange things" (1.2.155–7).[10] Likewise, as he eagerly buys into his role as long-lost favorite to his "aunt of *Faerie*" (1.2.149), Dapper too encounters an historical double: Queen Elizabeth's brilliant scapegrace godson, Sir John Harington, author of epigrams and letters, translator of Ariosto, but perhaps most lastingly remembered as inventor of the flush-toilet, which he popularized with his scatological mockencomium *The Metamorphosis of Ajax*. In 1611, only a year after the first performances of *The Alchemist*, Jonson clearly had Harington in mind, referring to the *Metamorphosis* in the last line of the last poem of his own book of *Epigrams* published in that year (133.196). As for Dapper, while he huddles in his outhouse awaiting the pleasure of his royal aunt, he seems almost deliberately designed to suggest the youthful Harington, whose exploits in the field of sanitary engineering established a particularly intimate connection between himself and his Faery godmother. For Harington in fact constructed two principal prototypes of his cloacal invention; retaining one for himself, he installed the other in Queen Elizabeth's palace at Richmond, where she kept a copy of Harington's *Metamorphosis* chained next to it, readily available as powder-room reading-matter.[11]

Thus it is appropriate that for Dapper himself, the outhouse he enters should not be simply a room of easement, but a means of conveyance into the royal presence. In this latter respect, the throne upon which he sits doubles and anticipates his aunt's own throne, and his privy chamber adumbrates yet another privy chamber, to which Harington had jokingly prophesied that his *Metamorphosis* would earn him special admission (Harington 1962: 61). Indeed, in its employment as a space of anticipation and deferred gratification, Dapper's privy recapitulates the palatial architecture of edifices like Richmond and Whitehall, which were constructed largely as a series of anterooms, waiting-spaces in which messengers and courtiers could cool their heels indefinitely while expecting an audience with the monarch of the moment. It is just this pose of reverent expectation that Dapper assumes in his outhouse; as Face assures Subtle, "Sir, he shall / Hold out, and 'twere this two houres, for her *Highnesse*" (3.5.69–70).

In this respect, Jonson's play arguably functions as autobiography, for the poet's career exhibits a lifelong commitment to self-promotion through royal patronage, as well as an intimate familiarity with the anterooms and waiting-chambers of White-hall. This commitment takes many forms, including not only acts of association with nobility but also repeated acts of symbolic separation from the stepfather who raised him, and scholars have discerned a pronounced anal impulse in these acts. David Riggs, for instance, has seen a reenactment of the Jonson family romance in *The Case Is Altered* (1597), whose unpleasant stepfather, Jacques de Prie, buries his gold in a midden only to lose it in the process (Riggs 1989: 30–1). Since psychoanalysts have long grounded their understanding of anality on symbolic equivalences between excrement and various substitute objects, such as dirt, mortar, buttons, and coins,[12] such equivalences are easy to discern in *The Case Is Altered. The Alchemist* requires a bit more historicization, however, not only because of the obvious parallels between Dapper's situation and the protocols of courtly behavior, but also because of the way it suggests Jonson's own career preoccupations; the play's scurrility seems not to have been merely an expression of Jonson's own peculiar temperament. At the very least, Jonson's fondness for coarse humor coincidentally mirrored that of his king, who grew rapidly famous among his English subjects for the indecorousness of his courtly behavior and sense of humor.[13] As James's court poet, Jonson was of course under a certain obligation to produce work that spoke to the royal tastes, and thus we may see the scatology of *The Alchemist* as central not only to Dapper's relation with his long-lost aunt, but also to the poet's relation with the royal patron who has, in effect, become a substitute father to him.

Certainly, when first produced, *The Alchemist* was a showpiece of upper-crust drama, composed by the king's house poet for performance by the king's personal troupe of players. This performance, in turn, was apparently designed to open the King's Men's second season at their private theatre in Blackfriars,[14] a theatre whose accommodations and entry prices deliberately narrowed the English public-theatre audience to a wealthier and trendier elite. By this measure, *The Alchemist* is in fact a more concert-edly anti-popular play than *Troilus and Cressida*, and in this it typifies Jonson's ambiva-lent relations with the popular element of his audience – the "vnderstanding Gentlemen o' the ground" (*Bartholomew Fair*, Induction 49–50), as he rather cattily describes them elsewhere. And when it concludes, *The Alchemist* addresses itself very specifically to a gentlemanly mode of understanding:

> Gentlemen,
> And kind Spectators, if I have out-strip
> An old mans grauitie, or strict canon, thinke
> What a yong wife, and a good braine may doe. (5.5.152–5)

> Gentlemen,
> My part a little fell in this last *Scene*,
> Yet 'twas *decorum*. (5.5.157–9)

But what actually counts, for this play, as gentlemanly understanding? Where *Troilus and Cressida*'s satire separates characters and audience in binary terms, differentiating between those with wit and those without, *The Alchemist* undertakes a detailed inventory of the gentlemanly attributes that might masquerade for wit, including wealth (for the megalomaniac Sir Epicure Mammon), roaring-boy behavior (for the bumptious Kastril), piety (for the hypocritical Puritan Tribulation Wholesome), commercial success (for the merchant Drugger), and family/patronage connections (for Dapper). The play's scatology works in large part to stigmatize these qualities as ersatz; yet at the same time it cannot help acknowledging their power to elicit admiration, a power without which they would be unworthy of contempt, and without which *The Alchemist* itself could not succeed as patronage drama.

Thus, in its treatment of its characters' social aspirations, in the audience and original performance setting it presupposes, and in the patronage context out of which it developed, *The Alchemist* offers us a model of scatological satire whose scatology is not simply allied to the abuses it condemns, but remains central to the social and political standards with which it identifies. As a further instance of this centrality, we might consider the royal office of Groom of the Stool, which has recently begun to attract an increased measure of scholarly attention.[15] By Jonson's day the Groom of the Stool, "whose original job [in the Middle Ages] had been to clean out the royal latrines," had grown to be "one of the most powerful and confidential of royal servants" (Girouard 1978: 58). The Black Knight in Middleton's *Game at Chess* boasts of having sold the position six times to different petitioners (4.2.41), and much of its desirability results from the intimate contact it affords between the groom of the moment and the sovereign he serves. As cloacal factotum, the Groom of the Stool presides over the offices of royal excretion; he maintains the royal close-stool and examines its products for signs of health or distemperature; he serves, in this sense, both as a royal confidant and an intermediary between the royal self in its private and public capacities. The Groom's office, in short, involves an "exquisite combination of intimacy, degradation, and privilege" (Paster 1993: 32); like Dapper in his closet of easement, the Groom of the Stool becomes both invisible and on display, marking, in the process, the equivalent doubleness of the royal body he serves.

Enshrined at the heart of this doubleness, and at the center of the Groomship of the Stool, is the royal turd itself, whose status as an object both to be hidden and to be exhibited suggests its disturbing liminality as a property of the self. As Hamlet might say, the king's body is with the turd, but the turd is not with the body; it is simultaneously an alienable and an inalienable manifestation of his royal majesty. In the former capacity, human waste was not only hoarded for use as fertilizer in early modern England, but middens were also, on at least some occasions, assigned financial value in legal documents of the day (Boehrer 1997: 153–61). Necessarily and inevitably extruded, our excrement is the part of us we can least help leaving behind; in this sense, alienation is its *raison d'être*. Yet extruded or not, it remains distinctively our own. As Freud long ago observed, we relate to our own excrement differently than we do to that of others, and the Groomship of the Stool extends this relationship by regarding one's feces as a double of one's self, marking one's state of health, one's rank, one's intestinal fortitude (as it were). One's stool, in short, both mirrors and reconfigures one's identity. It participates both in life and in art.

Gondomar's Fistula

Although produced some fifteen years after *The Alchemist* – and a quarter-century after *Troilus and Cressida* – Middleton's *Game at Chess* deserves notice alongside these earlier plays, if only to demonstrate the durability of the scatological element in early modern English satirical drama. Middleton's play resembles *The Alchemist* and *Troilus and Cressida* in belonging to the repertoire of the Lord Chamberlain's/King's Men, but it differs vastly from the two earlier plays in the nature and extent of its public appeal, having achieved the greatest celebrity of any play ever acted in the early English theatre, generating more ticket revenue, more consecutive performances, and more international notoriety in its day than anything by Shakespeare or Marlowe or Jonson. Yet Middleton's work – a vehement attack upon the abortive marriage negotiations between the Prince of Wales and the Spanish Infanta in 1623 – employs some of the same satirical techniques developed in *Troilus* and *The Alchemist*: recurrent scatological invective, prominent use of doubling and framing devices, a coincidence of alimentary and medical vocabularies. And like the earlier plays by Shakespeare and Jonson, *A Game at Chess* aims at establishing group identity through the construction of difference. In the case of Middleton's play, however, the group identity in question coincides not with gentility in the narrow sense, commensurate with notions of social rank or intellect, but rather with a "gentleness" of national character and religious affiliation that encompasses the entire public-theatre audience to which it is addressed.

Middleton's play manifests its doubleness on the broadest possible structural level. Saturated as it is with anti-Spanish sentiment, it concentrates its invective upon two larger-than-life characters, the Fat Bishop and the Black Knight, who act out an ambivalent relationship of mutual mimicry and antagonism. The two are drawn as blatant political caricatures: the Fat Bishop represents Marco Antonio de Dominis, Archbishop of Spalatro, who earned bitter English enmity when, after converting to the Church of England in the early 1600s, he recanted his conversion in 1622 and returned to the Continent; and the Black Knight famously lampoons the influential Spanish ambassador to England, Don Diego Sarmiento da Acuña, Count Gondomar, at whose urging Prince Charles had pursued the unpopular prospect of marriage to the Infanta. De Dominis and Gondomar, the Fat Bishop and the Black Knight, represent Catholic perfidy in the sacred and Spanish perfidy in the secular regiments respectively, and they are endowed with a carefully drawn somatic complementarity, embodying gross disorders of the mouth and of the anus.

In this latter respect, Middleton chose the objects of his satire well. During his years in England, de Dominis achieved notoriety for his greed and hedonism; remembered as "corpulent in his body" (Fuller 1868, 3: 343) and a "great-bellied-Doctour, made fat vnder Antichrist" (Floyd 1617: sig. S3r), he could figure the rapacious appetites of the Catholic church in the very folds of his flesh. As for Gondomar, he achieved equal fame both for his political cunning and for the chronic misery he endured from an anal fistula; this inglorious malady occasioned much English mirth, appearing again and again in the anti-Spanish tracts upon which Middleton drew in composing his play. Even more ingeniously, Middleton has made these two characters the primary mouthpieces for his play's anti-Catholic, anti-Spanish invective; instead of relying upon the members of the White House to denounce their Black House counterparts, Middleton contrives to have the Fat Bishop and Black Knight censure each other, locked in a mutual enmity that ultimately undoes them both.

Thus it is appropriate that the play's most severe attack upon gluttony, the Fat Bishop's signature vice, should issue from the Black Knight, who extols the temperance of his countrymen by reference to negative example:

> We do not use to bury in our bellies
> Two hundred thousand ducats and then boast on't,
> Or exercise th'old Roman painful-idleness
> With care of fetching fishes far from home . . .
>   . . . We commend rather
> (Of two extremes) the parsimony of Pertinax. (5.3.6–29)

The diatribe continues, in this vein, for half of the play's final act, and its applicability to the Fat Bishop is underscored when, a hundred lines later, the Bishop is taken by the White House and placed in the bag reserved, like a kind of hell-mouth, for the game's captured pieces. As he enters confinement, his fellow-prisoners complain of the Bishop's girth, and he responds with insolent pride: "The Bishop must have room, he will have room, / And room to lie at pleasure." The Black Jesting Pawn, pressed beneath the Fat Bishop's bulk, retorts that "All the bag, I think, / Is room too scant for your Spalato paunch" (5.3.19–95), thus reminding the audience again of the Bishop's iconic status as gluttony incarnate.

But if the Black Knight particularly condemns the Fat Bishop's overindulgent mouth, it is the Fat Bishop who most viciously derides the Black Knight's corrupt anus. The insult in question is de Dominis's own, from his time as an anti-Catholic polemicist,[16] and the Black Knight recalls it with indignation:

> I'll tell you what a most uncatholic jest
> He put upon me once, when my pain tortured me;
> He told me he had found a present cure for me
> Which I grew proud on, and observed him seriously.
> What think you 'twas? Being execution-day
> He showed the hangman to me out at window,
> The common hangman. (2.2.66–72)

The force of this insult derives from its conflation of the medical with the moral; the Black Knight's ulcerated anus manifests a corruption of character that can only be relieved by execution. Small wonder, then, that the Black Knight responds by dwelling on his counterpart's fatness: in the Knight's imagination, the Bishop becomes a "greasy-turn-coat, gourmandizing prelate" (2.2.54), a "thing swelled up with mingled drink and urine" (2.2.75) whose "fat and fulsome volumes" (2.2.56) of theological controversy bespeak an appetite in excess of the flesh that nurtures it.

Yet for all his denunciation of the Fat Bishop's gourmandizing, the Black Knight, too, is a slave to appetite. Having censured the Bishop's excesses of diet in the play's final act, he immediately figures his own political aspirations in extravagant culinary terms, as a "large Feast of our Vast Ambition" (5.3.83) in which Venice supplies the fowl course, Italy "the bake-meats" (5.3.89), Geneva "the chipped manchet" (5.3.90), etc. It is in terms of this overweening will to power that the Fat Bishop has earlier derided the Black Knight as "the fistula of Europe" (2.2.46); Gondomar's malady comes to stand synecdochically not only for Gondomar himself, but for his policies and aims in their broadest possible extent. Where de Dominis feeds "upon the fat" of the White "kingdom" (2.2.19), Gondomar vents his corruption across an entire continent.

Hence the Black Knight's ailment comprises the principal bodily referent for political intrigue in Middleton's play. Entering with a specially designed "chair of ease" (4.2.3) – a chair with cutaway seat like one used for comfort by Gondomar himself[17] – the Knight calls it his "chair of cozenage" (4.2.3); he cites the "foul flaw in the bottom of [his] drum" as evidence that he will make "sound treacher / With any he in Europe" (4.2.7–9);[18] he describes himself as a ship with "a leaking bottom" which has nonetheless "been as often tossed on Venus' seas / As trimmer fresher barks" (2.1.172–4). While Gail Paster (1993) has argued that early English drama often figures women as "leaky vessels" (p. 23), distinguished by a urinary, menstrual, and lacteal incontinence which betokens their essential imperfection, the Black Knight offers a case of masculine characterization in the same vein. The putrid discharge of his anus provides a visible index of his moral corruption, which can only be redeemed by hanging; still, his cunning excites "moral condemnation and abhorrence" more than the "ridicule" reserved for the Fat Bishop (Howard-Hill 1995: 74). The Fat Bishop is to the Black Knight not only as mouth is to anus, but as comedy is to tragedy; he remains merely loathesome and contemptible, whereas the Knight manages in contrast to be loathesome and threatening. His anality constitutes a threat and an affront to Englishness and true Christianity, as Middleton's play rallies its audience against a corrupt Catholicism emanating from the south.

A Second Fistula

In sustaining its fever-pitch of nationalist sentiment, *A Game at Chess* relies not just upon scatological invective, but also upon a broad range of particular associations between the anal and the political. If Gondomar is the "fistula of Europe," the privy flaw that usurps his identity recalls in turn a considerable array of Spanish and Catholic practices. Discovered in his attempts to seduce the White Queen's Pawn, the Black Bishop's Pawn exclaims in dismay, "Methinks I stand over a powder-vault / And the match now akindling. What's to be done?" (2.1.156–7), his language thus inevitably alluding to that most notorious of Catholic conspiracies, the Gunpowder Plot, built like the Black Knight's character upon a flawed and unsuccessfully concealed fundament. As the Black Queen's Pawn and the Black Knight convey the Black Bishop's Pawn to safety, they secure him within a "secret vault" (2.1.187), a back-door repository for spiritual infection that mimics not only the Black Knight's fistula but also the domestic architecture of certain crypto-Catholic homes in England.[19] But it is within the confessional that we see Gondomar's abscess writ most large. Thus the Black Bishop's Pawn, in the duplicitous role of spiritual adviser, counsels the White Queen's Pawn not to suppress the knowledge of her sins:

> You must part with 'em; to be nice or modest
> Toward this good action is to imitate
> The bashfulness of one coneals an ulcer,
> For the uncomely parts the tumor vexes
> Til't be past cure. (1.1.115–21)

Thus, while presenting confession in medical terms, as the figurative act of draining an ulcer, the Black Bishop's Pawn also uses it as the framework within which to develop a confidential, intimate relation that will provide him with privileged access to the White Queen's Pawn's "[un]comely parts."

This range of associations, simultaneously as broad as Europe and as narrow as the confession booth, retains its corrosive genius even at the present late date. And when *A Game at Chess* was first performed, at least one of its spectators saw the play as an act of specifically anal revenge, a satire that could literally bite its object on the bottom:

Lic{kfinger}. What news of *Gundomar*?
Tho{mas Barber}.   A Second *Fistula*,
Or an *excoriation* (at the least)
For putting the poore *English-play*, was writ of him,

To such a sordid vse, as (is said) he did,
Of cleansing his *posterior's*.
(Ben Jonson, *The Staple of News*, 3.2.207–11)

Ben Jonson, writing in 1625–6, could thus present Middleton's play as a return of the anal repressed, and in a sense the play itself is structured upon the very dynamic of revelation and purgation that the Black Bishop's Pawn uses to describe the sacrament of confession. Thus Middleton engineers the climactic checkmate of the Black House "by / Discouery" (5.3.161–2) – that is, by the White Knight's public revelation of his privileged conversations with the Black Knight on the subjects of ambition and political duplicity. Having insinuated himself into the Black Knight's confidence just as the Black Bishop's Pawn insinuates himself into that of the White Queen's Pawn, the White Knight is situated, at play's end, to disclose the cozenage of which Gondomar's fistula is itself only a physical, and still at least partially concealed, manifestation. To this extent, the White House out-Gondomars Gondomar; as the White Knight himself confesses to the Black Knight before placing the Black House in checkmate, "I'm an arch-dissembler, sir" (5.3.15). Black House and White House double one another much as do Black Knight and Fat Bishop. And if Middleton's play appealed to its audience, it would do so in large part by placing that audience itself in the privileged position of the confessor: the Black Bishop's Pawn as he listens to the White Queen's Pawn's self-disclosures, or the White Knight as he learns the secrets of the Black Knight's villainy. In this sense, *A Game at Chess* takes on the overall structure of a figurative anal purge. It is theatre as enema.

But to end where we began, with doubles: when Jonson reports the sighting of a "Second *Fistula*" on Gondomar's backside, we may perhaps discern within his words a meaning beyond that which he more obviously intended. For whether or not Middleton's play actually succeeded in excoriating Gondomar's bottom, there was most certainly a second fistula in existence already, within (upon?) the surviving body of the early English drama, and again it returns us to where we began: to Shakespeare.

As is well known, *All's Well That Ends Well* (1602–3) enacts a variation upon one of the most time-honored narrative motifs of fairy-tale and romance: the story of an unknown and improbable hero who, in the face of immense odds, rejuvenates a languishing kingdom by healing its ruler's seemingly incurable wound, and whom the grateful monarch rewards according to his request. The particular changes that Shakespeare works on this theme may in part be traced to his proximate source, Boccaccio's tale of Giletta of Narbonne in the *Decameron* (third day, ninth story), as Englished in William Painter's *Palace of Pleasure*.[20] There one may already discover the particular malady with which the King of France is afflicted in *All's Well*, and which Shakespeare's Helena cures, thereby securing marriage to Bertram as her dubious reward: a potentially "notorious" fistula (*All's Well*, 1.1.36) which, like Gondomar's after it, seems curable only by the offices of the hangman. Indeed, when we first hear in Shakespeare of the king's condition, it is in the context of the sufferer's own resignation: "He hath abandon'd his physicians, . . . under whose practices he hath persecuted time with hope, and finds no other advantage in the process but only the losing of hope by time" (1.1.13–16); this, too, may be traced to Boccaccio, whose king "had tried many physicians, none of [whom] had been able to cure him," with the result that "the King was driven to despair and no longer would consult with or seek assistance from any of them" (p. 227). To this degree, at least, the malady in question seems not to reflect much independent deliberation on Shakespeare's part; it is simply an inherited plot element.

But of course Shakespeare does make a number of changes to the tale he inherits, changes that seem primarily aimed at heightening the audience's sense of Helena's unrequited merit and of Bertram's inexcusable self-absorption.[21] For instance, the new figure of Parolles, doubling Bertram, enhances the latter's selfishness in the process, whereas Shakespeare all but erases the resistance to Helena's low birth that pervades Boccaccio's story. In *All's Well That Ends Well* the principal vestiges of this rank-based bigotry survive only in Bertram himself. Amid revisions of such an overt and calculated nature, the King of France's fistula undergoes a minor change of sorts, too, and while this change may simply be the product of coincidence or expediency, it nonetheless suggests something about the way in which Shakespeare has darkened and complicated his received subject-matter.

For Boccaccio, the abscess in question is clearly thoracic in nature. The King of France, we are told, developed his affliction "because of a tumor on his chest which had been badly treated" (p. 227); in Painter's version of the story, this detail has been carefully preserved (Bullough 1957–75, 2: 390). In Shakespeare, however, the precise location of the fistula is no longer clear; on the contrary, the only thing we learn about it, apart from the fact of its resistance to treatment, is that the king's courtiers do not want it to be the subject of conversation ("I would it were not notorious": 1.1.36). Given the breadth of discourse bestowed upon Gondomar's fistula two decades later, and given the fact that fistulas were typically associated with the anal region by medieval and early modern medical practitioners,[22] one may perhaps sympathize with the courtiers' reticence on this subject, and one may also conjecture that perhaps the fistula itself has migrated, in Shakespeare's reconstruction of his backstory, to a position below the belt.

This shift may not be monumental, but it certainly intensifies the darkness of Shakespeare's overall tone. When viewed from the standpoint of genre, *All's Well That Ends Well* makes a deliberate effort to transform the stock material of fairy-tale into something edgier and more equivocal, and we may perhaps regard the King of France's fistula, nestled securely in its new and unnamed location, as a little parcel of unpleasantness installed at the fairy-tale's core, signaling the turn to satire and raillery characteristic of Shakespeare in his problem plays. Likewise, the newly hidden nature of the king's malady may reflect upon the particular twist Shakespeare gives to the character of his leading man, Bertram, whose external gifts of breeding and youthful vigor disguise an appalling absence of honor and good judgment. Here, once more, the scatology of Shakespeare's problem plays reengages issues of social discrimination. Surely there is no drama more class-conscious than *All's Well*, and yet *All's Well* famously stands the markers of rank and class on their heads, juxtaposing a corrupt possessor of status and title like Bertram to the worthy but lowly Helena so as to adumbrate a relation between Bertram's weakness of character and his king's physical corruption. "Unworthy" the "good gift" of Helena (2.3.151), Bertram, as much as the king, requires physic in hidden places.

But what they – and we – get instead is theatre: a particular kind of theatre that seems determined not to heal the wounds it inflicts, but to keep them suppurating instead. The King of France's fistula is replaced by other maladies, of character and conscience, which escape the ameliorative virtue of Shakespeare's play; Gondomar's fistula remains curable only by the hangman; Dapper wanders off into plague-beset London with his ignorance as his greatest blessing; Pandarus bequeaths us his diseases. Shakespeare's participation in this form of drama – his figurative immersion in the pus and excrement that are its native element – has lastingly resisted critical efforts to associate his name with later, prissier notions of theatrical high culture. Like Gondomar's fistula, the problem plays survive as an unsettling extrusion on the backside of their author's *corpus*, refusing to be ignored or explained away.

NOTES

1　For Freud's original concept of anality, see "Character and Anal Erotism" (Freud 1959) and "The Disposition to Obsessional Neurosis" (Freud 1958). For further development of Freud's theory, see Ferenczi (1950: 319–31) and Jones (1949: 413–37). For recent discussions of anality that make particular reference to the Elizabethan and Jacobean drama, see Wilson (1948: 213–32), Pearlman (1979), and Boehrer (1997).

2　For the scatological element in Aristophanes' work, see Henderson (1991), especially pp. 63–75 and 187–203. For a helpful treatment of scatology in Greek and Roman epigram, see Richlin (1992: 127–51).

3　See Jamieson (1972) for a review of the genre's history and definition. For more recent comment, see Howard (1999: 306–8).

4　For Shakespeare's treatment of Hector's death (traceable to Caxton's and Lydgate's descriptions of the death of Troilus in *The Recuyell of the Historyes of Troye* 638–9 and the *Troy Book* 4.2647–779, respectively), see James (1997: 97–106) and Bevington (1998: 390). For the contrast between Shakespeare's and Chaucer's treatment of Cressida, see James (1997: 95, 106–12), who argues that "Shakespeare's play systematically repudiates its predecessors," in part by creating a Cressida who "does not shoulder full responsibility for the play's failures of value" (p. 95). See Dollimore (1984: 40–9) for support of this view. On the other hand, Thompson (1978) claims that "Shakespeare is . . . hostile [to] his heroine" (p. 142).

5　For additional scholarly discussion of this theme, see Muir (1955: 33–4), Kaufmann (1965: 153–7), and Thomas (1987: 127–31).

6　Thus Kenneth Muir (1955) asserts that "we do not know whether [*Troilus and Cressida*] was ever performed in Shakespeare's lifetime" (p. 28). Bevington (1998: 1–6) agrees. Leslie Fiedler (1985: 51), on the other hand, believes the play failed at the Globe. The editors of the *Norton Shakespeare* suggest, more conservatively, that it may have "never got[ten] beyond performance by university students" (Greenblatt et al. 1997: 717). This last conjecture, while unproven, would introduce a rank-specific doubling of audience into the play's textual and performance history.

7　For the effects of scopophilia on *Troilus* and its audience, see Charnes (1993: 100–2).

8   The editors of the *Norton Shakespeare*, following those of the Oxford edition, argue that Pandarus' Epilogue, the front-matter to the 1609 Quarto, and certain other passages should be suppressed (or at least bracketed) in conformity with the apparent aims of the "revised, more authoritative" Folio text of the play (Greenblatt et al. 1997: 725). This suppression effectively creates two different forms of *Troilus and Cressida*: an earlier Quarto version of the play designed for coterie performance and exhibiting a marked "satiric thrust" (p. 717), and a revised Folio version aimed at public-theatre performance and configured as tragedy. This argument renders explicit the doubling of audience (and genre) that typifies the play as a whole.

9   For Bakhtin's theory of carnivalesque laughter, see *Rabelais and His World* (1984), especially pp. 59–114. For discussion of Bakhtin in terms of the early modern English theatre, see Bristol (1985: 19–25), Stallybrass and White (1986: 9–79), and Boehrer (1997: 14–19).

10   The scenes involving Dapper have long been viewed as Jonson's attack upon "what he sees as the effeminate preciousness of Spenser's narrative" in *The Faerie Queene* (Moulton 2000: 96).

11   See Beal (1980: 124, 131–3, 138–41, 628) and Pops (1982: 46).

12   See, for example, Ferenczi (1950: 324–8) and Jones (1949: 25–7, 429–30).

13   As David Riggs (1989) has remarked, "Broadly speaking, the poet was in the employ of King James" (p. 118); thus, for Jonson, "Composing comedy [was] an adaptive . . . act" whereby he "had discovered how to turn manure into a valuable commodity" (p. 31).

14   *The Alchemist*'s first recorded performance took place in September 1610 in Oxford, while the London theatres were closed by the plague. Thus, Peter Womack (1986) conjectures, "since the script was new . . . it seems obvious that the company would do [the play] in London once the theatres reopened" (p. 117).

15   For recent scholarly interest in the Groom of the Stool, see Paster (1993: 139–40), Girouard (1978: 56–8), and Starkey (1987: 78).

16   The jest is ascribed to de Dominis in 1655 by Thomas Fuller (1868, 3: 336).

17   This chair is featured in the title-page engraving, by Crispin van de Passe, for Thomas Scott's *Second Part of Vox Populi* (1624), a work that influenced Middleton heavily. For the engraving and its influence, see Howard-Hill (1995: 126–30).

18   The first Quarto of *A Game at Chess* renders Gondomar's reference to the "fowl flaw in the bottom of [his] drum" by substituting "bum" for "drum." See Middleton (1999: 444, n. 4.2.7).

19   For the practice of providing English Catholic homes with priest-holes, see Coffey (2000: 88–9) and Morley (1978: 140–4).

20   For relations between Shakespeare's play, Boccaccio's *Decameron*, and Painter's *Palace of Pleasure*, see Daniell (1986: 115–17) and Cole (1981: 12–32, 72–89, 114–37).

21   As Daniell (1986) has remarked, "Shakespeare has complicated . . . Boccaccio . . . by making Helena more radiant and problematic, and Bertram without any redeeming feature at all" (p. 115). For Shakespeare's use of Boccaccio, see Cole (1981), esp. pp. 114–37.

22   In John Arderne's medieval manual for the treatment of fistulas, the anal variety take pride of place (Arderne 1968: 1–2); for a later treatment of the subject see De La Charrier (1695: 128–31). The association of fistulas with the anal region was so general in early modern England that by 1581 Walter Haddon could describe the Catholic practice of selling pardons as a "frettyng Fistula within the Bowels of the Christian commonweale" (sig. 2F5v).

References and Further Reading

Arderne, J. (1968). *Treatises of Fistula in Ano, Hemorrhoids, and Clysters*, ed. D'Arcy Power. Oxford: Oxford University Press.

Artaud, A. (1958). *The Theater and Its Double*, trans. M. C. Richards. New York: Grove Press.

——(1976). *Antonin Artaud: Selected Writings*, ed. S. Sontag. Berkeley: University of California Press.

Bakhtin, M. (1984). *Rabelais and His World*, trans. H. Iswolsky. Bloomington: Indiana University Press.

Beal, P. (ed.) (1980). *Index of English Literary Manuscripts*, Vol. 1: 1450–1625, Part 1. London: Mansell.

Bevington, D. (ed.) (1998). *Troilus and Cressida, by William Shakespeare*. Walton-on-Thames: Thomas Nelson and Sons.

Boas, F. S. (1896). *Shakspere and His Predecessors*. London: John Murray.

Boccaccio, G. (1982). *The Decameron*, trans. M. Musa and P. Bondanella. New York: New American Library.

Boehrer, B. (1997). *The Fury of Men's Gullets: Ben Jonson and the Digestive Canal*. Philadelphia: University of Pennsylvania Press.

Bristol, M. (1985). *Carnival and Theater*. New York: Methuen.

Bullough, G. (1957–75). *Narrative and Dramatic Sources of Shakespeare*, 8 vols. London: Routledge and Kegan Paul.

Charnes, L. (1993). *Notorious Identity: Materializing the Subject in Shakespeare*. Cambridge, MA: Harvard University Press.

Coffey, J. (2000). *Persecution and Toleration in Protestant England, 1558–1689*. Harlow: Longman.

Cole, H. C. (1981). *The "All's Well" Story from Boccaccio to Shakespeare*. Urbana: University of Illinois Press.

Daniell, D. (1986). Shakespeare and the Traditions of Comedy. In S. Wells (ed.) *The Cambridge Companion to Shakespeare Studies*. Cambridge: Cambridge University Press, 101–21.

De La Charrier, J. (1695). *A Treatise of Surgical Operations After the Newest, and Most Exact Method*. London.

Dollimore, J. (1984). *Radical Tragedy: Religion, Ideology, and Power in the Drama of Shakespeare and His Contemporaries*. Chicago, IL: University of Chicago Press.

Ferenczi, S. (1950). *Sex in Psychoanalysis*, trans. E. Jones. New York: Basic Books.

Fiedler, L. A. (1985). Shakespeare's Commodity-Comedy: A Meditation on the Preface to the 1609 Quarto of *Troilus and Cressida*. In P. Erickson and C. Kahn (eds.) *Shakespeare's "Rough Magic": Renaissance Essays in Honor of C. L. Barber*. Newark: University of Delaware Press, 50–60.

Floyd, J. (1617). *A Survey of the Apostasy of Marcus Antonius de Dominis*, trans. A. M. St. Omer.

Freud, S. (1958). The Disposition to Obsessional Neurosis: A Contribution to the Problem of Choice Neurosis. In *The Standard Edition of the Complete Psychological Works of Sigmund Freud*, Vol. 12, trans. J. Strachey. London: Hogarth Press, 315–26.

——(1959). Character and Anal Erotism. In *The Standard Edition of the Complete Psychological Works of Sigmund Freud*, Vol. 9, trans. J. Strachey. London: Hogarth Press, 167–75.

Fuller, T. (1868). *The Church History of Britain from the Birth of Jesus Christ until the year 1648*, 3 vols. London: William Tegg.

Girouard, M. (1978). *Life in the English Country House: A Social and Architectural History*. New Haven, CT: Yale University Press.

Greenblatt, S. et al. (eds.) (1997). *The Norton Shakespeare: Comedies*. New York: W. W. Norton.

Haddon, W. (1581). *Against Jerome Osorius*, trans. J. Bell. London.

Harington, Sir John (1962). *The Metamorphosis of Ajax*, ed. E. S. Donno. New York: Columbia University Press.

Henderson, J. (1991). *The Maculate Muse: Obscene Language in Attic Comedy*, 2nd edn. New York: Oxford University Press.

Hillman, D. (1997). The Gastric Epic: *Troilus and Cressida*. *Shakespeare Quarterly*, 48, 3 (fall), 295–313.

Homer (1951). *The Iliad*, trans. R. Lattimore. Chicago, IL: University of Chicago Press.

Howard, J. (1999). Shakespeare and Genre. In D. S. Kastan (ed.) *A Companion to Shakespeare*. Oxford: Blackwell, 297–310.

Howard-Hill, T. H. (1995). *Middleton's "Vulgar Pasquin": Essays on "A Game at Chess."* Newark: University of Delaware Press.

James, H. (1997). *Shakespeare's Troy: Drama, Politics, and the Translation of Empire*. Cambridge: Cambridge University Press.

Jamieson, M. (1972). The Problem Plays, 1920–1970: A Retrospect. *Shakespeare Survey*, 25, 1–10.

Jones, E. (1949). *Papers on Psycho-Analysis*. Baltimore, MD: Williams and Wilkins.

Jonson, B. (1925–52). *Ben Jonson*, 11 vols., ed. C. H. Herford, P. Simpson, and E. Simpson. Oxford: Clarendon Press. All references to Jonson's work are to this edition.

Kaufmann, R. J. (1965). Ceremonies for Chaos: The Status of *Troilus and Cressida*. *English Literary History*, 32, 2, 139–59.

Middleton, T. (1999). *Women Beware Women and Other Plays*, ed. R. Dutton. Oxford: Oxford University Press. All references to Middleton's work are to this edition.

Morley, A. (1978). *The Catholic Subjects of Elizabeth I*. Totowa, NJ: Rowman and Littlefield.

Moulton, I. F. (2000). *Before Pornography: Erotic Writing in Early Modern England*. Oxford: Oxford University Press.

Muir, K. (1955). *Troilus and Cressida*. *Shakespeare Survey*, 8, 28–39.

Parker, P. (1987). *Literary Fat Ladies: Rhetoric, Gender, Property*. London: Methuen.

Partridge, E. B. (1958). *The Broken Compass: A Study of the Major Comedies of Ben Jonson*. London: Chatto and Windus.

Paster, G. (1993). *The Body Embarrassed: Drama and the Disciplines of Shame in Early Modern England*. Ithaca, NY: Cornell University Press.

Pearlman, E. (1979). Ben Jonson: An Anatomy. *English Literary Renaissance*, 9, 364–94.

Pops, M. (1982). The Metamorphosis of Shit. *Salmagundi*, 56, 26–61.

Richlin, A. (1992). *The Garden of Priapus: Sexuality and Aggression in Roman Humor*, 2nd edn. Oxford: Oxford University Press.

Riggs, D. (1989). *Ben Jonson: A Life*. Cambridge, MA: Harvard University Press.

Schanzer, E. (1987). *The Problem Plays of Shakespeare*. New York: Schocken.

Shakespeare, W. (1987). *The Riverside Shakespeare*, ed. G. Blakemore Evans et al. Boston, MA: Houghton Mifflin. All references to Shakespeare's work are to this edition.

Sontag, S. (ed.) (1988). *Antonin Artaud: Selected Writings*. Berkeley: University of California Press.

Stallybrass, P. and White, A. (1986). *The Politics and Poetics of Transgression*. Ithaca, NY: Cornell University Press.

Starkey, D. (1987). Intimacy and Innovation: The Rise of the Privy Chamber, 1485–1547. In D. Starkey et al. (eds.) *The English Court: From the Wars of the Roses to the Civil War*. London: Longman, 68–92.

Taylor, G. (2001). Gender, Hunger, Horror: The History and Significance of *The Bloody Banquet*. *Journal for Early Modern Cultural Studies*, 1, 1 (winter/spring), 1–45.

Thomas, V. (1987). *The Moral Universe of Shakespeare's Plays*. London: Croom Helm.

Thompson, A. (1978). *Shakespeare's Chaucer: A Study in Literary Origins*. Liverpool: Liverpool University Press.

Tillyard, E. M. W. (1971). *Shakespeare's Problem Plays*. Toronto: University of Toronto Press.

Wilson, E. (1948). *The Triple Thinkers: Twelve Essays on Literary Subjects*. New York: Oxford University Press.

Womack, P. (1986). *Ben Jonson*. Oxford: Blackwell.

5
Hymeneal Blood, Interchangeable Women, and the Early Modern Marriage Economy in *Measure for Measure* and *All's Well That Ends Well*

Theodora A. Jankowski

This fellow has undone me endlessly.
Never was bride so fearfully distressed.
The more I think upon th' ensuing night,
And whom I am to cope with in embraces,
One who's ennobled both in blood and mind, . . .
Before whose judgment will my fault appear . . .
                      . . . There's no venturing
Into his bed, what course soe'er I light upon,
Without my shame, which may grow up to danger;
He cannot but in justice strangle me
As I lie by him, as a cheater use me.
'Tis a precious craft to play with a false die
Before a cunning gamester. (4.1.1–5, 7, 11–17)

The above quote is obviously not from Shakespeare. It is from Thomas Middleton and William Rowley's *The Changeling* (ca. 1622). Beatrice-Joanna is reflecting on the fact that she has married her true love, Alsemero, knowing she has given her virginity to the servant Deflores in payment for his having murdered her father's choice of suitor, Alonzo. I begin with this quote because it clearly focuses on the most important aspect of the early modern (so-called) "companionate" marriage – the bride's virginity – and the dire consequences attendant upon its loss. Claude Lévi-Strauss (1969) has pointed out that marriage is an alliance "between two groups of men" in which the intact woman/wife becomes the contractual signifier of an economic (later to be termed "familial") bond between two patriarchal families (p. 115).[1] I want to focus in this essay on how the fetishization of the hymen – resulting from the importance of its intactness up until its quasi-ceremonial penetration at the *right* time by the *right* man

– undergirds the entire structure of early modern marriage and deconstructs its "companionate" nature. It is important to consider how such fetishization is managed in various Shakespearean texts because these plays have become crucial for defining the concept of the early modern "companionate" marriage for us today, as well as defining its slightly later – and especially current – manifestation as marriage for "true love." Specifically, I want to look at how the "bed trick" – and its variations – in a number of Shakespeare's later plays demonstrates the slippery ground upon which the edifice of the companionate/true love marriage is constructed.

The particular "bed tricks" I am interested in exploring are those in *Measure for Measure* (ca. 1603) and *All's Well That Ends Well* (ca. 1604–5), two of Shakespeare's so-called "problem comedies" – plays which, while technically "comic," raise moral issues usually considered unsuited to comedy. While the substitution of one woman for another in a man's bed allows for the saving of a life, a marriage, and a vow of virginity, this plot-solving device poses innumerable problems regarding the morality of the male characters involved, as well as the morality of sexual substitution itself. Additionally, it is very difficult to consider plays whose denouements depend upon violations of basic honesty and social morality as comic. My interest in the bed trick, however, has little to do with issues of social morality but much to do with the troubling depictions of marriage in these two plays. I see the bed trick – and the various logistics necessary to its consummation – as a site where it becomes easier to examine women's problematical relationship to patriarchal marriage than in Shakespeare's "happy comedies." While I see the bed trick as problematizing the "companionate" nature of early modern marriage, I also see an understanding of it as a tool which we can use to reconsider the often unquestioned festive nature of the early comedies and their overall salvific depictions of marriage.

The economic understanding of marriage as a contract between two male individuals as representatives of their families proposed by Lévi-Strauss certainly undergirds all conceptions of marriage in early modern England, both "dynastic" and "companionate." Such a contractual understanding treats both potential spouses as property, used simply to establish political or necessarily dynastic connections between the families who sponsor the union. I want to stress that this sense of contractual obligation was present in the earlier form of early modern marriage often referred to as "dynastic" as well as in the later form referred to as "companionate."[2] The "dynastic" marriage can be seen as originating during the feudal period and being primarily concerned with insuring the consolidation/expansion of landholdings and political alliances. While the social structures of feudalism insured that women were subject to control by their fathers before and their husbands after marriage, potential grooms as well as potential brides were often the victims of their parents' desires to increase familial power through marital alliances. While such a marriage arrangement may have initially treated both sons and daughters as chattel, sons achieved actual power in the social system once they attained their majority and in the family once they were married. Women remained chattel – legally they were "covered" by their husbands as *femes covert* – for the duration of their marriage.[3]

Since the emerging early modern middle class did not base its wealth/power on inherited land and was not particularly concerned with establishing political alliances through marriage, it was considered to have been influential in reconceptualizing "dynastic" marriage and its deleterious effect on the partners concerned, especially the women. But while political considerations were virtually eliminated from middle-class unions, economic considerations were not. Lévi-Strauss's notion of marriage as a contract between men was as much a part of the "companionate" as the "dynastic" marriage. Indeed, the notion of a marriage *contract* was even more acceptable within the trade milieu of the middle class. Consequently, economic considerations in these marriages became paramount; decisions regarding the proposed union also involved more of the family than simply the parents of the betrothed couple. Sons, especially eldest sons, had a distinct stake in the financial viability of their potential brides. After all, they would inherit their fathers' business and substance and needed to be aware of any potential financial liabilities on the part of the bride's family. Second and subsequent sons had an even greater stake in the financial viability of the bride's family, since they were more dependent upon the provisions of the bride's marriage portion. Yet since middle-class wealth was not entailed land, fathers *could* (and apparently did) leave some of their substance – though perhaps not the business itself – to second and subsequent sons, and even daughters.[4]

While I have focused here primarily on the economic distinctions between the "dynastic" and the "companionate" marriage, I must acknowledge that there are critics who see the companionate marriage as originating from non-economic roots. Those who view it as a primarily *Protestant* creation (see note 2) see it as resulting directly from the Protestant reaction against the glorification of virginity in Roman Catholicism and what was viewed as the "selling" of daughters in dynastic marriage. For Protestants, marriage was considered to be "companionate" because they viewed " 'solitarinesse' [as] essentially not a state of mind demanding remedy, but a physical handicap" (Halkett 1970: 16). Indeed, Cornelius Agrippa von Nettisheim claimed marriage "was ordeyned for an helpe for propagation, and to avoid fornication" (sig. Biii).[5] Thus, for Protestant theorists, marriage was designed as a partnership whereby men and women were to provide help and consolation to each other, propagate (and educate) Christian children, and avoid the dangers of fornication by engaging in religiously/legally mandated sexual activity. The raising and education of Christian children assured both that future generations would *become* acceptable members of society and that they were inculcated in the necessary social ideologies by acceptable members of society.[6] The affection implicit in this idea of parents jointly raising children and spouses relieving each others' loneliness leads to the definition of this type of marriage as "companionate" and to the belief that it resulted in greater autonomy for wives. Indeed, William Gouge feels that "it is requisite that there should be some equality betwixt the parties that are married in *Age, Estate, Condition, Piety*" (cited in Halkett 1970: 43). But while this list of equalities seemed to be designed to eliminate some of the grosser excesses of dynastic marriage – brides married to men who were thirty or forty years their senior, much above or below them in class, vastly richer or poorer, less pious – nowhere in this list is equality of sex or gender mentioned. While we may rightly argue that the companionate marriage provided some improvement for women over the dynastic marriage, we should not at all equate the early modern companionate marriage with the late twentieth- or early twenty-first century "true love" match. While early modern parents were urged by Protestant sermons and marriage manuals to consult with their children regarding their potential partners and to pair their children to spouses who would treat them well, provide good parents for their children, and whom they could like and respect, parents *did* have the final say as to who married whom. And while one's partner may be a decent, upstanding, God-fearing person who was a good parent and provider and treated one with respect, that partner may also not be one's "true love." I will have more to say later on the issue of "true love."

Daughters of the middle class clearly had more autonomy, if not more legal standing, within the early modern "companionate" marriage paradigm than daughters of the nobility. Those women were essentially treated as breeding stock and their physical virginity was essential for insuring that the husbands' lands and title passed on to first sons of their own blood. Yet while the virginity of the potential middle-class wife was not essential to insuring the purity of the titled heir, most men – fathers as well as husbands – did not wish their substance to pass out of their blood. So whether she was contracted into a noble or a middle-class marriage, the bride was still expected to be a virgin on her wedding night. The importance of this for noble women is obvious in Beatrice-Joanna's dilemma, as indicated in the epigraph to this chapter. Not only has this character lost her virginity, but she has done so to a man who is a servant. The special and particular qualities of the virgin are so unique that the character does not feel she could "fake" her "defloration" when she and Alsemero consummate the marriage.[7] What exactly *are* the special and particular qualities of the virgin bride experienced by the husband during the defloration? Folk belief has it that the virgin bride is known by her intact hymen that tears and bleeds when her husband penetrates her. Whether or not her intactness makes her feel "tight" to her husband, the presence of enough blood to stain the wedding sheets provides the dramatic proof of the bride's once-virgin status. The bride *must* be known to bleed on her wedding night, or the groom has gotten a bad bargain, been sold "used" goods, been duped, or cuckolded before he was even "officially" married. Hence the development of the folk tradition of displaying bloodied wedding sheets to assure the community that the bride was, indeed, a virgin and her husband was, indeed, the first to penetrate her.

Yet the various "problems" inherent in the simple narrative of this tradition are suggested by the ending of the Isak Dinesen short story *The Blank Page*. This story is about a convent whose nuns grow and spin the flax and weave the linen for the bridal sheets of the royal house. As is the custom, the bloodied sheets are hung from the palace balcony after each royal wedding night. The convent gets to display permanently a framed portion of the wedding sheets complete with nuptial blood stains. Yet among this grotesque gallery of female intimacy hangs a frame whose portion of sheet is pure and unbloodied. The piece of unstained cloth suggests that bleeding did not occur because the bride was not a virgin. However, there are many other possibilities for that lack of stain. All hymens have some perforation (or women could not menstruate). Consequently, not all women bleed the first time they are penetrated by a penis. Some hymens have very small perforations. Therefore, some women could bleed while masturbating (self-penetration with a finger or other instrument) or by being penetrated by a man's finger. A woman could also bleed by being penetrated by another woman's finger or instrument. Such pre-marital bleeding would most likely eliminate the telltale blood from the bridal sheets. Other scenarios might also accomplish this non-event. The bride may have been frightened, or ill, and the groom may have respected her wish not to engage in intercourse at that time. A similar situation may have occurred to the groom. Or, he may not have been able to penetrate the bride, either because of an unusually tough hymen or his inability to have an erection. The bride may have successfully fought off the husband's attempts to penetrate her. Or he may simply have been rendered impotent by the mere thought of heterosexual intercourse. He might have been asexual or may simply have preferred sexual activity with men. Or any number of other scenarios.

Now, granted, consummation was required for the marriage to be rendered legal, and early modern couples would have had it drummed into their heads that they *had* to consummate the marriage so as not to render either or both of them — and their families — laughing stocks. Suddenly finding themselves in a situation where penetration could not occur, or bleeding did not, couples might want to insure the *appearance* of consummation by staining the sheets with *some* blood or bloody substance, no matter whose or what. Which makes the blank sheet/canvas of the Dinesen story so teasing. We are given no indication of what actually has occurred. I do not want to spend a lot of time in idle speculation, though I have indicated above several possible reasons for the lack of a stain. What I want to focus in on here is the *necessity* of the stain, the necessity of the bleeding hymen and the stained sheets, the necessity that whoever the bride is, whatever her title or fortune, what *really* matters is that the bride bleeds. Hence the curious circumstance that the identity of the character Alsemero penetrates is immaterial so long as, when he awakes the following morning, he sees blood on the sheets. Beatrice-Joanna now knows that the *only* thing that *really* matters in this marriage is her hymen, not Alsemero's love for her or hers for him.

I have been using the term "hymen" as it is used currently to describe "a fold of mucous membrane partially closing the external orifice of the vagina in a virgin" (*The Random House Dictionary of the English Language*). The word derives from the Greek *hymene*, *hymenos* meaning "thin skin," and comes into English in the sixteenth century via the French anatomist Ambroise Paré (*OED*). The word previously referred to the Greek god of marriage, and in the early seventeenth century referred to marriage or the wedding itself (*OED*, 1608, 1613).[8] The more usual term to refer to this membrane in the sixteenth and seventeenth centuries was the "maidenhead." Use of this word to describe the hymen goes back at least to 1300 and continues until the late seventeenth century and beyond (*OED*). The combining of "maid" plus "head" in the creation of the word serves to focus the object on women, though the *OED* also suggests that the term may be "said occasionally of a man" (def. 1).[9] The combination of words also allows for much punning, such as that occurring in *Romeo and Juliet*: "I will bee civill with the Maids, and cut off their heads . . . the heads of the Maids, or their Maiden-heads" (1.1.23, *OED*).

When I wrote of the bride having her hymen penetrated, I was also employing current usage. A more apt early modern usage would be to speak of "deflowering" a virgin. The euphemistic archaism of this word, though, hides a much nastier truth. While definition 1 in the *OED* defines the verb as "to deprive (a woman) of her virginity," it goes on to indicate, as synonyms, "to violate, ravage, desecrate, to rob of its bloom, chief beauty, or excellence, to spoil." Interestingly, both usages of the early modern term "deflower" are embedded within the discourse of rape. "Violation," "ravage," "desecration," and "spoil" are hardly phrases we would expect to be used to describe the consummation of a marriage of "true love," or even a marriage of "companions." While the above two phrases conceal the actual role of women in early modern dynastic or companionate marriages – as breeder or chattel – "deflower" continues the disconnect between an ideal consummation and what might feel to an early modern woman suspiciously like a rape.

But to return to Shakespeare. "Happy comedies" such as *The Comedy of Errors*, *The Taming of the Shrew*, *A Midsummer Night's Dream*, *Much Ado About Nothing*, and *As You Like It* serve an important purpose as regards the development of a *discourse* about the early modern companionate marriage. The valorized plot action of these playtexts is the successful courting and marriage of various pairs of "true lovers": Luciana and Antipholus of Syracuse, Bianca and Lucentio, Hero and Claudio, Hermia and Lysander, Helena and Demetrius, Rosalind and Orlando, and Celia and Oliver. Despite various pre-nuptial trials, the movements of these various plays assure us that parental whim – or the desire for an economically secure or upwardly mobile union – will not stop the movement of true lovers toward each other and toward marriage. We can locate the whim that makes Egeus insist that Hermia marry Demetrius, as well as the desire for political alliance that makes Leonato agree to Claudio's proposal. Yet these left-overs of the dynastic marriage paradigm tend to disappear as these happy comedies come to their coupled endings.[10] These plays imply that dynastic marriage, with its lack of input from the betrothed couple, is dead and marriage based on true love lives and triumphs.

Or does it? I would argue that the bitter reality of early modern marriage in either of its forms is vitally present in these plays, if seemingly overlaid with the veneer of blissful love. All of the happy comedies I have mentioned contain a counter-narrative of marriage which upholds the importance of dynastic/familial unity, the search for economic stability, or the necessity of retaining the social status quo. These plays may seduce us into believing that the companionate/true love marriage is the prevailing norm in the early modern period, yet they simultaneously deconstruct this "reality," revealing that previous forms of marriage have not totally disappeared. For example, we often forget that, in his first appearance in the play, the character Petruccio declares that he has "come to wive it wealthily in Padua" (1.2.72).[11] Orlando is a second son who will not inherit anything.[12] Antipholus of Ephesus, a grown-up orphan of the storm, manages to save Duke Solinus's life and is rewarded with the Duke's ward, the presumably wealthy and certainly well-connected Adriana. In all these cases, one individual of the prospective pair, or his/her family, clearly stands to gain from the marriage. Katherine and Bianca have a wealthy father. Rosalind is her father's heir. Celia's family may advance both politically and economically. Claudio and Hero are both heirs, though Claudio also holds a title. While some of these pairings may seem to come about as the result of true love, the playtexts also show that there are other – perhaps more profound – factors driving the marriage contract.

These early comedies also point out the interchangeability of bodies, especially women's bodies. The situation of the boy actor who plays girls' roles has been examined by a number of critics in terms of the kinds of erotic "charge" such substitution and play acting produces in the audience. I want to look at a different kind of interchangeability, that between various women characters in the early comedies. The love potion in *A Midsummer Night's Dream* allows Lysander and Demetrius to redirect their love back and forth between the seemingly interchangeable Helena and Hermia. Yet this "playful" exploration of the similarity between women does not negate the cruel redirection of Demetrius's love from Helena to Hermia – apparently without reason – before the play begins. Similarly, Proteus in *The Two Gentlemen of Verona* switches his affections from Silvia to Julia as though there is nothing to choose between any two women. Yet to my mind the most egregious example of female interchangeability in an early play occurs in *Much Ado About Nothing* where the servant Margaret is mistaken for Hero, resulting in the latter being accused of unchastity. These plays demonstrate that not only are women of the same class interchangeable, but apparently women of different classes as well. Darkness may be the "excuse" for the interchanging of Hero and Margaret, but Demetrius and Proteus find it easy to take one woman for another in broad daylight. I will have more to say later about this "curious" ability of women to resemble each other.

Though I have mentioned Katherine and Petruccio in the context of greedy suitor and wealthy potential wife, I want to consider them in another context along with a similar couple, Beatrice and Benedick. This latter couple does not fit the economic paradigm I have been examining above. While Beatrice is wealthy, there is no indication that Benedick is financially needy. Nor does he seem to desire a political alliance with Beatrice's uncle. Yet as much energy is spent by the company of *Much Ado About Nothing* in getting these two married as Petruccio spends in taming Katherine. By the end of each play we are led to believe that initial prejudices have been overcome and each pair forms a true love match. Jean Howard (1987), in a brilliant essay, has pointed out the fallaciousness of this conclusion as regards Beatrice and Benedick.[13] She argues that these two characters, in their opposition to marriage, challenge the early modern social structure. While Bianca and Hermia each may challenge social norms (as represented by her father) by insisting on marrying the man of her choice, Beatrice and Benedick challenge society at a far deeper level by refusing marriage itself. Their friends' plan to bring them together is more a plan to enfold them within the embrace of society than to "awaken" the dormant true love between them. I would adapt Howard's argument to Katherine and Petruccio. These characters are as rene-gade as Beatrice and Benedick, yet Petruccio realizes that marriage is necessary to his financial survival as well as a social demand. The character pragmatically marries a suitorless and undisciplined heiress knowing that his promise of marriage will be accepted simply because of its singularity. Yet Petruccio also knows that living within society is impossible – and dangerous – if one does not follow the rules. His taming of the character Katherine is an attempt, I would argue, to make her cognizant of the necessity of paying close attention to social norms and living as they dictate.[14] While a society may be willing to accept a certain amount of rebelliousness in a young man, it may be less willing to accept such behavior in a young woman, and even less in an old(er) woman. Such "abnormal" female behavior has often led, in the sixteenth and seventeenth centuries, to punishment as a witch.[15]

Yet while Katherine's and Beatrice's behavior may have been abnormal, and there-fore threatening, the characters never completely violate what is arguably the most important social norm for women. Neither sacrifices her virginity before marriage. Such a "crime" would place a woman completely outside the norms of society, as demonstrated in *Much Ado About Nothing*. Claudio's accusation of Hero results in her "death" (4.1). Despite the fact that she is belied, Hero suffers almost as great a fate as if she were guilty. While her fainting in church symbolizes her social death, if the plan to clear her name fails, she will actually "die" to society by being forced to relocate to a convent for the rest of her life. Thus early modern society imposed strict norms upon its female members regarding preserving their virginity for marriage. The fate almost suffered by the character Hero points out the importance of the intact hymen for "defining" women in early modern society. The blood Hero, or any woman, will shed at her socially sanctioned defloration stands in for/reinforces her familial "blood," the honor of her family, and her good name.

While the character Hero serves to demonstrate the social death suffered by women who have lost their honor inappropriately, her situation also points out how fragile female honor is. While that honor can literally be lost through the incorrect or inop-portune penetration of the woman's hymen, it can also be lost through the incorrect "description" of the woman as dishonorable. Here the hymen is figuratively pen-etrated – or the vagina invaded – by male speech.[16] Thus male descriptions or defin-itions of women as unchaste can have the same effect as actual inappropriate/illegal sexual activity. Claudio's words are not the only ones that destroy a woman's honor. Iago completely destroys Desdemona's honor through words that convince Othello that she is Cassio's mistress. Iago ventriloquizes both Desdemona and Cassio to create the fiction of the adulterous couple. Yet when Othello demands "ocular proof," the character Iago is stymied by stage conventions governing "the unrepresentable." Since Cassio cannot be shown on stage penetrating (the male actor playing) Desdemona – or a stand-in actor, since such an act never occurs – the presumed penetration is replaced by an acceptable representation: the strawberry-spotted handkerchief. A miniature bridal sheet, the handkerchief stands in for Desdemona's hymeneal blood/vagina, which is clearly compromised in the passage from Othello to Cassio, to Iago, and back to Othello.[17] A similar situation happens in *Cymbeline*. Giacomo convinces Posthumus that he has had intercourse with Innogen because he is able to describe her bedchamber, tell him about the mole on her breast, and gain possession of her bracelet. While Posthumus shrewdly points out that Giacomo could have heard the bedchamber and mole described by others, he is totally convinced once presented with the "ocular proof" of the bracelet. Again, the character Giacomo's presumed penetration of Innogen is unrepresentable. Her bracelet becomes the same sort of acceptable representation as the handkerchief. Yet where the blood-colored strawberries alluded to hymeneal blood which, in turn, calls to mind Desdemona's vagina, the open circle of the bracelet more directly represents the "penetrated" vagina.[18] Although the vagina and its penetration are unrepresentable on stage, objects like the handkerchief and bracelet stand in for them and allow the audience to "see" those fragile parts upon which wives' and husbands' honors rest. Desdemona and Innogen, like Hero, are never inappropriately/illegally penetrated by anything but a man's words, but the possession of the representable symbols of their vaginas figures their ownership by men who are *not* their husbands.

The various bed tricks in Shakespeare's plays – both actual and symbolic – are implicated in the folk traditions I have been exploring: the "fact" that the penetrated virginal hymen bleeds, the "fact" that any man can tell whether the woman he has just penetrated is a virgin, and the "fact" that all women are interchangeable in the dark. While readers/audiences today recognize that some virginal hymens *do* bleed, they have much more trouble accepting either a man's ability instantly to tell that a woman is a virgin or the interchangeability of women in a dark room. Yet *Measure for Measure* and *All's Well That Ends Well* specifically ask us to do just that. We are supposed to believe that Bertram cannot figure out that a woman who has lived in his own home for several years is in his arms, and not Diana. We are similarly supposed to believe that Angelo assumes Isabella is in his arms and not a woman to whom he has been betrothed. We are also simultaneously supposed to believe that the darkness and silence that allow these deceptions also allow the men in question to "know" they are with the correct women because their virginal hymens have been penetrated. The question I want to ask is, how: how are these deceptions *supposed* to work? In the cases of Iago and Giacomo mentioned earlier, the deceptions work both because sexual activity never occurred and because the husbands in question accept objects or other body parts as substitutes for the vagina. The strawberry-spotted handkerchief "becomes" Desdemona's vagina and Cassio's possession of it equals his sexual possession of Othello's wife. The mole on her breast, her bracelet, and her bedroom "become" Innogen's vagina, and Giacomo's view or possession of them signifies his sexual possession of Posthumus's wife.

Given this focus on the defloration of the bride to consummate a marriage (or legitimate a marriage contract) that can only be achieved through the grotesquerie of the bed trick,[19] the "problem comedies" *Measure for Measure* and *All's Well That Ends Well* seem to function almost solely as critique of the early modern companionate/true love marriage. If the companionate marriage is one which celebrates the existence of an affectionate relationship between men and women, then the presence of the success-fully accomplished bed trick interrogates whether such a relationship has any basis in fact or is even possible given how male–female relationships can degenerate to the manipulation of body parts in a patriarchal culture. *Measure for Measure* is set in a society that has no place for what we might consider *ordinary* male–female relation-ships. There are, in fact, no ordinary couples in the play. The characters easily fall into two categories: hypersexual and asexual. An exploitive culture of prostitution, rather than one connected to marriage, represents the status quo of sexual activity in Vienna and provides sexual partners for such hypersexual males as Lucio and, presumably, the Duke.[20] Yet this society contains virtually no female examples of this kind of hyper-sexuality. Indeed, we are forced to question whether the whores are as "traditionally" oversexed as folk culture would have us believe. Mistress Overdone's is the only one of these voices we hear, yet her desires are focused more on business than sex (1.2.54–93).[21] We hear the highly mitigated and ventriloquized voice of Mistress Kate Keepdown, yet in sifting through parts of what she purportedly has said, we "see" a woman who is more concerned with raising her child than with anything else (3.1.427–31). On the other side of the divide are Angelo and Isabella, both asexual or sexually repressed. Although Isabella retains her sexuality to serve God, Angelo seems to enjoy his ability to piss ice water purely for its own sake.

In fact, the only "normal" people in this society are the "criminals," Claudio and Juliet. Their sexual activity is heterosexual and monogamous. They are the ideal pair of true lovers that companionate marriage supposedly celebrates. Yet the society of the play presents no way in which their love can be legitimately consummated because of the failure of their parents to agree to the socially mandated contractual arrange-ments regarding their marriage. Given no legitimate outlet for their love, they have produced an almost illegitimate child. If this situation had not underscored the innu-merable problems inherent within the contractual aspects of the early modern mar-riage, Angelo's grotesque proposal that the virgin Isabella sleep with him to save her brother presents it in letters many stories high. Such a situation calls many aspects of the early modern sex–gender system into question. In a culture that allows men to be hypersexual, there is no safe place for women, even if they have entered a profes-sion that "guarantees" them freedom from male predation. But the bargain Angelo makes turns upon the same issue that marriage does: virginity. Angelo desires Isabella more because she is a consecrated virgin than because she is a woman. Had his desire been simply for a woman, he could have satisfied it with any of the sex workers who populate Vienna. And, of course, in desiring a virgin, Angelo desires possession of her hymen. Isabella's intact hymen separates her from all of the women we have previously encountered in Vienna, even the chaste – though now pregnant – Juliet.

All's Well That Ends Well similarly, and perhaps even more overtly, explores the problems attendant upon all types of marriage contracts and arrangements, whether dynastic or companionate. In fact, I would suggest that the marriage between Bertram and Helen is to be considered a conflation of the dynastic and companionate marriages: dynastic because it unites the woman who saved the King's life with a family close to him; companionate because of Helen's hope that her one-sided love of her churlish husband may lead to a union of mutual respect between the two. In the feudal world of this play, Helen is rewarded for saving the King's life with an appropriate gift for a dowryless woman: a husband. Yet her middle-class position as a physician's daughter seems to question whether the King's awarding of her to Bertram, a member of the nobility, is appropriate or an insult to his ward. Bertram suggests, perhaps rightly, that marriage with Helen will debase him.[22] Consequently, he challenges the social norms of the feudal/dynastic marriage in several ways: he refuses his ruler/guardian's request that he marry the woman chosen for him; he refuses to consummate the marriage; and he leaves the country and his wife without his overlord's permission. Yet in Bertram's obvious disloyalty and disobedience, we can clearly see the power that any ordinary man/husband has in patriarchal society to desert his wife or the women in his life. In just this way does Lucio repudiate Mistress Kate Keepdown and their child after promising to contribute to its raising. While husbands in all types of marriages did (and do) abandon their wives for licit or illicit reasons, Bertram's justification forces us to consider this marriage in light of the dynastic, rather than the companionate, tradition.

While Helen is the recipient of the King's largess as a reward for her cure, her reason for choosing Bertram is simple: she loves him (1.1.74–93). However, her dowryless state and middle-class condition would mean she would have to settle for a husband of much lower rank than the Count of Roussillon. Her lack of dowry alone would suggest that she accept *any* marriage offered to her. Yet the play clearly indicates that the character loves Bertram even before he is offered to her as a reward.[23] For her, companionate marriage is the goal, even though she has to achieve it through dynastic means. The character Bertram's desires are less clear. It is obvious that he finds the marriage arranged for him unacceptable, but he does so because he finds it debasing, not because he is in love with anyone else. In fact, it is necessary to realize that his desire for Diana also has nothing to do with love or affection.

Ultimately, Angelo and Bertram are completely deceived in their sexual partners. Each actually sleeps with a virgin; she is just not the virgin he expected. I want to consider how the deceptions succeed and what the ability of these deceptions *to* succeed says about early modern marriage. In describing the arrangement for "her" assignation with Angelo, Isabella indicates that

> ... I [have] made my promise
> Upon the heavy middle of the night
> To call upon him ...
>   ... a repair i' th' dark,
> And that I have possessed him my most stay
> Can be but brief, ...
>   Little have you [Mariana] to say
> When you depart from him but, soft and low,
> 'Remember now my brother'. (4.1.31–3, 40–2, 64–6)

The darkness and the short stay are predictable conditions, yet Isabella indicates that Mariana should plead for Claudio's life as she leaves, even going so far as providing stage directions that the voice she uses be "soft and low." I wonder how, after hearing her voice, Angelo would not know he bedded his former betrothed. Diana obtains Bertram's ring *before* "she" sleeps with him, thus eliminating the necessity of speech. Her specific instructions are simply:

> When midnight comes, knock at my chamber window.
> I'll order take my mother shall not hear.
> Now I will charge you in the bond of truth,
> When you have conquered my yet maiden bed,
> Remain there but an hour, nor speak to me . . . (4.2.55–9)

In that impenetrable midnight darkness, the characters Mariana and Helen lose their virginity to the men they love while simultaneously convincing them – Mariana with soft and low speech – that they are other women. Since the only thing the substitute woman has in common with the desired woman is virginity – the unpenetrated hymen – the virginal hymen that bleeds when penetrated is not only the marker of the generic virgin but the means by which women are marked as interchangeable. The virgins Mariana and Helen bleed on the sheets to prove their unpenetrated condition to Angelo and Bertram. Yet if this encounter happened in a room so dark the women's faces or bodies were invisible, how did the men know that the sheets were, indeed, bloodied without lighting a candle or lamp? Obviously such a lighting would render the bed trick ineffectual, but, beyond the feel of a tight vagina, neither man would know he had penetrated a virgin without *some* indication of blood. If ocular proof is unavailable or impossible, smell, taste, and perhaps touch are all that remain. Thus Bertram and Angelo, to assure that they are getting what they bargained for, need to become *very* intimate with their partners' vaginal blood, perhaps even more intimate than they were with the women themselves.

I have discussed the success of Isabella's deception. Yet why, beyond the necessity of having a woman willing to sleep with Angelo, is Mariana so necessary? I suggest that she is necessary because she is also a virgin. If Angelo wants to be assured of *Isabella's* participation in the assignation, he needs to be assured that the woman he *has* penetrated is a virgin. The only assurance of that is blood. And, since Angelo is satisfied that he has, indeed, deflowered a virgin, he demonstrates that the most (only?) important part of a woman's body *is* her hymen. But, again, why is Mariana necessary to this deception? I suggest this character is necessary because her previous history with Angelo reinforces the barren nature of early modern marriage and its legal arrangements already demonstrated by Juliet and Claudio. Like Juliet, Mariana's dreams of the ideal companionate marriage with her true love Angelo have been shattered by the inability of her family to uphold its end of the marriage contract. Mariana's dowry sank to the bottom of the sea in the storm that killed her brother (3.1.181–258). Yet the Duke also indicates that Angelo refused Mariana not only because of her lack of dowry, but "pretending in her discoveries of dishonour" (3.1.221). Focusing on Mariana's lack of chastity draws attention away from Angelo's real objection to the marriage, lack of a marriage portion. The character Angelo might seem a churl for repudiating his betrothed after her brother's death, yet the possibility that Mariana is not a virgin, that her hymen has bled for some other man, allows Angelo "graciously" to refuse to uphold his end of the contract. Even in terms of Juliet and Claudio, a couple deeply in love, the play's focus on the economic nub of marriage reveals it to be, at base, so sordidly financial that it destroys, rather than promotes, companionate relationships. Thus the play radically points out the commercial aspects of *all* marriages, even the companionate marriage that supposedly remedied the financial/political problems of the dynastic marriage. The importance of the hymen to the bed trick reinforces its importance to marriage as a whole. Women are not simply bodies to be traded between men, they are really only membranes that bleed to attest to the individual woman's purity.

Like Mariana, Helen needs to sleep with her husband to legalize her marriage. Without consummation, any marriage is unofficial and can be easily annulled. Thus while Bertram's and Angelo's assignations with Diana and Isabella are guilty and sinful from their point of view, Helen's and Mariana's actions in sleeping with their men are legitimate and, in Helen's case especially, legally mandated. Just as Helen, or any wife, cannot legally deny her husband the "marriage debt," her husband cannot legally deny it her. But, as in *Measure for Measure*, Helen's deflowerer has no idea that he has penetrated the wrong hymen, though he *does* know he *has* penetrated a virginal one. Consecrated virgin or destined for marriage, French or Italian, a hymen is a hymen and all hymens are the same, providing they bleed when penetrated by a penis. Where then does the notion of the companionate marriage, the marriage designed to protect men and women from loneliness and allow them to raise Christian children, lodge? How can we resolve the bizarre grotesquerie of the interchangeable hymen with the notion of the couple (and later the family) created by love and further creating love in the children who will be produced?

I am not sure we can do it without great difficulty. I think that grotesquerie is, to some extent, ingrained in the nature of patriarchal marriage and patriarchal society. If women are objectified in any way, it is a forgone conclusion that they will be objectified in *all* ways. If, as Peter Stallybrass has cogently argued, the woman's body becomes identified with her house, her mouth with her vagina, and her vagina with her open door, it is not so great a leap to see her reduced simply to a hymen, perforated or non-perforated as the case may be. Yet while the bed trick in and of itself as a folk-tale substitution motif *does* call into question the very nature of the early modern sex–gender system and marriage, the Shakespeare plays I have examined also question the nature of marriage. They are not content to demonstrate the fairy-tale perfection we usually encounter in the "true love" match. While some of this may be present in the "happy comedies," these same plays also present us with hints of the underlying "darkness" of the early modern marriage paradigm. *Measure for Measure* and *All's Well That Ends Well* with their bed tricks necessitated by various contractual difficulties strongly point out the destructive nature of any form of marriage based upon a patriarchal social construct. Further, I suggest that such bleak and demeaning portraits become examples of the necessity of redesigning existing marriage norms with a changed role for women, one that stresses their individuality rather than their interchangeability.

NOTES

1   Lévi-Strauss's concept is the basis for Eve Kosofsky Sedgwick's (1985, 1990) explication of male "homosocial" relationships. Similar definitions of patriarchal gender relationships are found in Hartmann (1981), Beechy (1979), Omvedt (1986), and Rubin (1975). For specific descriptions of early modern marriage, see Jankowski (1992, ch. 1; 2000, ch. 1), Callaghan (1994), and Dolan (1996).

2   The "dynastic" marriage is often thought of as a "Roman Catholic" form that was replaced by the later "Protestant" "companionate" marriage. I agree with the many critics – like John C. Bean (1974) and Kathleen M. Davies (1976–7) – who dispute this Catholic/Protestant dichotomy and see the "companionate" marriage as having a more middle-class – whether Roman Catholic or Protestant – inception and being more reflective of the social and economic structures experienced by the existing middle class, or changing as England became more capitalist. See Jankowski (1992: 31–5) and Belsey (1985, 1995).

3   Widows, however, did have a legal identity. This was necessary for the protection of any minor heirs by insuring that they always had a legal guardian to protect their inheritance. Widows also had the financial means to support themselves through the dower and jointure. Widows lost their legal identity as well as their dower and/or jointure if they remarried. Control of their minor children then passed to the new husband (Jankowski 1992: 35–6).

4   Amy Erickson (1995) has indicated that "The twin pillars of common law control over women's economic futures – primogeniture in inheritance and coverture in marriage – were draconian in theory, but had less impact in practice" (p. 224). She points out that the English system of inheritance, known as "primogeniture," was in effect from the mid-thirteenth century and remained unchanged until 1925 (p. 26). In this system, sometimes referred to as *tail male*, *entailed* land and property passed from eldest son to eldest son in order to keep large estates intact. Neither second nor subsequent sons – nor daughters – could inherit entailed property (Jankowski 1992: 35–6). However, Erickson argues that English law preferred, in the absence of sons, to pass inheritance on to daughters rather than a "collateral male" (p. 27). (This inheritance pattern is sometimes referred to as *tail général*.) She further indicates, as a result of her research into inheritance records in Cambridgeshire, Lincolnshire, Northamptonshire, and Sussex, that inheritance was often more balanced – that is, more equitably distributed between sons *and* daughters – than the laws of primogeniture would suggest (see chapter 4). While pointing out that the existence of wives' wills indicated that married women had some, albeit restricted, legal power to leave their property to whomever they chose, Erickson also reminds us that "we know virtually nothing from personal writing about ordinary women's lives" (pp. 139–43, 223).

5   *An Homily of the State of Matrimony* (1563), ordered to be preached at all weddings, reinforced this Protestant concept of marriage: "The word of almighty God doth testify and declare whence the original beginning of matrimony cometh and why it is ordained. It is instituted of God to the intent that man and woman should live lawfully in a perpetual friendly fellowship, to bring forth fruit, and to avoid fornication" (cited in McDonald 2001: 285). Shakespeare presents a version of the *Homily* in Kate's final speech (5.2.140–83) in *The Taming of the Shrew* (ca. 1592).

6   Gouge (1622) indicates that "a familie is a little Church, and a little Common-wealth, at least a lively representation thereof, whereby triall may be made of such as are fit for any place of authoritie, or of Subjection in Church or common-wealth" (sig. Cv).

7   Alsemero had earlier administered a bizarre potion-swallowing test for virginity to Beatrice-Joanna. Having discovered the test potion and the desired "virginal" reaction beforehand, she was success-fully able to fake the reaction and convince Alsemero of her virginity. Interestingly, though, that test does not – or perhaps *cannot* – replace the "true" test of virginity: the ruptured hymen and bloody sheet that Beatrice-Joanna must be sure to arrange.

8   The connection between Hymen, the god or the membrane, and marriage is obvious in a number of early modern English texts. Hymen himself – the god – appears at the end of *As You Like It* to solemnize Rosalind's wedding. Spenser also evokes Hymen in his "Epithalamion," though it is difficult to know whether he means *only* the god, or the membrane as well:

> . . . the boyes run up and downe the street,
> Crying aloud with strong confuséd noyce,
> As if it were one voyce.
> *Hymen iô Hymen, Hymen* they do shout,
> That even to the heavens theyr shouting shrill
> Doth reach, and all the firmament doth fill,
> To which the people standing all about,
> As in approvance doe thereto applaud
> And loud advance her laud,
> And evermore they *Hymen Hymen* sing. (ll. 137–46).

9   *OED* definition 2 provides figurative use of the word as "the first stage or fruits of anything; the first example, proof, trial, or use." Thus, no matter what usage, "maidenhead" retains the sense of primacy or "first time." This use was operative from at least the end of the sixteenth to the early seventeenth centuries. Ralegh, in fact, uses the phrase to describe the unexplored realm of Guyana which still "has her maidenhead."

10   See Belsey (1994), especially "Introduction: Reading Cultural History," for one explanation of the development of the discourse of "true love" and its relationship to Shakespeare's plays.

11   In fact, as he explains,

> As wealth is the burden of my wooing dance –
> Be she as foul as was Florentius's love,
> As old as Sibyl, and as curst and shrewd
> As Socrates' Xanthippe or a worse,
> She moves me not – or not removes at least
> Affection's edge in me, were she as rough
> As are the swelling Adriatic seas. (1.2.65–71)

We may also forget that wealth is the primary reason the impoverished Bassanio finds Portia attractive:

> In Belmont is a lady *richly* left,
> And she is fair . . . (1.2.161–2; my emphasis)

All references to Shakespeare's plays will be to the edition indicated in the list of references, and will appear in the text.

12   See Montrose (1981) for an example of how second sons' search for wealth is presented in Shakespeare's comedies.

13   See also Howard (1994: ch. 3).

14   The character Kate's internalization of early modern society's norms regarding marriage, and women's place in it, articulated in her final speech (5.2.140–83), shows just how much she has been tamed. See also note 5.

15   See Jankowski (1992: ch. 2).

16   Stallybrass (1986) argues that a woman's open mouth or open house door signifies a displaced opening of the vagina and its willingness to admit all comers.

17   Karen Newman (1987) gives a fine reading of the handkerchief and points out that the straw-
     berries embroidered on it can also refer to Desdemona's nipples, lips, or clitoris.
18   In this context, consider also the symbolism of Portia's ring.
19   See Ranald (1979) for *de praesenti* and *de futuro* marriage contracts and which legitimately allow
     sexual intercourse.
20   Interestingly, the prostitutes in *Measure for Measure* are not so much defined as sex workers –
     necessary accoutrements to a patriarchal society that, like early modern England, *does* fetishize vir-
     ginity – but as (lower-class) women who have lost their chance to be considered honorable by losing
     their virginity inappropriately. In this context we also need to consider the social position of some
     actual and potential children in the play. If she does not marry, Kate Keepdown's child will likely
     follow his/her mother into sex work. If the child is a girl, her actual virginity will almost not count,
     since she is the child of a whore and presumed not to be capable of honor. We might ask how that
     perception would (or should?) change once Kate marries Lucio. And what would happen to Juliet's
     unborn child? If Claudio were executed, their child would be illegitimate and destined for the same
     fate as Kate Keepdown's. If Juliet were not to be executed, her only option would probably be to
     become a sex worker like Kate. Presumably her family would not support her, since they have not
     shown any inclination to do so. If she were to be executed after her child were born – she is, after
     all, guilty of the same crime as Claudio – would this illegitimate orphan child's life be better or
     worse than that of its parents? Its mother, after all, has bled away her honor in dishonor with its
     father.
21   Dollimore (1985) provides a sensitive reading of the voiceless, yet often ventriloquized, whores in
     this play.
22

> *King.* Thou know'st she has raised me from my sickly bed.
> *Bertram.* But follows it, my lord, to bring me down
> Must answer for your raising? I know her well:
> She had her breeding at my father's charge.
> A poor physician's daughter, my wife? Disdain
> Rather corrupt me ever. (2.3.107–12)

23   There is, of course, the possibility that Helen cures the King so that she *can* win Bertram.

References and Further Reading

Agrippa [von Nettisheim], C. (1540). *The Commendation of Matrimony*, . . . STC 201, trans. D. Llapam.
    London: Thomae Berthes.
Bean, J. C. (1974). Passion versus Friendship in the Tudor Matrimonial Handbooks and Some
    Shakespearean Implications. *Wascana Review*, 9, 231–40.
Beechy, V. (1979). On Patriarchy. *Feminist Review*, 3, 66–82.
Belsey, C. (1985). Disrupting Sexual Difference: Meaning and Gender in the Comedies. In J. Drakakis
    (ed.) *Alternative Shakespeares*. London: Methuen, 166–90.
——(1994). *Desire: Love Stories in Western Culture*. Oxford: Blackwell.
——(1995). *Shakespeare and the Loss of Eden*. New Brunswick, NJ: Rutgers University Press.
Callaghan, D. (1994). The Ideology of Romantic Love: The Case of *Romeo and Juliet*. In D. Callaghan,
    L. Helms, and J. Singh (eds.) *The Weyward Sisters: Shakespeare and Feminist Politics*. Oxford: Blackwell,
    59–101.
Davies, K. M. (1976–7). The Sacred Condition of Equality: How Original Were Puritan Doctrines of
    Marriage? *Social History*, 1–2, 563–80.
Dolan, F. E. (1996). Introduction. In F. E. Dolan (ed.) *William Shakespeare: The Taming of the Shrew: Texts
    and Contexts*. Boston, MA: Bedford Books.

Dollimore, J. (1985). Transgression and Surveillance in *Measure for Measure*. In J. Dollimore and A. Sinfield (eds.) *Political Shakespeare: New Essays in Cultural Materialism.* Ithaca, NY: Cornell University Press, 72–87.

Erickson, A. L. (1995). *Women and Property in Early Modern England.* London: Routledge.

Gouge, W. (1622). *Of Domesticall Duties: Eight Treatises.* STC 12119. London: [J]ohn Haviland.

Halkett, J. (1970). *Milton and the Idea of Matrimony.* New Haven, CT: Yale University Press.

Hartmann, H. (1981). The Unhappy Marriage of Marxism and Feminism: Towards a More Progressive Union. In L. Sargent (ed.) *Women and Revolution: A Discussion of the Unhappy Marriage of Marxism and Feminism.* Boston, MA. South End Press, 2–41.

Howard, J. E. (1987). Renaissance Antitheatricality and the Politics of Gender and Rank in *Much Ado About Nothing.* In J. E. Howard and M. F. O'Connor (eds.) *Shakespeare Reproduced: The Text in History and Ideology.* New York: Methuen, 163–87.

——(1994). *The Stage and Social Struggle in Early Modern England.* London: Routledge.

Jankowski, T. A. (1992). *Women in Power in the Early Modern Drama.* Urbana: University of Illinois Press.

——(2000). *Pure Resistance: Queer Virginity in Early Modern English Drama.* Philadelphia: University of Pennsylvania Press.

Jones, A. R. and Stallybrass, P. (2000). *Renaissance Clothing and the Materials of Memory.* Cambridge: Cambridge University Press.

Lévi-Strauss, C. (1969). *The Elementary Structures of Kinship.* Boston, MA: Beacon Press.

McDonald, R. (2001). *The Bedford Companion to Shakespeare: An Introduction with Documents*, 2nd edn. Boston, MA: Bedford/St. Martin's Press.

Middleton, T. and Rowley, W. (1976). *The Changeling.* In R. A. Fraser and N. Rabkin (eds.) *Drama of the English Renaissance, Volume II: The Stuart Period.* New York: Macmillan; London: Collier Macmillan, 401–49.

Montrose, L. A. (1981). The Place of a Brother in *As You Like It*: Social Process and Comic Form. *Shakespeare Quarterly*, 32, 28–54.

Newman, K. (1987). "And wash the Ethiope white": Femininity and the Monstrous in *Othello.* In J. E. Howard and M. F. O'Connor (eds.) *Shakespeare Reproduced: The Text in History and Ideology.* New York: Methuen, 143–62.

Omvedt, G. (1986). "Patriarchy": The Analysis of Women's Oppression. *The Insurgent Sociologist*, 13, 30–50.

Ranald, M. L. (1979). "As marriage binds and blood breaks": English Marriage and Shakespeare. *Shakespeare Quarterly*, 30, 68–81.

Rubin, G. (1975). The Traffic in Women: Notes on the "Political Economy" of Sex. In R. R. Reiter (ed.) *Toward an Anthropology of Women.* New York: Monthly Review Press.

Sedgwick, E. K. (1985). *Between Men: English Literature and Male Homosocial Desire.* New York: Columbia University Press.

——(1990). *Epistemology of the Closet.* Berkeley: University of California Press.

Shakespeare, W. (1997). *The Norton Shakespeare*, ed. S. Greenblatt, W. Cohen, J. E. Howard, and K. E. Maus. New York: W. W. Norton.

Spenser, E. (1968). "Epithalamion." In H. Maclean (ed.) *Edmund Spenser's Poetry.* New York: W. W. Norton, 434–45.

Stallybrass, P. (1986). Patriarchal Territories: The Body Enclosed. In M. W. Ferguson, M. Quilligan, and N. J. Vickers (eds.) *Rewriting the Renaissance: The Discourses of Sexual Difference in Early Modern Europe.* Chicago, IL: University of Chicago Press, 123–42.

6

Varieties of Collaboration in Shakespeare's Problem Plays and Late Plays

John Jowett

I

"Alone I did it" cries Coriolanus, describing the attack on Corioles that gave him his name, with hubris and with partial truth (*Coriolanus*, 5.6.117). It is common to think of his author Shakespeare too as a man alone. But Shakespeare was also a collaborator. How does it matter that Shakespeare did not always write alone? This chapter, by showing a writer who participated with others, will bring Shakespeare out of monumental isolation as apparent sole author of a finite and known canon of texts. And it will suggest how the way we think about the texts themselves can be reshaped by an awareness of the contribution of others.

Though most of Shakespeare's plays were presumably written without the participation of another dramatist, there are significant exceptions. Earlier plays in which Shakespeare wrote as collaborator probably include *1 Henry VI* (Taylor 1987: 112–13), *Titus Andronicus* (Jackson 1996), *Edward III* (Hope 1994: 133–7), and *Sir Thomas More* (Taylor 1987: 124–5). Shakespeare's problem plays and late plays concern us most immediately here. Scholars are moving towards a consensus about the collaborative nature of *Pericles*, written with George Wilkins, and *Henry VIII* and *Two Noble Kinsmen*, both written with John Fletcher. They draw attention to a lost play by Shakespeare and Fletcher called *Cardenio*. The problematic *Timon of Athens* is now increasingly explained as a collaboration with Thomas Middleton. Middleton's hand as an adapter has long been recognized in *Macbeth*, and the more recent case for Middleton treating *Measure for Measure* in a comparable way is gaining momentum (Taylor and Jowett 1993).

Simply listing these eleven plays immediately revises the picture that prevailed over much of the twentieth century of Shakespeare as a dramatist who collaborated little. There is, after all, little documentation of Shakespeare as a collaborator – though it should not be forgotten that the very first known reference to Shakespeare as a playwright, *Greene's Groatsworth of Wit* (1592), seems to charge him with reworking the output of other dramatists. The 1623 Folio presents him as a non-collaborating dramatist, but, as will be explained below, it provides an inaccurate and commercially motivated account (De Grazia 1991: 14–48). Title pages of other books can similarly provide unreliable or deficient information. Most pre-1600 Quarto editions of Shakespeare do not name him or any other dramatist. Sometimes he is credited with the authorship of plays he evidently did not write – though critics have occasionally and speculatively sought for evidence of his hand in plays that fall in this category, such as *The London Prodigal* (1605) and *A Yorkshire Tragedy* (1608). In just one late case, *Two Noble Kinsmen* (1634), he is credibly named as collaborator with John Fletcher.

In principle, it is a sensible procedure to prefer documentary evidence such as title pages to "internal" evidence based on language and stylistic preferences. It is not, however, strongly justified in circumstances where the documentary record is absent or unreliable. The title pages of plays from the early modern public theatres drastically under-represent collaboration. Yet scholars are well aware of the dangers of an impressionistic approach to "internal" evidence. A number of studies in the early twentieth century sought aggressively to take away from Shakespeare any writing that sounded to the investigator's ear like George Peele, or Robert Greene, or John Lyly, or Christopher Marlowe. In 1924 they were rightly castigated by E. K. Chambers (1933). Schoenbaum's (1966) later and more detailed study of attribution techniques reinforced the skepticism that prevailed over much of the century. Hence what Chambers called the "disintegration" of Shakespeare came to be seen as a disreputable activity. Over the past half-century scholars have struggled to find more reliable ways of analyzing the texts themselves for evidence of collaboration. They have had some success, perhaps more than is generally realized, though they have not achieved the final and definitive clarity that one would wish for.

One factor here is the uneven and sometimes anxious take-up of attribution studies by editors and other scholars. Objections will be found to even the most convincing study of authorship attribution by those who disagree with its findings. An edition of *Timon of Athens* in the Cambridge series briefly dismisses the case for collaboration without looking at the appropriate evidence (Klein 2001: 63–5). In contrast, editors of three different *Complete Works* of Shakespeare appearing within a short span of time have accepted Shakespeare's authorship of "A Funeral Elegy" on the basis of work whose findings have subsequently been questioned (retracted by the author). Outside observers would be forgiven for thinking that there is so much tortuous and impenetrable disagreement in this field that it should be left well alone.

Consider, for example, these two influential but apparently wildly conflicting statements about *Titus Andronicus*: "the presence in the early part of the play of so many different features that are atypical of Shakespeare and typical of Peele is most plausibly explained as the legacy of Peele's having actually written Act 1 at least" (Jackson 1996: 147), and "the statistical probability of Peele's involvement is less than one in ten thousand million" (Bate 1995: 83; citing Metz 1985; citing Andrew Q. Morton's unpublished collaborative study). Something, somewhere, seems wrong. In fact, Jackson and Morton are not comparing like with like. Morton refers to the possibility, not that Peele was at all involved in *Titus*, but that *Titus*, *Julius Caesar*, and *Pericles* collectively belong to the same "population" as the works of Peele (quoted in Metz 1985: 155). Jackson would agree that no more than a good fraction of *Titus* can be by Peele, and would not be surprised that three plays that collectively may be less than 10 percent by Peele should be clearly distinguishable from Peele's writing.

Quite apart from the conclusions drawn in these studies, there are significantly different methodologies at work. Morton and Metz concern themselves with "function words," very common words that have no obvious stylistic impact on the text but that occur frequently enough in combinations such as "of the" to provide quantifiable evidence. They obtain their astonishing probability figure by multiplying together the individual probabilities obtained from each of five tests. Jackson accumulates evidence that may in an individual category be too small to be statistically quantifiable, but whose significance as a way of distinguishing the two (or more) writers in question will be readily explicable to the reader. One fundamental problem with stylometric tests is that sound results depend on figures that are large enough not to be local aberrations: as statistical figures, three and five do not discriminate as reliably as thirty and fifty. Tests that work well on entire plays may therefore break down when they are applied to mere parts of plays.

On the whole, the most widely applicable methods and the most coherent and consensualizable results in attribution studies have come from investigations which, like Jackson's, depend on establishing a broad profile of different kinds of data that conform in showing the same division of authorship, with each test having transparent evidence and procedures. The techniques were established by Cyrus Hoy in a series of investigations of the "Beaumont and Fletcher" plays, where the problem of distinguishing Beaumont from Fletcher was often compounded by the presence of other dramatists such as Philip Massinger and, indeed, Shakespeare (Hoy 1956–62). Hoy's concern was to avoid the impressionism of earlier studies that had relied on an unsophisticated and subjective use of verbal parallels between texts. He looked instead at grammatical and lexical choices that established an identifiable fingerprint for each writer. For example, a typical Fletcher characteristic is a high incidence of feminine endings to verse-lines, and, compared with other dramatists, he favors "ye" over "you." Hoy was able to show that such features fluctuated in accord with each other, in accord also with a sensible division of labor, and reasonably in accord with most critics' sense of what sounds like Fletcherian writing. The more recent studies of Jonathan Hope (1994) have added the sophistication of sociolinguistics to Hoy's approach. Hope sees linguistic variables as characteristic of certain social populations, defined by age, status, or geographical region. This approach allows the characteristics of a particular writer to be correlated with his or her social background.

There are, of course, limitations to this kind of testing (McMullen 1996: 443–53). Some writers have more strongly individualized habits. Hoy himself recognized, for example, that Beaumont's hand is sometimes identified more on the basis of an absence of Fletcher or other markers than specific positive evidence for his own hand. Moreover, it is rare to find absolute consistency of usage. Even the ratio between one usage (such as "ye") and its alternative ("you") can vary between different texts of the same authorship, sometimes for inexplicable reasons. Attribution studies therefore hope to find a goodness of fit between indicators that are reasonably stable within each author's habits, as well as significantly differentiated between authors. But Hoy's tests also assume, as do other forms of attribution study, that the writing of a play will break down into more-or-less self-contained sections, the typical unit being a scene. This premise is entirely reasonable, as shared playwrighting would usually begin with a division of labor so that each dramatist could write sections for which he held initial responsibility, and it often turns out to be valid in practice. But there is no fixed pattern for the sharing of work, scenes were sometimes split between more than one writer, and it is always possible that one writer revised the work of another, or eventually copied out the entire play, superimposing his preferences over those of his colleague as he did so. Such considerations weaken the empirical value of attribution testing, because contrary evidence is not invalidating: indications of hand A in a scene otherwise attributable to hand B can readily be explained, and so they do not refute hand B's authorship of the scene in the first instance. Difficulties such as these need careful and patient negotiation, and there is no doubt that the outcome will be to some extent influenced by the theoretical models of collaboration that the investigator deploys. This can be especially critical in the fine-tuning. In practice, however, such considerations often do not prevent a reasonably clear overall outline of the pattern of collaboration from being determined.

Other questions potentially complicate any simple division of a play between collaborators. Might the theory of "accommodation" apply, whereby participants might congenially shift their usages towards each other, as Hope proposes for the disputed sections of *Henry VIII*? Might a scribe have complicated the picture by eliminating some part of the authorial fingerprint and imposing his own characteristics? These are real problems to which there are no standard answers. But they do not amount to a theoretical objection to the whole enterprise. If, for example, a case arises where variation might reflect compositorial or scribal practices, such possibilities can be investigated. *Timon of Athens* is a good case in point. If, as has been suggested, a second compositor set one page, his presence does not dispose of the evidence cited to support Middleton's hand. One editor attempted to explain the distinctive profile of contractions over part of the play in terms of an overlay introduced by the scribe Ralph Crane (Oliver 1959: xix–xxi), but his findings have been decisively rejected by Lake (1975: 284–5) and Jackson (1979: 55–6). Here, an anti-disintegrationist was keen to find an alternative to co-authorship, but the alternative can be ruled out.

Lake, Jackson, and Holdsworth (1982) have developed the methods of Hoy and applied them to the Middleton canon, seeking always to broaden the range of significant variables. These might include grammatical preferences ("have" as against "hath," for instance), habits of metre and rhyming (Middleton favored rhyming couplets and was in the un-Shakespearean habit of mixing verse and prose in a single speech), preferred oaths and expletives, preferred contractions, and choice between doublets ("between" as against "betwixt"). Holdsworth's intensive study is the main basis for attributing parts of *Timon* to Middleton. As well as addressing linguistic and gram-matical preferences, Holdsworth refines a technique that fell into some discredit earlier in the twentieth century, the use of verbal parallels. His trained ear for genuinely dis-tinctive Middletonian idioms and his ability to show different parallels of word, phras-ing, and thought coinciding in the same paired passages in *Timon* and Middleton texts enable him to use such evidence persuasively. The availability of online databases can now often demonstrate just how precisely a word or phrase is associated with Mid-dleton and not with other writers. The validity of Holdsworth's claims for parallels can be tested by searching for equivalents in virtually the whole of early modern drama, or indeed all periods and all genres of English literature. New tests making similar use of electronic resources promise to make the findings of attribution study more reliable. It is not a precise science, as Gordon McMullen's (1996) incisively skep-tical study has shown, but even McMullen accepts that its methods are fully suffi-cient to determine that a play such as *Henry VIII* was written by Shakespeare in collaboration with Fletcher.

II

One reason why an aura of conflict sometimes surrounds attribution studies is that the critical and ideological reasons for undertaking such investigations are themselves profoundly in dispute. For example, when Masten (1997: 12–27) objects to the methods of the school of Hoy his criticisms sound as though they concern a failure to establish adequately grounded conclusions, but Masten's more fundamental concern lies elsewhere. He favors the principle of collaboration in that it erases authorial voice and turns the text towards a condition of non-individualized socially constructed lan-guage. His fundamental charge against attribution studies is that they act in accor-dance with the ideology of single authorship: they treat collaboration as abnormal, and cope with it by attempting to distribute the sections of a collaborative play into separate authorial canons.

In other words, what seems to be a dispassionate philological project turns out, in this view, to support a conservatively romantic notion of the author that is inappro-priate to early modern playwrighting. Yet it is only through seeking to describe the artistic, cultural, and material aspects of authorship and collaboration with respect to particular texts that any notion of the author can be founded, whether romantic or post-Foucauldian. Masten's rewardingly provocative critique finds its anchorings in the scholarship of Bentley, who demonstrated the extent to which early modern dra-matic authorship was shaped by the institutional circumstances of the theatre (Bentley 1971: 197–234). Bentley considered that up to half the plays of the period probably involved the work of more than one dramatist, though this includes adaptations that were originally written by a single dramatist. The figures are highly conjectural esti-mates, for a number of reasons. Most plays written in the period by far are now lost, and we know little or nothing about them. The plays that were preserved because they were published as printed books may be atypical of the drama as a whole, and, as we have seen, the preservation of a play does not ensure an accurate statement of its authorship. It is also by no means certain how typical are the practices uniquely recorded in the diary of Philip Henslowe, whose records as financial manager of the Admiral's Men and other companies are crucial evidence.

The magical watershed of 50 percent, in any case, is not entirely the point. There was probably not so much a normative practice of collaborative authorship in the early years of the professional theatre, as an acceptance and widespread practice of both single authorship and collaboration. The uplifting of the playwright to the status of literary author in the early seventeenth century took place most obviously in printed books that set themselves apart from the public theatre, and one of the ways they did so was by promoting the figure of the dramatic author.

Although modern approaches to collaboration need to take full cognizance of the practices of an earlier period, they are not bound passively to replicate those conditions. The authorship of a text is a matter of standard enquiry into one of the most fundamental matters we can expect to know of it, a central part of the question: how was this text produced? Moreover, as we will see below, attribution study can lead into new lines of critical and historical enquiry that are not focused on the authors in question to any significant degree. Work such as Hoy's can have many outcomes, not least of which is that it allows a critic such as Masten a firmer purchase on the very phenomenon of collaboration that he studies. It is Masten's achievement to have identified a way of discussing collaboration that relates to other critical concerns, in his case figurations of homosociality. In principle, a poetics or literary sociology of collaboration can be applied to virtually any critical approach to a play.

For reasons such as these, it is significant to know, as far as possible, who wrote what in a particular text. In cases such as *Henry VIII* this involves challenging the claim in the First Folio of 1623 that this play along with the others is, simply, "MR WILLIAM SHAKESPEARES." The distorted image of Shakespeare as a writer who did not practice collaboration found its most emphatic and influential early expression in the first collection of his plays that aspired to completeness, the First Folio. As Martin Droeshout's famous engraving of Shakespeare in the preliminaries testifies, the volume presented a strongly personalized author. The dramatic works and the man are locked as it were indissolubly together. The plays, perfect in their numbers, represent a complete picture of Shakespeare's dramatic achievement. Silence was maintained on the whole subject of divided authorship so as to separate an idealized image of Shakespeare from the contaminating and less prestigious activity of collaboration. And an effect of this process is actively to make collaboration a more lowly activity, it being the implicit abasement against which the solo author is exalted.

No book has been more influential to English literature than this publication, and the assumptions underlying its production came to be absorbed into our way of thinking about Shakespeare, about authorship, and about literature itself. A succession of Shakespeare editions over nearly five hundred years has perpetuated the image of Shakespeare as a genius who stands apart from his fellow dramatists, their feet clogged in the mud of contingency and early modernity which Shakespeare alone transcends. The tradition of including a special section of apocryphal plays, begun with the 1664 reissue of the Third Folio, suggests a more complex picture. These plays were all seen as having some claim to be of Shakespeare's authorship, but in most cases it was acknowledged that the claim was weak. Plays such as Middleton's *A Yorkshire Tragedy* stand alongside *Pericles* and *Two Noble Kinsmen*, both of which have a large Shake-spearean content. But a typical *Complete Works* of the twentieth century followed the Folio precedent of ignoring or diminishing the issue of collaboration. Only the Oxford Shakespeare systematically reevaluated the issue of collaboration (Taylor 1987: 69–144). In this edition the title pages of plays thought to be collaborative clearly state that the play is by Shakespeare and whomever his partner might have been. Here the reader will find that Shakespeare is presented as a working dramatist, and his shared labors are given recognition as such.

III

Since its publication in 1647, the Folio edition of plays attributed to Francis Beau-mont and John Fletcher has offered an iconic monument of collaborative dramatic authorship. The image it presents is cavalier, gentrified, and homosocial: terms that apply equally to the volume's figuration of dramatic authorship and some of the areas of experience represented in the plays. Beaumont and Fletcher, in John Aubrey's famous words, "lay together; had one Wench in the house between them, which they did so admire; the same cloathes, &c. betweene them" (Aubrey 1972: 184). Aubrey was writing after the 1647 Folio was published. He surely alludes to the sense in which the dramatists "lay together" in the book. But Fletcher's career as a dramatist was more diverse than the 1647 Folio suggests. It includes, for example, the three plays he wrote in collaboration with Shakespeare. After Shakespeare's retirement Fletcher became the regular dramatist for the King's Men, and his collaborations with Shakespeare, all written shortly before Shakespeare gave up writing plays, may have served as an induction into this role.

Doubts as to Shakespeare's single-handed authorship of *Henry VIII* began as a response to the play's variable style, and were later confirmed and modified by lin-guistic studies. It is now widely accepted that Fletcher co-authored the play, though some doubts remain as to the extent of his work. James Spedding (1850) first pro-posed that Fletcher had a part in the play and assigned various sections to him: the Prologue; from 1.3 to 2.2; 3.1; 3.2.204–460; act 4; and the rest of the play from 5.2. Spedding relied on the varying literary qualities of the play. Hoy's examination of linguistic forms considerably diminished Fletcher's contribution, restoring 2.1, 2.2, all of 3.2, and act 4 to Shakespeare. Though Hoy's evidence for Fletcher is weaker and is sometimes localized within the disputed scenes, these scenes likewise show little positive sign of Shakespeare, and the linguistic evidence for Fletcher now seems stronger than Hoy had realized (Hope 1994: 67–83). Though some intermittent contribution from Shakespeare remains possible, a "convergence" of Fletcher's preferences towards Shakespeare's provides another possible explanation. In either case Fletcher's hand is probably dominant in the play as a whole, and the ascription should be to "Fletcher and Shakespeare," as is established by both the alphabetical order of the dramatists' names and the proportion of their labor.

Two Noble Kinsmen presents a different initial situation, for the play is recorded on the title page as by "William Shakespeare and John Fletcher." The ascription is also made in the publisher's entry of the play in the Stationers' Register. As Taylor (1987) notes, "*Kinsmen* is the only play attributed to [Shakespeare] in the two decades between the First Folio and the Civil War, and the only play before the Restoration attributed to him as part-author" (p. 134). The ascription to two hands is made unexpectedly and reliably. Recent scholarship has confirmed that the shares of the two dramatists can be identified with more confidence and clarity than is the case with *Henry VIII*. Indeed, the distribution of material "seems designed to facilitate collaboration between two people who did not have much opportunity to talk about work in progress" (Potter 1997: 25). Shakespeare's part was evidently act 1; 2.1; 3.1–2; and all of act 5 except 5.1.1–33 and 5.4 (the final scene of plot about the Jailer's Daughter; 5.2 in some editions). Fletcher wrote all the scenes involving the Jailer's Daughter, and some sections of the Kinsmen plot. Shakespeare's authorship of the opening and closing scenes is a pattern found in *Timon* too, and might suggest in both cases that he, as senior dramatist, retained overall control – though the younger Fletcher was entrusted with the end of *Henry VIII*.

Masten addresses the early modern trope of male friendship as an informing model for collaboration. The metaphor is of homosocial bonding, and his approach favors the diadic union of two as its normative model. But Aubrey's account of Beaumont and Fletcher applies to Shakespeare and Fletcher, as far as we know, neither in life nor, metaphorically, to the arrangements for writing *Two Noble Kinsmen*. In the text itself there is dialogue between the dramatists, yet also separation, and circulation both around and away from male–male bonding.

It is Fletcher who expresses most fully the conflict between heterosexual love and male friendship:

> am not I
> Part of your blood, part of your soul? . . .
> Why then would you deal so cunningly,
> So strangely, so unlike a noble kinsman,
> To love alone? (2.2.187–94)

This is a Shakespearean theme that Fletcher develops from precedents such as *Two Gentlemen of Verona* and sonnet 42 (Potter 1997: 56). Fletcher writes his clear, unmetaphoric verse in dialogue with a remote and intertextual Shakespeare, as he did likewise in developing Shakespeare's depiction of Ophelia's madness into his portrayal of the Jailer's Daughter. For his part, Shakespeare takes as his intertext Montaigne's essay on man-to-man friendship and applies it to Theseus and Pirithous (Potter 1997: 55–6), paraphrasing Montaigne when he writes:

> Their knot of love,
> Tied, weaved, entangled with so true, so long,
> And with a finger of so deep a cunning,
> May be outworn, never undone. (1.3.41–4)

And Shakespeare gives Emilia by way of response an eloquent and quietly eroticized description of adolescent woman-to-woman friendship:

> The flower that I would pluck
> And put between my breasts – O then but beginning
> To swell about the blossom – she would long
> Till she had such another, and commit it
> To the like innocent cradle, where, phoenix-like,
> They died in perfume. (1.3.66–71)

To complete the circle, this past love has sufficient force to ensure that she will never "Love any that's called man" (1.3.85). If the text reflects the collaboration of its writing, it does so in such a way as to depict a world in which neither love nor friendship will find secure fulfillment.

IV

Notwithstanding a challenge from a stylometric study that yields no clear conclusions (Smith 1991) and a merely cautious endorsement from Hope (1994), the evidence for Middleton's hand in *Timon of Athens* is as strong as that for Fletcher's hand in *Henry VIII*. It is reinforced by a bibliographical consideration. The original plan for the 1623 Folio was to have *Troilus and Cressida* come after *Romeo and Juliet*. Difficulties in securing the copyright led to its removal from that slot, and *Troilus* was finally printed as a bibliographically separate subsection before the Tragedies. The gap – an unnegotiably fixed gap because the following play had already been printed – was filled with *Timon* (Hinman 1963: 2.231–85). In all probability, if *Timon* had not been inserted as a substitute for *Troilus* it would not have been printed at all. If so, it is a marginal member of the Shakespeare canon, a play perhaps initially rejected, like *Pericles*, *Two Noble Kinsmen*, and *Cardenio*, because it was a collaboration.

Middleton took responsibility for specific areas of the text: the banquet scene (1.2), the creditor scenes and the banishment of Alcibiades (all of act 3 except the middle part of the mock-banquet scene, 3.7), and most of the lines dealing with Timon's Steward (Flavius) in act 4. He may also have contributed oddments such as the closing ten lines of 1.1 and parts of 2.2 (Holdsworth 1982). Shakespeare's Timon, both in Athens and in the woods, defies all customary behavior; it is Middleton who most crucially articulates these opposite, social forms of expression. Where Shakespeare's language is metaphoric and hyperexpressive, Middleton's is satiric and reductive; most of his speakers fend off sincere self-expression rather than articulate their feelings. This is not to say that Shakespeare contributed no irony or satire to *Timon*, nor that Middleton contributed no emotional sincerity. Rather, Middleton gave the play a distinctive quality that is not Shakespearean, creating a dialogue or tension between different styles and areas of represented experience.

Whether by symptomatic luck or design, it transpires that almost every instance of the word "gold" in *Timon* occurs in a passage attributed to Shakespeare. Gold is not only a monetary means for exchange; it is the lustrous commodity in its own right, a symbol and embodiment of what is precious, representing Timon's fascination with the ideal. For his part, Middleton is the poet of debt. He understands debt moralistically, but he also evidently understands that in early seventeenth-century England there was a severe and growing shortage of hard coinage; debt and the social systems that regulated debt were ubiquitous. Middleton reproduces the language by which credit and trust were communicated in business dealings, subjecting it to cynical disbelief. He suggests not only the vulnerability of Timon, but also the vulnerability of a whole system based on trust in words, where the words themselves are based on commercial self-interest.

Interpretative considerations such as these play at best a minor confirmatory role in upholding Middleton's hand in the play; the point here is rather that a hypothesis about divided authorship can constructively feed into a critical, interpretative practice. Different parts of the play contrast in authorial idiolect, and also are differently rooted in early modern society and culture. To understand the play, it is helpful to understand it as a collaboration, while viewing collaboration itself as a valid and *different* mode of play production.

V

The word "collaboration" is etymologically grounded in the idea of "labor" – in the case of literature, the intellectual work of authorship. It is therefore grounded in the idea of agency; it relates to the origination of the text, and is virtually meaningless unless one is prepared to contemplate the text as a product of a complex set of material, intellectual, and emotional circumstances located most meaningfully in the persons of the authors. So it is that for critics such as Masten (1997) "collaboration," though it unpicks the perfection of match between author and text, still runs the risk of overemphasizing the agency of the individual. It remains impossible while focusing on authorial agency to do full justice to the extent to which the text is a product of culture and ideology.

Because collaboration between authors "reflects sociability in the textual realm" it inevitably leads on to a recognition of a broader view of collaborative textual production. This view includes solo-authored plays, and acknowledges the extent and limitations of other, non-authorial, presences that make every playtext a product of a more complex process of origination (McMullen 1996: 454). This widening of the terms of reference beyond the author(s) involves thinking of a play as it appears in, say, the First Folio of 1623 as the outcome of a process of textual production that has run through time. To think of collaboration as "labor" is entirely consistent with an approach of this kind. Indeed this part of the word's etymology usefully challenges the idea that authorship is sealed off from other activity; it encourages us to be receptive towards the input of the theatre, of scribes, of printers and publishers.

From the viewpoint of textual study, theatre is a notoriously destabilizing place. The text is always subordinate, a preliminary to the staging of the play. But performance is disturbingly ephemeral, changeable in detail from one day to another, and subject to larger alteration as the text migrates from original staging to revival, from Globe to Blackfriars, from public stage to court. Minor alterations might pass unrecorded; others might be written into an existing playbook; others again might require the preparation of a new manuscript. At no point do we have access to performance itself. And yet performance is crucial to an appropriate understanding of a play, setting it within the framework of a highly collaborative cultural institution. That institution itself operates in a wider sphere where it encounters specific outside intervention such as, most obviously and unnegotiably, theatrical censorship.

If we look at the printed text, we will find an artifact that is collaborative in another way. It embodies and indissolubly includes the work of those in the printing industry who contributed to its making, even as far away as the French and Flemish paper manufacturers who made the grained surface on which the ink is imprinted. The entity in question is here not simply the text as a sequence of words, but the material object of the book in which the text appears. As with performance, there are implications for how we conceptualize the existence of the text, and implications also for the actual words.

From what has been said so far, it still remains possible to think of the early modern playwright(s) as the point of origination. But there are ways in which even the script was not, after all, entirely of the playwright's making. The separation of pre-theatrical writing from post-authorial writing is immediately thrown into disarray when the common practices of authorial revision and theatrical adaptation by another dramatist are built into the picture. Shakespeare's revision of *King Lear*, for example, evidently came some time after the play's early performances and incorporates the company's experience of the play on stage. But the players were in the picture from the first inception of a new play. The ground for the new work was agreed between playwright and company (Bentley 1971: 62–5). Full-scale writing took place only after the dramatist had sketched an outline or "plot" that had been endorsed by the company. By the time the typical professional dramatist ceased to work on the script, it would already have had input from the actors. The fact that Shakespeare was an actor and leading member of his company, the King's Men, perhaps gave him more control over the process (Orgel 1981), but at the same time it potentially blurs further the boundary between authorship and the staging of plays.

Even the words the dramatist wrote as he sat (as we might imagine) alone in his lodgings are often not wholly his own. The language on which he drew – the *langue* out of which he constructed his *parole* – was not his but everybody's. He inhabited a preformed world of lexis and grammar (though it would not be left in quite the same form by the time he had finished writing). Ready-made phrases of everyday speech, proverbs, lines from the Bible, echoes of other poets, were available as raw material on which to work. When Shakespeare wrote "perpetual night" he was using an English form of a Senecan tag meaning "death," and by using these words he would be importing the resonance of Seneca into his text. The word usually used to describe such borrowing is "allusion." It is more appropriate to accept this term than to suggest that Shakespeare and Seneca were collaborating, but the sense of double authorship is undeniable. Calling such a phrase an "allusion" works in the same way as calling a theatrical or printing-house change a "corruption" of the text. In neither case is the term objective and neutral; both protect the idea of authorial autonomy. Words, phrases, thoughts, and feelings flow through textual culture, through authors who are readers and transmitters, through transmitters who are readers and authors, and through readers who are authors and transmitters, ever changing, ever recombining.

VI

Pericles offers the most complex example of collaboration of the plays discussed in this chapter. It first appeared in a Quarto edition as a play "By William Shakespeare" in 1609, but was excluded from the 1623 Folio. The Shakespearean quality of much of the writing has been widely accepted, and this, combined with the undivided ascription to Shakespeare on the Quarto title page, helped the play to be slowly absorbed into the mainstream Shakespeare canon. Yet, with a few exceptions, critics have agreed that the first two acts are written in a style completely unlike that of Shakespeare, and that impression has been confirmed in stylometric tests (Taylor 1987: 130). Recent investigations identify the collaborator as George Wilkins, the author of another play of the King's Men, *The Miseries of Enforced Marriage*.

Here the picture begins to grow complicated. In 1608 a prose novella on *The Painful Adventures of Pericles King of Tyre* was published; its author too was Wilkins, and the text not only tells the same story as the play but also has close echoes of its language. Of the two versions, the novella appears to be the derivative text. In "The Argument" Wilkins invites his reader "to receive this history in the same manner as it was under the habit of ancient Gower the famous English Poet by the King's Maiesty's Players excellently presented." It seems that Wilkins put together his prose account in order to exploit the popularity of the play (Taylor 1986). He evidently acted without the benefit of a manuscript copy, and recalled *Pericles* as best he could. The text he recalled was not, however, the same as the Quarto printed in 1609. The latter is in itself seriously corrupted, in that the Shakespearean section has an overlay of non-Shakespearean features of metre and language. Most critics agree that the Quarto is based on a memorial reconstruction.

The theory of memorial reconstruction, as it applies to a number of Shakespeare and non-Shakespeare playtexts, has come under criticism because for many plays the kinds of evidence that can be brought forward to demonstrate its presence can also be explained in other ways (Maguire 1996). In the case of *Pericles* the recurrent mangling of verse is one characteristic that does point to a break in direct document-to-document transmission; memorial reconstruction provides a plausible explanation of this and other peculiarities. So an actor or actors probably contributed to the 1609 text. The effect of their presence would inevitably be to devolve the text away from the form in which Shakespeare wrote it. Furthermore, comparison with *Painful Adventures* suggests that two entire episodes have been lost from the Quarto, though in one case the more plausible explanation is that some of Marina's speeches persuading Lysimachus to abandon brothel-going were censored because they questioned too radically the sexual morality of a prince.

The pattern of work between the two dramatists appears to be unusually straightforward. The most striking difference is stylistic: the clunking and lackluster verse of Wilkins as against the characteristically Shakespearean cadences that make themselves felt from scene 10 onwards. This, Gower's third chorus speech, is closely reminiscent of Robin Goodfellow's language in *A Midsummer Night's Dream*:

> The cat with eyne of burning coal
> Now couches fore the mouse's hole,
> And crickets sing at th' oven's mouth
> As the blither for their drouth. (10.5–8)

When Pericles enters in the following scene, his language clearly derives from the author of *King Lear* and *The Winter's Tale*:

> The god of this great vast rebuke these surges
> Which wash both heav'n and hell; and thou that hast
> Upon the winds command, bind them in brass,
> Having called them from the deep. (11.1–4)

As the Shakespearean part of the play unfolds, its action begins to anticipate Shakespeare's late plays, most obviously in the final scene of the main action in which Pericles has first his daughter and then his wife, both thought to be dead, restored to him as it were by a miracle.

VII

What is striking in the case of *Pericles* is that in the text as we have it the question of lateral collaboration between Shakespeare and Wilkins is closely tied up with questions relating to the text's passage through time. But perhaps *Pericles* is merely an exacerbation of normality; for playwrighting itself is enmeshed with the physical and intellectual contribution of others. The point can be elaborated with reference to the early sociotextual history of *The Tempest*, a play that might seem to be of impeccable authorial purity.

Unusually, the plot of *The Tempest* seems to have been of Shakespeare's devising. But it is – correspondingly – dense in intertextual material of various other kinds. The play includes moments where Shakespeare pulls his writing so close to another text that it is impossible to claim that the texture of the passage belongs simply to its immediate author. Here is an example from *The Tempest*, where the antecedent passage is, once again, from Montaigne's *Essays*. In Montaigne, as translated by John Florio, Shakespeare would have read:

> It is a nation . . . that hath *no kinde of traffike, no knowledge of Letters*, no intelligence of numbers, *no name of magistrate*, nor of politike superioritie; *no use of service, of riches or of povertie; no contracts, no successions, no partitions, no occupation but idle*; no respect of kindred, but common, no apparell but naturall, *no manuring of lands, no use of wine, corne, or mettle* . . . (Montaigne 1904–6, 2: 245)

From this catalog of negatives Shakespeare drew on the phrases emphasized above. They can be extracted and reordered to anticipate Shakespeare's arrangement:

> no kind of traffic,
> no name of magistrate
> no knowledge of letters
> no use of service, of riches or of poverty,
> no contracts, no successions,
> no partitions, no manuring of lands,
> no use of wine, corn, or metal.
> no occupation but idle

Every phrase here is still Montaigne. Shakespeare then reworked the passage into pentameters:

> no kind of traffic /
> Would I admit; no name of magistrate; /
> Letters should not be known; / riches, poverty,
> And use of service, none; / contract, succession, /
> Bourn, bound of land, tilth, vineyard, none; /
> No use of metal, corn, or wine, or oil; /
> No occupation; all men idle, all.

In terms of post-Enlightenment principles of intellectual property, perhaps even in the sense recognized in *Greene's Goatsworth of Wit*, Shakespeare is guilty of plagiarism.

In the early modern period, however, the idea of the author as an originator was still jostling against the older idea that poets merely reworked the literary models available to them. Yet Shakespeare's contribution lies more than merely in juggling Montaigne's prose to set up blank verse. He supplies a theatrical context that changes its meaning. Gonzalo is trying in vain to cheer up Alonso by intimating that all things, even utopian things, might be possible on the island where they are shipwrecked. He is frustrated by the cynical interruptions of Antonio and Sebastian, who point out the contradiction between a commonwealth with "No sovereignty" and Gonzalo's first premise that he "were king" of the island. To the Renaissance audience the premise "Had I plantation of this isle," redolent as it is of English schemes for colonizing and settling Ireland and America, would sit incongruously with the source material, in which Montaigne is presenting a description of indigenous Patagonian tribal culture untouched by European civilization.

Montaigne's own account is deeply intertextual, twining together Plato's description of the ideal republic and the Renaissance travel narrative of Amerigo Vespucci, old world and new, the mythical and the presumably extant. Once adopted by *The Tempest*, this conjunction of the geographical and historical planes of referentiality combines with others. In particular, the play draws on contemporary accounts of a shipwreck and salvation from disaster in the "Bermuda pamphlets," correlating them with moments from Aeneas' journey towards Rome in Virgil's *Aeneid*. The dramatic principle by which such material is organized and harmonized owes much to a form of drama that is foreign to the public theatre. The Jonsonian masque of the Jacobean court informs *The Tempest*'s music, its spectacle, its contrasting tableaux of comedy and sublimity, its movements between disorder and anxiously attempted order. This play, in which the idea of authorial control is more prevalent than in any other Shakespeare work, turns out to orchestrate a rich and diverse array of non-authorial cultural materials by means other than the usual conventions of Shakespeare's stage plays. No Jonson, no *Tempest*.

And in a similar spirit one might say "no king, no *Tempest*." The play was performed at court on November 1, 1611 and during the winter of 1612–13, and Shakespeare might well have written specifically with an eye to the royal favor that the play was to gain. Literary patrons gave authority to the texts they patronized. In the case of King James as patron of the King's Men, patronage would have been less direct than in the case of, for instance, a commissioned occasional poem – or, if the legend is true, Queen Elizabeth's request that Shakespeare write a play showing Falstaff in love. But some elements of *The Tempest* respond to court politics and voice the predilections of James. In the play's debate between courtly Platonism and debauchery, between self-effacement and political absolutism, between insularity and colonial expansion, between magic and secular authority, we see the imprint of royal ideology.

In a more specific and localized way, the scripting of the play also takes into account government regulations that had come into force in 1606 whereby profanity is forbidden on the stage. It would be quite possible to relate the play's forcibly chastened language with Prospero's attempts to control others' words and thoughts. Shakespeare was writing constructively within the institutional and legal limits set before him, the external constraints influencing the play's linguistic texture.

The material conditions of playing influence every aspect of the play. Most specifically, its character as a play written for indoor performance determines its structure. We have it on the word of John Dryden that *The Tempest* was performed at the Blackfriars, an indoor theatre which required artificial lighting from candles. The play's careful and meaningful structuring in five acts meets the requirement that there should be act intervals during which the spent candles could be replaced. *The Tempest* is a musical play, and a number of music manuscripts preserve one or more of the songs "Full Fathom Five" and "Where the Bee Sucks" (Orgel 1987: 220–6). Most of them derive from a single source, with settings by Robert Johnson as arranged by John Wilson. Both composers evidently worked for the King's Men. By combining words and music in one document, the manuscripts represent true collaborations between Shakespeare and Johnson (and Wilson). And, as the writing of scores was a usual aspect of play production, they testify to the wider collective nature of theatre. The music, of course, takes us beyond the specific textualization in the 1623 Folio, but reminds us that the Folio text is in this respect incomplete. Music too was textualized, and words in stage directions such as *"playing & singing,"* "Burthen dispersedly," "Burthen: ding dong," *"playing solemne Musicke,"* *"Sings in Gonzaloes eare,"* *"Solemne and strange Musicke,"* *"to soft Musicke,"* testify to the missing complement of the music manuscripts.

As printed in the 1623 Folio, *The Tempest* is one of a number of plays evidently set from a transcript prepared by an identifiable scribe, Ralph Crane (Howard-Hill 1972). He may indeed have been "Shakespeare's earliest editor" (ibid). The King's Men employed Crane in the early 1620s, and his transcripts might have been written out specifically to supply the Folio printers with copy. In the main run of dialogue, Crane's influence would have been limited, and he was in general a careful copyist. Hyphenated compounds such as "wide-chopt-rascall," "dark-backward," "peg-thee," "bemockt-at-Stabs," and "midnight-Mushrumps" are typical of his work, and he would have introduced brackets such as those in "my prime request / (Which I do last pronounce) is (O you wonder)."

Such features, sometimes rhetorically suggestive, sometimes downright misleading, usually disappear when editors modernize punctuation and spelling. What is of more significance to the modern reader is the attention Crane might have paid to the stage directions. The phrasing of expressions such as "with a quaint device," "several strange shapes," "they heavily vanish," "which Prospero observing, speaks" are completely atypical of stage directions in Shakespeare's plays (Jowett 1983). Some key words and phrases are, indeed, found nowhere else in Shakespeare's works. The style is that of the Jonsonian masque. It looks as though the stage directions were refashioned on this model. The sequencing phrase "after which," the describers of sound-effect "tempestuous" and "confused noise," the formula "here X discovers Y": such forms can be found in Jonson's stage directions rather than Shakespeare's. Other phrases such as "properly" followed by a past participle, "in like manner," and "helps to attire" are closely paralleled in the dialogue of Jonson's works. "With a frantic gesture" is closer to Jonson's "with other variety of ridiculous gesture" (stage direction) or "an antic gesture" than anything in Shakespeare's works. It is not impossible that Jonson rather than Crane was the editor.

The location note and the list of *"The Names of all the Actors"* printed at the end of the play are probably also editorial. Such lists are unusual unless there is space to waste (*2 Henry IV*, *Timon of Athens*) or the play was set from a Crane transcript (*The Tempest*, *Two Gentlemen*, and *Measure for Measure*). In other words, their presence relates to circumstances surrounding the printing of the Folio; they are unlikely to have been written by Shakespeare, and are particularly associated with Crane.

The Folio editors made one other major decision that had an effect on the presentation of the play. They placed *The Tempest* as the first play in the volume. The prominence it so achieved can be connected with its elegant presentation and clean printing. *The Tempest* was evidently chosen as a showpiece for the book, and as a shining example of Shakespeare's art. Its status as one of Shakespeare's last plays and its courtliness of tone are two possible reasons why it was singled out in this way.

The printing of the text brought in its own contribution from the typesetters. Anyone who reads the book stands in immediate proximity to the product of their labors, and at some remove even from Crane. On the whole, however, the compositors' influence was slight, limited to the imposition of house style for spellings and presentation, and a few accidental errors or deliberate miscorrections. But one reading deserves attention because it raises acute questions about the relationship between authorial and compositorial work. Depending on the reading of one letter, Ferdinand asserts that either "so rare a father and a wise" or "so rare a father and a wife" has the effect of making "this place paradise" (4.1.123–4). What is at issue is whether Ferdinand is including Miranda alongside his prospective father-in-law Prospero as object of his admiration. If he is doing so, there are further questions as to whether the reference to her is complimentary or incidental and patronizing. That discussion is beyond the present remit, but it serves as a reminder that the reading is consequential (Wayne 1998). And it hangs on the slightest evidence, the absence or presence of a damaged crossbar that would distinguish "f" from long "s," a type distinguished from "f" only by the latter's crossbar. In a few copies of the Folio a damaged crossbar has been supposed to be visible, though examination under an electron microscope suggests otherwise. The question that relates to collaboration lies in the status of the type as evidence of the compositor's intention. The most important criterion is not the existential nature of the matrix in which the type was manufactured, but the perception, intention, and execution of the compositor in setting it. He now becomes a quasi-authorial figure who shares in the making of the text, and who is invoked to confirm or correct what appears, or appears to appear, in the text itself.

The narrative that has just been constructed running from Plato to the figure known as Folio Compositor C may seem to string together a loose aggregate of information, and it is now time to bring the whole into focus with this claim: at every stage, the play's encompassing of the non-Shakespearean is critical to the determination of its status as an artwork. The paraphrase of Montaigne and the reenactments of Virgil establish the play's cultural territory and provide an agenda for its negotiation between past and present, imperial Rome and pre-imperial Britain. *The Tempest* therefore addresses the concerns of power elites. But it does so, like Virgil's *Aeneid*, by acknowledging the prerogatives of art and elegance, the role of the poet in the *res publica*. And *The Tempest* extends the matter of state to the wider audience of the public theatre. Masquelike spectacle and music are the means whereby the play echoes the techniques and ideological ambitions of court theatre, and it is by way of the dialogue between masque on the one hand, and the conventions of public stage plays on the other, that the play represents its political high concerns to a socially more middling audience. The play's aspirational quality and its affinity with court masque are exactly what Crane, or Jonson, or another Folio editor, chose to emphasize when reworking the functional stage directions of the theatre, turning them into elegant and complimentary descriptions not of what will happen but of what has happened on stage, as though the text recalled a single and wonderful moment in the past. And the decision to make *The Tempest* the first play in the volume is part of the editors' bid to place Shakespeare himself on a high cultural footing – admittedly a commercial author of stage plays, but also a writer whose art lifts itself above its humble origins. As for the pseudo-variant "wise"/"wife," it touches a theme that goes back to the classical myth of the Golden Age, which correlates with the biblical Paradise: is Paradise a place without marriage, a place with marriage, or a place in which women are incidental to the main business of binding fathers and sons, creators and male subjects? Ultimately, we understand, it is utopian art that makes Paradise, though *The Tempest* is always careful to stop pointedly short of the Platonic ideal and to reencounter bodily, comic, sexual, physical, postlapsarian reality – a world of contingency in which authors, like Prospero, have to make constant adjustments in order to accommodate and share with others.

VIII

But the diachronic, process-oriented aspect of collaboration does not end here. Ultimately, one would need to address what Jerome J. McGann describes as "the global set of all the texts and poems which have emerged in the literary production and reproduction process" in order to define the "work" as a changing entity that moves through time via new editions and new performances (McGann 1991: 31–2). From this perspective, later "collaborators" in *The Tempest* would include William Davenant and John Dryden, who wrote the first Restoration adaptation, and Thomas Shadwell and Henry Purcell, who produced an operatic version a few years later. Such an account would extend to the most recent editions, productions, and adaptations. And, bearing in mind the reader's role in the continuation of interpretation and meaning, it might include readers too. All this takes us dangerously close to *expansio ad absurdum*, and goes beyond the more modest scope of the present account. But it is relevant to mention in this context that our only access to the lost Shakespeare–Fletcher collaboration *Cardenio* is, in probability, by way of *The Double Falsehood*, an eighteenth-century play by Lewis Theobald on the subject-matter of Cardenio which Theobald claimed to have revised and adapted from a Shakespeare play in manuscript (Taylor 1987: 132–3).

Theatrical adaptation for a revival is a major element in process-oriented collaboration. As it was practiced in the early modern period, it can be studied as a phenomenon influencing the earliest printed texts of two Shakespeare plays, *Macbeth* and *Measure for Measure*; indeed in these plays it is improper to ignore it, because we have no access to the text in the more fully Shakespearean state it assumed before adaptation. Of the two, *Macbeth* lies outside the area of Shakespeare's works covered in the present volume, but is the better known and longer established example. It will be considered briefly before turning to *Measure*.

For a student of Shakespeare's text, the curious thing about *Macbeth* is that, as printed in the 1623 First Folio, it includes songs found also in a tragicomedy by Middleton called *The Witch* (Taylor 1987: 128–9). This play was evidently written in 1616, by which time Shakespeare either was living retired in Stratford or was already dead. Closer examination of the songs in the two plays shows that they seem to have originated in *The Witch* and to have been subsequently transferred to *Macbeth*. It seems, then, that these songs were imported into *Macbeth* as part of a revival performed probably after Shakespeare's death. Other Middleton characteristics have been identified in the Hecate scenes (3.5; 4.1.39–60 and 141–8) in which the songs are performed and, locally, elsewhere in the play. It has been widely accepted that Middleton adapted *Macbeth*, and the case for his involvement is considerably strengthened in his forthcoming *Collected Works*.

IX

The theory that in 1621 Middleton adapted *Measure for Measure* in a similar manner to *Macbeth* is newer and less familiar, but the evidence in its favor is if anything stronger (Taylor and Jowett 1993: 107–236). For reasons already mentioned in relation to *The Tempest*, the absence of offensive oaths points to a revival after 1606, and the presence of act breaks probably reflects staging at the Blackfriars theatre after 1609. On both counts, the Folio text would seem to derive indirectly from a manuscript prepared for a revival some time after the original stagings in 1603–4. The dating can be pushed markedly later by the appearance of the one conspicuously solitary song in *Measure*, "Take oh take those lips away," because the same song also occurs, with a second stanza, in *Rollo, Duke of Normandy* (alternatively known as *The Bloody Brother*). The situation is conspicuously similar to that with *Macbeth*. Every indication is that the song originated in the non-Shakespeare play, which was written in 1617–20, and that the first stanza was borrowed for *Measure*. A brief passage of dialogue after the song must have been added to lock it into the dramatic action. Adaptation evidently also entailed transposition of the Duke's soliloquies "O place and greatness" and "He who the sword of heaven will bear," so as to produce a stronger close to the new act 3.

By comparison, a passage at the beginning of 1.2 is a more straightforward and sustained piece of dramatic composition, but it too can be seen to date from after Shakespeare's death. Most of the play's editors have accepted that there is a duplication in the second scene, and it now seems that Middleton wrote the first 82 lines. It is Middleton who favors the linguistic forms that mark this passage out from the rest of the play and from Shakespeare's usage more generally. Moreover, an array of individual words, distinctive phrases, and idiosyncratic turns of thought can be paralleled in Middleton but not Shakespeare. There are also striking Middleton parallels for the passage's staging, structure, and dramatic function, all contributing to a strongly Shakespeare-negative, Middleton-positive profile.

Middleton evidently added a few other lines and short passages, including, it now seems, the short conversation between Escalus and the Justice at the end of 2.1 and Pompey's catalog of the prisoners at the beginning of 4.3; he also probably relocated the action from the Italian city of Ferrara to Vienna (Middleton, *Collected Works*). But the expansion of 1.2 and 4.1 was his main contribution. With the opening of 1.2 Middleton updated the play by inserting a passage that was intensely topical to the early 1620s. It both added to and thematized the play's participation in public debate, at a time when King James was attempting to stifle it, and when parliament was insisting on its rights to debate foreign policy. Lucio's conversation with his companions supplies a sensationalizing but localizing environment variously for the Duke's supposed urgent affairs out of Vienna, for Claudio's sexual misdemeanor as a topic for rumor-mongering, and for Lucio's role as news-bringer to Isabella in the convent, not to mention the rumors he later promotes about the Duke's sexual conduct. The allusions to the Thirty Years War are especially significant. Middleton seizes on the significance to the moment of the revival of the new location in Vienna, by 1621 the seat of the Catholic Emperor Ferdinand II, and a city at war. It is in this context that the audience would have understood the opening exchange:

> *Lucio.* If the Duke with the other dukes come not to composition with the King of Hungary, why then, all the dukes fall upon the King.
> *First Gentleman.* Heaven grant us its peace, but not the King of Hungary's! (1.2.1–5)

The Hungarian prince Bethlen Gàbor had joined the Protestant alliance; as a gesture of defiance towards the Emperor's title of King of Hungary, he was elected king in 1620, so making a "King of Hungary" an enemy of Vienna. His troops made incursions against Austrian strongholds in Bohemia, and into Austria itself; by mid-September 1621 they were within sight of the walls of Vienna.

War in Europe prompted the innovation of newspapers, in the form of news-sheets or "corantos" presenting regular reports from Vienna and other centers of conflict. The news-sheets of 1621 gave constant reminders of the Hungarians' progress, new cities besieged, new villages burnt. But dispatches from Vienna in the news-sheets of September 12 and October 6 note a new move towards peace. *Measure* was probably revised after October 6, when a news-sheet was issued with details of lords of the Catholic League negotiating with Bethlen (Jowett 2001). If so, Middleton was writing at a time when the outcome was in the balance. Bethlen was in the midst of a rapid about-turn that could lead to a settlement. The pacifist King James and others in England were dismayed by the alliance between James's son-in-law Frederick, the Elector Palatine, and Bethlen, a prince supported by the Turks. A treaty between the Hungarians and Vienna would, however, be a deep disappointment to those who favored a united military campaign against the Catholic Empire.

The revision was concerned not only to make the play topical, but also to make the play's structure, style, and fascinations match the dramaturgy of an indoor hall theatre in the early 1620s. Critics have described the moment when the Duke steps forward in 3.1 to take control of Isabella's destiny as a crucial hinge that divides the play in two. From the point of view of a reviser establishing five acts, this mid-scene hinge was unusable. The introduction of a unique song at the beginning of the new fourth act imposes a new two-part structure in which the song is a formal marker. The act-interval moats the grange from Vienna; the song that follows it reinforces that separation and affirms a new turning point. "Take, oh take those lips away" presents in tableau fashion the new figure of the jilted Mariana. The song opens on a realm of experience remote from Vienna's rigorous nexus between sexual crime and punishment.

Mariana's role as a keynote figure for the final two acts of the play corresponds with that of Lucio for the first three acts. In this respect the interpolated episode near the beginning of the play works in a remarkably similar way to the interpolated song. In the earlier episode too, a minor figure, Lucio, is presented so as to give him representative status, and the mode of dramatic writing is again almost exaggeratedly appropriate to the role. Here too, nothing much happens in the episode, but it gives a strong coloration to our view of the play's world; this is, after all, our first introduction to Vienna's street-life. The two major interventions, despite their differences of method and the contrast in their tone, are therefore of a piece. These and the other changes addressed important peripheries. Though they neither perceptibly added to nor perceptibly detracted from the roles of Isabella, Angelo, and the Duke (notwithstanding the latter's moved speeches), the adaptation touches upon major aspects of *Measure*.

X

This discussion has steered clear of the technicalities of attribution study in order to present collaboration as an issue for criticism of Shakespeare's problem and late plays. The study of collaboration has various possible outcomes. It can affirm or interrogate the authorial context of a particular text, and affirm or interrogate the contents and complexion of an authorial canon. It can question the nature of authorship itself, especially in an environment where the modern concept of literary authorship had relatively little purchase and collaboration was common, such as was the early modern professional theatre. It can study figurations of collaborative authors and the homosocial relationship between them. It can lead towards analysis of a collaborative text as a harmonized or contestatory dialogue between different authorial voices within it. It can identify different contiguities between the text and the culture in which it participated. It can offer a means to explore the palimpsestic and diachronic development of a text that presents itself in a simultaneous and linear fashion. It can restore a text to historical contexts through which it has passed between its original writing and its publication.

As has been shown, all these outcomes can be explored in relation to Shakespeare's problem plays and late plays. And what is left of Shakespeare? If one measures Shakespeare by the yard, attribution study somewhat shortens him, certainly as regards his dramatic works. Less may, of course, be more, but there is no legitimacy in "improving" Shakespeare by removing the supposedly inferior parts and handing them to another dramatist in the manner of the disintegrators. The sense in which Shakespeare emerges as a better dramatist by identifying the hands of sharing dramatists lies elsewhere. As we have seen in the particular case of *Timon*, and as in a different way Masten argued in relation to *Two Noble Kinsmen*, a collaboration demands a different kind of critical response, a response that legitimizes dividedness and finds interest in the tension of dialogue. Critics learnt long ago not to cite the views of Shakespeare's characters as representative of the views of Shakespeare himself. We can equally learn to read Shakespeare's collaborative plays as dialogues of another kind.

REFERENCES AND FURTHER READING

Aubrey, J. (1972). *Aubrey's Brief Lives*, ed. O. L. Dick. Harmondsworth: Penguin Books.

Bate, J. (ed.) (1995). *Titus Andronicus*. London: Routledge.

Bentley, G. E. (1971). *The Profession of Dramatist in Shakespeare's Time, 1590–1642*. Princeton, NJ: Princeton University Press.

Chambers, E. K. (1933). The Disintegration of Shakespeare. British Academy Shakespeare Lecture, 1924. Reprinted in *Aspects of Shakespeare*. Oxford: Clarendon Press, 23–48.

De Grazia, M. (1991). *Shakespeare Verbatim: The Reproduction of Authenticity and the 1790 Apparatus*. Oxford: Clarendon Press.

Hinman, C. (1963). *The Printing and Proof-Reading of the First Folio of Shakespeare*, 2 vols. Oxford: Clarendon Press.

Holdsworth, R. V. (1982). Middleton and Shakespeare: The Case for Middleton's Hand in *Timon of Athens*. University of Manchester. Unpublished Ph.D. thesis.

Hope, J. (1994). *The Authorship of Shakespeare's Plays: A Socio-Linguistic Study*. Cambridge: Cambridge University Press.

Howard-Hill, T. H. (1972). *Ralph Crane and Some Shakespeare First Folio Comedies*. Charlottesville: University Press of Virginia.

——(1992). Shakespeare's Earliest Editor: Ralph Crane. *Shakespeare Survey*, 44, 113–29.

Hoy, C. (1956–62). The Shares of Fletcher and his Collaborators in the Beaumont and Fletcher Canon, 7 parts. *Studies in Bibliography*, 8 (1956), 129–46; *SB* 9 (1957), 143–62; *SB* 11 (1958), 85–106; *SB* 12 (1959), 91–116; *SB* 13 (1960), 77–108; *SB* 14 (1961), 45–68; *SB* 15 (1962), 71–90.

Jackson, M. P. (1979). *Studies in Attribution: Middleton and Shakespeare*. Salzburg: University of Salzburg.

——(1996). Stage Directions and Speech Headings in Act 1 of *Titus Andronicus* Q (1594): Shakespeare or Peele? *Studies in Bibliography*, 49, 134–48.

Jowett, J. (1983). New Created Creatures: Ralph Crane and the Stage Directions in *The Tempest*. *Shakespeare Survey*, 36, 107–20.

——(2001). The Audacity of *Measure for Measure* in 1621. *Ben Jonson Journal*, 8, 1–19.

Klein, K. (ed.) (2001). *Timon of Athens*. Cambridge: Cambridge University Press.

Lake, D. J. (1975). *The Canon of Thomas Middleton's Plays*. Cambridge: Cambridge University Press.

McGann, J. J. (1991). *The Textual Condition*. Princeton, NJ: Princeton University Press.

McMullen, G. (1996). "Our whole life is like a play": Collaboration and the Problem of Editing. *Textus*, 9, 437–60.

——(ed.) (2000). *King Henry VIII*. London: Thompson Learning.

Maguire, L. E. (1996). *Shakespearean Suspect Texts*. Cambridge: Cambridge University Press.

Masten, J. (1997). *Textual Intercourse: Collaboration, Authorship, and Sexualities in Renaissance Drama*. Cambridge: Cambridge University Press.

Metz, G. H. (1985). Disputed Shakespearean Texts and Stylometric Analysis. *Text*, 2, 149–71.

Middleton, T. (forthcoming). *Collected Works*, 2 vols., ed. G. Taylor et al. Oxford: Clarendon Press.

Montaigne, Michael, Lord of (1904–6). *Essayes*, trans. John Florio [London, 1603], 3 vols. London: Oxford University Press.

Oliver, H. J. (ed.) (1959). *Timon of Athens*. London: Methuen.

Orgel, S. (1981). What is a Text? *Research Opportunities in Renaissance Drama*, 24, 3–6.

——(ed.) (1987). *The Tempest*. Oxford: Clarendon Press.

Potter, L. (ed.) (1997). *The Two Noble Kinsmen*. London: Thomas Nelson and Sons.

Schoenbaum, S. (1966). *Internal Evidence and Elizabethan Dramatic Authorship: An Essay in Literary History and Method*. London: Edward Arnold.

Shakespeare, W. (1986). *Complete Works*, gen. eds. S. Wells and G. Taylor. Oxford: Clarendon Press.

Smith, M. W. A. (1991). The Authorship of *Timon of Athens*. *Text*, 5, 195–240.

Spedding, J. (1850). Who Wrote Shakespeare's *Henry VIII*? *Gentleman's Magazine*, n.s., 34, 115–23, 381–2.

Taylor, G. (1986). The Transmission of *Pericles*. *Papers of the Bibliographical Society of America*, 80, 193–217.

——(1987). The Canon and Chronology of Shakespeare's Plays. In S. Wells and G. Taylor, with J. Jowett and W. Montgomery, *William Shakespeare: A Textual Companion*. Oxford: Clarendon Press, 69–144.

——(1995). Shakespeare and Others: The Authorship of *Henry the Sixth Part One*. *Medieval and Renaissance Drama in England*, 7, 145–205.

Taylor, G. and Jowett, J. (1993). *Shakespeare Reshaped 1606–1623*. Oxford: Clarendon Press.

Wayne, V. (1998). The Sexual Politics of Textual Transmission. In T. L. Berger and L. Maguire (eds.) *Textual Formations and Reformation*. Newark: University of Delaware Press.

"What's in a Name?" Tragicomedy, Romance, or Late Comedy

Barbara A. Mowat

The story of the generic placing of four of Shakespeare's late plays – *Pericles*, *Cymbeline*, *The Winter's Tale*, and *The Tempest* – began as an unintended consequence of the founding in 1874 of the New Shakspere Society, which had as its purpose the "very close study of the metrical and phraseological peculiarities of Shakspere, to get his plays as nearly as possible into the order in which he wrote them" (Furnivall 1874: vi). Among its first accomplishments, the Society established the existence of a group of late Shakespeare dramas in need of generic classification. Until 1874 there had been little thought that these four plays had much in common, either chronologically or generically. Earlier in the century, Malone, Knight, and others had attempted to arrange Shakespeare's plays in the order of their writing, and Malone (who recognized that "the versification of [*Cymbeline*] bears . . . a much greater resemblance to that of the Winter's Tale and the Tempest, than to any of our author's earlier plays") (Malone 1821: 453), at one point tentatively placed *Cymbeline* among the later plays, but his and others' belief that *Cymbeline* showed marked connections with *Macbeth* and, especially, *King Lear* occluded any evidence that would have separated it chronologically from *Lear* and the other Holinshed-based plays.[1] Thus, until 1874 *The Tempest* had been identified as "late" (ca. 1610–12); *The Winter's Tale*, after considerable uncertainty about possible early dates, had also been identified as "late";[2] *Cymbeline* had been classified as "middle" (ca. 1604–6); and *Pericles* sometimes as "late" and sometimes as "very early" (with Charles Knight placing its writing in the late 1580s) (Knight 1854: 844). Only the mounting evidence of metrical tests supported and published by the New Shakspere Society brought together these four plays as a chronological group.[3]

Until that moment, the plays' generic classifications had been determined by the Folio's division of the plays into "Comedies, Histories, and Tragedies." Heminge and Condell (or whoever edited or designed the Folio) had placed *The Tempest* as the first of the "Comedies" and *The Winter's Tale* as the last, and this classification had raised no significant generic questions. Samuel Johnson (1765), for instance, viewed *The Tempest* as like *A Midsummer Night's Dream*, the two comedies representing "the noblest Efforts of that sublime and amazing Imagination, peculiar to Shakespeare," and he found *The Winter's Tale*, "with all its absurdities, very entertaining" (1: 3; 2: 349). Had the Folio not placed *Cymbeline* as the last of the "Tragedies," surrounding it with misleading para-textual matter[4] ("The Tragedie of Cymbeline" as title and running head), Johnson might well never have attacked the play for "the folly of the fiction, the absurdity of the conduct . . . and the impossibility of the events in any system of life" (Johnson 1765, 7: 403). But "The Tragedie of Cymbeline," printed as it was in the Folio in the climactic position after "The Tragedie of King Lear," "The Tragedie of Othello, the Moore of Venice," and "The Tragedie of Anthonie and Cleopatra," could hardly have presented itself to Johnson as, "with all its absurdities, very entertaining."[5] *Cymbeline*'s identification as a Tragedy drew scholarly attention to its Holinshed-based material, separated it defini-tively from the "Comedies," and made of the play a generic puzzle, though scholars did not expressly address the genre issue. *Pericles*, because it was excluded from the First Folio, received little serious scholarly attention – again, until 1874, when the applica-tion of metrical and verse tests placed the "Shakespearean" parts of the play in the same group as *Cymbeline*, *The Winter's Tale*, and *The Tempest*.

Once these plays were linked through the metrical tests and the group was assigned to the final years of Shakespeare's productive life, its first generic "naming" followed almost immediately. G. G. Gervinus, in his 1874 *Shakespeare Commentaries*, used the newly determined chronological positions of Shakespeare's plays to place them in significant "periods," and he accepted the evidence that put the writing of *Pericles*, *Cymbeline*, *The Winter's Tale*, and *The Tempest* in Shakespeare's last productive years. But he did not give a name to these late plays,[6] nor did he seek for similarities among them. Indeed, while acknowledging that *Cymbeline* was probably written in 1609, he placed his discussion of the play not with the other late plays but, instead, "next after *Lear*, on account of its internal relation with this tragedy" (p. 644). It was Edward Dowden who, building on Gervinus's "periods," discussed the late plays as a distinct group and found a name for them. In his 1875 *Shakespeare: A Critical Study of His Mind and Art*, Dowden writes that, despite the "remarkable" positions in which the Folio places *Cymbeline*, *The Winter's Tale*, and *The Tempest*, "characteristics of versification and style, and the enlarged place given to scenic spectacle, indicate that these plays were pro-duced much about the same time. But the ties of deepest kinship between them are spiritual. There is a certain romantic element in each" (p. 403).[7] By 1877 he was ready to go further. He added *Pericles* to his list and wrote of the now-four plays:

> There is a romantic element about these plays. In all there is the same romantic inci-dent of lost children recovered by those to whom they are dear . . . In all there is a beau-tiful romantic background of sea or mountain. The dramas have a grave beauty, a sweet serenity, which seem to render the name "comedies" inappropriate . . . Let us, then, name this group, consisting of four plays, . . . Romances. (Dowden 1877: 55–6)

It would be interesting to know where Dowden found the name "Romances" for this set of plays. As a generic label, *romance* had long since been used to describe a particular kind of verse or prose narrative, one usually set in opposition to *epic* or, especially in the eighteenth and nineteenth centuries, to other kinds of serious prose fiction. In letters written in 1876 Dowden himself used the term *romance* to refer to a just-published novel, describing George Eliot's *Daniel Deronda* as an "ideal romance, almost," calling it a "companion" of the "realistic, satirical" *Middlemarch*, and pointing out correspondences between the "*natural* mystery and marvel" of *Daniel Deronda* and the "interpositions of the miraculous" in medieval "Legends and Romances" (Dowden 1914: 99–101). In the early nineteenth century the term *dramatic romance* had appeared. William Hazlitt, for example, wrote in 1817 that *Cymbeline* "may be considered as a dramatic romance" (though he also called it "one of the most delightful of Shakespear's historical plays") (p. 1) and in 1820 he wrote a review of "The new Dramatic Romance (or whatever it is called) of *The Vampyre*" (which he also described as a "melodrama") (Hazlitt 1971: 204–5).[8] It is possible that Dowden, like Hazlitt, thought of plays like *Cymbeline* as stories to be read and thus properly describable as "romances,"[9] or it is possible that the theatrical spectacle that accompanied such dramatic romances as *The Vampyre* led Dowden to endow the late plays with the generic name *romance*. (Compare, for example, Dowden's list of the "romantic" elements in the late plays: their "scenic spectacle," their "beautiful romantic background of sea or mountain," their "grave beauty" and "sweet serenity," with Hazlitt's description of the theatrical setting for *The Vampyre*: the "hue of the sea-green waves, floating in the pale beam under an arch-way of grey weather-beaten rocks," a description that concludes: "In the scene where the moonlight fell on the dying form of Ruthven (the Vampyre) it was like a fairy glory, forming a palace of emerald light") ("The Drama," 1820, p. 205).[10]

Whatever led Dowden to choose the name "Romances" for this group of plays, the name itself has been remarkably durable. In contrast, his comments characterizing the plays and their author did not long stand unchallenged. Dowden had focused on the fact that the four "Romances" were written at the end of Shakespeare's working life, and for him the central fact about the plays was their relationship to Shakespeare as author, particularly to Shakespeare's state of mind as he approached retirement and death. The common features Dowden found in the plays indicated to him an authorial mind that had recently emerged from the despair which had produced the tragedies. Dowden's conclusions about the plays and about their author were attacked both by critics who found in the plays something other than "grave beauty" and "sweet serenity" (see, for example, Strachey 1922) and by those who noticed the potential significance of the years 1608–12, the dates assigned the plays as a result of the metrical tests. These years, scholars pointed out, were far more than the final period of Shakespeare's working life. They were also the years in which Beaumont and Fletcher wrote a new and amazingly popular kind of drama, the years in which Shakespeare's company acquired and began to play at a private indoor theatre, and the years in which the court masque flourished and the anti-masque developed.

As the connection between Shakespeare's "romances" and the 1608–12 theatrical scene awakened increasing interest, scholars urged the importance of Fletcherian influence, the importance of the Blackfriars venue, and the possible influence of the court masque. In 1901 A. H. Thorndike placed the chronological results of verse tests for Shakespeare's plays against those he established for the Beaumont and Fletcher plays, and, excluding *Pericles* from the group, argued that Shakespeare's "romances" were surely written in imitation of the new "heroic romances" created by Shakespeare's younger colleagues writing for the King's Men (p. 6 *passim*). While Thorndike adopted Dowden's term *romance* to identify not only *Cymbeline*, *The Winter's Tale*, and *The Tempest* but also the "tragi-comedies and tragedies" written by Beaumont and Fletcher in "the romance mode" (p. 5), he did not accept Dowden's explanation of the impulse that led Shakespeare to write the plays. "It is stated," Thorndike writes,

> that [Shakespeare] passed out of a period of life, gloomy, passionate, full of suffering, into one of philosophic calm, renewed optimism, and final reconciliation: or as Mr. Dowden puts it, he passed "out of the depths" and rested "on the heights."

While "it would be stupid to deny the possibility of such a change," he continues, "we are on far safer grounds when we study objective influences" (p. 6). He found such influences primarily in the dramas of Beaumont and Fletcher, but he also urged the influence of the court masque and the significance of the new Blackfriars venue (a suggestion fully developed in 1948 by Gerald Eades Bentley).

From 1901 onward, then, the impulse that scholars perceived as leading Shakespeare to write his late plays can only be described as overdetermined: Shakespeare wrote the plays when he was himself in his final productive years; in the same years, a style of drama developed that may have suggested to Shakespeare a change in direction for his talents, and, simultaneously, a new kind of theatre space offered Shakespeare the opportunity to write in a different style. In other words, the years assigned the plays as a result of the metrical tests offered a rich assortment of biographical and theatrical influences, any one of which could be (and often was) used as the full explanation for the differences that scholars could suddenly see linking these plays and separating them from Shakespeare's earlier dramas. By 1910 those scholars wanting to emphasize theatrical influences were beginning to suggest that Dowden's name for the plays should be replaced with the name "tragicomedies," emphasizing in this renaming the perceived resemblances to Beaumont and Fletcher's works (some of which had been called "tragicomedies" in the 1679 Folio).

For scholars today, the existence of a group of late Shakespeare plays that belong together in a single genre is a given. As Philip Edwards put it, "*Cymbeline*, *The Winter's Tale*, *The Tempest*, with (sometimes) *Pericles* and (sometimes) *Henry VIII* as outriders . . . seem more closely related than any other group of Shakespeare's plays" (Edwards 1958: 1), and few would disagree with Gerald Eades Bentley's claim that "No competent critic who has read carefully through the Shakespeare canon has failed to notice that there is something different" about these plays. Indeed, most scholars today assume that the late plays "have commonly been discussed as a distinct genre," as Bentley states, and that their "peculiar characteristics . . . have generally been recognized, whether the plays are called Shakespeare's Romances, or Shakespeare's Tragi-Comedies, or his Romantic Tragi-Comedies, or simply the plays of the fourth period" (Bentley 1948: 47–8).[11] As we have seen, the generic similarity has been "commonly . . . discussed" and "generally . . . recognized" only since the late nineteenth century, but the present-day agreement that links the plays chronologically and generically is so widely accepted as to seem self-evident.

Even so, scholars have not yet reached agreement about what the plays should be called. This impasse results in part, I suggest, from problems inherent in the generic names themselves. The term *romance* does not designate a dramatic genre today, nor did it in Shakespeare's time – the category is strikingly absent from Polonius's comically comprehensive list of such genres, and, indeed, from Shakespeare's works generally – and when the term was used in Shakespeare's day it referred primarily to verse tales of chivalry. To apply it as a genre designation to a set of his plays, then, is to some extent anachronistically Victorian and inapposite. Nor is the name *tragicomedy* completely apt. F. H. Ristine whose 1910 *English Tragicomedy: Its Origin and History* supported Thorndike's argument that Shakespeare probably followed the lead of Beaumont and Fletcher as they created sophisticated tragicomedies, confessed that Shakespeare's plays do not fit the new pattern. *Cymbeline*, for example, follows the "older epic method of construction." In this play,

> apparitions appear among the *dramatis personae*, war comes to the foreground and a battle is represented on the stage, and the final defeat of villainy and triumph of romantic love has left death behind it.

"*The Winter's Tale*," Ristine continues, is "related to the old school of rambling romance even more than *Cymbeline* is"; and *The Tempest*, "Shakspere's third and last romance," is "even further removed from the world of fact and reality" (pp. 113–14). Marvin Herrick's *Tragicomedy: Its Origin and Development in Italy, France, and England* also indicates that the label *tragicomedy* sits uneasily on Shakespeare's late plays. While he finds "tragicomic qualities and devices" not only in the late plays but also in "most of Shakespeare's romantic comedies," he sees *Pericles* as a "romantic history" and *Cymbeline* as "a tragedy with a happy ending" (pp. 249, 255). Joan Hartwig makes an extensive case for calling *Pericles*, *Cymbeline*, *The Winter's Tale*, and *The Tempest* tragicomedies, but at the center of her argument is the acknowledgment that "Shakespeare's work in the genre differs from that of other dramatists": it shares with Beaumont and Fletcher an emphasis on artifice and a tragicomic denouement, but even in these similarities it exhibits "the vast difference in the purpose each had in using the mode" (Hartwig 1972: 15, 29). Indeed, her work demonstrates that Shakespeare's late plays differ so markedly from the definitions put forth by Guarini and Fletcher and from the plays written by Beaumont and Fletcher that her claim that Shakespeare's late plays are tragicomedies applies finally to the vision she sees the plays conveying and the experience she sees them providing for the audience. And Robert Henke, who has recently argued that Shakespeare's late plays "should be seen in the light of the generic practices of tragicomedy in the pastoral mode," neverthe-less distinguishes the plays from "the Italian pastoral tragicomedies and those of Guarini's English imitators" (Henke 1997: 31, 27; see also pp. 53–5).

The names *romance* and *tragicomedy*, then, do not place the plays in recognizable categories of Jacobean drama, nor do they fully distinguish the late plays from Shakespeare's works in general. (Madeleine Doran has long since shown how romance story is at the heart of all of Shakespeare's plays – indeed, of much Elizabethan and Jacobean drama (Doran 1954: 171–90 *passim*) – and critics from Samuel Johnson to W. B. Yeats have pointed out that all of Shakespeare's plays are, in effect, tragicome-dies (Yeats 1953: 286; 1961: 240; Johnson 1765, 1: v–lxxii, esp. xii–xvi).) In other words, as generic labels the names are of questionable utility – if one wishes, that is, for a label that clearly demarcates the class within which the plays belong. Yet schol-ars continue to use both *romance* and *tragicomedy* to designate these plays – and not, I suggest, simply because no other genre designation is available. The term *late Shake-spearean comedy*, for example, could certainly serve the purpose, properly categorizing the plays in terms of their overall comic design and their chronological placement by assigning them to a subset of the subgenre "Shakespearean comedy." Yet scholars, not content with such a label, continue to fall back on the *romance/tragicomedy* dyad, some-times combining the terms, as in "romantic tragicomedy" or "tragicomic romance," sometimes insisting on the supremacy of one term over the other. I would argue that the durability of these rather unsatisfactory names for Shakespeare's late plays is itself a clue worth our following.

Alastair Fowler, reworking Wittgenstein's "theory of family resemblance" – a theory that, in Wittgenstein's words, recognizes in related phenomena "a complicated network of similarities overlapping and criss-crossing: sometimes overall similarities, sometimes similarities of detail" (Wittgenstein 1988: 32) – has suggested that "genres appear to be much more like families than classes," and has proposed that represen-tatives of a genre "be regarded as making up a family whose sets and individual members are related in various ways, without necessarily having any single feature shared in common by all" (Fowler 1982: 41).[12] This looser definition of genre allows us to see *romance* and *tragicomedy* as pointing toward characteristics of the plays that link them both to romance (as a kind of story and a type of structure) and to tragi-comic methodologies and modes – to recognize the names, in other words, as signal-ing generic resemblances, indicating "families [rather] than classes" – from which point we can begin to discover the family or families within which these plays are most at home. Particularly helpful for the critic of Shakespeare's late plays is Fowler's discussion of "literary tradition" as the basis of "family resemblances" in literature: "What produces generic resemblances," he writes, "is tradition: a sequence of influ-ence and imitation and inherited codes connecting works in the genre. As kinship makes a family, so literary relations of this sort form a genre" (p. 42).

Within the context of inherited codes, of genre as a set of works connected by family resemblances, *romance* and *tragicomedy* become truly useful names for Shakespeare's late plays. Neither name, as already noted, serves to fix the plays in a recognizable category of Jacobean drama, but both names – or, better, the names in combination – lead us to a family of works within which Shakespeare's late plays clearly belong.[13] Not that they are at home in this genre exclusively. One of the attractive features of the "family resemblance" school of genre theory is that it helps us see how genres overlap, how a work, or set of works, can be in several genres simultaneously. Shakespeare's late plays belong, for example, in the category of "Shakespeare's plays" in general (as the names *late Shakespearean comedies* or *Shakespeare's late plays* indicate); at the same time, they share many features with the subgenre of Fletcherian tragicomedy and with that of non-dramatic romances such as the *Aethiopica* and the *Arcadia* (as the names *tragicomedies* and *romances* suggest). But the family of works with which the plays share the most numerous and most intriguing connections is that set of dramas that trace back to the English miracle plays and then forward through the dramatic romances from *Clyomon and Clamydes* through *Mucedorus*. Like Shakespeare's late plays, these earlier plays are simultaneously dramatized romances and tragicomedies; they are linked by the kinds of stories they dramatize, the characters and incidents they include, and the way they dramatize the stories. Scholars have noticed similarities between *Cymbeline* and *The Rare Triumphs of Love and Fortune*, for instance, and between *Pericles* and the Digby *Mary Magdalene*, and between *The Winter's Tale* and *The Old Wives Tale* (see, for example, Nosworthy 1955: xxiv–xxviii; Hoeniger 1963: lxxxviii–xci; Edwards 1986), but they have not pursued the idea that "a sequence of influence and imitation and inherited codes" draws this set of plays into a genre, a family within which Shakespeare's late plays are comfortably at home.[14]

There are two good reasons why this line of investigation has not been pursued. First, there are very few plays in the genre that have survived. J. M. Manly (1927), who traces the tradition of romantic drama in England back to the *miracula* – "plays of the lives and sufferings and miracles of saints and martyrs" – bemoans "the scantiness of the texts and the records" (p. 134). C. R. Baskerville (1916–17), too, whose interest is in romantic drama up until the time of Elizabeth, acknowledges the fact of the "meager remains of the drama" (p. 43), and Patricia Russell confesses that

> generalisations about the romantic narrative plays of 1570 to 1590 are based on a few remaining plays, no two of which are quite alike, which makes a strict classification "popular romantic narrative drama" impossible. (Russell 1966: 111)

Second, few critics, especially of Shakespeare's works, have been willing to admit that this particular tradition is worth exploring. As J. M. Nosworthy most tellingly puts it, "a tradition that rests on things no better than *Mucedorus* or Peele's *Old Wives Tale* scarcely merits the name of tradition" (Nosworthy 1955: xxx).

Yet – to address first the issue of the scarcity of extant plays – evidence indicates that the scarcity is simply the result of poor survival rates and that romantic drama was for centuries extremely popular in England. "Scanty as the records are," writes Manly, "their number, their distribution and their nature prove conclusively . . . that . . . the miracle play properly so-called flourished in every part of England" and led directly to "the romantic plays which we find holding the stage . . . in the sixteenth century," there being no line that one can draw "between saints' legends and romance: the incidents are the same; the material is identical" (Manly 1927: 136–7, 142, 153). Baskerville, too, finds "evidence of a fairly fully developed taste for romantic plays during the reign of Henry VIII," and argues that "the extensive use of romantic motives [in entertainments] at [Henry VIII's] court . . . and the frequent repetition of conventional romantic settings suggest that many a lost romantic drama is recorded in the annals of the time simply as 'a play' or 'an interlude'" (Baskerville 1916–17: 94, 85). And Betty J. Littleton begins her discussion of *Clyomon and Clamydes* as an "early romantic drama" by arguing that "*Clyomon and Clamydes*, *Common Conditions*, and *The Rare Triumphs of Love and Fortune* are the only surviving representatives of a large group of romantic plays which were produced during the period from about 1570 to about 1585," noting "the titles of 27 lost plays" that are clearly dramatized romances (Littleton 1968: 53).

As for scholars' dismissal of these earlier dramas, I would argue that the rewards for examining this admittedly scanty collection of less-than-stellar early dramatized romances are, for the student of Shakespeare's late plays, considerable. When we place his plays within this particular genre, we are rewarded first by a clearer recognition of the kind of romance story that his "romances" dramatize. The Romance mythos proposed by Northrop Frye would have it that "the complete form of the romance is clearly the successful quest" in which the "hero is analogous to the mythical Messiah or deliverer who comes from an upper world and his enemy is analogous to the demonic power of a lower world," and in which there is "a crucial struggle" followed by "the exaltation of the hero" (Frye 1957: 187). This definition of romance story clearly has almost no bearing on Shakespeare's late plays.[15] Except for Prospero, the late-play "heroes" are quite passive, playthings of fortune, impulse, or obsession. Their prototypes in non-dramatic romance are to be found in the ancient romances of Heliodorus and Achilles Tatius,[16] but prototypes can also be found on the English stage at least as early as the performance of "Placy Dacy, alias Saint Eustacy" at Braintree in 1534. J. M. Manly, in his study of the link between the miracle plays and sixteenth-century romantic drama, draws particular attention to this play because, dramatizing as it does "the well-known legend of Placidus (or Placidas), who after his conversion was renamed Eustachius," it illustrates "admirably the romantic character of medieval legend, and the close relationship between the miracle play and such Elizabethan dramas as 'Common Conditions' [and] 'Sir Clyomon and Sir Clamydes'" (Manly 1927: 147).[17] The presence of Eustace-type plots in all of Shakespeare's late plays (as well as in the frame-story for *Comedy of Errors*) suggests that the influence of the Eustace story on the English stage is perhaps even more extensive than Manly suggests, threading its way as an "inherited code," "overlapping and criss-crossing" within the "network of similarities" that makes up the genre of early dramatic romances.

The Eustace story as recounted in the *Golden Legend* (see Jacobus de Voragine 1993, 2: 266–71) and as presumably dramatized in 1534 tells the story of the conversion of Placidus, the commanding general of Emperor Trajan's army, who with his wife and two sons was baptized and given a new name. As Eustace, he was told by God that he would suffer much, would indeed "become another Job," but that once he had "been humbled," God would restore him to his "erstwhile glory." Eustace's "trials" begin with a plague that destroys his servants and herds and turns Eustace and his family into "fugitives." They flee toward Egypt, but onboard ship the captain seizes Eustace's wife and puts the father and sons ashore. As they attempt to cross a river, one son is taken by a wolf and the other by a lion. Eustace is left to "mourn and tear his hair." He works as a laborer "for a pittance," while his sons, saved by shepherds and huntsmen, grow up in a neighboring village, unaware that they are brothers. After fifteen years the Emperor Trajan, in need of the military expertise of his former commander-in-chief, has Eustace sought for throughout the land. When Eustace is found, he is "clothed in fine garments" and put in command of the Roman army. He orders "recruits to be called up from every city and village," and among the recruits are his two lost sons. "By God's will" the youths are quartered in an inn where "their hostess was also their mother." The mother overhears the two share their life stories and, as they come to realize they are brothers, she begins to suspect they are her lost sons. She in turn goes to the commander, recognizes him as her husband, and reveals herself as his wife. "Tears of joy and mutual embraces followed and he glorified God who comforts the afflicted." The youths in turn are summoned and tell their stories. "He and their mother embraced them, floods of tears were shed, and kisses exchanged time after time" (ibid: 270–1).

Eustace's story is included in the *Golden Legend* because of the spectacular nature of his conversion (Jesus appeared to him as a stag) and because Eustace and his family are later martyred for refusing to sacrifice to idols, but at the core of the legend is the romance story of the trials he endures, his loss of wife and children, and the subsequent restoration of his family and his "erstwhile glory."[18] Because of the scarcity of extant early romantic plays, it is impossible to be certain of the lines of influence that connect the dramatizations of Eustace-like romances.[19] But the motifs of the hero's suffering as a test or trial, the separation of the hero from his wife and children, the tracing of separate family members' adventures, and the overwhelmingly emotional reunion that concludes the drama are reflected in part in the dramatic romance of *Common Conditions* (where God as the controlling force in the action is replaced by the Vice figure) and can be found in varying iterations in *Pericles*, *Cymbeline*, *The Winter's Tale*, and *The Tempest*.

In *Pericles* the plot of the separated family is central: the hero/king loses his wife, then his child, suffers miserably for years, then is given back both daughter and wife and returns to his throne. The fact that these plot features also characterize the Apollonius of Tyre story on which *Pericles* is directly based illustrates, for our purposes, the usefulness of Fowler's "family resemblance" theory of genre, in that we need not exclude the Eustace similarities from our consideration of *Pericles* nor search for a common source for the Eustace and Apollonius legends simply because the two stories are frequently parallel. As Wittgenstein pointed out, in "family resemblance" theory lines simply overlap and crisscross, forming a network of resemblances. The Apollonius story itself and its retelling in *Pericles* overlap significantly, in fact, not only with the legend behind "Placy Dacy, alias Saint Eustacy" but also with the story of Mary Magdalene (as it is told in the *Golden Legend* by Jacobus de Voragine, 1: 374–83, esp. 377–80) and with its dramatic rendering in the Digby *Mary Magdalene* (Furnivall 1930: 53–136, esp. 109–30), in both of which versions a ruler's wife gives birth aboard ship in a storm, dies, is cast overboard (or abandoned on a rock) in an attempt to save the ship from sinking, and is then miraculously saved and restored to her husband and supposedly dead child. *Pericles* itself thus stands as a network of connections linking various stories of families separated and reunited, at least two of which stories (that of Eustace and that of the King of Marcylles in *Mary Magdalene*) were already, by the early sixteenth century, part of the dramatized romance tradition.

Pericles is linked also to Shakespeare's other late plays by the "inherited code" of the Eustace story, a "sequence of influence" that pulls the four plays into a subgeneric family. The plays are remarkably different, especially in structure, but one can discern in their shared story of loss, suffering, and joyous reunion a distinct family resemblance. In *Cymbeline* the Eustace-like story is given interesting elaborations and twists: the king has lost his wife and sons and has, in effect, replaced them with the Queen and her son Cloten before the play's action begins; in the course of the play he loses his daughter, the stepson, and the Queen; finally, in a notoriously complex reunion scene, his daughter and his two long-lost sons are restored to him and he and the succession are secure. In *The Winter's Tale* (largely a dramatization of Greene's *Pandosto* but closer to the Eustace legend than is Greene's novel),[20] the king/father himself causes the violent rending of the family: he sentences his baby daughter to banishment, where she barely escapes destruction by a storm and then by a wild animal; he denounces his chaste wife and loses her to death/concealment and loses his son to death; sixteen years later Jove's oracle is fulfilled and a humbled Leontes, like Eustace before him, regains his lost wife and one child, though his dead son returns only in the guise of the new son-in-law. (Because his wife "dies" almost immediately after the birth and abandonment of her baby, her story also overlaps with that of the Queen of Marcylle in *Mary Magdalene* and Thaisa in *Pericles*; Hermione "dies" but, like her forerunners, she is "preserved" – or has "preserved [her]self" – "to see the issue": 5.3.128–9).[21] *The Tempest* dramatizes the Eustace story by, in effect, dividing the protagonist into two figures: the king, Alonso, loses his son in the shipwreck, repents of the "trespass" that, according to the Harpy, has led to this loss, and is rewarded at the end by the return of the prince and the gift of a daughter-in-law; the restoration to "erstwhile glory," however, is the reward not of the erring and penitent king but of the banished Duke Prospero. In each of the plays a Eustace-like story is shaped into a drama in which a king/father suffers, loses, mourns, and regains much if not all of what he had lost, and in each play the succession turns on the recovery of the royal children.

This story-pattern may be related to at least one of the plot motifs that overlap and crisscross within the late plays as well as within the larger generic family of dramatized romances, the motif of romantic love across lines of social rank, or what Paul Yachnin calls "cross-rank" wooing and marriage (see chapter 3, this volume). In the early dramatic romances (as well as in Shakespeare's late plays) the motif occurs sometimes as peripheral to the main action and sometimes as the crucial precipitating device. In *Clyomon and Clamydes* it triggers one of the two major plot lines. Princess Neronis rescues a nameless knight cast up on the shore of her father's kingdom and falls in love with him, immediately chiding herself for this weakness:

> Ah wofull Dame, thou knowest not thou, of what degree he is,
> Of noble bloud his gesters showe, I am assured of this.
> Why belike he is some runnagate that will not show his name.
> (Littleton 1968: ll. 1016–18)

Like Imogen in *Cymbeline*, Neronis is pursued by a loathsome royal suitor; like Imogen, she dresses as a page and falls into despair at finding a corpse that she thinks is that of her lover; unlike Imogen, Neronis learns that her love is not cross-rank: the nameless knight turns out to be Prince Clyomon, son of the King of Denmark. In *The Rare Triumphs of Love and Fortune* the plot turns on the love of Princess Fidelia for a supposed "upstart fondling [i.e., foundling]" brought up at court and then banished at the instigation of Fidelia's boorish brother. The play's happy ending comes about after Venus appears onstage and announces that the "fondling" "is not borne so base, / As you esteeme, but of a noble race" (Greg 1930: ll. 323, 1757–8). And in *Mucedorus* the hero/prince ("Mucedorus, the King's Son of Valencia") disguises himself as a shepherd and in this role wins the heart of the princess ("Amadine, the King's Daughter of Aragon").[22] Later, disguised as a hermit, he warns Amadine that a shepherd is "Sure a man unfit to match with you" (5.1.29) and, having resumed his shepherd's garb, he spells out all the reasons a princess should not marry a shepherd such as he (5.1.135–44). When she continues to protest her love and her determination to take on the life of a shepherd's wife, he reveals himself as "born of royal blood," to which she responds: "Ah, how I joy my fortune is so good" (5.1.151–4).

The most conspicuous cross-rank couple in Shakespeare's late plays is *Cymbeline*'s Imogen and Posthumus, but the situation of Florizel and Perdita in *The Winter's Tale* – their mutual anxiety about their love, their flight in the face of King Polixenes' fury, their despair when Leontes learns that Florizel's "bride" is not royal – turns on the presumed difference in their rank. In *Pericles* the princess Thaisa falls in love with the "stranger knight" (2.3.69), who is allowed to woo her only because the king recognizes something royal in him beneath his unpromising exterior (2.5.78–80); and *The Tempest* plays with cross-rank wooing by having Prospero accuse Ferdinand of usurping a royal title while, at the same time, Prince Ferdinand, thinking himself now King of Naples, finds himself wooing the daughter of a crabbed exile about whom (until past mid-play) Ferdinand knows nothing except that he's "composed of harshness" (3.1.8–9). In each of these Shakespeare plays, as in *Clyomon and Clamydes*, *Rare Triumphs*, and *Mucedorus*, a prince or princess is in love with a supposed or actual commoner – a plot situation that does not occur in the Shakespeare canon outside of these four late plays.[23] While the device is undeniably an example of what Fowler terms "literary tradition," part of a "sequence of inherited codes" found throughout the early dramatic romance genre, it can also be seen as worth scholarly attention as one of the elements (one linked, perhaps, to the larger stories of bereaved and penitent kings) in the kind of tragicomic drama Shakespeare chose to present at the Globe and presumably at the Blackfriars during the years that Beaumont and Fletcher were also experimenting with tragicomic forms.

In suggesting that Shakespeare chose to present a particular kind of tragicomic drama in his late plays, I am not abandoning my larger argument that the plays belong in the genre of dramatized romance. Romance stories as dramatized on the early English stage are in essence tragicomic – not, as Madeleine Doran has demonstrated, tragicomic in the formal sense proposed by Guarini and adapted by Beaumont and Fletcher, nor even as a deliberate mixture of tragic and comic forms, but as preceding formal "breakdown" into tragedy and comedy. As Doran writes,

> romantic story, neither tragic nor comic in the classical sense, was not a breakdown of these forms but antecedent to them in medieval and early renaissance stage practice. It was romantic story which, under the influence of inherited conceptions of ancient drama, got pulled about and shaped into the separable forms of tragedy and comedy. (Doran 1954: 186).[24]

What is immediately clear about the Eustace-type plot that we find in Shakespeare's late plays is how well it fits Doran's description of the romance story that is in its essence tragicomic. The stories at the heart of Shakespeare's late plays are, as Ben Jonson accused them of being, "mouldy tales" – with Jonson's phrase referring not only to their "use of romance traditions" but also to their "being old-fashioned" (Hattaway 1984: 206, ll. 21–2n.).[25] Jonson used the term to condemn *Pericles*, but, as he indicates in his attack on those who beget "Tales, Tempests, and such like drolleries," he was aware that other of Shakespeare's late plays were also based on unrealistic old stories that "make Nature afraid" (instead of showing her her own image).[26] These stories – tragicomic in essence, not yet "pulled about and shaped" into either comedy or tragedy – are, as Doran points out, what we find in "medieval and early renaissance stage practice" – and, I would add, in Shakespeare's late plays.

Shakespeare's practice in these plays (as it is in Peele's *The Old Wives Tale*) is to draw repeated attention to the moldiness of the tale and to the lack of credibility attaching to the story (see Mowat 1976: 36–68; Ewbank 1975: 125). In many of the other early dramatized romances the practice instead is to foreground the pull and tug of comedy and tragedy, of Eros and Fortune, in the shaping of the story. Sometimes the plays simply gesture toward the embedded conflicting forms. The Prologue to *Clyomon and Clamydes*, for instance, introduces the audience to a play "Wherein the froward chances oft, of Fortune shall you see . . . / Wherein true Lovers findeth joy, with hugie heaps of care" (ll. 7–9). Often, though, the battle between the life-promoting and life-destroying forces of comedy and tragedy is represented in some detail. The romance action of *The Rare Triumphs of Love and Fortune*, for instance, is represented as growing out of a debate between Venus and Fortune about which is more powerful in human life; Jupiter orders the two goddesses to "prove" their "sovereinties" on the princely couple whose stories the play will dramatize, with Venus ordered to "encrease their joy" and Fortune to "destroye" their "pleasures and their pastimes" (ll. 260–3). As the lovers suffer setbacks or overcome obstacles, Fortune and Venus alternately claim "soverainty," and the play ends happily only after Jupiter orders the two goddesses to combine forces to bring the young couple joy and prosperity (ll. 1564–83).

In *Mucedorus* it is the figures of Comedy and Envy who, in the Induction, seek control over the action and outcome of the play they introduce. Comedy's boast that the day and place are hers, and that therefore the play will bring the audience joy and laughter, is interrupted by the entrance of Envy, "*his arms naked, besmeared with blood*": "I'll interrupt your tale," says Envy, "And mix your music with a tragic end" (ll. 8–10). The debate that follows suggests that the tragicomedy will be a hard-fought battle between these two conflicting powers. Comedy delights "in mirth, mixt all with lovely tales, / And bringeth things with treble joy to pass" (ll. 39–40), while Envy "Delights in nothing but in spoil and death" (l. 43). When Comedy urges Envy to "Give me the leave to utter out my play / . . . And mix not death amongst pleasing comedies, / That treats naught else but pleasure and delight," Envy responds by threatening to "make thee mourn where most thou joyest, / Turning thy mirth into a deadly dole, / Whirling thy pleasures with a peal of death" (ll. 48–51, 56–8), and he promises that he will "with threats of blood begin thy play" (l. 62). Their concluding dialogue describes the coming action as a struggle between comedy and tragedy:

> *Com.*   . . . [T]hough thou think'st with tragic fumes [i.e., fits of anger]
>   To prave [i.e., ruin] my play unto my deep disgrace,
>   . . . I scorn what thou canst do.
>   I'll grace it so, thyself shall it confess
>   From tragic stuff to be a pleasant comedy.
> *Envy*. Why, then, Comedy, send thy actors forth,
>   And I will cross the first steps of their tread,
>   Making them fear the very dart of death.
> *Com.*   And I'll defend them maugre all thy spite. (ll. 66–74)

Envy gets the last word in the Induction:

> *Envy*   . . . I'll go spread my branch,
>   And scattered blossoms from mine envious tree
>   Shall prove to [i.e., become] monsters, spoiling of their joys. (ll. 77–9)

The version printed in the 1598 Quarto (Q1) gives us an immediate taste of Envy's power, with the first action in the play proper fulfilling Envy's promise to begin the play "with threats of blood": "*Enter Segasto running, and Amadine after him, being pursued with a bear.*"[27] But Comedy has the last word in the play's action, with the King of Aragon's "Come on, my lords, let's now to court / Where we may finish up the joyfullest day / That ever hapt to a distressed king" (5.2.84–6), and with Envy, in the Epilogue, explicitly yielding the day to Comedy: "Indeed, Comedy, thou has overrun me now" (l. 23).

The early dramatic romances are often linked to Sidney's attack on plays that he saw as absurd minglings of tragedy and comedy, plays that he called "mungrell Tragycomedies" (Sidney 1595: I4^v–K2^v, esp. K2^r), but they give evidence of being presented as quite deliberate battlegrounds on which comedy and tragedy are themselves forces that direct the action toward happiness or sorrow. This early form of tragicomedy – based on romance story and self-conscious about the roles of Eros and Fortune in shaping the fates of the story's protagonists – did not disappear with the advent of the new Jacobean Italianate tragicomedy; indeed, as Lois Potter notes, even the name "tragicomedy" continued to be used to describe this popular, public drama. "The evidence suggests," she writes, "that the term 'tragicomedy,' in the public theatre, never quite lost its sixteenth-century meaning: a play which contained both tragic and comic elements" – a play, as she notes, that is quite distinct from that tragicomedy "whose immediate context was the court and its circle of gentlemen amateurs" (Potter 1987: 197). But Potter's remark needs to be qualified: the "sixteenth-century" kind of tragicomedy that persisted alongside the Italianate form was often much more than "a play which contained both tragic and comic elements." As we have seen, it was often a play that consciously dramatized romance story as a contest between cosmic forces, usually Eros and Fortune, that drive the protagonists hither and yon, providing them with "joy," but only after they have experienced "hugie heaps of care." But Potter's statement that this "sixteenth-century" kind of tragicomedy existed well into the seventeenth century and that it is distinct from Fletcherian Italianate tragicomedy is indisputable. In comparison with *The Rare Triumphs of Love and Fortune* and *Mucedorus*, Shakespeare's experiments with shaping romance story into tragicomic drama are perhaps less overt in setting tragedy against comedy, Eros against Fortune, but the resulting forms of his late plays, varied as they are, show their kinship with their generic forerunners.

That Shakespeare's "romances" present tragicomedies that differ in kind from those created by Beaumont and Fletcher has been pointed out by many critics, from Ristine (who, as noted earlier, cites their relation to the "old school of rambling romance," along with their inclusion of "apparitions" and "death") to Hartwig (who mentions, in her list of Shakespeare's crucial differences, the presence onstage of supernatural figures and "the pressure of the actual . . . upon the dramatic illusion" through "the occurrence of deaths") (Hartwig 1972: 30; see also Henke 1997: 53–5 *passim*). Recently, Lee Bliss, examining plays written for the King's Men in 1609–11, has contrasted Shakespeare's "scope" with Fletcherian "concentration," and has pointed out Shakespeare's extension of space and time to include the "cycles of human generation" and the "healing effects of time" (Bliss 1986: 152). She has noted as well the sharply different explanations for the unexpected happy endings offered by the two sets of plays. In *Cymbeline, The Winter's Tale*, and *The Tempest*, she writes, "the benevolent coincidences that provide the occasion for final resolution . . . all seem part and parcel of a providence that has operated throughout." In contrast, "in Beaumont and Fletcher's conclusions the gods remain offstage and uninvolved, and events are more fully explicable by rational means . . . The resolutions seem less wondrous than arbitrary and wittily surprising" (pp. 156–8). Her conclusion is that

> while Shakespeare's last three plays look back to the very roots of romance, and to *Pericles* and the unearthly tone of its conclusion, Beaumont and Fletcher's Sidneian choreography of movement and speech remains detached and frequently satiric . . . Structurally as well as thematically, Shakespeare gradually submerges us in romance. (pp. 158–9)

To recognize that *Pericles, The Winter's Tale, Cymbeline*, and *The Tempest* are part of a larger family of dramatized romances, that they "submerge us in romance," and that they present highly sophisticated versions of an old form of tragicomedy with native rather than Italianate roots, does not answer the question underlying so much twentieth-century debate about the late plays: namely, what led Shakespeare to create these plays? But it does point us toward a fruitful way of asking questions about the place of these plays not only within Shakespeare's own work but also within what Jean Howard calls "the overarching system of dramatic genres" of the early seventeenth century. Howard argues that "in the early modern theatrical milieu, the loosely differentiated system of dramatic kinds in play at any time was always in motion" and that it would be a useful exercise "to put Shakespeare's plays in conversation with those of other playwrights and sometimes to see them in relation to generic forms not foregrounded in the first folio" (Howard 1999: 304). It seems unlikely that Howard was thinking of such plays as *Clyomon and Clamydes* and *Mucedorus* as interesting conversational partners for Shakespeare's dramas. But to place *Pericles, Cymbeline, The Winter's Tale*, and *The Tempest* in dialogue with such early dramatic romances, to conceive of his late plays as deliberate transformations of very old forms that appear in new guises as part of the King's Men's repertory, in competition with the more Italianate, courtly forms produced by Shakespeare's fellow playwrights, is to better position ourselves for deciding, for example, in what ways these sophisticated "mouldy tales" were, in Howard's words, "implicated in social transformations and struggles" (p. 304). We are also better placed for determining how best to read, perform, and respond to these creakily old-fashioned, deeply resonant, Shakespearean tragicomic romances.

NOTES

1   For an account of attempts to place *Cymbeline* chronologically, see Furness (1913: 443–54). For Malone's discussion of *Cymbeline*'s similarities to *Macbeth* and *King Lear*, see Malone (1790, 1: 354).

2   In 1790 Malone wrote, "In the first edition of this essay I supposed *The Winter's Tale* to have been written in 1594" (1: 349; a footnote at 1: 261 specifies that "the first edition of this essay" was published in 1778); in the 1790 "edition" of the essay he placed *The Winter's Tale* in 1604 (Malone 1790, 1: 348). In the 1821 version he placed it in 1611 (Malone 1821, 2: 459).

3   For an account of the use of metrical tests in the early 1870s, see Furnivall (1877). The controversies that later surrounded the use of metrical tests in constructing the chronology of the plays seem to have had no impact on the acceptance of the chronological grouping of Shakespeare's "late plays." For a summary of the vexed late nineteenth- and early twentieth-century history of attempts to bring metrical tests to bear on the construction of a Shakespeare chronology, see Chambers (1930, 1: 255–69). I am grateful to Paul Werstine for helpful conversations about scholarly reception of the metrical tests.

4   For a discussion of paratexts, see Genette (1997).

5   In his edition of the plays, Johnson prints *Cymbeline* as *Cymbeline: A Tragedy*.

6   Gervinus speaks of the Third Period plays [i.e., those written between 1600 and 1612] as being divided into "groups, in which we see tragedy, history, and romantic plays appearing in much more pure and more refined forms than before." But this is the extent of his "naming" of the plays generically – and he does not specify which plays fall into the categories of "tragedy, history, [or] romantic plays." Gervinus (1883: 477, 481).

7   For Dowden's dependence on Gervinus, see Dowden (1875: ix). F. J. Furnivall's *Succession of Shakspere's Works* (originally printed in 1874 as an "Introduction" to Gervinus, and hence seeming to predate Dowden), discusses the late plays in terms very like Dowden's, but Furnivall warmly acknowledges Dowden's then "forthcoming" book and includes a lengthy quotation from lectures of Dowden that Furnivall had attended. See Furnivall (1877), esp. pp. xlv–xlvii.

8   Robert Browning also used the name "Dramatic Romances" for a collection of his poems written in the 1840s and 1850s.

9   Hazlitt writes of *Cymbeline*: "The *reading of this play* is like going a journey with some uncertain object at the end of it"; "as the impression [of all the plot lines tending to the same point] exists unconsciously *in the mind of the reader*, so it probably arose in the same manner in the mind of the author." Hazlitt (1817: [1], 10; italics added).

10 Stage directions from Victorian dramas show that the "romantic" theatrical spectacle described by Hazlitt was not at all unusual. See, for example, Rowell (1978), esp. pp. 43–5. I am grateful to John Ripley for helpful conversations about Victorian stage productions and other possible Romantic and Victorian contexts for Dowden's adoption of the generic label *romance* for Shakespeare's late plays.

11 Bentley limited his own list to *Cymbeline, The Winter's Tale*, and *The Tempest*, and occasionally added *Two Noble Kinsmen*. Several other scholars – beginning with Thorndike – who want to emphasize the influence either of Beaumont and Fletcher or of the Blackfriars venue exclude *Pericles* from the group because it appeared too early to be accounted for as the result of these influences.

12 Fowler's "family resemblance" genre theory has been criticized by Earl Miner, but I agree with Lewalski that "Fowler's metaphor of 'family resemblance'" is "particularly useful . . . as the basis for identifying works in a given historical genre" (Lewalski 1986: 4).

13 I am most grateful for many conversations on this topic with the late Susan Snyder, whose insights were, as always, invaluable.

14 Leo Salingar, in his *Shakespeare and the Traditions of Comedy* (1972), makes a general connection between the late plays and the early romantic dramas. He notes that many of the motifs in the early romantic dramas are found "singly in Shakespeare's early writing and intertwined together in his last plays," and he suggests that "it seems very likely that in choosing romantic plots and reshaping them for his early comedies, [Shakespeare] was responding to some of the plays he had seen from his boyhood on" (p. 30). Salingar's argument is closest to mine when, in challenging Nosworthy's assertion that Shakespeare drew specifically on *The Rare Triumphs of Love and Fortune* in writing *Cymbeline*, he writes: "it seems more likely that Shakespeare would have recalled the

general style of a whole group of similar old plays than that he would have singled out this one in particular" (p. 38).

15 The disjunction between Shakespeare's late plays and Frye's influential definition of romance is central to D. T. Childress's argument that it is inaccurate and misleading to call Shakespeare's late plays "romances." See Childress (1974: 47–8).

16 See, for example, Roderick Beaton's (1989) discussion of "the ancient romances" and their emphasis on "Chance and the passive hero": "The inactivity of the main characters in the face of Chance and of a domineering god of love amounts in the ancient romances to the status of a theme" (pp. 58–62, esp. p. 59). For discussions of Shakespeare's late plays and Greek Romance, see Gesner (1970) and Mowat (1976), esp. pp. 129–32.

17 Only the title of "Placy Dacy, alias Saint Eustacy" survives, but, as Manly (1927) explains, "as there is only one legend concerning [St. Eustace] we can be sure of the material used by the dramatist" (p. 147). Gordon Hall Gerould's (1904) exhaustive examination of the "Forerunners, Congeners, and Derivatives of the Eustace Legend" emphasizes the wide popularity of that legend, stresses "its extraordinary popularity with all classes," and points to the "fact that it was retold in the vernacular during the centuries of romance" (pp. 342, 406, 446).

18 Gerould (1904), in studying the widely dispersed legend exemplified by the story of St. Eustace – a legend that Gerould calls "The Man Tried by Fate" – formulates "the essential motive . . . thus. A man for some weighty reason, often religious or resulting from religion, departs from home with his family. He loses his sons (usually twins) and his wife by accident or human violence, or both. After various adventures and considerable suffering, the several members of the family are at last reunited" (p. 338). Gerould is able to trace this legend far back into Eastern literatures and forward in the West into the sixteenth century. The stories that follow the pattern he delineates "group themselves about the legend of *St. Eustace*; and considering the immense popularity of that legend throughout the Middle Ages there is a good deal of antecedent probability that it was largely influential in molding the form of the Occidental members of the cycle" (p. 342). He concludes that "there is very good reason for supposing that we have to do with a case of actual transmission from Orient to Occident by means of a saint's legend, that on *Eustace* all the European tales converge, and that *Eustace* can be grouped with its relatives from Asia" (p. 379). Gerould does not consider the use of the legend in drama, either in the miracle plays or in later romance drama.

19 C. R. Baskerville (1916–17) argues for the widespread popularity of the Eustace legend onstage across Europe, noting that the Eustace theme not only "prevailed in the earliest English romantic drama known," but that it and the Constance theme "of calumniated women cast away and wrecked at sea" were "possibly the most popular themes among the Basque and Breton plays in both miracles and in purer romantic form" (p. 124). Salingar notes that the story of St. Eustace "was an enduring subject for the stage," and adds several examples to those mentioned by Baskerville (Salingar 1972: 64–5).

20 Stanley Wells (1966) makes a persuasive case for Shakespeare's having moved the story farther away from romance than does Greene. I agree with Wells's careful argument, but note that in two major respects – the sense that Shakespeare's hero is tried and tested and changed and the fact that he regains his lost wife – *The Winter's Tale* is closer to the Eustace and the Mary Magdalene legends (and dramas) than is *Pandosto*.

21 Quotations from Shakespeare's plays are from Bevington (1992).

22 The title of the play is "A Most Pleasant Comedy of *Mucedorus*, the King's son of Valencia, And *Amadine*, the King's Daughter of Aragon." See Jupin (1987: 76). All quotations from the play will be from this edition, which edits the 1598 Quarto, adding the Q3 (1610) additions in an appendix.

23 Shakespeare, of course, played with a fantasy situation of a queen in love with a commoner in *A Midsummer Night's Dream* (in the Titania–Bottom plot).

24 Ristine (1910) also discusses at some length the inseparability of romance and tragicomedy, writing, for example, that "The ruling spirit of romance is the very essence of tragicomedy" (pp. 73–6).

25   David L. Frost (1986), placing *Cymbeline* within the context of such early dramatic romances as *Mucedorus*, argues that *Cymbeline* should be understood as a kind of parody of such plays. Since he sees no connection between the "mouldy tales" and *The Winter's Tale* and *The Tempest*, he argues that it is inappropriate to consider *Cymbeline* in the same category as Shakespeare's other late plays. The quotation from Ben Jonson is from his "Ode to himself" published at the conclusion of *The New Inn* (1631).

26   Jonson's attack on Shakespeare's late plays is in "The Induction on the Stage" for *Bartholomew Fair*. (See Horsman 1960: 6–13, esp. p. 2, and Horsman's note to Induction ll. 129–33, pp. 11–12.)

27   The version of *Mucedorus* performed at Whitehall in 1610 and printed in the 1610 Quarto (Q3) inserts a scene between the Induction and the entrance of Amadine and the bear. In Q3 the entrance immediately following the Induction reads "*Sound. Enter Mucedorus and Anselmo, his friend,*" and the scene shows us Mucedorus's decision to seek the love of Amadine in the disguise of a shepherd. Because *Mucedorus* was presented at Whitehall and because it was a tremendously popular play – especially after the 1610 performance and printing – the play has been more widely studied than many of the other early dramatic romances. See, for example, Frost (1986), Reynolds (1959), Thornberry (1977).

References and Further Reading

Baskerville, C. R. (1916–17). Some Evidence for Early Romantic Plays in England. *Modern Philology*, 14, 37–59, 83–128.

Beaton, R. (1989). *The Medieval Greek Romance*. Cambridge: Cambridge University Press.

Bentley, G. E. (1948). Shakespeare and the Blackfriars Theatre. *Shakespeare Survey*, 1, 38–50.

Bevington, D. (1962). *From Mankind to Marlowe: Growth of Structure in the Popular Drama of Tudor England*. Cambridge, MA: Harvard University Press.

——(ed.) (1992). *The Complete Works of Shakespeare*, 4th edn. New York: HarperCollins.

Bliss, L. (1986). Tragicomic Romance for the King's Men, 1609–1611: Shakespeare, Beaumont, and Fletcher. In A. R. Braunmuller and J. C. Bulman (eds.) *Comedy from Shakespeare to Sheridan: Change and Continuity in the English and European Dramatic Tradition*. Newark: University of Delaware Press.

Brooke, T. (ed.) (1915). *Common Conditions*. Elizabethan Club Reprints, 1. New Haven, CT: Yale University Press.

Browning, R. (1964). Dramatic Romances. In *The Poetical Works of Robert Browning*. Oxford: Oxford University Press.

Chambers, E. K. (1930). *William Shakespeare: A Study of Facts and Problems*. Oxford: Clarendon Press.

Childress, D. T. (1974). Are Shakespeare's Late Plays Really Romances? In R. C. Tobias and P. G. Zolbrod (eds.) *Shakespeare's Late Plays: Essays in Honor of Charles Crow*. Athens, OH: Ohio University Press.

Colie, R. L. (1973). *The Resources of Kind: Genre-Theory in the Renaissance*, ed. B. K. Lewalski. Berkeley: University of California Press.

Danson, L. (2000). *Shakespeare's Dramatic Genres*. Oxford: Oxford University Press.

Demaray, J. G. (1998). *Shakespeare and the Spectacles of Strangeness: The Tempest and the Transformation of Renaissance Theatrical Forms*. Pittsburgh, PA: Duquesne University Press.

Derrida, J. (1980). The Law of Genre. *Glyph*, 7, 55–81.

Doran, M. (1954). *Endeavors of Art: A Study of Form in Elizabethan Drama*. Madison: University of Wisconsin Press.

Dowden, E. (1875). *Shakespeare: A Critical Study of His Mind and Art*. London: Henry S. King.

——(1877). *Shakspere*. London: Macmillan.

——(1914). *Letters of Edward Dowden and his Correspondents*, ed. E. D. Dowden and H. M. Dowden. London: J. M. Dent.

Edwards, P. (1958). Shakespeare's Romances: 1900–1957. *Shakespeare Survey*, 11, 1–18.

——(1986). "Seeing is Believing": Action and Narration in *The Old Wives Tale* and *The Winter's Tale*. In E. A. J. Honigmann (ed.) *Shakespeare and His Contemporaries: Essays in Comparison*. Manchester: Manchester University Press.

Ewbank, I.-S. (1975). "What Words, What Looks, What Wonders?": Language and Spectacle in the Theatre of George Peele. In G. R. Hibbard (ed.) *The Elizabethan Theatre*, vol. 5. Toronto: Macmillan of Canada.

Felperin, H. (1972). *Shakespearean Romance*. Princeton, NJ: Princeton University Press.

Foakes, R. A. (1986). Tragicomedy and Comic Form. In A. R. Braunmuller and J. C. Bulman (eds.) *Comedy from Shakespeare to Sheridan: Change and Continuity in the English and European Dramatic Tradition*. Newark: University of Delaware Press.

Fowler, A. (1982). *Kinds of Literature: An Introduction to the Theory of Genres and Modes*. Cambridge, MA: Harvard University Press.

Frost, D. L. (1986). "Mouldy tales": The Context of Shakespeare's *Cymbeline*. *Essays and Studies*, 39, 19–38.

Frye, N. (1957). *Anatomy of Criticism: Four Essays*. Princeton, NJ: Princeton University Press.

Furness, H. H. (ed.) (1913). *The Tragedie of Cymbeline: A New Variorum Edition*. Philadelphia, PA: Lippincott.

Furnivall, F. J. (1874). Opening Meeting at University College. *Transactions of the New Shakespeare Society*, series I, v–xii.

——(1877). *The Succession of Shakspere's Works and the Use of Metrical Tests in Settling it, etc. Being the Introduction to Professor Gervinus's Commentaries on Shakspere* . . . London: Smith, Elder.

——(ed.) (1930). *The Digby Plays*. Early English Text Society. London: Milford. (Original work published 1882.)

Genette, G. (1997). Genre Indications. In *Paratexts: Thresholds of Interpretation*, trans. J. E. Lewin. Cambridge: Cambridge University Press.

Gerould, G. H. (1904). Forerunners, Congeners, and Derivatives of the Eustace Legend. *Publications of the Modern Languages Association*, n.s. 12, 335–448.

Gervinus, G. G. (1883). *Shakespeare Commentaries*, trans. F. E. Bunnett. London: Smith, Elder. (Original work published 1874.)

Gesner, C. (1970). *Shakespeare and the Greek Romance: A Study in Origins*. Lexington: University of Kentucky Press.

Greg, W. W. (ed.) (1930). *The Rare Triumphs of Love and Fortune*. London: Malone Society Reprints.

Griffin, N. E. (1923). The Definition of Romance. *Publications of the Modern Languages Association*, 38, 50–70.

Hartwig, J. (1972). *Shakespeare's Tragicomic Vision*. Baton Rouge: Louisiana State University Press.

Hattaway, M. (ed.) (1984). *The New Inn, by Ben Jonson*. Manchester: Revels.

Hazlitt, W. (1817). *Characters of Shakespear's Plays*. London: Reynell.

——(1971). The Drama. In G. Rowell (ed.) *Victorian Dramatic Criticism*. London: Methuen. (Original work published in *The London Magazine*, September 1820.)

Henke, R. (1997). *Pastoral Transformation: Italian Tragicomedy and Shakespeare's Late Plays*. Newark: University of Delaware Press; London: Associated University Presses.

Herrick, M. (1955). *Tragicomedy: Its Origin and Development in Italy, France, and England*. Urbana: University of Illinois Press.

Hillman, R. (1992). *Intertextuality and Romance in Renaissance Drama: The Staging of Nostalgia*. New York: St. Martin's Press.

Hirst, D. L. (1984). *Tragicomedy*. London: Methuen.

Hoeniger, F. D. (ed.) (1963). *The Arden Edition of the Works of William Shakespeare: Pericles*. London: Methuen.

Horsman, E. A. (ed.) (1960). *Bartholomew Fair, by Ben Jonson*. Cambridge, MA: Revels.

Howard, J. E. (1999). Shakespeare and Genre. In D. S. Kastan (ed.) *A Companion to Shakespeare*. Oxford: Blackwell.

Jacobus de Voragine (1993). *The Golden Legend: Readings on the Saints*, 2 vols., trans. W. G. Ryan. Princeton, NJ: Princeton University Press.

Jameson, F. (1975). Magical Narratives: Romance as Genre. *New Literary History*, 7, 135–63.

Johnson, S. (ed.) (1765). *The Plays of William Shakespeare*, 8 vols. London: Tonson.

Jupin, A. H. (ed.) (1987). *Mucedorus: A Contextual Study and Modern-Spelling Edition*. New York: Garland.

Kermode, F. (1963). *William Shakespeare: The Final Plays*. London: Longmans Green.

Kirsch, A. C. (1967). *Cymbeline* and Coterie Dramaturgy. *English Literary History*, 34, 285–306.

Knight, C. (ed.) (1854). *The Works of William Shakspere*, 6th edn. London: Bohn.

Lewalski, B. K. (1986). Issues and Approaches. In B. K. Lewalski (ed.) *Renaissance Genres: Essays on Theory, History, and Interpretation*. Cambridge, MA: Harvard University Press.

Littleton, B. J. (ed.) (1968). *Clyomon and Clamydes: A Critical Edition*. The Hague: Mouton.

Malone, E. (1790). An Attempt to Ascertain the Order in Which the Plays of Shakespeare were Written. In E. Malone (ed.) *The Plays and Poems of William Shakspeare*, 10 vols. London.

——(1821). An Attempt to Ascertain the Order in Which the Plays of Shakespeare were Written. In E. Malone (ed.) *The Plays and Poems of William Shakespeare*, 22 vols. London.

Manly, J. M. (1927). The Miracle Play in Mediaeval England. In M. L. Woods (ed.) *Essays by Divers Hands, Being the Transactions of the Royal Society of Literature of the United Kingdom*, new series VII. London: Humphrey Milford.

Miner, E. (1986). Some Issues of Literary 'Species, or Distinct Kind.' In B. K. Lewalski (ed.) *Renaissance Genres: Essays on Theory, History, and Interpretation*. Cambridge, MA: Harvard University Press.

Mowat, B. A. (1976). *The Dramaturgy of Shakespeare's Romances*. Athens, GA: University of Georgia Press.

——(1987). Shakespearean Tragicomedy. In N. K. Maguire (ed.) *Renaissance Tragicomedy: Explorations in Genre and Politics*. New York: AMS Press.

Nosworthy, J. M. (ed.) (1955). *The Arden Edition of the Works of William Shakespeare: Cymbeline*. London: Methuen.

Orgel, S. (1979). Shakespeare and the Kinds of Drama. *Critical Inquiry*, 6, 107–23.

Parker, P. A. (1979). *Inescapable Romance: Studies in the Poetics of a Mode*. Princeton, NJ: Princeton University Press.

Pettet, E. C. (1949). *Shakespeare and the Romance Tradition*. London: Staples Press.

Potter, L. (1987). The 'Whole Truth' of Restoration Tragicomedy. In N. K. Maguire (ed.) *Renaissance Tragicomedy: Explorations in Genre and Politics*. New York: AMS Press.

Reynolds, G. F. (1959). *Mucedorus*, Most Popular Elizabethan Play? In J. W. Bennett, O. Cargill, and V. Hall, Jr. (eds.) *Studies in the English Renaissance Drama*. New York: State University of New York Press.

Ristine, F. H. (1910). *English Tragicomedy: Its Origin and History*. New York: Columbia University Press.

Rowell, G. (1978). *The Victorian Theatre: 1792–1914. A Survey*, 2nd edn. Cambridge: Cambridge University Press.

Russell, P. (1966). Romantic Narrative Plays: 1570–1590. In *Elizabethan Theatre*. Stratford-upon-Avon Studies 19. London: Edward Arnold.

Salingar, L. (1972). *Shakespeare and the Traditions of Comedy*. Cambridge: Cambridge University Press.

Sidney, Sir Philip (1595). *An Apologie for Poetrie*. London: Olney.

Smith, H. (1972). *Shakespeare's Romances: A Study of Some Ways of the Imagination*. San Marino, CA: Huntington Library.

Snyder, S. (2001). The Genres of Shakespeare's Plays. In M. de Grazia and S. Wells (eds.) *The Cambridge Companion to Shakespeare*. Cambridge: Cambridge University Press.

Strachey, L. (1922). Shakespeare's Final Period. In *Books and Characters: French & English*. New York: Harcourt, Brace. (Original work published in the *Independent Review* III, 1904.)

Strelka, J. P. (ed.) (1987). *Theories of Literary Genre*. University Park: Pennsylvania State University Press.

Thornberry, R. T. (1977). A Seventeenth-Century Revival of *Mucedorus* in London before 1610. *Shakespeare Quarterly*, 28, 362–4.

Thorndike, A. H. (1901). *The Influence of Beaumont and Fletcher on Shakspere*. Worcester, MA: Oliver B. Wood.

Tillyard, E. M. W. (1938). *Shakespeare's Last Plays*. London: Chatto and Windus.

Turner, J. (1995). Reading by Contraries: *The Tempest* as Romance. In N. Wood (ed.) *The Tempest*. Theory and Practice Series. Buckingham: Open University Press.

Wells, S. (1966). Shakespeare and Romance. In J. R. Brown and B. Harris (eds.) *Later Shakespeare*. Stratford-upon-Avon Studies 8. London: Edward Arnold.

Wittgenstein, L. (1988). *Philosophical Investigations*, trans. G. E. M. Anscombe. New York: Macmillan.

Yeats, W. B. (1953). *Autobiography*. New York: Macmillan.

——(1961). *Essays and Introductions*. London: Macmillan.

8

Fashion: Shakespeare and Beaumont and Fletcher

Russ McDonald

In the middle of Joseph Mankiewicz's *All About Eve* (1950), the aging actress Margot Channing, famously, brilliantly played by Bette Davis, explodes with rage on learning that Eve Harrington, the mousy and apparently naive fan who works as her assistant, has been auditioned as her understudy. Margot's ferocity is directed particularly at the playwright Lloyd Richards, who exclaims that hearing Eve speak his words is a revelation, that the lines sound new, as if someone else had written them. Most readers will be sufficiently familiar with Davis's style to supply the proper inflections in a transcription of Margot's reply: "When you hear someone else's lines, who is it you hear? Arthur Miller? Sherwood? Beaumont and Fletcher?" Introducing Beaumont and Fletcher as the most distant, recondite example Margot can summon, the sarcastic question not only measures how much movie dialogue has changed over the past half decade but also establishes the obscurity into which the two Jacobean dramatists had fallen by the middle of the twentieth century. In that vale of neglect, the occasional attempt at illumination notwithstanding, they have remained almost undisturbed to the present day.

Changing Fortunes

Modern indifference to Beaumont and Fletcher is striking given the popularity of their work in the seventeenth century and the respect it commanded. As implausible as it may seem, they were at one time considered the most successful playwrights of their age, as a single passage from John Dryden's *Of Dramatic Poesy* conveniently indicates:

> I am apt to believe the *English* language in them arriv'd to its highest perfection; what words have since been taken in, are rather superfluous than necessary. Their Playes are now the most pleasant and frequent entertainments of the Stage; two of theirs being

acted through the year for one of *Shakespeare's* or *Johnsons*: the reason, is because there is a certain gayety in their Comedies, and Pathos in their more serious Playes, which suits generally with all mens humours. *Shakespeares* language is likewise a little obsolete, and *Ben Johnson's* wit comes short of theirs. (Dryden 1971: 56–7)

Dryden's remarks must be seen in light of his changing and perhaps contradictory views of the work of Fletcher and Shakespeare (Markley 1984), but in any case they attest to the esteem in which the literary establishment of his age had come to hold Beaumont and Fletcher. And a glance at the 1647 Folio confirms Dryden's assessment.

Comedies and Tragedies written by Francis Beaumont and Iohn Fletcher, Gentlemen. Never printed before, and now published by the Authours Originall Copies, an obvious effort to situate the two playwrights on the same artistic plane as Shakespeare and Jonson, opens with a gallimaufry of praise, thirty-five commendatory poems contributed by the theatrical and literary luminaries of the day.

> *Let* Shakespeare, Chapman, *and applauded* Ben
> *Weare the Eternall merit of their Pen,*
> *Here I am love-sicke: and were I to chuse,*
> *A Mistress corrivall 'tis* Fletcher's *Muse.*

This is George Buck, in "To the desert of the Author in his most Ingenious Pieces" (Beaumont and Fletcher 1905–12: xxxii), and the celebratory tenor is typical of most of the verses, the majority written specifically for the volume, although a few reprints of earlier tributes were also included. Some of the poems contain what we would consider helpful critical insights, and a few offer hints about the process of collaboration that have become part of literary legend: William Cartwright, for example ("Upon the report of the printing of the Dramaticall Poems of Master *John Fletcher*, collected before, and now set forth in one volume"), contributed the notion that Fletcher submitted his abundant poetic imagination to Beaumont's sober judgment and that after Beaumont's retirement Fletcher continued to impose that restraint on himself (Beaumont and Fletcher 1905–12: xxxviii).

Although theatre companies throughout the eighteenth century regularly performed and frequently adapted the plays, a reliable sign of popular (and in this case critical) esteem, the simultaneous rise in Shakespeare's popularity was an ominous sign of things to come. Beaumont and Fletcher seem to have been submerged in the flood of European Romanticism and never to have quite surfaced: at the beginning of the nineteenth century, Coleridge summoned them as whipping boys, using their "mechanical" work to demonstrate the superior humanity and "organic" art of Shakespeare. Moreover, his censure seems, at least in part, politically motivated. He famously dismissed them as "the most servile *jure divino* royalists," as "high-flying passive-obedience Tories," and as demonstrating "a servility of sentiment, a partisanship of the monarchical faction" (Coleridge 1936: 69, 77, 95). This judgment apparently stuck, and critics have only recently begun to contest it. Coleridge's apodictic successor, T. S. Eliot, damned them, in a celebrated formulation, with superficiality: "the blossoms of Beaumont and Fletcher's imagination draw no sustenance from the soil, but are cut and slightly withered flowers stuck in the sand" (Eliot 1932: 135).[1] Such romantic and post-romantic views of Beaumont and Fletcher would determine critical responses throughout most of the twentieth century.

Lately critical fashion has begun to change, and the former court toadies are now often seen, by some of the few who have begun to look, as brilliant and subtle subverters of Jacobean absolutism. Walter Cohen, referring often to Beaumont and Fletcher while writing about tragicomedy in general, insists on "the prerevolutionary character – in the strong sense – of all early Stuart drama" (Cohen 1992: 123). Specifically, he asserts that "the more popular plays deepen the critique of the crown by moving partly or wholly outside the courtly milieu and by challenging the aristocratic, often absolutist representational assumptions about the form" (p. 128). Similarly, Philip Finkelpearl begins his *Court and Country Politics in the Plays of Beaumont and Fletcher*, a title that is in itself telling and that would not have been possible a century ago, by stating his "belief that political criticism of court and king was a central urge in the most important plays of Beaumont and Fletcher" (Finkelpearl 1990: 7). And Jonathan Hope and Gordon McMullan, introducing a collection of essays called *The Politics of Tragicomedy*, maintain that "Fletcherian tragicomedy, the dominant mode of the period 1610–1650, can in fact be characterized more accurately as anti-court drama rather than courtly" (Hope and McMullan 1992: 10–11). Clearly, at the beginning of the twenty-first century critical opinion – what little there is of it – has moved to the opposite end of the spectrum from Coleridge.

But most remarkable is the widespread neglect. Beaumont and Fletcher's plays are almost never performed: the Swan Theatre in Stratford-upon-Avon, opened in 1986 for the express purpose of presenting the works of Shakespeare's contemporaries, had in its first fifteen years produced not a single play by Beaumont and Fletcher (although the company did produce Fletcher's two surviving collaborations with Shakespeare). Despite the publication over some thirty years of the Cambridge edition of *The Dramatic Works in the Beaumont and Fletcher Canon*, the plays are rarely read, rarely taught, and rarely written about, this last fact especially striking in an academic field noted for the energy of its participants and the perpetual need for new projects. It is probably not an exaggeration to say that some specialists in early modern drama are acquainted with no more than a handful of texts to which either dramatist contributed. Beyond two or three obvious titles lurk a host of plays that ideally one ought to know, but since nobody else knows them and since they are no longer performed and hardly even referred to, they can safely be ignored. A senior scholar recently suggested to a graduate student seeking a dissertation topic that the most valuable contribution she could make to the study of early modern drama would be to prepare and submit a detailed plot summary of each of the plays in the Beaumont and Fletcher canon.

Obstacles

The effort to establish the intertextual relations between Beaumont and Fletcher's work and Shakespeare's final plays has been impeded chiefly by this neglect of the two younger playwrights, but other factors have contributed too. First, modern criticism has been inhibited by widespread uncertainty about how to think about an authorial team, especially one in which the two members' professional accomplishments are so thoroughly interwoven with the work of several other contemporaneous playwrights. While acknowledging intellectually that the Jacobean theatre was a collaborative enterprise, few critics have accorded that fact much weight in their consideration of Shakespeare's late work, and much of the attention devoted to Beaumont and Fletcher in the middle of the twentieth century has represented an effort to assign authorial shares and thus undo the fact of collaboration by assigning just who wrote what. Jeffrey Masten has recently approached the topic with a fresh perspective, although it is still too early to tell whether others will follow his lead (Masten 1997). With respect to Shakespeare's unfortunate participation in such cooperative efforts, the mix of bardolatry with collaboration makes the Fletcher–Shakespeare union especially unsettling. The usual defensive maneuver, therefore, has been to assign *Henry VIII* solely to Shakespeare's pen, to dismiss the one undeniable collaboration, *The Two Noble Kinsmen*, as an ill-advised product of the master's old age or a dutiful endeavor to help the junior playwright of the company, and to be silently grateful that the third joint effort, *Cardenio*, was lost.

The second obstacle to joint study is the problem of attribution and definition. Any effort to relate the two bodies of work requires caution since those "two bodies of work" are by no means discrete entities. It might be said that there are five textual categories available for study: the first three would be the unaided plays of Shakespeare, of Fletcher, and of Beaumont, the fourth comprises the collaborations between Beaumont and Fletcher, and the last the collaborations between Fletcher and Shakespeare. But to insist too rigidly on delineation and discrimination tends to stifle one of the principal benefits of broad intertextual study, i.e., a more vivid sense of the outlines of Jacobean theatrical taste and cultural values. A related problem is that of terminology, especially agreement on generic categories. Did Fletcher actually introduce tragicomedy to the English theatre, or did it exist under another name before *The Faithful Shepherdess*? Should Shakespeare's late plays be so categorized? They are not called tragicomedies in the Folio, and they were not called romances until the nineteenth century when Edward Dowden, following a suggestion of Coleridge, so grouped and described them.

Next is the apparently intractable difficulty of dates. No one has established indisputably when or in what order Shakespeare wrote the last of his unaided plays, nor when Fletcher (with and without Beaumont) wrote his of the same period. The origins of the collaboration between Beaumont and Fletcher are likewise uncertain. It is generally agreed that Beaumont's *The Knight of the Burning Pestle* (1608) and Fletcher's *The Faithful Shepherdess* (ca. 1608) were unaided plays. But there is much that we do not know. A lost play, *Madon, King of Britain* (Chambers 1923, 3.223), has been attributed to Beaumont, but the evidence is skimpy. *The Woman Hater* was apparently written for the Children of Paul's in 1606 and published anonymously in 1607; although it seems to have been mainly Beaumont's work, it may have been the initial collaboration.[2] Or *Love's Cure* (ca. 1606), revised by Philip Massinger in 1625, may have been the first joint effort. *Cupid's Revenge* (ca. 1607–8) is thought to be originally Beaumont's work touched by Fletcher (Hoy 1958: 90–1), but the date of this doctoring is unknown: did it occur before production, or after production but before publication in 1615? Evidently the pair began to collaborate in earnest about 1608 or 1609 on *Philaster*, written for and performed by the King's Men both at Blackfriars and the Globe. Over the next three or four years they worked together on a number of plays, certainly *The Maid's Tragedy* and *A King and No King*, and perhaps *The Captain*, *The Coxcomb*, and *The Scornful Lady*. Fletcher during these years was also working independently (on *The Woman's Prize*, a response to *The Taming of the Shrew*), and around 1612 embarked on his three collaborations with Shakespeare. Beaumont seems to have been less industrious than his colleague. After writing *The Mask of the Inner Temple and Gray's Inn* in early 1613, he decamped, marrying an heiress, giving up the theatre for the more relaxed world of Leicestershire, and thereby simplifying matters somewhat for literary critics and theatrical historians.

Intertextual study has been further impeded by the hamfisted work of some of the early practitioners who overstated their view that Beaumont and Fletcher are responsible for Shakespeare's shift from tragedy to romance or tragicomedy. An early advocate of this position was Ashley H. Thorndike, who attempted to redress the excesses of Victorian bardolatry by publishing *The Influence of Beaumont and Fletcher on Shakespere* in 1901. But in an effort to cinch the connection, he proscribes any other influence, seeming to suggest that the period produced only three playwrights. Thorndike's absolute view of indebtedness provoked caustic rebuttal, such as Harold S. Wilson's: "To select certain stock romance situations from two plays like *Philaster* and *Cymbeline* and to conclude from this that one play must be imitated from the other is like comparing, let us say, the David of Verocchio and the Statue of Liberty and concluding that because they contain similar materials the one must be imitated from the other" (Wilson 1961: 252–4). Wilson's condescending dismissal of possible influence was one of the few sustained discussions of the question in the twentieth century. Mostly, the increasing dominance of Shakespeare and the fact that Beaumont and Fletcher's plays went unperformed made hyperbolically stated claims all the easier to ignore.

A final problem is bardolatry and its concomitant depreciation of other early modern dramatists. For all the historicizing and reevaluating and recontextualizing that have characterized early modern studies, we still cling to dated prejudices about many of Shakespeare's contemporaries. In the case of Beaumont and Fletcher, the verdict of the twentieth century was that they were superficial, trivial, meretricious, sensational, shallow. Building on Eliot's condemnation of their verse as "hollow . . . superficial with a vacuum behind it" (Eliot 1932: 135), Muriel Bradbrook deplored the "outrageous stimulation . . . and the grosser exhibitions of physical pain" (Bradbrook 1935: 247); Robert Ornstein was affronted by "ethical frivolity . . . far more disturbing and reprehensible than Marston's inane amalgam of Senecan horror and religious sentiment" (Ornstein 1960: 163, 166–7); and Arthur Kirsch, commenting on the woodland scene in *Philaster*, complains that "the whole situation is false and improbable" (Kirsch 1971: 41). Such censure is typical of twentieth-century criticism, and while some defenders have recently come forward, such as Lee Bliss, Philip Finkelpearl, and Gordon McMullan, the more telling fact is that many books on early modern drama no longer even mention Beaumont and Fletcher. Bradbrook stuffed them into a final chapter titled "The Decadents," but nowadays even that dismissive gesture is considered unnecessary. The most common critical response is silence.

Why should we care about plays that are never performed and dramatists that even pedants ignore? The proper answer is that we cannot expect to understand Jacobean theatre without understanding their distinctive contribution. The more immediate and practical answer, then, given the volume in which this essay appears, is that to study the interrelations of Beaumont and Fletcher with their senior colleague is to extend the still incomplete project of reading Shakespeare historically. Shakespeare and Beaumont and Fletcher entertained their audiences – the same audiences, at both the Globe and at Blackfriars, played to by the same actors, the King's Men – with many of the same theatrical means and topics. The demise of the children's companies led to the King's Men's taking possession of the hall theatre in Blackfriars in 1608, and that commercial expansion coincided with Beaumont and Fletcher's invitation to supply the company with scripts. The theatre came into full use probably in late 1609 or early 1610, and it is significant that for the entire period with which this essay is concerned, the company was performing at both Blackfriars and the Globe. In other words, *Philaster, The Maid's Tragedy, A King and No King, Cymbeline, The Winter's Tale, The Tempest, Cardenio, The Two Noble Kinsmen,* and *Henry VIII* were all performed in both the "public" and the "private" theatre.[3] Focusing on the period from 1607 to 1612, I want to propose some areas that warrant further intertextual study, interdependencies that will ultimately teach us more about the playtexts, the dramatists, the audience, the theatres, and the culture from which the works sprang.

These artistic interrelations fall into three categories: sex, politics, and theatrical self-consciousness. In developing these topics, I assume familiarity with Shakespeare's late plays and thus devote a greater proportion of space to Beaumont and Fletcher. If my discussion at times seems excessively descriptive, I would submit that a good deal of summary and illustration are warranted by the widespread unfamiliarity with Beaumont and Fletcher, the product of decades of neglect. One of my purposes in addressing these topics is to point to some fruitful areas of future research. Another is to encourage a fresh approach to less familiar works in light of some familiar ones. A third is to establish even more specifically than we have some of the theatrical preferences of the Stuart audiences. And my overriding goal is to suggest that the present critical moment is especially appropriate for a reconsideration of two very talented playwrights.[4]

Sex on the Stuart Stage

Beaumont and Fletcher seem obsessed with sex. As even their earliest works disclose, both appear to have regarded the libido as the most potent of motivating forces, or at the very least one of the most theatrically compelling subjects. It is clear from seventeenth-century commentary that the public recognized and admired this gift for representing the erotic. William Cartwright, in his prefatory poem for the 1647 Folio, makes the point by comparison: "Johnson . . . writ things lasting, and divine, / Yet his Love-Scenes, Fletcher, compar'd to thine, / Are cold and frosty . . ." (Beaumont and Fletcher 1905–12: xxxix). Beaumont and Fletcher people their works with an unending parade of sexual adventurers, abstainers, victims, novices, predators, prudes, perverts, prostitutes, and other permutations of taste and experience. Reading through the plays with an ear for the erotic is, to adapt a phrase of Noel Coward's, like piling Pelleas on Melisande.

In 1602 Francis Beaumont published anonymously a long Ovidian poem called *Salmacis and Hermaphroditus*. He was 17 years old. The choice of form and subject indicates an awareness of the public taste for erotic poetry and a wish to satisfy it: to name only the most obviously pertinent examples, *Hero and Leander* and *Venus and Adonis* had been often reprinted throughout the 1590s and had provoked a host of imitations. By opening *The Woman Hater* with the nocturnal rambles of a sexually adventurous Duke, the young playwright alludes mockingly to Vincentio's high-mindedness in *Measure for Measure*.

> *Lucio.*   I think your grace
> Intendes to walke the publique streetes disguised,
> To see the streetes disorders.
> *Duke.*   It is not so.
> *Arrigo.* You secretly will crosse some other states,
> That doe conspire against you.
> *Duke.*   Waightier farre:
> You are my friendes, and you shall have the cause;
> I breake my sleepes thus soone to see a wench. (1.1.23–9)

This Duke has no intention of cleaning up vice or closing the brothels, in and around which several of the later scenes take place; in fact, the crucial encounter resolving the action occurs in a bawdy house into which Oriana, the virtuous heroine, has been lured. Gondarino, the eponymous woman-hater who seeks to ruin her, impugns her as one "that itches now, and in the height / Of her intemperat thoughts, with greedy eyes / Expects my comming to allay her lust" (4.2.312–14). Such lechery apparently is common among the aristocracy, as Oriana's brother admits: "as great lords as I, have had knowne whores to their sisters, and have laught at it" (4.2.323–4). The play's subplot explores the problem of desire in another key: Lazarello's exorbitant appetite for food serves as a thematic surrogate for other, baser appetites prevalent in the court.

Passion also dominates Fletcher's first unaided theatrical effort, that audacious and complex anatomy of erotic desire, *The Faithful Shepherdess*. Although it might appropriately be considered below in connection with theatrical forms, the tragicomedy is pertinent here because it prefigures the various sexual situations and multiple characters that Fletcher will continue to develop, both alone and with Beaumont and other collaborators. The pastoral setting is the backdrop for the representation and evaluation of a wide range of amorous energy, from the rapacious Sullen Shepherd –

> be they faire, or blacke, or browne,
> Virgin, or carelesse wanton, I can crowne
> My appetite with any (2.3.11–13) –

to the available Cloe –

> It is Impossible to Ravish mee
> I am so willing (3.1.212–13) –

to the chaste Clorin and the steadfast Amoret, both virtuous but manifesting their purity in different forms. Fletcher's thematic goal is the promotion of temperance, and he does so by creating a vast and intricate dramatic structure illustrating the dangerous extremes. *The Faithful Shepherdess* not only confirms his fascination with and attraction to the erotic but also presages his antithetical or complementary method of representing it.

Rampant appetites also drive many of the characters in *Cupid's Revenge*. Its two plots attest to the dramatists' attraction to Elizabethan fiction in that the principal stories are dramatizations of episodes from the *Arcadia* (Finkelpearl 1990: 128–35). The play opens with a spectacular error on the part of the two earnest offspring of Duke Leontius: arguing that worship of Cupid has corrupted the youth of Licia, they succeed in persuading their father "That these erected obsceane Images / May be pluckt down and burnt" (1.1.74–5). The twin stories, then, develop the consequences of this naive effort at policing the bodies of the body politic. Cupid's revenge is, first, that the Duke's daughter Hidaspes falls passionately in love with the court dwarf, a figure so grotesque that, in the words of one of the court ladies, he "will hardly / Serve i' th' darke when one is drunke" (1.4.66–7). When her father refuses her request to marry the dwarf and instead has him executed, Hidaspes falls ill and dies. As for her brother Prince Leucippus, the angry god sees to it that he fares no better: the old Duke, his father, falls for Bacha, the beautiful widow who is the Prince's mistress. After marrying the old Duke, the dissolute Bacha does not abandon her desire for Leucippus but repeatedly taunts him with sexual advances. At the same time, Bacha's daughter by her first marriage falls in love with Leucippus (her new stepbrother as well as object of her mother's passion) and, in a preview of *Philaster*, disguises herself as a boy to serve her beloved. At the end of the play, everyone stabs everyone else, the carnage a direct consequence of the impossible attempt to suppress the carnal.

Philaster, like *The Faithful Shepherdess*, presents an exceptionally wide range of sexual exemplars, from Pharamond, the randy Spaniard, at one end, to the chaste, spiritual Euphrasia/Bellario at the other. The action arises initially from the irrepressible physical drives of Arathusa's suitor, Pharamond, who cannot manage for long without "sport," his term for sexual satisfaction: "The constitution of my body will never hold out till the wedding: I must seeke else-where" (1.2.200–1). When the foreigner is caught *in flagrante* with Megra, the promiscuous lady-in-waiting, the King reviles her in ugly detail:

> Thou most ill shrowded rottennesse: thou piece
> Made by a Painter and a Pothicary:
> Thou troubled sea of lust: thou wildernesse,
> Inhabited by wild thoughts: thou swolne clowd
> Of Infection: thou ripe mine of all diseases:
> Thou all sinne, all hell, and last, all Divells . . .
> By all the gods, all these, and all the Pages,
> And all the Court, shall hoote thee through the Court,
> Fling rotten Oranges, make ribal'd rimes,
> And seare thy name with candles upon walls:
> Doe ye laugh, Lady *Venus*? (2.4.136–41; 144–8)

The speech is notable not only for its sexual content but also for the ostentation of its rhetorical schemes ("Thou . . . Thou . . . Thou . . . Thou . . ."), a typical stylistic trait that Fletcher never abandons. At this outburst, the defiant Megra declares herself no more licentious than any other lady at court, including the King's daughter, Arathusa herself:

> The Princesse your deare daughter, shall stand by me
> On walls, and sung in ballads, any thing:
> Urge me no more, I know her, and her haunts,
> Her layes, leaps, and outlayes, and will discover all;
> Nay will dishonor her. I know the boy
> She keepes, a handsome boy: about eighteen:
> Know what she does with him, where, and when. (2.4.155–61)

This is the baseless charge that prompts the primary action. Philaster believes the slander, rejects Arathusa, and vilifies the page, Bellario. The charges against the beautiful youth turn out to be risible when, at the end of the play, it is revealed that Bellario is in fact female, a courtier's daughter who has dressed as a young man to be near her adored Philaster. Again the playwrights work by means of contraries and especially extremes: Euphrasia represents spiritual passion and self-denial, qualities antithetical to the erotic chicanery and intemperance characteristic of this court.

The sexual spectrum might even be said to include the Country Fellow, that rural gawker out to see the King at the hunt, who finds himself caught up in the most tonally complex episode of the play. After rescuing Arathusa from Philaster, who has just wounded her, and bullying the Prince into flight, the Country Fellow himself, in one of the most memorable theatrical turns in the play, makes a pass at her: "I cannot follow the rogue: I preethee wench come and kisse me now" (4.5.106–7). This sudden, shocking demand makes for one of the most notorious moments in the canon, a line that is surprising, amusing, and disgusting all at once. To complicate the sexual range even further, Beaumont and Fletcher go beyond their *dramatis personae* and invent imaginary figures. As Philaster reflects on the corruptions of court life and the infidelities of its sophisticated women, he comforts himself with a pastoral fantasy – actually a loose translation of Juvenal's sixth satire – in which he has taken as a partner "some mountaine girle" who would "have borne at her big breasts / My large course issue" (4.2.7, 11–12). As they do with the related topic of honor, the collaborators seek to exhibit their subject from several points of view, taking particular care with the process of the revelation. Such variety amounts to a kind of theme and variation, a technique that Andrew Gurr, speaking of other themes in *Philaster*, has described as "situational puns," parallel or contrasting episodes or relationships that call attention to both their likeness and difference (Gurr, in Beaumont and Fletcher 1969: lxiii).

The typical court in a Beaumont and Fletcher play is peopled not only with hot-blooded princes and ladies but also with gentlemen (and gentlewomen) who comment suggestively on the courtiers' affairs.

> *Enter two* [Gentlemen] *of the Bed-chamber.*
> *1. Gentleman.* Come, now shees gone, lets enter, the King expects it, and will be angry.
> *2. Gentleman.* 'Tis a fine wench, weele have a snap at her one of these nights as she goes from him.
> *1. Gentleman.* Content: how quickly he had done with her, I see Kings can doe no more that way then other mortall people. (5.1.113–18)

This interlude is from *The Maid's Tragedy*, and the King, of course, is dead, stabbed moments before by the "fine wench" who has just departed. The central conflict of the play involves the revelation of sexual iniquity: the idealistic Amintor, reneging on his engagement to Aspatia, discovers that Evadne, the bride chosen for him by the King, is actually the King's mistress and that she defiantly expects to continue in that role.

In the teasing moments leading up to the bedroom scene, the commentators are women: the pathetic Aspatia, who enters to profess her fidelity to Amintor, and the bride's entourage, who contribute a stream of bawdy remarks: "A dozen wanton words put in your head / Will make you livelier in your husband's bed" (2.1.20–1). These conventional comments, which seem mildly tasteless before the bedroom encounter, are rendered juvenile and naive by the revelation of the bride's corruption. According to Kathleen McLuskie, the preliminaries of the wedding-night scene increase the sexual and theatrical titillation of a promised consummation rendered impossible by conditions of representation; expectations are then exploded by Evadne's sordid surprise (McLuskie 1992: 95). Other such annotators, male and female, respond sardonically to the words and actions of the major characters in play after play:

> *Gallatea.* 'Tis late.
> *Megra.* 'Tis all,
>   My eyes will doe to lead me to my bed.
> *Gallatea {aside}.* I feare they are so heauy, youle scarce finde
>   The way to your owne lodging, with um to night. (*Philaster*, 2.4.4–8)

Ribald marginalia of this kind is one of the main guarantors of the erotic atmosphere for which Beaumont and Fletcher were becoming known.

Although the topic of incest has made *A King and No King* perhaps the most notorious of the collaborations, the play is not about "real incest" at all, of course. Rather, it is about amorous desire which the parties only believe to be incestuous but which proves (technically) not to be. The provocative treatment the dramatists give their subject, teasing their audience with forbidden desire, has contributed significantly to twentieth-century disapproval of their work. When King Arbaces falls in love with the woman he believes to be his sister and, after a moral struggle, resolves to yield to his passion, he is essentially guilty of the sin of incest although intercourse never occurs. As a prominent Stuart divine put the theological point, "though the sinne be an *act*, yet it is denominated from the *thought* . . . The principall part thereof, lyeth in the purpose of the heart, not in the outward performance by our body . . . the inward lust is the greatest part of fornication and incest" (Arthur Lake, quoted in McCabe 1993: 200). Theatrical tension is produced by the possibility of forbidden love, by the moral struggle that Arbaces and Panthea, especially he, must endure, as in his complaint to the gods:

>   . . . give me sorrow, that will render me
>   Apt to receive your mercy; rather so,
>   Let it be rather so, then punish me
>   With such unmanly sinnes: Incest is in me
>   Dwelling alreadie, and it must be holie
>   That pulles it thence. (3.1.327–32)

And the submission, to which all has been building, is calculated to provoke shock and wonder.

Beaumont and Fletcher have been frequently disparaged for solving the dramatic dilemma by means of a secret. According to McCabe, "The play demands, but fails to produce, an answer in affection rather than plot contrivance. There remains to the end what Clifford Leech terms a 'double impulse' towards orthodoxy and subversion" (McCabe 1993: 200). This is seen as an instance of Ornstein's "ethical frivolity," and it is an opinion shared by many. The disapproval probably also arises from critics' anger at having been tricked. But as playwrights concerned mainly with telling an effective story, Beaumont and Fletcher treat incest as a dramatically provocative element, a useful tool in the narrative medium. Their indifference to the moral question is entirely characteristic, and while it has offended some important twentieth-century readers, their own audiences were apparently less sensitive.

If Beaumont and Fletcher tease their audiences with sexual situations and problems such as Evadne's guilt, Shakespeare makes the absence of sex the source of trouble. A character imagines an act of infidelity only to find that the real depravity lies in the strength and detail of the suspicion, that the reviled woman – the focus of the charge is of course female – is innocent. Posthumus in *Cymbeline* is representative in imagining Imogen's yielding to Iachimo, who "Perchance . . . spoke not, but / Like a full-acorn'd boar, a German one, / Cried 'O!' and mounted" (2.5.15–17). Leontes is equally vulgar, with his puns on "play," his image of his wife as "sluic'd," and his misogynistic assaults on both Hermione and Paulina. These suspicious figures inflict great pain on themselves, their victims, and even – in Leontes's case – the kingdom by imagining sexual perfidy, by supposing, in other words, that they inhabit the moral realm of Beaumont and Fletcher. Even in *The Tempest*, with only one human female in the cast, there is concern about non-existent intercourse as Prospero repeatedly enjoins Ferdinand to self-restraint.

Sexual activity in Shakespeare's plays is not *only* imaginary: some characters are sexually active, such as Thaisa and Pericles, or will soon be, such as Miranda and Ferdinand. Some of the most vivid characters are sexually obsessed – Boult and his employers in *Pericles*, Cloten in *Cymbeline*, and Caliban in *The Tempest*. Iachimo's overpowering lust for Imogen, although he is unable to act upon it, is expressed in powerfully imagined language, particularly in the voyeuristic scene in her bedchamber. Henry VIII's weakness for what Wolsey calls Anne Bullen's "fair visage" (3.2.88) partly motivates his divorce of Katherine, and the nature of the King's relationship with Anne is specified in the Old Lady's crack that for a crown Anne would "venture an emballing" (2.3.47). In the Mytilene segment of *Pericles* we learn of the masturbating Spaniard who, upon hearing Boult's advartisment of Marina, "went to bed to her very description" (4.2.98–101).

Incest for Shakespeare seems to be more than a marketable topic but an abiding moral threat. All his last plays are haunted by the specter of endogamous sexual desire. *Pericles* opens with the incestuous relationship between Antiochus and his daughter: "Bad child, worse father" as Gower puts it. And from that point the principal relationships depicted are refractions or countervailing instances of the wicked union, Simonides and his daughter Thaisa being the first. Indeed the source of *Pericles* gives Simonides a wife, which Shakespeare seems to have omitted to sharpen the comparison and contrast between the two kings and their daughters. In the final act Marina's reunion with her despairing father serves as the healthy complement to the perverse coupling in Antioch. A quick review reminds us that while the succeeding plays offer less obvious cases of potential incest, the topic will not go away. *Cymbeline* glances at the problem in a number of ways: Posthumus and Imogen, now married, were reared essentially as brother and sister, and Cloten, who has sexual designs on her, is Imogen's step-brother. When she leaves the court for Wales, she unknowingly encounters her lost brothers, prompting some mildly salacious talk, despite her boy's disguise, about her good looks. Although *The Winter's Tale* is distanced from its source, *Pandosto*, by Shakespeare's distinctive treatment of the story, Greene's fiction concludes with the king's suicide upon discovering that the young woman to whom he is attracted is his lost daughter. The isolation of Prospero and his maturing daughter on the island has raised eyebrows, although Shakespeare doesn't make much of the potential danger. Henry VIII divorces Katherine on grounds of incest, since she had first been married to his dead brother Arthur. There needs no ghost come from the grave to tell us that people like plays about sex, especially about forbidden forms, but the consistency in the repertory of the King's Men at this period implies an exceptional enthusiasm for the topic on the part of the Jacobean audiences.

Politics and Plays

Everybody seems to think that politics is fundamental to the works of Beaumont and Fletcher, although nobody can agree on their allegiances. The contradictory views of their political affiliations – Coleridge belittling them as royalist toadies, a recent critic describing them almost as radicals – reveals more than the mutability of critical opinion over time. It suggests that politics is fundamental to their work in the strict sense, that it serves as a foundation for narrative and dramatic structures that the playwrights use to attain their principal goal, entertaining their audiences. The oppositional nature of politics makes it especially valuable as a basis for dramatic conflict in any age: the playwrights may set progressive against conservative, city against country, old guard against young hotheads, king against parliament. The last of these oppositions had become especially contentious at the moment that Beaumont and Fletcher began their collaboration. The gloss of novelty had worn off James Stuart's crown, his idiosyncratic, irregular style of rule having become familiar and distasteful to many of his subjects. By 1609 or so the monarch's devotion to absolutist principles had become so exaggerated, his manner of expressing those views so blunt, and the reaction of many members of parliament so violent, that it is possible to discern the outlines of the conflict that four decades later would lead to regicide (Davies 1959: 10–15). These issues must have been of compelling interest to most members of the audience at the Blackfriars and many at the Globe, most of them citizens of the capital in which these disputes were raging. In fact, some of the spectators at Blackfriars must have been themselves major players in some of these political scenarios.

Virtually every Beaumont and Fletcher play may be said to have a "political" setting. *The Woman Hater* opens with its prowling Duke and moves on to its wronged aristocratic lady, *Cupid's Revenge* explicitly attributes Cupid's revenge to the state's attempt to police the hearts of the people, and *The Maid's Tragedy* explores in detail the problem of tyranny, with the King's tainted sexual arrangements an image of his self-serving style of government. Virtually every scene of *A King and No King* contains debate about court politics, flattery, foreign policy, intrigue, who's in and who's out, and other such topics. From the start Arbaces is seen as erratic in the performance of his royal duties – "vain-glorious, and humble, and angrie, and patient, and merrie, and dull, and joyfull, and sorrowfull, in extreamities in an houre" (1.1.81–3) – and this capriciousness is shown to have direct political consequences. The most obvious reversal is his treatment of Tigranes, the Armenian prince whom Arbaces has just defeated when the play opens. The King promises that Tigranes shall marry Panthea, Arbaces's sister, and then reneges on that promise when he falls in love with her himself. But in terms of the playwrights' interest and emphasis, the personal and the theatrical outweigh the political.

Although the typical setting is a royal court, we are occasionally afforded glimpses of the citizenry. Returning to the capital after his military triumph, Arbaces ceremoniously speaks to the people:

> All the account that I can render you
> For all the love you have bestowed on me,
> All your expences to maintaine my warre,
> Is but a little word: you will imagine
> 'Tis slender payment; yet 'tis such a word
> As is not to be bought without our blouds;
> 'Tis peace. (2.2.82–8)

His subjects' response to this pretty speech would probably disappoint him, but he doesn't hear it, having left the stage before they comment and disperse:

> *1. Citizens Wife.* . . . Come *Philip*, walke afore us homeward: – did not his Majestie say, he had brought us home Peaes for all our money?
> *2. Citizens Wife.* Yes marry did he.
> *1. Citizens Wife.* They are the first I heard on this yeere by my troth, I long'd for some of um; did he not say we should have some?
> *2. Citizens Wife.* Yes, and so we shall anon I warrant you, have every one a pecke brought home to our houses. (2.2.152–9)

The people are capricious, self-absorbed, proud, and prone to error – that is, very much like their leader. The King's will receives much emphasis, especially his tendency to change his mind and to manipulate others for the satisfaction of his own wishes.

For all this attention to government and the nature of those who rule, the political in *A King and No King* seems to yield to the erotic and the histrionic. Whether the Jacobean audience felt this way is difficult to tell, and since the play is almost never performed we have had few opportunities for testing its effect on modern spectators. But the relative importance of politics and desire seems indicated by the progress of the action, which moves towards Arbaces's joy at having become "No King" and having found Panthea available to him after all. Likewise, the mysterious assassination plot pursued by the Queen Mother is, politically speaking, nugatory. The same balance can be said to characterize *Philaster*. As is often pointed out, it is a play that owes much to *Hamlet*, particularly since Philaster, the "right Heire" to the crown of Sicily, has never attained the throne: his "father . . . was by our late King of *Calabria*, unrighteously deposed from his fruitfull *Cicilie*" (1.1.23–4). In both plays the political yields, I believe, to the personal. Even when in the last act the citizens rebel and place Philaster on the throne, what matters most to him (and probably to the audience) is clearing up the scandal surrounding his relations with Arathusa and Bellario/Euphrasia. In short, the political leanings of Beaumont and Fletcher have been so difficult to discern – one age reviles them for their politics while another applauds them for the same views – because they don't really matter. Harold S. Wilson may overstate the case, but his intuition is sound where politics is concerned:

> *Philaster* is a lively series of incidents contrived with great ingenuity to provide con-
> stant excitement and surprise and to issue agreeably with the recognition and reward of
> virtue, the dismissal of the wicked in disgrace. And it is nothing more. (Wilson 1961:
> 259)

The play's the thing.

In giving up tragedy around 1608 or 1609, Shakespeare appears to be turning away from a serious engagement with politics. The tragedies he wrote in the three or four years before devoting himself to romantic tragicomedy, i.e., *King Lear*, *Macbeth*, *Antony and Cleopatra*, *Coriolanus*, perhaps *Timon*, were among the most political works he had produced since the history cycles of the 1590s. These are plays that give serious attention to some of the most pressing questions of the day: tyranny, familial division, self-interest, neglect of duty, public versus private, the individual versus the community, the problem of communication. But the move to tragicomedy or romance may be seen less as a stylistic rupture than as a metamorphosis. For the last plays are also concerned with the problem of government in its various senses, i.e., control of the self and control of the state. A recent critic makes a very strong case "that Shakespeare's late plays can be understood as political drama. Depicting conflict in royal households, kingdoms, and finally within the expansive terms of empire, these plays are informed by contemporary ideas of government at all levels of society and under the laws of nations and nature" (Jordan 1997: 211). But even here "political" is the adjective, "drama" the noun.

Obviously some of these texts respond more readily to political analysis than others. Many readers have found *Cymbeline* quite hospitable to political interpretation, especially the scenes given over to the tribute dispute with Rome, and James's pretensions as European peacemaker must have augmented the resonance of that narrative strain for the original audiences (Bergeron 1986: 136–56). These days *The Tempest* is read almost exclusively in political terms, as a meditation on imperial ambition, expansion, foreign alliance, master–servant relations, and neglect of civic duty. It is important to remember, however, that the nineteenth century saw it as a spiritual journey from a fall, through a period of hatred, to forgiveness. Although *Pericles* and *The Winter's Tale* depict rulers whose personal conflicts have political import, even the most thorough political readings can seem forced, as if special pleading were required to place politics center stage.

Shakespeare is arguably more concerned with the problems of politics than are Beaumont and Fletcher. Their use of political situations and themes clearly is calculated to amplify the theatrical impact of their narrative reversals, conflicts, and surprises, whereas Shakespeare seems to want to engage his audience in political problems: the conditions of a healthy state, the nature of tyranny, and the complex relationship between character and office. But he too is even more concerned with drama. In *Cymbeline* theatrical history suggests that the tribute scenes pale next to Iachimo's nocturnal prowl through Imogen's bedchamber, the grotesque scene in which she awakens from "death" next to the headless corpse of Posthumus/Cloten, the spectacular descent of Jupiter, and the lovers' reconciliation ("hang there like fruit, my soul, till the tree die"). Constance Jordan admits that it is difficult to determine "whether or not [the late plays] endorse a political position with respect to alternative systems of rule" (Jordan 1997: 211). And once again I suspect that the difficulty arises from the primacy of the stage in the thinking of all three playwrights.

The Virtuosos

The self-consciousness that Beaumont and Fletcher exhibit in virtually all their theatrical efforts must be attributable, at least in part, to youth. As talented youngsters new to the stage, they quickly absorbed the conventions that Shakespeare, Jonson, Marston, Dekker, Chapman, and others had been developing over the course of several years. They arrived on the scene, in other words, with a knowing attitude, an awareness of current theatrical tastes and practices, and they began to build upon that awareness, appropriating and shaping the theatrical medium to their own ends. What is vital is that they set out to make their audience aware of their awareness of conventions. Like composers or painters or filmmakers – like artists in any field – the two dramatists seem to have been bent on making a name for themselves by broadening the limits of their discipline, in their case by identifying and exaggerating some of the topics and strategies of their contemporaries. The acute sense of audience is apparent in *The Woman Hater*, which has "a special Jacobean flavor" (Finkelpearl 1990: 73), every scene attesting to familiarity with prevailing theatrical modes and their chief practitioners. An even more obvious case is *The Knight of the Burning Pestle*, a play which springs from its author's familiarity with the public's familiarity with what was selling on the contemporary stage. *The Knight* was apparently not a success, nor was *The Faithful Shepherdess*, but notwithstanding these disappointments, the two young playwrights rose to professional prominence rather swiftly, and one way of explaining that success is to say that they quickly learned to give the public in abundance what it had come to the theatre for.

Beaumont and Fletcher knew that theatrical success depends to a large extent on good storytelling, and their canniness is apparent both in the nature of the stories they select and in their way of telling them. "Sensational" is probably the term that best captures their sense of what their audiences might like to see. Any number of examples suggest that the playwrights chose their narratives with the box office in mind: Megra's filthy accusations in *Philaster*, Evadne's hideous revelation in *The Maid's Tragedy*, the incest in *A King and No King*. But their stories are less important than the telling of them, a feature that has been recognized since the middle of the seventeenth century. Robert Herrick, in his prefatory poem for the 1647 Folio, recorded his admiration for "that high designe / Of *King and No King*" (Beaumont and Fletcher 1905–12: xli), and Dryden also thought that play "the best of their designs" (Waith 1952: 28). In Eugene Waith's study, *The Pattern of Tragicomedy in Beaumont and Fletcher*, "pattern" is as important as "tragicomedy." A stylistic analysis, particularly of Fletcher's verse, reveals a delight in syntactical and other kinds of poetic and rhetorical patterning (Hoy 1984).

Every play exhibits their awareness of an audience's taste for architectural intricacy, for symmetrical structures, mirroring characters, complementary ideas, and other such evidence of pleasing arrangement. In *The Maid's Tragedy* Aspatia's innocent candor and fidelity to Amintor balance Evadne's secret corruption and her depraved use of him. In *A King and No King* Arbaces turns to his twin Iberian captains, Mardonius and Bessus, to arrange the sexual encounter with his supposed sister: "I would desire her love / Lasciviouslie, leudlie, incestuouslie" (3.3.76–7). The placement of the two responses, consecutively in the same scene, emphasizes both their likeness and difference. First Mardonius refuses:

> there's your Ring againe; what have I done
> Dishonestlie in my whole life, name it,
> That you should put so base a businesse to me? (3.3.80–2)

And a few moments later Bessus enthusiastically consents:

> Ile doe your businesse . . . and when this is dispatcht, if you have a minde to your
> Mother tell me, and you shall see Ile set it hard. (3.3.166–9)

Such contrasts and parallels abound – two kings (Arbaces and Tigranes) and two women (Panthea and Spaconia), an antagonistic parent in each of the plots (the mother in one and the father in the other), the courtiers versus the citizens, a king and no king. What matters is the self-consciousness with which such obvious patterns and strategies are employed. It is as if the playwrights have identified the fundamentals of dramatic success – political conflict, amorous entanglement, theatrical confrontations, parallel stories and structures, heightened speeches – and exaggerated those characteristics, pleasing the spectators with the basic trope and with the punctuation or underscoring of it.

A related structural device is the "big scene," Beaumont and Fletcher's patented strategy for whipping up dramatic anxiety and then resolving the threat in a surprising fashion. The wedding-night scene in *The Maid's Tragedy* has already been mentioned in this respect, and once Amintor learns of his wife's status, the audience is led to anticipate and fear the consequences. First comes the great confrontation between the bridegroom and his best friend, Evadne's brother, Melantius. Then follows Evadne's act of contrition and revenge:

> I take my leave my Lord,
> And never shall you see the foule *Evadne*
> Till she have tried all honoured meanes that may
> Set her in rest, and wash her staines away. (4.2.279–80)

This is succeeded by Aspatia's attempt, by dressing as a male and challenging Amintor – *She kickes him* – to die by the hand of her lover. All the plays are similarly constructed to take advantage of expectations (Waith 1952: 38–41), fulfilling them predictably and surprisingly, as a glance at *A King and No King* confirms. We witness the big moment that we expect, the declaration of love between Arbaces and Panthea, but we are also given a denouement that, while it has been hinted at, we cannot have specifically anticipated.

This taste for patterning and arrangement helps to explain the condescension with which Beaumont and Fletcher have been treated in twentieth-century critical discourse. The use of such terms as "superficial," "false," "frivolous," "meretricious" derives in part from the frequency with which the plays depend on surprise, peripety, sudden revelation, and other such narrative trickery or bravado. When at the end of *Philaster* everyone learns the sex of Bellario, the revelation produces the following outburst from the relieved hero:

> It is a woman Sir; harke, Gentlemen,
> It is a woman. *Arathusa* take
> My soule into thy bres't that would be gone
> With joy: it is a Woman . . . (5.5.137–40)

It is notable, in light of the topic of revelation and reversal, that this moment of jubilation occurs exactly five lines after the stage direction, *{Philaster} offers to stab himself.* Moreover, the extravagant rhetoric which greets the discovery is both ironic and not: by concealing the disguise until the very end, the dramatists aim for the genuine effect of surprise while at the same time nudging the audience at the trick they have succeeded in bringing off. *A King and No King* concludes with a similar surprise ending presented in a similarly self-conscious manner. The theatre of Beaumont and Fletcher has, for much of the nineteenth and twentieth centuries at least, been maligned for being theatrical.

A similarly complex mixture of *naïveté* and sophistication accounts for the tonal ambiguity of Shakespeare's late plays. Such complementarity is perhaps most obvious in *Cymbeline*, since the scope of the play means that the various elements – multiple locations, Italian villainy, stolen children, paired hero and clown, Jupiter descending – are not as integrated and polished as they are in *The Winter's Tale* and *The Tempest*. The wager plot is an old standard, borrowed from Boccaccio, and the romance staple of the royal brothers stolen at birth is also commonplace. And yet all these materials are treated in a thoroughly up-to-date, knowing, presentational fashion (Mowat 1976). The cardboard quality of some of the villains, notably the Queen and Cloten, sharpens this sophisticated tone, as does Imogen's finding herself in the Welsh mountains with her brothers, or the knowing use of such an ancient device as the *deus ex machina*. The grotesquerie of Imogen's awaking next to the headless corpse of Cloten and mistaking it for that of Posthumus seems like one of Beaumont and Fletcher's big scenes, as does the extravagant finale, with its serial revelations and reversals. Although *Cymbeline* is usually considered most like a play by Beaumont and Fletcher and is often discussed with *Philaster*, *The Winter's Tale* is also dependent upon old-fashioned elements set forth in a thoroughly fashionable manner. The big scene, of course, is the trial of Hermione, whose speech of self-defense is both immensely moving and unusually lengthy: Shakespeare clearly expects the audience to take pleasure in the delayed resolution. Once that speech is completed (and belittled by Leontes), the action hurtles forward with the opening and reading of the judgment from the oracle, Leontes's dismissal of it, the servant's entrance to announce the death of Mamillius, and Hermione's swoon. The scene is as contrived, as "theatrical," as melodramatic, and as knowing as any in Beaumont and Fletcher.

Shakespeare too seems to be gratifying his audience's taste for being in the know: the late work is exceptionally self-conscious, even for Shakespeare. *Pericles* gives us Gower's winking, confidential relationship with the audience. In *Cymbeline* the asides spoken serially by the wicked Queen, Cornelius the doctor, and Pisanio, all about the box of poison, are writ extremely large, as if the playwright is exaggerating the convention as a means of guying it, yet using it seriously at the same time. The masque in *The Tempest*, Prospero's clock-watching, and the Epilogue all expose the strings of the puppeteer. Time's soliloquy in *The Winter's Tale* is perhaps the most pointed instance of self-consciousness. While asserting the omnipotence of Time and, by extension, his authorial power abruptly to shift the temporal scene, the dramatist contrasts the fashionable status of his audience ("what is now received") with the creaky, old-fashioned quality of his story: Time promises to despoil "th' freshest things now reigning, and make stale / The glistering of this present, as my tale / Now seems to it" (4.1.13–15). This series of receding moments acknowledges the taste of the audience and Shakespeare's sly manner of catering for that taste, providing a story to which the audience can both condescend as outmoded or ridiculous and respond with surprise and delight.

Conclusions?

The question of "influence" between the young collaborators and the experienced dramatist, as I have indicated, is unlikely to be adequately answered. The early work of Beaumont and Fletcher must have attracted Shakespeare's favorable notice, since their invitation to write for the King's Men would likely have depended upon his approval, as shareholder and principal dramatist. Depending on chronological priority, it may be that Fletcher's domestication of Italian pastoral tragicomedy stimulated Shakespeare's imagination, or that *Pericles* encouraged the two collaborators to experiment further with the form of tragicomedy. It is possible that Beaumont and Fletcher's look back to Elizabethan fiction prompted Shakespeare to review the stories of his young manhood for usable material. But even the discovery of a cache of reliable data about exactly who wrote which play in which year would not significantly enlarge our understanding of these Jacobean artistic relations. In a sense, *Cymbeline* could not have been written without *Philaster*, nor *Philaster* without *Cymbeline*. This is what McMullan means when he declares that "determining exact precedence for Shakespeare's 'late plays' and Fletcher's early work is largely futile: the point is that both playwrights were aware of, and in a sense collaborating with, each other's work for several years before they finally began to write plays together" (McMullan, in Shakespeare 2000: 116). The impossibility of assigning priority or determining influence is in fact liberating because it permits us to look in more profitable directions. Neutral study of the intersections between the two bodies of work may not tell us a great deal about the authors but does tell us something about the fashions of the early modern English stage.

What seems more pertinent is the influence of the audiences. Ultimately they were the arbiters, the companies were in business to attract and please them, and their likes and dislikes shaped the work not only of the three dramatists considered here but of everyone who wrote plays in the period, even those who, like Jonson, had an especially vexed relationship with them. The constitution of these audiences was the topic of much debate among the theatre historians of the twentieth century (Harbage 1941: 87–90; Finkelpearl 1990: 61–3). Although claims were made for the determinative power of the court on the drama of the period, such notions have been discounted by more recent criticism (Finkelpearl 1990: 50–1), and discussion has centered on the two principal bodies, those who frequented the public and the private theatres, represented here by the Globe and Blackfriars. Without addressing all the conflicting evidence and subtle distinctions raised in the debates over class, education, wealth, youth, and other such considerations, it seems fair to conclude that: (1) there were differences between the two audiences, (2) these differences were neither negligible nor enormous, so that there might have been some overlap in the two groups, (3) the private theatres, generally speaking, housed a wealthier, better educated, slightly more fashionable crowd, while (4) the public theatres, by virtue of their lower prices, served a segment of the public that did not frequent the private houses. It is worth considering that the conventional, simplified accounts of the tastes of these two groups might be accurate, that the Blackfriars audience, particularly those members of the literary and social elites, preferred a more sophisticated and aggressively "modern" style of drama, whereas the Globe patrons enjoyed a simpler, perhaps old-fashioned, more generally "popular" kind of play. Since most of the plays discussed herein were performed at both the Globe and Blackfriars, it is possible that the divergent tastes of this double audience are partly responsible for their unusual mixture of elements, the modish and the outmoded, and particularly the complex tone, with its combination of artlessness and sophistication.

Study of these theatrical interdependencies also tells us a good deal about ourselves and our own critical prejudices, particularly when we come to recognize that Beaumont and Fletcher have been derided for exploiting some of the same dramatic tropes for which Shakespeare has been acclaimed. Their long critical eclipse surely has much to do with Victorian bardolatry, with the High Modernist emphasis on seriousness and skepticism of the popular, with New Critical taste for poetic complexity, and with New Historicism's uncertainty about the politics of the plays. The collaborators may prove beneficiaries of the poststructuralist dispersal of textual responsibility. Now that Foucauldian pressures have begun to reshape our sense of *the author*, the fact of collaboration seems to have become somewhat more palatable, emerging as one alternative to the outmoded image of the solitary artist and serving as a bridge between the notion of a single writer and a thoroughly cultural approach to the problem of literary origin. And we must frequently remind ourselves that different periods value different kinds of art, that works and schools go in and out of fashion for any number of good and bad reasons, and the time may now be right, as critical fashion continues to change, to reevaluate writers and texts that we have been taught by an earlier age to dislike.

For much of the twentieth century it was axiomatic to speak of Beaumont and Fletcher as "baroque" dramatists, and even though the term described a legitimate category of much important seventeenth- and eighteenth-century visual art and music, it usually had pejorative associations when applied to literature.[5] *Baroque* "denote[s] something exaggerated, overblown, capricious," or "dramatic, at times bombastic, and manipulative of the spectator" (Langmuir and Lynton 2000: 48–9); the style is characterized by "discords and suspensions," "grotesqueness and contortion" (Holman and Harmon 1992: 46); "baroque was tormented by doubts, shot through with conflicts and tension. Not a happy and unreflective pleasure of the senses, but gross sensuality alternating with pangs of conscience become the dominant note. The baroque age was torn between extremes" (Friedrich 1952: 41). The applicability of such rhetoric to the drama of Beaumont and Fletcher is easy to discern, and if we ignore the evaluative connotations it can be surprisingly helpful in thinking about Jacobean tragicomedy.

It may be, however, that we need a new set of terms. At the risk of seeming glib, I would propose that the same characteristics of Beaumont and Fletcher – and

Shakespeare also – that suggested the label of "baroque" may now prompt us to think of their work in the context of the postmodern.

> When everything is simulacra, when there are neither criteria for judgment nor shared goals for shaping audiences, and when serious gestures seem inseparable from self-advertisement, postmodernism finds it difficult to distinguish resistance to the dominant social order from complicity in its hunger for media events. Sympathetic critics in turn have enormous difficulty in deciding which features of the art are genuinely "oppositional" – either as counterassertions or as exposures of basic contradictions in the established order – and which actually reinforce the subjectivist multiplicity on which late monopoly capitalism feeds. (Preminger and Brogan 1993: 795)

The value of such a formulation – once adjustments are made for temporal differences – is that our familiarity with cultural developments at the end of the twentieth century may help us to understand puzzling works of an earlier age. The difficulties critics have had in identifying the political sympathies of Beaumont and Fletcher may be a function of something like a postmodern resistance to certainty or "meaning." The dramatists seem to have occupied a cultural moment rather like our own, one in which the relative certainties of a previous age, and the artistic instruments for expressing them, had begun to dissolve in the face of various political, social, and scientific challenges. The tragicomic mode represents a borrowing from established forms, a kind of pastiche in which something new and playful is fashioned from the stricter artistic modes of the previous age. G. K. Hunter, after noting the mid-twentieth century view of Beaumont and Fletcher's "decadence," suggests a shift like that I describe: "The 'modernist' position . . . seems to be giving way to a 'post-modernist' one . . . [and recent work] shows the post-modernist taste for indecidability operating to the advantage of Fletcher and the whole tragicomic genre" (Hunter 1997: 512n.). The combination of the old-fashioned and the new-fangled, the frequent use of exaggeration and parody, self-consciousness and reflexivity, fictions within fictions, an emotionally distanced audience, an uncertain moral or political thrust – all these indicate the utility of the postmodern aesthetic for thinking about their style.

This category also supplies a way of discriminating between the similar work of Shakespeare and his new colleagues. We might say that Shakespeare is to the end of modernism as Beaumont and Fletcher are to the beginning of postmodernism. The same materials are used, many in the same ways, but a difference is sill discernible between the effects of the two styles. Putting it crudely, we might say that Shakespeare seems still to retain belief in a mysteriously ordered world, a realm "open to the possibilities for renewal offered by chance, the operations of time, and youth's natural innocence" (Bliss 1986: 152), a universe of natural cycles and time that heals as well as destroys, whereas Beaumont and Fletcher show no faith in such an order. Evidence of similar division exists also in our own age. It may be that critical fashion has changed so that the time is right for a reconsideration of Beaumont and Fletcher.

NOTES

1 Philip Finkelpearl has noted that Eliot seems, consciously or unconsciously, to have taken this image from Richard Flecknoe's *A Short Discourse of the English Stage* (1664): "Beaumont and Fletcher first wrote in the Heroick way, upon whom Suckling and others endeavored to refine agen; one saying wittily of his *Aglaura* that 'twas full of fine flowers, but they seem'd rather stuck than growing there" (Finkelpearl 1990: 6).

2 Cyrus Hoy believes that, while both dramatists worked on the play, Beaumont copied out the final version of the text and thus his contribution seems perhaps a bit more prominent than that of Fletcher (Hoy 1958: 98–9).

3 Hunter (1997) indicates that evidence exists for dual performances in all cases except *The Winter's Tale*, which we know Simon Forman saw at the Globe, and which was performed at court: it seems reasonable to conclude that this play, like the others in repertory at the time, was performed in both theatres.

4 I hope to avoid rehearsing many of the distinctions and likenesses established by Lee Bliss (1986) in her excellent analysis of Shakespeare and Beaumont and Fletcher. This piece should be mandatory reading for anyone interested in Jacobean theatre. Second, I have paid little attention to the two collaborative efforts of Shakespeare and Fletcher, *Henry VIII* and *The Two Noble Kinsmen*, because these two texts have recently benefited from excellent Arden editions by Gordon McMullan and Lois Potter, who both write helpfully on the issue of collaboration.

5 An admirable exception to the disapproval is found in the work of Herbert Blau (1986).

REFERENCES AND FURTHER READING

Appleton, W. W. (1956). *Beaumont and Fletcher: A Critical Study*. London: Allen and Unwin.

Beaumont, F. and Fletcher, J. (1905–12). *Works*, 4 vols., ed. A. Glover and A. R. Waller. Cambridge: Cambridge University Press.

——(1966–96). *The Dramatic Works in the Beaumont and Fletcher Canon*, 10 vols., ed. F. Bowers et al. Cambridge: Cambridge University Press.

——(1969). *Philaster or Love Lies a-Bleeding*, ed. A. Gurr. London: Methuen.

Beckson, K. and Ganz, A. (1993). *Literary Terms: A Dictionary*. New York. Noonday.

Bergeron, D. (1986). *Shakespeare's Romances and the Royal Family*. Lawrence: University of Kansas Press.

Blau, H. (1986). The Absolved Riddle. *New Literary History*, 17, 539–54.

Bliss, L. (1986). Tragicomic Romance for the King's Men, 1609–1611: Shakespeare, Beaumont, and Fletcher. In A. R. Braunmuller and James Bulman (eds.) *Comedy from Shakespeare to Sheridan*. Newark: University of Delaware Press.

——(1987). *Francis Beaumont*. Boston, MA: Twayne.

——(1990). Pastiche, Burlesque, Tragicomedy. In A. R. Braunmuller and M. Hattaway (eds.) *The Cambridge Companion to English Renaissance Drama*. Cambridge: Cambridge University Press.

Bradbrook, M. C. (1935). *Themes and Conventions of Elizabethan Tragedy*. Cambridge: Cambridge University Press.

Chambers, E. K. (1923). *The Elizabethan Stage*, 4 vols. Oxford: Oxford University Press.

Cohen, W. (1992). Prerevolutionary Drama. In J. Hope and G. McMullan (eds.) *The Politics of Tragicomedy*. London: Routledge.

Coleridge, S. T. (1936). *Coleridge's Miscellaneous Criticism*, ed. T. M. Raysor. London: Constable.

Danby, J. (1952). *Poets on Fortune's Hill*. London: Faber and Faber.

Davies, G. (1959). *The Early Stuarts, 1603–1660*. Oxford: Oxford University Press.

Dryden, J. (1971). *The Works of John Dryden: Prose, 1668–1691*, vol. 17, ed. H. T. Swedenberg, Jr. Berkeley: University of California Press.

Eliot, T. S. (1932). *Selected Essays, 1917–1932*. New York: Harcourt Brace.

Finkelpearl, P. J. (1990). *Court and Country Politics in the Plays of Beaumont and Fletcher*. Princeton, NJ: Princeton University Press.

Friedrich, C. J. (1952). *The Age of the Baroque: 1610–1660*. New York: Harper.

Harbage, A. (1941). *Shakespeare's Audience*. New York: Columbia University Press.

Holman, C. H. and Harmon, W. (1992). *A Handbook to Literature*, 6th edn. New York: Macmillan.

Hope, J. and McMullan, G. (eds.) (1992). *The Politics of Tragicomedy: Shakespeare and After*. London: Routledge.

Hoy, C. (1956–62). The Shares of Fletcher and His Collaborators in the Beaumont and Fletcher Canon. *Studies in Bibliography*, 7 articles, vols. 8, 9, 11, 12, 13, 14, 15.

——(1984). The Language of Fletcherian Tragicomedy. In J. C. Gray (ed.) *Mirror Up to Shakespeare*. Toronto: University of Toronto Press, 99–113.

Hunter, G. K. (1997). *English Drama 1586–1642*. Oxford: Oxford University Press.

Jordan, C. (1997). *Shakespeare's Monarchies: Ruler and Subject in the Romances*. Ithaca, NY: Cornell University Press.

Kirsch, A. (1971). *Jacobean Dramatic Perspectives*. Charlottesville: University of Virginia Press.

Langmuir, E. and Lynton, N. (2000). *The Yale Dictionary of Art and Artists*. New Haven, CT: Yale University Press.

Leech, C. (1962). *The John Fletcher Plays*. Cambridge, MA: Harvard University Press.

McCabe, R. (1993). *Incest, Drama and Nature's Law, 1550–1700*. Oxford: Oxford University Press.

McLuskie, K. (1992). "A Maidenhead, *Amintor*, At My Yeares": Chastity and Tragicomedy in the Fletcher Plays. In J. Hope and G. McMullan (eds.) *The Politics of Tragicomedy*. London: Routledge, 92–121.

McMullan, G. (1994). *The Politics of Unease in the Plays of John Fletcher*. Amherst: University of Massachusetts Press.

Maguire, N. K. (1987). *Renaissance Tragicomedy: Explorations in Genre and Politics*. New York: AMS Press.

Markley, R. (1984). "Shakespeare to thee was dull": The Phenomenon of Fletcher's Influence. In R. Markley and L. Finke (eds.) *From Renaissance to Restoration: Metamorphoses of the Drama*. Cleveland, OH: Bellflower Press, 88–125.

Masten, J. (1997). *Textual Intercourse: Collaboration, Authorship, and Sexualities in Renaissance Drama*. Cambridge: Cambridge University Press.

Mizener, A. (1941). The High Design of *A King and No King*. *Modern Philology*, 38, 133–54.

Mowat, B. A. (1976). *The Dramaturgy of Shakespeare's Romances*. Athens, GA: University of Georgia Press.

Natoli, J. and Hutcheon, L. (eds.) (1993). *A Postmodern Reader*. Albany: State University of New York Press.

Ornstein, R. (1960). *The Moral Vision of Jacobean Tragedy*. Madison: University of Wisconsin Press.

Preminger, A. and Brogan, T. V. F. (1993). *The New Princeton Encyclopedia of Poetry and Poetics*. Princeton, NJ: Princeton University Press.

Proudfoot, G. R. (1966). Shakespeare and the New Dramatists of the King's Men. In J. R. Brown and B. Harris (eds.) *Later Shakespeare*. London: Edward Arnold, 235–61.

Shakespeare, W. (1974). *The Riverside Shakespeare*, ed. G. B. Evans. Boston, MA: Houghton-Mifflin.

——(1997). *The Two Noble Kinsmen*, ed. L. Potter. London: Thomson.

——(2000). *King Henry VIII*, ed. G. McMullan. London: Thomson.

Smith, E. (2001). Studying Shakespeare and his Contemporaries. In D. Cartmell and M. Scott (eds.) *Talking Shakespeare*. New York: Palgrave.

Thorndike, A. (1901). *The Influence of Beaumont and Fletcher on Shakespere*. London: Russell and Russell.

Waith, E. M. (1952). *The Pattern of Tragicomedy in Beaumont and Fletcher.* New Haven, CT: Yale University Press.

Wilson, H. S. (1961). *Philaster* and *Cymbeline.* In M. Bluestone and N. Rabkin (eds.) *Shakespeare's Contemporaries.* Englewood Cliffs, NJ: Prentice-Hall.

Yoch, J. J. (1987). The Renaissance Dramatization of Temperance: The Italian Revival of Tragicomedy and *The Faithful Shepherdess.* In N. K. Maguire (ed.) *Renaissance Tragicomedy.* New York: AMS Press, 114–37.

9
Place and Space in Three Late Plays

John Gillies

It should not be necessary to point out that time and place are as essential to the action as husk is to kernel, and yet these are what provoke the loudest outcry. If Shakespeare discovered the godlike art of conceiving an entire world of the most disparate scenes as one great event, then of couse it was part of the truth of his events also to idealise time and place for each scene in such a way that they too contributed to the illusion. Is there anyone in the world who is indifferent to the time and place of even trivial events in his life? And are they not particularly important in matters where the entire soul is moved, formed, and transformed? . . . The individual quality of each drama, of each separate universe, pulses through place and time in the composition of all the plays.

(Herder 1985: 170–1)

Shakespeare in a play brought in a number of men saying they had suffered shipwreck in Bohemia, where there is no sea near by some 100 miles.

(Jonson 1985: 599)

What kind of account can be given of "place" in Shakespeare's late plays? As these citations suggest, place can be thought of as looking two ways. In Herder's formulation, it turns towards the play-world as a fully assimilated (if secondary) imaginative feature. In Jonson's formulation, it looks outward: begging for confirmation in the scientific discourse of geography, a discourse in which place was becoming progressively bled of its singularity within what Henri Lefebvre calls a systematized and gridded "production of space" (Lefebvre 1991).

I begin by suggesting that the meaning of "place" is not only, nor even primarily, geographic. The three plays in question each have a "geography," but Jonson's jibe at Shakespeare's carelessness in providing Bohemia with a sea-coast has a certain justice. Ever since, it has been hard to take the geography of the late plays seriously. Apart from the sheer illiteracy betrayed (or flaunted?) here, one can imagine these plays offending Jonson's geographic conscience in other ways. Like Sidney who lamented the failure of the native English drama to observe the unities, Jonson was averse to its geographic *hubris*: both to the showing of "places" too tremendous to fit plausibly onto a stage (Jonson's dramaturgy shied away from "the vasty fields of France") and also to the rapid interchange between different countries. Rather than swell or shift a scene, Jonson is careful to "report" actions that must (given the strict time-frame) happen somewhere else, and is likewise careful to confine his stage locations to contiguous interiors, streets or meeting places, that – famously in *The Alchemist* and *Volpone* – can then be reconciled with a factual civic topography. Where Jonson's insistence on the unities was so plainly bolstered by an educated awareness of the new cartography (to the extent surely of informing his whole idea of spatial dimension and placial quality), how much more averse was he to the late plays, where Shakespeare had apparently abandoned his own brand of dramaturgical sophistication for the moldy tales and servant monsters of the earlier tradition; for plays in which wandering and scene shifting are as obtrusive as they are superfluous?

There are, conceivably, other ways in which the late plays might yet be found to have geographical interest. Elsewhere I have suggested that the theatre had more than one response to the emergence of the new cartography. The first was simply to jump onto the cartographic bandwagon. Thus in his own way (if not quite in Jonson's) Marlowe plays up to the new cartography – celebrating, rivaling, appropriating it – in the two parts of *Tamburlaine* (Gillies 1998: 19–45). Another response was to apologize – as Shakespeare does (however disingenuously) in the opening chorus of *Henry V*. Yet another response was to represent the new cartography by introducing a map or globe to the stage, only to challenge its spatial idiom with another idiom: as Shakespeare does in *King Lear*, where the spatial allure of the map (internalized by Lear and Goneril) is challenged by a more primal and phenomenological modality (such as "inside" vs. "outside") and by a more "tragic" modality in which "perspective" is eschewed as a way of intellectual and emotional coping (Gillies 2001: 109–37). Further instances of the "challenge" response are furnished by Garrett Sullivan, particularly in the case of plays such as the anonymous *Arden of Faversham* and Brome's *A Jovial Crew*, in which a cartographically entailed idea of "absolute property" is opposed by a more traditional (and cartographically independent) ethic of stewardship (Sullivan 1998). In short, a play does not need to ape the new cartography to be of cartographic interest. Notwithstanding, the spatial and placial idiom of the later plays strikes me as neither emulative, apologetic, nor oppositional. How then does it work?

I would like to begin with two propositions regarding place. First, that place is without geographic interest as conventionally understood. This is to say that the most interesting way in which place inhabits these plays owes little or nothing to the new cartography, or to a conventional embeddedness within cartographic space. To this end, I adapt some insights of the philosopher Edward S. Casey who – noting the tendency of "place" to translate itself into a subset of "space" with the growing authority of cartographic science in fifth-century Athens and seventeenth-century Europe – argues that "place" reemerges as an authoritative domain independent of space from the moment that the human body (rather than Cartesian "extension") is taken as its origin (Casey 1997). This is not to say that the geography of the later plays is without rough coherence, merely that it is without point. Place in the later plays should be understood primarily in relation to the embodied self and its needs, rather than to some abstract mathematized order. My second proposition regarding place follows from this: namely, that the predominant structural modality of place here is not that of "setting" (Herder's "husk"). The various settings of the late plays tend, like the Near-Eastern cities of *Pericles* (Antioch, Tyre, Pentapolis, Tharsis, Mitilene), to be qualitatively "thin" and virtually interchangeable. One reason we do not care that Bohemia has a sea-coast is that it is already a geographic wraith. What, then, are the ways in which place is important in these plays? Instead of being boxed into "settings," I prefer to think of the placial imagination as informing the whole narrative, symbolic and dramatic life of the plays; and moreover inspiring a rethinking of the "idea of theatre" – indeed the experience of theatre – within which the plays have their being. This placial imagination operates, I suggest, at roughly two levels, dramatic and metatheatrical.

At the first level – one mainly of fictional, symbolic, and dramatic structure – it operates in terms of opposed movements of "exposure" and "return." Exposure is precisely a displacement of the body, an abandonment to placelessness in the sense of some actively inhospitable domain, typically imagined in terms of the sea, the wilderness, or a desert island. Placelessness – the negation of place by an ungrounded or abyssal extension – is precisely what I mean by "space." Space then in my usage is not the abstract dimensionality of the new cartography, but a refusal to environ, a refusal of the body's need for accommodation or emplacement. I prefer the term "body" to the term "self" here because the body's need for emplacement is more primordial and less plastic than the self's. The self, as we shall see in *The Tempest*, has its own potential for abstraction, for a virtual and quasi-technological extension into spatiality that must remain flawed in ways suggested by Hamlet's gnomic observation: "I could be bounded in a nutshell and count myself a king of infinite space, were it not that I have bad dreams" (2.2.256–8).[1]

The term "exposure" was suggested in the course of reading Otto Rank's acount of the *Apollonius* story and associated medieval incest myths in *The Incest Theme in Literature and Legend* (Rank 1992: 271–300). What seems valuable in this entirely conventional usage is the way in which the movement of dispersal, wandering, travel/travail tends to occur in the context of attempts to escape the danger of incest (typically in the form of a prophecy of patricide). Though the "danger" will not be so narrowly defined in the late plays, use of the term "exposure" will help to foreground what might otherwise be obscure: that the motif of travel–travail is always linked to some form of pollution, abjectiveness, or malaise – if not (as in *Pericles*) to incest as such. In *Cymbeline* and *The Winter's Tale* the pollution takes the form of adultery, even if this is imagined rather than real (in the latter a hint of incest survives transition from the source, Greene's *Pandosto*). Whereas sexual pollution has no overt connection to the exposure of Prospero and Miranda in *The Tempest*, it is peculiarly an obsession with Prospero. Its avoidance is a condition of the match between Ferdinand and Miranda, and thus a condition of "return" to Italy. Sexual pollutiveness is moreover involved in the shipwreck of Alonso (who has just married his daughter to an African), and again in Caliban's attempted deflowering of Miranda. It is again (and darkly) adverted in Caliban's whole relationship with Prospero – the reluctant foster parent forced to acknowledge "this thing of darkness" (5.1.277). The point I wish to stress here is that there is a willed and abjectional element to what may sometimes strike us as unmotivated wanderings in these plays, a sense of illegitimacy. The god that rules these gulfs is not just Fortune but a dark god of sexual anxiety; whereby the body in some sense conspires in its own abandonment, its own lostness. To find oneself displaced in these plays is in some sense to have fallen.

"Return" is the opposite of exposure, returning the body to a "kindly" environment, the family bosom, the hearth and home. The forlorn are not merely made happy by the rediscovery of loved ones but led toward some form of higher or deeper "emplacement," or in a word, "home" (a 1548 *OED* entry for "home" reads: "a place, region, or state to which one properly belongs, in which one's affections centre, or where one finds rest, refuge, or satisfaction"). On rediscovering his daughter, Pericles hears the music of the spheres (among other things, an image of cosmic emplacement). Having matched Miranda with Ferdinand and consolidated his grip on the island, Prospero needs to return to Milan (where "every third thought" will be an ironic version of home – the grave). Posthumus and Imogen are reunited in the context of a new realization of what it is to inhabit "Britain." The abandoned daughter and ostracized wife of Leontes return to the bosom of Sicilia.

The "homing instinct" has another dimension. This amounts to the second of the two ways in which I find the placial imagination informing the late plays. The moments of return tend to have a metatheatrical quality. Typically, the emotions of return are so consuming, thalassic, and all-embracing as to dissolve the elastic but always tensile Elizabethan equivalent of the "fourth wall" between actors and audience. At such moments, I want to suggest, the carefully nurtured Shakespearean "idea of the theatre" worked out in plays such as *A Midsummer Night's Dream*, *Hamlet*, and *Henry V* – plays proposing a subtle dialectic between stage and auditorium – is replaced by an apparently less structured idea (or experience) of theatre, something close to what the anthropologist Victor Turner means by "communitas." Communitas, according to Turner, is to be understood as an all-but-complete state within a rite of passage in which the initiands (in our case, an audience) experience an intense, unstructured and evanescent sense of communal belongingness:

> Communitas breaks in through the interstices of structure, in liminality; at the edges of structure, in marginality . . . It is almost everywhere held to be sacred or "holy," possibly because it transgresses or dissolves the norms that govern structured and institutionalized relationships and is accompanied by feelings of unprecedented potency. The processes . . . often appear to flood their subjects with affect. (Turner 1969: 128)

Seen from the vantage of such end-crowns-all moments, the whole play appears as a rite of passage, the modality of exposure becoming the liminality or separateness necessary for reintegration and return: "Was Milan thrust from Milan that his issue

/ Should become kings of Naples? O rejoice / Beyond a common joy!" (5.1.208–10). Characteristically, such communitas moments involve a metatheatrical homecoming: an opening out from the fictive placial domain (Prospero's island, Pericles's Mediterranean) to an environing domain expressive of deeply "local" and generally "English" communal bonds. Thus, Prospero begs a notionally pious English audience to release him from the island (the desert of exposure, the stage considered as site of transitional dramatic illusion), to return him "home" (to Italy) and to "release" him into the cultural and spiritual domain of the audience itself. The communitas effect is not necessarily confined to the conclusion. Thus, the story of *Pericles* is framed by the choric figure of Gower whose "homely" voice authorizes the performance in terms of a native English story-telling tradition and "returns" the audience to a deep cultural root:

> It hath been sung at festivals,
> On ember-eves and holy-ales;
> And lords and ladies in their lives
> Have read it for restoratives (1.5–8)

Aspects of the same "homely" metatheatrical framing are also to be found in *The Winter's Tale* (the rural festivities of the fourth act) and *Cymbeline* (with its mythos of "Britain"). In what follows, I should like to elaborate placial complex in three plays: *Pericles*, *The Winter's Tale*, and *The Tempest*. I do not expect to systematically extort the entire complex from each text alike, but to focus on those aspects of it that appear to best advantage.

Pericles

Perhaps unsurprisingly for what is the seminal play of the group, *Pericles* exhibits all aspects of the complex with equal force. The fact that it is only partly Shakespearean should not prevent us from taking an archetypal view of it, as it is quite possible that Shakespeare discovered what would become the formula for the other late plays in the process of writing this play.

I suggest that the logic of "place" in *Pericles* is bound up with the original attraction of the *Apollonius* story for Shakespeare. This in turn seems to have been inseparable from the cultural image of Gower. One attraction was that the story (like Gower) was old: "*Et bonum quo antiquius eo melius*" (1.10) – the older a good thing is the better it is. We may therefore suppose that Shakespeare's conception of the story differs from Gower's own (in the *Confessio Amantis*) by virtue of the very different cultural authority with which each invests it. Where Gower had taken a relatively commonplace moral view of the story (as a warning against incest and an exhortation to base one's love on the laws of "kind"), Shakespeare takes a mystical view of it as the bearer of an ancient and perhaps vanishing cultural heritage. This story *resembled* a medieval saint's legend – "the purchase is to make men glorious" (1.9) – without, like the legend of Constance in the second book of the *Confessio*, quite being one.[2] It was sanctified by age, assimilated to an idea of a native tradition (it is surely significant that Gower's "homely" and unrhetorical style is recreated to serve as a narrative medium), and – more than one might expect of a moral tale – is oddly credited with having "restored" generations of readers.

If the age and near-sacred character of the story clearly exercised one form of attraction for Shakespeare, there was perhaps another – a paradoxical modernity. Again, the germ of this quality would appear to have originated in Gower. One of the striking qualities of Gower's version of the *Apollonius* story is the awkwardness of its logic in the context of the *Confessio*, where the story is followed by a discussion between Gower's two moralizing personae, in which "Amans" (the pupil) is enjoined to heed the warning against incest by "Confessor" (the teacher). Amans replies that whereas the negative moral of the story is clear enough (and indeed superfluous in the sense he has never harbored incestuous desires in his life) the positive moral is unclear.[3] Whereas, in other words, Amans can see why the evil are punished in this instance, he cannot understand why the good end happily. This is because, without being a saint's life as such, the story relies inconsistently on an equivalent *deus ex machina* – here called "Fortune." Hence Amans is unconvinced – not of the morality of the moral but of its efficacy. Why and how exactly does "Fortune" work to make good people happy? What is the connection between fortune and simple decency? (Neither Gower's Apollonius nor Shakespeare's Pericles is depicted as outstandingly virtuous; neither has remarkable patience or saintly charisma.) It is (I am suggesting) the very intransigence of the *Apollonius* story to Gower's purposes – its transitional quality (part saint's life, part secular romance) – that results in the proto-modern quality. Where it differs from a true saint's legend such as that of Constance, is that the element of exposure has no mooring in the authority of the sacred. Where, in other words, Constance's driftings at sea are always under divine guidance, Apollonius's voyages – his travels and travails – are relatively ungrounded. Gower's response to this anomalousness is to work it into the moral logic of the story. Though Apollonius is a king, explains the Confessor, his situation is that of every man: his ship is emblematic of the self, his kingdom – and indeed the "wyde world" that he traverses – are emblems of common domestic sway.[4] What then keeps him from miscarrying? For Gower, it is his simple decency and the fact that his love is "grounded" on the laws of kind:

> Lo, what it is to be wel grounded:
> For he hath ferst his love founded
> Honestliche as forto wedde,
> Honestliche his love he spedde
> And hadde children with his wif . . . (viii, 1993–7)

Inconsistently, Gower presents the sea and winds behaving with a kind of random malignancy during the period of Apollonius's miserable "exposures," but under divine control from the moment that Apollonius is reunited with his daughter. The timing of all this, as indeed the hero's eventual happiness itself, has patently little to do with the fact that the father's love is well grounded.

What, I suggest, was anomalous for Gower, presented an opportunity for Shakespeare. In *Pericles* the *Apollonius* story is further secularized and (without detracting from its carefully cultivated impression of antiquity) modernized. The opposing effects are, so to speak, separated out into different economies. Thus the providential effect is associated with the genius-like figure of Gower and assimilated to his culturally inflected act of choric narrative. At the level of the fiction or drama itself, however, the randomness effect is unrelieved and indeed heightened. Unlike in Gower (or indeed Petrarch, where such galleys are in principle guidable if not "charged with forgetfulnes") the ship-of-the-self here is ungrounded. It has no in-built homing mechanism. The sea of *Pericles* is stormy and calm without reason; without, that is to say, a character motive. In this respect, the fictional and dramatic pattern of *Pericles* is an extreme version of that in *King Lear* – abjection from love into the wilderness, descent into madness, eventual recognition of the lost daughter – but with the difference that the abjection of Pericles is effectively unmotivated, and to that extent more arbitrary and (potentially) more absurd. It is thus not merely the *extremity* of the relationship between exposure and return (the lack of any half-way position), but also its arbitrariness and potential absurdity that make for the modernity of this play.

What we find in *Pericles*, I suggest, is an emotive and magic-realist version of the spatial economy of Cartesian physics. In Descartes, place has been swallowed up by space. There is simply space ("extension") on the one hand and the subject on the other. *Pericles* enacts the drama of the feeling subject rather than the reflecting *cogito*. From the standpoint of human need, a placial vacuum is intolerable. While *Pericles* predates Descartes's *Discours de la Méthode* (1637) by some quarter century, there is no shortage of contemporary English expressions of spatial anxiety. Donne, for example, conveys a haunting vision of lostness in a number of poems (particularly the *Second Anniversary* and the *Hymn to God my God in my Sickness*) in which the soul attempts to reorientate itself in a world stripped of the older placial logic which had once directed it. The anxiety of lostness is if anything heightened by the sheer unlikeliness of the "homing" directions that the soul now improvises, mostly from scraps of the outmoded sacred geography (Gillies 1994: 182–8).[5] A less intellectualized but no less haunting sense of homelessness is conveyed in Isabella Whitney's *Her Will to London*, with its combination of Gower-like plainness and emotional bereftness (Whitney 1998: 1–10). This is the homeless (or barely accommodated) person's celebration of "home," a proprietorial circumambulation and mock-bequeathing of streets that refuse to acknowlege their "owner":

> And now has time put me in mind
> Of thy great cruelness,
> That never once a help would find
> To ease me in distress.
> Thou never yet wouldst credit give
> To board me for a year,
> Nor with apparel me relieve
> Except thou payed were. (ll.17–24)

The modernity of *Pericles* consists of the starkness with which it dramatizes the exposure of an ordinary man to sheer contingency, one which finds no guarantee other than in the act of story-telling itself. The greater modernity of Shakespeare's play relative to Gower's poem is suggested by two alterations to emotional character and narrative symbolism. Shakespeare's hero is emotionally frail in a way that Gower's is not. Thus, where Gower's Appolonius flees Tyre for the purely practical purpose of escaping Antiochus's vengeance, Shakespeare's Pericles is overcome by a self-conscious melancholy.

> Why should this change of thoughts,
> The sad companion, dull-ey'd melancholy,
> Be my so us'd a guest as not an hour
> In the day's glorious walk or peaceful night,
> The tomb where grief should sleep, can breed me quiet?
>
> . . .
>
> Then it is thus: the passions of the mind,
> That have their first conception by misdread,
> Have after-nourishment and life by care . . . (1.2.2–13)

While fear of Antiochus is perfectly rational in the circumstances, the tendency to reflective melancholy is morbid, hypochondrial, and excessive to dramatic needs.[6] Rank might have explained this passage as an internalization of the incest motive, a transference of guilt from Antiochus to Pericles. What I find interesting at the level of narrative symbolism is the way it links the incest episode with the theme of wandering, lending an abjectional quality to the multiple exposures that follow, and manifesting that abjection in the image of emotional disorder. Can it be accidental that the phrase "the passions of the mind" echoes the title of a popular contemporary handbook on the emotions (Wright 1601)?

The second alteration to Gower's hero and to the symbolic structure concerns the emotional prostration of the hero in relation to his reunion with the daughter. The emotional abandonment of Shakespeare's Pericles is more striking than that of Gower's Appolonius. At the news of Marina's death, Pericles *"makes lamentation, puts on sackcloth, and in a mighty passion departs"* (18.22ff.). When next we see him, within a curtained pavilion on board ship at Mitilene, he is exhibited *"reclined on a couch, unkempt and clad in sackcloth"* with the words, "Behold him. This was a goodly person" (21.28). By comparison, Gower's Appolonius is not ritually unkempt (he had vowed not to shave but this was until his daughter's marriage), nor ritually clad in sackcloth. He is "esmaied"; he curses fortune and takes to his cabin. The greater emotional prostration of Shakespeare's hero is related to a difference in the reunion with the daughter. Where Appolonius is drawn towards his daughter by an instinct of kind *before* hearing the corroborating details of her life story ("Lo, what it is to be wel grounded"), Shakespeare's Pericles is left in doubt until the whole story is told.[7] The added suspense allows emotional tension to build and elaborate itself in terms of the sea-symbolism of the name of Shakespeare's daughter. By changing the daughter's name to Marina ("For I was born at sea"), Shakespeare connects her to the principal symbol of exposure, of spatial immensity and of ungrounded contingency – the sea. Through that she is also linked to Pericles's melancholic addiction to travel (his constitutional ungroundedness), and to the incest episode behind it (his psychological ungroundedness). Hence, perhaps the startling (almost shocking) expression of the reunion in terms of an inverted begetting:

> O Helicanus, strike me, honour'd sir! . . .
> Lest this great sea of joys rushing upon me
> O'erbear the shores of my mortality,
> And drown me with their sweetness. O, come hither,
> Thou that beget'st him that did thee beget;
> Thou that wast born at sea . . . (5.1.192–6)

Where Rank would read this moment as a sentimentally disguised resurgence of the incest motive, its theatricality gives it an entirely different character. The emotional investment of this moment – in which two hopelessly ungrounded castaways "return" to each other – is made by the audience, a casual assembly of mutual strangers suddenly yoked in a delerium of closeness.

The Winter's Tale

At the level of its action, *The Winter's Tale* shows a broadly similar structural movement of abjection, exposure, and return. As in *Pericles*, the movement is precipitated by an incest-like motive, in this case an intensely imagined "adultery" with incestuous overtones in that the offending party is a bosom friend or "brother." There is in fact an eerie sense in which the adultery is felt as a direct expression of the friendship rather than a perversion of it. Thus, Leontes muses: "to mingle friendship farre is mingling bloods" (1.2.111). Again – with his eye on Mamillius but his mind perhaps on Polixenes – Leontes muses that "we are / Almost as like as eggs" (1.2.131–2). Mingling of bloods (adultery in the technical sense of exotic commixture) has a clear homology with the yolk-like mingling of friendship. The dangers of an overly close friendship are again adverted to in Leontes's idea of the sexually trespassing friend who recognizes "no bourn 'twixt his and mine" (1.2.136). Seeming to prefigure Gonzalo's invocation of the golden age topos in *The Tempest* (no "bourn, bound of land": 2.1.159), the phrase connotes the topos of golden age communism with an overtone of the sexual communism routinely attributed to the natives of the New World. It thus connotes the clearest equivalent of this idea in the play: namely, the prelapsarian friendship between Leontes and Polixenes as children.

Psychologically, too, Leontes's adultery-anxiety seems related to the felt danger of a promiscuously close friendship. Leontes convinces himself that his wife is unfaithful with his friend precisely because he is less assured of Hermione's intimacy than he is of Polixenes's. Thus, where Polixenes has been "close" to him from the beginning, Hermione has not. As Leontes bitterly remarks, Hermione had opened her hand to him only after a protracted and agonizing three-month suit. How is it possible for Polixenes to refuse the request of his intimate friend, yet bow to the request of the friend's wife (unless of course, he was more intimate with the wife than he was with the friend)? Such suggestions are underlined by the fact that Hermione is heavily pregnant, and that the term of her pregnancy has coincided exactly with Polixenes's nine-month visit. Is Polixenes's initial anxiety to leave occasioned by a fear of looking on the child? Alternatively, is his decision to stay occasioned by a reassurance that he can look on the child without danger?

Again as in *Pericles*, but far more subtly and powerfully, the incest motive (or its adulterous equivalent) is spatialized or geographized. Exposure of the notionally misbegotten child requires a sea voyage not merely to "some remote and desert place, quite out / Of our dominions" (2.3.176–7), but to the haunt of strangers:

> As by strange fortune
> It came to us, I do in justice charge thee,
> . . . That thou commend it strangely to some place
> Where chance may nurse or end it. (2.3.179–83)[8]

Having transgressed, Polixenes is no longer an intimate but a foreigner. This symbolic relation of the intensely intimate and the extensively spatial is adverted to early in a strikingly baroque image:

> Sicilia cannot show himself over-kind to Bohemia. They were trained together in their childhoods, and there rooted betwixt them then such an affection which cannot choose but branch now . . . that they have seemed to be together, though absent; shook hands, as over a vast; and embraced, as it were, from the ends of opposed winds. (1.1.20–30)

The two friends embrace from opposite ends of a "world" map or its ornamental frame, positions conventionally occupied by personified Winds.[9] Unlike those, however, the friends reach out over the "vast" cartographic surface, simultaneously adverting to and annulling it. It is noteworthy that this playfully climactic image should begin the play rather than end it. What this tells us is that the play begins where it should end: with a "return," a species of "homecoming" after a long and geographically mediated separation. Shortly afterwards, Leontes imagines a morbid inversion of this cleverly conceited marriage of bodies and cartographized spaces: "'tis powerful, think it, / From east, west, north and south; be it concluded, / No barricado for a belly" (1.2.203–5).

Again, as in *Pericles*, this spatialized pattern of abjection, exposure, and return is mediated at a self-consciously theatrical level. Unlike in *Pericles*, however, where the metatheatrical element is relatively transparent, in this play it is so audacious and original as to almost defy interpretation from our belated historical standpoint. I suggest that the three spatial movements of *The Winter's Tale* – from Sicilia to Bohemia and back to Sicilia – are accompanied by three different species of theatrical self-consciousness, effectively three different "ideas" of theatre. The first is an anti-theatrical idea of theatre, the second a localized idea of theatre, and the third a "sacred theatre."

To begin with, I want to suggest that Leontes's jealousy is theatrically problema-tized in the sense of having little plausibility or pretext. Where, in other words, it was open to Shakespeare to provide a naturalistic "motivation" or pretext – such as that provided by Robert Greene in *Pandosto*, where Pandosto's wife is so fond of the friend "that her countenance bewrayed how her mind was affected," and so familiar with the friend as to visit him in his bedchamber – Shakespeare conspicuously with-holds a naturalizing pretext, thereby creating a theatrical "problem" (Pafford 1976: 185–6). Why? Part of the answer, I suggest, is that Shakespeare is interested in the wider problem of what Stanley Cavell calls "scepticism" (Cavell 1987). Leontes sus-pects Hermione not because he has "evidence" of her infidelity (all he has are baseless circumstantial cues) but because he makes the mistake of seeking an evidentiary basis for his faith in her. Instead, therefore, of believing in Hermione, in the absence of a reason *not* to believe in her, Leontes suspends belief because such belief can never be justified in evidentiary terms. What Leontes demands is certain *knowledge* of another mind, exactly what Cartesian skepticism recognized to be impossible. In attempting to *see* the truth (Othello's "ocular proof") rather than *feel* it, Leontes begins to "the-atricalize" Hermione and Polixenes (as Cavell would have it), treating them as a kind of spectacle, a play of mere surfaces and gestures. Because the gestures are treated as feigned and because the eye penetrates no further than the surface, the resulting "show" ("paddling palms and pinching fingers": 1.2.117) is skeptically overdeter-mined ("All's true that is mistrusted": 2.1.50). It is surely no accident that Leontes's skeptical reading of this compulsively theatricalized spectacle should coincide closely with the terms in which the theatre was read by antitheatrical pamphleteers. Here too is an obsessive focus on surfaces: "such wantone gestures, such bawdie speaches: such laughing and fleering: such kissing and bussing: such clipping and culling: such winckinge and glancinge of wanton eyes" (Stubbes 1972). On the one hand, the the-atrical body is skeptically drained of its ostensible meaning. On the other hand, it is reinvested with oceans of complicitous promiscuity. Hence, surely, Leontes's compul-sive repetitions of the word "play" ("Go play, boy, play, thy mother plays and I / Play too . . .": 1.2.188–9). Fidelity is played rather than truly meant. The word "playing" is preferred to the word "acting" for the reason that "playing" was the derogatory, morally questionable, equivalent of "acting" – and hence routinely preferred by the antitheatricalists in their denunciations of the stage.

This "Sicilian" species of theatrical self-consciousness gives way to a "Bohemian" phase towards the end of the third act. Before explaining what I mean by the latter, however, I would like to note two revealing oddities about "Sicilia" and "Bohemia." The first is that while Shakespeare borrowed these names from the source, he reversed the order in which he found them. In *Pandosto* the first movement of the story is located in "Bohemia" and the second in "Sicilia." The second oddity is that whereas both locations are equally notional in Greene, they are not equally notional in Shakespeare. What I mean by this is that whereas "Sicilia" is placially "thin" in Shakespeare, "Bohemia" is placially "thick" or marked by a strong local accent: that which an English audience (and probably only an English audience) must have located in the England of rural tradition. This adds a whole structural dimension to Shakespeare's play relative to the source, with the countrified "Bohemia" relating to the courtly "Sicilia" in the pastoral way that the Forest of Arden relates to the court in *As You Like It*. This in turn suggests an interesting reason for Bohemia's being given a sea-coast in Shakespeare. While Shakespeare may just have been echoing Greene ("the mariners described the coast of Bohemia"), it is more likely that he was indulging a theatrical joke (Pafford 1976: 217). Shakespeare's reversal of the two locales means that the journey of exposure is in a northerly direction rather than a southerly (the direction in Greene). What this suggests is that Shakespeare's Bohemia has a sea-coast because it is, for all theatrical purposes, England.

What does localization mean, and what is its logic in *The Winter's Tale*? I have borrowed this term from the Japanese performance tradition where it suggests a Shakespeare performance which is not merely "contemporized" but "localized"; injected with elements of local meaning that only a local would find meaningful.[10] Typically this takes the form of lighthearted in-joking. The effect is furtive rather than sustained, in keeping with its inherently "ludicrous" premise (that assimilating Shakespeare to Japan is more of a jest than an article of faith).[11] Unlike "setting," localization tends not to work in terms of standardized nor universalized signs (it is more code than sign, essentially for local consumption). Again unlike setting, localization works characteristically by breaking the frame of representation. It is more *plataea* than *locus* (to adopt Robert Weimann's understanding of the medieval distinction between the stage domain of audience address, and the stage domain of illusion) (Weimann 1978: 73–85). The first irruption of the local is signaled by the stage direction "*Exit, pursued by a bear*" (3.3.56ff.). The bear is local not because bears were native to England at the time of the play but because bears were local to the Bankside. In a sense the joke works by contrasting the levels of *locus* and *plataea*. The bear is thus simultaneously "distant" ("places remote enough are in Bohemia") at the level of placial illusion or *locus*, and uncannily "local" or "here" at the level of *plataea*. The shepherd and the clown are similarly localized and similarly irruptive: the storm, the sinking of the ship, the devouring of Antigonus are all turned into a theatrical joke as the *locus* of exposure becomes the *plataea* of return, of "kindliness," of "home."

In the fourth act proper, localized theatrical values become the norm. The songs, the references to cony-catching, the sheep-shearing feast, the flower ritual, the suggestion of "Whitsun pastorals" all create a mood which is self-consciously theatrical as well as pastoral. As in the first act, the modality of "playing" is underlined. Again, this connotes something mysteriously conspiratorial. The gods "conspire" with Autolycus in his knavery. The "borrowed flaunts" (costumery) worn by Perdita as queen of the feast conspire to "alter" her "disposition." Here, however, the theatricalized body is transfigured rather than emptied. Playing partakes of the sacred, the kindly. Playing too is less a discrete object of skeptical view than an enveloping form of "entertainment," a *communitas* in which auditorium and stage become as one.

These energies are carried back to Sicilia where they prepare us for a third and patently sacred form of theatre. While the discovery of Perdita is like a ballad or old tale "to be hooted at," the statue scene is a kind of Miracle play. Again, as in the first act, Hermione presents herself to Leontes as a theatricalized object of vision. Again, too, the bodily surface becomes the focus of close attention ("What fine chisel / Could ever yet cut breath?" 5.3.79–80). The homology with the theatricalized body in the first act is of course reversed. In place of a full body threatened with skeptical emptying, Leontes confronts an apparently empty or artifactual body awaiting the touch of faith.

The Tempest

At one level, *The Tempest* represents a return to the radical and ungrounded tension between the self and spatiality that I have posited in *Pericles*. Exposure is the dominant modality. The self is exposed to or poised over a threatening and abyssal spatiality (sea, storm, oceanic distances) from a tenuous placial vantage point that is more "site" than place (the island, the cell, the stage). While the possibility of reaching "home" is adverted to in the last act and in the Epilogue, nobody – neither characters nor audience – finds their way home in the moment of the play. Unlike in *The Winter's Tale*, the ludic element does not of itself redeem. While – as "rough magic" and the masques of Ariel – no doubt vital in resurrecting Prospero's fortunes, it is too heavily invested in a single character's agenda and to that extent too circumscribed to be redemptive in the wider existential sense of the two earlier plays. Instead of reaching out to embrace the audience's communal being, the stage is as limited, anonymous, temporary, and provisional a site as the island is. Neither place nor theatre have the value of "home."

The Tempest is a play of multiple exposures. In chronological order first Sycorax, next Prospero and Miranda, and finally the castaways of the opening scene are exposed on the island. While Caliban was born on the island, he had been carried there in Sycorax's womb and was the reason for her exposure. So he too is a castaway. Only Ariel seems native to the island, yet at the end of the play he returns to the elements rather than to the island. In this sense then, the island is essentially "bare." It has no natives. Its life is provisional upon the exposures and exposing to which it plays host. Even considered as a *locus*, the island is more site than place. Anonymous, simultaneously barren and fertile, desert and paradise, Atlantean and Mediterranean, it has the qualities of many islands but the identity of none. It is the site or condition of a curiously solipsistic and proactive exposure. Prospero's ability to turn exposure from a passive to an active state has something to do with another site within the island:

his "cell." At once a shelter and an interior, the cell is an inner sanctum, a laboratory, a factory, and a back-stage. While the cell does not have the value of "home," it does have the value of a "room." It guarantees a vital measure of privacy. It is where Prospero can see but not be seen – not even by the audience.

Defining (and to some extent interpenetrating) the island is an abyssal and devouring space: "the never surfeited sea," the ocean, the tempest, the whole elemental world. Vastness – the impression of a spatiality beyond human grasp; a temporality beyond human recall – is a repeated effect. Distances are so vast as to be phantasmal. Tunis is "so far from Italy removed" that Alonso despairs of seeing his daughter again. For Antonio and Sebastian, that same daughter seems yet further. Claribel,

> She that is Queen of Tunis; she that dwells
> Ten leagues beyond man's life; she that from Naples
> Can have no note, unless the sun were post –
> The man i' th' Moon's too slow – till newborn chins
> Be rough and razorable; she that from whom
> We were all sea-swallowed. (2.1.251–6)

As in Donne's "That Unripe Side of Earth," where the new world is so far off as to be insulated from the Fall, distance confounds revelation and history. Distance, however, is not the only form of vastness. Prospero speaks of his urchins working in "that vast of night," suggesting a cosmic spatial depth (a vision of the night sky perhaps). Time too – "the dark, backward and abysm of time" across which Miranda's memories come – has this quality. Abyssal too is the tendency for figures to be swallowed up by or imprisoned in matter or in nature. Ships are "sea swallowed." The sea is "never surfeited." Alonso lies "full fathom five" where his body is subject to undreamed-of mutations. Ariel is confined by Sycorax within a pine, and threatened by Prospero with imprisonment in "the knotty entrails of an oak." Also abyssal is the use of the word "hollow" in relation to sounds on the island. Antonio and Sebastian report "a hollow burst of bellowing." Thunder is continually heard as an aural signifier – detached from its conventional signified, a storm. Finally, and most mysteriously of all, the dance of nymphs and reapers that was to have concluded the masque of Ceres dissolves to "*a strange, hollow and confused noise*" (4.1.142ff.).

The tension between this actively menacing spatiality and the self is thus extreme. While suggesting *Pericles* to this extent, however, *The Tempest* differs to the extent of radically altering the meaning of this tension. Here – rather as in the cartographic conceit of the two friends at the ends of opposed winds in *The Winter's Tale* – the self is the master of the abyss rather than its slave. While the extent of Prospero's control over space is unique within Shakespeare, he does have a certain kinship with a class of "closet warriors" (mathematicians, military cartographers, model-drawers) from earlier plays; men who, like Cassio and Ulysses, model the turbulence of the real world from a position of closeted but all-seeing detachment (Gillies 1998: 30–1). Prospero's command over space, however, is far greater than theirs. His "prescience" is celestial as well as geographical. He "reads" the track described by Alonso's voyage from Tunis and also its conjunction with the "most auspicious star" of his own fortunes. In addition to merely reading space of course, Prospero is able to bend it to his will. He causes storms (or appears to cause them). He sinks ships (or appears to sink them). In Ariel, moreover, he commands an athlete of metamorphosis; a being whose intelligence and will are at once a projection of his own and yet interpenetrable with space and the elements.

If Prospero's "rough magic" is not exactly reducible to the new cartography, it does have a powerful resonance with it via what we may call the construction of the subject in cartographic discourse. Thus Prospero's control or oversight of space is linked with his temperance and self-control while the spatial impotence of his enemies is linked to their emotional and intellectual infirmity:

> Who was so firm, so constant, that this coil
> Would not infect his reason? (1.2.207–8)

The contrast between Prospero and his victims recalls a cartographic commonplace whereby the cartographer is imagined cozily insulated from the dangers of travel in the real world by the virtuality of cartographic "travel."[12] But it more particularly recalls a stronger statement of the same idea in contemporary treatises on the emotions where the passions are imagined in terms of a tempestuous seascape, while temperance is imagined in the image of cartographic foresight:

> Wherefore the waves of passion, and billows of apparent reasons, so shake the sandy shelfe of a weake will, that they mingle it with them, and make all one . . . wee may compare the soule without passions, to a calme sea . . . but the passionate to a raging gulfe swelling with waues, surging by temptests, minacing the stony rockes, and endeuoring to ouerthrow mountaines.

> An angry man raiseth brawles . . . men had neede of an Astrolabe alwayes, to see in what height or eleuation his affections are. (Wright 1601: 100, 10)

Prospero's spatial mastery then is due not just to a superior technology but also to a superior mental and emotional equilibrium. While just as ungrounded as in *Pericles*, then, the subject is upheld here by a combination of technological "extension" and moral vision.

"Rough magic" is also a metaphor of theatre. Having stranded his enemies on the island, Prospero splits them into different groups – respectively, Ferdinand, Alonso's court, and the servants – and then subjects each to a tailored mix of temptation, moral ordeal, and physical progress around the island. As with the storm, the object is to provoke a passionate response. Once raised or smoked out, however, these passions form the raw ingredients of three morality plays in which the erring mortals are confronted with masquelike "discoveries" of their own shortcomings or achievements. Prospero's "theatre of the self," however, is not quite coincident with the wider play or indeed with the overwhelming tendency of Shakespearean dramaturgy.

Shakespeare's drama is not in general consciously "redemptive" or "reformative" in the narrow terms of the theatrical *autos sacramental* to which Prospero subjects the castaways on the island.[13] There is another important difference. Whereas Shakespearean plots tend to arise indifferently from the actions of many characters while belonging to none in particular, the plot of *The Tempest* is projected by a single character onto others. Prospero choreographs the other characters, he plots them in the cartographic sense as well as the fictive sense, he maps them.

For all its mapping and all its self-control, however, the Cartesian self is not finally insulated from abyssal spatiality and passion. Prospero's control of extensive and interior domains is as haunted as Hamlet's fantastic kingdom of "infinite space." The effort to control seems inseparable from anger, anxiety, and possibly bad conscience. The most compelling image of his emotional frailty comes after the dissolution of the masque of Ceres:

> Your father's in some passion
> That works him strongly
>
> . . .
>
> Never till this day
> Saw I him touched with anger so distempered.
>
> . . .
>
> Sir, I am vext.
> Bear with my weakness; my old brain is troubled.
> Be not disturbed with my infirmity . . .
> . . . A turn or two I'll walk
> To still my beating mind. (4.1.143–63)

The moment is a notorious crux. Why should Prospero start "suddenly" and speak as the masque is concluding in a "graceful dance"? We are invited to look beyond the immediate pretext ("I had forgot that foul conspiracy / Of the beast Caliban": 4.1.139–40) to the acknowledgment of mortality in the "Our revels now are ended" speech. Our life is founded over the abyss – "the dark, backward and abysm of time" – and must eventually be swallowed by it. So too the symbols of Prospero's art – the staff and the book – are swallowed by the earth and the sea respectively. Ultimately there is no ground, no home, and no insulation from the abyss. There is only the possibility of a prayer in the mind of the departing playgoer.

NOTES

1   All references to playtexts are from William Shakespeare, *The Complete Works*, ed. Stanley Wells and Gary Taylor (Oxford: Clarendon Press, 1994).

2   For a true Saint's legend, Shakespeare needed to look no further than the legend of Constance in Book 2 of the *Confessio*. The story resembles *Apollonius* closely but for its explicitly Christian and

miraculous content, and for the fact that the hero is female. Constance, the saintly daughter of the emperor, has a talent for converting and winning the love of pagan kings. She is set adrift ("exposed") at various stages of her story by the detraction of evildoers, but overcomes all adversity by patience and miraculous power. Her son Moris (fathered by the converted Saxon king) eventually becomes emperor. The story incorporates implicitly incestuous material. Two of Constance's rivals are mothers of converted kings. Each is murderously opposed to this female rival for their son's love. When the mother of the Saxon king informs him that his wife has given birth to a monster, Constance is set adrift with the baby. Before dying she is joyfully reunited with her royal Saxon husband.

3 The passage bears quoting in full:

> Mi fader, hou so that it stonde,
> Youre tale is herd and understonde,
> As thing which worthi is to hiere,
> Of gret ensample and gret matiere,
> Whereof, my fader, god you quyte.
> Bot in this point miself aquite
> I mai riht wel, that nevere yit
> I was assoted in my wit,
> Bot only in that worthi place
> Wher alle lust and alle grace
> Is set, if that danger ne were.
> Bot that is al my moste fere:
> I not what ye fortune accompte . . . (viii, 2029–41)

4

> For conseil passeth alle thing
> To him which thenkth to ben a king;
> And every man for his partie
> A kingdom hath to justifie,
> That is to sein his oghne dom.
> If he misreule that kingdom,
> He lest himself, and that is more
> Than if he loste Schip and Ore
> And al the worldes good withal:
> For what man that in special
> Hath noght himself, he hath noght elles. . . .
> Thogh he hadde at his retenue
> The wyde world riht as he wolde,
> Whan he his herte hath noght withholde
> Toward himself, al is in vein . . . (viii, 2109–25)

5 For an analysis of the *Hymn to God my God in my Sickness*, see Gillies (1994).

6 This scene has been thought so odd by Philip Edwards and F. D. Hoeniger as to reflect textual corruption. Edwards (1952: 25–49) has attempted a reconstruction along more logically consistent lines, which is followed by Hoeniger (1969: 180–2). Even allowing for the reconstruction, however, Pericles's emotional self-absorption is remarkable.

7

> With that he sobreth his corage
> And put away his hevy chiere.
> Bot of hem tuo a man mai liere
> What it is to be sibb of blod:

> Non wiste of other hou it stod,
> And yit the fader ate laste
> His herte upon this maide caste,
> That he hire loveth kindely,
> And yit he wiste nevere why.

8   Pafford (1976: 52) explains that "Polixenes was a stranger and he . . . brought the child. Therefore it is but justice that it be committed 'as a foreigner'; or, 'to some foreign place'."

9   "World" here is intended in the elastic sense of the conventional "Orbis Terrarum," which could mean anything from the Mediterranean-centered Ptolemaic world to the truly global world of the Discoveries (Gillies 1994: 1–39).

10 This sense of "localization" might be distinguished from a more overtly "Japanized" form, in which the local element is invested with a kind of "brand label" level of recognizability, such that it is readable by foreigners as well as native Japanese. *Ninagawa Macbeth* would be a case in point. The samurai setting is a universally recognizable "Japanese" signature.

11 A fine example of this kind of localization is a production of *A Midsummer Night's Dream* by Norio Deguchi. This is set in the school that the director attended, and in the period in which he attended it (the late 1940s). Far from being universally accessible, this setting requires – and works by invoking – a deep and intimately nuanced local knowledge.

12 Thomas Cunningham celebrates the cartographer's ability to "drawe a Carde for Spaine, Fraunce, Germany, Italye, Graece, or any perticular regio: yea, in a warme & pleasant house, without the perill of the raging Seas: danger of enemies: losse of time: spending of substaunce: werines of body or anguishe of minde" (Cunningham 1968: fol. 120).

13 I use the term loosely. The *auto sacramental* was a Spanish form of sacred drama often with a mytho-logical and allegorical caste. According to *The New Princeton Encyclopedia of Poetry and Poetics*, "one of the most typical autos is *El gran teatro del mundo*, based on the *theatrum mundi* metaphor, in which God is the Director of the play of human life, distributing costumes and dividing the performance into three acts" (Preminger and Brogan 1993: 112).

References and Further Reading

Casey, E. S. (1997). *The Fate of Place: A Philosophical History*. Berkeley: University of California Press.

Cavell, S. (1987). *Disowning Knowledge in Six Plays of Shakespeare*. Cambridge: Cambridge University Press.

Cunningham, W. (1968) [1559]. *The Cosmographicall Glasse* (London, 1559). *The English Experience* No. 44. Amsterdam: Theatrum Orbis Terrarum; New York: De Capo Press.

Descartes, R. (1976a). *Discours de la méthode*, ed. E. Gilson. Paris: Librairie Philosophique.

——(1976b). *Discourse on Method*, trans. L. J. Lafleur. Indianapolis, IN: Bobbs-Merrill.

Donne, J. (1980). *The Complete English Poems*, ed. A. J. Smith. Harmondsworth: Penguin Books.

Edwards, P. (1952). An Approach to the Problem of *Pericles. Shakespeare Survey*, 5.

Gillies, J. D. (1994). *Shakespeare and the Geography of Difference*. Cambridge: Cambridge University Press.

——(1998). Introduction: Elizabethan Drama and the Cartographizations of Space. In J. Gillies and V. M. Vaughan (eds.) *Playing the Globe: Genre and Geography in English Renaissance Drama*. Madison, WI: Fairleigh Dickinson University Press.

——(2001). The Scene of Cartography in *King Lear*. In A. Gordon and B. Klein (eds.) *Literature, Mapping, and the Politics of Space in Early Modern England*. Cambridge: Cambridge University Press.

Gower, J. (1957). *Confessio Amantis*. In G. C. Macaulay (ed.) *John Gower's English Works*, vol. 2, Early English Text Society. Extra Series, LXXXII. Oxford: Oxford University Press.

Herder, J. G. (1985) [1773]. Shakespeare. In H. B. Nisbet (ed.) *German Aesthetic and Literary Criticism: Winckelmann, Lessing, Hamann, Herder, Schiller, Goethe*. Cambridge: Cambridge University Press.

Hoeniger, F. D. (ed.) (1969). *Pericles, The Arden Shakespeare.* London: Methuen.

Jonson, B. (1985). Conversations with Drummond. In I. Donaldson (ed.) *Ben Jonson.* Oxford: Oxford University Press, 599.

Lefebvre, H. (1991). *The Production of Space,* trans. D. Nicholson-Smith. Oxford: Blackwell.

Pafford, J. H. P. (ed.) (1976). *The Winter's Tale, The Arden Shakespeare.* London: Methuen.

Preminger, A. and Brogan, T. V. F. (eds.) (1993). *The New Princeton Encyclopedia of Poetry and Poetics.* Princeton, NJ: Princeton University Press.

Rank, O. (1992). *The Incest Theme in Literature and Legend: Fundamentals of a Psychology of Literary Creation.* Baltimore, MD: Johns Hopkins University Press.

Shakespeare, W. (1994). *The Complete Works,* ed. S. Wells and G. Taylor. Oxford: Clarendon Press.

Stubbes, P. (1972) [1583]. *The Anatomie of Abuses. The English Experience,* No. 489. Amsterdam: Theatrum Orbis Terrarum; New York: Da Capo Press.

Sullivan, G. A., Jr. (1998). *The Drama of Landscape: Land, Property, and Social Relations on the Early Modern Stage.* Stanford, CA: Stanford University Press.

Turner, V. (1969). *The Ritual Process: Structure and Anti-Structure.* London: Routledge.

Weimann, R. (1978). *Shakespeare and the Popular Tradition in the Theater.* Baltimore, MD: Johns Hopkins University Press.

——(2000). *Author's Pen and Actor's Voice: Playing and Writing in Shakespeare's Theatre.* Cambridge: Cambridge University Press.

Whitney, I. (1988). *Her Will To London.* In M. Wynne-Davies (ed.) *Women Poets of the Renaissance.* London: Dent, 1–10.

Wright, T. (1601). *The Passions of the Minde.* London.

10
The Politics and Technology of Spectacle in the Late Plays
David M. Bergeron

Andrew Gurr briefly contrasts the staging demands of *The Winter's Tale* and *The Tempest*: "as a general rule the better the playwright the less spectacle there was likely to be in his plays . . . The one play of Shakespeare's that makes great use of stage spectacle and business is *The Tempest*, a play in which Shakespeare seems almost to have been mocking his own art by the closeness with which he observed the neoclassical unities of time and place" (Gurr 1992: 191). This reliance on the unities certainly sets this play apart from *The Winter's Tale*. Gurr concludes this paragraph: "The stage business in *The Tempest* operates as a metaphor of Prospero's and Shakespeare's arts, of course, and is closed to our questions for that reason. But it does raise a suspicion about how deeply Shakespeare's tongue was embedded in his cheek in the last plays." I find these final two sentences cryptic and puzzling.

I do not know why we cannot question the way that the spectacle of *The Tempest* may serve as a metaphor about Shakespeare's art, nor do I embrace the notion that Shakespeare had his tongue firmly embedded in his cheek in the last plays. Such an idea raises doubt about the seriousness of these plays and the relevance of their spectacle. I will be arguing just the opposite: namely, that the spectacle of the late plays does not function as an idle ornament, nor is it a sign of a lesser playwright, but rather spectacle contributes to the serious purpose of these plays, including political issues. I take my cue from Samuel Daniel in his dedication to *The Vision of the Twelve Goddesses*, a 1604 masque, in which he suggests that ornaments concur "to the decking and furnishing of glory and majesty as the necessary complements requisite for state and greatness" (Daniel 1967: 25). The seemingly redundant doubling of terms – decking–furnishing, glory–majesty, necessary–requisite – calls attention to the intertwined nature of display and purpose. Such spectacles as complements make majesty and greatness complete.

We rightly ask why this preoccupation with spectacle at the end of Shakespeare's career. I will venture a few reasons that the subsequent discussion will examine. At least since the 1870s with Edward Dowden's naming of these final plays as "romances," scholars have grouped them together in part because they share characteristics common to traditions of romance. Spectacle does not equal romance, but it certainly contributes to and resides in romance. I think especially of the presence of the supernatural in romance, which often leads to spectacular event, as in, for example, the Greek romance *Daphnis and Chloe* or the English medieval chivalric romance *Sir Gawain and the Green Knight*. Such spectacle may be part of a theophany in romance; therefore, spectacle complements romance. Northrop Frye writes: "Romance has its own conception of an ideal society, but that society is in a higher world than that of ordinary experience" (Frye 1976: 150). This "higher world" to which romance may aspire can be epitomized in transcendental, supernatural events. I am suggesting that spectacle in the late plays may grow out of romance conventions and that Shakespeare's decision to pursue romance opens his narratives to the supernatural and spectacle. Gods and goddesses as presiding spirits over the final plays give rise to certain stage business that represents their power beyond ordinary experience.

Clearly, various productions of masques and pageants and their spectacular events influenced Shakespeare's Romances. The early years of King James's English reign resonate with multiple entertainments, public and private, not occurring in ordinary theatre buildings but rather at court or in London's streets. We have reason to think that Shakespeare, with other members of the King's Men, stood along London's streets for the magnificent royal entry pageant honoring James on March 15, 1604. If so, he could have seen an exceptional array of technical displays, including the seven extravagant and exquisite triumphal arches. Several decades ago Glynne Wickham observed that pageantry constitutes the "quintessence of emblematic art" (Wickham 1963, 2: 209). It takes no extraordinary leap of imagination to see Shakespeare's final plays as participating in emblematic art with their frequent disregard for neat, unfolding narrative lines. The nearest practical source would have been masques and pageants. Frye has cogently argued that "the structure of the romances thus approximates the complete polarity of the anti-masque and masque" (Frye 1978: 30). He even makes the startling suggestion that Shakespeare "may have been temperamentally closer to the masque than Jonson was." The nuptial masque in *The Tempest* shows its indebtedness to other dramatic forms.

The anthropologist Clifford Geertz, writing about kingship and pageant celebrations, observes: "A world wholly demystified is a world wholly depoliticized" (Geertz 1983: 143); that is, to strip the world of symbolism and spectacle (mystification) renders it politically empty. To turn Geertz's statement around: creating a mystery, a mythology, leads to a fully political world. This Shakespeare does in the final plays. Political display, Daniel reminds us, thus embraces spectacle and evokes romance. As I have argued elsewhere, the politics of the Stuart royal family permeates Shakespeare's Romances (Bergeron 1985). The events in this political family form a "text" that Shakespeare knew and appropriated. Certainly the celebratory spectacles associated with the royal family loom large in the public imagination in the early seventeenth century, and they help mystify this family. For Shakespeare, romance does not constitute an escape but rather an elevation of political issues. And spectacle complements political matters in his plays as in the Jacobean world.

Spectacle: Masques and Pageants

A dramatic text contemporaneous with Shakespeare's final plays includes this description:

> In a goodly Island styled *Insula Beata*, or the land of Happynes, we suppose that true *Majesty* holdeth her government: This island is round engirt with rich Rockes of Gold Oare and Chrisolytes, the maine Ocean also running naturally about it . . . There, in a golden Feild or Garden . . . where all the Trees and Fruites are of pure golde, do we erect *Majesties* watch Tower, which being square, consisteth of very artificial Colloms, Arches, Cornish, Freeze and other skilfull Architecture, but the whole bodie therof being so transparant, as both she and her royall attendants may be easily therein discerned. (Munday 1985: 27)

The figure Majesty sits in a rich throne, emblematically costumed and carrying a mound in her left hand and a golden scepter in her right. Directly beneath her sits Religion, "in a Virgin vesture of pure white." Other allegorical figures accompany them. On the back side reside Tranquility and the Three Graces, elaborately costumed, each carrying a symbolic shield. Four Tritons dance upon the billows of the sea "at the severall corners of the Island" (p. 28). What do we read here; what dramatic form gives rise to such spectacle? The technology of this spectacle, perhaps contrary to our expectations, belongs not to a court masque but to Anthony Munday's Lord Mayor's Show of 1609, *Camp-bell, or The Ironmongers Faire Feild*, performed in the streets of London for the inauguration of the new Lord Mayor on October 29. The intersection of built structures, emblematic costuming, and allegorical purpose defines the technology of spectacle, whether in masque or pageant.

In what follows I concentrate on performances of masques and pageants in two key years, 1604 and 1610. On March 15, 1604, as noted above, James made a procession through the City of London, starting at the Tower and moving westward. This civic pageant, long delayed because of the plague, captures our attention for several reasons, including the performance by the well-known actor Edward Alleyn, and the principal writing by Ben Jonson and Thomas Dekker (with one speech by Thomas Middleton). The City spent extravagantly and labored for months to make this spectacle possible. Dekker and Jonson produced texts, and so did the architect Stephen Harrison.[1] Harrison produced his *Arches of Triumph* (1604), which includes engravings by William Kip of the seven triumphal arches – the primary pictorial evidence that we have of civic pageants from this period. Harrison oversaw the construction of the arches, arranged for Kip to do the engravings, and in the text included the speeches, a description of what happened at the arches, and added some details not found in the other texts. Furthermore, the colophon says: "Imprinted at London by John Windet, Printer to the Honourable Citie of London, and are to be sold at the Authors house in Lime-street, at the signe of the Snayle. 1604" (sig. K1). Harrison thus adds to his tasks the selling of copies of the book from his own house – a busy man indeed, involved in all the technical functions of the pageant.

John Peacock has assessed the achievement of these triumphal arches: "In fact the arches are teeming farragos of infelicitous detail, their chaos emphasised by a busy, rebarbative Flemish mannerist style" (Peacock 1995: 63). This heavy-handed, overwrought evaluation fails to recognize Harrison's accomplishment. I will comment briefly on Harrison's technical, practical skills that served the purposes of spectacle and politics, including not only designing the arches but also figuring out how and where they would fit in London's narrow streets. In sometimes brilliant ways, Harrison solved technological problems. The first arch, for example, designed by Jonson and executed by Harrison, contained the City of London carved in realistic miniature on its top. Placed in Fenchurch Street, the arch, Harrison says, had its "backe . . . leaning on the East ende of the Church, that it overspread the whole streete" (sig. C1). He demonstrates his practical knowledge of the ancient orders of architecture when he describes this arch: "This Gate of *Passage*, then . . . was derived from the *Tuscana* (beeing the principal pillar of those 5. upon which the *Noble frame of Architecture* doth stand." Harrison uses Corinthian columns in the second and third arches, pyramids in the New Arabia arch, four great French terms in the Garden of Plenty arch, and round towers and ballisters in the New World arch. The Garden of Plenty Harrison situates at the Little Conduit in Cheapside, "which joyning to the backe of it, served (or might bee supposed to have bene) as a Fountain to water the fruits of this *Garden of Plenty*" (sig. G1). Art appropriates its real-world setting for symbolic purposes. In the difficult environment of London's cramped streets Harrison solved technical problems, making the spectacle dazzle in this greatest public appearance by the new king. Actors, playwrights, musicians, workers, and architects join together in the City's efforts to honor the king artfully.

The year began with Daniel's masque, *The Vision of the Twelve Goddesses*, performed at Hampton Court on January 8 at the request of Queen Anne, who favored Daniel for years. This masque set in motion a pattern of elaborate court masques that prevailed in the Stuart era. This one included a performance by the queen and other aristocratic women who portrayed the twelve goddesses. Like civic pageants, masques move back and forth across boundaries between fiction and reality; indeed, the culmination of a masque comes with dancing by the courtly audience. Daniel offers a spare text, in terms of stage directions that clarify the spectacle required. But he makes up for this with a long epistle dedicatory addressed to Lucy, Countess of Bedford, the epistle exceeding in length the masque itself. In this intriguing document Daniel makes clear that his spectacle serves larger moral and political purposes.

Daniel describes his method of spectacle: "And to this purpose were these Goddesses thus presented in their proper and several attires, bringing in their hands the particular figures of their power which they gave to the Temple of Peace, erected upon four pillars, representing the four Virtues that supported a globe of the earth" (Daniel 1967: 26). Juno, the goddess of empire, appears first, "in a sky-colour mantle embroidered with gold and figured with peacocks' feathers, wearing a crown of gold on her head." And thus Daniel indicates the costume of the goddesses. The action begins when Night awakens her son Somnus, sleeping in a cave. Iris "descends from the top of a mountain raised at the lower end of the hall, and marching up to the Temple of Peace, gives notice to the Sibylla of the coming of the Goddesses" (p. 29). The Three Graces "in silver robes with white torches appeared on the top of the mountain, descending hand in hand before the Goddesses," who followed them. Torch-bearers, "their heads and robes all decked with stars," intersperse among the procession. After several songs and dances, the goddesses ascended the mountain from whence they had come, as Iris gave the closing speech. This spectacular illusion paradoxically underscores the distinction between fiction and reality; it also corresponds precisely to Northrop Frye's observation that romance has a conception of an ideal society that exists in a higher world than that of ordinary experience. And it makes literal Frye's idea in *Secular Scripture* that romance contains ascent and descent motifs.

During the period from January 1610 to January 1611, Prince Henry, created Prince of Wales that summer, became the focus of an extraordinary array of civic and court entertainments, including tilting barriers, masques, street pageants, water pageants, and fireworks displays. Politically, these entertainments give striking testimony to Henry's rising status as heir apparent and the increasing hopes that fastened onto his destiny, all of which crashed, of course, with his untimely and unexpected death on November 6, 1612. This heightened interest in the prince corresponds in time with Shakespeare's writing the Romances, roughly 1608–11. An interest in spectacle cannot ignore the celebratory events of 1610, which begin with Jonson's speeches written for Prince Henry's Barriers, performed on January 6. This indoor entertainment opens with an appearance of the Lady of the Lake, who calls attention to the "ample lake" that has near it Merlin's tomb (Jonson 1969: 142). Henry has chosen the name "Meliadus" for this tournament, a name that derives from chivalric romances; and when Arthur appears, "discovered as a star above," we know that Jonson has appropriated romance conventions. Merlin becomes one of the principal speakers and lays out the case that this event is not just about romance but has political overtones. Meliadus (Henry) and his six assistants appear from St. George's portico. And just before the indoor jousting begins, Chivalry rouses herself from the House of Chivalry to speak in Henry's honor. Drawings by Inigo Jones, who designed the spectacle, survive (Jones 1973).

On April 23 the citizens of Chester presented a street pageant to celebrate Henry, although in all likelihood he was not present. But a text of the event, printed in London, allowed others to learn of this show. Allegorical figures dominated the scene in Chester, although several figures simply carried banners or other properties alluding to St. George. Fame with a trumpet in her hand speaks in praise of the day; a song follows that urges the descent of Mercury, who obliges by "descending from heaven in a cloud, artificially Winged, a Wheele of fire burning very cunningly, with other Fire-workes" (*Chester's Triumph* 1610: sig. A3v). Mercury says that he has come down from the throne of immortal gods, commanded to visit this place and honor the prince. Plenty, wearing a garland of wheat and strewing wheat as she rides, accompanies Peace. But the allegory moves in a more strident way with the entry of Envy, a wreath of snakes about her head and her face besmeared with blood, who contests the presence of Love. Joy and the other virtues join battle against Envy, however, and drive her away. Emblematic costume and spectacle enhance the moral battle that occurs in Chester's streets in honor of Henry.

Munday's *London's Love to Royal Prince Henry*, staged on May 31, opens the series of events immediately connected with Henry's installation. The trade guilds of London and the mayor lined the Thames in their barges in anticipation of Henry's arrival from Richmond. Munday wrote two speeches, the first spoken at Chelsea by John Rice, representing Cornwall, and the second, by Richard Burbage, representing the Genius of Wales. Small wonder that Munday refers to "the two absolute Actors, even the verie best our instant time can yeeld" (Munday 1985: 40). One can imagine that Burbage may have been rehearsing or performing one of Shakespeare's Romances in this late spring 1610. Having such actors represent Cornwall and Wales leads Munday to justify this artistic decision: "For such representations and misticall understandings, have alwayes bin reputed lawfull" (p. 40). "Misticall understandings," one might suggest, become the function of romance, masque, pageant, and Shakespeare's late plays; the powers of representation and spectacle help make such understandings possible. At Whitehall, Amphion (Burbage), "a grave and judicious Prophet-like personage . . . with his wreathe of Sea-shelles on his head, and a harp hanging in fayre twine before him" (p. 42), referred to the "Sunne of true-borne Majestie" that shines in Henry's bright eyes. When Amphion concluded his brief speech, shots sounded, "and such a triumphall noyse of Dromes and Trompets, as made the very ayre to Ecchoe" (p. 43). Munday's text also reports the intense mock sea battle that occurred a few days later.

Daniel's *Tethys Festival*, performed on June 5, provides copious detail about the staging and spectacle of this masque, celebrated at Whitehall at the request of the queen, on the day after Henry's official installation. Daniel includes a "Preface to the Reader," laying out a case for what he has done, expressing his reluctance to have the text published, and linking himself with the "poore Inginers for shadowes" who frame the images (Daniel 1963, 3: 306). He concludes with praise for Inigo Jones in a way that Jonson would have resisted, and his text gives priority to a lavish description of the spectacle. With Queen Anne as Tethys, Princess Elizabeth as the Nymph of Thames, and Arbella Stuart as Nymph of Trent, the masque gets underway with a description of the first scene, "which figured a darke cloude, interior with certaine sparkling starres" (p. 310), which gave way to a discovery of two 12-feet high statues of Neptune and Nereus. "These Sea-gods stood on pedestalls, and were al of gold" (p. 311). This scene contains a "Port or Haven . . . and the figure of a Castle

commanding a fortified towne" (p. 311), from which emerged Zephirus, impersonated by Charles, Duke of York, "in a short robe of greene satin imbrodered with golden
flowers." Another scene revealed an opening of the heavens in which "appeared 3
circles of lights and glasses, one with[in] another . . . [that] began to moove circu-
larly." Other caverns, sea scallops, fountains, a "Tree of victory" (also known as Apollo's
Tree), a grove, and a sudden flash of lightning help round out the spectacular artifice
of the masque, which also contained the usual music and dances. At the end of Triton's
speech, "*Mercury* most artificially, and in an exquisite posture descends, and summons
the Duke of Yorke, and six young Noblemen to attend him" (p. 322). Only concern
for the condition of the room prevented Daniel from adding Pages with torches, which
"might have added more splendor" (p. 323).

On January 1, 1611 the court celebrated a masque written by Jonson and designed
by Jones: *Oberon, the Fairy Prince*. This masque serves as a fitting conclusion to the
several events that have commemorated Henry's creation as Prince of Wales. With
Jonson's imagination and Jones's elaborate costuming, Henry becomes Oberon. Jones's
extant drawings make clear this spectacle. His technology included the "*scena ductilis*,
the 'tractable scene,' a device he had occasionally used before. Basically this was a
series of flats set in grooves in the stage, which could be swiftly and quietly drawn
aside into the wings to reveal the setting behind them" (Jonson 1969: 18). Orgel
(ibid) continues: "And while the *machina versatilis* could turn, say, a cave into a temple,
only the *scena ductilis* could wholly transform the entire stage."

Jonson begins his text with these directions: "The first face of the scene appeared
all obscure, and nothing perceived but a dark rock, with trees beyond it and all wild-
ness that could be presented; till at one corner of the cliff . . . the moon began to
show" (p. 159). Such a stark setting releases the satyrs, who become the skillfully integrated anti-masque element, as they look with excitement and anticipation for
Oberon. "'Within was discovered the frontispiece of a bright and glorious palace
whose gates and walls were transparent" (p. 163). Out of the dark rock emerges this
glorious palace, gleaming with Jones's familiar focus on light and transparency. After
an "antic dance full of gesture and swift motion" by the satyrs, the whole palace
opened; "and the nation of fays were discovered, some with instruments, some bearing
lights" (p. 167) with the Knights Masquers seated about the device. Then "Oberon
in a chariot . . . [with] a loud triumphant music began to move forward, drawn by
two white bears and on either side guarded by three sylvans." After Oberon and the
Knights dance and songs fill the air, Phosphorus "the day star, appeared and called
them away" (p. 172). His speech concluded, "they danced their last dance into the
work; and with a full song the star vanished, and the whole machine closed" (p. 173).
The jealous morning has come, the final song says, "Lest, taken with the brightness
of this night, / The world should wish it last, and never miss his light." Worlds of
such romance and spectacle must vanish into the thin air from whence they have come.
This vanity of Jonson and Jones's art must recede, even as the months of celebration
draw to a fitting close, wrapped in the illusions that art can produce and that technology can sustain.

Spectacle: The Late Plays

Shakespeare's last plays occupy the contextual space of masques and pageants, such as outlined above. In that theatrical climate, quite apart from explicit indebtedness, one would be surprised only if these plays did not exhibit similar spectacle. Indeed, at moments the plays' spectacle resembles masques, as in Jupiter's descent in *Cymbeline* and the masque in *The Tempest*. Even grotesque features echo anti-masques. Shakespeare incorporates spectacle in stage business, but it exists briefly, in contrast to masques and pageants. The chief distinction comes in Shakespeare's use of language to *report* spectacle, most obviously in the reunion of Leontes and Perdita; he therefore builds in a textual quality that can represent spectacle. Shakespeare's choice of romance as his subject focus opens the narratives to wondrous stage business, as presiding gods and goddesses increase the likelihood of supernatural intervention. Rather than having his tongue embedded in his cheek, Shakespeare uses spectacle purposefully to serve narrative and political ideas. I return to Frye's idea about the polarities that characterize masques and Shakespeare's Romances; spectacle reinforces this dichotomy.

This tension obviously occurs in *Pericles*, an ongoing conflict between demonic, night worlds and idyllic ones. This battle Shakespeare epitomizes in the places that he chooses for action. The incestuous relationship between King Antiochus and his nameless daughter that occupies the play's early moments in Antioch propels Pericles to continue his search for a suitable marriage partner. For all of her beauty, the daughter in Antioch cannot fulfill this expectation, as Pericles reports to Helicanus: "Her face was to mine eye beyond all wonder; / The rest, hark in thine ear, as black as incest" (1.1.75–6). "Beyond all wonder" may at moments define spectacle, but Pericles's experience warns about uncritically accepting all such display.

Marina's experiences at Mytilene reinforce a dark world that romance also embraces. Having survived birth at sea, the loss of her mother, abandonment by her father, attempted murder, abduction by pirates (an incident strongly reminiscent of *Daphnis and Chloe*), and being sold into a brothel, Marina needs a change of luck, if nothing else. Life in the brothel, the principal business of act 4, reinforces the descent motif for Marina. She cries out: "Diana, aid my purpose!" (4.2.147). Marina glimpses a world beyond herself, one that might include spectacular rescue. But the spectacle we see in 4.4 provides a dumb show: "Enter Pericles at one door, with all his train; Cleon and Dionyza at the other. Cleon shows Pericles the tomb; whereat Pericles makes lamentation, puts on sackcloth, and in a mighty passion departs" (4.4.22ff. SD). The spectacle of the glittering tomb, its epitaph inscribed in "glitt'ring golden characters" (4.3.44), cannot offer hope. But Marina remains expectant "That the gods / Would safely deliver me from this place!" (4.6.178–9). They do not swoop down and deliver her in some stunning stage business.

The spiritual darkness of Antioch gives way to the moral brightness of Pentapolis where good king Simonides presides in a wholesome relationship with his beautiful daughter, Thaisa, whose birthday the king wants to celebrate with spectacle and feasting. Into this happy place Pericles literally washes ashore, greeted by fishermen who rescue his rusty armor, a reminder of his father's legacy. Armed only with this armor, Pericles nevertheless becomes a participant in the tournament that Simonides has established. "There are," a Fisherman says, "princes and knights come from all parts of the world to joust and tourney for her [Thaisa's] love" (2.1.107–9). Scene 2 focuses on the tournament where the King and his daughter sit and watch the six knights present themselves and their shields to the princess. Each brings an emblematic shield, except Pericles who appears only with his armor but with a device, which Thaisa characterizes: "A wither'd branch, that's only green at top; / The motto, *In hac spe vivo*" (2.2.42–3). The scene closes with shouts from the lists of the tournament, "and all cry 'The mean Knight!'" (59 SD). Pericles has won at the tilting; and a banquet scene follows, continuing the spectacle, where the king orders: "Even in your armours, as you are address'd, / Will well become a soldier's dance" (2.3.94–5). Like a court masque, the spectacle dissolves into dance, as it offers hope for the future.

Darkness in Mytilene gives way to the unexpected reunion there of Pericles and Marina aboard a ship; and Pericles can say of her: "Thou that wast born at sea, buried at Tharsus, / And found at sea again" (5.1.196–7). In this ecstasy – "I am wild in my beholding," Pericles says – he begins to hear strange music, which he calls "the music of the spheres" (228). This music, unheard by others, becomes the prelude to the vision of Diana, who suddenly appears to Pericles and commands him: "My temple stands in Ephesus; hie thee thither, / And do upon mine altar sacrifice" (238–9). As suddenly as she has appeared, Diana disappears. Pericles responds to this theophany: "Celestial Dian, goddess argentine, / I will obey thee" (248–9). In Ephesus the final reunion occurs, that between Pericles and Thaisa, the follower of Diana. Certainly this spectacle carries us beyond the narrow confines of the natural world. But for all the glory of Ephesus, the characters cannot remain there and indulge themselves in Diana's temple; instead, they ready themselves to re-enter the political world of Pentapolis and Tyre.

Early in the action of *Cymbeline* Imogen cries out in exasperation: "Would I were / A neatherd's daughter, and my Leonatus / Our neighbour shepherd's son" (1.1.149–51). If this bucolic situation were true, Imogen would no longer face the obstinance of her father and his resistance to Posthumus; and the two lovers would be living the life of *Daphnis and Chloe*, removed from the harsh political world. Instead, Imogen and Posthumus must endure several permutations of this play's night world, including separation and presumed death. A curious spectacle occurs in 2.2 in Imogen's bedchamber, where she suddenly appears in bed, reading a book, and a trunk has also been placed on stage. The stage business in this perplexing scene constitutes a visual rape of Imogen, innocently sleeping and unaware of Iachimo's emergence from the trunk and his survey of the room and of her body. He discovers that she has been reading the story of Tereus's rape of Philomel, which Iachimo's activity here reinforces, albeit in a different key. Iachimo takes her bracelet and notices the mole on her left breast. As the clock strikes, he exits into the trunk, and the spectacle ends. But only for the moment. Another version, a textual one, occurs in 2.4 when Iachimo returns to Rome and tells a credulous Posthumus of his adventure in Imogen's bedchamber. Iachimo textually recreates the room through his description of all its accoutrements, such as the hanging tapestries of silk and silver that depicted the story of Cleopatra, the chimney piece of "Chaste Dian bathing" (82), and the "roof o' th' chamber / With golden cherubins . . . fretted" (87–8). The bracelet and the description of Imogen's body offer the most convincing "evidence" of what Iachimo has presumably done. He has thus recreated a spectacle, now played out in his discourse and triggering Posthumus's active imagination.

Imogen in male disguise has wandered into Wales in search of Posthumus, but the drug that she takes renders her lifeless and seemingly dead. When she awakens, she discovers a headless body next to her and believes it to be Posthumus; but actually it is Cloten, who has himself dressed in Posthumus's garments in order to pursue Imogen. This transfixing stage business seems only to deepen the demonic world that Imogen has entered. As Imogen spies the body, she cries out: "O gods and goddesses!" (4.2.296). "I hope I dream," she adds a few lines later. A dream world might clarify the spectacle, or gods and goddesses might provide rescue. As she embraces the body, this stage image sears into our consciousness.

Imprisoned and asleep, Posthumus has a most rare vision in act 5:

Solemn music. Enter, as in an apparition, Sicilius Leonatus, father to Posthumus, an old man, attired like a warrior, leading in his hand an ancient matron, his wife . . . with music before them. Then, after other music, follows the two young Leonati, brothers to Posthumus, with wounds as they died in the wars. (5.3.123 SD)

They circle Posthumus and speak to him as he continues to sleep, and invoke Jupiter, Sicilius crying: "Peep through thy marble mansion, help" (181). Then suddenly: "Jupiter descends in thunder and lightning, sitting upon an eagle. He throws a thunderbolt. The ghosts fall on their knees" (186 SD). Shakespeare nowhere else surpasses the sheer spectacle of this entire moment with a god descending among the dead family members, creating an experience far beyond the confines of this world, indeed beyond wonder. Jupiter chides Posthumus's family and explains: "Whom best I love, I cross, to make my gift, / The more delayed, delighted. Be content" (195–6). He leaves behind a riddling tablet for Posthumus, then "ascends into the heavens"; and soon the ghosts also vanish. The descent of the god Jupiter makes possible Posthumus's ascent, as this spectacle fulfills the promise of offering unusual hope. Surely we have been in the presence of those "misticall understandings" to which Munday referred. The play's final scene with its multiple reunions ratifies the godly vision and spectacle that Posthumus has had.

Although Apollo presides over *The Winter's Tale*, he never appears. I have argued that nevertheless he makes his presence felt in powerful and rewarding ways (Bergeron 1995). Hermione invokes Apollo in the trial scene (3.2); and his oracle message, preserved in a scroll, enters at a timely moment, condemning Leontes as a jealous tyrant and exonerating Hermione. When Leontes learns of Mamillius's death

and sees Hermione's apparent death, he cries out: "Apollo, pardon / My great pro-
faneness 'gainst thine oracle" (151–2). Exactly: Leontes has violated the god's will,
challenging his wisdom and justice. Cleomenes and Dion, having been dispatched by
Leontes to Delphos to receive Apollo's message, return in 3.1 at some unspecified location and recount the spectacle of their visit to the oracle's sacred place. Cleomenes
found impressive "the ear-deaf'ning voice o' th' oracle, / Kin to Jove's thunder" (9–10).
Dion notes the "celestial habits" and the "sacrifice" that they apparently saw.
Contrary to the theophanies of *Pericles* and *Cymbeline*, this play settles for a report of
messengers who have been in the presence of the god's representatives and bring with
them, in Dion's apt phrase, "Apollo's great divine sealed up" (19). But, of course,
Apollo cannot be contained: his power erupts in the trial and affects most of what
happens in the remainder of the play. Shakespeare keeps us at an aesthetic distance
from the god's presence, perhaps because he has more spectacular events in mind.

If not Apollo, then the allegorical figure of Time, who makes his single appearance
at the beginning of act 4.[2] If Shakespeare needed a model for Time, he could have
chosen from numerous pageants, masques, and emblem books. Indeed, he provides
Time with the standard equipment: wings and an hour glass. Time serves as part of
the transition from the fever-pitch of the trial in Sicilia to a different, yet in some
ways similar, world of Bohemia. He also indicates that sixteen years have passed:
"Impute it not a crime / To me or my swift passage that I slide / O'er sixteen years"
(4–6). This spectacle remains lawful business, even as it fulfills a basic characteristic
of romance to move rather abruptly to some other place or some other time without
attending causal links – the "and then" narrative structure that Frye has identified
(Frye 1976: 47–8).

The songs and dances of the great sheep-shearing festival of 4.4 remind us of
progress pageants and masques. The "dance of twelve satyrs" (337) may have been
inspired by a similar dance in *Oberon*, as scholars and editors delight in pointing out.[3]
If the King's Men performed the anti-masque in *Oberon*, this would offer a strong
probable link to this play. The feasting, song, and dance in Bohemia make it seem
the anti-masque to Sicilia, but jealousy and familial conflict eventually erupt in
Bohemia as fiercely as they had in Sicilia. As Camillo, surely one of the play's Apollo
representatives, had safely led Polixenes away from the poisoned world of Leontes's
court, he now will lead the son Florizel away from this father's wrath and to Sicilia
with Perdita in tow. We will receive in 5.2 the glorious account of the spectacle of
the reunion of father and daughter, long presumed dead. The Third Gentleman also
reports of the curious artifact in Paulina's possession: a statue of Hermione executed
by the Italian artist Giulio Romano: "He so near to Hermione hath done Hermione
that they say one would speak to her and stand in hope of answer" (5.2.98–100).
Paulina, according to the Second Gentleman, "hath privately twice or thrice a day
ever since the death of Hermione visited that removed house" (103–5). To that
"removed house" everyone goes in 5.3 in order to see this artwork.

Everything in the play points now to a special place of performance, this removed
location outside the normal boundaries of the play world – fit for extraordinary

spectacle. Paulina draws a curtain and reveals Hermione standing like a statue. Leontes first notes her "natural posture" (5.3.23). We are "mocked with art," Leontes adds later (68). "It is required," Paulina insists, "You do awake your faith. Then all stand still – / Or those that think it is unlawful business / I am about, let them depart" (94–7). But in producing "misticall understandings" all may be "lawful," as Anthony Munday pointed out just a couple of years before *The Winter's Tale*. With halting music, the seeming statue begins to move. We join the stage audience in joyful incredulity: Hermione indeed lives; Leontes's tears have been his "recreation," his suffering, efficacious. No other spectacle in Shakespeare surpasses this one in its powerful effect on everyone; it lifts us out of ourselves to a removed mystical understanding.

Curiously, it did not seem to register with Simon Forman who saw the play performed at the Globe in May 1611; or at least, he recorded no information about Hermione's transformation. I and others have suggested that perhaps in the version that Forman saw Hermione did *not* seemingly come back to life (Bergeron 1978). If that were true, then Shakespeare would be observing the narrative confines of his source *Pandosto*, which he otherwise follows closely. If Shakespeare changed the text to include Hermione's survival, then this play would have resonated with unusual force when performed before the royal family during the wedding festivities of February 1613 for Princess Elizabeth and Frederick, Elector Palatine of Germany, given the recent death of Henry. Munday's Lord Mayor's Show of October 1611, *Chruso-thriambos*, includes a "resurrection" of Nicholas Faringdon, a fourteenth-century mayor of London. The character Leofstane, played by John Lowin of the King's Men, greeted Time at Faringdon's tomb, where he has lain for several centuries. Time recounts his accomplishments and those of his fellow Goldsmiths. Then "*Time striketh on the Tombe with his silver wand, and then Faringdon ariseth*" (Munday 1985: 56). Faringdon responds: "Cannot graves contain their dead, / Where long they have lien buried, / But to Triumphs, sports, and showes / They must be raisd?" Here in London's streets spectators could have witnessed the spectacle of one presumably dead now brought to life through Time's efforts. Or court audiences in February 1613 could have seen two masques that include statue figures that come to life: the first antimasque of Beaumont's *Masque of the Inner Temple and Gray's Inn* includes four statues who dance with the nymphs and stars, and Thomas Campion's *Lords' Masque* has two sets of four statues which the gods transform into women. The spectacle of a transformed Hermione would fit easily in theatrical events of 1611 and 1613.

The wedding festivities of 1613 included *The Tempest*. Prospero has magical, transforming powers that reach beyond the earthly world, tying the action to romance traditions and to illusory spectacle of many masques and pageants. The setting on a removed island encourages the sense of a self-conscious performance, which Prospero has arranged by bringing travelers from Naples and Milan to this place for a single afternoon. We share Miranda's puzzlement at the opening storm. We learn, however, in 1.2 that the storm has been a spectacle, as Prospero insists: "There's no harm done" (15). "I have," he says to a distraught Miranda, "done nothing but in care of thee, / Of thee, my dear one, thee, my daughter, who / Art ignorant of what thou art"

(16–18). We may rightly hear in that statement that Miranda is "ignorant of art." Ariel later confirms the technology that he has used to create the conditions of the storm and seeming disaster. When Prospero asks: "But are they, Ariel, safe?" the spirit responds: "Not a hair perished. / On their sustaining garments not a blemish, / But fresher than before" (217–19). Gonzalo reinforces this idea in 2.1, when he, too, refers to their garments as having a "freshness and gloss" (63).

"Soft music"; "Enter Iris" – so begins the nuptial masque in 4.2 (59 SD). We, along with Ferdinand and Miranda, become the recipients of what Prospero calls "Some vanity of mine art" (41). Orgel lists the various nuptial masques that had occurred in recent years in the Jacobean court, such as Jonson's *Hymenaei* (1606) and *The Hadding-ton Masque* (1608), and Campion's *Lord Hay's Masque* (1607) (Shakespeare 1987: 173n.). We see in the presence of Iris, Ceres, and Juno a recollection of Daniel's *The Vision of the Twelve Goddesses*; one can imagine that Prospero's masque had these god-desses similarly costumed. When Ceres, referring to Juno, says, "Her peacocks fly amain" (74), Orgel includes this stage direction: "Juno's chariot appears suspended above the stage." Certainly this makes sense, even if not completely necessary since the goddess does not appear until a bit later. But this stage direction calls attention to the technology of the event. When Ceres asks Iris why they have been summoned to this place, Iris says: "A contract of true love to celebrate, / And some donation freely to estate / On the blessed lovers" (84–6).[4] Juno descends in her chariot and says: "Go with me / To bless this twain, that they may prosperous be, / And honoured in their issue" (103–5). As Juno and Ceres sing, they urge blessings on this political and social union. Ferdinand, struck by the beauty of this spectacle, refers to it as "a most majestic vision" (118); but Prospero reminds everyone that we see only the product of artistic fancy. Iris summons the "naiads of the windring brooks," recalling the naiads of Daniel's *Tethys Festival*. Nymphs do appear, along with "certain reapers"; all join in a graceful dance, until Prospero cuts short the entertainment, and the spirits vanish into the thin air from whence they came.

"The cloud-capped towers, the gorgeous palaces, / The solemn temples, the great globe itself" (152–3): these items, to which Prospero refers, sound like an inventory of properties for recent pageants and masques. How fitting that he should recall them, fixed as they must be in Jacobean theatrical imagination. And Prospero reminds us that they can only produce an "insubstantial pageant faded" (155) that leaves not even a cloud or mist ("rack") behind. So much for spectacle. But in fact Shakespeare indulges in spectacle regularly in these late plays because it can serve multiple purposes. It produces a brave new world that has such creatures in it, even if they are only illusions. Reality intrudes, as does Caliban's proposed rebellion. "Let me live here ever" (122), Ferdinand says in his delight at this spectacle; but in fact the group will depart from the island and return to the rough and tumble world of Italian pol-itics. Whatever else Prospero's Epilogue may say, it certainly points to the limitations of theatrical art: "Now my charms are all o'erthrown" (5.1.319). We cannot remain in the masquing hall, in the pageant streets, or in the theatre. But we may have gained a glimpse of some other world that spectacle assists us in understanding.

Politics

To call attention to the politics of masques and pageants risks examining the obvious. As David Bevington and Peter Holbrook have observed, masques are "unavoidably and consciously political" (1998: 4). It could not be otherwise. The occasions that gave rise to masque and pageant entertainment resonate with political significance: the Christmas festivities of the court, the installation of a prince as Prince of Wales, the wedding of a royal child or courtly aristocrat, the procession of a monarch through the city, the inauguration of the new Lord Mayor of London. By definition the simple physical presence of the sovereign or other royal family member equals politics, and the drama with its vivid spectacle reinforces this truth. Spectators busily watch the monarch as they simultaneously observe the drama. Dekker writes effectively of how the royal entry pageant of 1604 needed only the physical presence of the king to complete it and give it significance. In the middle of this fictional representation the Recorder of London greets the royal family, addresses them, and presents them with cups of gold: political reality intrudes into the fictional display. Or King James stands at the first triumphal arch and watches as the silk curtain that had hidden the arch of the City of London vanishes at the moment of his arrival, implying, as Jonson explains, a new day of political hope in the kingdom. Pageants and masques routinely fulfill propaganda purposes as they celebrate royal person or mayor. If we can recall the struggle among the foreign ambassadorial corps for precedence at masques and even at street pageants, we gain yet another political angle.

Daniel in the epistle dedicatory to *The Vision of the Twelve Goddesses* explains the "intent and scope of the project," which served to represent the blessings "which this mighty kingdom now enjoys by the benefit of his most gracious Majesty, by whom we have this glory of peace, with the accession of so great state and power." The goddesses embody those blessings of peace, as Iris confirms in the closing speech: "ever more to grace this glorious monarchy with the real effects of these blessings represented" (Daniel 1967: 37). The mid-March royal entry pageant and James's first address to parliament on March 19 reinforce the political idea of peace that James has brought to his new kingdom, both domestic and foreign peace. Holbrook (1998) sees Daniel's masque in the context of James's pursuit of peace with Spain, which would be ratified by treaty in August 1604. Holbrook comments: "For all its stiffly formal action in which the twelve goddesses approach the Temple of Peace and dedicate their various attributes to that ideal, Daniel's masque registers, in its preface and elsewhere, the conflicting discourses that attended James's controversial policy" (p. 72). Therefore, an unease, an uncertainty about the pursuit of peace resides in Daniel's masque even as it ostensibly celebrates the virtues of peace.

James as unifier of the kingdoms became a central political doctrine of his early years in England; indeed, he set out to make such union a legal accomplishment, but parliament thwarted his every effort. The concept seemed self-evidently worthy to James, and certainly masques and pageants pursued the ideal of union. Munday's 1605 Lord Mayor's Show, *The Triumphes of Re-United Britannia*, represents the concept of union in the historical figures of Brutus and his sons, in whose time the kingdoms were divided; but under James, the second Brutus, the kingdoms had achieved a new union. Jonson's *Hymenaei* (1606), although celebrating a wedding, gains much of its energy from a conscious reflection on the union of the kingdoms, the wedding becoming an analogy for the joining of the kingdoms (Gordon 1980: 157–84). Arthur in *Prince Henry's Barriers* insists that "Merlin's mystic prophecies are absolved / In Britain's name, the union of this isle, / And claim of both my scepter and my style" (p. 145). Britain experiences a new union and a new style, as in fact James had begun to refer to himself as King of Great Britain. Near the end of his long speech Merlin refers to a new golden age: "Henry but joined the roses that ensigned / Particular families, but this hath joined / The rose and thistle, and in them combined / A union that shall never be declined" (p. 155). Merlin's concluding prophecy calls attention to each member of the royal family as a means of extending the union in both time and space: "Whilst you [James] sit high, / And led by them behold your Britain fly / Beyond the line, when what the seas before / Did bound, shall to the sky then stretch his shore" (p. 158). This raises the prospect not only of union but also of expansive empire, an idea just beginning to gain some traction in Stuart political thinking.

Oberon, culminating Henry's year-long celebration, heaps praise on the young prince, who arrives as Oberon, we recall, in a chariot drawn by two white bears. The mythologizing of Henry competes, however, with indulgent attention paid to James, a situation captured in the song that follows Oberon's arrival: "we in tunes to Arthur's chair / Bear Oberon's desire, / Than which there nothing can be higher, / Save James, to whom it flies" (p. 168). Tom Bishop offers this analysis: "Novelty, prophecy, change and the future tend to become the domain of the Prince, while tradition, stasis and the received remain with the King. Between these two sets of terms, and perhaps the object of their struggle, lies the present, the moment of *Oberon, the Fairy Prince*" (Bishop 1998: 104). The masque thus oscillates between the opposing points of interest, creating what Bishop calls a "delicate hermeneutic spiderweb" (p. 104). The politics of the occasion have everything to do with an understanding of the dazzling spectacle that unfolded in January 1611: established king pitted against the rising star of a son who has begun to make his own way, who has gathered around him people and ideas in conflict with his father. The masque cannot mask these differences: its removed mysteries sound to the present occasion. Martin Butler (1998) concludes: "The legitimation of Prince Henry had consequences for the legitimation of King James, and *Oberon*, I wish to suggest, was centrally involved in this legitimation crisis" (p. 31). Butler adds: "If Oberon is Henry, he is James's son and heir to the British crown, but if Henry is Oberon, so to speak, he is heir to Elizabeth, whose moon illuminates the whole event" (p. 31). Therefore, this "night of homage to the British court," to cite Sylvan's words in the masque (p. 168), this construction of a Fairy Land replete with Knights Masquers, this celebration of "the high-grac'd Oberon" (p. 172), yields finally to Phosphorus, the day star. The idyllic world surrenders to the political world, which, paradoxically, permeates it. The vision of the future cannot escape the present.

Although Shakespeare's late plays remain fictions, they nevertheless contain serious internal political problems, some of which resonate in the real world of Jacobean politics. Some critics have in fact drawn explicit connections (see Jones 1961; Yates 1978; Wickham 1973; Marcus 1988), offering a kind of "King James Version" of the Romances. Marcus, for example, interprets *Cymbeline* as a political and topical allegory. The "text" of the Stuart royal family, its political and domestic life, surely influenced Shakespeare's writing, but I do not believe that Shakespeare writes these final plays in order to offer commentary on or guidance about current political realities. Royal families in fiction or in real life necessarily encounter some of the same issues. Swerving from his sources, Shakespeare nevertheless intensifies the political issues in the Romances. Two in particular surge through the late plays: *succession* and *union* (usually manifested in reunion). From the time of his arrival in England, King James underscored the importance of a peaceful succession to the throne, his progeny that seemingly secured the kingdom's future, and the union that he had achieved. Shakespeare's late plays at moments mirror these political concerns.

In *Cymbeline* the King must solve two major political problems: internal dissolution of the royal family and external threat from Rome. Only a successful resolution can assure peaceful succession. Cymbeline's status seems relatively secure, if problematic, at the beginning: he has somewhat recently married a widowed woman, who brings with her a disturbing son, Cloten; the King's healthy daughter could succeed him, if only she were obedient in marrying someone worthy; and Cymbeline has two sons, but they have been stolen away from the court for twenty years. Imogen's determination to marry Posthumus the King finds offensive: "Thou took'st a beggar, wouldst have made my throne / A seat for baseness" (1.1.142–3). Finding a suitable marriage partner for a royal child preoccupies all the father-kings in the Romances, as it also does King James. Shakespeare greatly complicates the narrative and political worlds. Thus, by the opening of 4.3, Cymbeline redefines his situation: Imogen, "The great part of my comfort, gone; my queen / Upon a desperate bed, and in a time / When fearful wars point at me; her son gone" (5–7). One would not wish Cymbeline's predicament worse; his assessment spells out what must be overcome, if peace and security can be enjoyed. This romance underscores the potentially precarious situation even for an absolute monarch.

The external Roman world enters with the arrival of Caius Lucius, who has come to urge the payment of tribute due Augustus Caesar (3.1). In one of Shakespeare's great ironies, the Queen and Cloten speak, resisting payment largely on nationalistic grounds, and for the moment they persuade Cymbeline. This leaves Lucius with few options; he thus tells Cymbeline: "War and confusion / In Caesar's name pronounce I 'gainst thee" (64–5). The brief, fifteen-line 3.7 takes place in Rome and certifies Caesar's intention to conduct war against Britain: "our wars against / The fall'n-off Britons" (5–6). In an unexpected development, Lucius encounters the disguised Imogen (Fidele) in 4.2 and enlists her in the Roman military cause, which succeeds. The Soothsayer has even had a dream about victory, having envisioned "Jove's bird, the Roman eagle" which "vanished in the sunbeams," all portending "Success to th' Roman host" (349–53).

With imagination and spectacle, as we have seen earlier, Shakespeare works on these political and military problems, getting rid of the Queen and Cloten, making Posthumus worthy of Imogen, and discovering and redeeming Guiderius and Arviragus into the royal family. The poignant reunion of father and daughter, the acceptance of Posthumus by Cymbeline, and the revelation of the lost sons (all happening in the last scene) point to peace and harmony in the private life of the royal family, thereby opening the prospect for domestic peace as they assure the kingdom's future through orderly familial succession. Even the battle with the Romans ends in peace and reconciliation.

Symbolizing this new peaceful condition, Philharmonus, the Soothsayer, comes to interpret Jupiter's text left for Posthumus, unfolding the political implications of the spectacle. Lucius orders: "Read, and declare the meaning" (5.4.435). The cedar of the riddle is Cymbeline, the two lopped branches, his lost sons. The tree now revives, "whose issue / Promises Britain peace and plenty" (458–9). The Soothsayer also reinterprets the vision that he had had in 4.2. This dream now yields different results: the soaring eagle means that imperial Caesar "should again unite / His favour with the radiant Cymbeline" (475–6). As peacemaker, Cymbeline now submits to Rome from his position of strength and magnanimity: "And in the temple of great Jupiter / Our peace we'll ratify, seal it with feasts" (483–4). The last line of the last speech in James's 1604 pageant wished for the King the lasting glory of Augustus's state. Cymbeline and the kingdom stand ready to enjoy such peaceful glory.

Unlike Cymbeline, Leontes in *The Winter's Tale* causes his own disruption in the political world of Sicilia; he faces no inherent disturbing forces from within the kingdom or from without. The problems emanate from within his psyche, and with enormous political consequences. But the play begins hopefully, full of promising royal children. Camillo and Archidamus in the play's opening scene not only talk about the great love that persists between Leontes and Polixenes but also of the delight in Leontes's son and heir. Archidamus says: "You have an unspeakable comfort of your young prince Mamillius" (1.1.32–3). Camillo concurs: "I very well agree with you in the hopes of him. It is a gallant child, one that, indeed, physics the subject, makes old hearts fresh" (35–7). Archidamus closes: "If the King had no son, they would desire to live on crutches till he had one" (42–3). Immediately, a pregnant Hermione enters, assuring an additional royal child and the health of the kingdom. Orderly succession seems guaranteed.

When Hermione urges Polixenes to remain in Sicilia, he responds with worry about the political well-being of Bohemia: "I am questioned by my fears of what may chance / Or breed upon our absence" (1.2.11–12). He adds a few lines later: "My affairs / Do even drag me homeward" (23–4). But he agrees to stay a bit longer, furthering Leontes's irrational suspicion and jealousy. Leontes asks Polixenes: "Are you so fond of your young prince as we / Do seem to be of ours?" (162–3). He answers affirmatively: "He's all my exercise, my mirth, my matter" (164). Shakespeare weaves together the two fathers' regard for their royal sons, even as he intersperses Leontes's inexplicable concern about the paternity of Mamillius. When Mamillius dies and

Florizel disobeys his father, we return to this opening to understand how important these sons should be for the state's political welfare.

Leontes's request that Camillo poison Polixenes terrifies Camillo, who reluctantly agrees to carry out the crime. He exacts a promise from Leontes: "Provided that when he's removed your highness / Will take again your Queen as yours at first, / Even for your son's sake, and thereby for sealing / The injury of tongues in courts and kingdoms / Known and allied to yours" (332–6). This double-faceted bargain rests on political realities: first, that the royal family of Sicilia be reunited, and second, that this harmony would prevent disparagement from other courts. Similarly, the Lord and Antigonus urge caution on Leontes who has just accused Hermione of adultery and ordered her to prison. Antigonus warns: "Be certain what you do, sir, lest your justice / Prove violence, in the which three great ones suffer, / Yourself, your Queen, your son" (2.1.127–9). His words echo through the rest of the play with prophetic power as Leontes indeed inflicts violence on the political state and harms the royal family.

In the trial scene Apollo's oracle indicates the innocence of Hermione, Polixenes, and Camillo; and it adds an ominous note: "the King shall live without an heir if that which is lost be not found" (3.2.132–4). Within a few short moments Leontes lashes out at Apollo, word comes that Mamillius has died, and then Hermione faints and presumably dies. The daughter has already been dispatched by Leontes to a foreign land and anticipated death. Suddenly Leontes, utterly alone, becomes apparently no longer a royal father or a royal husband. The question of succession becomes then a major motif in the play, underscoring the inextricable link between royal family and politics. In a lightning flash the kingdom that had been so secure teeters on the brink of uncertainty: no heir exists.

The Old Shepherd says to his son, on discovering the baby Perdita in Bohemia: "thou metst with things dying, I with things newborn" (3.3.109–10). This rhetorical hinge closes down the winter's tale of Sicilia and opens the play to new possibilities, which spectacle reinforces in act 4. But in the midst of the sheep-shearing festival the disguised Polixenes confronts his impertinent son, intent on marrying Perdita. When Polixenes asks: "Have you a father?" (4.4.387), the son shoots back: "I have, but what of him?" Polixenes reveals his identity and disinherits the son: "we'll bar thee from succession, / Not hold thee of our blood, no, not our kin" (426–7). Shakespeare goes out of his way to create this political conflict between father and son and stir the issue of succession, none of which appears in *Pandosto*. He complicates and intensifies politics in this play.

At the beginning of act 5 we hear Dion urge Leontes to remarry: "consider . . . / What dangers by his highness' fail of issue / May drop upon his kingdom and devour / Incertain lookers-on" (26–9). Dion rightly seizes on the peril of an issueless state, not anticipating that Paulina will provide a way out in a spectacle that reunites the royal family and solidifies the country's politics. In the glorious reports of 5.2 we learn that Leontes now knows Perdita's identity, and that which was lost has been found: an heir appears in the kingdom. When the statue-like Hermione descends into the loving arms of Leontes and Perdita, she says: I "have preserved / Myself to see the issue" (5.3.127–8). Sicilia and Bohemia now experience dynastic union through Florizel and Perdita, and the political future returns to the hopefulness of the play's opening in ways that *Pandosto* manifestly did not. Shakespeare's play makes old hearts fresh and kingdoms secure.

Pericles begins his quest for a suitable wife by first going to Antioch with nearly disastrous results; he seeks a wife "From whence an issue I might propagate" (1.1.73). He wants a successor to stabilize Tyre's government. Through all of his peregrinations, Pericles remains focused on the political status of his kingdom; fortunately, he has the good Helicanus in Tyre who staves off insurrection and urges patience. As the seemingly poor knight who washes ashore in Pentapolis, Pericles improbably tries and wins Thaisa's hand, the suitable wife who bears his child. Good King Simonides stands as a political model of how to govern well. Storm and shipwreck, of course, interrupt Pericles's intention to resume authority in Tyre with issue. The remainder of the play teases out this fundamental political and narrative problem. The unexpected reunion with first Marina and then Thaisa brings not only unrivaled joy for Pericles (and us) but also brings political security for both Pentapolis and Tyre. By virtue of his marriage Pericles has become heir apparent in Pentapolis, a claim that he presses at the play's end; and his royal child, the kingdom's heir, will rule at Tyre. Tacitly united, these kingdoms have solved the succession problem; a royal child makes this possible, a point not lost in Jacobean England.

The King of Naples in *The Tempest* says: "Would I had never / Married my daughter there [Tunis], for coming thence [to the island] / My son is lost, and, in my rate, she too / Who is so far from Italy removed / I ne'er again shall see her" (2.1.105–9). We might hear Cymbeline or Leontes in this. Alonso, now storm-tossed onto Prospero's magical island, had journeyed with the others to Claribel's wedding in Tunis only presumably to lose his son in the storm. The political heirs of Naples have been lost; further, Alonso has little reason to think that he himself will safely return to his kingdom. It turns out that Alonso is wrong about his son Ferdinand, but Claribel remains out of the picture. This political turmoil Antonio and Sebastian underscore in their plan to kill Alonso on the island, and thus reenact the deposition of Prospero twelve years earlier in Milan. This will be a cold-blooded attempt at political gain. If Ferdinand is dead, Antonio purposefully asks Sebastian, "Then tell me, / Who's the next heir of Naples?" (242–3). Sebastian rightly answers, "Claribel." And then Antonio astutely defines her political position: "She that is Queen of Tunis; she that dwels / Ten leagues beyond man's life" (244–5). It dawns on Sebastian that "'twixt which regions [Naples and Tunis] / There is some space" (255–6). They intend to rush into that space and claim political power. Only an alert Ariel thwarts their attempt at regicide. In a play heavily given over to spectacle, political issues pervade almost every fiber of its design.

Prospero has indeed brought this traveling party to the island to satisfy his own lingering political desire. Deposed twelve years earlier, he has apparently been waiting for this moment to torment them and alter the political landscape back in Italy. He not only reveals to Miranda her identity in the play's second scene; but he also reveals that he has been Duke of Milan, a "prince of power" (1.2.55), although a neglectful ruler. He unfolds to her incredulous ears a horrible story of political intrigue and betrayal by his brother Antonio with the assistance of Alonso. Antonio "did believe / He was indeed the duke, out o' th' substitution" (102–3). This past usurpation becomes the model, as Antonio makes clear to Sebastian, for the attempted coup on the island. Caliban also lives on this island, and he seeks revenge on Prospero, claiming that the island is rightfully his. His scheme, also a design for political power, becomes an amusing parody of Antonio and Sebastian; for Caliban unwisely links his plan to the aid of Stephano and Trinculo, who agree that if they are indeed in charge, then the state totters. Each group defines politics.

But unlike Pericles, Cymbeline, or Leontes, Prospero has magical power. He will use his royal daughter to recover control of Milan and to gain a measure of control of Naples through her marriage to Ferdinand, which the nuptial masque celebrates. Like other such spectacles, this one has political purpose despite its mythological figures. The royal daughter has found a suitable marriage partner, one who helps solve the problems of succession and who will bring about union of the kingdoms. Gonzalo rightly asks: "Was Milan thrust from Milan that his issue / Should become kings of Naples? O rejoice / Beyond a common joy" (5.1.205–7). Not all in the play agree with that sentiment, whatever we may think of it. Antonio, for example, expresses no contrition or any reaction to Prospero's offer of forgiveness. This strange afternoon on this strange island does not touch him deeply, but others do respond to the power of the spectacles that they have experienced and accept the shifting political tide. Prospero, his purpose fulfilled, abandons his magic and returns to the world of Italian politics, a world redefined by the royal children.

The "misticall understandings" to which Munday refers become essential in the spectacular representation of masques, pageants, and Shakespeare's late plays. Mystification of the world, real or fictional, heightens the political understanding of it. Ben Jonson writes at the opening of *Hymenaei* of his craft and purpose: "though their voice be taught to sound to present occasions, their sense . . . should always lay hold on more removed mysteries" (p. 76). Spectacle and politics unceasingly intertwine in these art forms as romance explores transcendental understandings beyond wonder. The "lawful business" that Paulina conducts in *The Winter's Tale*'s final scene can stand as an emblem for the late plays as spectacle creates a path toward "more removed mysteries," which nevertheless take part of their meaning from the political world. As spectacle complements state and majesty in masques and pageants, so it completes romance in Shakespeare's last plays.

NOTES

1 For discussions of this pageant see Bergeron (1971: 71–89; 2000: 164–92).
2 The production of this play at the Royal National Theatre, London, directed by Nicholas Hytner, which opened in May 2001, disappointed in its representation of Time because the director did not

present an allegorical figure, but rather dispersed Time's lines among several different characters. No one unfamiliar with the play would have readily understood that this was supposed to be the figure of Time.

3 See, for example, Orgel's suggestion in his edition of the play (Shakespeare 1996: 186n.; 79–80).

4 Campion's *Lords' Masque* certainly fulfills this purpose. For an extensive and convincing discussion that links *The Tempest* with Campion's masque, see Bevington (1998).

REFERENCES AND FURTHER READING

Bergeron, D. M. (1971). *English Civic Pageantry 1558–1642*. London: Arnold; Columbia: University of South Carolina Press.

——(1978). The Restoration of Hermione in *The Winter's Tale*. In H. E. Jacobs and C. M. Kay (eds.) *Shakespeare's Romances Reconsidered*. Lincoln: University of Nebraska Press.

——(1985). *Shakespeare's Romances and the Royal Family*. Lawrence: University Press of Kansas.

——(1995). The Apollo Mission in *The Winter's Tale*. In M. Hunt (ed.) *The Winter's Tale: Critical Essays*. New York: Garland, 361–79.

——(2000). Pageants, Masques, and Scholarly Ideology. In D. M. Bergeron, *Practicing Renaissance Scholarship: Plays and Pageants, Patrons and Politics*. Pittsburgh, PA: Duquesne University Press, 164–92.

Bevington, D. (1998). *The Tempest* and the Jacobean Court Masque. In D. Bevington and P. Holbrook (eds.) *The Politics of the Stuart Court Masque*. Cambridge: Cambridge University Press, 218–43.

Bevington, D. and Holbrook, P. (1998). Introduction. In D. Bevington and P. Holbrook (eds.) *The Politics of the Stuart Court Masque*. Cambridge: Cambridge University Press, 1–19.

Bishop, T. (1998). The Gingerbread Host: Tradition and Novelty in the Jacobean Masque. In D. Bevington and P. Holbrook (eds.) *The Politics of the Stuart Court Masque*. Cambridge: Cambridge University Press, 88–120.

Butler, M. (1998). Courtly Negotiations. In D. Bevington and P. Holbrook (eds.) *The Politics of the Stuart Court Masque*. Cambridge: Cambridge University Press, 20–40.

Chester's Triumph in Honor of Her Prince (1610). London.

Daniel, S. (1963). *The Complete Works in Verse and Prose of Samuel Daniel*, ed. A. B. Grosart. New York: Russell and Russell.

——(1967). *The Vision of the Twelve Goddesses*, ed. J. Rees. In T. J. B. Spencer and S. Wells (eds.) *A Book of Masques*. Cambridge: Cambridge University Press, 19–42.

Frye, N. (1976). *The Secular Scripture: A Study of the Structure of Romance*. Cambridge, MA: Harvard University Press.

——(1978). Romance as Masque. In C. M. Kay and H. E. Jacobs (eds.) *Shakespeare's Romances Reconsidered*. Lincoln: University of Nebraska Press, 11–39.

Geertz, C. (1983). Centers, Kings, and Charisma: Reflections on the Symbolics of Power. In *Local Knowledge: Further Essays in Interpretive Anthropology*. New York: Basic Books, 121–46.

Gordon, D. J. (1980). *Hymenaei*: Ben Jonson's Masque of Union. In S. Orgel (ed.) *The Renaissance Imagination: Essays and Lectures by D. J. Gordon*. Berkeley: University of California Press, 157–84.

Gurr, A. (1992). *The Shakespearean Stage 1574–1642*. Cambridge: Cambridge University Press.

Harrison, S. (1604). *Arches of Triumph*. London.

Holbrook, P. (1998). Jacobean Masques and the Jacobean Peace. In D. Bevington and P. Holbrook (eds.) *The Politics of the Stuart Court Masque*. Cambridge: Cambridge University Press, 67–87.

Jones, E. (1961). Stuart Cymbeline. *Essays in Criticism*, 11, 84–99.

Jones, I. (1973). *Inigo Jones: The Theatre of the Stuart Court*, 2 vols., ed. S. Orgel and R. Strong. Berkeley: University of California Press.

Jonson, B. (1969). *Ben Jonson: The Complete Masques*, ed. S. Orgel. New Haven, CT: Yale University Press.

Marcus, L. (1988). *Puzzling Shakespeare: Local Reading and Its Discontents*. Berkeley: University of California Press.

Munday, A. (1985). *Pageants and Entertainments of Anthony Munday: A Critical Edition*, ed. D. M. Bergeron. New York: Garland.

Orgel, S. (1975). *The Illusion of Power: Political Theater in the English Renaissance*. Berkeley: University of California Press.

Peacock, J. (1995). *The Stage Designs of Inigo Jones: The European Context*. Cambridge: Cambridge University Press.

Shakespeare, W. (1963). *Pericles*, ed. F. D. Hoeniger. London: Methuen.

——(1987). *The Tempest*, ed. S. Orgel. Oxford: Oxford University Press.

——(1996). *The Winter's Tale*, ed. S. Orgel. Oxford: Oxford University Press.

——(1998). *Cymbeline*, ed. R. Warren. Oxford: Oxford University Press.

Wickham, G. (1963). *Early English Stages: 1300 to 1660*. New York: Columbia University Press.

——(1973). From Tragedy to Tragi-comedy: *King Lear* as Prologue. *Shakespeare Survey*, 26, 33–48.

Yates, F. (1978). *Majesty and Magic in Shakespeare's Last Plays*. Boulder, CO: Shambhala.

11

The Tempest in Performance

Diana E. Henderson

What does *The Tempest* perform? Clearly *not* a realistically compelling story, given the absence of major struggle or action-based conflict carried forward through its narrative: Prospero, we learn from 1.2 onwards, controls the action fairly completely, and even scenes of attempted struggle against his island rule are presented with ironic detachment. Nor would focusing on narrative account for much of the play's kinetic energy, which emanates from Prospero's magical manipulations. Instead, *The Tempest* works – when it works – as an allegory of some sort.[1] Its performance becomes an occasion to meditate on some of the many issues suggested by the characters stranded in its imaginary terrain; it also provides an opportunity to rename Prospero's magic as that of the artists who imaginatively recreate its island adventure on stage, in print, and on screen. Be its symbolic resonance colonialist, theatrical, dynastic, or spiritual, *The Tempest* is most definitely a "meta"-event, and as such has inspired centuries of delight and debate. As a result, too, some of the most powerful productions have been the least "faithful," challenging or translating the text's logic and sympathies to create brave new worlds. In this, *The Tempest* has managed to outshine the other late plays of Shakespeare with which it shares so many textual affinities. Indeed, it has come to perform so much and so differently for so many, that one can easily feel tempest-tossed by the reams of historical and interpretive evidence we inherit: perhaps best then to follow in the footsteps of the play's own weary inheritor, Ferdinand, as he follows his spirit-guide "unto these yellow sands." For in Ariel's most haunting and haunted song, we may find moorings that befit a play defying simple definitions and easy comforts. And perhaps, like Ferdinand, we may become blessed with a better understanding of how and why we find ourselves here, where *The Tempest*'s performance continues to haunt imaginations on distant shores.

Full Fathom Five Thy Father Lies

What does *The Tempest* perform? One obvious answer would be: a version of Shakespeare's written text. Some would go further and say performance itself makes

Shakespeare's imagination real, for audiences removed in time and place. Since the nineteenth century, at least, critics and theatrical artists alike have tried to capture and perform what they believe are the author's intentions. Authorship is like paternity, in a simile dating back to the Renaissance; thus while Prospero and Alonso are fathers within *The Tempest*, the father of *The Tempest* is William Shakespeare. And one way to discover his intentions involves returning to the original text and performance.

Unfortunately, even if one were to accept this associative logic, both origins are shrouded in uncertainty. The first text we have appears at the front of the First Folio of 1623, by which time its "father" lay dead – not at the sea-bottom but under the stones of Holy Trinity Church in Stratford-upon-Avon.[2] The printing chronology might please those who prefer "live" theatre to "dead" text, since we know *The Tempest* was performed during Shakespeare's lifetime: on November 1, 1611 in the old banqueting house at Whitehall Palace before King James I, and again as part of the celebration for Princess Elizabeth's (ill-fated) marriage to the Elector of Palatine. Thus theatrical traces precede the script. Whether these are any more "originary" in their domain than the Folio is in the textual one, however, remains moot. Although some scholars have attributed the play's emphasis on stage spectacle and music – and especially the act 4 "masque" Prospero conjures for the betrothed lovers – to its courtly performance setting, others have countered that all this could just as easily have derived from public performances at the indoor Blackfriars' stage, or even at the great Globe itself.[3] And while the play's allusions to the Bermuda shipwreck imply that the script was completed after 1610, we do not know the exact type or time of its first performance.

We do know it pleased the court enough to be revived. Glynne Wickham and others have built arguments linking Prospero with England's royal father, a scholarly ruler who faced insurrections (the Gunpowder Plot), did not always attend to court corruption, and was marrying his daughter to a foreign prince. Whether or not one agrees with this particular claim,[4] the play's investigation of the involvement of family bonds and political rule, challenging but ultimately confirming the law of the fathers, gave the play a level of "realistic" involvement in the politics of its day that has disappeared only in its particulars: the terms of *The Tempest*'s political performance have shifted to questions of masters, servants, and imperial domination, but the seriousness of those themes continues to balance the play's equally apparent elements of musical comedy.

Another allegorical interpretation that has had widespread influence, if little more contextual evidence to support it (as Orgel stresses), connects the author–father analogy with Prospero's narrative authority and verbal dominance within *The Tempest*. This is the biographical reading in which Prospero stands for Shakespeare himself, wielding his theatrical arts but then concluding his career by breaking his pen/wand and retiring to Stratford, where every third thought would be his grave. Reaching its zenith in the late nineteenth-century writings of Edward Dowden, this interpretation nevertheless persists in consciously postmodern *Tempests* such as Peter Greenaway's experimental film, *Prospero's Books* (1991), in which Prospero himself composes the text that will become part of Shakespeare's Folio. A biographical reading calls special attention to Prospero's "Our revels now are ended" speech as a theatrical farewell from the playwright; some productions have moved the speech from act 4 to create an alternative Epilogue.[5] The association of the playwright with the magician continues to resonate in Giorgio Strehler's extravagantly metatheatrical 1978 staging at the Piccolo Teatro de Milan and then on a world tour; and in Derek Jarman's 1980 punk-alternative film in which Heathcote Williams's Prospero never renounces his magic. Belief in *The Tempest* as Shakespeare's last word likewise confounds historical counter-evidence. In Peter Brook's *The Empty Space* (the 1968 volume so influential on late twentieth-century directors), he writes that "when we begin to unearth the themes that Shakespeare so carefully buried, we see that it is his complete final statement, and that it deals with the whole condition of man" (Brook 1980: 96).

The theatrical power of these originary myths is unlikely to be undone (if indeed it should be undone) by scholarly corrections, unless those who create performances come to feel that the seeming authority and confidence they provide has been overborne by the weight of the father's dead hand. Some turgidly reverential *Tempest*s in recent years suggest that performers are finding this Shakespearean inheritance too heavy a burden (for instance – at the risk of citing "the usual suspects" – the BBC–Time/Life television version). Certainly it is harder nowadays to presume audience sympathy with the white-bearded Prospero who dominated the eighteenth-century stage and still occasionally returns, acting more like God-the-father than like the vexed single parent of a teenaged daughter, himself once victimized by a hostile takeover. One might note the actual practice of director Brook, and his attempts to capture not the letter but the spirit of what he sees as "Shakespeare" (and which some would say is just as much "Brook"). His 1957 *Tempest* – appearing a year after John Osborne's *Look Back in Anger* shook the English theatre with its "angry young man" – presented a vengeful rather than serene Prospero. It disturbed audiences by shifting away from the dominant tradition of a benign patriarch in a grandly ordered world. Clifford Williams, working with Brook in 1963, defended the choice, arguing that these days "you can't present a romance in romantic terms – the baroque, the rococo; we don't respond to them any more" (Hirst 1984: 47).

In performance, the play must translate "Shakespeare" to a new material setting, and the most innovative and successful productions have tended to be those that allow the father to rest in peace while they imagine the script anew. Within the fiction, Prospero once found his "library was dukedom large enough" – yet in doing so he lost his social power and grew unsatisfied. Even as he makes the book his weapon, he recognizes he must forgo it to return to society. The theatre is a social space rather than a library, and has other resources beyond the book: from the start, visual and aural technologies and kinetic energy have played a major part in the play's success. Perhaps for this reason as well as to fit their particular political emphases, when William Davenant and John Dryden radically adapted the play as *The Tempest, or The Enchanted Island* in 1667 – the version of "Shakespeare's play" that would dominate the English stage for 150 years – they cut this now-famous line from Prospero's first-act recollections.[6] From the Restoration well into the nineteenth century, *The Tempest* performed not only Shakespeare but Dryden and Davenant (and later Shadwell, with music by Lawes and then Purcell – not to mention the stage gestures of David Garrick's Prospero, Charles Bannister's Caliban, and a host of female Ariels). By the standard of authorial fidelity, this might be deemed treason akin to Antonio's. But Dryden and Garrick and Kemble would certainly not recognize themselves in the role of treacherous brother to the Bard; they were the makers of bardolatry.

Delight in old words and ways continues to jostle with the present moment. It took longer to recast the First Folio as an actor's scripture than it did to create the figure of the Bard; to a great extent, it was the twentieth century's achievement, though Garrick and Macready got the process rolling by performing Shakespeare rather than Dryden/Davenant. William Poel and Harley Granville Barker picked up the pace by honoring the text over turn-of-the-century spectacle, and finally the post-World War II Royal Shakespeare Company directors made "words first" their house style. Coming to the US, Shakespeare & Company's Kristen Linklater and Tina Packer made explicit their commitment to the Folio as Bible. Shakespeare the divinely inspired man became Shakespeare the theatre's holy text.

But in *Prospero's Books* there is more than one book at the core of this "magic." The film presents 22 digitally imagined Renaissance "books," plus the rest of the Folio (no. 23) and the manuscript of *The Tempest* itself (no. 24). The Folio is still there: for all his radical reconception Greenaway keeps it and "Prospero's" playscript sacral, with Caliban saving them from watery destruction. Yet the book's status is aptly confused, in a way magnified by the use of digital and film media. Even as Prospero literally composes and voices *The Tempest* (respectively, writing by hand and acting as the film's single speaker of its lines through four acts), coming to social maturity requires that he sacrifice univocal control of both text and voice: a trinity of Ariels guides him from vengeance to virtue by writing their own lines, and subsequently Prospero "lets" the other actors speak. Only then is dialogue, the stuff of drama, possible. And even the Folio seen at the end of the film, the remnant retrieved from the conflagration of history and time, contains not the "original" manuscript of *The Tempest* which Caliban likewise recovers but the printed "copy" of Shakespeare's other plays. The only "actual" book we inherit, the Folio, thus post-dates Prospero's in a frame invented by Greenaway. In playfully rethinking the logic of origins – while preserving both the Folio and the voice of one of the century's most important Prosperos, Sir John Gielgud, on film – *Prospero's Books* carries forward the dialogue with Shakespeare's words that has made *The Enchanted Island* as well as the Folio part of what *The Tempest* performs.

Of His Bones are Coral Made

Over Shakespeare's grave appears the warning: "curst be he that moves my bones." The threat may have spared them from human removal, but the bones remain subject to nature's transformations: the processes of historical change go on. From a material being, Shakespeare has been made into an aesthetic and functional object to fit the times.

The material theatre changed as well. Both the Globe and the old Whitehall banqueting house were consumed in flames before *The Tempest* appeared in print. Thirty-seven years after eleven-year-old Prince Charles attended its first court performance, King Charles I would be beheaded at the same spot (Law 1920: 2). *The Tempest's* popularity during the early years of his reign was followed by the Civil War, Commonwealth government, and the closing of the theatres. When they reopened in 1660, they catered to a far less diverse audience than the one that had encouraged Shakespeare's writing.

Dryden and Davenant's *Enchanted Island* adapted *The Tempest* to address its Restoration audience of London courtiers, eager for frivolity and comfort after years of war and exile. First performed at the Duke's Theatre, Lincoln's Inn Fields on November 7, 1667, it mocked its non-aristocratic characters' aspirations in a parody of republicanism – the same year John Milton, the great poet and bitter defender of such out-of-favor ideals, published *Paradise Lost*. Trinculo and Stephano, joined by Mustacho and Ventoso, quarrel as they attempt to challenge Prospero's regime of power, thus deflating the pretensions of less elevated citizens to wield social authority. Focusing on fraternal treachery at the higher levels of government would not have suited King Charles II, so the playwrights shifted attention by adding new characters and more sexual comedy (though to the lusty diarist Samuel Pepys it remained "the most innocent play that ever I saw").[7] The introduction of actresses to the English stage encouraged this and allowed more women's parts: not only did Miranda get a sister, Dorinda, but Ariel gained a beloved, Milcha. Even Caliban got a companion, a sister inheriting the name of Shakespeare's dead witch-mother, Sycorax. Adding a Mantuan prince, Hippolito, whom Prospero had hidden from all sight of women since infancy (yet who was played by an actress) allowed yet more romance and humor. It also expanded upon the trope of Miranda's naïveté at meeting a "brave new world" of old world courtiers – and further shifted attention to erotic rather than political irony. Even so, a form of social contract evolves in the relationship between the occasionally discontented Ariel and his errant master Prospero, whose plans go awry when Hippolito and Ferdinand fight with near-mortal consequences. This magician is not so firmly in control – a dramaturgical alteration likely spurred by changes in the monarchic state as well as by desire for more significant stage conflict.

Seven years later, Thomas Shadwell elaborated on Davenant and Dryden's framework by producing a musical drama or "opera" with settings by numerous composers (some later reset by Purcell). Emphasis on music, spectacle, and romantic comedy kept these versions exceedingly popular for decades to come, replacing the Folio text onstage. Indeed, attempts by James Lacy (1746) and Garrick (1756) to tip the balance back towards Shakespeare's text (though with many added musical and spectacular elements) were rebuffed by audiences. Garrick did perform a highly edited version of Shakespeare's *Tempest* sixty-one times over the next twenty years, but the Restoration additions of more masquing, singing, and stage machinery (including an elaborate shipwreck) remained dominant.[8] John Philip Kemble's 1806 Theatre Royal text, which became the standard acting version for decades, retained much of the spectacle, though he did cut some songs to allow proportionally more spoken text. In 1821 Frederic Reynolds and H. R. Bishop produced an operatic version adding still more "modern" music by Haydn, Mozart, and Rossini.

While the words of most productions remained a mixture culled from several seventeenth-century writers, not only the music but, more profoundly, the meanings attached to *The Tempest* continued to change with the times. The reputation of "Shakespeare" as England's national poet grew during the second half of the eighteenth century, due in great part to Garrick's vigorous promotion; along with his elevation of the Bard, he developed the cult of the great actor. An illustration of Garrick reciting Prospero's lines as the world crumbles behind him ("the cloud-capped towers, the gorgeous palaces . . . all which it inherit") captures not only (if at all) his appearance in a theatrical performance, but also the sense in which he had become the Bard's spokesperson, sustaining "culture" against threatening change. By the 1830s a similar painting by Samuel Colman places Shakespeare himself in the stance of Garrick (derived from engravings of the Stratford Jubilee), as massive buildings collapse around him. The need for a national poet in times of revolution and imperial war would create new associations for Shakespeare, and would lead to new perceptions of *The Tempest*. In political engravings from the 1790s, when Britain feared the consequences of the French Revolution and Napoleon's rise, "The Enchanted Island" was no longer a utopian fairyland or even a place for comic jabs at social upstarts; it became a label for England itself, as John Bull looked out at the French fleet threatening invasion. In later years the events on Prospero's island would come to stand for other problems on other shores, legacies of the colonizing project that had transformed Shakespeare's England into the British Empire.

In the interval, 1838 marked a watershed date in the movement back to the Folio. A year after Queen Victoria ascended the throne, William Charles Macready (having played Prospero several times before) decided to stage *The Tempest* without the Dryden and Davenant additions. Many lines were cut in the interest of spectacle (such as the entire first scene's dialogue during the shipwreck); nevertheless, from this time forward it was Shakespeare's text that would be interspersed with song and magnificent visual effects. And interspersed they were. Since its inception, *The Tempest* had involved music and magic as well as fine poetry, delighting ear and eye. The sensory experiences that so pleased past eras are gone, leaving us only textual traces that often prompt scoffing and charges of "sentimentality" from modern critics focused on the words. But the argument with those who are now bones seems too obviously stacked: of course the words carry on, while the stage machines and bodies that created shipwrecks and banquets have left not a wrack behind. Was it a failure of their aesthetic discernment that generations loved the operatic spectacle they called *The Tempest*? Or is it a failure of our imagination not to understand why they did?

Those are Pearls that were His Eyes

What did nineteenth-century viewers see with those vanished eyes, and how did it mesh with the pearls of poetry that transform the material into the magical? Beginning with the Romantic writers who preferred their solitary imaginations to theatrical performance, many have argued that elaborate shows distract from the sublime possibilities of Shakespeare – especially in plays such as *The Tempest* that feature unlocatable landscapes, metamorphic spirits, gods, and monsters. Yet this presumption disregards the kinetic energy that contributes to the theatrical sublime, and begs the question of how visual pleasure might participate in, rather than rival or quash, the audience's imagination. While much wonder within *The Tempest* is a verbal fiction, a serious "look" at the most overtly, even willfully, spectacular *Tempest* might give word-worshippers pause.

Charles Kean's 1857 *Tempest*, like the pageants he constructed out of Shakespeare's histories, displayed an epic sensibility and delight in antiquarian detail. Kean's Prospero dressed as a medieval courtier, and was ultimately transported back to Italy in a precise replica of an early fourteenth-century Neapolitan ship. Greek vases provided the design for the play's mythical elements. But added to this somewhat predictably literal mid-Victorian aesthetic of historical translation was an unusual sense of theatrical imagination in the "magic" scenes. Others had mounted fantastic opening storms before, from the Restoration onward. But Kean used lighting to produce a new strobe-like effect that dazzled the audience, as Ariel "flits among the frantic mariners as with flashing axe they hew the mast. Ariel is seen darting into the cabin, surrounded by white globules of ethereal fire contrasting admirably with the mortal red of the lamps" (*Era* review, July 5, 1857; in Nilan 1975: 198). And indeed the magical Ariel would remain the guiding spirit of the production from first to last, when he was left alone onstage.

For all the wonder of this extensive "prologue," the most innovative and what we would now call "theatrical" tableau was the act 3 banquet scene – too often a turgid and artificial mid-play interruption. Here it became a tribute to all the sensory possibilities of the nineteenth-century stage. It began with a set change from a barren landscape to one that literally "grew": "Gradually the effect of fertilization grows upon the spectator . . . Slowly, and by degrees, the evidence of luxuriant vegetation arises on every side while at length, from the land dividing, a river flows forth through the scene and fountains . . . spring up" (*Daily Telegraph*, July 2, 1857; in Nilan 1975: 199). Into this theatrical Bower of Bliss enter nymphs balancing fruit baskets on their heads, who then come "together, so that they themselves form the banquet table, the illusion being perfected by the festoons of flowers that conceal their figures" (*Times*, July 3, 1857; in Nilan 1975: 200). Having lured the audience into a state of wonder akin to that of the shipwrecked noblemen, the appearance of Ariel as harpy amidst thunderclaps and darkness no doubt startled: but more unusual was the swift "disappearance" of the banquet itself. The baskets fell through a trapdoor along with Ariel, while the "table" immediately dissolved when the nymphs rolled apart. This last effect, using the bodies of actors rather than machines alone, would please a modern performance artist. It indicates one of many ways in which spectacle did not necessarily mean the replacement of actor by machinery, but rather a synergy between them. Although the first night's running time took five hours due to the elaborate mechanics (cut by an hour subsequently), few thereafter complained about the time passing slowly.

What some *did* lament, however, was the loss of time for lines and thought, comments anticipating the turn-of-century "spectacle vs. text" debate. Nonetheless, the power of the stage pictures tellingly resurfaces even in critical chastisement: witness Hans Christian Andersen, who argued that "Shakespeare was lost in visual pleasure: . . . the living word had evaporated. No one tasted the spiritual banquet – it was forgotten for the golden platter on which it was served" (Marker 1971: 23). Whereas Romantic critics had argued the verbal imagination could not be captured onstage, here the show's visual vocabulary permeates the language of its opponents, obliquely confirming that it too could spur the mind and spirit.

During the early twentieth century, as the new medium of film began to provide wider access to certain forms of visual spectacle, the theatrical debate intensified. While critics and practitioners such as William Poël argued for pared-down representation and more attention to the word, however, audiences continued to enjoy the lush visual emphasis of Herbert Beerbohm Tree's 1904 *Tempest*. The gap between the "in-crowd" and the public may have been just that: often the avant-garde of one decade only gradually becomes acceptable and even standard fare for a larger audience. But it also seems that the terms of argument were not nuanced enough to account for the range of visual pleasure, and the multiple sources of imaginative engagement, that theatre affords to different viewers. A *Vogue* reviewer preferred a spare 1916 Amateur Drama Society of New York production of *The Tempest* because it "affords the poet an unimpeded appeal to the imaginations of the public" (Pearson and Uricchio 1994: 249). The notion that words alone inspired the imagination was not the only suspect claim here – though certainly it was easier in words than action to create the illusion that one was resurrecting a dead poet who wished to be granted space for such an appeal. Tellingly, Tree himself used the same sleight-of-hand conjuration of the author-figure (though at least in simile form) to argue in favor of detailed, literalist visuals: "The public of to-day demands that, if acted at all, Shakespeare shall be presented with all the resources of the theatre of our time – that he shall be treated, not as a dead author speaking a dead language, but as a living force speaking with the voice of a living humanity. And it will be my further endeavor to show that in making this demand the public is right" (ibid: 258).

Perhaps it is not surprising, then, that Tree was also amenable to experiments with film. Theatre historians tend to regard him as the last gasp of nineteenth-century aesthetics and might cringe at my placing him in a sentence with Giorgio Strehler and Robert Lepage, yet Tree was involved in the first attempt at "multimedia" Shakespeare: Charles Urban's 1905 attempt to film his opening storm scene, to be projected behind live actors. Some critics considered Tree's mode of theatricality itself akin to cinema in its "suggestion of overwhelming mechanism, of excellent craft but not of art" (*New Republic*, 1916; in Pearson and Uricchio 1994: 256). These words convey not just an anti-visual bias, but latent fears about modernity itself: its "overwhelming" scale of mechanization, and its obliteration of the aura of art by merely skillful forms of "mechanical reproduction" (to invoke Walter Benjamin's famous essay). No wonder, then, that the terms of these debates continue to appear (often in equally confused, imprecise forms) in critical responses to the mechanized mass art form of Shakespeare on screen: distress when images replace words; worries that sensory representation will thwart imaginative engagement, that box-office appeal will preclude spiritual edification, and that the art of "Shakespeare" is disappearing.

Arguably the screen has made more plausible some of the old worries about the effacement of language, or at least has tilted the balance so far towards visual apperception that words no longer do have the same sensory power and performative potential that they do onstage (and that is so underrepresented in the schema of text vs. performance). But this remains a moot point, and before leaping to that "rich and strange" domain, I want to reconsider one last spectacle, performed in 1916. This is Percy MacKaye's New York extravaganza, *Caliban by the Yellow Sands*. It has been invoked negatively by progressive critics from Lawrence Levine, whose bemusement verges on disdain, to Thomas Cartelli, who discredits at length its putatively democratic ethos. But while far from *The Tempest*'s text or the sophisticated political criticism it now prompts, the explicit allegory of this celebration of art – the level so quickly dismissed by scholars – helps account for the ongoing power of both communal spectacle and aesthetic romanticism in productions of *The Tempest* and beyond.

Caliban by the Yellow Sands was part of the extensive tercentenary celebration of Shakespeare's death on both sides of the Atlantic. With a huge supporting cast of ethnically diverse New Yorkers performing in a stadium for crowds of 135,000 people over ten nights, this show – like Tree's *Tempest* – was clearly "popular" in at least two senses.[9] Perhaps for this reason Levine stresses its variance from Shakespeare's words (i.e., even if it testifies to Shakespeare's mass appeal at the very moment Levine argues the Bard had become "highbrow," it isn't *really* Shakespeare and hence is not counter-evidence). Cartelli prefers to tar by association this large-scale community drama, emphasizing the privileged status of its author, MacKaye, and citing contemporary pseudo-inclusive events (i.e., even if the scriptwriter declared "Caliban" to be an every-man figure applicable to himself, and even if everybody thought they were participating in a collective celebration, they were duped or in bad faith, not realizing the prejudices inherent in their social location). Finally, its popularity can be seen as the last gasp of a tradition of burlesques and stage tributes endemic to the nineteenth century. Rightly noting that its representation builds on the Victorian association of Caliban with a Darwinian Missing Link, the Vaughans thus conclude, "In 1916 Caliban's aspiration to build a new world of truth and beauty still seemed plausible to New York audiences, but like Prospero's insubstantial pageant, they were a final vestige of Victorian belief in the inexorable progress of humankind" (Vaughan and

Vaughan 1991: 98). Ironically, these views of *Caliban* as a naive or unenlightened throwback curiously mimic the patronizing view of the Shakespearean character Caliban which these scholars would contest.

Certainly the pageant was not *The Tempest*, but rather a spin-off using Shakespeare's characters as allegorical figures to comment on contemporary society. As such, it resembled modern criticism and many performances of *The Tempest* on stage and screen. Caliban, debased by the magic of his parents Sycorax (a "Super-puppet," *à la* Bread and Circus) and the Tiger-Toad God Setebos, is "educated" by Prospero through the process of watching scenes from Western history and drama, especially the works of Shakespeare. However, he repeatedly backslides into lust and violence – as when riled by the "Once more unto the breach" speech from *Henry V* – and must be humbled into penitence. Shakespeare himself finally appears and recites Prospero's act 4 speech, while Caliban, "with gesture of longing, . . . crouches at Shakespeare's feet, gazing up in his face, which looks on him with tenderness" (MacKaye 1916: 145).

What fascinates me about the event, and the scholarship analyzing it, is the respective presence and absence of World War I in accounting for its particular aesthetic vision. While Cartelli cites MacKaye's explicit comments on the war and remarks upon the "masque's frequent references to the Great War and its identification of warlike behavior with the forces of Setebos," it is to highlight the "problematic" use of *Henry V* so close to its climax (Cartelli 1999: 70). That is, he perceives this might undermine what he takes to be an unalloyed, elitist devotion to the Bard as a means of "elevating" less assimilated, mob-like New Yorkers. Yet the show is premised upon our identification with, as well as disgust and sadness at, Caliban's only intermittently successful attempt to be a right-interpreting human being. *Caliban* is not written from the superior position of either Prospero or Shakespeare as Renaissance magus, but rather from the position of a man well aware of the seeming "backsliding" of all civilization, as evidenced by the ongoing slaughter in Europe. Indeed, as Caliban listens to Henry V he is overtly being seduced by the figure of War, the last of an infernal trinity of Setebos's priests (Lust and Death having been dispatched more swiftly). Thus the placement of *Henry V* indicates a more textured understanding of Shakespeare's cultural uses at a precarious political moment: it conveys the limits of human understanding and a dawning consciousness of how deeply the Great War undermined nationalist complacency. This would be, after all, the war's impact upon the "Lost Generation," and MacKaye's own preface overtly honors Shakespeare for his "world-constructive art" within a "self-destroying world."

Cartelli accentuates the predictable Anglo-American biases of MacKaye (who is, in fact, more broadly Eurocentric and critically informed than Cartelli implies, given the impressively learned appendices, the positive images of Egypt and India [in the original plans] and the negative portrayal of Caligula's Rome). But considering the moment of composition, this should be balanced by attention to the overt pacifism of his invocation of Shakespeare's "uninterable spirit" in order "to create new splendid symbols for peace through harmonious international expression" (MacKaye 1916: xiii). *Caliban by the Yellow Sands* was performed the very spring that Woodrow Wilson was being pushed vigorously towards war with Germany: having resisted military involvement after the 1915 sinking of the *Lusitania*, he was forced to issue an ultimatum in April when the Germans declared they would use submarines without restriction. They backed down until the following winter, after which Wilson finally felt compelled to declare war. Thus it was at a moment of great conflict and a sense of threat within the United States that MacKaye turned to Shakespearean mass spectacle as a means of opposing militarism and putting forth an alternative "faith" in the communal powers of art. Caliban concludes:

> A little have I crawled, a little only
> Out of mine ancient cave. All that I build
> I botch; all that I do destroyeth my dream.
> Yet – yet I yearn to build, to be thine Artist
> And stablish this thine Earth among the stars –
> Beautiful! (MacKaye 1916: 145)

Neither as complacent nor as certain of humankind's progress as the Vaughans imply, this pageant seems only in part vestigial. In fact, MacKaye is thoroughly pacifist and quite up-to-date in his theatrical knowledge and vision, employing one of Granville Barker's designers and taking steps "for the immediate translation of the Masque into Italian, German, and Yiddish" in his desire to realize a true "community theater" (ibid: 152). His selections from Shakespeare are consistent with this goal: Egypt and Greece are honored, for example, by choosing moments that idealize romantic love and reconciliation from *Antony and Cleopatra* and even *Troilus and Cressida* – pointedly dismissing the importance of martial glory in the process. The speech from *Henry VIII* recalling the Field of the Cloth of Gold becomes a crucial signifier of historical accord intersecting with art: as the printed volume's cover image, the masquing of that event exemplifies MacKaye's belief that bringing a community together through social art epitomized the best of human history, and his hope that it could thwart the forces of destruction. Thus his title and title-page epigraph from *The Tempest*: "Come unto these yellow sands, / And then take hands!" Aware of the tenuousness of the moment, however, the masque itself ends after the Spirit of Time, the Lady of the Yellow Sands, vanishes in darkness, leaving a longing Caliban, a wistful Miranda, and "the pensive form of Shakespeare" (belated inheritor of Prospero's cloak, in a nice *hysteron proteron* prefiguration of *Prospero's Books*) listening to Ariel's spirits reiterate "We are such stuff / As dreams are made on, and our little life / Is rounded with a sleep." Even the Master artist ultimately foretells dissolution rather than triumph in a world where War could use the art of *Henry V* to his destructive ends; and thus after *Caliban*'s production, the United States would be lured into the famously mis-billed War-to-End-All-Wars.

Though MacKaye was no great poet and might be surprised where such impulses could lead, his spectacle nevertheless prefigures a quite active strain – only sometimes escapist and utopian – within twentieth-century theatre, one which has claimed Shakespeare as a force for artistic internationalism against a backdrop of war, totalitarianism, and potential annihilation of the species. When Peter Brook, director of the "angry" 1957 production, returned to *The Tempest* in 1968, it was in a Roundhouse production commissioned by the classic French actor Jean-Louis Barrault, and was less a performance of "the text" than an experiment in cross-cultural communication among actors from different nations. And it is precisely the non-verbal dimension of theatre that has animated some of the bolder experimental versions of *The Tempest* invoking this aesthetic (in later Brook, in Strehler, in Japanese puppet theatres). Viewed thus, the legacy of theatrical spectacle is not so easy to dismiss.

Nothing of Him That Does Fade

Across the Atlantic from MacKaye, the Englishman Ernest Law wondered whether his studying *The Tempest* had any meaning during his "nation's struggle for existence and freedom"; less ambitious than the New Yorker, he turned for "solace and distraction" to "our great national poet" (Law 1920: 1). Like many others, he asked what was the "most loyal, as well as the most effective and convincing mode of presenting his plays on the modern stage?" (pp. 1–2). While modernists would argue that a radical break with history required new art forms and theatrical methods, old loyalties continued to appear in stage *Tempest*s. The elaborate spectacles of Kean and Tree gave way to the more abstract designs of artist–directors from Gordon Craig to Jennifer Tipton, but still theatre provided a place for visual as well as verbal pleasures. To keep Shakespeare from fading, each generation finds new strategies for making his play resonant. Sometimes the balance of loyalty and liveliness has led to explicitly historicist productions, as well: when Peter Hall directed Sir John Gielgud at the National Theatre in 1974, he returned to the Jacobean context of *The Tempest*'s first performance, using masque devices based on the designs of Inigo Jones and garbing Gielgud like Doctor John Dee, the Elizabethan "magus."

Sir John's own career as Prospero captures the dynamic of loyalty and change in twentieth-century performance. He rethought the particulars of his characterization through radically different productions, while retaining his distinctly melodic and mannered vocal style: that trademark voice also serves as a reminder how words can function not only as tools of representation but as a form of performance, as sensuous as spectacle. More than any other actor, Gielgud could claim to be "the" Prospero of the twentieth century – but unlike earlier definitive performers, he earned this distinction by constantly revising the part. When he first played it at the Old Vic in 1930, he followed the advice of Komisarjevsky, who told him to change the image from the bearded Old Testament sage of prior centuries. Modeling himself after representations of Dante in a set described as "Persian-cum-Japanese," his Prospero, said director Harcourt Williams, was a "being of great beauty" (Hirst 1984: 46). A decade later, Gielgud was a more irascible figure, signaling a shift that would become more generally pronounced in late twentieth-century *Tempest*s. When he appeared in Peter Brook's 1957 Stratford production, he was compared to a hermit or tortured saint within a tough, vengeful world. While Gielgud thus helped establish several new ways of playing Prospero, counterculture theatre of the 1960s went well beyond desacralization of the father-figure; by the time of the Hall *Tempest*, Gielgud struck some as having an air as antiquarian as the production itself. He had always avoided looking at Ariel, seeing the spirit as a projection or aspect of his own magical character, but now the action seemed aloof and politically evasive. However, his last appearance as Prospero, in Peter Greenaway's film, took advantage of Gielgud's double image, placing him within a flamboyantly avant-garde context where unglamorous naked bodies engaged the eye, while the soundtrack still honored Sir John's elegant, aristocratic articulation. And of course Gielgud himself ultimately chose to meld two performance traditions, daring to employ his knightly aura, derived from his theatrical heritage and classical technique, within an experimental medium that was commercially marginal. In so doing, he reinvented not only his own image but also what it means for a venerable British actor to "honor" Shakespeare.

Gielgud's willingness to play with his image recalls another way performance has kept *The Tempest* alive across generations: through burlesques and satires. While purists might say that Davenant and Dryden's *Tempest* was itself a burlesque, it quickly spawned a lowlife parody, *The Mock Tempest* (1675) by Thomas Duffett. The opening "storm" turns out to be a riot in a brothel, and pimps and bawds get the final Chorus. In 1850 a satire transformed the title of a successful opera, *La Tempesta*, into *La! Tempest! Ah!* Rather than mocking the play, this comedy was part of a debate about the appropriateness of making an opera out of *The Tempest*, a sign of the great reverence that had accrued to the figure of Shakespeare over the centuries. The ramparts scene from *Hamlet* was restaged featuring Shakespeare himself as the ghost; using his words, the prologue denounced *La Tempesta* as a form of "murder most foul" (Roche 1987: 459). Far more "foul" from our perspective is the "humorous" use of characters and lines from *The Tempest* to mock the Emancipation Proclamation in the English magazine *Punch* (January 24, 1863). Called "Scene from the American 'Tempest',", a cartoon presents Caliban as a slave inciting Abraham Lincoln, "You beat him 'nough, massa! Little Time, I'll Beat him too," with the grotesque subscript, "Shakespeare (Nigger translation)." Making Shakespeare "alive" in this way helps explain why so many colonized people would subsequently turn to Caliban as a figure to redeem and would regard aestheticized praises of Shakespeare, identified with Prospero's position, as repugnant. For long before academic criticism coined the term "postcolonial," actual cultural performances of *The Tempest* involved Shakespeare in systems of racism and oppression that worked against the idealistic vision of art undergirding *Caliban by the Yellow Sands*. Let us turn to this "sea-change" in the performance of *The Tempest*.

But Doth Suffer a Sea-Change

Crossing oceans since its original performance, *The Tempest* has traveled to the United States, Europe, and around the world; at the same time, masses of people were forced across oceans by the slave trade, moving to new islands and nations, and giving rise to new perspectives on this play. Caliban, seen (perhaps with willful blindness) by Davenant and Dryden as a comic buffoon, gradually became the symbol of "other" people – be they racially, culturally, or prehistorically differentiated. As slave, colonized subject, and Darwinian ape-man, Caliban has himself undergone sea-changes in performances that make it impossible to generalize about "his" role. The nineteenth-century actress Fanny Kemble characterized Caliban as a "gross and uncouth but powerful savage" and associated him with "the more ponderous and natural elements" (Slights 2001: 360), yet by century's end Beerbohm Tree chose to play this character rather than Prospero, and ended his staging with Caliban at center stage, pining as the Italians' ship left him behind. A play that had always provided some comedy now contained a subtext of unmitigated tragedy as well.

Few Shakespearean characters – and certainly no such "minor" characters, in terms of lines and narrative centrality – have sparked as varied and significant an afterlife as Caliban. Alden and Virginia Vaughan's book-length study captures the complexity of his "Cultural History," and one must look there to do justice to a character now emblematic of justice denied. But to write about the performance of *The Tempest* without noticing Caliban would be to reenact the nightmare of history. For while Shakespeare could hardly know how emblematic his puppy-eared monster would become, Britannia did indeed proceed to rule the waves, and when she did, she made the subjugation of peoples imagined to be like Caliban part of "all that we inherit." No one can perform *The Tempest* now "innocent" of those world systems intervening between Shakespeare's day and our own.

Caliban truly came into his own in the nineteenth and twentieth centuries. Of course the seeds were there in the Folio: in the mixture of brutality and poetry, in his poignant wish for "freedom" and the crassness of his imagined exploitation by Stephano and Trinculo, in his defiance and pursuit of grace. But only with the emergence of a rhetorically justified global system of slavery and colonialism did the hag-born whelp come to bear witness to massive numbers of dehumanized non-Europeans. As well as reinstating the Folio text, Macready's production also presented new empathy for Caliban, as represented by George Bennett. In an 1839 talk reflecting upon the production (and on the superiority of his day to the benighted middle ages), Patrick Macdonnell captured the uneasy feelings of a "civilized" Englishman which accompanied appreciation of a fine acting performance. Noting that "I have never read, or witnessed this scene, without experiencing a degree of pity, for the poor, abject, and degraded slave," he continues: "The part of Caliban, has generally been exhibited on the stage, in a manner, so as to excite feelings, almost approaching to a painful *and disagreeable kind*; but it has remained for the excellence of Mr. G. Bennett, to delineate, the rude and uncultivated savage, in a style, which arouses our sympathies, in behalf of those, whose destiny, it has never been, to enjoy the advantages of civilization" (Macdonnell 1840: 18). The halting hyperpunctuated description of this actor "at the acme of his art" (p. 19) reflects the mixed response of many at a time when Caliban was not usually viewed as a figure of political critique, yet clearly struck a nerve by reminding the "civilized" theatregoer of others who were denied his privileged position.

While the *Punch* cartoons testify that some saw more direct links to contemporary politics, for the most part nineteenth-century theatre kept its distance, preferring (gradually) to connect Caliban with less immediately disturbing associations – at least for those who considered themselves scientific and did not think metaphorically. Not until the mid-twentieth century would Caliban be performed by a black actor. Instead, in the wake of Darwin and Daniel Wilson's book *Caliban: The Missing Link* (1873), leading actor–managers Frank Benson (1891) and Beerbohm Tree (1904–8) took the part and transformed it into a star turn.[10] By conceptualizing the monster as an ancient ancestor, they could conjure sympathy that was not politically challenging to the Empire, and could also add absurd stage business. Benson appeared ape-like and swung from trees upside-down, in a costume his wife Constance called "half monkey, half coco-nut" (Vaughan and Vaughan 1991: 185). He famously entered with a real fish hanging out of his mouth. Presumably some of this business made up for the absence of the usually elaborate storm scene, which he cut (his budget was limited). Tree took full advantage of his resources, stressing the use of lighting and acrobatics, and adding the famous finale: after the ship sails and Ariel flies away, a tableau presented Caliban with arms outstretched towards the ship "in mute despair." Tree's description ends: "The night falls, and Caliban is left on the lonely rock. He is king once more" (Nilan 1972: 122). Tree made his point explicit in his edition's preface: "we feel that from the conception of sorrow in solitude may spring the birth of a higher civilization" (Vaughan and Vaughan 1991: 187). The long sweep of evolutionary history allows these *Tempests* to both feel for Caliban and sustain an unquestioning sense of cultural superiority. At least, for most viewers: W. T. Stead in "What About Rhodesia?" made a (fairly confused) case that expressed worries on behalf of white colonizers in Africa alongside comments about Caliban as the Jingoism-drunk representative of democracy during the Boer War (Griffiths 1983: 189–90). But a theatrical newspaper, *Era*, responded dismissively to such allusion-making.

By the mid-twentieth century, as colonial empires unraveled, the theatre began to perform Caliban in a way that showed more overt political engagement. Not that the first steps in the transition from Darwinian to postcolonial were particularly encouraging: Roger Livesey "blacked up" while retaining fur and scales, and the first actual black Caliban, Canada Lee, took the part in Margaret Webster's 1945 New York production likewise wearing scales, a mask, and crouching like an animal. Earle Hyman (1960) and James Earl Jones (1962), African-American actors who would later personify dignity, played Caliban as monster, with grotesque costumes and lizard-like makeup: in this, they resembled their Welsh vocal peer Richard Burton, who performed on US television (1960, Hallmark Hall of Fame) with floppy fin-feet and huge ears (though his poetry rang true). In other words, a radical rethinking of the play's politics did not emerge simply with changes in racial casting – at most, critics such as Ivor Brown saw a connection with "aboriginal" or "Backward and Underprivileged" people that *should* inspire more sympathy than was generally accorded (Griffiths 1983: 195–6).

Liberation writers and sociologists were in fact the ones who first made an explicit analogy between *The Tempest* and the dynamics of colonialist imperialism. As a result, it took a self-consciously intellectual director who read such works to introduce the political allegory into stage performance. Jonathan Miller, influenced by Octave Mannoni's *Prospero and Caliban: The Psychology of Colonization* (English translation, 1956), directed the breakthrough production at the Mermaid in 1970. He cast black actors for both Ariel and Caliban (Norman Beaton and Randolph Walker), and made Prospero (Graham Crowden) a district governor rather than awe-inspiring magus. Indeed, there was no stage magic at all, keeping the attention on the play of human power. The choice to make Ariel the "good subject" rather than an ethereal spirit was actually the most startling change. The emphasis shifted to his and Caliban's contrasting ways of aspiring to freedom: thus as Prospero's ship sails off this time, Ariel silently retrieves Prospero's damaged wand and repairs it, whereas Caliban shakes his fist at the departing white man. It was not the outright rebel who would become king of this island, but the "educable" assimilating neocolonialist.

However, if we consider performance to include adaptations and spinoffs, the theatrical credit for revolutionizing interpretation shifts – away from a white Englishman. *Une tempête*, by Martiniquan Aimé Césaire, was performed in 1969 in Tunisia, then in Avignon and Paris. Described by its author as a "psychodrama," it also drew explicit parallels with the fractured African-American rights movement (Caliban being aligned with Malcolm X, while the mulatto Ariel was linked with Martin Luther King). By its conclusion (in Philip Crispin's 1998 translation), Prospero is old, stiff, and alone on the island with Caliban, locked in a dynamic of mutual loathing as he continues to proclaim himself the guardian of civilization. But far away, amidst sounds of the sea, the last word – or rather, note – goes to Caliban, who sings "Liberty, Oh-Ay! Liberty!" (Hulme and Sherman 2000: 156).

Many variations on the imperial theme followed, including novels – such as Marina Warner's *Indigo* (the story of Sycorax as a Caribbean islander) – that go beyond *The Tempest*'s cast-list in endeavoring to reimagine the histories that colonialism effaced.[11] Philip Osment's *This Island's Mine* shifts attention to issues of homosexuality and oppression in Thatcherite Britain. Raquel Carrio and Flara Lauten's *Otra Tempestad*, playing not only in Cuba but at the London Globe (1998), invoked Afrocuban deities and made the tempest Sycorax's creation. Rather than align with Caliban against empire, it seeks (as the combination of performance venues might suggest) a new interplay of texts that absorbs the complex mixed heritage of the postcolonial subject. When Robert Lepage produced *La Tempête* in 1992, his Caliban was a woman, Anne-Marie Cadieux. A sea-change in power relations, involving gender as well as race and nationalities, has made both nostalgic reenactments of "Shakespeare's intentions" and simpler Caliban-focused counter-arguments seem inadequate to many. Meanwhile new energies and angles have emerged through reconceived *Tempests* – in Bali and Japan, in Canada, South America, and India.

"Straight" *Tempests* within the English-speaking tradition likewise continue to explore different frames of political references, such as Native American conquest (Ben Kingsley as Ariel in Barton's 1970 Stratford production) and Caribbean rebellion (David Suchet as Caliban in 1978, at Stratford). In 1981 at the Guthrie, Liviu Ciulei surrounded the stage with a moat of blood containing broken artifacts of Western civilization, while Simon Russell Beale's Ariel spat in Prospero's face in Sam Mendes's 1993 Stratford production (at least early on; the controversial action was later cut). Then the mood seemed to change: George C. Wolfe's New York Shakespeare Festival production (Central Park and Broadway, 1995), starring Patrick Stewart as Prospero, mixed the colonial structure – a female black Ariel (Aunjanue Ellis) and a male black Caliban (Teagle F. Bougere) – with multicultural celebratory theatre in which all could participate. Given an African-American director was working with a British actor famous as the French Captain Picard on *Star Trek* (and who balanced uneasiness at his own master-status with an energetic desire to play), the metatheatrical context abetted the theatrical concept. In a similar vein, Ron Daniels's ART production (1995) made the act 4 masque into Carnival, with goddesses representing the Americas, Europe, and Africa. It aspired to symbolize "la raza cosmica" (borrowing from José Vasconcelos) with Ferdinand and Miranda as "the new multicultural children" (Program commentary). How one could blithely assert that the privileged white European couple fit this role boggles the mind; but then again, this was the mid-1990s when a quick phrase sufficed to "feel your pain" if the show was enjoyable to watch. The political sting of critique was being supplanted by feel-good internationalism, at least on the Anglo-American commercial stage – not so very far away, a cynic might remark, from the world of Percy MacKaye. Perhaps it is time not only to challenge orthodoxy yet once more, but to look to new media.

Into Something Rich and Strange

Leaping from stage to screen calls attention to their different expressive powers and raises that tempestuous question, what is "real"? What exactly does it mean to perform *The Tempest* on film? Translation and adaptation seem inadequate words to describe this process: it is truly a transformation. And just as some of the most compelling stage productions have been those where directors (Brook, Miller, Strehler) felt free to reconceptualize the play, so too the film versions of *The Tempest* – unlike a fairly undistinguished group of video performances – have succeeded to the extent that they have transformed Shakespeare's play into something rich and strange.

Perhaps it is not surprising that the filmic history of *The Tempest* began with its storm scene. The photorealistic possibilities of the medium would seem ideal for giving extra power to a scene that is designed, after all, to deceive its audience into believing it is "real": only after we have watched scene 1 will Miranda and Prospero arrive to explain that we have been misled by the conventions of theatre. That bit of late Shakespearean bravura has often been undone onstage, by calling special attention to the magical presence of Ariel onboard or even by reversing the scenes so we know of Prospero's art in advance. But film provides extra incentive to honor the title.

Yet the three major films – Derek Jarman's *The Tempest*, Paul Mazursky's *Tempest*, and Peter Greenaway's *Prospero's Books* – prove that the medium and the text benefit from something other than the obvious moves. In none of these versions is the "realistic" use of spectacle a source of power, nor (with the possible exception of Mazursky) do they appear to anticipate it would ever be appropriate. Instead, the films play against realism from the start, making consciousness of the medium and its "unreality" part of their most "potent art." (Obviously in even looser "spinoffs" than Mazursky's such as the western *Yellow Sky* (1948) and the science-fiction classic *Forbidden Planet* (1956), the narrative and style depart from anything like "literalism.") Only a few instances will suffice here: fortunately, these films have prompted enough analysis to let these remarks serve as a supplement.[12]

Most would say Mazursky's *Tempest* (1982) is at best a partial success, enlisting some excellent actors (John Cassavetes, Gina Rowlands, Susan Sarandon) in the interests of a fairly complacent narrative about male mid-life crisis forgiven. But one sequence stands out, in part because it is a narrative interlude that does not involve Philip/Prospero at all (directly), in part because its frivolity sparks a wild change in style. This is a goat dance, literally, inspired by Raúl Julia's island native Kalibanos piping the tune, "New York, New York." Given that the film's Greek island serves as the escapist alternative to the angst-ridden Big Apple, one can argue that the song is there to demonstrate the yearning of the Caliban-figure to join "civilization," in the great *Tempest* performance tradition. Certainly the already commercialized goatherd Kalibanos tries to make money off his visitors and buys a television with which to entice Miranda into his cave. But during this sequence, none of it seems to matter much. Rather, sheer enjoyment temporarily relieves the film's tendentious psychodrama once Kalibanos begins to play. At the first strains, the goats prick up their ears; then, as Liza Minnelli's voice begins to overlay his piping, they careen down the cliffsides, culminating in a buoyant parody of the Beatles leaping through the air in *A Hard Day's Night*. Julia makes the most of a simple soft-shoe in front of his goat-chorus line, and as a result the liveliest visual sequence is not the "realistic" storm but this consciously absurd scene. Moreover, the viewer's new allegiance to these lively dancing creatures means that the slaughter of one, to provide a scapegoat and banquet for the fifth act's equivalent forgiveness scene, gives a bit more consequence to the otherwise sentimental conclusion. Reconciling the two domains, the song anticipates the film's final return to New York City – though without Kalibanos (and landing near the World Trade Center, which now carries its own poignance). Even here in a dominantly naturalistic film, spectacle works best not as literalist visualization but as an occasion for imaginative intertextuality.

As if to defy the medium's possibilities for storms and magic on a grand scale, Jarman and Greenaway both emphasize spatial enclosure in their films. Jarman's *Tempest* takes place primarily in a ruined stately house (Stoneleigh Abbey, in Shakespeare's home county) seemingly emblematic of post-imperial Britain's decline, while Greenaway creates a surreal palace for Prospero, claustrophobically peopling the screen with naked figures. Inverting *Titanic*-style epic movie-making, in which models become larger than life, *Prospero's Books* begins with a travesty storm: a boy's urine stream capsizing a toy boat. For Jarman's storm and other outdoor sequences he uses a blue filter as a kind of alienation effect. Each director plays with film reality to create alternative forms of audience engagement. Jarman's casting of the magician Heathcote Williams as Prospero and Jack Birkett ("The Great Orlando") as Caliban plays with the boundary between fiction and filmed performance art, while Greenaway dazzlingly superimposes digitized images of Renaissance books come to life, and highlights the balletic beauty of Caliban's movements. Each film also reveals the inadequacy of evaluating the medium by fidelity to the text: drastically different from each other and from "traditional" stage versions, each is also quite careful in following the Folio text. (Playfully, Jarman concludes by adding the song "Stormy Weather" – as well as dancing sailors rather than goats.) What they perform is a conceptual and visual fantasia on *The Tempest*: as Jarman's subtitle reminds us, this is a play "as seen through the eyes of Derek Jarman." Greenaway's creativity is so obvious that even had he not changed the title, no announcement would be necessary.

What none of these films manages, however, is a dialogue with the postcolonial critiques of the twentieth century. Postmodern style may have implicit links with such challenges to received common sense, and Jarman had explicit reasons for political coalition with other marginalized social groups. But *The Tempest* on film has yet to perform the dimension of intercultural work most important in its late twentieth-century stage life. Indeed, when Greenaway (like Jarman) visualizes Alonso's daughter Claribel married to the King of Tunis, his choice to render the Neapolitan courtiers' perspective on alliance with an African results in his camera replicating not just sixteenth-century textual beauty but racism as well.

Sea-nymphs Hourly Ring His Knell

And what of gender? Long before Walt Disney's *The Little Mermaid*, Ariel became a female acting part. Originally a boy actor who could appear as a harpy and sea-nymph at will, with the advent of actresses during the Restoration this soon seemed a role amenable to adaptation. By the nineteenth century, the norm was a Tinkerbell fairy: Miss Horton, Kate Terry, and Julia St. George all fit the bill. In the early twentieth century Earnest Law was indignant at "our modern ineptness of setting a grown-up young woman to personate that 'spirit of air'," arguing that "this part, indeed, ought never to be played at all except by a boy in his early 'teens'" (Law 1920: 18). Yet it must have been easier for audiences to accept Prospero's affectionate address to a female in those centuries of idealized heterosexuality, and the women's parts in the classical repertory were limited indeed. Moreover, Law's assumption that it would be more apt for a boy to play an airy spirit reveals his own rootedness in a gender system that associates women with the base and earthly. Ariel continues to be an androgynous role, played by both sexes successfully. In Strehler's production, he was a graceful Pierrot;[13] Jarman made him the focus of homoeroticism; Greenaway created a trinity of male youths; and Mazursky renamed him/her Aretha, invoking the Queen of Soul.

Nor has Ariel's own struggle been entirely overshadowed by revolutionary Calibans: Greenaway makes much of the tri-Ariel's assumption of the pen, and Miller, Wolfe, and Strehler all – in diverse ways – emphasized the moment of freedom. While the twentieth-century shift to male Ariels to some extent coincided with greater seriousness and political resonance being accorded the part, recent female Ariels have become more than Tinkerbells: in George Wolfe's *Tempest*, the imbrication of race and gender politics created an overdetermined figure whose doubled oppression historically has been underrepresented. Even in less political productions such as Jennifer Tipton's 1991 *Tempest* at the Guthrie, a female Ariel now works differently. For Hans Peter Kuhn, Tipton's sound designer, "Ariel is to my way of thinking the rightful possessor of the island . . . whenever Ariel appears something strange will open in sound" (Shyer 1992: 30). And it is Ariel, after all, whose song we follow here: while Prospero may be the puppeteer/director, he leaves the details to his spirit-worker, and he/she not only reminds him of the plot but creates the artistic interludes that enchant.

But there is another creature Prospero loves, originally played by a boy actor but never after challenged as being female. Miranda has been idealized (especially in eighteenth- and nineteenth-century illustrations; see Kromer 1998) and yet dismissed by many as a thankless part: even her harsh berating of Caliban's attempted rape was often transferred to her father in the past, that bit of rage for the actress deemed too unladylike. The problem in playing Miranda, however, is more structural than characterological: she (like Juliet, Imogen, and some other beloved Shakespearean heroines) may defy her father's orders, but the audience knows in advance that he not only realizes it but planned it: so much for agency. Nevertheless, Carrie Preston played against type as an island tomboy in Wolfe's production, and Toyah Wilcox (in Jarman) and Molly Ringwald (in Mazursky) likewise found ways out of the Sleeping Beauty straitjacket. Miranda is, after all, the one who shows concern and suspicion about the storm from the start, immediately establishing a perspectival connection with the audience. If Prospero's cynicism about her "brave new world" eventually trumps her view, she is nevertheless the only indisputably female character represented in a man's world: it is not a comfortable position to be in. The implied alternatives, only present in words, are witches (Sycorax), dead mothers (Prospero's nameless wife), and vanishing goddesses. If Miranda can hold her own onstage, she is doing quite well.

(Burden) Ding Dong

Who bears the burden of *The Tempest*? Caliban obviously, but there are others who do the dirty work in this play as well. While the nineteenth-century stage drowned out his words, the surly seaman who begins the play reminds us that aristocratic authority has limits – imposed by nature as well as magic. And as the comical undersong to Prospero's search for vindication and Caliban's for grace, there is the motley carousing and ding-dong inanity of Stephano and Trinculo, the servants at court. Jan Kott noted that *The Tempest* was the most Italian of Shakespeare's plays, and certainly these *commedia* clowns give some grounding for the claim. (In Strehler's metatheatrical production, Trinculo became the Neapolitan Pulcinella and Stephano was the Bergamot Brighella.) But they also remind an audience, after the seamen go aground, of the ongoing class distinctions upon which Shakespearean "civilization" is constructed. When hauling logs becomes a young suitor's knightly trial and a would-be rapist's punishment, alienation from labor surely becomes a parenthetical burden to the play's magical escapism. The "rude mechanicals" of *A Midsummer Night's Dream* have been recast as twentieth-century heroes; but few productions have yet taken the challenge of rethinking class, as well as race and gender, when staging *The Tempest*.

Hark, Now I Hear Them, Ding Dong Bell

What does the audience hear and perceive? Does *The Tempest* perform enchantment for them? And do they attend as well to the fraud and falsity of this entire song? For Ariel's song, like the dirge in *Cymbeline*, destabilizes easy conclusions. After all, while the spirit leads Ferdinand to yellow sands and sings a dirge, the father is alive. Within the fiction, Alonso has not been transformed into art, but remains a man of bones, in thrall to Prospero's rough magic. He, like Ferdinand, is led astray. But Alonso is also led by magical performances to the self-examination and condemnation that, arguably, will allow his eventual reconciliation and the partial repair of society. A song that can be deemed cruel to the naive prince, awakening him to grief and loss, also brings him wonder and love – and his "fated" political alliance. The lyrical lie, then, is no less ambiguous than the tempest itself: deceptive, miraculous, destructive, and comical. What audiences have a chance to witness depends in great part on the choices of theatrical and film artists, who can pull our strings as if we were all Ferdinand. Pawns in their plotting, do we attain any freedom of mind or growth of sensibility as a result? Or do we rebel like Caliban, believing we could do better? Do we hear the words we want to, and follow our own song?

In Jennifer Tipton's staging *The Tempest* was a world of mirrors and shadows, of neon lights that reflected dark souls. In the Folio Caliban is left seeking for grace, which is only a letter away from Prospero's final progress towards the grave. Are they one and the same, found in an other/afterworld that cannot quite be represented, but towards which *The Tempest* always aspires? Giorgio Strehler's grand *coup de théâtre* had the stage itself collapse as Prospero recited his Epilogue: theatrical magic, like the great Globe itself, leaving not a wrack behind. But then, as the audience clapped hands at Prospero's request, they became the play's ultimate conjurors: the stage gradually came "back to life," resurrected from the sea-depths in tribute to human agency – or society – or art. Harder to construct than destroy, the performances of *The Tempest* remain our conjurations and memories, the stuff that dreams are made on. In witnessing, and witnessing to, its performances, perhaps we should all seek for grace.

NOTES

1   Often produced, *The Tempest* can be painful when done badly. To cite the great director Peter Brook at his most scathing: "As a straight-forward plot it is uninteresting; as a pretext for costumes, stage effects and music it is hardly worth reviving; as a pot-pourri of knockabout and pretty writing it can at best please a few matinée-goers – but usually it only serves to put generations of school children off theatre for life" (Brook 1980: 94). This from a man who loves the play.

An essay of this kind cannot adequately acknowledge its debt to scholars who have come before. Besides those listed in the bibliography, I thank Tony Dawson for sharing work in draft. A special note of gratitude is due my researcher Lianne Habinek, whose insights have contributed immeasurably. *Tempest* citations refer to the Vaughan edition (Shakespeare 1999).

2   The Folio's *Tempest* begins in some copies with an elaborate but backwards "B," epitomizing the hazards distancing any printed text from Shakespeare's brain; the inversion was corrected early in the print run. A more substantial textual debate concerns Ferdinand's wise/wife line; see Orgel's edition (Shakespeare 1987). For more on the theoretical issues involved in textual editing, see Donaldson (1997a).

3   On early performances, see Orgel's edition of the play, and Gurr (1989), Demaray (1998), and Bruster (1995).

4   The latter choices might as easily recall the play's other father, Alonso – hardly a parallel to please the king. Moreover, the death of Prince Henry between the first and second recorded court performances eerily inverts the play's movement from loss to recovery of the putatively dead son. It would seem grossly insensitive to create specific connections with the royal family in this context, and we have no evidence that the audiences so perceived this entertainment.

5   The spectacular tribute *Caliban by the Yellow Sands*, discussed below, likewise concludes with this speech placed in the mouth of Shakespeare "As Prospero," after an exchange of identity between magician and playwright. Such use of this speech also illustrates the importance of textual cuts in shaping performance, since as written it concludes with Prospero far from transcendent, instead confessing to Ferdinand, "Sir, I am vexed."

6   They did however retain his other line prizing some volumes "above my Dukedom," which conveys the value without privileging the space.

7   Cited from Bevington's edition of Shakespeare (1988: 513).

8   Stone (1956) argues that Garrick's 1750 production was the "swan song of the Dryden–Davenant–Shadwell play"; while he shows just how much local changing went on subsequently and stresses Garrick's role in returning to (part of) Shakespeare's text, this remains a vast overstatement, falsely reducing the length of *The Enchanted Island*'s stage reign.

9   The New York venue was Lewisohn Stadium; it was later staged at the Harvard stadium in Boston. MacKaye's original plan had been a Central Park performance, but some concerned citizens opposed it (playing against Cartelli's emphasis on MacKaye's privileged sponsorship – as if any production of this scale could have gone forward without corporate sponsors, then or now). But the City College came through with Lewisohn, leaving MacKaye to lament the lack of "democratic equipment" for "the people's expression in civic art-forms" (MacKaye 1916: xx, xix) in New York – and Shakespeare in the Park to wait forty years for Joe Papp.

10   Pearce (1995) defends Tree's directorial concept, whereas most scholarship dismisses it as self-serving spectacle. A 1903 touring production by Frederick Warde and Louis James, originating in San Francisco and reaching Chicago, likewise presented Caliban (played by James) as a Missing Link. So did Tyrone Power in Augustin Daly's 1897 New York production, with a mixture of scales and fur. Later Darwinian Calibans included Russell Thorndike and Robert Atkins at the Old Vic (1919 and 1920–5 respectively) and G. Wilson Knight in Toronto (1938). For more, see Griffiths (1983) (reprinted in Palmer 1991) and Vaughan and Vaughan (1991); but for a very different view that could qualify our smugness about this "antiquated" tradition as much as the spectacular one it emerged within, see the work of writer–primatologists Peterson and Goodall (1993).

11   The number of novelistic as well as theatrical spinoffs is too large to catalog here. See Vaughan and
     Vaughan (1991), Hulme and Sherman (2000), Fischlin and Fortier (2000), and Indra Ganesan's *The
     Journey* for starters.
12   See Cavecchi (1997), Donaldson (1997b), Cartmell (2000), Jackson (2000), Kennedy (1992), Harris
     and Jackson (1997), and Tweedie (2000).
13   On Strehler, see Warren (1986: 263), Kennedy (1993: 309), and Hirst (1984).

REFERENCES AND FURTHER READING

Anderson, R. L. (1993). Shakespeare at the Guthrie: *The Tempest* Through a Glass, Darkly. *Shakespeare
     Quarterly*, 44, 1, 87–92.
Beerbohm-Tree, H. (1913). *Thoughts and After-thoughts*. New York and London.
Brook, P. (1980). *The Empty Space*. New York: Atheneum.
Bruster, D. (1995). Local *Tempest*: Shakespeare and the Work of the Early Modern Playhouse. *Journal of
     Medieval and Renaissance Studies*, 25, 1, 33–53.
Cartelli, T. (1999). *Repositioning Shakespeare: National Formations, Postcolonial Appropriations*. New York:
     Routledge.
Cartmell, D. (2000). *Interpreting Shakespeare on Screen*. London: Macmillan.
Cavecchi, M. (1997). Peter Greenaway's *Prospero's Books*: A Tempest Between Word and Image.
     Literature/Film Quarterly, 25, 2, 83–9.
Cholij, I. (1998). "A Thousand Twangling Instruments": Music and *The Tempest* on the Eighteenth-
     Century London Stage. *Shakespeare Survey*, 51, 79–94.
Demaray, J. G. (1998). *Shakespeare and the Spectacles of Strangeness: The Tempest and the Transformation of
     Renaissance Theatrical Forms*. Pittsburgh, PA: Duquesne University Press.
Donaldson, P. (1997a). Digital Archive as Expanded Text: Shakespeare and Electronic Textuality. In K.
     Sutherland (ed.) *Electronic Text: Investigations in Method and Theory*. Oxford: Clarendon Press, 173–97.
——(1997b). Shakespeare in the Age of Post-Mechanical Reproduction: Sexual and Electronic Magic
     in *Prospero's Books*. In L. E. Boose and R. Burt (eds.) *Shakespeare: The Movie*. New York: Routledge.
Dymkowski, C. (ed.) (2000). *Shakespeare in Production: The Tempest*. Cambridge: Cambridge University
     Press.
Fischlin, D. and Fortier, M. (eds.) (2000). *Adaptations of Shakespeare: A Critical Anthology of Plays from the
     Seventeenth Century to the Present*. London: Routledge.
George, D. E. R. (1989). *The Tempest* in Bali. *Performing Arts Journal*, 11–12, 3–1, 84–107.
Griffiths, T. R. (1983). "This Island's Mine": Caliban and Colonialism. *The Yearbook of English Studies*,
     13, 159–80. Reprinted as "Caliban on the Stage" In D. J. Palmer (ed.) (1991) *Shakespeare: The Tempest*.
     London: Macmillan, 184–200.
Gurr, A. (1989). *The Tempest*'s Tempest at Blackfriars. *Shakespeare Survey*, 41, 91–102.
Harris, D. and Jackson, M. (1997). Stormy Weather: Derek Jarman's *The Tempest*. *Literature/Film
     Quarterly*, 25, 2, 90–8.
Hirst, D. L. (1984). *The Tempest: Text and Performance*. Basingstoke: Macmillan.
Hulme, P. and Sherman, W. H. (eds.) (2000). *"The Tempest" and Its Travels*. Philadelphia: University of
     Pennsylvania Press.
Jackson, R. (ed.) (2000). *The Cambridge Companion to Shakespeare on Film*. Cambridge: Cambridge
     University Press.
Kennedy, D. (1993). *Looking at Shakespeare: A Visual History of Twentieth-Century Performance*. Cambridge:
     Cambridge University Press.
Kennedy, H. (1992). Prospero's Flicks. *Film Comment*, 28, 1, 45–9.
Kromer, B. (1998). *Embellished with Beautiful Engravings: Visualisierungen von Shakespeares Tempest in
     Großbritannien 1790–1870*. Trier: Wissenschaftlicher Verlag Trier.

Law, E. (1920). *Shakespeare's Tempest as originally produced at Court.* London: Chatto and Windus.

Levine, L. W. (1990). *Highbrow/Lowbrow: The Emergence of Cultural Hierarchy in America.* Cambridge, MA: Harvard University Press.

Macdonnell, P. (1840). *An Essay on the Play of the Tempest, with Remarks on the Superstitions of the Middle Ages . . .* London: John Fellowes.

MacKaye, P. (1916). *Caliban by the Yellow Sands: Shakespeare Tercentenary Masque.* New York: Doubleday.

Marker, F. J. (1971). The First Night of Charles Kean's *The Tempest* – from the Notebook of Hans Christian Andersen. *Theater Notebook,* 25, 20–3.

Nilan, M. M. (1972). *The Tempest* at the Turn of the Century: Cross-Currents in Production. *Shakespeare Survey,* 25, 113–23.

——(1975). Shakespeare, Illustrated: Charles Kean's 1857 Production of *The Tempest. Shakespeare Quarterly,* 26, 2, 196–204.

Palmer, D. J. (ed.) (1991). *Shakespeare: The Tempest.* London: Macmillan.

Pearce, B. (1995). Beerbohm Tree's Production of *The Tempest,* 1904. *New Theatre Quarterly,* 11, 44, 299–308.

Pearson, R. E. and Uricchio, W. (1994). "Shrieking from below the gratings": Sir Herbert Beerbohm-Tree's *Macbeth* and his Critics. In A. J. Hoenselaars (ed.) *Reclamations of Shakespeare. DQR Studies in Literature,* 15, 249–71.

Peterson, D. and Goodall, J. (1993). *Visions of Caliban: On Chimpanzees and People.* Boston, MA: Houghton Mifflin.

Roche, S. W. (1987). *Travesties and Burlesques of Shakespeare's Play on the British Stage during the Nineteenth Century.* Unpublished dissertation, University of London.

Shakespeare, W. (1987). *The Tempest,* ed. S. Orgel. Oxford: Clarendon Press.

——(1988). *The Late Romances,* ed. D. Bevington. New York: Bantam.

——(1999). *The Tempest,* ed. V. Mason and A. T. Vaughan. Arden Shakespeare. Walton-on-Thames: Thomas Nelson and Sons.

Shewing, M. (ed.) (1998). *Shakespeare and the Japanese Stage.* Cambridge: Cambridge University Press.

Shyer, L. (1992). Disenchanted: A Casebook on the Making of Jennifer Tipton's *Tempest. American Theatre,* January, 24–31, 64–5.

Slights, J. (2001). Rape and the Romanticization of Shakespeare's Miranda. *Studies in English Literature,* 41, 2, 357–79.

Stone, G. W. (1956). Shakespeare's *Tempest* at Drury Lane During Garrick's Management. *Shakespeare Quarterly,* 7, 1, 1–7.

Tweedie, J. (2000). Caliban's Books: The Hybrid Text in Peter Greenaway's *Prospero's Books. Cinema Journal,* 40, 1, 104–26.

Vaughan, A. T. and Vaughan, V. M. (1991). *Caliban: A Cultural History.* Cambridge: Cambridge University Press.

Warren, R. (1986). Shakespeare on the Twentieth-Century Stage. In S. Wells (ed.) *The Cambridge Companion to Shakespeare Studies.* Cambridge: Cambridge University Press, 257–72.

12

What It Feels Like For a Boy: Shakespeare's *Venus and Adonis*

Richard Rambuss

Upon entering the Forest of Arden, Rosalind, the crossdressing heroine of Shakespeare's *As You Like It* and the play's nexus of erotic desire, renames herself after a mythic boy beauty. "I'll have no worse a name than Jove's own page," she informs her companion in exile, Celia, "And therefore look you call me Ganymede" (1.3.118–19).[1] Intending to "suit me all points like a man," Rosalind dons "A gallant curtal-axe upon my thigh" and "A boar-spear in my hand" (110–12). In so doing, however, Rosalind may seem less to resemble Ganymede, who was simply a shepherd boy in the field before a smitten Jove ravished him away to heaven, than she does the other great male beauty of classical legend, Adonis, a huntsman who likewise armed himself with the boar-spear. Shakespeare retells this beautiful boy's own story – another narrative of male ravishment, but also death – in *Venus and Adonis*, an erotic mini-epic or epyllion, as the genre came to be known. He dedicated this by turns comic and tragic, earthy and elevate piece of Renaissance erotica to Henry Wriothesley, Earl of Southampton, a rich, 19-year-old aristocrat, who was known for his own good looks, as well as his sophisticated literary tastes. Published in 1593, early in the period in which he was writing his comedies, *Venus and Adonis* was Shakespeare's debut in print. The poem, a showy display of rhetorical brilliance, was an immediate sensation, its popularity warranting numerous editions during Shakespeare's lifetime.

In *As You Like It* Rosalind, notwithstanding her "swashing and . . . martial outside" (1.3.114), hopes never to need to use the masculine props she brandishes. By contrast, Shakespeare's Adonis desires only to hunt and, apparently, to hunt only the boar at that. "I know not love, . . . nor will not know it, / Unless it be a boar, and then I chase it" (409–10), the boy hunter declares to Venus, who has in effect here been hunting him. Shakespeare culls the story of Venus and Adonis from Book 10 of Ovid's *Metamorphoses*, a pervasive influence throughout Shakespeare's writings.[2] In Ovid, Adonis is inclined toward love as well as hunting. He even allows the goddess of love to join him on the chase. Together they stalk, Ovid specifies, timid creatures such as deer and rabbits. When Venus grows tired of this sport, she initiates another, directing her not unwilling paramour into a shady grove. There, making a pillow for him of her breast, she relates a cautionary tale, intermixed with kisses, meant to warn her beloved away from the more savage beasts of the forest, from hunting the wolf, the bear, the lion, and, of course, the wild boar. "Beauty and youth and love / Make no impression on bristling boars and lions, / On animal eyes and minds," Venus cautions (10.549–51). But Adonis recklessly disregards her warning, takes after the first wild boar he comes upon, and dies upon its tusk.

Shakespeare's Adonis not only scorns Venus's admonition; he scorns her. In Ovid's rendering, Adonis readily assumes a submissive role in relation to Venus' advances, which is to say that he does not reject them. Shakespeare retools the passivity of Ovid's Adonis into active resistance: "Hunting he loved, but love he laughed to scorn," we learn as soon as the poem opens (4). Adonis' willful, resolute disdain for love – or, more precisely, for Venus – is Shakespeare's principal revision of the Ovidian original, a point registered in nearly every critical treatment of the poem. But Shakespeare wrought other, related alterations, which, though less remarked upon or even unnoticed, also prove significant. We have already seen how in Ovid Venus hunts both for and with Adonis. Not so in Shakespeare. There, from the very beginning of the poem, Venus' wooing interrupts Adonis' hunting. And instead of passively succumbing to her charms, Adonis spends most of the poem endeavoring to escape them in order to resume the hunt – though not with Venus, but rather, he says, with his friends (585–8). Even after the goddess of love has captured him in her arms and aggressively plied him with kisses, Adonis reiterates his eagerness to rejoin his male companions: "The night is spent," he declares, and "I am . . . expected of my friends" (717–18). The mention of these friends, these fellow huntsmen, is Shakespeare's innovation; they are not in Ovid. Their addition to the realm of the hunt, in tandem with Venus' exclusion from it, entails that the hunt, Adonis' singular desire in Shakespeare's poem, remains a distinctly male domain.

Whereas Shakespeare adds mention of Adonis' friends, he subtracts from the story the range of wild beasts that are named in Ovid. Shakespeare's Venus cautions Adonis against the wild boar alone, and it is the boar alone that Adonis remains intent upon pursuing, notwithstanding the goddess's dire oracle: "I prophesy thy death, my living sorrow, / If thou encounter with the boar tomorrow" (671–2). But why *just* the boar in *Venus and Adonis*, as though the forest afforded only one wild quarry worth the chase, only one way for a young man to earn his spurs? We will be returning to the boar's significance throughout this essay. Here, at its beginning, it seems important to remark the association in medieval and Renaissance mythography of the wild boar with jealousy, rivalry, lust, and male passion more generally. The boar, as one earlier critic succinctly put it, is an emblem of "overmastering virility" (Hatto 1946: 354). Like the addition of Adonis' companion huntsmen and his reiterated desire to rejoin the company of men, the narrowing down of the hunt to a single quarry – one whose mythographic resonance is markedly male – functions to hyper-masculinize the hunt. What is more, the poem charges the masculine world of the hunt with eroticism. The homoeroticism of this pursuit is apparent in the very terms of Adonis' rejection of

Venus for the wild boar, which at once oppose the hunt to love and eroticize it: "I know not love, quoth he, nor will not know it, / Unless it be a boar, and then I chase it." Here the wild boar serves both as a foil to Venus and her designs on the boy, and as an eroticized alternative to her for him. I foreground the masculine textures of Shakespeare's poem – its overtones of male friendship, male initiation or coming of age, male homoeroticism, and hyper-masculinity – in view of, to some extent even against, prevailing readings of the poem that principally turn on role reversal and gender inversion. Inversion, subversion, reversal, androgyny, effeminacy: these, I will suggest here, are not the only, or perhaps any longer even the most interesting, terms with which to treat *Venus and Adonis* as a piece of early modern erotica.[3]

To be sure, *Venus and Adonis* works a witty transposition of the Petrarchan conventions that inform so much of the period's love poetry, in which a painfully enamored man casts about to woo a reluctant, often unobtainable woman, who is all the more desirable as such, as unobtainable. Here, however, the pursued – an unwilling, high-minded, sullen, virginal Adonis – turns out to be male, and the pursuer – a sweating, lustful, incorrigible, sexually experienced Venus – female:

> He burns with bashful shame; she with her tears
> Doth quench the maiden burning of his cheeks.
>
>   . . .
>
> He saith she is immodest, blames her miss;
> What follows more she murders with a kiss. (49–50, 53–4)

In the typical Petrarchan scenario, the fervor of the lover's desire for the beloved is matched only by the icy disdain of her rebuff. Shakespeare, we see here, waggishly represents both wooer and her wooed as enflamed. Adonis' boyish bashfulness ignites the "maiden" or virginal (*OED* 2c) burning of his rosy cheeks. Yet his chiding, his blaming of her "miss" – her misbehavior, but also her mistake in believing that she could ever seduce him – serves only to heat the passion of his "bold-faced suitor" (6): "Being so enraged, desire doth lend her force" (29).

The poetic conventions traditionally associated with an eager, appetitive male lover and a reluctant, even adverse female beloved are not simply upended in *Venus and Adonis*: their reassignment is comically hyperbolized. Shakespeare's Venus appears to dwarf Adonis, whom she freely manhandles throughout the poem. "You hurt my hand with wringing," he exclaims at one point (421). The goddess is so much larger, so much stronger than the mortal target of her affections that she is able "to pluck him from his horse" (30) and handily tuck him under her arm: "Over one arm, the lusty courser's rein; / Under her other was the tender boy" (31–2). The goddess of love is so coercive in her pursuit of Adonis, the power differential between them so great, that Jonathan Crewe argues that we take this seriously as a case of classical sexual harassment.[4] Here, too, we might make note of another of Shakespeare's rewritings of Ovid. In *Metamorphoses* Adonis is an exceedingly beautiful boy now become "a man, more handsome / Than he had ever been" (10.523–4). Shakespeare's Adonis, however, is still very much a youth. "The tender spring upon thy tempting lip," Venus herself admits, "Shows thee unripe" (127–8). She also describes the young hunter as "Thrice fairer than myself" (7): a "Stain to all nymphs, more lovely than a man, / More white and red than doves or roses are" (9–10). Venus' blazon of her "sweet boy" (155) is echoed in *Twelfth Night*, when Orsino tells his page Cesario (the crossdressed Viola) that

> . . . they shall yet belie thy happy years
> That say thou are a man. Diana's lip
> Is not more smooth and rubious; thy small pipe
> Is as the maiden's organ, shrill and sound,
> And all is semblative a woman's part. (1.4.29–33)

In *Twelfth Night* the "semblative" or seeming androgyny of Viola/Cesario, around whom cluster desires both heterosexual and homosexual, is a function of crossdressing. That is, Viola's assumed male attire and manner, renders her not exactly masculine, but rather effeminate. Since there is no crossdressing in *Venus and Adonis*, from what does Adonis' androgynous beauty derive? Venus finds him "more lovely than a man." What might this mean? What is lovelier than a man? An exceptionally beautiful boy? A maid? An androgyne? One like Ovid's Hermaphroditus, who was "half a man, / With limbs all softness" (4.381–2)? Or like Leander, the luscious male youth in Marlowe's epyllion, *Hero and Leander*, who seeks to put off an amorous Neptune by declaring, "I am no woman, I" (2.192)? Or might Venus be praising Adonis as a male mortal so lovely that he seems more like a god? The goddess's encomium is ambiguous in its hyperbole.[5] Insofar as androgyny is an element of Adonis' allure in Shakespeare's poem, that quality may derive from the temporarily liminal gender status of the beardless boy in Elizabethan culture. As Stephen Orgel (1996) observes, attractive male youths "were praised in Renaissance England by saying that they looked like women – 'A women's face, by Nature's own hand painted / Hast thou, the master-mistress of my passion'" (p. 51). "Eroticized boys," Orgel adds, "appear to be a middle term between men and women" (p. 63). Perhaps it is this very liminality that Adonis looks to throw off by way of his single-minded pursuit of the fearsome boar, making the hunt a kind of masculine rite of passage.[6] In any event, the cross-genderings that we find in *Venus and Adonis* are not so straightforwardly crossed, not so neatly inverted as to substantiate, at least in any unproblematic way, what appears to be the prevailing consensus in every critical quarter, traditional to "queer." Namely that here Venus "plays the part of the male lover" (Evans 1989: 8) and Adonis, as if by default or even necessity (but necessity according to what view of eroticism?) that of the "passively 'feminine' boy" (DiGangi 1997: 136).

For, as we have already seen, the depiction of Adonis as a passively feminine boy would first need to be complicated by his ineradicable, almost mechanical drive toward the "hard hunt" of the wild boar, instead of the "soft hunt" of "timorous creatures" like the hare, fox, and roe advocated by Venus.[7] Second, as William Keach usefully points out, most of what we know about Adonis we know from Venus (Keach

1977: 67). Essentially all that we know about Adonis from Adonis himself is that he loves to hunt, that he wants to rejoin his friends, and that he knows, even though he won't or can't coherently articulate why, that he does not want Venus: "More I could tell," he tries to explain, "but more I dare not say" (805). We may then want to consider the extent to which the poem's renderings of Adonis as a pouty, delicate, fair — that is, effeminate — male beauty do not simply correspond to, but may in fact derive from Venus' own desire. A number of critics, Catherine Belsey (1995) most brilliantly among them, have read Shakespeare's poem — particularly Venus' position in it: "She's Love; she loves; and yet she is not loved" (610) — as a kind of poetic phenomenology of erotic desire. As such, as a lyric meditation on the subjective conditions of desire, might not *Venus and Adonis* be about, among other things, desire's propensity to fashion its love-object *as it would have it*, that is according to the desirer's own desire? Hence Venus is able to hear Adonis' increasingly testy refusals as what she calls "Thy mermaid's voice" (429), recasting his chaste refusal as a winsome siren song of seduction. Adonis corrects Venus on this account later in the poem — in a sense reinverting her gender inversion of him — by repudiating *her* amorous entreaties as "wanton mermaid's songs" (777). Such strains, he insists, have no effect upon him: "For know, my heart stands armèd in mine ear, / And will not let a false sound enter there" (779–80). Adonis answers Venus' enticement to erotic play with a martial figure; he regards himself as a soldier not a lover.

We are now in a better position to see how Shakespeare's chief reworking of the story — he makes Adonis say no — actually cuts in the other direction from the transgender interpretations that predominate in the criticism, even as the poem's revision of Ovid works its witty play with Renaissance Petrarchanism. Indeed, it could be said that Ovid's is really the more effeminate Adonis. For whereas Shakespeare's Adonis remains "unapt to toy" (34), actively seeking to escape Venus, Ovid's Adonis dallies with her, languorously submitting to her advances and readily abandoning the hunt for a time. Of course, "active" and "passive" are not so univocally gendered, either in Shakespeare's poem or according to the Petrarchan love tradition that it parodies, where even as the male lover actively pursues his female beloved, he bitterly complains of his hapless passivity in view of her power to reject him, of his tender mistress's hard heart. Similarly in Shakespeare's poem, Venus entitles Adonis "love's master" (585), notwithstanding the domineering role she takes in the courtship of a beloved who is named both the "tender boy" (32) and the "flint-hearted boy" (95). If active and passive, hard and soft are not so uniformly gendered as amorous attributes here or elsewhere, why should the narrative feature of Venus wooing Adonis redound to his effeminacy? Similarly, why should Adonis' erotic apathy for the very goddess of love herself come (as so many critics have cast it) at the cost of his masculinity? It clearly need not, at least to those who can conceive of masculinity and male sexuality apart from heterosexuality, that is, apart from Venus: to those, in other words, who can grasp that a boy *as a boy* might desire something else.

Nor am I any more convinced that Shakespeare's poem renders a transsexual Venus, who, as though this were a necessary corollary to a passively feminine Adonis, can simply be said, as Evans puts it, to play "the part of the male lover." Just as the notion of Adonis' youthful effeminacy is complicated by his staunch devotion to the hypermasculine boar hunt, so too is the belief that Venus is effectively regendered in her aggressive pursuit of him at odds with the poem's representation of her as the instantiation, if not hyperbolization, of the desirable female figure. Or at least that is how the goddess of love, understandably enough, regards herself: "Thou canst not see one wrinkle in my brow," she challenges Adonis (139). What follows is a blazon of female beauty that is conventional in every respect — except, of course, that it issues from its subject's own mouth: "Mine eyes are grey, and bright, and quick in turning. / My beauty as the spring doth yearly grow. / My flesh is soft and plump, my marrow burning" (140–2). Venus further amplifies her own desirability in a second self-blazon, which pornographically surveys the terrain of her outsized female form, metaphorizing it as a delightful, if inescapable, pastoral playpen for the boy hunter:

> Fondling, she saith, since I have hemmed thee here
> Within the circuit of this ivory pale,
> I'll be a park, and thou shalt be my deer.
> Feed where thou wilt, on mountain or in dale;
>   Graze on my lips, and if those hills be dry,
>   Stray lower, where the pleasant fountains lie.
>
> Within this limit is relief enough,
> Sweet bottom-grass, and high delightful plain,
> Round rising hillocks, brakes obscure and rough,
> To shelter thee from tempest and from rain.
>   Then be my deer, since I am such a park;
>   No dog shall rouse thee, though a thousand bark. (229–40)

Once again, the poem sets the call of the hunt ("No dog shall rouse thee") in opposition to a distinctly female domain of amorous pleasure: Venus' own female body. The metaphorical park to which Venus would confine Adonis evokes the pastoral delicacies of the woodlands to which Titania, queen of the fairies, imprisons Bottom, her own mortal paramour, in *A Midsummer Night's Dream*. "Out of this wood, do not desire to go," she enjoins him; "Thou shalt remain here, whether thou wilt or no" (3.1.134–5).

Even the poem's renderings of Venus' desire at its most voracious remain markedly female in their gendering. Here is, for instance, how the poem describes her as she is about to kiss Adonis, having strong-armed him off his horse and onto his back:

> Even as an empty eagle, sharp by fast,
> Tires with *her* beak on feathers, flesh, and bone,
> Shaking *her* wings, devouring all in haste
> Till either gorge be stuffed or prey be gone,
>   Even so *she* kissed his brow, his cheek, his chin,
>   And where *she* ends *she* doth anew begin. (55–60; my emphasis)

No conceits of inverted, doubled, or blurred gender here. The image of a lustful Venus as a starved female eagle ripping into her prey – of Venus as raw animal appetite – is remarkable for its sheer intensity, for the "downright violence" of female desire as Shakespeare here renders it. No less interesting is how this representation of the goddess of love alludes to and recasts that other Ovidian narrative of male ravishment: Jove's abduction of Ganymede, for which to accomplish the king of the gods assumed the form of a giant eagle, "the only bird / Able to bear his thunderbolts" (10.158–9). Here, then, is indeed an instance of sexual inversion in *Venus and Adonis*, but it has little to do, I would argue, with any notion of gender indeterminacy. Rather, the poem's figurative metamorphosis of Venus into a female eagle, able to pluck Adonis from the hunt as easily as Jove snatched Ganymede from his flock, inverts a classical emblem of male homoerotic desire into a drama of (failed) heterosexual seduction. It should be evident by now that I have been regarding Shakespeare's Venus – who attempts to bolster her suit with procreative arguments ("Thou was begot; to get it is thy duty": 168), in tandem with an indictment of Adonis' male narcissism ("Is thine own heart to thine own face affected?": 157) – not simply as the goddess of love, but as the font and the fulfillment of a certain kind of love, of *heterosexual* love.[8] For even in this sixteenth-century text – written centuries before the great Victorian divide posited by Foucault of sexuality into heterosexuality and homosexuality – sexuality and heterosexuality, sexuality and Venus, are not construed to be fully coextensive: "I know not love, quoth he, nor will not know it, / Unless it be a boar, and then I chase it."

Later in the poem, after the sunset, Adonis offers Venus a goodnight kiss as a "fee" (538) for his release:

> He with her plenty pressed, she faint with dearth,
> Their lips together glued, fall to the earth.

> Now quick desire hath caught the yielding prey,
> And glutton-like *she* feeds, yet never filleth.
> *Her* lips are conquerors, his lips obey,
> Paying what ransom the insulter willeth,
>   Whose vulture thought doth pitch the price so high
>   That *she* will draw his lips' rich treasure dry. (545–52; my emphasis)

The detail of this kissing couple falling backwards to the earth bespeaks another repointing of the Ganymede myth, a myth that was imbued in the Renaissance with a spiritual, as well as a homoerotic, significance as an emblem of the transumption of the devout soul from earth to heaven.[9] Here that trajectory is dramatically reversed downward, as the poem further accentuates the carnal, indeed bestial aspects of sexual desire, even when it emanates from a divinity. In doing so, Shakespeare coarsens the image of Venus as a bird of prey, figuratively metamorphosing her yet again, this time turning her in the throes of her passion from a Jove-like eagle into a ravenous vulture and vampire. Notably, the figuration remains distinctly female. Maurice Evans reminds us that the Ovidian tradition, in contrast to the Petrarchan, produces a number of impassioned, aggressive women who undertake all the wooing: Echo with Narcissus, Salmacis with Hermaphroditus, and Myrrha (Adonis' own mother) with Cinyras.[10] Nor are such powerful female aggressors unknown in Shakespeare, as *A Midsummer Night's Dream* illustrates. Like *Venus and Adonis*, that play stages an anxiety about – or maybe an interest in – female erotic domination: "Tie up my love's tongue; bring him silently," Titania instructs her fairy minions as they carry off Bottom to her bower (3.1.182). Indeed, the queen of the fairies and the goddess of love seem, in Shakespeare's conception of them, to share a taste for men and boys in bondage, restraint being a principal component of their amorous repertoires. Thus at the beginning of the poem, Venus having already tethered Adonis' male charger to "a ragged bough," looks next "To tie the rider" (37, 40). She also boasts to him of having led Mars, "the stern and direful god of war, / Whose sinewy neck in battle ne'er did bow," as (in one of the poem's most famous lines) her "prisoner in a red-rose chain" (98–9, 110). "Lie quietly, and hear a little more," Venus tells the squirming boy as he tries to break away; "Nay, do not struggle, for thou shalt not rise" (709–10). He doesn't.

My point is that the panting, sweating, rapacious Venus of *Venus and Adonis*, for all the poem's erotic plethora, is more a representation of aggressive female sexuality – or, really, aggressive heterosexuality – than she is a figure of gender inversion or indeterminacy. Rather than simply "reversing female and male roles," as Philip Kolin (1997: 31) and so many other critics have framed it, the poem, it may be more accurate to say, instead shows Venus taking on both roles herself: "Backward she pushed him, as she would be thrust, / And governed him in strength, though not in lust" (41–2). Venus, that is, does to Adonis what she wants done to herself. That she is constrained to enact all the amorous roles within the poem's at once exaggerated and parodically dysfunctional Petrarchanism – to be both lover and would-be beloved, both blazoner and blazoned beauty – moreover seems to me to have less to do with the kind of theatrical destabilization of gender wrought in Shakespeare's crossdressing comedies than it does with the simple fact of Adonis' unresponsiveness to her charms – that, and his contrasting obsession with the boar.

When Adonis tells her he still intends to seek the boar the next day, Venus says that she is jealous (649, 657). She then endeavors to dissuade him from the hunt by insisting that his singular beauty will be unappreciated by the "churlish swine" (616), who, the goddess informs him by means of yet another blazon, could never love him as she does (631–6). Venus makes her case from flat on her back, having excitedly pulled Adonis down on top of her at his mention of the boar. And in her jealousy and her alarm, she prophetically envisions a supine Adonis, wounded and bleeding, in the very same, hence erotic, position underneath her masculine rival:

> And, more than so, presenteth to mine eye
> The picture of an angry chafing boar,
> Under whose sharp fangs on his back doth lie
> An image like thyself, all stained with gore. (661–4)

For just as the poem has been consistent in specifying that Venus remains in female form throughout each of her figurative animal metamorphoses, so too is Shakespeare's boar, in keeping with literary tradition, a male boar. Given that bestiality and buggery were so closely associated in English Renaissance erotic discourse (sodomy might name either species of sexual crime), it is striking that Venus conceives the threat that the boar poses to Adonis in terms of penetration, and this multiply so, seemingly from every point of the beast's body. His tusks, she thus warns, "never sheathed, he whetteth still" (617). "On his bow-back he hath a battle set," she continues, "Of bristly pikes that ever threat his foes," while "His snout digs sepulchres where'er he goes" (619–20, 622). "[H]aving thee at vantage," Venus concludes, he "Would root [your] beauties as he roots the mead" (635–6). Of course the boy hunter wields his own "pike," the boar-spear, but his weapon, he is plainly told, is no match for the boar, whose "brawny sides with hairy bristles armed / Are better proof than thy spear's point can enter" (625–6). Venus' figuration of the wild boar *as penetration* can be linked up with a blazon of Adonis earlier in the poem, in which the poet renders the boy's beauty in curiously orificial terms. There his "pretty dimple[s]" are cast as "These lovely caves, these round enchanting pits, / Open[ing] their mouths to swallow Venus' liking" (242, 247–8). Love (Cupid), we are told, "made those hollows," not so much to capture Venus' fancy but to suit his own, so that if he

> . . . himself were slain,
> He might be buried in a tomb so simple,
>   Foreknowing well, if there he came to lie,
>   Why, there love lived, and there he could not die. (243–6)

This passage signals, well before the appearance of the "rooting" boar, that Adonis' beautiful, penetrable boy's body, with its amorously alluring hollows and openings, is a site of homoerotic interest as well. Which is also to say that the poem reminds us here, if only obliquely, that there is another god of love – a male one – who seems in fact to enjoy more intimate access to Adonis' body than his mother Venus ever gains.

Like the male god of love, "the hunted boar" (900) is himself little more than a trace presence in *Venus and Adonis*, appearing *in propria persona* only momentarily, for three lines near the poem's end. The boar crosses Venus' path on her way the next morning to her discovery of Adonis' body, and she notes with horror that the beast's "frothy mouth" is "bepainted all with red, / Like milk and blood being mingled both together" (901–2). Then she comes upon Adonis. Here white and red – the color scheme of the blazon – again mingle, this time around the "wide wound" the boar has just "trenched" into Adonis' "soft," "lily-white" flank, a wound that Venus finds still to be weeping bloody "tears" (1051–6). The trauma of this sight redoubles itself – literally so, Venus seeing two corpses ("behold two Adons dead!": 1070), both multiply penetrated: "Upon his hurt she looks so steadfastly / That her sight, dazzling, makes the wound seem three" (1063–4). The reduplicating violence of the traumatic gaze – of "her mangling eye, / That makes more gashes where no breach should be" (1065–6) – prepares the way for the stunning self-identification of Venus (whose desire the poem repeatedly figures, we have seen, in animal terms) with her erotic rival several stanzas later: "Had I been toothed like him, I must confess / With kissing him I should have killed him first" (1117–18). As Venus comes to embrace the boar's violence as a reflection of her own desire for the boy, she reciprocally recasts that violence as a form of sexual climax: "He thought to kiss him, and hath killed him so" (1110). Suddenly unsaying all that she had said before about the boar as a blind, furious enemy of beauty, Venus renames him "the loving swine":

> 'Tis true, 'tis true; thus was Adonis slain;
> He ran upon the boar with his sharp spear,
> Who did not whet his teeth at him again,
> But by a kiss thought to persuade him there,
>   And, nuzzling in his flank, the loving swine
>   Sheathed unaware the tusk in his soft groin. (1111–16)

As rendered by Venus with such palpable, voluptuous detail, the coupling of the boar and the boy stands as one of the most graphically sexual figurations in Renaissance poetry of male/male penetration, of tusk in groin, of male body "rooting" male body.

But why does Shakespeare's Adonis die? Or, "since all Adonises must die," as Don Cameron Allen (1959: 111) reminds us, what does his death here mean? Surely there is more to his death on the point of the boar's tusk than simply a scoring of the familiar Renaissance pun on dying as climax, as orgasm. Indeed, the meaning of Adonis' death has puzzled many of *Venus and Adonis's* readers, especially the poem's most moralizing allegorists. We expect Adonis to die in Ovid (so the moralist accounts go) because there we find that beauty has succumbed to lust. There, Adonis' death is a form of punishment for the youth and the goddess both. But here, in Shakespeare's poem, Adonis does no more than sample Venus' lips, that kiss ultimately serving only to confirm his decided indifference. So why should Shakespeare's Adonis, who ultimately spurns Venus, and with her what he censures as "sweating lust" (794), have to die?

According to Coppélia Kahn, this is precisely the reason that Adonis dies, and apparently deservedly so. In an enduringly influential essay, she argues that Adonis meets his death precisely because he refuses Venus' love, because he "scornfully rejects the easier, more overtly pleasurable and normal course for the fatal one" (Kahn 1981: 44). Kahn sees Adonis as caught between the poles of adulthood and youth, between "intimacy with Venus, which constitutes entry into manhood, and the emotional isolation of narcissism, which constitutes a denial of growth" (p. 21). Asserting that "for a man sexual love of woman is vital to masculinity" (p. 42), Kahn's reading collapses sexuality – more precisely, sexual object choice – into gender identity:

The boyish Adonis, whom Venus, the very incarnation of desirable femininity, presents with an enviable chance to prove his manhood, sternly rejects that opportunity, meets death in the boar hunt, and metamorphosed into a flower, ends up as a child again, sheltered in Venus's bosom. (p. 22)

What Kahn here terms "mature sexuality" (p. 22) is simply and only heterosexuality. Although she is unapt to treat what the boar represents in the poem's allegory as a homoerotic or even a homosocial alternative to Venus, Kahn's explanation of why Adonis rebuffs "the very incarnation of desirable femininity" nonetheless turns out the usual suspects thought to be responsible for male homosexuality in psychoanalytic accounts that look to render it a form of deviancy. Hence Kahn predicates of Adonis male narcissism, effeminacy, infantilism, castration anxiety, and what she simply terms "the fear of woman" (p. 23).[11]

What Kahn does say of the wild boar is that he "embodies all that is inimical to life, beauty, and love" (p. 44). The goddess of love, we found, thought so too, but then she changed her mind. Why can't the critic? As we have seen, Kahn's orthodox psychoanalytic feminism, with its developmental model of maturation into heterosexuality, simply will not allow for "life, beauty, and love" deriving from any other kind of desire. "Venus," Kahn flatly declares, "is the queen of love, the supreme object of desire for any man, whose manliness is defined by his desire for a woman" (p. 34). Not only is this a reductive view of desire that ignores desire's incorrigible waywardness in Shakespeare (not to say Ovid), but Kahn's definition of masculinity is also strikingly unhistorical. Virility may be demonstrated a number of ways in Renaissance culture – prowess in the hunt or on the battlefield among them, but acceding to the amorous advances of an aggressively desirous woman would hardly rank very high among them. On the contrary, unbridled passion for women was widely seen to have an effeminizing effect upon a man. *Romeo and Juliet*, written just a few years after *Venus and Adonis*, provides the most pointed registration of this anxiety in Shakespeare. After his part in the botched street fight that leaves his friend Mercutio mortally wounded, Romeo exclaims "O sweet Juliet, / Thy beauty hath made me effeminate / And in my temper softened valour's steel" (3.1.108–10).

Kahn may be the most influential, but she is by no means the only critic to cast Adonis' lack of interest in Venus as more or less aberrant. For every critic like Allen, who lampoons Venus as "a forty-year-old countess with a taste for Chapel Royal altos" (Allen 1959: 101) (and thereby justifies Adonis' disdain for her), there is another like Evans who takes Shakespeare's huntsman to task for choosing "the sterile chase of the boar in preference to the kiss of Venus" (Evans 1989: 14). "Adonis," Evans finds, "is drawn as callow, petulant, curiously literal and unpoetic: above all, narcissistic," and his motives in rejecting Venus "have nothing to do with the idealism about love of which he is made the mouthpiece, and in all respects he falls short of the Platonic conception of beauty" (p. 13). William Keach (1977), who astutely recognizes that Shakespeare's handling of the myth is too ambivalent to yield "a conventionally moral interpretation" (pp. 52–3), nonetheless determines that "there is something mean and perverse in Adonis's aversion to love as such" (p. 70). Heather Dubrow (1997), while wholly disapproving of Venus' "tendency to see love not as 'mutual render' (Sonnet 125.12) but rather as an aggressive struggle for domination" (p. 225), is hardly less suspicious of Adonis' resistance to her. "Recognizing that Adonis does not fully understand his own behavior," she writes, "we begin to suspect subterranean motives that he cannot or will not face, such as the narcissism of which Venus accuses him" (p. 240). Even Richard Halpern (1997) has recently suggested in his gynocentric reading of the poem that Adonis' indifference to Venus signals sexual deficiency. Halpern repeatedly refers to "the strategic absence of Adonis' erection," although, in an interpretive twist, he reads this phallic lack as a "viciously misogynist" joke staged more at Venus' expense than the boy's (pp. 382, 378).

The critics I have been citing represent widely divergent interpretive methods, and the readings they forge of Shakespeare's poem are ultimately quite different. Yet their estimations of Adonis (to the extent that they are concerned with him) all seem to me to be predicated upon the view, as Kahn (1981) puts it, that "in repudiating [Venus] he repudiates love itself" (p. 29). In contrast, the impetus of my reading is to consider how Adonis' intractable disregard for Venus begins to point in the direction of another kind of love. Whereas Kahn posits that "hunting serves Adonis's deepest unconscious need, which is to keep eros out of his life" (p. 39), I see the hypermasculine world of the boar hunt as being shot through with eros, an eros that is at once different from and like what Venus proffers. To summarize what I have been arguing thus far, then, I regard Shakespeare's poem as less monolithically heterosexual in its conception of love than the criticism concerned with the poem has tended to be. Second, the expression of homoerotic desire here is not exclusively, or even primarily, beholden to tropes of gender inversion or reversal, tropes that tend to reinscribe homoerotic desire onto a heterosexual template (Adonis in the feminine or androgynous role and Venus in the masculine). And third, I find that Adonis can refuse Venus – just as a man may refuse, may turn away from the love of women – and that refusal be neither deviant nor necessarily tantamount to an expression of misogyny.

So what do we say about a beautiful male youth whose passion cannot be roused by "the very incarnation of desirable femininity" herself? I have been arguing that Adonis' eschewal of Venus – the pivotal feature of Shakespeare's rendering of the story – points in the direction of another kind of love. Moreover, I would say that it does so in a way that makes *Venus and Adonis* something other than simply one more illustration of the fluidity of desire (now much discussed in the criticism) so prevalent in Renaissance literature, and perhaps nowhere more so than in Shakespeare's own writings. There we find that erotic desire tends to be a highly mobile affective impetus: cross-sex, same-sex, and not infrequently both at once, Shakespeare's comedies, in particular, stage sustained explorations of what Valerie Traub (1992) nicely terms "the flexibility of erotic attraction" (p. 128). In *As You Like It* we saw that when Rosalind crossdresses as a young man, she takes the homoerotically charged name of Ganymede as her alias in exile. Thus disguised, she meets Orlando in the forest and offers to impersonate his beloved (who happens to be Rosalind herself), while schooling him in courtship. Orlando quickly falls in love with Ganymede-cum-Rosalind, even as Rosalind-cum-Ganymede also becomes the beloved of another woman, the shepherdess Phoebe. The fact that Rosalind, a girl who plays a boy playing a girl, is herself of course played by a boy actor in drag (a convention of the English Renaissance stage the play's Epilogue highlights) further complicates this comedy's multiply crossed and recrossed vectors of desire. As Traub (1992) describes it, "distinctions between homo-erotic and heterosexual collapse" (p. 127). Erotic attraction may be even more transitive in *Twelfth Night*, Shakespeare's last comedy, which produces interchangeable male/female twins, Viola and Sebastian, as its doubly sexed, hetero-/homoerotic universal object of desire.

In contrast, Adonis' desire – to the extent that it finds expression in the poem (a matter to which I will shortly return) – flows in only one direction: toward the boar. Adonis wants to rejoin his friends so that he can resume the hunt. In this respect, the characters from the comedies that he ultimately most resembles are not Rosalind, Orlando, Viola, Sebastian, and the like: characters crisscrossed by hetero- and homoerotic desires before, and in some cases even as, they are eventually paired off in marriage. Rather, Adonis seems to me more to resemble two figures from the comedies who are not folded into the heterosexual closure toward which romantic comedy as a genre seems inexorably to be pointed, however ambivalently in many of Shakespeare's own comedies. The two figures I have in mind curiously share the same name: Antonio. They appear in plays – *The Merchant of Venice* and *Twelfth Night* – that abound in crossdressing and crossed desires, but there seems to be nothing pluralistic about their own erotic longings. They both love other men. Passionately.[12] As Stephen Orgel (1996) observes of the latter play: "What the presence of Antonio and Sebastian acknowledges, in a play that has at its center a man wooing a man, is that men *do* fall in love with other men" (p. 51). To this I would only add that – even as early on as on the early modern stage – some men who fall in love with other men do not *also* fall in love with women at the same time, or even eventually thereafter. This is what makes the Antonios different from Shakespeare's other lovers, including the Antonios' own male beloveds, Bassanio and Sebastian, respectively. At the conclusion of both *The Merchant of Venice* and *Twelfth Night*, an Antonio notably remains outside the conventional comedic closure wrought by marriage. But apart as what? Not as a homosexual *per se*, surely, inasmuch as early modern same-sex desire has yet to coalesce into the distinctive subjectivity connoted by that term.[13] Yet the monovalently homoerotic love voiced by the Antonios – who together represent perhaps more a "desire position" than a characterology – signify, if only nascently, something different from the erotically transversal sexual desire of the other characters around them, characters who nonetheless all choose or are made to marry.

Shakespeare's Antonios thus seem to me to be figurations of a proto-gay male desire, just as *Venus and Adonis* can be read, at least *vis-à-vis* Adonis and the boar, as a proto-gay text. Jonathan Goldberg's *Sodometries* (1992), still the most sophisticated discussion of the vagaries of early modern homoeroticism, brilliantly explicates "how relations between men (or between women or between men and women) in the period provide the sites upon which later sexual orders and later sexual identities could batten" (p. 22). I hope that I have at least shown that Shakespeare's epyllion should be seen as one such site. But might the poem's place as a small, but not insignificant part of the still to be fully unfolded "history of sexuality" be something still more?

Here let us turn to the jumble of reasons that Adonis himself provides as to why he wants nothing to do with Venus. As I remarked earlier, those reasons are not fully coherent. Adonis first declares his hostility to love as he understands it – that is, as Venus – in a chiasmus that paradoxically renders his repudiation of love in amorous terms: "My love to love is love but to disgrace it" (412). Adonis later gainsays his own claim when he informs his pursuer that "I hate not love, but your device in love" (789). He then contrasts lust and love, maintaining that the latter "to heaven is fled" (793–804). The youth's indignant Platonism quickly founders, however, upon his own lack of experience. "The text is old, the orator too green," he admits (806). Yet even when Adonis seems implicitly to concede the possibility that his relation to eros may change as he grows older, the poem offers no indication that it will ever come to embrace Venus, "Fair queen" (523) though she may be.

Adonis' explanations of why he cannot return Venus' love may be incoherent. There may even be a vector of misogyny that crosses through some of his expressions of scorn for her, though, unlike Halpern, I do not find male contempt for woman to be the poem's predominant charge. Yet however muddled, Adonis' anti-venerian discourse remains stubbornly anti-heterosexual. This aversion is pointedly registered in his curt, contemptuous dismissal of Venus' attempts to win him with arguments (recurrent in the period's love poetry) about beauty being sterile and wasteful until it is deployed in the service of reproduction. "You do it for increase – O strange excuse," Adonis retorts distastefully (791). Even more remarkable is Adonis' hostile indifference to what is presented to him as a natural emblem of the naturalness of heterosexual desire, of the animal attraction that every male is supposed to feel for the female. Spying "A breeding jennet, lusty, young, and proud," Adonis' instantly aroused charger "Breaketh his rein, and to her straight goes he" (259–64). The poem devotes fifteen stanzas, yet more virtuosic blazons, and some of its most exuberant poetry to this didactic erotic set piece. "Thy palfrey, as he should, / Welcomes the warm approach of sweet desire" (385–6), Venus endeavors to instruct "the wayward boy" (344) of whom she has laid hold. Pedagogy then becomes pornography: "Who sees his true-love in her naked bed, / Teaching the sheets a whiter hue than white, / But when his glutton eye so full hath fed / His other agents aim at like delight?" (397–400). "O, learn to love!" Venus continues; "The lesson is but plain. / And, once made perfect, never lost again" (407–8). This sexy exemplum of how the sexes are meant to respond to each other – no doubt one of the bits responsible for *Venus and Adonis's* contemporary reputation as a lover's Bible and a literary aphrodisiac (Kolin 1997: 12) is, however, wholly lost on Adonis himself. His only thought "Is how to get my palfrey from the mare" (384).

Renaissance homoeroticism, as groundbreaking work by Goldberg (1992), Orgel (1996), and Eve Sedgwick (1985) has demonstrated, seldom poses as a distinct opposite to heterosexual forms of desire or as adversarial to marriage. In *The Merchant of Venice* Antonio materially enables Bassanio's marriage by funding, at great personal cost, his beloved's trip to Belmont, where Bassanio wins Portia's hand. (Antonio's reward for this service comes not only in the form of his deliverance from his bond to Shylock by Portia, but also as an invitation from her to live with the newlyweds back in Belmont.) It is a different matter in *Venus and Adonis*, however; there Adonis' repudiation of Venus and his corresponding eroticized devotion to the hunt *is* effectively anti-heterosexual. Here, too, we should consider Shakespeare's final revision of Ovid. In Shakespeare's poem, Venus never gets Adonis, not even in the end, not even after death, the way that she does in *Metamorphoses*: that is, her beloved and loving Adonis transformed into a flower. In Ovid, Venus sprinkles "sweet-smelling nectar" over his spilt blood and an anemone springs forth, a flower as frail as Adonis' life was brief (10.731–9). In Shakespeare, however, Adonis' corpse melts into the air like a vapor, and the purple flower that sprouts from his blood, seemingly of its own accord (here Venus plays no role in the transformation), is identified not as Adonis metamorphosed, but as his offspring. "Poor flower," Venus laments, "this was thy father's guise – / Sweet issue of a more sweet-smelling sire –" (1177–8). She then plucks the bloom (yet another change from Ovid) and plants it in her bosom, there to wither: "Here was thy father's bed, here in my breast. / Thou art the next of blood, and 'tis thy right. / Lo, in this hollow cradle take thy rest" (1183–5). These alterations are subtle, but telling. In *Venus and Adonis* the goddess never gets her boy, but rather gets *his* boy. Any form of heterosexual congress or closure is here replaced by the odd couple of a compensatory erotic maternalism and male parthenogenesis.[14]

Joel Fineman's *Shakespeare's Perjured Eye* (1986), his commanding reading of Shakespeare's sonnets, essentially credits the sequence, published a decade-and-a-half after *Venus and Adonis*, with the invention of heterosexual literary subjectivity. This claim's obverse – namely that in *Venus and Adonis* Shakespeare "invents" homosexual poetic subjectivity – is not exactly what I am looking to set forth here. Adonis does not seem fully to understand what his relationship to love should or will be. He may not, as Dubrow (1997) wonders, even know exactly what he wants or what it means. Indeed, I would further argue that Adonis' desire – what it feels like for a boy – is, in fact, just what the poem does not deliver. W. B. C. Watkins voices a complaint prevalent in the criticism when he dubs Adonis "an incomplete sketch of what might, in a less confusing poem, have been a characterization" (cited in Keach 1977: 68). The sense that Shakespeare's Adonis remains unrealized, especially in comparison to the poem's rendering of its other titular character, derives, I think, from more than the relatively few lines (only eighty-eight) that he speaks. Even Venus finds him as a "Well painted idol, image dull and dead," a "Thing like a man, but of no woman bred" (212–14). Adonis seems a cipher to Venus, a "Thing like a man" but no man, because he remains so perversely impervious to what every man, even a young one, is supposed to respond to. "What are you then?" the goddess seems to be asking here. Shakespeare's poem looks ahead to, anticipates, but does not distinctly realize what a boy like Adonis – a boy who feels that whatever he wants or will want, it will not be Venus, will not be a female lover, even if she is the goddess of love herself – what a boy like this might want *instead*. Hence Adonis' desire can only be rendered here in negative terms: "I know not love, quoth he, nor will not know it, / Unless it be a boar, and then I chase it."

This recognition may open another vantage onto the meaning of Adonis' death in Shakespeare's poem. Perhaps the question of why Adonis dies here should be recast along the lines of: What else do we envision the story doing with him? In this respect, *Venus and Adonis* evokes another of those "beautiful male young men who die (and are transfigured)" narratives. There are, of course, the stories of Narcissus, Hyacinthus, and Apollo's male beloved Cyparissus (who himself fell in love with a great stag), all in *Metamorphoses*. There is also Marlowe's Leander. We might even think here of Christ. But the particular story I have in mind is Melville's *Billy Budd*, another, though much later, piece of proto-gay literature. As soon as Billy, who is simply called "Beauty" throughout the novella — "the flower of his flock" (1357) — is taken aboard the *Bellipotent*, he becomes the ship's cynosure of erotic desire.[15] From that point on, we sense that Melville's "childman" (1393), however much an innocent, is not long for this world. Whereas in his death Shakespeare's Adonis generates a flower, Melville's beautiful male youth — an Adonis rearticulated into an all-male setting — is already a flower, a "bud," a "buddy," a friend, who becomes a Christ-like figure after his execution. And that, of course, is one of the ways Renaissance moralizers of Ovid liked typologically to view the mutilated Adonis: as a pagan prefiguration of the slain and resurrected Christ.

What a boy like Adonis wants remains gestural, allegorical in Shakespeare's poem. Adonis never articulates a view of love that is a coherent alternative to Venus. Nor do we ever find him happily back in the company of the friends whose mention Shakespeare adds to the story. Nor do we ever actually see Adonis coming together with the wild boar. Rather, the poem elides a direct representation of that encounter, instead mediating it through the divinely visionary powers of Venus. Even Venus' own desires, then, cannot be entirely circumscribed within the normative heterosexuality that she is principally made (no doubt reductively at times) to represent in this argument. For, we may ask, what kind of erotic desire is *female* desire for a soft, effeminate boy — if that is indeed what Adonis is here, or even simply what Venus wants him to be? But that is another story. Yet even in this story, one about Adonis and male homoeroticism, the poem's most explicitly sexual expression of male homoerotic desire — the boar attempting to kiss Adonis as he sheaths his tusk in the youth's soft groin — is planted by Shakespeare in Venus' imagination and cast, "cross-voice" by the male poet, in her words.[16] In so doing, however, Shakespeare enhances the erotic force of the encounter. For what transpires between "the loving swine" and his Adonis is something that someone no less than the goddess of love herself can recognize and ordain as erotic love.

ACKNOWLEDGMENTS

I would like to express my gratitude to the volume's editor, Jean Howard, who surmised that I would have something to say about this poem well before I could conceive what it might be. I also enjoyed discussing this essay as it unfolded with Charles V. O'Boyle, Jr., and I am grateful for all that he brought to the scene of its writing.

NOTES

1 All references to Shakespeare's works are according to the *Norton Shakespeare*, ed. Stephen Green-blatt et al. (New York: Norton, 1997).

2 Arthur Golding's 1567 translation of the *Metamorphoses* made Ovid's work available in an English verse edition.

3 The homoeroticism that I am arguing is amplified in Shakespeare's rendering is by no means absent in the Ovidian original. The context there too is homoerotic. As Bate (1993) reminds us, Ovid's story of Venus and Adonis is narrated by Orpheus – "the patron saint of homosexuality, or, more precisely, of pederasty" – in his extended lament to the trees and the wild beasts after his loss of Eurydice (pp. 82–3). Afterwards, Ovid tells us, Orpheus' love "was given / To young boys only" (X.82–3).

4 Crewe (1999: xxxv and xl–xli) argues, "To imagine that a powerful older woman's persistent, coer-cive advances cannot count as damaging in Shakespeare's judgment (or be taken seriously even now as a form of sexual violence) is again to refuse a consideration of what the poem is about. Refusing to take *Venus and Adonis* seriously may also entail the sexist assumption that while coercive or threat-ening advances by a man are serious, such advances by a woman, especially an older one, cannot be taken seriously, women being by definition powerless, so to speak, and their desires merely embar-rassing" (p. xxxvii).

5 Keach (1977) also remarks the ambiguity of "more lovely than a man," but he does not conceive of its meaning apart from androgyny: "This ambiguity is richly expressive of the way in which the soft, effeminate male became for the Renaissance an ideal type of human beauty" (p. 67).

6 Cf. Berry (2001): "Adonis's quest to 'know' himself through the boar hunt is thus an initiatory quest. The boy becomes a man in the conquest of death, taking on the warrior-status of the fero-cious beast he kills" (p. 47). Berry's book provides a valuable cultural history of the hunt in early modern England and Shakespeare's writings more specifically.

7 I derive the terms "soft hunt" and "hard hunt" from Allen (1959).

8 Maus (1997) makes a similar point: "Venus, the goddess of love, is supposed to be the apex of het-erosexual desirability, both source and goal of every man's desire" (p. 605).

9 On Ganymede's spiritual significance, see Saslow (1986). While he considers both the erotic and the religious significance of Ganymede, Saslow scrupulously keeps these categories of meaning sep-arate. See also Bush (1963: 168–9). For an account that treats the religious and the homoerotic meanings of Ganymede in relation to each other, see Rambuss (1998).

10 Evans (1989: 9). As many critics have noticed, Shakespeare absorbed elements of the story of Nar-cissus and Echo and the story of Salmacis and Hermaphroditus into his rendering of the Venus and Adonis story. See Bush (1963: 138–9); Kahn (1981: 26–7); Keach (1977: 56); and Bate (1993: 89–92).

11 Feminist theory, psychoanalytic literary criticism, and Shakespeare studies have all certainly come a long way in the decades since Kahn's essay first appeared, especially in their ability to address sexuality, and homosexuality in particular. Yet Kahn's essay, which continues to be widely cited and reprinted in critical anthologies, has eluded sustained critique. It recently appears, for instance, as one of the five recommended critical texts on *Venus and Adonis* in the *Norton Shakespeare*. Even so, Kahn's insistent pathologization of any desire that parts company with heterosexuality would, one hopes, now have little critical currency. That said, the essay's ascription to Adonis of a perverse, even lethal inclination to foreswear "the easier, more overtly pleasurable and normal course" of desire "for the fatal one" still rankles. Indeed, the notion that non-heterosexual male desire is essentially suicidal in nature has acquired an especially pernicious resonance in our own time, in the midst of the ongoing AIDS epidemic.

12 Antonio, facing his imminent execution in *The Merchant of Venice*, enjoins Bassanio: "Commend me to your honourable wife. / Tell her the process of Antonio's end. / Say how I loved you. Speak me

fair in death, / And when the tale is told, bid her be judge / Whether Bassanio had not once a love" (4.1.268–72). The Antonio of *Twelfth Night* speaks no less passionately of his love and desire for Sebastian. See, for instance, 3.3.1–13.

13 In a much-cited summary passage, Foucault (1990) writes: "The nineteenth-century homosexual became a personage, a past, a case history, and a childhood, in addition to being a type of life, a life form, and a morphology, with an indiscreet anatomy and possibly a mysterious physiology. Nothing that went into his total composition was unaffected by his sexuality. It was everywhere present in him . . . It was cosubstantial with him, less as a habitual sin than as a singular nature" (p. 43).

14 The poem's Dedication offers another scene of male/male procreation. There Shakespeare offers *Venus and Adonis*, "the first heir of my invention," to his patron the Earl of Southampton, who is named "so noble a godfather" to the male poet's offspring.

15 As with Shakespeare's Adonis, Billy Budd's beauty is described in ambiguously gendered terms:

> He was young; and despite his all but fully developed frame, in every aspect looked even younger than he really was, owing to a lingering adolescent expression in the as yet smooth face all but feminine in purity of natural complexion but where, thanks to his seagoing, the lily was quite suppressed and the rose had some ado visibly to flush through the tan. (1359–60)

Is Billy's "all but feminine" beauty so lovely that it is nearly feminine in quality? Or are his masculine, seafaring good looks anything but feminine? Interestingly, Benjamin Britten's *Billy Budd*, the canon's only all-male opera, casts Billy as a baritone, not a tenor.

16 I take the term from Enterline (2000). See also Harvey (1992).

REFERENCES AND FURTHER READING

Allen, D. C. (1959). On *Venus and Adonis*. In *Elizabethan and Jacobean Studies Presented to Frank Percy Wilson*. Oxford: Clarendon Press, 100–11.

Barkan, L. (1986). *The Gods Made Flesh: Metamorphosis and the Pursuit of Paganism*. New Haven, CT: Yale University Press.

Bate, J. (1993). Sexual Perversity in *Venus and Adonis*. *Yearbook of English Studies*, 23, 80–92.

Belsey, C. (1995). Love as trompe-l'oeil: Taxonomies of Desire in *Venus and Adonis*. *Shakespeare Quarterly*, 46, 257–76.

Berry, E. (2001). *Shakespeare and the Hunt: A Cultural and Social Study*. Cambridge: Cambridge University Press.

Bush, D. (1963). *Mythology and the Renaissance Tradition in English Poetry*. New York: W. W. Norton.

Crewe, J. (1999). Introduction. In *William Shakespeare: The Narrative Poems*. The Pelican Shakespeare. New York: Penguin Putnam, xix–liv.

DiGangi, M. (1997). *The Homoerotics of Early Modern Drama*. Cambridge: Cambridge University Press.

Dubrow, H. (1997). "Upon misprision growing": *Venus and Adonis*. In P. C. Kolin (ed.) *Venus and Adonis: Critical Essays*. New York: Garland, 223–46.

Enterline, L. (2000). *The Rhetoric of the Body from Ovid to Shakespeare*. Cambridge: Cambridge University Press.

Evans, M. (1989). Introduction. In *William Shakespeare: The Narrative Poems*. London: Penguin Books, 1–24.

Fineman, J. (1986). *Shakespeare's Perjured Eye: The Invention of Poetic Subjectivity in the Sonnets*. Berkeley: University of California Press.

Foucault, M. (1990). *The History of Sexuality: An Introduction. Volume 1*. New York: Vintage Books.

Goldberg, J. (1992). *Sodometries: Renaissance Texts, Modern Subjectivities*. Stanford, CA: Stanford University Press.

Golding, A. (1567). *Metamorphosis, translated oute of Latin into English meter*. London.

Halpern, R. (1997). "Pining their maws": Female Readers and the Erotic Ontology of the Text in Shakespeare's *Venus and Adonis*. In P. C. Kolin (ed.) *Venus and Adonis: Critical Essays*. New York: Garland, 377–88.

Harvey, E. D. (1992). *Ventriloquized Voices: Feminist Theory and English Renaissance Texts*. London: Routledge.

Hatto, A. T. (1946). *Venus and Adonis* – and the Boar. *Modern Language Review*, 41, 353–61.

Hulse, C. (1981). *Metamorphic Verse: The Elizabethan Minor Epic*. Princeton, NJ: Princeton University Press.

Kahn, C. (1981). *Man's Estate: Masculine Identity in Shakespeare*. Berkeley: University of California Press.

Keach, W. (1977). *Elizabethan Erotic Narratives: Irony and Pathos in the Ovidian Poetry of Shakespeare, Marlowe, and their Contemporaries*. New Brunswick, NJ: Rutgers University Press.

Kolin, P. C. (ed.) (1997). *Venus and Adonis: Critical Essays*. New York: Garland.

Marlowe, C. (1971). *The Complete Poems and Translations*, ed. S. Orgel. New York: Penguin Books.

Maus, K. E. (1997). Introduction: *Venus and Adonis*. In S. Greenblatt et al. (eds.) *The Norton Shakespeare*. New York: Norton, 601–5.

Melville, H. (1984). *Billy Budd, Sailor*. In *Herman Melville*. Library of America edition. New York: Penguin Books.

Orgel, S. (1996). *Impersonations: The Performance of Gender in Shakespeare's England*. Cambridge: Cambridge University Press.

Orgel, S. and Keilen, S. (eds.) (1999). *Shakespeare's Poems*. New York: Garland.

Ovid (1955). *Metamorphoses*, trans. R. Humphries. Bloomington: Indiana University Press.

Rambuss, R. (1998). *Closet Devotions*. Durham, NC: Duke University Press.

Saslow, J. M. (1986). *Ganymede in the Renaissance: Homosexuality in Art and Society*. New Haven, CT: Yale University Press.

Sedgwick, E. K. (1985). *Between Men: English Literature and Male Homosocial Desire*. New York: Columbia University Press.

Smith, B. (2000). *Shakespeare and Masculinity*. Oxford: Oxford University Press.

Traub, V. (1992). *Desire and Anxiety: Circulations of Sexuality in Shakespearean Drama*. London: Routledge.

13

Publishing Shame:
The Rape of Lucrece
Coppélia Kahn

The story of Lucrece, celebrated by Livy, Ovid, Chaucer, and Shakespeare, is a founding myth of patriarchy.[1] It entails the heroine's death, in this case accomplished by her own hand. While suicide marks Lucrece's exit from the story, though, it does not constitute narrative closure. That is accomplished with the expulsion of the Tarquins (the ruling dynasty, to which the heroine's assailant belongs) from Rome, the abolition of the monarchy, and the inauguration of the republic. Thus Lucrece's story marks a key turning point in Roman history, in which the personal is surely the political. Rape authorizes revenge; revenge comprises revolution; and revolution establishes the republic.

In Shakespeare's time, like Pompey, Cato, or Julius Caesar, Lucrece was a Roman hero familiar even to common folk; an exemplar embodying the single virtue of chastity, whose name called up her story. Shakespeare's version of that story begins with a prose Argument telling how Tarquin's father got his throne by murder, a violent, illicit "possession" that mirrors the rape his son commits (Belsey 2001: 6). The Argument then recounts the precipitating incident of the rape, briefly alluded to in the poem: during a military siege outside Rome, in Tarquin's tent Collatine "extolled the incomparable chastity of his wife." The soldiers post to Rome to verify his claims, and find all the women save Lucrece "dancing and revelling," while she is spinning with her maids. Tarquin, inflamed with lust, secretly returns to Collatine's house with the intention of raping Lucrece: at this point the poem proper begins. Innocently welcomed by Lucrece as her husband's friend and kinsman, Tarquin holds an agonized debate with himself (lines 126–356), then forces his way into Lucrece's chamber. If she resists him, he says, he will kill her and then slander her as an adulteress; if she yields peaceably, he will keep the deed secret (511–39). She pleads with him at length (561–666); he rapes her and departs. She laments the loss of her chastity in the high style of the complaint poem, addressing Night (764ff.), Opportunity (764ff.), and Time (925ff.), then sends a letter to Collatine summoning him to Rome but not explaining the reason. In the most famous set-piece of the poem, as she waits for him to arrive, she surveys a painting of Troy's destruction, searching for ways to comprehend her own disaster (1366–1568). When Collatine and other lords arrive, she reveals the rape but insists that they swear to avenge it before she finally names Tarquin as the rapist (1611–1723). Thereupon, she stabs herself and dies (1723–9). Brutus urges the men to revenge, and in the last stanza they "publish Tarquin's foul offence" (1852), which results in his banishment.

The focus of this poem is rape – a moral, social, and psychological problem that is rooted in Roman patriarchy but persists in the twenty-first century. Until the advent of feminist criticism in the 1970s, however, scholars didn't treat rape as a critical issue in the poem. J. W. Lever's (1962) summary of criticism on *Lucrece* lists as its major concerns the poem's relationship to Shakespeare's other narrative poem, *Venus and Adonis*; his use of dramatic as opposed to narrative modes; his relationship to the Earl of Southampton, the patron to whom he dedicates both poems; anticipations of his later works in this early one; the poem's use of rhetoric; and its possible tragic dimensions. If, as Barbara Baines holds, the history of rape is in effect the reluctance to acknowledge "the reality of rape" by "troping, metaphorizing, rationalizing" it, then the critical history of *Lucrece* has followed the same path (Baines 1998: 69).

For critics writing before the 1970s, the poem's self-conscious use of rhetoric invited critical attention for its own sake, and offered a happy escape from the insistent concern with the relationship between sex and power in its representation of rape. Yet they were also made uneasy by that rhetoric, particularly by Lucrece's meditations after the rape. This comment by F. T. Prince, the Arden editor of Shakespeare's poems, is representative: "Not only is she a less *interesting* character than Tarquin; she is forced to address herself in a way which dissipates the real pathos of her situation . . . After her violation, Lucrece loses our sympathy exactly in proportion as she gives *tongue* [emphasis mine]" (Prince 1969: xxxvi). Prince's phrase links Lucrece's speech with a physical organ and makes it sound unseemly (even faintly obscene) for her to use that organ to speak about her violation. That violation, of course, brings into prominence physical organs about which it is unseemly to speak. To be raped and to "publish" it are thus similarly indecorous, alluding to matters about which women in particular, according to early modern canons of femininity, ought to be silent.

Now that feminist criticism has made rape germane to our understanding of the poem, it is generally acknowledged that a contradiction centering on speech in fact constructs the very idea of rape. In the Middle Ages, little distinction was made between rape on the one hand, and abduction or elopement on the other. Thus "Rape was a crime against property and a threat to the class structure and thus very much 'between men'" (Baines 1998: 72). But two important statutes written in 1555 and 1597, by treating rape separately from abduction, in effect placed greater emphasis on woman's will. Whether or not the woman consented became increasingly important in defining the crime as a crime against the person rather than a crime against property. But, in the (usual) absence of witnesses to the act, how could a woman prove that she had not consented to it? What was taken as consent, and what demonstrated resistance? Only physical rather than verbal resistance left traces that could be construed as evidence. Furthermore, in the courts and in literature, a woman had to speak up, to publish the very act that had violated her modesty, when "silence, the closed mouth, was made analogous to chastity" in the cultural discourses that defined her very womanhood (Stallybrass 1986: 127). In defending her chastity, a woman risked impugning it. Furthermore, in Catherine Belsey's influential formulation, even though early modern women were "able to take up a subject-position in discourse . . . [they] were denied any single place from which to speak for themselves . . . [so that] they speak with equal conviction from incompatible subject-positions" (Belsey 1985: 149). This is the case in *Lucrece*, as I will argue, and it is this instability that has inspired a stringent, thoughtful debate among critics about the extent to which Lucrece speaks for herself or, given her adherence to the codes governing women in patriarchy, speaks – however valiantly – from the script it has written for her.[2]

In this early modern context, then, speech and rhetoric are inextricably related to gender, sexuality, and power. Rather than affording an escape from the poem's central act, speech and rhetoric take us to the heart of it. Like other early modern rape victims, Shakespeare's heroine enacts "the contradictions . . . of all women in her society. She is a man's possession, yet a responsible, human agent" (Williams 1993: 94). Drawing on Ovid and Livy but significantly changing their emphasis, Shakespeare constructs Lucrece's dilemma so as to expose not only the contradictions she experiences as a woman in patriarchy, but the thinking and the institutions that create them. Lucrece's suicide, long a subject of intense debate, is inspired if not mandated by the contradictions of her position. Thus she has as much claim as Hamlet or Macbeth to be considered a tragic hero.

Rape

The central metaphor in the poem is that of a stain, which Lucrece experiences as an indelible mark on her very being. The words "stain" or "stained" are mentioned eighteen times in 1,855 lines, and synonyms such as blot, spot, blur, blemish, attain, scar, and pollution are often used. Other words denoting either moral fault, social disgrace, or both occur with great frequency: shame, blame, infamy, offence, disgrace, sin, guilt, crime, trespass, defame, fault, and corruption. Tarquin introduces the metaphor as he contemplates the rape: "Let fair humanity abhor the deed / That spots and stains love's modest snow-white weed" (195–6).[3] After the rape, the idea that she is "stained" becomes the leitmotiv of all Lucrece's laments, and the motivation for her suicide. In the poem as in Ovid and Livy, however, Lucrece is wholly innocent of any provocation or complicity in the crime; therefore, it would seem that the stain cannot represent her guilt. Nonetheless, Lucrece believes that she is indelibly "stained," and tragically lives out the implications of that belief. To understand it, we must understand the function of chastity within the institution of marriage and the Roman state.

The poem deals with the rape of a *married* woman. Lucrece's chastity is emphatically that of a wife, whose dedication of her body to her husband has sacralized it. She is called "This earthly saint" (85), "heavenly image" (288), "so pure a shrine" (194); her breasts are "maiden worlds" (408) as though she is still a virgin, untouched by her participation in the sexual act. As Shakespeare would have known from Ovid's *Fasti* and Livy's history of Rome, the national cult of Vesta, goddess of the hearth, interestingly placed the virgin, rather than the mother, at the symbolic center of the home. This cult duplicated on a national scale the values and rituals of the ancient Roman domestic religion, in which the household altar fire was identified with the ancestral gods of the family. Numa, the Roman king who founded the temple of Vesta, entrusted the tending of the sacred altar fire specifically to virgins, who enjoyed high public honors. It was believed that catastrophe would befall the state if the vestal fire were ever allowed to go out, and any breach of chastity by the vestals was punished by their being buried alive.[4] Thus the very existence of the state was made symbolically dependent on the confinement of women's bodies – specifically, of their reproductive capacities, their wombs – within the institutional boundaries of marriage, family, and *domus*.

Shakespeare announces in the first stanza that Tarquin "lurks to aspire / And girdle with embracing flames the waist / *Of Collatine's fair love, Lucrece the chaste*" (5–7; emphasis mine) – signaling that it is not simply Lucrece's beauty that arouses Tarquin: it is her chastity and, moreover, her husband's possession of her body (as in Livy, *cum forma tum spectata castitas incitat*: I.57.10). The metaphor of jewels, treasure, or wealth to represent the lady's value to her lover, common to the courtly love tradition, Petrarchan poetry, and the Bible, thus takes on a more specific meaning in Shakespeare's poem. Collatine's possession of Lucrece as his treasure and his alone makes her a prize in the incessant rivalry among men inherent to Roman culture, as represented in the boasting contest that is the precipitating event of the poem:[5]

> For he [Collatine] the night before, in Tarquin's tent
> Unlock'd the treasure of his happy state:
> What priceless wealth the heavens had him lent,
> In the possession of his beauteous mate. (15–18)

If Collatine speaks of Lucrece to another man, he invites competition for possession of her, because she is "that rich jewel he should keep unknown / From thievish ears, because it is his own" (34–5). When Tarquin considers "his loathesome enterprise" before departing for Lucrece's chamber, he mainly views it as a violation not so much of Lucrece's chastity but rather of his and Collatine's honor: it is an affair among men. Mark Breitenberg identifies the contradiction underlying the interlocking set of binary terms, male/female, honor/chastity, that structures the poem: "If female chastity functions as the basis of masculine honor, both terms accrue value only within a public exchange system – they must be published," yet "female chastity must at the same time remain the private possession of men, indeed of women too" (Breitenberg 1996: 100). It is this contradiction that Lucrece heroically lives out.

When Tarquin draws aside a bed-curtain to view the sleeping Lucrece, it isn't erotic desire that configures his view of her, but rather her status as Collatine's wife:

> Her breasts like ivory globes circled with blue,
> A pair of maiden worlds unconquered;
> Save of their lord, no bearing yoke they knew,
> And him by oath they truly honoured.
> These worlds in Tarquin new ambition bred . . . (407–11)

These lines portray Lucrece as "virgin territory" that, like the New World, invites rival powers to compete for dominion. In lines 409–10 the marriage of Lucrece to Collatine is metaphorically a feudal contract in which she owes fealty to him as her lord, but his "yoke" over her incites rather than checks Tarquin's "new ambition."

Ironically, Tarquin is driven to risk all in raping Lucrece *because* the law makes her taboo to anyone but her husband: thus forbidden, she acquires a high erotic potency totally extraneous to her own sense of her body as properly dedicated to Collatine. Many critics see male rivalry, or "emulation," as the determining factor in the rape. For Patricia Klindienst Joplin, writing on Livy's account of Lucretia (which Shakespeare follows closely), the core of the story isn't lust but rather "violent political rivalry among princes," evidenced in the prior acts of violence by which Rome was founded: the rape of the Sabine women, the rape of the vestal virgin Rhea Silvia by Mars which produced the twins Romulus and Remus, and finally, the murder of Remus by Romulus, through which he became Rome's first king (Joplin 1990: 53). Nancy Vickers, focusing on the rhetorical tradition of the blazon that organizes Tarquin's elaborate description of the sleeping Lucrece, comes to much the same conclusion. The blazon, she holds, is "in large part, the product of men talking to men about women . . . a battle between men that is figuratively fought out on the fields of woman's 'celebrated' body" (Vickers 1985: 209–10). This agonistic subtext, she argues, marks not only the poem's beginning but also its end, when Lucrece's husband and father incongruously argue over which one has most right to call the dead woman "his."

Joel Fineman, Heather Dubrow, and Catherine Belsey all regard the rhetorical figure of chiasmus or syneciosis, in which opposites switch places in a sentence to form oxymoronic and paradoxical assertions, as a key figuration of the poem's tensions.[6] Fineman calls it the "expression of an eros whose contrapposto energy, the resistance to resistance, simulates the action of a rape" (Fineman 1987: 32, 42). Numerous images of hindrance, he finds, spur the rapist on, as does Lucrece's chastity and her resistance to the rape, but unlike Joplin and Vickers, Fineman isn't concerned with the politics of gender that might underlie such representations. Dubrow calls syneciosis "a linguistic analogue to the competitiveness that . . . is the primary characteristic of the world Shakespeare evokes" (Dubrow 1987: 82). Catherine Belsey makes syneciosis the link between the expropriability of material possession and the instability of desire. As the poem frequently reminds us, "Honour and beauty in the owner's arms / Are weakly fortress'd from a world of harms" (27–8): the more secure Lucrece's chastity makes Collatine's possession of her seem, the less secure it actually is because chastity inflames Tarquin's desire to possess her. Belsey also traces a more overtly political counter-movement in the poem, in which the self-determination of her suicide leads to the republican institution of consent.

The political dimensions of the rape are dramatized right from the beginning in the threat by which Tarquin overpowers Lucrece, a threat that exposes the devious nexus of coercion and resistance, speech and silence, in the construction of rape:

> 'Lucrece,' quoth he, 'this night I must enjoy thee.
> If thou deny, then force must work my way;
> For in thy bed I purpose to destroy thee;
> That done, some worthless slave of thine I'll slay,
> To kill thine honour with thy life's decay;
>   And in thy dead arms I do mean to place him,
>   Swearing I slew him, seeing thee embrace him. (512–18)

As Tarquin speaks these words, "he shakes aloft his Roman blade" (505), a transparent symbol of his power over Lucrece as husband, nobleman, and soldier. The "force that must work [his] way" (513) echoes the language of military conquest that has framed the rape all along. But the most potent, disabling element in his threat isn't death by physical force but rather the insidious coercion of slandering her chastity. In this threat he appears to understand Lucrece from her point of view. He sees that she has perfectly identified herself with her husband as the seal of his honor, and that therefore she fears dishonoring him more than she fears death. To save her husband, Tarquin guesses, she will yield herself. But if she does, then – according to the definition of rape that prevailed in early modern England – she is understood to consent, and there is no rape. Rather, she has as it were violated her own chastity. Two stanzas later, Tarquin adds a further inducement: if she does yield, he will keep the rape a secret, reasoning that "The fault unknown is as a thought unacted" (527). Here, of course, he misjudges Lucrece who, incapable of deception, can only view her chastity as both a material condition and a state of mind.

Actually, Lucrece *does* resist Tarquin, in twelve stanzas of passionate argument terminated by the rape (568–665). The inner consistency and dramatic intensity of her verbal struggle against him arises from its anatomy of marriage as an institution that effects male control of women's sexuality. She appeals to religion, the social hierarchy, friendship between men, the sacred bonds of marriage, etc. – all of which reinscribe Collatine's claim to her body rather than making any claim of her own.[7] Lucrece can't find any stable subject-position that is hers from which to speak. In fact, the narrative moment in which the rape takes place specifically associates men's domination of women by force with the domination established through men's control of language. Tarquin interrupts Lucrece's pleas in mid-sentence at line 666, and in five succinct lines reiterates the terms of his threat. Then, with the conventional ellipsis, these lines narrate the act:

> Shame folded up in blind concealing night,
> When most unseen, then most doth tyrannize.
> The wolf hath seized his prey, the poor lamb cries,
>   Till with her own white fleece her voice controll'd
>   Entombs her outcry in her lips' sweet fold. (675–9)

Two kinds of suppression are imaged in these lines: the stifling of Lucrece's voice and the shaming of her sexuality. The word often used for women's sexual parts, *pudenda*, derives from *pudere*, to be ashamed. According to the norms of chastity by which Lucrece is governed, a woman's sexuality is her shame, and must be modestly concealed. Even when the shame of the rape is concealed by darkness, that shame "most doth tyrannize," because for Lucrece it resides not in what can be seen of her but in her awareness of what Tarquin has done to her body. When Tarquin seizes her "white fleece" (her nightgown) and "entombs her outcry in her lips' sweet fold," in a single gesture he both strips her of modest concealment and stifles her voice. "Her lips' sweet fold" can be read as an upward displacement of that "sweet fold" below, which – naturally, as it were – constitutes the concealment dictated by Roman mores. Though his act is brutal and unlawful, though he penetrates what ought to remain closed, at the same time he but repeats and reinforces the culture's dominant mode in concealing, sealing off, muffling women's sexuality and women's speech.

Suicide

Tarquin's suppression of Lucrece's voice, however, is only half the story: it is equally true that after the rape Lucrece finds a voice she didn't have before. Whether the authority behind that voice can be called hers and not that of the patriarchal values she upholds is a question that has prompted critical debate, as has the closely related question of her agency in taking her own life. Ian Donaldson is troubled by a lack of univocal logic and consistency in Lucrece's deliberations, "an alternation of Roman and Christian viewpoints, which generates constant uncertainty as to the way in which the poem is to be read," and makes it waver between "the idea of Lucrece's tragic loss" and "the idea that essentially she is untouched by the rape" (Donaldson 1982: 45–6, 49). However, I would argue that the incoherence of Lucrece's view of the rape in her apostrophes perceptively dramatizes the actual incoherence of the position in which the rape places her as a Roman woman, which doesn't differ markedly from that of an early modern woman in similar circumstances.[8]

As Lynn Enterline suggests, "In the Ovidian tradition, rape is the call that interpellates the female subject" (Enterline 2000: 158). Only after Tarquin threatens Lucrece with rape does the poem quote Lucrece's words directly, and in the aftermath of the rape, for almost 1,000 lines (747–1722), Lucrece's is the only voice we hear, explaining her complex – and necessarily contradictory – understanding of her position, which becomes her rationale for suicide. Her voice is thus tantamount to her agency as one who freely wills her own death. In Rome, suicide was known as *voluntaria mors*, a voluntary death, and honorably associated with freedom of the will and rationality. Orthodox Christian thought, in contrast, made suicide a sin on two grounds: it violates the first commandment, and it constitutes a rejection of God's grace.

The suicide of Lucrece was controversial long before Shakespeare wrote his poem. In Book I of *The City of God* Augustine questions and rejects Livy's representation of it as the proof of her virtue, drawing a sharp distinction between his own Christian point of view and that of the Roman historian. Augustine's conception of chastity is based on the dichotomy of mind and body:

> In the first place, it must be firmly established that virtue, the condition of right living, holds command over the parts of the body from her throne in the mind, and that the consecrated body is the instrument of the consecrated will; and if that will continues unshaken and steadfast, whatever anyone else does with the body or to the body, provided that it cannot be avoided without committing sin, involves no blame to the sufferer. (Augustine 1972, I.16: 26)

For Augustine, the only important consideration involves Lucretia's will: whether she steadfastly opposed the rape, or whether she consented to it. If she remained "unshaken and steadfast," then as far as Augustine is concerned, her chastity is intact, and she has no defensible reason for committing suicide. If she consented, then she sinned and added to her guilt by the sin of self-murder. Augustine is not convinced that she did not consent, but assuming for the sake of the argument that she did not, he concludes:

> Her killing of herself because, although not adulterous, she had suffered an adulterer's embraces, was due to the weakness of shame, not to the high value she set on chastity. She was ashamed of another's foul deed committed *on* her, though not *with* her, and as a Roman woman, excessively eager for honour, she was afraid that she should be thought, if she lived, to have willingly endured what, when she lived, she had violently suffered. (Augustine 1972, I.19: 30)

Augustine regards Lucretia as a moral agent whose will is free and ought to determine her actions, whereas Shakespeare's Lucrece finds herself trapped by the values underlying her role as wife, a role crucially important to the Roman social order. She is indeed "a Roman woman," who is "ashamed of another's foul deed committed *on* her, though not *with* her," but she isn't "greedy of praise" in suicide. Rather, she dies not merely or even mainly to save her honor, but to save Collatine's. In the immediate aftermath of the rape, she thinks of her honor as existing for his sake, and believes that the rape has stained that honor permanently. When she finally works out her rationale for suicide, however, she arrives at a nuanced perspective that takes account of both her innocence and her shame, and she acts not only to restore his honor but to preserve chastity as an institution crucial to the Roman state. It is as though Shakespeare dramatizes, in the contradictions of her discourse, the clash between pagan and Christian values that concerns Augustine.

The first words she speaks after the rape voice a despairing sense of what she calls "disgrace," "sin," "guilt," and "shame," using all four terms within six lines (751–6). She laments her "loathesome trespass" precisely as it affects Collatine: "The orator to deck his oratory / Will couple my reproach to Tarquin's shame" (815–16). This vision of the public consequences of the rape for Collatine fills her with a yearning for concealment and impels her apostrophe to Night (764ff.). Out of that apostrophe, however, emerges a complex sense of responsibility and agency, in which Lucrece distinguishes herself as victim from Tarquin as criminal:

> If, Collatine, thine honour lay in me,
> From me by strong assault it is bereft . . .
> Yet am I guilty of thy honour's wrack;
> Yet for thy honour did I entertain him:
> Coming from thee I could not put him back,
> For it had been dishonor to disdain him. (834–5, 841–4)

Though Lucrece assigns the responsibility for loss of her honor to him who took it "by strong assault" she assumes the guilt, but qualifies it (by the successive use of "Yet" in lines 841–2), noting that in receiving Tarquin as her guest, she acted on behalf of her husband's "honor" in a different sense, that stands for the totality of her dedication to his honor.

In the apostrophes to Opportunity (876–924) and Time (925–1015), on the other hand, rather than trying to articulate the particulars of her situation, Lucrece turns outward to blame forces she holds responsible for "all sins past and all that are to come" (923) and "never-ending woes" (935). This level of abstraction blurs the focus of her dilemma, and peters out in a salvo of futile curses on Tarquin (967–1015). Nonetheless, that expression of hostility toward her assailant seems to effect a kind of catharsis impelling her to reject words in favor of action: "This helpless smoke of words doth me no right," she exclaims, "The remedy indeed to do me good / Is to let forth my foul defiled blood"(1027–8).

The rich symbolism of Lucrece's suicide matches the cunning of Tarquin's coercion. Tarquin used the threat of dishonor, rather than physical force, to coerce Lucrece into yielding physically to the rape even as she resisted it verbally. Thus he precluded the accumulation of any physical evidence that could have proven that she did not consent to it. As in so many instances of rape, it is her word against his. Her only recourse to this lack of evidence, therefore, is suicide, which she manages expertly. First of all, she implicitly relies on the Roman ethos of suicide, well known to Shakespeare's readers through the humanistic revival and revalidation of Roman history and literature. By reading about exemplars such as Cato, Brutus, and the Lucretia of Livy and Ovid, many early modern readers understood suicide as the defense of honor and the preservation of a good name into posterity (Kahn 1997: 121–36). Addressing the hand that will hold the knife (Romans spoke of the performance of suicide as death *sua*

manu, death by one's own hand, signifying the dignity of an action freely willed),
Lucrece inquires,

> Poor hand, why quiver'st thou at this decree?
> Honour thyself to rid me of this shame:
> For if I die, my honour lives in thee,
> But if I live, thou liv'st in my defame.
> Since thou could'st not defend thy loyal dame,
>   And wast afeard to scratch her wicked foe,
>   Kill both thyself and her for yielding so. (1030–6)

The neat oppositions of living and dying, honor and "defame" in lines 1032–3
represent suicide as canceling out shame and restoring her honor and her husband's.
"Since" in line 1034 makes it clear that suicide stands in for the physical resistance
of which Lucrece was deprived through the terms of Tarquin's threat.

At first Lucrece seems to conceive the blood she plans to shed as the literal equivalent of the stain which she so laments, declaring that she will "let forth [her] foul
defiled blood" (1029). But she recasts her understanding of the act, in terms akin to
Augustine's:

> 'To kill myself,' quoth she, 'alack what were it,
> But with my body my poor soul's pollution? . . .
> My body or my soul, which was the dearer,
> When the one pure, the other made divine? . . .
> Ay me, the bark pill'd from the lofty pine,
>   His leaves will wither and decay;
>   So must my soul, her bark being pill'd away.' (1156–7, 1163–4, 1167–9)

The image of soul and body as tree and bark expresses Lucrece's understanding of the
complexity of her situation and her feelings: shame at what Tarquin did to her body,
along with honor in resisting and withholding consent to it. She employs Augustine's
clear-cut hierarchy of distinctions, in which the mental resistance exerted through will
supersedes the merely accidental condition of the body, only to rebut it with her own
experience. As a Roman wife, by virtue of a forbidden contact (however unavoidable)
she has become a polluted object and cannot escape that (self) perception or its consequences. At the same time, she bravely and independently maintains her understanding of herself as having preserved her chastity in spirit, by taking the course that
best protected her husband's honor:

> Though my gross blood be stain'd with this abuse,
> Immaculate and spotless is my mind . . .
> The poisoned fountain clears itself again,
> And why not I from this compelled stain? (1655–6, 1707–8)

Her discourse reflects the tragic duality of her awareness (she vows to bequeath her stained blood to Tarquin and the suicidal knife, representing her unstained honor, to Collatine: 1181–5).[9] But it also demonstrates her increasing autonomy and self-confidence, epitomized in the declarations, "I am mistress of my fate" (1069) and "My tongue shall utter all" (1076).

Lucrece stage-manages her death so as to maximize its effectiveness in purging her shame and protecting Collatine's honor. For two reasons, in the letter by which she summons him, she doesn't mention the rape. First, to tell him she was raped is *ipso facto* to "publish" her shame; she fears that even he would suspect her of "gross abuse"; that even to recount the extenuating circumstances would be a "stain'd excuse" (1314–16). Second, by delaying the full revelation to the moment preceding her suicide, she immediately supplies the "evidence" of her absolute commitment to chastity that Tarquin's threat prevented her from demonstrating. Anticipating her status as exemplar, she declares, "No dame hereafter living / By my excuse shall claim excuse's giving" (1714–15).

Revolution

From my perspective as a twenty-first-century feminist critic, the rape of Lucrece is always already a political act that depends on and brings into play the ideology and the institutions of patriarchy. But the poem's unfolding of the rape involves a significant movement from the innermost chamber of Collatine's house and the innermost places of Lucrece's body to the public forum, a movement from the intense modesty of chastity in a feminine, domestic setting, to the glare and clamor of publicity and political conflict. The Argument prefacing the poem begins with an account (derived from Livy's history) of the outrages perpetrated by the king, Tarquin's father, who had caused his father-in-law to be murdered and, "contrary to the Roman laws and customs, not requiring or staying for the people's suffrages, had possessed himself of the kingdom." The poem, in contrast, explores with intense subtlety the thoughts and feelings of rapist and especially, victim, a focus on interiority more in concert with Ovid than with Livy. But the poem ends in the political arena, with the intervention of Brutus, who transforms revenge into revolution.[10] Moreover, if we follow Michael Platt's suggestion, and read the Argument as "an indispensable part of the poem," *Lucrece* becomes a brief condensed epic that "begins in kings and ends in consuls," the rape being an action *in medias res*, an egregious example of the Tarquins' tyranny that providentially leads to their downfall and the establishment of the republic (Platt 1975: 64).[11]

Yet it is impossible to ignore Shakespeare's debt to the complaint poem, a genre enjoying great popularity in the 1590s when he wrote *Lucrece*.[12] Like Lucrece, complaint heroines lament the injuries they suffer from abuses of male power; their highly rhetorical style dilates their emotions and plays on the reader's sympathies. Standing at the margins of history, they can do no more than bewail their fates. As Mary Jo Kietzman remarks, however, complaint narrators are nonetheless "characters who create themselves not by acting but by talking" (Kietzman 1999: 23). Given the fact that Lucrece's complaint-style apostrophes culminate in the highly public act of her suicide, an act that supplies the grounds for revolution, it would seem that rather than posing complaint against epic, private against public, Shakespeare is bending the terms of each genre to suggest, instead, connections.

A key site of such connections in the poem, which prepares the reader for the final scene of uprising against the Tarquins, is one of its most famous passages: the *ekphrasis* or description of a painting of the destruction of Troy (1366–1568). The literary genealogy of this scene is indisputably epic: two descriptions of Troy from the *Aeneid*. In the first, Aeneas gazes at scenes of the war painted on the doors of Juno's temple in Carthage (Book 1, 456–95); in the second, at Dido's banquet he narrates the destruction of Troy (Book 2, entire). By positioning Lucrece as viewer of the fall of a great city and as the consciousness through which we understand the tragedy of that fall, Shakespeare parallels her with a revered epic hero who is impelled to save the remnants of his culture, thus enabling its perpetuation. In two complementary ways, her extended meditation on the painting serves as "the means of providing Lucrece with an appropriate heroic dimension" (Roe 1992: 31). First, Shakespeare looks back and, as it were, inward, to suggest parallels between the rape of a woman and the destruction of a city. He had already used this familiar trope in comparing Tarquin to an army marching implacably "To make the breach and enter this sweet city" of Lucrece's body (469; see also 407–13, 435–41). Later, at some length she compares the traitor Sinon to Tarquin:

> For even as subtle Sinon here is painted . . .
> To me came Tarquin armed to beguild . . .
>   As Priam did him cherish,
> So did I Tarquin, – so my Troy did perish. (1541, 1544, 1546–7)

Second, Lucrece's identification with the image of Hecuba moves her toward the performative speech and the suicide that empower the Romans to rout the Tarquins. Hecuba, like Lucrece, has suffered a crime "that lies beyond the power of words to tell" (Enterline 2000: 153).[13] In projecting her own voice onto the silent figure of Hecuba mourning her dead husband, Lucrece actually analyzes the causality of the war and, moving from Helen as "the strumpet that began this stir" (1471), to Paris and his "heat of lust" (1473), demands "Why should the private pleasure of some one / Become the public plague of many moe?" (1478–9). The parallel with her own experience is all too clear, but she concludes her response to Hecuba even more trenchantly, by locating the ultimate cause of the catastrophe in the abuse of patriarchal authority: "Had doting Priam check'd his son's desire, / Troy had been bright with fame and not with fire" (1490–1).

At this point, we may recall that the Argument begins the poem by recounting the abuses of monarchical power committed by Tarquin's father, who surely didn't check his son's desire. In this poem, however, the ruin of Troy suggests the restoration of Rome. Though patriarchy allows Lucrece no legitimate avenue to seek redress for the rape in her own right, the manner in which she demands retribution forms a template by which Brutus leads her kinsmen not simply to private revenge but rather to collective justice. Before she reveals the wrongdoer's name, she demands that her kinsmen swear an oath of vengeance – a gesture that Brutus repeats after her death, when he urges them to kneel and to swear "by the Capitol that we adore . . . [and] / By all our country rights in Rome maintained" to "revenge the death of this true wife" (1835–41). Brutus configures the rape not as a domestic matter, but a political one. As I have argued, throughout the poem, marriage, female chastity, and male honor are understood to be cornerstones of the *res publica*, the Roman state. Even more tellingly, Brutus plucks from Lucrece's side the very knife with which she kills herself (1734–5, 1807), and kissing it as he concludes the oath, makes it a symbol of the action they have vowed to carry through (1842–3).

Finally, the exposure or "publishing" of Lucrece's "shame" – variously understood as her sexuality *per se*, the rape, the stigma she acquires from it, public knowledge of it, or simply naming it – acquires a new meaning in the overtly political context of the finale:[14]

> When they had sworn to this advised doom,
> They did conclude to bear dead Lucrece thence,
> To show her bleeding body thorough Rome,
> And so to publish Tarquin's foul offence;
> Which being done with speedy diligence,
>   The Romans plausibly did give consent
>   To Tarquin's everlasting banishment. (1849–55)

Collatine's unwise "publishing" of Lucrece's chastity as a "rich jewel" that he "owned" made her the fatal object of male rivalry (33–5), but this final "publishing" reconfigures her shamed body as the honorable symbol of republican Rome. Another key word in this concluding stanza of the poem, Catherine Belsey points out, is "consent," which appears twice in the Argument, both times with reference to the general political will that constitutes the republic in opposition to the monarchy: "with one consent" Rome "changed from kings to consuls." Lucrece's refusal to consent leads to her suicide, but her suicide leads to government by consent: the republic (Belsey 2001: 21–4). Yet because Shakespeare has "given tongue" to a heroine who hardly speaks at all in Livy or in Ovid, because he has endowed her with such keen insight into the patriarchal meanings of the rape, her "bleeding body," understood by the Romans as an icon of their newly won republican liberty, must also be read as a disturbing after-image of how patriarchy – whether in monarchical or republican form – configures the feminine.

NOTES

1   Parts of this essay are adapted from my article "The Rape in Shakespeare's *Lucrece*," *Shakespeare Studies*, 9 (1976), 45–72 and my book *Roman Shakespeare: Warriors, Wounds, and Women* (London: Routledge, 1997).

2   Positions regarding the extent to which Lucrece possesses voice and agency vary widely. Maus argues that "Lucrece's language persistently obscures the crucial question of agency," by reinforcing her "paradoxical sense of herself as both guilty and innocent" (Maus 1986: 73, 75). Dubrow (1987), who thinks Lucrece is subject to a naive belief in absolutes and is above all passive, nonetheless sees her suicide as an act of taking control. In my chapter on *Lucrece* in *Roman Shakespeare*, I argued that her understanding of the rape is based on the same patriarchal ideology that generated Tarquin's act. In this essay, I have changed that position considerably, influenced mainly by Philippa Berry, Lynn Enterline, and Catherine Belsey. Berry makes a strong claim for Lucrece's apostrophe to Night as an attempt to "figuratively seize control of history, rather than remaining its passive victim . . . through a highly poetic use of language which stresses language's magical, incantatory properties." Yet, she concedes, Lucrece is only a "partially independent" and "somewhat unorthodox (and confused) historical agent" (Berry 1992: 34, 35). Enterline, exploring Ovidian and Petrarchan treatments of female voice and agency, views Lucrece as a figure for the necessarily fleeting and fragmentary vocal agency of the poet, but offers a rich and compelling account of her interpellation as a subject of rape (Enterline 2000: 152–97). Through the issues of possession (of property and of self) and consent (in rape and in politics), Belsey (2001) brilliantly links sexual politics to state politics, and makes a trenchant argument for Lucrece's suicide as a challenge to the cultural values that authorized the rape. See also the valuable work of Williams (1993), Baines (1998), and Kietzman (1999).

3   This and subsequent quotations are taken from *The Poems* by William Shakespeare, ed. F. T. Prince (1960, rptd. 1992).

4   In Book I, chapter 20 of *The History of Rome*, Livy notes that Numa gave the virgin priestesses "a public stipend so that they might give their whole time to the temple, and made their persons sacred and inviolable by a vow of chastity and other religious sanctions" (Livius 1926, I.24). Ovid's *Fasti* (Ovid 1931), in addition to the story of Lucretia (II.721–852), includes descriptions of the observances pertaining to Vesta and discusses Numa's founding of her cult (III.141–4, IV.949–54, VI.249–348).

5   For a discussion of emulation, defined in the *OED* as "to copy or imitate with the object of equalling or excelling," in Shakespeare's Roman works and in Roman society, see Kahn (1997: 15, 88–96). For emulation in *Lucrece*, see Dubrow (1987: 84–9).

6   In *The Arte of English Poesie* George Puttenham defines syneciosis as "The Crosse-Couple, because it takes me two contrary words, and tieth them as it were in a paire of couples, and so makes them agree like good fellowes" (Puttenham 1970: 206). Syneciosis abounds in *Lucrece*. For example, covetous people "by hoping more . . . have but less" (134–7); Tarquin after the rape is "a captive victor that hath lost in gain" (730).

7   For an argument that Lucrece's resistance is vitiated by the terms in which it is posed, see Kahn (1997).

8   Baines remarks that with regard to rape, the Renaissance "both re-presents medieval and classical assumptions and lays the foundation for what we recognize as our own modern concerns" (Baines 1998: 69). In sixteenth-century England the law began to place more importance on women's consent, but since men could easily employ coercion rather than outright force, and since resistance or non-consent could only be proven if force were applied, the new criteria for consent only served to make rape less rather than more visible.

9   Commenting on the assertions made by Lucrece's male kin that "Her body's stain her mind untainted clears" (1709–10) as driven by an Augustinian (and later, Cartesian) mind–body dualism,

Belsey states, "Rape . . . violates flesh as well as self-respect, organic integrity at the same time as self-determination. Rape, in other words, deconstructs the opposition between mind and body" (Belsey 2001: 19). The division of Lucrece's blood after her death into a red stream denoting healthy blood and a black one denoting diseased blood (an event not found in the sources), would seem to reiterate her sense of her innocence coexisting with guilt, her pure mind contending with her polluted body (1737–50). In line with Belsey's reading, Shakespeare represents this dualism within her body, rather than between her body and her mind. For fuller discussion of the meanings of Lucrece's blood, see Kahn (1976).

10   Brutus's name means dull, heavy, insensible in Latin, and refers to the persona he assumed to protect himself against his uncle, the king Tarquinius Superbus mentioned in the Argument, who murdered Brutus's two brothers. Feigning idiocy, Brutus cleverly waited for the chance to strike back; thus he is a precursor for Hamlet, who feigned madness to further vengeance against Claudius. The figure of Brutus is also linked to *Julius Caesar*, which was written around the same time as *Hamlet*, 1599–1600. Cassius makes the Brutus of the poem an ancestor of Marcus Brutus and a symbol of the republic when he persuades his compatriot to take action against Caesar. For a reading of Shakespeare's Brutus, see Dubrow (1987); for Livy's Brutus, see Joplin (1990); for Brutus's role as "castigator" and analogies between the founding of the Florentine republic in the fifteenth century and the founding of the Roman republic, see Jed (1989).

11   Annabel Patterson connects the popularity of *Lucrece* (by 1640 there were eight editions) with its "bearing on political issues," pointing out that the idea of consent in the Argument draws on the vocabulary of early republican sentiment in England (Patterson 1993: 301, 306). Martin Dzelzainis argues, on the basis of Shakespeare's dedication of the poem to Southampton, that the poet wrote *Lucrece* to appeal to the earl's interest in republican thought (Dzelzainis 1999).

12   Between 1592 and 1594 seven complaint poems, including *Lucrece*, were published. See Dubrow (1987: 142–51) for an account of how Shakespeare departs from the conventions of the complaint in *Lucrece*, and Kietzman (1999) for the interesting argument that "Shakespeare presents the complaint in *The Rape of Lucrece* as a means to transformative action through deliberation" and, more broadly, that complaint poems "interrogated . . . fictions of masculine selfhood and desire . . . while experimenting with the creation of other modes of subjectivity" (ibid: 23, 26).

13   As in Lucrece's identification with Philomel, who is portrayed leaning on a thorn to prolong her song of "ravishment" (1128–55), in Lucrece's voicing of Hecuba Shakespeare evokes only part of her story, specifically effacing the gruesome revenge she later exacts for the murder of her last surviving son, and emphasizing empathetic sorrow instead. For a challenging critique of Shakespeare's treatment of Philomel in *Lucrece*, see Newman (1994); on Hecuba, see Kahn (1997: 62–3).

14   Wendy Wall connects the fact that "*Lucrece* was Shakespeare's second publication and one of his few known premeditated forays into print" with the story's central concerns: "sexual shame . . . linked to dangerous speech" (Wall 1993: 217). Similarly, Mark Breitenberg calls attention to Shakespeare's publication of the poem as "another version of publishing [Lucrece's] chastity and violation, analogous to Collatine's within the poem" (Breitenberg 1996: 117).

REFERENCES AND FURTHER READING

Augustine (1972). *The City of God*, trans. D. Knowles. Harmondsworth: Penguin Books.

Baines, B. J. (1998). Effacing Rape in Early Modern Representation. *English Literary History*, 65, 69–98.

Belsey, C. (1985). *The Subject of Tragedy*. London: Methuen.

——(2001). Tarquin Dispossessed: Expropriation and Consent in *The Rape of Lucrece*. *Shakespeare Quarterly*, 52, 3, 315–35.

Berry, P. (1992). Woman, Language, and History in *The Rape of Lucrece*. *Shakespeare Survey*, 44, 33–9.

Breitenberg, M. (1996). *Anxious Masculinity in Early Modern England*. Cambridge: Cambridge University Press.

Donaldson, I. (1982). *The Rapes of Lucretia: A Myth and Its Transformations.* Oxford: Oxford University Press.

Dubrow, H. (1987). *Captive Victors: Shakespeare's Narrative Poems and Sonnets.* Ithaca, NY: Cornell University Press.

Dzelzainis, M. (1999). Shakespeare and Political Thought. In D. S. Kastan (ed.) A *Companion to Shakespeare.* Oxford: Blackwell, 100–16.

Enterline, L. (2000). *The Rhetoric of the Body from Ovid to Shakespeare.* Cambridge: Cambridge University Press.

Fineman, J. (1987). Shakespeare's Will: The Temporality of Rape. *Representations,* 20, 25–76.

Jed, S. (1989). *Chaste Thinking: The Rape of Lucretia and the Birth of Humanism.* Bloomington: Indiana University Press.

Joplin, P. K. (1990). Ritual Work on Human Flesh: Livy's Lucretia and the Rape of the Body Politic. *Helios,* 17, 1, 51–70.

Kahn, C. (1976). The Rape in Shakespeare's *Lucrece. Shakespeare Studies,* 9, 45–72.

——(1997). *Roman Shakespeare: Warriors, Wounds, and Women.* London: Routledge.

Kietzman, M. J. (1999). "What is Hecuba to him or he to Hecuba?": Lucrece's Complaint and Shakespeare's Poetic Agency. *Modern Philology,* 97, 21–45.

Kramer, J. and Kaminski, J. (1977). "These Contraries Such Unity Do Hold": Structure in *The Rape of Lucrece. Mosaic,* 10, 143–55.

Lever, J. W. (1962). The Poems. *Shakespeare Survey,* 15, 18–30.

Livius, Titus (1926). *The History of Rome.* London: J. M. Dent.

Maus, K. (1986). Taking Tropes Seriously: Language and Violence in Shakespeare's *Rape of Lucrece. Shakespeare Quarterly,* 37, 66–82.

Newman, J. O. (1994). "And let mild women to him lose their mildness": Philomela, Female Violence, and Shakespeare's *The Rape of Lucrece. Shakespeare Quarterly,* 45, 304–76.

Ovid (1931). *Fasti,* trans. J. G. Frazer. Loeb Classical Library. London: William Heinemann.

Patterson, A. (1993). *Reading Between the Lines.* London: Routledge.

Platt, M. (1975). *The Rape of Lucrece* and the Republic for Which It Stands. *Centennial Review,* 19, 2, 59–79.

Prince, F. T. (1969). Introduction. In William Shakespeare, *The Poems.* Arden Shakespeare. London: Methuen.

Puttenham, G. (1970) [1936]. *The Arte of English Poesie,* ed. G. D. Willcock and A. Walker. Cambridge: Cambridge University Press.

Roe, J. (1992). Introduction. In William Shakespeare, *The Poems,* The New Cambridge Shakespeare. Cambridge: Cambridge University Press.

Stallybrass, P. (1986). Patriarchal Territories: The Body Enclosed. In M. W. Ferguson, M. Quilligan, and N. Vickers (eds.) *Rewriting the Renaissance: The Discourses of Sexual Difference in Early Modern Europe.* Chicago, IL: University of Chicago Press, 123–42.

Vickers, N. (1985). "The Blazon of Sweet Beauty's Best": Shakespeare's *Lucrece.* In P. Parker and G. Hartman (eds.) *Shakespeare and the Question of Theory.* New York: Methuen, 95–115.

Wall, W. (1993). *The Imprint of Gender.* Ithaca, NY: Cornell University Press.

Willbern, D. (1991). Hyperbolic Desire: Shakespeare's *Lucrece.* In M. R. Logan and P. L. Rudnytsky (eds.) *Contending Kingdoms: Historical, Psychological, and Feminist Approaches to the Literature of Sixteenth Century England and France.* Detroit, MI: Wayne State University Press.

Williams, C. (1993). "Silence, like a Lucrece knife": Shakespeare and the Meaning of Rape. *Yearbook of English Studies,* 23, 93–110.

14

The Sonnets: Sequence, Sexuality, and Shakespeare's Two Loves

Valerie Traub

"Two loves I have of comfort and despair"

Sonnet 144

"Stage love will never be true love while the law of the land has our heroines played by pipsqueak boys in petticoats"

Shakespeare in Love

In recent years many scholars have come to accept that the desires articulated in Shakespeare's sonnets to the young man are not adequately addressed through invocations of Platonic love. A positive appraisal of the homoeroticism of the sonnets was broached explicitly by scholars in the mid-1980s (Sedgwick 1985; Pequigney 1985) and defended in increasingly historicist terms in subsequent years (Crosman 1990; Smith 1991, 2000; Bredbeck 1991).[1] On the eve of our new century, the idea had gained sufficient academic credibility to be marketed to undergraduates, as three recent publications attest. "And as for the compromising or 'disgraceful' elements of the sonnets," remarks Katherine Duncan-Jones in her preface to the Arden edition of *Shakespeare's Sonnets*, "their homoeroticism is here confronted positively, and is newly contextualized within the powerfully 'homosocial' world of James I's court" (Duncan-Jones 1997: xiii). Reference to the poems' "striking verbal and thematic originality organized around the daring representation of the speaker's homoerotic and adulterous passions" is the way Walter Cohen of the *Norton Shakespeare* begins his introduction to the sonnets (Cohen 1997: 1915). And "gay and bisexual readings of the Sonnets" are promoted as "perhaps the most interesting development of the last decade or so" in James Schiffer's introduction to Garland Press's *Shakespeare's Sonnets: Critical Essays* (Schiffer 2000: 45). Whatever overt controversy currently attends Shakespeare's sonnets, it no longer is focused primarily on their erotic content.

But is the homoeroticism of the sonnets so easily assimilated into and accommodated by our academic – and more general – culture? One only has to read the letters
to the editor of the *New York Times* following Stephen Greenblatt's Op Ed piece on
the 1998 film *Shakespeare in Love* to recognize that agreement is far from universal.
Greenblatt begins his commentary on the film by noting the irony of the fact that

> moviegoers who have seen "Shakespeare in Love" must now be convinced that
> Shakespeare's ravishing sonnet "Shall I Compare Thee to a Summer's Day?" was written
> for a fair-haired, wealthy young woman, Viola de Lesseps, who bore a striking resem-
> blance to the actress Gwyneth Paltrow.

Greenblatt demurs:

> one of the few things that scholars know about Shakespeare . . . is that this poem (No.
> 18 in the 1609 edition) is one of a group of 126 sonnets apparently written to a fair-
> haired, wealthy young man. (Greenblatt 1999)

Although Greenblatt never asserts anything directly about Shakespeare's erotic practices (the closest he comes is to term Shakespeare's sexuality "ambiguous"), several of
the letters to the *Times* protest the (to them apparent) implication that, as Earl
Dachslager puts it, "the relation between Shakespeare and the young man was homosexual." This retired English professor from the University of Houston maintains:

> In fact, there is no evidence of this at all. It is well to remember that Shakespeare spent
> 20 years of his life in a profession in which he was surrounded by men, mostly young,
> assuming the roles of women . . . That he might have become attached to one of them,
> mentored one of them, been in love with one of them, without necessarily having a
> sexual relationship, is not only plausible but most likely. (Dachslager 1999)

For Shakespeare to have loved another man is plausible, even likely; for Shakespeare's
body to have been implicated in such love apparently is unthinkable – or at least
subject to a burden of proof that is impossible, at this historical distance, to attain.

The "commonsensical" division of love from genital sexuality upon which
Dachslager implicitly grounds his (ahistorical) definition of "homosexuality" circu-
lates widely in US and British culture. Its applicability to the sonnets and to
Shakespeare, however, has been problematized by much of the recent scholarship on
male–male relations in the early modern period (Goldberg 1992; Orgel 1996;
DiGangi 1997; Masten 1997), as well as by readings of the sonnets themselves
(Crosman 1990).[2] The effort to divorce sex from love is, at any rate, no longer an issue
that much troubles Shakespeareans, in part because, with the exception of certain psychoanalytic critics, few ground their interpretations of the lyric in biographical
speculation.[3] Duncan-Jones succinctly states what I take to be, in part, the new conventional wisdom:

The homoerotic thrust of [sonnets] 1–126 . . . may also be construed as designed to gratify the literary culture of James's court, rather than (necessarily) to reflect or express any personal preference on the part of Shakespeare "the man." (Duncan-Jones 1997: 50).[4]

Reformulating under the auspices of historicism Stephen Booth's oft-cited New Critical quip of 1977 – "William Shakespeare was almost certainly homosexual, bisexual, or heterosexual. The sonnets provide no evidence on the matter" (Booth 2000: 548) – Duncan-Jones affirms the homoeroticism of the sonnets while remaining agnostic on the matter of "the man." We can interpret this agnosticism two ways: whatever bodily practices Shakespeare may or may not have performed, the poems demonstrate his ability to imagine a range of emotional affects, including carnal desire, for other men; or, whatever homoerotic desires the poems represent, they may or may not have anything to do with Shakespeare's own bodily practices. The new critical consensus thus retains ambivalence, not about the *sonnets* but about *Shakespeare.* As long as the sonnets are viewed as representations of homoerotic desire rather than biographical expressions of it, their erotic affect is deemed unexceptional, indeed, as indicative of broader social patterns.

In positing the existence of a new (albeit ambivalent) critical consensus, I would seem to be in disagreement with Bruce Smith, who begins his essay in Schiffer's volume: "on the subject of homoerotic desire, people are willing to say yes to Shakespeare's plays. But they are inclined to say no to Shakespeare's Sonnets" (Smith 2000: 411). Citing previous generations of critics along with Anthony Hecht's introduction to the New Cambridge edition of *The Sonnets* (1996), Jonathan Bate's *Shakespeare's Genius* (1997), and an essay by Heather Dubrow originally published in *Shakespeare Quarterly* (Dubrow 2000), Smith observes that the sonnets operate as "a site of resistance" (p. 414) to homoeroticism.[5] On the one hand, I believe that Smith underestimates the influence of his own scholarship – as well as that of other critics – on the academic Shakespeare industry. On the other hand, he is certainly right to query the strategies by which certain critics attempt to keep "the Sonnets safe for heterosexual enjoyment" (p. 412). Although Smith, like Duncan-Jones, notes that anxieties about Shakespeare's personal reputation contribute to readerly resistance,[6] the "more complicated" cause, he maintains, is revealed by exposing the transactions among pronouns, both within the poems and between the poems and their readers. In Smith's phenomenological reading, "I," "you," "he," "she," and "we" function as indicators or "reference points" for the subject-positions and identifications of readers today (p. 415). Because of the high proportion of the first-person singular, "to read Shakespeare's Sonnets is . . . to acquire a certain identity as 'I' " (p. 414);[7] at the same time, because the "mode of Shakespeare's sonnets is confessional," the poems are "set up as revelations of private experience" (p. 416). The result is a lack of distance between the reading "you" and the speaking "I" – and this potential for a collapse of identification means that "too many people have too much personal investment in that 'I' to be able to own the desire that 'I' expresses for a person of the same sex" (p. 427).

If critics as diverse as Katherine Duncan-Jones, James Schiffer, and Walter Cohen all readily acknowledge the homoeroticism of the sonnets, however, it may be that the hold of the first-person singular on the reader is more flexible, or at least less anxiety-provoking within the current critical climate, than Smith suggests. Nonetheless, Smith's insight that pronominal address offers a point of access to readers' identifications with, and disavowals of, the sonnets' homoeroticism is echoed in work on what would at first appear to be an unrelated topic: the sonnets' intended arrangement. With the authorization of the 1609 Quarto perennially in dispute, most contemporary critics feel it incumbent to confess their position on the sonnets' status as a sequence before proffering their interpretations of the poems.[8] Despite the fact that a New Critical orthodoxy – still powerful in approaches to the lyric – would treat each poem as a unity separate unto itself and thus render irrelevant the question of sequence, the majority of contemporary critics, even the most formalist, tend to accept the Quarto's ordering, even if they judge the narrative resulting from that order to be obscure, inconsistent, incomplete, and in many respects unsatisfying. Included within this general acceptance is the division of the sonnets, common since Malone's edition of 1780, into two subsequences: the first 126 poems addressed to the fair young man and the remaining 28 directed to the so-called "dark lady."

In 1996 Heather Dubrow waged a frontal attack on the terms of this acceptance by deploying an eclectic mix of poststructuralist, formalist, and feminist arguments (Dubrow 2000). The lack of surety regarding the intended sequencing of the poems, she contends, necessarily disrupts any certainty regarding the narrative enacted, and the number of sonnets that lack gendered pronouns compounds this narrative uncertainty. Without a prior assumption of narrative sequence or "story" that would stabilize their meaning, the objects of address in many poems, if read as independent lyrics, remain indeterminate. The combined indeterminacies of the "plot" of the sonnets and their gendered address, Dubrow maintains, can be pressed into the service of a feminist and queer agenda.

Yet, as students of deconstruction have recognized, indeterminacy is as amenable to conservative politics as to progressive ones, and it is in part because of such a possibility that Smith includes Dubrow in his list of those who resist the sonnets' homoeroticism.[9] But the question of the sonnets' narrativity is more central to Smith's concerns about sexuality than a focus on the politics of indeterminacy would imply. As a second letter to the *Times* protesting Greenblatt's remarks reveals, the problem of narrative sequence and the problem of "same-sex love" are often closely related:

> [Greenblatt] assumes that Shakespeare wrote the sonnets in his own person and addressed them to real people. He also assumes that the sonnets are a narrative sequence, when actually no coherent story can be agreed upon by the critics. Though Mr. Greenblatt hedges his assertions, he creates the impression that he finds the "same-sex love" to be Shakespeare's. The truth is that neither Shakespeare's own sexuality nor anything else about his life is revealed by his plays or poems. For all we know, the Dark Lady and the young gentleman may be as fictional as Ophelia and Hamlet. (Bennett 1999)

And neither Ophelia nor Hamlet, the assumption goes, would tell us anything about Shakespeare's sexuality.

This is an assumption with which I largely concur. Nonetheless, I am struck with the repeated linkage of (at least) two out of three ideas – biography, narrative sequence, and sexuality – not only in statements defending Shakespeare's reputation but also in scholarship indifferent to such concerns. For Dubrow, indeterminacy in the order of sequence results in indeterminacy in the order of sexuality. Whereas her formalist inclinations preclude direct consideration of Shakespeare's sexuality, the logic of her assumptions is indicated by fellow formalist Stephen Booth, whose sardonic "Facts and Theories about Shakespeare's Sonnets" moves, albeit dismissively and rapidly, from the issue of the poems' "Arrangement" to "Biographical implications, the 'story' behind the sonnets" to "Homosexuality" (Booth 2000: 543–9). Although the association of biographical affairs with erotic desire is obvious enough, it is less clear why narrative arrangement would lead analytically to either.[10] Indeed, in criticism even more dismissive of authorial intention than Booth's commentary, a rhetorical linkage of biography, sequential order, and sexuality still creeps in: for instance, Howard Felperin's brief for "what deconstruction can do for Shakespeare's Sonnets" characterizes the efforts of positivist criticism "to propose numerous re-orderings of the sequence to force its latent narrative out of its closet" (Felperin 1988: 70); in thus construing the *narrative* as "latent" and in need of coming out of the "closet," Felperin unwittingly collapses the issue of Shakespeare's sexuality into the sexuality of the sequence. Why does the question of biography so often butt up against the question of narrative, even in criticism that delegitimates one or both concerns? And why does the question of sequence so often refer back to the question of sexuality? Biography, sequence, sexuality – these seem to be the raw materials, as it were, out of which many interpretations of Shakespeare's sonnets over the past thirty years have been fashioned.

In what follows I propose to explore the relations among biography, sequence, and sexuality through a contemporary representation of a highly fictionalized "Shakespeare": that of Marc Norman and Tom Stoppard's 1998 film, *Shakespeare in Love*. Through the lens of this mass culture film, the very title of which proclaims a link between biography and sexuality, we are given the opportunity to analyze not only how homoerotic desire is treated in a popular culture "Shakespeare," but how ideas about narrative sequence are implicated in representations of eroticism. Despite the mainstreaming of the sonnets' homoeroticism within the Shakespeare establishment, *Shakespeare in Love* reveals that anxiety about the homoeroticism of the sonnets and, by extension, of Shakespeare, has not disappeared – rather, it is taking other forms. What interests me is less the presence of such anxiety (I would be more surprised if the new critical consensus had permeated Hollywood studios) than the particular strategies by which homoeroticism is displaced – kept at a distance from Shakespeare, as well as from Shakespeare's sonnets. It is part of the aim of my essay to suggest that the sonnets themselves, along with some of Shakespeare's plays, produce the terms by which the film's strategies of displacement are authorized. By staging a cross-dialogue about the status of sequence among *Shakespeare in Love*, Shakespeare's sonnets, and some of his plays, I hope to show that the syntactical arrangement of erotic paradigms in the film is indebted to a logic of sequence which continues to constrain our sexual lives.

Before I embark on this analysis, however, I too must confess: I accept the 1609 order of the sonnets – not because I am confident that it represents Shakespeare's "intent," but because intention is impossible to determine in this case. Such a pragmatic recognition of impossibility is not a wholesale acceptance of textual indeterminacy, however. Indeed, given the vagaries of early modern publication practices, the 1609 Quarto provides us with a remarkably stable text – one that is inclusive, well printed, and, for the majority of poems, without a textual rival. Even if the Quarto is not "authoritative" (and on this point I am as indifferent as I am agnostic),[11] it is the only Shakespearean "sonnet sequence" we have – and I propose to read it for what it can tell us about the interarticulation of sequence and sexuality.

Shakespeare in Love (Miramax, directed by John Madden) apparently had its origins in a screenwriter in possession of a subject but in search of a story. According to Greenblatt, screenwriter Marc Norman consulted him about "what in Shakespeare's life might make a good plot." In response to this call for a compelling narrative, Greenblatt offered two ideas, one of which was: "Why not have Shakespeare, whose sexuality was ambiguous, have an affair with Marlowe and then become involved, in some way or other, with Marlowe's death?" (Greenblatt 1999). Not only did the screenwriters *not* take Greenblatt's advice ("No dice, Mr. Norman said. No studio would buy it"), they went overboard in the opposite direction. *Shakespeare in Love* redeems the sexuality of Will Shakespeare (played by Joseph Fiennes) by representing him as a romantic hero who comes, quite literally, into his own genius through the experience of love and sex with a woman. Departing significantly from what little historians have been able to document of Shakespeare's life (and thus causing no small consternation on the part of reviewers concerned with historical fidelity), Norman and Stoppard created star vehicles for Gwyneth Paltrow and Joseph Fiennes by appropriating Shakespeare's language of love for a liberal feminist love story.

I do not oppose taking historical liberties with "Shakespeare" nor do I want to deride the film, which I rather enjoyed. Exuberantly acted and bustling with the creative energies of Elizabethan London, its love of the theatre is palpable, its portrayal of the theatrical marketplace brilliant. As moneylenders, theatre owners, players, Puritans, and the queen all battle for the soul of the stage – not to mention its ideological and financial profits – the material conditions of the drama as a commercial enterprise are made abundantly clear. From the narcissism of actors to the presence of the plague, there is much that this film got right, in spirit if not in fact. I do, however, want to raise questions about the means by which certain historical liberties are taken, and in particular, about the terms by which the enjoyment of spectators, my own included, is solicited by the film. What are the strategies and costs of the film's depiction of "Shakespeare" in love?

Through the cinematic apparatus of montage, crosscuts, doubling, and substitution, *Shakespeare in Love* mines a popular association between poeticizing and lovemaking, creative inspiration and inspiriting sex. Unsurprising for a film so invested in romantic ideals of genius and love, eroticism is woven inextricably into its depiction of literary creativity.[12] In our first glimpse of "Shakespeare," we encounter a primal scene of authorship: in a garret littered with crumpled sheets of paper, as the title of the film is written across the screen, the camera zeroes in on a hand in the act of writing. What is the hand writing? A name, scrawled obsessively and spelled variously, but a name that we all know: "Will Shagsbeard . . . W Shakspur . . . William Shasper . . ." (Norman and Stoppard 1998: 5).[13] As a "notorious identity," this name necessarily possesses a history that precedes it (Charnes 1993). Evidently, playwriting begins with signing, and signing is a sign (and performance) of identity. But Will Shakespeare, quite pointedly, is *not* really writing, since he is not producing anything other than his signature – and even this is an object of dissatisfaction and is tossed into waste paper balls. The visual pun on wasted balls supplements the punning equation implied between the experience of writer's block and a stalled will, a pun made immediately available by the foreshortening of the dramatist's name. A few scenes later, Will's visit to Dr. Moth (apothecary and "priest of psyche") makes his impotence comically over-explicit: "my quill is broken . . . the proud tower of my genius has collapsed," says the sexually and artistically frustrated poet (p. 10) – and this is just the beginning of a long litany of complaints that derive their impact from an analogy between sexual and creative prowess.[14]

Through such scenes, the film sets up a correlation (initially, a negative one) between Will's creative and sexual state and that of the poet–speaker of Shakespeare's sonnets who also puns (obsessively, some would say) on his own name, using it as both noun and verb to multivocally convey and compound appetite, desire, the genitals (both male and female), and self-presence. It is as if the manic "Will in overplus" represented in sonnet 135 – "Think all but one, and me in that one Will" – never quite gains access to the genital body of the mistress, whose own will, already "large and spacious," will receive *his* will – at least, if the poet–speaker's sophistic persuasions are effective.[15] Nonetheless, the recursive (and increasingly frenetic) energy of the companion sonnet 136, whereby "Will will fulfill the treasure of thy love" by exploiting the nature of the number "one" and its affinities with "none," is fulfilled in the film as we watch Will's will circle in and collapse on itself, as if in literal compliance with the tautology of the final couplet: "Make but my name thy love, and love that still, / And then thou lov'st me for my name is Will."

Despite the semantic multivalence achieved by the sonnets' dedication to repetition and wordplay, the significations of embodiment – of situated, gendered bodies – limit the free play of the signifier. Sonnets 135 and 136 overtly thematize the poet–speaker's name in order to assert its coherence and commensurability with the will of his mistress; in essence, these poems attempt to bend *her* will to his. The film, in contrast, depicts Will obsessively writing his name, isolated and alone, because, without a sufficiently inspiring lover, he cannot write his play. As the scene fades, the theatre owner Philip Henslowe, his feet recently roasted by the moneylender Fennyman, begs Will in desperation for his play. Will's offhanded reply, "As soon as

I have found my muse" (p. 6), articulates the mystical relation between sexual and artistic inspiration that motivates the film's plot. Initially believing his muse to be Rosaline, the lower-rank mistress of famed actor and theatre owner Richard Burbage, Will manages to write one scene; but when he discovers Rosaline inexplicably in bed with the nemesis of the theatre, Mr. Tilney, Master of the Revels, he tosses the torn pages he has composed into the fire. It is only after the creative prod of rival playwright Christopher Marlowe (Rupert Everett), that words again begin to flow.

One of the few out gay actors in mainstream cinema, Rupert Everett slyly inserts a "gay" Kit Marlowe into the film – less through the fact of his public identity than by means of his ironic performance of detachment from Will's romantic and creative angst.[16] When Kit, considered by all (except Viola) to be the best poet of the age, hands the despairing Will the plot and characters of Romeo and Mercutio, Shakespeare's play begins to take shape. This cooperation between the confident avatar of poetic genius and the talented but struggling hack is later echoed twice: first when the solipsistic tragedian Ned Alleyn (Ben Affleck) succumbs to an uncharacteristically generous impulse, giving Will the title "Romeo and Juliet" to replace the bathetic "Romeo and Ethel the Pirate's Daughter" – "just a suggestion," he murmurs wryly (p. 86) – and again when Alleyn responds thoughtfully to a rehearsal of the climax of the play: "Yes – it will serve. But there's a scene missing between marriage and death" (p. 115). Collectively, these moments dramatize in subtle but nonetheless important ways what Jeffrey Masten has termed the "collaborative homoerotics" of the early modern theatre: a homosocial and homoerotic milieu whose condition of possibility begins in the material conditions of all-male acting companies (Masten 1997).

Such collaboration, however, is intermittent and fleeting. Slowly but surely, the film leaves behind these male sources of artistic support, productive rivalry, and inspiration in order to promote a fantasy of authorial genius originating in the authentic experience of heterosexuality. After falling in love with Viola at first sight while in search of the mysterious boy actor, "Thomas Kent," Will "is inspired" (p. 47), and poetry quickly begins to cover sheets of paper. The entire middle of the film is one long montage of love talk, sex, writing, and performing as Viola and Will exchange in bed the same words that "Thomas Kent" speaks while rehearsing the role of Romeo with Sam Goose, the boy actor playing Juliet. As the camera crosscuts from stage to writing desk to bedroom, love poetry spoken lyrically on the stage merges with love poetry spoken ecstatically between the sheets. The ability of good sex to make the creative juices flow fulfills the historical destiny of the name written so obsessively in the opening scene: apparently, Shakespeare would not be Shakespeare without love. Displacing the self-doubting orthography of the author's variable signature with a masterful script composed, without a blotted line, in the hot flush of true love, the film nonetheless comes close to privileging sex acts over creative acts: as Viola muses after the lovers' first stolen night together, "I would not have thought it. There is something better than a play" (p. 70).

The film's concept of authorial genius, established through the equation of writing, sex, and love, is permeated throughout by the anxiety of Marlovian influence. The repeated mention by sundry characters of Marlowe's poetic prominence sets the stage; Will's assumption of Marlowe's name in an effort to deceive and elude Viola's betrothed, the mercenary Lord Wessex (Colin Firth), rams the point home. Believing he has caused Kit's barroom death by telling Wessex that Marlowe was Viola's lover, Will is haunted by the thought of his culpability. His reaction – "demented, grieving . . . kneeling, praying, weeping, banging his head, in his private purgatory" (p. 108) – may seem like cheap theatrics (reviewers complained about the element of psychodrama), but it is consistent with the logic of substitution and displacement consistently deployed by the film. Indeed, when Viola first hears from Wessex of a playwright's death, she assumes it is that of Will; and when Wessex sees a "spectral, bedraggled figure" in church (p. 110), he assumes it is Marlowe's ghost. With Marlowe's death, the film abandons all pretenses of collaborative homoerotics, replacing the male nexus of creative rivalry and support with the collaborative heterosexuality of playwright–poet and his actress–muse. Assuming the mantle of Marlowe's genius, Will dispenses with his self-protective tactics of impersonation and imitation. Romantic genius, born of the authentic experience of romantic love, is exalted, as male homoeroticism and homosociality are rendered obsolete.

This movement of the male protagonist away from the relative safety, familiarity, and pleasure of male homosocial bonds into a threatening yet compelling domain of heterosexual otherness mimics the basic plot structure of many of Shakespeare's plays, from *The Merchant of Venice* and *All's Well That Ends Well* to *Othello* and *Antony and Cleopatra*. As Bruce Smith notes, "all of Shakespeare's comedies and tragicomedies end with male friendship yielding place to heterosexual love" (Smith 1991: 72),[17] and, as many psychoanalytic critics have contended, the process by which this "transition" occurs can be seen to correspond to a psychosexual narrative of male development (Kahn 1981; Wheeler 1981; Adelman 1985; Erickson 1985; MacCary 1985). Given this ready mapping of a tendentiously normalizing understanding of psychosexual development onto the structures of dramatic plot, "yielding" is perhaps too easeful a word to convey the emotional intensities and traumas enacted in the plays, not to mention the ideological stakes involved. The extreme exigencies of this process are voiced succinctly if bluntly in *Much Ado About Nothing*, when the grieving Beatrice responds to the hyperbolic offer of her newly minted lover Benedick, "Come, bid me do anything for thee," with the steely demand, "Kill Claudio" (4.1.286–7). The stakes for male friendship involved in the embrace of heterosexual marriage are immediate and horrifying. If Benedick's reply, "Ha! Not for the wide world" (4.1.288), exploits this moment of emotional realignment for its comic potential, the plot endorses the lethal demands of heterosexual necessity when Benedick acquiesces to Beatrice's demand and challenges Claudio to a duel. The wonder of it all is that the violence and aggression implicit in these confrontations are negotiated with such dramatic and psychological finesse, as the transition from male homosociality to marital heterosexuality is accomplished, at least in the comedies, without the shedding of blood. Indeed, the reorientation of the hero's affective commitments is dramatized so plausibly, so seamlessly, that it seems, above all, to be *natural*.

The finesse of Shakespeare's strategy of imposing romantic and marital closure characterizes the sleight-of-hand accomplished in Norman and Stoppard's film as well, as all that might be conjured poetically and erotically by Marlowe's "mighty line" is deftly overwritten by the lyricism of Shakespeare's "sugared sonnets." Yet, even as the film endorses the equation of authenticity, creativity, and heterosexuality, it also implies that authorial autonomy is difficult to maintain: if, in the "killing" of Marlowe, Shakespeare comes into his own, his "own" remains stubbornly dependent on the creative ideas of another. Although the film's substitution of the promiscuous Rosaline by the chaste heiress Viola positions Viola as Shakespeare's muse, the film's feminist commitments demand that she assist him as co-equal. At the film's denouement, heartsick and claiming that he is "done with the theatre" (p. 151), Will is given by Viola the beginnings of a plot and the names of characters in *Twelfth Night*. The ghost of Marlowe returns. The collaborative dependencies of playwriting have not disappeared; rather, as Viola's authorial voice counterpoints and merges with Will's, they are regendered.

If Marlowe's death is the most obvious instance of the film's logic of substitution and displacement, the most egregious moment is when Will, in a flash of inspiration, composes sonnet 18 for his new beloved. Describing this replacement of the object of desire, Greenblatt maintains that the screenwriters "simply moved 'Shall I compare thee to a summer's day?' from its sequence and redirected it to a recipient whom modern film audiences, or at least the studios that try to reach these audiences, deem acceptable." Greenblatt's explanation is fine as far as it goes, but in suggesting that the crucial substitution is of girl for boy, it does not address the fact that the film's blond Viola de Lesseps bears little resemblance to the sonnets' so-called "dark lady." The differences extend beyond the obvious physical distinctions of light and dark, blond and brunette, into the very heart of what it means, within the claustrophobic erotic triangle of the sonnets, for a man to love or desire a woman. As sonnets 127–54 abundantly attest, such love is for the most part degraded, abject, full of loathing of the other as well as of the self – in short, infiltrated throughout by a misogyny (and masochism) that has troubled many contemporary readers.

Differentiating Shakespeare's "dark lady" from the female beloveds of his (largely Petrarchan) predecessors, Duncan-Jones, for instance, stresses that Shakespeare's treatment is "really horribly different, for this woman also has a muddy complexion, bad breath and a clumsy walk." She compares Shakespeare's cynical depiction of the poet–speaker's mistress to Touchstone's disparaging treatment of Audrey in *As You Like It*:

> the sonnets celebrat[e] her in swaggering terms which are ingeniously offensive both to her and to women in general . . . there could surely be no question of the woman described in *Sonnets* either reading or understanding what is said about her, let alone receiving any pleasure from it. Shakespeare's speaker seems, like Touchstone, to brag to other men in his audience that he can make satisfactory sexual use of a woman too stupid to realize that she is also being set up as the butt of his wit. (Duncan-Jones 1997: 48)

As much as I share Duncan-Jones's distaste for the misogyny of the sonnets, I believe that their representation of the mistress, as well as the poet–speaker's relationship to her, is more complicated than her literalist reading would suggest. In the first place, there is little in the poems to support the contention that the lady is particularly dense; indeed, in sonnet 138 the lady's sexual and moral turpitude, represented by her "false-speaking tongue," is likened, through a carefully extended rhetorical symmetry, to the poetic and erotic "lying" of the poet: "Therefore I lie with her, and she with me, / And in our faults by lies we flattered be." The implication of stupidity seems to derive more from Duncan-Jones's own aversion to identification with the mistress and her ability to stand for "women in general" than from anything internal to the poems. Perhaps more important, by calling the lady "no more than a sexual convenience" (p. 51), Duncan-Jones aligns her interpretation with a system of value that sees in women's sexualization their necessary victimization; motivated by a defense of female virtue, Duncan-Jones never considers whether it might be the poet–speaker who is being sexually "used."

It is just such "use" at the hands of an erotically compelling woman that I have elsewhere suggested helps to explain the misogyny of sonnets 127–54 (Traub 2000b). Charting throughout the sequence a taxonomy of related oppositions (male/female, homoerotic/heterosexual, fair/dark, love/lust, angel/devil, similitude/difference, reproductive/sterile),[18] I argued that the possibility of a woman capable of producing in the poet–speaker unwanted desires (against his "will," as it were) creates an image of woman that, as Margreta de Grazia also has argued, is terrifying in its ability to upset early modern social hierarchies (de Grazia 2000). Despite whatever affection the poet–speaker feels for the lady, the images of the "fair, kind, and true" young man (sonnet 105) and the duplicitous "dark lady" function tropologically as aesthetic, moral, and erotic opposites. Contrary to an expectation raised by the male beloved addressed in sonnets 1–126, it is not the poet–speaker's desire for men that is depicted as sodomitical; rather, sodomy is the early modern term that best describes the experience (for this man) of sex with women; further, "its potential to mark erotic practices as illicit and threatening provides a governing structure for the poems' negotiations of gender and erotic difference" (Traub 2000b: 435). Conveying the poet–speaker's confused intermingling of desire and horror, lust and disgust, misogyny and masochism, the image of the woman-as-sodomite, I argued, is deployed in order to compensate for, and defend against, the sexual power of women over men.

The second subsequence, in other words, works to contain and disavow female erotic agency (including female infidelity and duplicity) under the sodomitical image of the "dark lady." But, rather than enact a critical practice that is complicit with the poems' efforts to contain female "promiscuity" under the sign of "sodomy," the reading I proposed exposes the linguistic and cultural *work* involved in forging this link. Identifying with neither the poet–speaker (in Smith's terms, the subjective "I") nor the mistress (Smith's objective "she"), but viewing both of these subject-positions as mutually constitutive, the critic is freed from the prism of identification to treat both

"I" and "she" as placeholders for ideological and affective contradictions that exist at the core of early modern sexuality.

Focused on elucidating the relations between male homoeroticism and heterosexuality, I did not pay particular attention to the modes of readerly response generated by the sonnets' abjection of the "dark lady." But when David Schalkwyk asks whether "the formalism of so much contemporary criticism [of the sonnets] obscure[s] a revulsion, signaled by sonnet 129 among others, at the embodiment of this woman specifically and women in general," his implied affirmative suggests that Duncan-Jones's disidentification with the mistress is widely shared.[19] Asserting that a new kind of biographical criticism might generate insight into the social context of gendered embodiment, Schalkwyk notes that

> to confine the dark lady to the limits of Shakespeare's text is to refuse to hear her voice, to neglect to imbue her with a humanity that would belie her status as a mere sign of difference or symbol of duplicity.

Further, he remarks pointedly,

> asked what the history of the dark lady in conventional accounts of the Sonnets is, we would have to reply, with Viola/Cesario: "A blank . . . she never told her love" (2.4.110). Instead she has it told for her, as a lie. (Schalkwyk 1994: 396, 399)[20]

That the mistress, represented as a figure of duplicity, is also subject to lies told about her in "conventional accounts of the Sonnets" likewise would seem to motivate Dubrow's desire to expand our "interpretative options" through highlighting the benefits of textual indeterminacy (Dubrow 2000: 123). Dubrow's essay is motivated as well by a desire to reveal the unacknowledged "plots . . . that attract the academy" (p. 117), including anxieties about the growing feminization of the literary professorate. Yet Dubrow's essay reveals an unacknowledged plot of its own when she comes to the defense of the sonnets' lady:

> Suppose, for example, the generations of undergraduates who have assumed a female addressee for the frequently anthologized lines of sonnet 18 ("Shall I compare thee to a summer's day?") are right and it is the Dark Lady who is celebrated as "lovely and . . . temperate" (1.2)? The tortured and tortuous love staged in the later sonnets may be but one of several responses to her . . . Our assumption that she is unremittingly evil would be complicated . . . (p. 124)

Attacking the academy's "gendering of evil" (p. 130), Dubrow enacts a form of readerly identification that depends on the same investment in female virtue motivating Duncan-Jones's *dis*identification:

> Critics' unacknowledged anxieties about the possible homoerotic undertones in this text may have led them to replicate one of the most common narratives our culture scripts:

the regendering of guilt. That is, by imposing on the Sonnets the plot I have outlined, Shakespeareans can deflect onto the Dark Lady's corruption anxieties about homoerotic corruption and betrayal. (pp. 129–30)

Purportedly exposing homophobic anxiety while redeeming the female image, Dubrow's unacknowledged "plot" in fact plays feminist and queer agendas off of one another.

It is no accident, I want to suggest, that the widely anthologized sonnet 18 functions as a linchpin in this effort. However we strive to train our students in methods of feminist criticism, the way is not to affirm readings of this sonnet as a conventional love lyric addressed to a female beloved. (Nor is it necessarily to search for or endorse positive images of women.) The ability of Shakespeare's sonnets to disrupt students' widely held assumptions about "Shakespeare" as a cultural icon and the often mystified genre of "love lyric" through their manipulation of gendered address is an added benefit to their inclusion on an undergraduate syllabus. Precisely because it is so often anthologized, and thus decontextualized from both the sonnet sequence and from history, sonnet 18 plays a particularly vital role in this pedagogical aim, as Mario DiGangi implies:

> Although the enigmas of the *Sonnets* are palpable and immediate, many students will have been guided by previous teachers or textbooks to regard these poems as transparent yet profound expressions of heterosexual love. They may be surprised to discover that the "mistress" praised in the oft-anthologized sonnet 18 ("Shall I compare thee to a summer's day?") is actually the young man addressed in the early poems. (DiGangi 2000a: 175)

Writing about the procreation sonnets (1–18), Robert Crosman likewise remarks:

> First-time readers of the sonnets typically assume that they are addressed to a woman. Conventionally they *should* be addressed to a woman, so it is not necessarily homophobia that makes one feel a shock at discovering that they are addressed to a man. Once that discovery has been made, probably the most urgent question the reader has is about the nature of the relationship between the two. (Crosman 1990: 474–5)

This moment of shock and discovery provides teachers with an opportunity not only to disrupt heterosexist assumptions,[21] but to do so in the name of history:

> The goal . . . is not to convince students that Shakespeare was "homosexual" or "gay" (which are modern identity categories) but to establish the historical distinctness of Renaissance sexual ideologies and to convey the idea that multiple, contradictory understandings of same-sex desire existed in Shakespeare's culture, as in our own. (DiGangi 2000a: 176)[22]

The desire to render adequately the complexity and alterity of early modern sexuality is, I would maintain, simultaneously a feminist and a queer goal. Because of sonnet

18's culminating role in the procreation sequence, marking the place where the poet—speaker shifts from deploying a rhetoric of marital persuasion to a poetics of homoerotic praise, from enjoining heterosexual procreation to immortalizing male love, it provides in the span of its fourteen lines a particularly dense site for considering the interarticulation of literary form with ideologies of gender and sexuality — ideologies that in the poem are complexly represented and slyly negotiated.

Unmindful of the harm done to this hermeneutic and pedagogical project by displacing male—male desire from the critical conversation, Dubrow's advocacy of gender indeterminacy is uncannily similar to the appropriation of sonnet 18 on behalf of the mistress by *Shakespeare in Love*. Yet my point is not so much the shared obliviousness of criticism and cinema as what their lack of concern tells us about the intimate relations between sequence and sexuality in contemporary culture. The displacements revealed in the film and in scholarship are, I want to suggest, symptomatic of broader exigencies at work, not only in the sonnets, but in the modes of identification currently practiced by readers. These modes of identification appear to be structured by a strangely overdetermined asymmetry: on the one hand, readers, male and female, who align themselves with the aims of feminism tend to disavow any identification with the "dark lady"; on the other hand, readers, male and female, who align themselves with the aims of gay/lesbian/queer studies tend to participate in an identification with, if not the young man, then those desires expressed for him. Within the gendered paradigm proffered by the sonnets, it apparently is difficult to profess, along *with* Shakespeare, a simultaneous appreciation, however ambivalent and strained, for both of his "two loves."

It is with a view toward understanding this asymmetry of identifications between "a man right fair" and "a woman coloured ill" (sonnet 144), as well as the displacements this asymmetry apparently invites, that I want to look more closely at the representation of the female beloved in *Shakespeare in Love*. In contradistinction to the silent mistress of the sonnets (whose voice, unlike that of other female beloveds in Elizabethan sonnet sequences, is not even ventiloquized), the mistress of the film proclaims her love — both in ardent speeches to her lover and, through her rebellious actions, to her loathed fiancé and esteemed queen. Viola's principal modes of defiance — fulfilling her dream of acting by crossdressing as a boy and engaging in premarital sex with "a Bankside poet and player" (p. 66) — are represented as parallel acts of resistance to dynastic marriage and to the exclusion of women from dramatic production. The analogies forged between the patriarchal marriage market and the patriarchal theatrical marketplace run deep. Just as the material motivations of aristocratic betrothals are depicted through crass monetary transactions between the wealthy "shopkeeper" Sir Robert de Lesseps and the well-born but impecunious Lord Wessex, "bargaining for a bride" (p. 37), the financial burdens of the theatrical market are thematized by reference to the physical torture of theatre owners by usurers and investors. Self-reflexive jokes about the insignificance of the playwright — "Who is that? Nobody, the author" (pp. 49–50) — mirror the insignificance of a daughter's desire in the choice of her spouse. Even Queen Elizabeth (Judi Dench), the final arbiter of Viola's fate, gives no ground on this point: "Those whom God has joined in marriage, not even I can put asunder" (p. 150), she proclaims, even as she appreciatively eyes Viola's disobedience in pursuing, and Shakespeare's talent in depicting, "the very truth and nature of love" (p. 148). Perhaps most importantly, Viola's newfound opportunities for theatrical and sexual adventure enable this otherwise dutiful daughter to discover her "voice." This discovery, the film implies, will have far-reaching ramifications – for when Viola steps in to play Juliet at the moment of Sam's vocal crisis, an authentic female voice is first heard on the Elizabethan stage. The theatre, we are meant to infer, will never be the same.

There are, then, multiple interconnected registers in which Viola speaks. Far from being associated with the dark lady, she is an amalgam of Shakespeare's most attractive romantic heroines: the crossdressed Viola of *Twelfth Night*; the similarly crossdressed and performance-enthralled Rosalind of *As You Like It*, whose wit rivals that of her lover's; and the ardently desiring Juliet, whose tragic motto easily could be "all for love." This last connection is the most sustained, as the story of Will and Viola's love affair is interlaced with, and provides the raw material for, scenes from "Romeo and Ethel the Pirate's Daughter": a moment of love at first sight during the father's ball (p. 42); a suitably comic balcony scene later that night (pp. 45–6); and a reluctant aubade to the dawn (pp. 71–2). Fused together in Viola's body, Shakespeare's intelligent, resourceful, desiring, verbally proficient, and above all, chaste female characters displace the duplicitous and promiscuous dark lady of the sonnets, whose "looseness" is all in body, not in tongue.

Viola's literary heritage does not stop with Shakespeare, for a more modern icon of female aspiration, Virginia Woolf's Orlando, informs Viola's characterization as well. Echoing Orlando's romantic quest for life, literature, and a lover, Viola remarks to her Nurse: "I will have poetry in my life. And adventure. And love. Love above all" (p. 21). *Shakespeare in Love* thus forges a lineage of transvestite female adventure from *Twelfth Night* through *Orlando* (1928) and then back again in order to appropriate Shakespeare for a modern performance of female empowerment. Further endorsed by the depiction of a regal if sardonic Elizabeth ("not even *I* can put asunder"), the film promotes a brand of liberal feminism in which social and political power go hand in glove with women's expression of creativity, zest for adventure, and quest for romantic love.[23]

It is a seductive combination, made all the more so, given the recent popularity of gender bending in academia and the mainstream media, by the film's multiple uses of gender disguise.[24] As Richard Burt notes in enumerating what he calls the film's "Shakesqueer" scenes, Viola's transvestism, like that of her namesake, disturbs "the film's equation of literary creativity and well-oiled heterosexual desire" (Burt 2000: 214). The fact that during the first performance of "Romeo and Juliet" the queen also is disguised in order to attend the public theatre incognito, and explicitly aligns herself with Viola with her remark, "I know something of a woman in a man's profession, yes, by God, I do know about that" (p. 148), underscores the extent to which gender passing is represented as offering women a means of both theatrical and political power: as one reviewer put it, pulling on this thematic strand, Elizabeth is "the biggest role player and drag artist of them all" (Combs 1999: 33).

The queerest moment in the film, however, is when Will speaks the lines of Juliet while lying in bed with Viola. This verbal impersonation, performed under the pretense of a director rehearsing his actress, temporarily abandons strict gender alignments in the interest of merging life with art. The presence of the lovers' naked bodies, however, helps to resecure gender difference: Gwyneth Paltrow never is convincing as a boy, least of all when lounging in bed.[25] So, too, a distinction between fiction and life is subtly maintained via the juxtaposition of two proximate scenes during the montage of lovemaking and acting. When Will in bed speaks Juliet's lines, "Stay but a little, I will come again," the stage direction reads: "VIOLA slaps him playfully for his vulgarity, and then kisses him." Regardless of his verbal impersonation of Juliet, Will is a guy, punning about his orgasm. Crosscutting to Sam as Juliet rehearsing the very same lines, the following scene in the theatre suggests no vulgarity, only lyricism, and the dialogue passes quickly to Viola as Romeo intoning, "Oh blessed blessed night" (pp. 83–4).

These queer moments ask us to consider the extent to which boys and women function as interchangeable objects of male erotic attraction, an idea much discussed in recent Renaissance scholarship. Stephen Orgel, for instance, argues that because adolescent males were considered less threatening than women in early modern patriarchal society, the "interchangeability of the sexes" operates "on both the fictive and material level" as "an assumption of [the Renaissance] theatre" (Orgel 1996: 18). Lisa Jardine links the employment of boy actors to prostitution, claiming that the crossdressed heroine played by a boy actor was viewed as a young androgyne who, in his "submissiveness, coyness, dependency, passivity, exquisite whiteness and beauty" echoes feminine traits of attractiveness (Jardine 1983: 18; 1992). This gender bending at the level of embodied performance destabilizes the conventional displacement of homo by hetero, as material bodies trouble the marital resolution enforced by the plot.

However pervasive this logic of substitution may have been in the theatre, the sonnets insist on the difference between men and women. They do so by asserting embodied dualisms that preclude any possibility of successful substitution:

> Despite some gender ambiguity in modes of linguistic address, male and female *bodies* are cathected quite differently in these poems; whereas pronouns attached to each erotic object may be absent or indeterminate, the emotional affects attached to their bodies are neither . . . Rather than celebrating a polymorphously perverse desire that can find satisfaction anywhere with anyone, or a gender transitivity that masculinizes women and feminizes men, the Sonnets apotropaically defend against the possible substitution of women for men. (Traub 2000b: 442)

In its insistence on such gender divisions, the film follows the logic not of the transvestite stage, its ostensible model, but of the sonnets, whose binary designation of "two loves" — one of comfort, one of despair — articulates a compelling, if rigid and misogynist, definition of gender difference. Indeed, the trajectory of the film is to persuade that boys and women are *not* interchangeable, either on stage or in bed. Not only is Sam Goose, the boy actor, not particularly convincing as a girl; at the critical moment, his voice breaks. In a parallel manner, the breasts of Viola, the woman disguised as a boy actor, are revealed. In addition to the privileging of the gendered body over disguise. When Viola says that "stage love will never be true love" as long as heroines are played by "pipsqueak boys" (p. 20), she reiterates Cleopatra's oft-cited complaint about the inadequacy of female impersonation ("I shall see / Some squeaking Cleopatra boy my greatness / I' th' posture of a whore": 5.2.15–17), using a discourse of authenticity to trump a male homoerotic theatrical economy. The import of this privileging of authenticity is intensified when it becomes the focus of Wessex's wager, as interpreted by Elizabeth: "Can a play show us the very truth and nature of love?" (p. 95). Will's winning of the wager, presided over by the queen herself, resolves in typical Shakespearean fashion the conflicts that Viola's disguise initially sought to circumvent, while linking a discourse of authenticity to romantic love, and both to Shakespeare's genius. In essence, Viola, whose efforts at gender passing ultimately fail, becomes the prime spokesperson for heterosexuality and authenticity, leaving the male homoeroticism and female impersonation of the Elizabethan theatre – dominated as it was by the memory of Marlowe's mastery of the masculine poetic line – behind. Through his success in meeting the terms of the wager, the playwright ultimately attains the acclaim and royal patronage he seeks, while Viola is delivered from a loveless marriage. If Will's fantasy of a shipwreck is taken literally (as the privileging of creativity throughout suggests it should be), Viola steps onto an entirely new shore – one that, we know from *Twelfth Night* and *The Tempest*, evoked for Shakespeare the imaginative possibility of an entirely brave new world.[26]

Together, the heroine and monarch of *Shakespeare in Love* join hands to enact a form of feminism well suited to a late twentieth-century consumer culture, where freedom is often construed as an abundance of material and affective choices.[27] Differently situated as queen and heiress are, they portray variations on the theme of women "having a voice," with the trope of voice functioning, in the mainstream and in academia, as an easily recognizable metonymy of female power.[28] The emergence of this voice in the realms of poetry, the theatre, sexuality, and state governance comprises one of the film's definitions of narrative development or "progress." Nonetheless, the displacements accomplished by the film make it difficult to celebrate this progress unreservedly. Like the scholarly and pedagogical appropriation of sonnet 18 on behalf of the "dark lady," the film's version of feminist progress is purchased, deliberately and without irony, at the expense of male–male desire. *Shakespeare in Love* thus participates in and promotes and ideology that positions feminist and gay/queer interests as antithetical. Further, by overwriting Renaissance formations of gender and eroticism with the wish-fulfillment of modern romantic love, the film occludes the alterity and complexity of the meanings of love and eroticism, both hetero and homo, in the early modern period. Within the terms of mainstream feminist thought underlying the film, there is no way to do justice to Shakespeare's "two loves." Replacing the "dark lady" with a blond and allowing her to speak, however lyrically, does not suffice. The film thus begs two

questions: How is female erotic agency so readily pressed into the service of normative heterosexuality? And how might those of us who find our affiliations disallowed
and deformed by this ideological press-ganging, resist this double bind?

The impasse born of this logic is explicitly thematized in sonnet 42, the lyric
which, along with sonnet 41, first confronts the possibility that Shakespeare's "two
loves" might desire one another: "That thou hast her, it is not all my grief, / And yet
it may be said I loved her dearly; / That she hath thee is of my wailing chief, / A loss
in love that touches me more nearly." The poet–speaker's tortured attempt to think
himself out of "los[ing] both twain" results in what is arguably the most specious reasoning of the entire sequence: "Thou dost love her, because thou know'st I love her,
/ And for my sake ev'n so doth she abuse me." Via the conventional friendship trope
of erotic similitude, the final couplet unconvincingly extends the narcissistic self-
delusion: "But here's the joy: my friend and I are one. / Sweet flattery! Then she loves
but me alone." With such manifest casuistry directed toward himself, we scarcely can
look to the poet–speaker to help us find a way out of this dilemma. Nor is our mis-
trust misguided; sonnets 133 and 134, which return to the anguish of erotic trian-
gulation, demonstrate the results of this zero-sum game: "Of him, myself, and thee I
am forsaken," bemoans the poet–speaker in sonnet 133, articulating a self-canceling
grief that is partially mitigated only if one countenances the aural genital/anal pun
that concludes sonnet 134: "Him have I lost; thou hast both him and me; / He pays
the whole, and yet am I not free."

Although I do not know the way out of this impasse, I want to suggest that the logic
of sequence – by which I mean the temporal and structural relations of precedence,
chronology, substitution, displacement, and supersession – offers us one way to analyze
the construction and perdurability of this double bind. In its multi-layered vision of
"progress" – the progress of a love affair, the unfolding of Shakespeare's poetic genius,
the evolution of theatrical innovation toward gender inclusivity – *Shakespeare in Love*
doggedly deploys a logic of sequence that is simultaneously temporal, developmental,
and ideological. From Will's misguided infatuation with Rosaline to Viola's deliverance from a loveless marriage, from the poet's waste paper balls to his drama of immortal verse, from an all-male transvestite stage to the birth of the female actor, the film
defines the workings of "plot" as a sequential operation whereby certain ideologically
freighted terms are cannily delegitimized and replaced by others. Because of the pervasive analogies forged between creativity, authenticity, and sexuality, a movement in
one register pulls on and jogs an adjustment in another. This synchronicity of realignment is overdetermined, propelled by the quiet strength of ideological conviction mas-
querading as necessity. Crucially, such displacements are not a matter of positive or
negative representations (they do not occur at the level of semantics); rather, they are
enabled and enforced through syntactical arrangements. They are an effect of sequence.

By invoking sequence, I mean to build on two central insights shared by post-
structuralism and feminism: that constructions of difference tend toward opposition
and that binary oppositions are not innocently complementary but coercively hierar-

chical. Such a conception of hierarchical opposition, however, can unwittingly hypo-statize binary terms into an atemporal, structural inevitability, suggesting that the hierarchies embedded in oppositions simply *are*. By inserting the operations of sequence into this theoretical paradigm, I hope to mobilize an understanding of the *workings* of hierarchy as a successive progression of terms – with "progression" understood as a movement along a syntactical line that, despite its retrospective appearance of enacting a foregone teleology, a conclusion imbued with necessity, is in fact a temporal and contingent operation that can be exposed, interrupted, contested, and redirected.

My invocation of sequence is motivated as well by Annamarie Jagose's assertion that "a sequential logic organizes modern categories of sexual identification," whereby "the cultural weighting of heterosexuality as first-order and homosexuality as second-order is secured" (Jagose 2002: ix). The logic of sequence, she argues, especially informs representations of lesbianism as inconsequential, imitative, and belated – a deviation of a deviation. Jagose's particular aim in *Inconsequence* is to connect the work-ings of sequence to the regime of visibility that many lesbian scholars have proposed as *the* problem of lesbian representation and thus "to demonstrate the strategic value in lesbian derivation" (p. 144).

Given that (with the possible exception of Nature in sonnet 20) the figure of the homoerotically desiring woman is conspicuously absent from both Shakespeare's sonnets and *Shakespeare in Love*, one may well wonder how Jagose's project intersects with the displacements I have tracked. It does so precisely in its contention that close attention to the logic of sequence reveals *all* sexual identifications to be "always sec-ondary, always back formations, always belated" (p. 145). (Thus, the derivativeness ascribed to lesbianism masks a "disavowal of precisely that derivativeness which . . . is at the heart of sexuality itself"; p. x). Focusing on "sequential switch points of first and second" (p. x), on those detours that destabilize the ontological superiority of origin and endpoint, Jagose's theorization of sequence offers one model for scrutiniz-ing the technical procedures and achievements of displacement and supersession. Because the chronological is "also always the hierarchical" (p. xi) and the temporal is "also always the precedential" (p. 36), sequence assumes a "self-licensing" power to function "as its own imprimatur" (pp. ix, xi). Relations of hierarchy and precedence are not only a *matter* of sequence; they are *enforced* by it. Sequence, one might say, pos-sesses its own constitutive power, its own form of agency.

The regulatory effect of sequence is felt not only when male homoeroticism is seam-lessly displaced by heterosexuality, but when feminism is slyly conscripted to prop up and enforce this displacement. Yet *Shakespeare in Love* did not develop its mode of enforcement out of thin air; it drew on the powerful precedents of the plot structure of Shakespeare's plays and, in a more complex manner, on the gender arrangement of his sonnet sequence. The film's appropriation of these materials functions simultane-ously on different registers. Its use of the plays, for instance, is straightforwardly mimetic at both the temporal and thematic level: in both film and plays, male homoeroticism is shoved to the sidelines, rendered less deficient than defunct as its emotional intensities are redirected toward heterosexual love. The film's appropriation of the sonnet sequence, in contrast, is more complex. On a thematic level, while the sonnets idealize male homoeroticism, privileging it over a degraded heterosexuality, the film idealizes heterosexuality, celebrating it over a superannuated male homoeroticism. The film thus inverts the semantic values the sonnets bestow on Shakespeare's "two loves." *Syntactically*, however, the sonnets, the plays, and *Shakespeare in Love* all deploy the same exclusionary logic of supersession, whereby the ascendance of one mode of erotic engagement is predicated upon, indeed, stipulates the loss of the other. Deliberately exploiting sonnet 18 to invert Shakespeare's tropological hierarchy of gender and erotic difference, the film nonetheless retains the sonnet sequence's logic of either/or. Exacting a stiff price, the preemptive logic of sequence precludes the possibility of thinking through, much less honoring, feminism and male homoeroticism simultaneously.

The difficulties of interarticulating the concerns of feminist, lesbian, gay male, and queer agendas are oft noted in contemporary cultural criticism, generally taking the form of charges of gay male sexism or queer theory's *de facto* privileging of maleness (Butler 1993b; Martin 1996). In the face of such difficulties, some lesbian feminists would separate the projects of queer men and women altogether (Faderman 1997). My own strategy has been to reject the gendered assumptions that underlie that trend: by attending to the costs of a liberal feminist stance to gay male representation, I have tried to respond in kind to that gay male/queer cultural criticism that successfully integrates a feminist critique of patriarchy into its theorization of male subjectivity (and which does so without making a performance of masculine guilt or abjection) (Crimp 1993; Jackson 1995). This response proceeds less from a Pollyannish good will than from a belief that our collective future lies in an enhanced ability to identify *across*, rather than solely by means of, the vectors of gender and erotic identification. Theoretically as well as experientially, such cross-identifications – and the broadening of alliances that *might* ensue from them – could be based as much on an appreciation of differences (including contradictions internal to the desiring subject) as on an apprehension of similarities.

In an effort to critically mine such cross-identifications, I have tried to suggest that certain tensions between feminist and gay male (or lesbian and queer) identities are not peculiar to our own cultural moment, but have a long history. My point, however, is not so much historical as genealogical. If, as I have argued, the logic of *Shakespeare in Love* replays the syntax of Shakespeare's sonnets and plays, then this recognition provides an opportunity to assess the ways in which, despite the gulf of time and changes in the meanings of gender and sexuality separating us from the Renaissance, the logic of sequence in the domain of sexuality continues to operate as a little-noticed form of interpellation. Such an assessment would have as its aim not simply a syntactical (as opposed to semantic) reading of texts or a judicious tally of the costs of heteronormativity. As important as each of these aims is, they need to be supplemented by the exposure of those moment-by-moment sequential procedures that enforce the logic of mutually exclusive, antithetical sexualities.

One available method for exposing such procedures is the queer use of the Derridean *supplement*, which provisionally privileges the displaced term in an effort to destabilize its supersession. Aligned with Judith Butler's (1993a) exposition of heterosexuality as a melancholic disavowal of a prior, abjected homosexuality, this mode of analysis tends to stress the insecurity that attends the "achievement" of heterosexuality by demonstrating how efforts at naturalization are profoundly unstable, subject to a return of the repressed that amounts to a deconstruction from within. Kathryn Schwarz, for instance, enacts such a strategy when she argues, in the context of an analysis of female intimacies in *A Midsummer Night's Dream*, that a

> transition into heteroeroticism implies a possible transition out, and in constructing a female homoerotic past tense, *A Midsummer Night's Dream* defines its present state in relative and contingent terms . . . preoccupation with homosocial and homoerotic bonds makes heterosexuality an awkwardly subjunctive third term. (Schwarz 2000: 220, 221)

Although Schwarz is highlighting the ways in which "consummated relations between men and women recede into the future" in the play (p. 221), her insight into the subjunctive status of heterosexuality troubles the teleology of displacement I have adduced thus far. Following her example, for instance, we might substitute in the quotation above "male" for "female" and *Shakespeare in Love* for *A Midsummer Night's Dream* in order to challenge the integrity and self-assurance of the film's imposition of heterosexual closure. In *Shakespeare in Love* the hetero clearly *is* a back formation of the homo, a dependent and subjunctive term that never achieves total stability. Will, after all, must give up Viola, displacing his desire onto a virtual object (at the end of the film we see him, pen in hand, murmuring ". . . and her name will be . . . Viola": p. 155). Likewise, Viola, enjoining her lover in her final words to "Write me well" (p. 153), is left to seek her fortune alone. Heterosexuality recedes into the future of creative imagining.

As useful as this deconstructive reading is for revealing and destabilizing the hierarchy of terms, it nonetheless perpetuates the articulation of sexuality as a matter of sequence; by reprioritizing homoeroticism, this tactic remains, like many deconstructive maneuvers, caught within the logic it seeks to undermine. I want to close by suggesting that it is not just that the hetero is a backformation of the homo or that the hetero is a subjunctive term, but that the process of hierarchical succession which privileges either homo or hetero must be unpacked, and the glue that holds this syntax together dissolved. Only as we disarticulate sequence from sexuality will we be able to envision a protocol for synchronizing multiple forms of gender and erotic difference. Although I do not know the precise way such a disarticulation and syntactical realignment might occur, we might follow Jagose's lead by emphasizing the potentially subjunctive − that is, hypothetical, contingent, dependent, *queer* − status of *all* erotic identifications and practices. Such a protocol would studiously avoid granting priority to either of Shakespeare's "two loves," in the radical conviction that it is *necessary* to honor them both.

We might push, then, in the direction opened up by Alan Sinfield when he generated out of a historical understanding of early modern erotic practices some provocative performance possibilities for Shakespeare's plays. Sinfield offers an alternative ending to *Twelfth Night*, for instance, in which "Sebastian's marriage to a stranger heiress need not significantly affect Antonio's relationship with him . . . a director might show [Antonio] delighted with his boyfriend's lucky break" (Sinfield 1996: 137). He proposes a similar *ménage a trois* to conclude *The Merchant of Venice*: Bassanio need not choose between Portia and Antonio, but all three happily enter Portia's house together.[29] Based on the erotic possibilities envisioned by Shakespeare's sonnets as well as my own work on early modern lesbianism (Traub 2002), my own response to screenwriter Norman's request for a "Shakespeare plot" would go something like this: Shakespeare and Marlowe do have an affair, as do Shakespeare and the (initially cross-dressed) Viola. Rather than these liaisons leading to Marlowe's death, they lead to Viola's infatuation with Kit. Kit, however, continues to prefer the company of boys and men, while Will, feeling betrayed by both of his two loves, contemplates how much more he liked Viola when she was dressed as a boy. When a transvestite "female husband" arrives at the Globe seeking work as a stagehand, Shakespeare finds in the successfully passing woman a refreshing twist to sonnet 20's expressed desire for a "master–mistress" – a recognition that prompts the plot's exploration of *this* woman's desire, as well as Shakespeare's creation of a whole new body of poetry.

ACKNOWLEDGMENTS

I thank Jeffrey Masten for providing me with the original impetus, Holly Dugan for her research assistance, and Patsy Yaeger and David Halperin for helping me with the denouement of this essay.

NOTES

1   For an annotated bibliography of scholarship on the homoeroticism of the sonnets since 1980, see Traub (2000a). Homoerotic interpretations had been offered previously by Oscar Wilde and Samuel Butler, but were not widely circulated or accepted.

2   As Cohen puts it, to deny the sexual component of the sonnets, an interpretation "must ignore or explain away the many explicit expressions of love as well as the powerful evocation of a range of feelings ordinarily associated with love. It also cannot do justice to the repeated comparison of the youth to a 'rose' – a traditional symbol of female genitalia and arguably the speaker's name for his object of desire" (Cohen 1997: 1920).

3   Schiffer notes, for instance, that "since Rollins's *Variorum* (1944), a virtual *Dunciad* of scholarly folly, and certainly since Booth's appendix to his 1977 edition, there has been a marked decrease in the number of readings that touch directly on biographical issues" (Schiffer 2000: 42). Schalkwyk (1994: 398) also points to a "revulsion against biography" in recent criticism. Crosman is even more pointed about the exclusion of "biographical contextualizing," arguing that "most editions of the sonnets are downright schizophrenic on the subject: first they give us the biographical background of the sonnets, then they warn us not to use it" (Crosman 1990: 478, n. 7).

4   I say "in part" because Duncan-Jones's dating of certain sonnets to the Jacobean period remains controversial.

5   To Smith's list one might add the comments of Helen Vendler (1997) who notes that "over time there has evolved . . . an increasing willingness to admit, about the first subsequence, that its controlling motive is sexual infatuation." Simultaneously aligning herself with, and distancing herself from, this admission, Vendler continues, "the infatuation of the speaker with the young man is so entirely an infatuation of the eye – which makes a fetish of the beloved's countenance rather than of his entire body – that gazing is this infatuation's chief (and perhaps best and only) form of intercourse" (p. 15).

6   Duncan-Jones writes that "a fear that a personal interpretation of the 'young man' sonnets might link Shakespeare . . . with criminalized activity seems to have operated as a powerful disincentive. Most serious critics and scholars have studiously resisted, or side-stepped, the temptation to connect *Sonnets* with Shakespeare's own life and personality" (Duncan-Jones 1997: 82).

7   The assumption that such an invitation to identification forms the basis of Shakespeare's art is widely shared; see Crosman (1990: 473) and Dubrow (1981): "the primary effect of the lyrical mode of these poems is to intensify our identification with the speaker" (p. 66). The assumption of the subjective nature of lyric's address is pervasive throughout the critical history of the lyric; for critiques of this presumption, see Jackson and Prins (1999) and Hôsek and Parker (1985).

8   Useful summaries of the authorization debate can be found in Schiffer (2000) and Booth (2000) [1977]; most recently, Duncan-Jones (1997) has made an influential case for considering the dating of many of the sonnets as Jacobean and the Quarto as authorized by Shakespeare. In regards to narrative, Schiffer remarks, "most commentators acknowledge the presence of narrative elements in the Sonnets, ranging from individual poems structured at least in part as narrative . . . to sonnets in which there is a rich interplay . . . of narrative, lyric, and dramatic modes . . . to references in other sonnets to an imperfectly rendered story that may have relevance to all the sonnets" (unpublished manuscript).

9   Smith (2000) charges that Dubrow's invocation of indeterminacy "disables any attempt to settle the Sonnets in a particular sexual scenario" (p. 413).

10 My ideas about the relation between narrative sequence and sexuality have been spurred by Annamarie Jagose's *Inconsequence*, as well as by working with Theresa Braunschneider on her Ph.D. dissertation, "Maidenly Amusements" (2002).

11 In this respect, I agree with Howard Felperin (1988) that both the desire to "pin down the personal experience of an originary author" and the related "dream of reconstructing an authoritative text of the *Sonnets*," are "baffled from the onset by the uncooperative aloofness of their freestanding autonomy" (p. 70). Once we divorce our engagement with the sonnets from a concern with authorial authorization, we can move, in the terms of Roland Barthes (1977), from "work" to "text."

12 My discussion of the film is indebted to discussions with Jeffrey Masten, whose unpublished writing on the film sparked many of my ideas.

13 For ease of demonstration, quotations from the film, hereafter noted parenthetically by page number, are taken from the published screenplay, which sometimes deviates in minor ways from the lines spoken in the film.

14 The published screenplay uses a close-up of a hand writing with a quill to adorn its title page (Norman and Stoppard 1998).

15 All references to the sonnets and plays are from the *Norton Shakespeare* and are hereafter cited parenthetically in the text.

16 Everett has played gay roles in several films (*My Best Friend's Wedding* and *The Next Best Thing*) as well as a campy bachelor in the cinematic adaptation of Oscar Wilde's *An Ideal Husband* and *The Importance of Being Earnest*.

17 Incorporating Shakespeare's plot design into his own typology of early modern homoeroticisms, Smith contends that "Shakespeare plays out the sexual conflict that the Myth of Combatants and

Comrades poses for that other Renaissance ideal of human relations, the Myth of Companionate Marriage" (Smith 1991: 64). Smith further notes of *The Two Noble Kinsmen* that "on the issue of male bonding versus marriage Shakespeare finished his career, not with one of the reconciliations that are the common theme of his other late plays, but with a fresh recognition of the impasse between the two" (p. 72).

18   These binaries are analyzed brilliantly, if problematically, by Fineman (1986), whose work provided the basis of my own interpretation.

19   Historically, the scholarship on the "dark lady" poems has been obsessed with establishing her identity – as if that knowledge would somehow lay to rest all that is disturbing about these poems. Marvin Hunt (2000), who elaborates on de Grazia's suggestion that the dark lady is of African descent, provides a useful survey of efforts to establish the mistress's identity.

20   It should be noted, as Smith does, that "the desired male object in the sonnets" likewise "has no voice" (Smith 2000: 420).

21   Crosman's rhetoric of "shock" would seem to imply not only surprise but dismay – a reading that fails to account for the presence of gay/queer identified readers in the classroom, for whom any "shock" might be the pleasurable shock of identification.

22   See also DiGangi (2000b).

23   On the possibility of feminist popular culture versions of Shakespeare opening up new avenues for female authority over representation, see Burt (2000).

24   The work on early modern transvestism is vast; for starters, see Garber (1992) and Orgel (1996).

25   Likewise, Will's impersonation of a laundry woman, who chaperones Viola to her Greenwich audience with the queen, could be seen as gender bending, if it weren't such a clichéd instance of transparent drag.

26   The final words of the screenplay are, "DISSOLVE slowly to VIOLA, walking away up the beach towards her brave new world" (p. 155).

27   With the exception of Viola and Elizabeth, the film's depiction of women rests on some unfortunate stereotypes, apparently authorized by the idea that none would be a suitable creative partner to Will. The existence of Anne Hathaway, mentioned briefly to Dr. Moth, is narratively dispatched when Will confronts Viola's charge of deception with the words, "I have a wife, yes, and I cannot marry the daughter of Sir Robert de Lesseps. It needed no wife come from Stratford to tell you that" (p. 112). Viola's mother, complicit with her husband's monetary investment in their daughter, is drawn from the vacant Lady Capulet. Viola's nurse, who, like the Nurse of "Romeo and Juliet" genuinely cares for her charge, demands the spectator's interest precisely insofar as she deviates from the role created by Shakespeare; part of the fun is watching just how far she will aid and abet Viola's desires.

28   My ideas on "voice" have been informed by the work of Gina Bloom (2001). Focused on the distinction the film enforces between "good" and "bad" capitalism, Courtney Lehmann (2002) takes a harsher view of the film's feminism, pointing out that Viola's authorial collaboration is "reduced to copulation" (p. 223) and that she ultimately becomes "the feminized object of exchange" (p. 226) within an economy that mystifies labor even more than love.

29   The campy pleasures that attend such alternatives are playfully displayed in Jonathan Dollimore's (1990) arch proposal for a cross-gender production of *Antony and Cleopatra* starring Shakespeare critics Marjorie Garber as Antony and Peter Stallybrass or Gary Taylor as Cleopatra.

References and Further Reading

Adelman, J. (1985). Male Bonding in Shakespeare's Comedies. In P. Erickson and C. Kahn (eds.) *Shakespeare's "Rough Magic": Renaissance Essays in Honor of C. L. Barber.* Newark: University of Delaware Press, 73–103.

Barthes, R. (1977). From Work to Text. In *Image-Music-Text*, trans. S. Heath. New York: Hill and Wang, 155–64.

Bate, J. (1997). *Shakespeare's Genius*. London: Picador.

Bennett, K. C. (1999). Shakespeare in Love? *New York Times*, February 12, section A, p. 26, column 6.

Bloom, G. (2001). Choreographing Voice: Staging Gender in Early Modern England. Unpublished Ph.D. dissertation, University of Michigan.

Booth, S. (2000). *Shakespeare's Sonnets*. New Haven, CT: Yale University Press.

Braunschneider, T. (2002). Maidenly Amusements: Narrating Female Sexuality in Eighteenth-Century England. Unpublished Ph.D. dissertation, University of Michigan.

Bredbeck, G. (1991). *Sodomy and Interpretation: Marlowe to Milton*. Ithaca, NY: Cornell University Press.

Burt, R. (2000). *Shakespeare in Love* and the End of the Shakespearean: Academic and Mass Culture Constructions of Literary Authorship. In M. T. Burnett and R. Wray (eds.) *Shakespeare, Film, Fin de Siècle*. New York: St. Martin's Press, 203–31.

Butler, J. (1993a). *Bodies That Matter: On the Discursive Limits of "Sex"*. London: Routledge.

——(1993b). Critically Queer. *GLQ: A Journal of Lesbian and Gay Studies*, 1, 1, 17–32.

Charnes, L. (1993). *Notorious Identity: Materializing the Subject in Shakespeare*. Cambridge, MA: Harvard University Press.

Cohen, W. (1997). The Sonnets and "A Lover's Complaint." In S. Greenblatt (ed.) *The Norton Shakespeare. Based on the Oxford Edition*. New York: Norton, 1915–21.

Combs, R. (1999). Words, Words, Words. *Film Comment*, 35, 3, 32–5.

Crimp, D. (1993). Right On, Girlfriend! In M. Warner (ed.) *Fear of a Queer Planet: Queer Politics and Social Theory*. Minneapolis: University of Minnesota Press.

Crosman, R. (1990). Making Love Out of Nothing at All: The Issue of Story in Shakespeare's Procreation Sonnets. *Shakespeare Quarterly*, 41, 4, 470–88.

Dachslager, E. L. (1999). Shakespeare in Love? *New York Times*, February 6, section A, p. 26, column 6.

de Grazia, M. (2000). The Scandal of Shakespeare's Sonnets. In J. Schiffer (ed.) *Shakespeare's Sonnets: Critical Essays*. New York: Garland, 89–112.

DiGangi, M. (1997). *The Homoerotics of Early Modern Drama*. Cambridge: Cambridge University Press.

——(2000a). "Love is not (heterosexual) love": Historicizing Sexuality in Elizabethan Poetry. In P. Cheney and A. L. Prescott (eds.) *Approaches to Teaching Shorter Elizabethan Poetry*. New York: Modern Language Association, 173–8.

——(2000b). "Shakespeare's Sexuality: Who Needs It? In W. Spurlin (ed.) *Lesbian and Gay Studies and the Teaching of English: Positions, Pedagogies, and Cultural Politics*. Urbana, IL: National Council of Teachers of English, 147–67.

Dollimore, J. (1990). Shakespeare, Cultural Materialism, Feminism, and Marxist Humanism. *New Literary History*, 21, 3, 471–93.

Dubrow, H. (1981). Shakespeare's Undramatic Monologues: Toward a Reading of the Sonnets. *Shakespeare Quarterly*, 31, 1, 55–68.

——(2000) "Incertainties now crown themselves assur'd": The Politics of Plotting Shakespeare's Sonnets. In J. Schiffer (ed.) *Shakespeare's Sonnets: Critical Essays*. New York: Garland, 113–33.

Duncan-Jones, K. (1997). *Shakespeare's Sonnets*. London: Thomas Nelson and Sons.

Erickson, P. (1985). *Patriarchal Structures in Shakespeare's Drama*. Berkeley: University of California Press.

Faderman, L. (1997) Afterword. In D. Heller (ed.) *Cross-Purposes: Lesbians, Feminists, and the Limits of Alliance*. Bloomington: Indiana University Press, 221–9.

Felperin, H. (1988). The Dark Lady Identified, or What Deconstruction Can Do for Shakespeare's *Sonnets*. In G. D. Atkins and D. M. Bergeron (eds.) *Shakespeare and Deconstruction*. New York: Peter Lang, 69–93.

Fineman, J. (1986). *Shakespeare's Perjured Eye: The Invention of Poetic Subjectivity in the Sonnets*. Berkeley: University of California Press.

Garber, M. (1992) *Vested Interests: Cross-Dressing and Cultural Anxiety*. New York: Routledge.

Goldberg, J. (1992). *Sodometries: Renaissance Texts, Modern Sexualities*. Stanford, CA: Stanford University Press.

Greenblatt, S. (ed.) (1997). *The Norton Shakespeare. Based on the Oxford Edition*. New York: Norton.

——(1999). About that Romantic Sonnet. *New York Times*, February 6, section A, p. 15, column 1.

Hecht, A. (1996). Introduction. In C. B. Evans (ed.) *The Sonnets*. Cambridge: Cambridge University Press, 1–28.

Hôsek, C. and Parker, P. (ed.) (1985). *Lyric Poetry: Beyond New Criticism*. Ithaca, NY: Cornell University Press.

Hunt, M. (2000). Be Dark but Not Too Dark: Shakespeare's Dark Lady as a Sign of Color. In J. Schiffer (ed.) *Shakespeare's Sonnets: Critical Essays*. New York: Garland, 369–89.

Jackson, E., Jr. (1995). *Strategies of Deviance: Studies in Gay Male Representation*. Bloomington: Indiana University Press.

Jackson, V. and Prins, Y. (1999). Lyrical Studies. *Victorian Literature and Culture*, 27, 2, 521–30.

Jagose, A. (2002). *Inconsequence: Lesbian Representation and the Logic of Sexual Sequence*.

Jardine, L. (1983). *Still Harping on Daughters: Women and Drama in the Age of Shakespeare*. Brighton: Harvester.

——(1992). Twins and Travesties: Gender, Dependency and Sexual Availability." In S. Zimmerman (ed.) *Erotic Politics: Desire on the Renaissance Stage*. New York: Routledge, 27–38.

Kahn, C. (1981). *Man's Estate: Masculine Identity in Shakespeare*. Berkeley: University of California Press.

Lehmann, C. (2002). *Shakespeare Remains: Theater to Film, Early Modern to Postmodern*. Ithaca, NY: Cornell University Press.

MacCary, T. (1985). *Friends and Lovers: The Phenomenology of Desire in Shakespearean Comedy*. New York: Columbia University Press.

Martin, B. (1996). *Femininity Played Straight: The Significance of Being Lesbian*. New York: Routledge.

Masten, J. (1997). *Textual Intercourse: Collaboration, Authorship and Sexualities in Renaissance Drama*. Cambridge: Cambridge University Press.

Norman, M. and Stoppard, T. (1998). *Shakespeare in Love: A Screenplay*. New York: Hyperion for Miramax Film Corp. and Universal Studios.

Orgel, S. (1996). *Impersonations: The Performance of Gender in Shakespeare's England*. Cambridge: Cambridge University Press.

Pequigney, J. (1985). *Such is My Love: A Study of Shakespeare's Sonnets*. Chicago, IL: University of Chicago Press.

Schalkwyk, D. (1994). "She never told her love": Embodiment, Textuality, and Silence in Shakespeare's Sonnets and Plays. *Shakespeare Quarterly*, 45, 381–407.

Schiffer, J. (2000). Reading New Life into Shakespeare's Sonnets: A Survey of Criticism. In J. Schiffer (ed.) *Shakespeare's Sonnets: Critical Essays*. New York: Garland, 3–71.

——The Sonnets as Anti-Narrative. Unpublished manuscript.

Schwarz, K. (2000). *Tough Love: Amazon Encounters in the English Renaissance*. Durham, NC: Duke University Press.

Sedgwick, E. K. (1985). *Between Men: English Literature and Male Homosocial Desire*. New York: Columbia University Press.

Sinfield, A. (1996). How to Read *The Merchant of Venice* Without Being Heterosexist. In T. Hawkes (ed.) *Alternative Shakespeares*, Vol. 2. London: Routledge, 122–39.

Smith, B. R. (1991). *Homosexual Desire in Shakespeare's England: A Cultural Poetics*. Chicago, IL: University of Chicago Press.

——(2000). I, You, He, She, and We: On the Sexual Politics of Shakespeare's Sonnets. In J. Schiffer (ed.) *Shakespeare's Sonnets: Critical Essays*. New York: Garland, 411–29.

Traub, V. (2000a). Recent Studies in Homoeroticism, 1970–1999. *English Literary Renaissance*, spring, 284–329.

——(2000b). Sex Without Issue: Sodomy, Reproduction, and Signification in Shakespeare's Sonnets. In J. Schiffer (ed.) *Shakespeare's Sonnets: Critical Essays*. New York: Garland, 431–52.

——(2002). *The Renaissance of Lesbianism in Early Modern England.* Cambridge: Cambridge University Press.

Vendler, H. (1997). *The Art of Shakespeare's Sonnets.* Cambridge, MA: Harvard University Press.

Wheeler, R. (1981). *Shakespeare's Development and the Problem Comedies.* Berkeley: University of California Press.

Woolf, V. (1956). *Orlando: A Biography.* New York: Harcourt Brace (original work published 1928).

15

The Two Party System in
Troilus and Cressida
Linda Charnes

No progress can be made on the political front until the cycle of violence is crushed and broken.

George W. Bush, *New York Times*, June 2001

Political and cultural weapons are customarily deployed to maintain in operation an identity structure which, if laid out as doctrine, would be absurd.

Tom Nairn, *Faces of Nationalism*

In his statement to reporters about the ineffectual Palestinian–Israeli "ceasefire" of June 2001, George W. Bush deploys, with unusual precision, the same rhetoric that fuels the situation he condemns. To speak of ending a cycle of violence by "crushing" and "breaking" it is purely tautological – yet Bush's choice of words reveals how difficult it is to escape the logic of a system once its form has overdetermined, if not overtaken, its content. Whatever national identity Palestinians currently have has been constituted, in their view, by being denied statehood by Israel; and although many Israelis believe the time has come to abandon such terms, it is difficult to imagine an Israeli national identity that isn't on some level underwritten by the threat of "exterminations" past, present, or future. Both sides are locked together in a kind of vicious parody of a two party system that, while not equally balanced in power or justification, nonetheless provides the rhetorical equilibrium of the classic claim/ counterclaim structure. The ideological content of those claims is difficult to discern through their repeated formalizations as a "war," which may be one reason why compromises over "content" seem to be ineffective.

On a less explosive but no less entrenched front, the structure of American politics has calcified into a series of cyclical and redundant battles between the Democratic and Republican parties. If Election 2000 proved anything, it was that even though Americans are nearly evenly divided between the two parties, the ideological positions each represents have never been closer. With the exception of the "far right,"

Democratic and Republican centrists are virtually indistinguishable from each other (as Senator Jim Jeffords's "defection" from the Republican Party into "independence" graphically demonstrated). One would think that the result would be a greater ability to work across party-lines, but the opposite seems to have happened: as the two parties look more alike, they seem more invested than ever in ferreting out differences, many (though not all) of them trivial, and building them into implacable monsters.

Nothing in the Constitution of the United States requires us to carve our political landscape into two such blocs. Nevertheless, partisans on each side claim to possess the political equivalent of the Lacanian *Objet A*: that obscure object of desire usually referred to as *What the American People Want*. In this political rhetoric the complex subjectivities of a vast and diverse nation are reified into that well-known chimera "the American People," recruited by both sides as a rhetorical weapon in the real battle, which is not about delivering what "the people" really want (Freud couldn't unravel it) but rather, about maintaining *at any cost* the two party system itself.

In a world in which global politics are rearranging, for better and worse, territorial allegiances, American politics – with its gridlocked two party system – seems increasingly caught up in something inarticulable, something irrational. Stuck in a cycle of campaigning that never ceases, not even in the weeks immediately following an election, politicians look for any opportunity to launch surprise attacks on each other, whether armed with "evidence" of financial corruption or of sexual impropriety. With citizens beaten senseless by redundant bombast, citizens who can no longer believe either in the nobility or the honor of their most prestigious representatives, American politics has come to look alarmingly like the Trojan War in Shakespeare's *Troilus and Cressida*.

I

Over the last thirty years the poststructuralist project of "decentering" the humanist subject has made *Troilus and Cressida* less a "problem play" than a litmus test for measuring Shakespeare's own skepticism about the ideological investments that constitute subjectivity. The play's de-idealizing discourse gave critics a nice jump start on their critiques: no other play in the corpus more relentlessly deconstructs its own "ideological apparatuses," exposing the "traffic in women," the cultural logic of the commodity fetish, the reification of social values, and the diseases and wastefulness of war. Taking their cues from the play, scholars have productively emphasized topics such as the "heteronormativity" of the play's romance motif; the homoerotics of warfare; representations of gender and class in relation to Elizabethan court politics; masculine identity and the deep misogyny of patriarchy, and the critique of emergent capitalist market relations. Several critics have focused on the play's self-referentiality or "citationality": the way the story of the Trojan War and its epic figures are gradually emptied of any meaning that is not "about" rhetoric itself; others have concentrated on how the play gets around the abstraction of citationality by, for example, relocating rhetorical material in the body and its dis-eases. Others have written about how the play maps dislocations and fictions of desire, both hetero- and homoerotic.

This scholarship has more than demonstrated the play's relevance to poststructuralist, feminist, materialist, historicist, and psychoanalytic concerns at the end of the twentieth century and, perhaps significantly, most of it deals, in one way or another, with issues of subjectivity. In my own earlier work on the play, I explored how Shakespeare used the notorious Troy story to demonstrate the tenuous and tortured relationship between public identity, personal subjectivity, and political historiography in a culture that turns people into commodities and fetishizes famous "names" (Charnes 1993). With the obsessive cult of celebrity that characterized the last twenty years, this emphasis seemed appropriate to its cultural moment.

But I believe that moment has changed. Notoriety, of course, hasn't – if anything, what Leo Braudy calls "the frenzy of renown" has grown more frenzied (Braudy 1986). But recent developments in politics have subtly altered the relationship between "subjectivity" and how philosophers and academics have been theorizing systems. While politicians and market advertisers continue to trumpet the rhetoric of individual choice, something in American culture is starting to function ever more discretely, as if it were an entity in its own right. In saying this, however, I am not, strictly speaking, talking about the kinds of "autonomous" structural systems exhaustively posited by theorists such as Marx, Althusser, Bourdieu, Foucault, Luhmann, Adorno, and Habermas, because the function I'm addressing doesn't (as their models do) disqualify "intentionality." Certainly structural-systems models have been applied persuasively to the interpretation of Shakespeare, and the discussion that follows will dance around the edges of these readings. For example, in *Shakespeare's Universal Wolf* Hugh Grady's concern is with how Shakespeare anticipates and participates in the systemic discourses of modernity. Grady finds that

> The common concept, at least in the most central of these theories – those from Foucault, Althusser, the Frankfurt School, and Habermas, and one which they seem to share with Shakespearean motifs – is an emphasis on reifications which are socially produced but *outside of any subjective intentions*. For example, Foucault's paradox of power's status as a system of intentionality without a subject precisely restates the paradoxical quality of instrumental reason, defined by Horkheimer and Adorno as a "blind domination" at work. (Grady 1996: 54; my italics)

Grady makes a strong case for regarding *Troilus and Cressida* as "a play displaying . . . a metaphoric structure linking power, desire, autonomous rationality, and the market" (p. 56). However, I think it is possible and even critically desirable to rethink structural systems in ways that take into account the active force of individual agency and personal choice. Thus I'm not interested in deconstructing these other theoretical models, which are useful and share considerable areas of overlap. Instead, I want to situate my discussion on ground closer to what Jon Elster calls "methodological individualism," a proposition that he readily admits cannot be nailed down:

It implies neither an atomistic perspective (it grants that relations between individuals are not always reducible to their monadic predicates) nor egoism (it is compatible with any specific set of motivations), nor rational choice (here again it is perfectly neutral), nor the innate or "given" character of desires (it is consistent with the view that desires are shaped by society, that is, by other individuals) . . . methodological individualism tells us to study the individual human action as the basic building block of aggregate social phenomena. (Elster 1993: 7–8)

As slippery as Elster's provisional model may be, its value resides in its refusal to disconnect individual agency and structural systems. The key term that allows Elster to adjudicate between them is "mechanism," a usefully inchoate word that I'll appropriate here in order to talk about something that is both systematic *and* individual, and thus must be kept distinct from such *structural* poststructures as "ideological state apparatuses," hegemony, "lifeworld," "habitus," or even the usual critical whipping post, "the cultural logic of late capitalism."

What I'll address is neither "blind domination" nor "false consciousness." The 2000 presidential election offers a valuable illustration. To briefly recap events: the outcome of the election was that one candidate, Al Gore, Jr., won the "popular" vote, while the other candidate, George W. Bush, won the "electoral" vote. The former – the individual vote – is our only political mechanism for giving voice to citizens as individuals; the latter – the electoral college – is an antiquated mechanism that gives small groups of political constituents the right to "stand for" individual citizens. With respect to the 2000 election, the status of the individual vote in Florida was determined to be so close that the electoral vote was virtually undecidable without extended review, which the intervention of the Supreme Court cut short. Given that less than half the qualified voting population bothers to vote at all, the one indisputable fact to come out of Election 2000 is that the United States has a President whom the majority of its *individual* citizens did not elect.

Knowing this – and knowing that the balloting system has considerable discrepancies in form and procedure, that the ratio of voters whose votes were "disqualified" were disproportionately black, that different standards were applied to the acceptance of overseas and absentee ballots, that the butterfly ballot is technically illegal in Florida but was used anyway, that one candidate's brother "happened" to be governer of that state, and that the Secretary of State in Florida was a campaign partisan, and lastly, knowing that the US Supreme Court overrode the Florida State Supreme Court's constitutional right and decision to permit counting to continue – we are now proceeding as if George W. Bush won the vote of "the American People." While there are certain virtues in moving on to communal acceptance of the *fait accompli*, the entire tortured process raised, for this critic at least, and in a new light, serious questions about the relationship between individual knowledge and communal action.

Obviously what I've described above is not false consciousness, nor is it interpellation, or structuring structures reproducing structured structures. The models of Marx, Althusser, and Bourdieu render citizens dupes, largely "unconscious" of what they are doing; each presumes that the System is "smarter" than the subject. But the situation I've been describing speaks to a profound *knowingness* to political subjectivity, an "intentionality" within the system, however perverse. The consequences and implications of knowing what's going on and subscribing to it anyway will be pursued in this essay. In our simultaneously over-informed and underthought Information Age, the "hermeneutics of suspicion" are performed by everyone; we live, as Bruno Latour (1993) puts it, in "the Age of Denunciations." If Latour is correct, it would be a peculiarly Marxist form of elitism not to realize that concepts such as interpellation, false consciousness, or even old stand-bys such as "cognitive dissonance" or "bad faith" have to a large extent lost their explanatory power. Instead, as critics we're faced with a much more flexible, and therefore murky phenomenon, one that renders ideology critique useless even as it emerges as its unacknowledged offspring. In this essay I'll call this mechanism "cynical essentialism": an ontology in which everyone has always-already performed ideology critique on everything, or had it performed for them by media pundits, advertisers, public intellectuals, and academic critics. Under the conditions of cynical essentialism, the demystified future, and not the past, is Prologue to an excessively knowing present.

The relevance to Shakespeare's *Troilus and Cressida* is I hope beginning to appear. Critics have often observed that the play is nihilistic; and even the Prologue makes no pretense of honoring its celebrated matter:

> In Troy, there lies the scene. From Isles of Greece
> The princes orgulous, their high blood chaf'd
> Have to the port of Athens sent their ships
> Fraught with the ministers and instruments
> Of cruel war: sixty and nine that wore
> Their crownets regal, from th' Athenian bay
> Put forth toward Phrygia, and their vow is made
> To ransack Troy, within whose strong immures
> The ravish'd Helen, Menelaus' queen,
> With wanton Paris sleeps – and that's the quarrel.
> (The Norton Shakespeare 1997: Prologue 1–10)

Abruptly dropped into the *mise-en-scène*, one might expect the epic material to generate a bit of *frisson*. But there is no seduction here: Helen sleeps with Paris and that's the quarrel. Compare these lines with those of another Shakespearean Prologue:

> O for a muse of fire, that would ascend
> The brightest heaven of invention:
> A kingdom for a stage, princes to act
> And monarchs to behold the swelling scene.
> But pardon, gentles all,
> The flat unraised spirits that hath dared
> On this unworthy scaffold to bring forth

> So great an object. Can this cock-pit hold
> The vasty fields of France? Or may we cram
> Within this wooden O the very casques
> That did affright the air at Agincourt?
> O pardon . . .
> (*Henry V*, Prologue, 1–15)

The rapturous *exhortatio* of the Chorus in *Henry V* works its audience into a mood, not unlike a John Williams score to a Steven Spielberg movie. The first act stages Henry's bishops delivering a ludicrous genealogy justifying an invasion of France, a litany the absurdity of which is, as the play continues, progressively forgotten as the audience's investment in the construction of "Harry England" is complete. *Henry V* begins by declaring its intention to mystify war and ends by celebrating its success at having done so. In *Troilus and Cressida*, however, the opposite is the case: not only is no effort made to induct the audience into the play's ideological project, but the Prologue sends us leaping "o'er the vaunts and firstlings of those broils" to "begin in the middle," where the whole stale business has become stalled.

Following such a set up, it is no surprise that in 1.1 we're introduced to a Troilus sorely in need of distraction, which is being nicely provided by his fixation on Pandarus' niece Cressida. As he and Pandarus banter about Troilus's campaign to "win" her, Troilus claims he is "mad / In Cressid's love," an incongruous choice of words given that his soliloquy at the end of 1.1 reveals a fully sane view of his world:

> Peace, you ungracious clamours! Peace, rude sounds!
> Fools on both sides, Helen must needs be fair
> When with your blood you daily paint her thus.
> I cannot fight upon this argument;
> It is too starv'd a subject for my sword. (85–9)

In these lines we hear a Troilus who is *anything but* naive and idealistic and, furthermore, has a sophisticated understanding of the triangulated dynamics of mimetic desire. And if Troilus isn't a hopeless romantic (and therefore in need of enlightenment) he cannot later be "disillusioned," not really: for here is a figure who knows exactly what he is doing and why. This is the dilemma cynical essentialism creates for its subject: the only alternative, the only escape from the flat landscape it creates, is into a willfully chosen self-mystification, evident in Troilus' sudden change of topic and tone:

> Tell me, Apollo, for thy Daphne's love,
> What Cressid is, what Pandar, and what we.
> Her bed is India; there she lies, a pearl.
> Between our Ilium and where she resides,
> Let it be call'd the wild and wand'ring flood,
> Ourself the merchant, and this sailing Pandar
> Our doubtful hope, our convoy and our barque. (1.1.94–100)

These are not simply the clichéd musings of a lovestruck post-adolescent. Troilus chooses the hackneyed trope (yes even in Shakespeare's time) of woman as pearl and treasure *precisely because* it is a cliché. The image has the convenience of being readily available for use, a prefabricated refuge from having to see things the way they really are. Here Troilus perfectly demonstrates what philosopher Peter Sloterdijk calls "enlightened false consciousness," a frame of mind Sloterdijk describes as "cynicism in a crystalline state" (Sloterdijk 1987: 5). Somewhere on the spectrum between *meconnaissance* and hypocrisy, enlightened false consciousness belongs to neither; rather, it integrates mutually exclusive positions into a new form that Sloterdijk dubs "cynical idealism": a deliberate choice to "believe" in something one knows full well one doesn't believe in.

Troilus's opening salvo may be a panegyric to Greek skill, but later, when Aeneas arrives to tell him that Paris has been hurt, Troilus betrays his contempt for the Greeks: "Let Paris bleed, 'tis but a scar to scorn: / Paris is gor'd with Menelaus' horn" (1.1.112). Given this immediate demonstration of Troilus' grasp of *realpolitik*, it stretches credulity to imagine that Troilus then "unwittingly" lapses into naive consciousness when dealing with matters of his own heart. As his attitude towards Helen and Paris shows, Troilus is fully able "to take into account the particular interest behind the ideological universality, the distance between the ideological mask and the reality" and still retain the mask (Žižek 1989: 29). Again, Sloterdijk's analysis is pertinent to this scenario:

> For cynics are not dumb, and every now and then they certainly see the nothingness to which everything leads. Their psychic apparatus has become elastic enough to incorporate as a survival factor a permanent doubt about their own activities . . . Well-off and miserable at the same time, this consciousness no longer feels affected by any critique of ideology; its falseness is already reflexively buffered. (Sloterdijk 1987: 5)

Instead of providing an epistemological break from the "unhappy consciousness" that cynical essentialism brings, Troilus' love lyrics become, as the play unfolds, more an example of "artful stupefaction": a condition in which one is simultaneously "naive and cunning" (ibid: 30). In a slightly different spin, Timothy Bewes calls this mode of consciousness *instrumental stupidity*: "a manifestation of ignorance adopted wilfully, for pragmatic reasons, in order to maximize the rhetorical impact of subjectivity and the potency of individual volition" (Bewes 1997: 105).

The combined effect of the Prologue and first scene, then, is to signal to the audience that whatever else the play has in store, its characters certainly do not need anyone outside the "diegesis" to critique their activities. Instead, as audience and as critics, we are presented with a bizarrely mortifying challenge: what do we do *after the moment for critique has passed?* This is the intellectual dilemma the play proposes, and surely one of its most perplexing qualities as a "problem" play. In other words, how, as critics, do we proceed to analyze or "interpret" what we are seeing? Since cynical essentialism is *formal* – that is to say does not offer its own positive propositional content –

it cannot be addressed in the same way that the particular views of individual cynics can, since views involve *ideas* that can be examined, revised, rebutted, or debated. Cynical essentialism, on the contrary, is concerned not with *what* people think but with the form in which they think it, what Freud would call the "dreamwork."

One would suppose that in a world emptied of persuasive ideological force, both individual and collective agency would be fatally hobbled. Paradoxically, however, cynical essentialism produces the opposite effect: a system evacuated of *believable content* makes any proposition equally supportable and thus, perversely, even more deserving of total investment (since there is no possibility of being proven either wrong or right). We see this effect operating clearly in the famous Trojan debate about "value" in 2.2. The Trojans have reached a moment of crisis, in which reality threatens to over-power their ideological mask. This scene is not, I would suggest, about how they are going to proceed but rather about consolidating and reaffirming their commitment to a shared ideological fantasy in which no one actually believes. Priam begins the debate:

> After so many hours, lives, speeches spent,
> Thus once again says Nestor from the Greeks:
> 'Deliver Helen, and all damage else –
> As honour, loss of time, travail, expense,
> Wounds, friends, and what else dear that is consum'd
> In hot digestion of this cormorant war –
> Shall be struck off.' Hector, what say you to't? (2.2.1–7)

Like Nestor and Agamemnon, Priam is of the "old school." How can we tell? His question involves real consequences – hours, lives, loss of time, travail, expense – in short it issues from the pre-cynical realm of ethical pragmatism. When the question is put in this way, there can be only one answer, which Hector provides: that Helen is not worth to them "the value of one ten" and they must "Let Helen go" (15–24).

The problem, however, is that this isn't news – *everyone* knows Helen is not worth the cost of keeping, but that isn't what this debate is about. It's about declaring the demise of real ethics under the guise of honor; and here Troilus emerges as the master spokesman for cynical idealism. When Hector challenges them all by asking "What merit's in that reason which denies / The yielding of her up?" Troilus replies (with palpable sarcasm),

> Fie, fie, my brother:
> Weigh you the worth and honour of a king
> So great as our dread father's in a scale
> Of common ounces? Will you with counters sum
> The past-proportion of his infinite,
> And buckle in a waist most fathomless
> With spans and inches so diminutive
> As fears and reasons? Fie for godly shame! (25–32)

One might expect that given Troilus' denunciation of them all in 1.1 as "fools on both sides," he would support Hector's position; but instead Troilus argues that reason (a touchstone of ethics) itself is unreasonable:

> . . . Nay, if we talk of reason,
> Let's shut our gates and sleep: manhood and honour
> Should have hare hearts, would they but fat their thoughts
> With this cramm'd reason: reason and respect
> Make livers pale, and lustihood deject. (46–50)

With simultaneous sarcasm and sincerity, cunning and *naïveté*, Troilus' words evince the double-voicing that cynical essentialism produces, and its most strange and powerful effect: the fusion of denunciation and investment.

For no less than the nature of investment itself is at stake, as Hector reminds Troilus: "Brother, she is not worth what she doth cost the keeping" (50–1). As the debate between them continues, the concept of investment shifts from one of fungible resources – the aforementioned men, money, time, etc. – to a different logic, driven home by Troilus:

> Why keep we her? – The Grecians keep our aunt.
> Is she worth keeping? – Why, she is a pearl
> Whose price hath launch'd above a thousand ships,
> And turn'd crown'd kings to merchants.
> If you'll avouch 'twas wisdom Paris went –
> As you must needs, for you all cried 'Go, go;'
> If you'll confess he brought home worthy prize –
> As you must needs, for you all clapp'd your hands
> And cried 'Inestimable?': why do you now
> The issue of your proper wisdoms rate,
> And do a deed that never Fortune did –
> Beggar the estimation which you priz'd
> Richer than sea and land?

Troilus reminds them all that Helen was from the beginning only scaffolding: that "political and cultural weaponry are customarily deployed to maintain in operation an identity structure which, if laid out as doctrine, would be absurd" (Nairn 1997: 103). In effect Troilus is calling everyone's bluff, saying, if *now* you want to "lay out" Helen as a doctrine, if *now* you want to acknowledge her absurdity, well, our entire identity structure, not to mention political and cultural weaponry, would collapse. His eloquence makes its point with brutal clarity: to disinvest now would not simply mean cutting losses but being forced to admit the *originary* bankruptcy of their entire cultural currency. By pointing out the "collateral" on the other side (the Trojan aunt), and how much both sides have already invested in her, Troilus "coins" Helen as "The Helen": a kind of Trojan version of the "Euro" – an international (Greek/Trojan) currency the value of which can only be maintained in relation to another political identity structure acknowledged as equivalent. Hence the hall of mirrors these two warring states present to each other is precisely what sustains their difference. Troilus is the most vocal defender of what is in fact the two party system of Greeks and Trojans: through Helen they create a shared currency that enables the open competition of "free enterprise." Far from weakening the Trojan commitment to fight, her very insufficiency, Troilus suggests, should intensify their affective investment in the war – her surplus value, in other words, resides in her obvious insufficiency. What thus seems counterintuitive makes perfect sense in the framework of cynical essentialism that sustains this two party system: *investments grow increasingly vehement as the perceived value of an object diminishes.*

II

The Trojan debate on "value" is a casebook on how to enshrine the irrational power of trivial stakes. In this respect they are, ideologically speaking, on slightly more stable ground than their opponents, who seem to have reached a dangerous point in their own cynical essentialism. In the other famous set-piece in the play, the Greek debate about "degree," the mechanism of consensus seems to have broken down. Most notably, Ulysses complains that

> The great Achilles, whom opinion crowns
> The sinew and the forehand of our host,
> Having his ear full of his airy fame,
> Grows dainty of this worth, and in his tent
> Lies mocking our designs: with him Patroclus
> Upon a lazy bed the livelong day
> Breaks scurril jests,
> And with ridiculous and awkward action
> Which, slanderer, he imitation calls,
> He pageants us. (1.3.142–50)

The danger here is that cynical idealism will revert to mere cynicism, which no matter how apparently disengaged, always retains a residual attachment to ideology critique and therefore has the potential to be critical of the powers-that-be. Patroclus' performance of the "parts" of Agamemnon and Nestor for Achilles turns Achilles' "tent theatre" into burlesque, the lowest form of parody that treats its objects as grotesque caricatures. Unlike our own contemporary political leaders, Agamemnon and Nestor haven't learned that being the objects of mimetic disrespect can be turned to one's advantage. Even Ulysses, the craftiest of Greeks, doesn't realize that in a political world in which justifications of power are *constitutively* demystified, parody becomes homage, an *acknowledgment* of the rules of cynical decorum and an expression of "solidarity" with them. All three of these Greeks could learn something from Janet Reno, who during her four years as the United States Attorney General was the object of a scathing *Saturday Night Live* parody called "Janet Reno's Dance Party." In this popular skit, actor Will Ferrell (dressed in what became known as the "signature" Janet Reno blue dress) "hosted" a party in her basement for naive young people whom she then wouldn't let leave. On the last day of the Clinton Administration, *SNL* offered "Janet Reno's Final Dance Party"; but this time, with a surprise visitor: the real Janet Reno. In what was literally her final "act" as Attorney General, she punched her way through the prop-basement wall to confront and "arrest" her impersonator. A complete shock to the audience (though presumably not to the actors), her unannounced appearance within the parody as her real self confronting her parodic self with her "official" self completely subverted the subversion and outparodied the parody. If Ulysses were really smart, he'd advise Agamemnon and Nestor to lighten-up – just go to the tent, play "yourselves," and take it out of Patroclus' hands.

Ulysses, however, is incapable of self-irony and well beyond the kind of humor that still maintains a link, however removed, to political idealism. The Dick Cheney of the Greek camp, Ulysses is the man-behind-the-scenes who's responsible for making sure that the ideological fantasy of "degree" remains up to code. As long as Achilles and Patroclus are stuck at the level of disenchantment (which still tethers them, perhaps against their will, to belief) they represent a threat, since disenchantment is vastly less productive than fetishistic disavowal.

Which may be the reason that this play is disguised as a love story, organized around a legendary tale of romantic betrayal. We've already seen that there are no "dupes" in this play. Why, then, the eleventh hour reconstruction of Troilus as disenchanted idealist and Cressida as betrayer? Cressida is every bit as canny as Troilus in matters of love; she cannot be read merely as a victim of the "traffic in women." During Pandarus' running commentary on the "parade" of Trojan soldiers in 1.2, Cressida shows herself a witty and experienced skeptic, unswayed by the opinions of others. In the brief soliloquy that ends the scene, she reveals her interest in Troilus, and her simultaneous understanding that this attraction is her greatest weakness:

> Yet hold I off. Women are angels, wooing:
> Things won are done; joy's soul lies in the doing.
> That she belov'd knows naught that knows not this:
> Men prize the thing ungain'd more than it is. (1.2.291–4)

As prescient about commodification as Troilus, Cressida knows that the only reason the Trojans remain "interested" in Helen is because the Greeks want her back; thus she realizes that triangulated desire is the only thing that reproduces the value of the conquest. However unhappy she may be about it, Cressida is a "daughter of the game" long before Ulysses makes this observation about her; not because there is anything wrong with her "character" but because everyone in the Trojan camp is a daughter or son of the game, except perhaps Cassandra – and she is classified as insane.

When Troilus and Cressida finally achieve their assignation in 3.2, Cressida's brief deviations from her script of "knowingness" bring her only self-humiliation; there is neither joy nor relief in finally "confessing" her love.

Troilus. What offends you, lady?
Cressida. Sir, mine own company.

Aware that the only ground safe to inhabit is performative disinterest, Cressida feels she's given the game away, and in truth she has. All of Troilus' rhapsodies about the quality of his love for her amount, after all, to nothing. When Aeneas informs him in 4.2 that "We must give up to Diomedes' hand / The Lady Cressida," Troilus' response is anemic at best: "Is it so concluded?" (68): "How my achievements mock me!" (71).

Catherine Belsey has argued that the play's relentless linkage of love and disease reinforces its dominant heterosexual theme of desire as excessive:

Troilus and Cressida shows a world where desire is everywhere. Here the condition commonly exceeds its outward motive, its object . . . The play stages the extent to which objects of desire, always only a succession of stand-ins, are ultimately interchangeable for the subject. But obsession here is indiscriminate: the characters lose all distinction as desire becomes the element in which they have their being.

Belsey is right that the play "stages the extent to which objects of desire . . . are ultimately interchangeable." But not, I think, that "desire is the element in which [the characters] have their being" (Belsey 1992: 93). That elemental place, as I have been arguing, belongs to cynicism. The play's inflated *rhetoric* of desire signals perhaps an even more frightening scenario – a world in which desire is nowhere to be found. This is not a play in which desiring subjects seek viable objects for their desire but one in which cynical subjects seek viable desire to attach to available objects. No play in the canon works harder to generate the impression of a world driven by desire; but in most respects no play more fully explores the failure of excessive rhetoric to bring *believable* desire back to the site of production.

Or perhaps I should say believable heterosexual desire. In the context of the obvious fascination Greek and Trojan men have for each other, the most convincing erotic desire in the play is also the most "campy." Pandarus, the play's designated drag queen, has the bifold job of "acting out" desire on others' behalf. Providing the breathless reportage about who said what to whom, how Helen and Paris cracked wits, how hard Hecuba and Hector laughed, and so forth, Pandarus achieves an apotheosis of high camp during the parade of Trojan soldiers in 1.2, as he exclaims to Cressida the qualities of each. When Hector goes by, Pandarus sounds alarmingly like Dame Edna:

That's Hector, that, that, look you, that; there's a fellow! Go thy way, Hector – there's a brave man, niece – O brave Hector! Look how he looks, there's a countenance: is't not a brave man? (201–4)

'Tis Troilus! There's a man, niece! Hem, Brave Troilus, the prince of Chivalry!

Whether Pandarus is "ventriloquizing" the desire of others or expessing his own is not important; in either case he is clearly "modeling" what he supposes are the sounds of a presumably feminine desire. Cressida is understandably embarrassed by this display, but Pandarus cannot contain himself:

> Mark him, note him. O brave Troilus! Look well upon him, niece, look you how his sword is bloodied, and his helm more hacked than Hector's, and how he looks, and how he goes! O admirable youth; he never saw three and twenty. Go thy way, Troilus, go thy way.

His words raise the bar for all the language of desire in the play, and suggest that any "love story" set against a "backdrop" of militarism can only be a parody of the conditions that make it possible. In the figure of Pandarus, *desire itself is in Drag*: a constitutively parodic relationship to a presumed "authentic" but absent original.

And the original discourse of desire that founded the war, insofar as it was based on a sexual predation, has long since been replaced by the erotic attachments the Greek and Trojan men have to each other. The insistence that Helen remain the designated object of desire permits the collective disavowal that keeps the war going on both sides, and turns Troilus and Cressida's "private" heterosexual romantic disenchantment into nothing more than a minor mockery. After all, Love may disappoint but War between oppositional groups is the gift that keeps on giving. Community, masculine identity, cultural production, the traffic in women, each is sustained by the fuel that cynical essentialism provides. This fuel continues to drive every two party opposition long after its original passions have been subsumed by its formal reproduction. Jon Elster, in his discussion of Alexander Zinoviev's farce of Soviet life, *The Yawning Heights*, points out that

> Marx said that history repeats itself, the first time as tragedy, the second time as farce. Zinoviev turns him around: "a farce which constantly repeats itself is actually a tragedy" . . . "One triviality," Zinoviev writes, "just gives place to another . . . but the system of trivia remains." (Elster 1993: 82)

Shakespeare's "problem play" *Troilus and Cressida* brilliantly represents an originary farce "as if" it were a tragedy, and clearly shows us how a legendary war, begun for a trivial cause, is tragic *only* in its inability, and unwillingness, to transcend its own astonishing triviality. In this respect, Shakespeare presciently anticipates the inevitable endgame of any rigidly entrenched two party system that refuses to give up its constitutive differences, no matter how outrageous and expensive the ultimate costs.

References and Further Reading

Adelman, J. (1985). This Is and Is Not Cressid. In S. N. Garner, C. Kahane, and M. Sprengnether (eds.) *The (M)Other Tongue: Essays in Feminist Psychoanalytic Interpretation*. Ithaca, NY: Cornell University Press.

Belsey, C. (1992). Desire's Excess and the English Renaissance Theatre: *Edward II, Troilus and Cressida, Othello*. In S. Zimmerman (ed.) *Erotic Politics: Desire on the Renaissance Stage*. London: Routledge.

Bewes, T. (1997). *Cynicism and Postmodernity*. London: Verso.

Braudy, L. (1986). *The Frenzy of Renown: Fame and Its History*. Oxford: Oxford University Press.

Bruster, D. (1992). *Drama and the Market in the Age of Shakespeare*. Cambridge: Cambridge University Press.

Cartelli, T. (1991). *Marlowe, Shakespeare and the Economy of Theatrical Experience*. Philadelphia: University of Pennsylvania Press.

Charnes, L. (1993). *Notorious Identity: Materializing the Subject in Shakespeare*. Cambridge, MA: Harvard University Press.

Cook, C. (1986). Unbodied Figures of Desire. *Theatre Journal*, 38.

Dollimore, J. (1984). *Radical Tragedy: Religion, Ideology and Power in the Drama of Shakespeare and His Contemporaries*. Chicago, IL: University of Chicago Press.

Elster, J. (1993). *Political Psychology*. Cambridge: Cambridge University Press.

Engle, L. (1993). *Shakespearean Pragmatism: Market of His Time*. Chicago, IL: University of Chicago Press.

Fineman, J. (1980). Fratricide and Cuckoldry: Shakespeare's Doubles. In M. Schwarz and C. Kahn (eds.) *Representing Shakespeare: New Psychoanalytic Essays*. Baltimore, MD: Johns Hopkins University Press.

Freund, E. (1985). "Ariachne's Broken Woof": The Rhetoric of Citationality in *Troilus and Cressida*. In P. Parker and G. Hartman (eds.) *Shakespeare and the Question of Theory*. New York: Methuen.

Girard, R. (1985). The Politics of Desire in *Troilus and Cressida*. In P. Parker and G. Hartman (eds.) *Shakespeare and the Question of Theory*. New York: Methuen.

Grady, H. (1996). *Shakespeare's Universal Wolf: Studies in Early Modern Reification*. Oxford: Clarendon Press.

Greenblatt, S., Cohen, W., Howard, J., and Maus, K. (eds.) *The Norton Shakespeare*. New York: Norton.

Greene, G. (1980). Shakespeare's Cressida: A Kind of Self. In C. Lenz, G. Green, and C. Neely (eds.) *The Woman's Part: Feminist Criticism of Shakespeare*. Urbana: University of Illinois Press.

Hillman, D. (1997). The Gastric Epic: *Troilus and Cressida. Shakespeare Quarterly*, 48, 3.

Latour, B. (1993). *We Have Never Been Modern*. Cambridge, MA: Harvard University Press.

Mallin, E. (1990). Emulous Factions and the Collapse of Chivalry: *Troilus and Cressida. Representations*, 29.

Nairn, T. (1997). *Faces of Nationalism: Janus Revisited*. New York: Verso.

Parker, P. (1996). *Shakespeare from the Margins: Language, Culture, Context*. Chicago, IL: University of Chicago Press.

Paster, G. K. (1997). Nervous Tension: Networks of Blood and Spirit in the Early Modern Body. In D. Hillman and C. Mazzio (eds.) *The Body in Parts: Fantasies of Corporeality in Early Modern Europe*. New York: Routledge.

Sloterdijk, P. (1987). *Critique of Cynical Reason*. Minneapolis: University of Minnesota Press.

Traub, V. (1992). *Desire and Anxiety: Circulations of Sexuality in Shakespearean Drama*. London: Routledge.

Žižek, S. (1989). *The Sublime Object of Ideology*. London: Verso.

16
Opening Doubts Upon the Law:
Measure for Measure
Karen Cunningham

From its biblical title in the Revels Accounts of December 26, 1604, to its controversial denouement in the streets of Vienna, *Measure for Measure* invites its audiences to think about the law. Anyone attempting to navigate the play's relationships to the law or the scholarly tradition documenting those relationships, however, soon discovers that "the law" turns out to be laws, neither so clear nor so cohesive as a singular designation suggests. In the process of dramatizing "the properties" of government (1.1.3), the play alludes to a plural and contradictory collation of jurisdictions and spiritual and legal sources.[1]

Early arguments for the play's links to the gospels (Knight 1949) have been followed by assertions that the play "depends on certain Pauline ethical and psychological formulations" (Berman 1967: 142); that it dramatizes a dialectic between love and duty and so "must be read as a parable, like the parables of Jesus" (Bache 1969: 9); that it evokes "natural law" as expressed by Calvin and Hooker, which recognizes "God's ordering principle and law eternal" in both statutory and divine law (Gless 1979: 35); and that it rejects the Old Law of the Catholic church in favor of new Protestant views shared by its early Jacobean audience (Harper 1998: 26–8). Its debates about the proper relationship between justice (understood in terms of a spiritual and legal absolutism) and mercy have led scholars to discover a contention between Old Testament and New Testament positions toward divine and human law (Lever 1965: lxiv), and a contemporary battle between the common law courts, rumored to be literalist in their adjudications, and the courts of Chancery, especially the "equity" courts that were created primarily as a reaction to what was perceived to be an excessive rigidity in common law courts (Cohen 1999: 439). The historical questions have multiplied with the knowledge that common law courts also claimed to work on principles of equity.[2]

The critical and performance histories of *Measure for Measure* are a testament to these controversies and irresolutions, and Shakespeare's play itself invites these disputes. Incorporating "dialectical" (Bache 1969) or "antithetical" (Hawkins 1987: 11) "contrarieties" (Harper 1998: 3) as the basis for its plot and characterization, it provides evidence for nearly every perspective it evokes. Depending on one's point of view, the Duke can be seen as a benign magistrate who, in the tradition of the disguised ruler genre, conceals his identity to gain anonymity so that he can educate himself and test the moral resolve of the citizens of his city, or as a duplicitous, evasive figure who, like the popular stage Machiavel derived from *The Prince*, exercises the coercive powers of "terror" and "love," extending their reach even to his public proposal to Isabella. The Duke's surrogate, Angelo, who appears initially to adhere to a rigid austerity ("a man whose blood / Is very snow-broth": 1.4.57), routs the law he is entrusted with administering and the morality he so self-righteously proclaimed and only belatedly suffers exposure, punishment, and an unmerited forgiveness. Isabella, a young novice apparently committed to a cloistered life and wishing "no farther privileges" (1.4.1) than those allowed by the order of St. Clare's, emerges from the convent to plead for her brother's life, suffers the legal rejection and sexual threats of Angelo, and, instead of returning to the sanctity of the convent, discovers a capacity for forgiveness and a social role in marriage. The Duke's distribution of the concluding four marriages (including his own to Isabella) bears the arbitrariness of a *deus ex machina* ending: the enforced marriages either belie what has gone before and represent marriage as punishment, or attest to the quasi-divine ruler's ability to bring about legitimate personal and social order.

That these disputes are irresolvable is part of *Measure for Measure*'s distinction and appeal. The play requires its characters and audiences to consider and evaluate competing views of the elements of city life, yet these evaluations produce little consensus. Instead of resolving its debates, Shakespeare's story ends. Both its conjectural basis and its denial of resolution link *Measure for Measure* to a contemporary sixteenth- and seventeenth-century legal ritual: the practice of mooting (see Baker and Thorne 1990; Smith 1860: 21–40). In the imaginary cases performed by aspiring young benchers at the Inns of Court, the English common law was figured not as a self-interpreting code that could be "applied" to particular cases – whether by a literalist like Angelo or interpretationists like Escalus and Isabella – but as a prompt for speculating, for imagining challenges to its operations and disasters befalling the citizens it organizes.

Tudor–Stuart culture did not bracket off its imaginative practices from each other, and Shakespeare would certainly have run across mooting and could easily have exploited its imaginative potential. There was an effortless transit between writers of all kinds and members of the Inns of Court. Tradition has it that both Chaucer and Gower were members, and in the sixteenth and seventeenth centuries a surprising number of popular writers occupied the Inns at some point, including Thomas More, George Gascoigne, Thomas Sackville, and Thomas Norton, Walter Ralegh, John Donne, Francis Bacon, John Marston, John Ford, Francis Beaumont, William Carew, John Suckling, and William Congreve, among others (Finkelpearl 1969: 19).

Moreover, wherever lawyers gathered, they put cases to each other, extending the arguments about moral and legal points beyond the confines of the law school and the lawcourt to various informal locations. In addition to official sites, London taverns

were among the places where legal opinions were often argued and where mootmen
and playwrights might readily contest imaginary cases. In what became known as
"table cases" in pubs, London locals used mealtimes to debate current proceedings
(Abbott 1973: 184–95). The audience for Shakespeare's theatre might well have
included many of these figures, already interested in the radically conjectural processes
of adjudicating, as well as others interested in old and new thinking, folks with business interests in London, well-to-do citizens and merchants, and the greater nobility
(see Cook 1981; Gurr 1987).

Considered as an instance of dramatic mooting, *Measure for Measure* directs its audience away from the idea that character and personality are fixed, individualized things
that "change," and toward the idea that identity is fundamentally improvisational and
social. Focused on the process of forging communal selves in a common language,
Shakespeare's speculative tragicomedy aims more at raising than at resolving important points about contemporary issues such as pregnancy and marriage or leniency
and rigidity in executing the law. It would have been a provocative play, a theatrical
moot that staged versions of, and challenges to, "the terms / For common justice"
(1.1.10–11).

I

Mooting emerged as an identifiable practice late in the fourteenth century; it enjoyed
its heyday during the decades from 1450 to 1550; it persisted throughout the late
sixteenth and early seventeenth centuries; and it slowly faded until its curtailment in
1642 (Baker and Thorne 1990: xxviii). Attempts to revive the practice in 1660 failed,
and it never recovered its former importance as a site where doctrine was performed,
fabricated, and challenged (Baker 1986: 281).

Deliberately devoted to irresolution and contestation, the basic structure of moot
cases included four parts: (1) the problem; (2) the question arising from the problem;
(3) the disputation, arguments pro and contra; and (4) the solution, any authoritative
answer or ruling given by the teacher (Baker and Thorne 1990: xvii).[3] The generic
outline, however, is deceptively tidy. Mooters were rewarded for their inventiveness
and encouraged to fabricate what legal historian J. H. Baker labels "mind-stretching
remote contingenc[ies]" and extemporaneous exceptions to pleadings (Baker 1986:
280; see also Smith 1860: 21–2). As law teachers conveyed legal principles through
extensive discussions of cases that were "sometimes real, sometimes imaginary," the
purpose of judicial playing became calling to mind exceptions to traditional frames
of reference (Baker and Thorne: 1990: xv).

Before they settle their issues, these legal inventions require the disputants to
deliberate a wide range of imaginary, anomalous events that need not be antithetical
to each other, but that nonetheless demand accommodation. In the process, these
imaginative practices introduce into circulation elusive ideas – ideas about affiliations

among kin, about sexuality and its management, and about the sudden liquidity of a city or village – that are not wholly contained by the discourse that elicited them. Because the purpose of mooting was to show how legal principles might work in hypothetical situations, there was no necessary relationship between the events represented in moots and their probability of occurring in social life, nor was there any necessary relationship between the position the mootman argued and his personal opinions. "It does not seem to have mattered too much whether they were examples ever likely to be met with in the real world, though of course the law teacher's most unlikely academic fantasies have a habit of coming true" (Baker 1986: 276). The mooters' typical method was to list copious examples to illustrate the subject. The more, and the more comprehensive the examples, the better.

Like other fictions, specific moots advance plots, suggest character (typically in archetypal terms), arrange space, and develop imaginative landscapes. One often-repeated, classic case can offer a partial glimpse of the England imagined in moots. In order to preserve its distinctive flavor, I quote it here at length:

> Two brothers, who are villeins, purchase jointly certain land to which an advowson is appendant; the lord enters and leases the same land with the appurtenances to the two of them to hold in villeinage; the elder brother dies, his wife being secretly pregnant; the lord marries the same woman, who is delivered of a son and dies; the lord takes another wife and dies, his wife being secretly pregnant; the younger brother marries the same woman, who has a son, and then the wife dies; he takes another wife, who is pregnant by him before the espousals; the husband dies; the woman is delivered of two twin sons, namely Jacob and Esau; the elder brother's son enters in one moiety, and the three sons in the other moiety, but the attendancy is made to the elder brother's son; the three sons enter and make partition among themselves; the twin son grants what belongs to him and what belongs to his younger brother to an abbot, unto him and his successors; the lord's son brings a writ of right of advowson against him, and after the mise joined he is nonsuited; then the elder twin son enters into religion in the same abbey; the abbot is deposed, and he is elected abbot; then the church becomes vacant; the abbot presents; and he is hindered by the three. Etc. Discuss. (Baker and Thorne 1990: 17–18)[4]

As this case suggests, moots resemble the popular chronicle histories contemporary with them: organized by temporal sequence and divided into units that represent the ownership of successive husband–fathers, moots tell the histories of the commonwealth in its analogous form of the family. In doing so, they comprehend the commonwealth not only as a geographical entity, but also as a temporal and imaginative process.

Entitled "Jacob and Esau," this case takes its name from the narrative in Genesis in which Esau sold his birthright to his younger twin, Jacob, who became father of the twelve tribes of Israel (Genesis 25: 21–34; 27). It depicts the siblings as rivals, and the rivalry rests on the relationship between birthright and changes in land possession. If we set aside the technicalities of law and the unfamiliar language, however, and focus on the story "Jacob and Esau" tells, we discover a vision in which the security of the community is sustained even as alliances shift swiftly and devotions dissolve briskly one into another. Like the mooting genre more generally, "Jacob and Esau" is anticipatory and predictive: it perceives threats and challenges that *will* occur almost inevitably at unspecified times. In anticipating challenges, moots are surprising in allocating an authoritative, disruptive agency equally to a wide range of subjects across genders, ranks, and occupations: nieces, daughters, widows, abbots, strangers, as well as wives, husbands, brothers, and fathers, initiate actions that are shown to have the potential to sustain or subvert the community. Yet this genre is founded on actions more than on motives, on doing more than on desiring, and it is silent about the individual emotional lives of its figures. The purposes of the agents remain obscure, elusive, and inferential: things happen, people act, but the reasons are inscrutable or irrelevant. As it is figured in these stories, the law does not care about inwardness one way or another, and selfhood is represented as occupying a place in a perpetual process of preserving the community.

Like many moots, this one's recurring event is pregnancy. When the female first appears, she is already both married and pregnant: "the elder brother dies, his wife being secretly pregnant," "the lord takes another wife and dies, his wife being secretly pregnant," "he takes another wife, who is pregnant by him before the espousals." When the female emerges into visibility, it is as a representative of the category "wife" and, more precisely, as "pregnant wife"; in two cases, she is "secretly pregnant wife." Why does the moot keep these pregnancies "secret"? To whom are they unknown? The husband? The village? In these patterns the moot demonstrates the remarkable mobility of legal practice; it is never stagnant. Here, in addition to preserving land transmission, it wards off the social consequences of adultery and cuckoldry, acknowledges secrecy as a fact of being in the world, and sustains the subject's honor and authority. The imaginative process takes the legal concept of the *feme covert* and enlivens it, and we witness an endlessly repeatable performance of subsuming a wife; neither being pregnant nor having children renders her unmarriageable. Visible primarily in transit toward a husband, the female is always an element in a teleology of matrimony that both privileges heterosexuality and equates it with reproduction.

This recurring association between women and pregnancy carries us to the moot's concern with paternity. In the legal imagination paternity is primarily a matter of attribution, of assigning the position of father to the man to whom each woman was wed at the time of childbirth. It is not the representation of male sexuality or desire *per se* that is crucial; instead, the presence of desire is represented as an effect, pregnancy. Instead of privileging interior or private emotion and intention, moots privilege solutions to social problems, in this case, the specification of a birth father for each child. In the language of *King Lear*'s Gloucester, sons are differentiated as Edgar and Edmund were, by "order of law" (1.1.19) or by "breeding" (1.1.9). What becomes apparent are the operations of the marriage contract itself: it legitimates whoever is born under its authority. And insofar as it makes a potential "bastard" into a "son" under the law, the contract forges a particular social identity.

Like many moots, "Jacob and Esau" was formed prior to the Reformation and continued to be used after the Henrician parliaments had recast the position of religious figures. The genre is fascinated with the equivocal position of abbots, which may reflect an earlier anxiety that is, like those associated with pregnancy and marriage, multivocal and continuously transformed. Baker notes that moot books "are full . . . of landowners becoming monks and then inconveniently coming back to life when claimed by deserted fiancées" (Baker and Thorne 1990: lxxii). In general, moots represent abbots and monks as common men, changeable mortals who might at any minute renounce a worldly family in favor of the church, then renounce the church in turn and return to the worldly, tacking restlessly between the temporal and eternal.[5]

In contrast to the sequential momentum of their events, the intellectual or imaginative properties foregrounded in moots are largely *non sequiturs*, and their themes are the precariousness of life, the vulnerability of marriage, the changeability of the self, and the mortality of humankind. And there is no apparent closure within the moot. It stops rather than concludes. It imagines a place in constant jeopardy from undisclosed pregnancies, from arbitrary deaths, from men suddenly struck by religion then struck again by worldly aspirations, and the force of the repetition makes it seem that the community will continue well after an individual's claims on it end. Moreover, it is not only the student's psyche or the English law that comes to seem mobile, but the community itself, as it is verbally transported from figure to figure.

Although the content of moot cases enthusiastically exploited the improbable and unpredictable, the conditions for performance limited that latitude. Exercises were highly regulated by a strong sense of history revived, performed by "the ancient custom of the house" (Smith 1860: 29), and mooters were assigned two positions from which to argue, which they did before an assembled audience of fellow Innsmen and senior barristers. At their conclusion, an elder barrister would make the legal points that ended that day's practice (Baker and Thorne 1990: lxi). In these performances the Innsman discovered himself not by a process of differentiation or personalization, but by a process of affiliation. He immersed himself in a communal identity and a legal discourse that evoked a sense of a collective, anonymous voice: "Une gent dient"; "ascuns diont"; "semble a auters"; "moy semble." This anonymity casts the mooting disputes themselves as what "some" and "others" say, normalizing anonymous speaking subjects as voices in a shared imagination. "Our laws are not individual, but communal and positional," this anonymity suggests; "they do not see or make visible prejudices of nature, nurture, and politics." In this practice, to become an English person meant to affiliate oneself with what an historically generated "some" continued to "say" about the realm in legal rituals.

II

From the moment it begins, *Measure for Measure*, like "Jacob and Esau," imagines a world in flux. With a plot structured to keep doubts alive, it opens with dramatic and specific change that evokes immediate uncertainty. Beginning to expound on "the properties" of government (1.1.3), the Duke indicates that he need not go on, for Escalus, to whom he is speaking, in this "science" already exceeds whatever the Duke may say. The talk is unsettling, however, as the Duke plans to transfer his authority, and we are led to assume Escalus will be deputized. But instead of Escalus, the Duke commissions Angelo. In a triple pattern of change, Shakespeare directs our attention from ruler (the Duke) to potential ruler (Escalus) to potential ruler (Angelo) in a matter of sixteen lines. Like moot cases, which structure the life of the community as a pattern of transience in which the city is sustained not despite but *because* of changes from person to person, *Measure for Measure* develops a structure of deferral from character to character and from scene to scene: presiding over legal matters, the Duke defers to Angelo (1.1.16); Angelo defers to Escalus (2.1.137); and Escalus defers to Elbow to make the case against Pompey (2.1.88–132). Shakespeare's play is animated by substitutions, and he intersperses them throughout, realizing them most sharply in the exchange of Mariana for Isabella in the bed trick and Ragozine's head for Claudio's (see Maus 1995: 207–11; Wheeler 1981: 120–38; Leggatt 1988).

This structure of exchange, which carries with it the momentum of change for the commonwealth, becomes more explicit and urgent with Claudio's arrest; its very unpredictability is cause for confusion and discussion. Nothing in Claudio's character or in the city's operations had anticipated the arrest, and even naming the crime is troublesome.[6] Lucio speculates, "what, is't murder?" (1.2.129); Claudio describes too much "liberty"; Lucio queries, "Lechery?" (1.2.129); Claudio concedes "Call it so" (1.2.129); and yet later, Lucio recasts it again: "Claudio is condemned for untrussing" (3.2.173). Each designation reveals something about the character who uses it – speaking to Angelo, Isabella invokes a moral category, "There is a vice that most I do abhor" (2.2.29) – and each attempt to name the crime also suggests something about the elusive particularity of the deed. In the world of Vienna crime is not self-identifying; it does not announce itself, but comes into being (or does not) through naming. In Elbow, who cannot differentiate between "benefactors" and "malefactors" or "detests" and "protests" (2.1), as in the many characters who struggle to describe crimes, Shakespeare dramatizes the instability of the principles and concepts that ostensibly found religious and secular laws; neither the meanings of actions, such as consummating marriages, nor the meanings of words are self-evident. Naming is a kind of evaluating, a means of positing similarities and differences that are subject to judgment: is the sex between Claudio and Julietta the same as that between Angelo and Mariana? Does that activity need to be called something different in each case? Is Claudio's crime "groping for trouts in a peculiar river" (1.2.90), or is it, as he would have it, "most mutual entertainment" (1.2.154)? As the characters "moot" Claudio's case throughout the play, shifting positions with the demands of the story, the audience shares the process. What is important to note, in the context of mooting, is that Claudio's arrest is represented as an anomalous event, so unlikely that Lucio and the Gentlemen refuse to believe it has occurred until Overdone offers her eyewitness authority: "I saw him arrested; saw him carried away" (1.2.61–2). The play insists that this prosecution, like the proclamations ordering the tearing down of houses of prostitution, represents an abrupt "change indeed in the commonwealth" (1.2.96–7). In this play, indeed, change *is* the commonwealth.

Like moot cases, Shakespeare's play deliberately evokes the language of conjecture and conditionality in order to heighten the point that every view is provisional and under construction. "If" Angelo is a "seemer," then his new authority will bring it to light (1.3.54). "If" Isabella is Claudio's sister and a virgin, then Lucio has an errand for her (1.4.16–17). "If" Isabella yields her virginity to Angelo, then Claudio will be freed (3.1.96–8). "If [Angelo's] own life answer the straitness of his proceedings, it shall become him well: wherein if he chance to fail, he hath sentenced himself" (3.2.249–51). This motif of the "if" is contagious and appears centrally in the later comic scenes, when the Provost lays out the terms of Pompey's punishment "if" he will become a hangman or "if" he will not (4.2.8–10 and 4.2.40–5). Claudio tries to pit what appears to be a certain legal point against these uncertainties: claiming "a true contract" with Julietta, he explains "she is fast my wife, / Save that we do the denunciation lack / Of outward order" (1.2.134–8). And although many scholars turn to the *sponsalia de praesenti* common law marriage contract (see Lever 1965: 16; Cohen 1999: 440) to argue that Shakespeare agrees with Claudio, it seems more likely that the contract, too, is under scrutiny. When a marriage contract reappears, recast as the *sponsalia de futuro* (see Lever 1965: 78) in the Duke's revelations about Mariana's relationship to Angelo (3.1.212–13, 4.1.72), the characters and audience again are asked to moot the case: the Duke first assures Isabella (3.1.207, 237), then Mariana (4.1.71–4), of the virtue of the bed trick (3.1.207, 237), yet Shakespeare has made his audience aware that such justification is necessary. Repeatedly telling his story in hypothetical terms, Shakespeare brings out the basis of life in Vienna: in this city, everything is temporary, dependent on a mutating series of "ifs." This motif of rhetorical conjecture stretches from the play's early scenes to its comic ending, sweeping up Angelo's solicitation of Isabella in mere supposition – "Admit no other way to save his life . . . but that either / You must lay down the treasures of your body / To this suppos'd or else to let him suffer: / What would you do?" (2.4.88–98) – and carrying through to Claudio's unmasking –" If he be like your brother," he is pardoned (5.1.488). Yet the relationships implied here between the tentative and the certain are troublesome and variable: Angelo is *not* speculating, though Claudio *is* Isabella's brother.

Earlier in his career Shakespeare had adopted this same motif to satirize the notion that law could somehow manage human behaviors. In *As You Like It* Touchstone comically parodies petty legalism in describing how one might conduct a duel by the book, concluding "All these [parries] you may avoid but the Lie Direct; and you may avoid that too, with an If. I knew when seven justices could not take up a quarrel, but when the parties were met themselves, one of them thought but of an If, as 'If you said so, then I said so;' and they shook hands and swore brothers. Your If is your only peacemaker; much virtue in If" (5.4.95–102). In *Measure for Measure*, however, instead of making peace, the "if" and its cousin, supposition, make trouble. The equivocations crystallize in the satirical story of Elbow's wife, which might have been torn from the pages of some Innsman's notes. In part, the scene implies Elbow's unfitness for the role of constable: he cannot manage the language of the law, riddling it with "misplacings" that extend literally to his misplaced wife. In part, it implies a more general illiteracy of the lower-class village constables as a group, betraying a class prejudice in suggesting that those figures were not as capable as city authorities in managing legal process. And in part, it satirizes legal language itself, reducing legal practice to malapropisms and doggerel reminiscent of Dogberry's in *Much Ado About Nothing*. But the point of the scene also is the evocation of the sort of "mindstretching remote contingencies" to which a mootman is challenged to aspire. In the case of Elbow's wife, legal authority in Escalus yields to legal imagination, and Elbow bases his testimony on a list of contingencies and verbal errors that sustain (but do not resolve) the audience's awareness of what "might" have happened: "if" his wife "had been a woman cardinally given, [she] might have been accused in fornication, adultery, and all uncleanness" in Mistress Overdone's house (2.1.78–80). Pompey's mythic explanation of what happened with Elbow's wife, however, stretches the boundaries of what the law could have anticipated, as it moves from Mistress Overdone's house to Mrs. Elbow's longing for stewed prunes to the only two prunes in a fruit dish; from the fruit dish to its price (three pence) and its quality ("not china dishes, but very good dishes"); from the dishes to Froth having eaten the prunes; from Froth having done so to their efficacy in curing certain unnamed illnesses; and so on (2.1.88–185). The scene is crafted precisely of the kinds of imaginative details that were deliberately evoked in order to challenge statute law by querying its self-evidence, and Escalus signals the power of this kind of imagination to defeat resolution and judgment, finally telling Elbow the prosecution will be deferred "'till thou knows't what" Pompey's offenses are (2.1.184).

Shakespeare's play, like comedies in general and like moots in particular, is devoted to telling the story of the commonwealth in the analagous form of the family. The play evokes many forms of familial relationships: the sisterhood of St. Clare's; the brotherhood of friars; the "brother-justices" Escalus and Angelo (3.2.252); the siblings Mariana and her drowned brother; the siblings Isabella and her imprisoned brother. Unlike comedies, however, but nonetheless like moot cases, *Measure for Measure* offers a proliferation of pregnancies, more than occur in any other Shakespeare play. Initially, Shakespeare puns on the term "pregnant": the Duke acknowledges Escalus's knowledge of the people and the city's institutions, "y'are as pregnant in / As art and practice hath enriched any / That we remember" (1.1.11–13); and Angelo debates Escalus about what the law sees, using the same diction: "'Tis very pregnant, / The jewel that we find, we stoop and take't / Because we see it" (2.1.23–5). In both cases the puns link "pregnancy" with kinds of knowledge, intellectual and carnal, in which fullness of thought is sister to fullness of the womb. Moreover, all the cases that come into court or that the law "sees" are related to family matters. Julietta is "with child" (1.2.66); Elbow's wife is "great with child" (2.1.87); Mariana's night with Angelo introduces the idea that she might become with child; Kate Keep-down "was with child" (3.2.193); and Mistress Overdone is a surrogate mother, caring for Kate Keep-down's child. Isabella, who is introduced at a liminal point as a votarist of St. Clare's "yet unsworn" (1.4.9), and whose celibacy is an extreme in a city of sexuality, holds her position only temporarily. Lucio's initial greeting casts her in speculative terms before turning to a blazon that allies her more to the sonnet convention than to the convent, and that proleptically signals her transit toward marriage: "Hail virgin, if you be – as those cheek-roses / Proclaim you are no less" (1.4.16–17). More than chastity, it is pregnancy that is the social problem of the play.

As it is in moots, so in *Measure for Measure* generally, male sexual desire is represented primarily not as an emotion but as an effect: it is implied in the overdone fecundity of the female characters, it is "writ on Juliet" (1.2.144), and it is embodied in Kate Keep-down's child. It is the driving force behind Mistress Overdone's thriving business: labeled "Madam Mitigation" (1.4.16–17), Overdone lives by trading in women. And it is a source of disease and imprisonment in Vienna, its moral theme of slavery to lust translated into social imprisonment in Pompey's survey of the prison: "I am as well acquainted here as I was in our house of profession; one would think it were Mistress Overdone's own house" (4.3.1–3). In these cases, as in moot cases generally, problems associated with male sexuality are represented primarily socially, as events that threaten the stability of the community.

Marking the eruption of personal desire simultaneously in the male character and the governing of the city, Shakespeare differs substantially from moot cases in his treatment of Angelo. Represented as erotic and sexual, male interiority is also represented as an abdication of social responsibility, something that separates a man from his role as an authority. In his first aside, Angelo formally claims a kind of private rhetorical space to express his private emotion at Isabella's words: "She speaks, and 'tis such sense / That my sense breeds with it" (2.2.142–3). Like the puns on pregnancy, these on "sense" evoke the intertwining of the conceptual meaning and physical desire, both of which "breed" in Angelo's imagination. Like the other surprises and unpredictable events that overtake the characters, desire startles and overtakes Angelo: "What's this? What's this?" (2.2.163). And although the character tries initially to pass off some of the responsibility for what he feels – "Is this her fault or mine? . . . Who sins most, ha?" (2.2.163) – he turns suddenly to an awareness of himself as the center of unruly desire: "Not she; nor doth she tempt" (2.2.165). In the same moment when he acknowledges his sexual desire (or lust) he also raises a question about his own identity: "What dost thou, or what art thou, Angelo?" (2.2.173). As Shakespeare writes it, this eruption of specifically male erotic desire constitutes Angelo's individual identity: none of the other male characters speaks in such terms about his relationship to women. Further, what makes Angelo individual is, in Shakespeare's view here, what makes him personally unfit to rule and professionally dangerous to the commonwealth: out of this desire, which is associated with a secret interior self, springs the contract Angelo offers Isabella, sacrifice her virginity or sacrifice her brother (2.4.96–7). Significantly, Angelo's interiority is itself at issue in the play's final scene, when Isabella pleads for his pardon on the basis of a distinction between the inner and outer man: "His act did not o'ertake his bad intent, / And must be buried but as an intent / That perish'd by the way. Thoughts are no subjects; / Intents but merely thoughts" (5.1.449–52). Resonating with the logic of "if" as the great peacemaker, Isabella's words evoke one contemporary view, that intent is not legally actionable under common law,[7] and realign Angelo's destructive interiority with the thematics of mooting, silencing the secret erotic self in the interests of sustaining the city.

The Duke's role has prompted a wide range of interpretations, most of which understand him as either a conventional benign ruler of comedy or a divine ruler of early Jacobean political theory.[8] Such interpretations assume that the legitimate authority of the Duke is a settled matter, and that he sets up a series of "tests" for other characters: he explains to Friar Thomas about Angelo, "Hence shall we see, / If power change purpose, what our seemers be" (1.3.), and he deliberately misleads others to enable them comically to expose themselves, like Lucio, or to rise to their higher spirituality, as is the case with Julietta, Claudio, and even Isabella at the play's end (see Bevington 1980: 465). Accompanying this view is a tendency to read the Duke's authority at the end as reflecting James I's absolutist views of a godlike ruler; as Angelo expresses it, "your Grace, like a power divine, / Hath looked upon my passes" (5.1.367–8). If we consider the play in terms of moot cases, however, the Duke's authority and control over events appear more equivocal. Throughout much of the plot, he is less a quasi-divine orchestrator of events than a figure whose reach and authority are circumscribed: he resolves none of the disasters voiced by the citizens of Vienna, whether the prospect of peace that threatens to make soldiers unemployed (1.2.15–16), or the prospect of tearing down the houses of ill-repute and depriving Overdone and others like her of a livelihood (1.2.88); Overdone's pertinent question, "What shall become of me?" (1.2.97), goes unanswered. Often Shakespeare positions the Duke at the receiving end of accident and coincidence: his match up with Julietta in prison; his discovery that Claudio is condemned; his learning that Angelo propositioned Isabella; his awareness of Kate Keep-down's child (the child itself unplanned, like Julietta's) – all these come to him accidentally, immersing him in the pervasive activity of improvising.

Far from upholding the divine legitimacy and power of the Duke's authority, Shakespeare uses the Duke's limitations to emphasize authority's temporal and temporary reach. And Elbow's case amplifies this radically circumscribed notion of authority's capacity to resolve what it meets: the case produces more befuddlement than resolution, driving one judge from the room (Angelo) and thwarting the other's attempts simply to learn what happened (Escalus). In these representations of the Duke, Angelo, and Escalus, the play seems to say that a ruler's authority is provisional, sustained only through cooperation, consensus, and that most uncertain of things, coincidence.

Even in the representation of the Duke as a wooer, Shakespeare constrains the ruler within the communal confines set for others in the play. In *Measure for Measure*, as in moot cases, marriages ward off adultery, accommodate secrecy, and sustain individual honor. But the play has told us not to seek individual erotic desire and interiority, if by that we mean avowals of emotional attachment; the figure who does so betrays his personal and social responsibilities. In a city where male sexuality is equated provisionally with unruliness, immorality, and at least potential pregnancy – as with Claudio, Angelo, and Lucio – the solution to preservation of the community depends on marriage. So by the Duke's order, Claudio is returned to Julietta, resolving the threat of their child being born outside the law; Angelo is returned to Mariana, resolving the threat of their secret sexual encounter shaming her (the Duke echoes this view to Mariana: "He is your husband on a pre-contract": 4.1.72); Lucio is promised to Kate Keep-down, the mother of his child; and the Duke is promised to Isabella.[9] In *Measure for Measure*, however, the conditional phrasing of the Duke's proposal makes it no sure thing, echoing ambiguously with Angelo's earlier speculative proposition: "Dear Isabel, / I have a motion much imports your good; / Whereto if you'll a willing ear incline, / What's mine is yours, and what is yours is mine" (5.1.531–4). There are unresolved tensions here between elusive ideas of authority and interiority and narrow conceptions of "the law" as a repressive system. These irresolutions have contributed, in turn, to a dissatisfaction with the play's ending, which is seen as failing to reconcile the inner human being with the external forces of an arbitrary legalism.[10] But Shakespeare's own play has demonstrated not the desirability but the disruptive force of secret inwardness. Instead, he dramatizes the communal force of the marriage contract itself, as it forges new public identities by turning bawds into bridegrooms. These challenges to probability are present and accounted for in the playwright's own request voiced by Isabella, "Make not impossible / That which but seems unlike" (5.1.54–5).

The communal identity being forged by the practice of mooting, and the immersion of the self in the tradition of collective speaking that characterized the performance, carries us to the communal language of *Measure for Measure*: the proverb. In Quintillian's view, proverbs were the "common property" of the people and of uncertain authorship. Conveying memorially the "testimonies" of shared opinions, they forged notions of common knowledge not committed to ideas of accuracy or truth (Tilley 1926: 19). As Morris P. Tilley argues, at the time of *Measure for Measure* proverbs were credited with authority not because they were tied to a historical fact, but because they were perceived as speaking with the common voice (ibid: 40–1). And the idea being offered as a proverb need not have been in fact in common coinage; the notion that an idea *might* be proverbial prompted a kind of authority and believability in it as a repository of common knowledge. "Writers of the Renaissance were fond of introducing a statement by some such phrase as, 'The Prouerb goeth . . . ,' 'As the Proverbe is . . . ,' 'As we say,' 'We say . . .'" (Tilley 1983: v).[11] Displaying "the popular mind at work on variants of the same idea," proverbs came from different sources, often contradicted each other without eliminating each other, and served routinely as "the small change of conversation" (ibid: vi–vii). In such prefatory phrases the playwright could "invent" the proverbial.

The common voice of proverbs sounds throughout *Measure for Measure*: in the Duke's "be absolute for death" (3.1.5) and "The hand that hath made you fair hath made you good" (3.1.179–80); in Angelo's "we must not make a scarecrow of the law"

(2.1.1); in Isabella's "That in the captain's but a choleric word, / Which in the soldier is flat blasphemy" (2.2.131–2), and in her more controversial phrase, "More than our brother is our chastity" (2.4.184). The easy transit between the proverbial and the legal is suggested by common lawyer Edward Coke's collection of aphorisms and by its place in Shakespeare's play: Angelo quotes Coke, "The law hath not been dead, though it hath slept" (2.2.91). A proverb's popularity and familiarity as well as its power are suggested by Angelo's attempt to ward off Isabella's arguments: "Why do you put these sayings upon me?" (2.2.134). As there is in the practice of mooting, so there is throughout *Measure for Measure* an implied ideology of community mediated by these sayings: by trading in the proverbial, characters affiliate themselves with certain (remembered) traditions and with each other. Instead of privileging the individual voice and the implied distinctive subjectivity that accompanies that voice, this communal language allies the speakers more with a shared "we" than with a distinguishable "I." Like the common law, this common language is community property, its plural possessives not only attributes of majesty but possessions of the subject. At stake in this communal vision is "the nature of *our* people" and "*our* city's institutions" (1.1.9–10).

III

Like moot cases, *Measure for Measure* is engaged in forging communal identities, accustoming audience members to ways of thinking about the conjectural, the arbitrary, the improbable. This emphasis on the collaborative and communal need not be understood as necessarily repressive; it need not, for example, be wholly in the service of a royalist program. Instead of representing law as serving court-centered power,[12] mooting constituted a counterprocess that had long been perceived as troublesome because it undermined and threatened royal authority. Complaining about the unofficial influence of the Inns, Henry VIII had tried to discourage mooting and Elizabeth tried to have the Inns shut down (Baker 1986: 283). "Although they did not make law in the sense of establishing statutes, readers of moots did contribute to consolidation and explanation of unwritten principles, establishing a tradition as to what was received learning and what was dubious. The influence of the law schools, though unofficial, was deep" (see Baker 1986: 278, 283).

Writing retrospectively under James I, Francis Bacon, himself a resident of the Inns in the sixteenth century, concluded that although originally mooting had a noble intention, by the early seventeenth century its most visible effect was to cloud rather than to shed light on legal principles; its conjectural bases challenged legitimate authority and obscured rather than illuminated the law. He contrasts what he imagines to have been a superior ancient practice with that of the earlier Tudor era: "for the use then was substantially to expound the statutes by grounds and diversities . . . and not to stir concise and subtle doubts, or to contrive a multitude of tedious and intricate cases, whereof all, saving none, are buried, and the greater part of that case, which is taken, is commonly nothing to the matter in hand; but my labour shall be in the ancient course, to open the law upon doubts, and not to open doubts upon the law" (quoted in Smith 1860: 31–2). Perceived as influential in shaping legal judgments, mooting's capacity to open "doubts upon the law" was also perceived as undermining parliamentary and royal prerogatives, disseminating among a wide range of subjects an equally wide range of ways of imagining issues of social and political importance. The position of mooting, then, was outside of and often against what parliament or a monarch might prefer.

Nonetheless, the play leaves open questions of its relationship to the new James I, for whom it was staged in 1604. Although it has become a commonplace to assert an identity between James I's views and an interpretation of the play's ending as absolutist, we know too little to support such views. More to the point, as Jonathan Goldberg has argued, "the opinions that the Duke and James share can be found readily in many political treatises of the time; [and] much as some of the Duke's acts may recall James's, more do not" (Goldberg 1983: 232).[13]

The relationship I want to propose is not one of duplication but of audience to moot case. *Measure for Measure* positions itself to dramatize, in a speculative vein, the transience of the community and the effect of permanence that attends on social contracts, in this case, specifically marriage. In doing so, though its nominal setting is Vienna, its codes and values are more accurately London's. It simply stakes a claim: to be one of "us" means to enter into a process of achieving a social identity conveyed in proverbial terms. James was not, from the point of view of the native Briton, one of "us"; he did not trade in the same laws, preferring his own version of politics articulated in the *Basilicon Doran* and *True Lawes of Free Monarchies*; he did not share the common language, one in which a communal identity of the realm had been historicized in terms of what "some say" and "others say." In the presence of this new, alien rule, *Measure for Measure* asserts its own identity as an English play about "our" institutions and "the terms for common justice"; it invites its audiences to imagine themselves proprietors of a continuously mutable realm; and it makes its political commentary by indirection, evoking "mind stretching remote contingencies." Neither anti-Jacobean nor pro-divine right, the play perhaps makes its strongest statement simply by "opening doubts upon the law."

NOTES

Portions of this chapter are taken from *Imaginary Betrayals* by Karen Cunningham. Copyright © 2002 University of Pennsylvania Press. Reprinted with permission.

1   *Measure for Measure* was first printed in the Folio of 1623; on the textual history, see J. W. Lever (1965: xi–xxxv). Citations from the play are from this edition and appear in the text. The title alludes to Matthew 7: 1–2: "Judge not, that ye be not judged. For with what judgement ye judge, ye shall be judged; and with what measure ye mete, it shall be measured to you again."

2   For diverse readings that take up the play's religious subtexts and biblical allusions, see for example Schleiner (1982), Lupton (1996: 110–40), and Battenhouse (1946). For a full sense of the

intertwining of some of the theological and political issues in the period, with the tensions and similarities between canon and civil law, see Shuger (2001).

3   On rhetorical form and exploratory comedy, see Altman (1978: 229).

4   Questions of blood kinship in law are related to issues of who can inherit, which kind of inheritance will be allowed, and the proportion one might be eligible to receive. The recurring legal issue underwriting this pattern is the feudal distinction in inheritance between fee simple and fee tail. Fee simple describes a freehold estate of virtually infinite duration; inheritance is free from conditions, limitations, or restrictions to particular heirs. In contrast, fee tail identifies a conveyance created by a deed or will to a person and "the heirs of his body" specifically. For definitions of these and other legal terms, see Gifis (1991: 187, *passim*).

5   For an argument that references to abbots were an indirect means of talking about the monarch's prerogatives, see Kantorowicz (1957: 406). I am indebted to R. A. Foakes for suggesting this view of the abbot, and to Debora Shuger for pointing out the references in Kantorowicz.

6   See also Isabella 1.4.45 and 2.2.29; Pompey 1.2.83; Claudio 1.2.143; and Escalus 2.1.40.

7   This argument is Ernest Schanzer's (1963: 101–4); see also Cohen (1999: 453). On judges refusing to consider a felon's thoughts, see William Holdsworth (1942, 3: 373–4). Contra Schanzer's argument, legal case history shows that the question of intent in common law prosecutions is inconsistent and contradictory. Richard Firth Green has shown that common law first begins to consider intentions in the context of institutional treason, but its appearance in other legal areas, such as private obligation and contract, is less clear (Green 1999: 119).

8   On the Duke at the end representing royal power in the mode preferred by James I, see Cohen (1999: 446–55).

9   The idea that Isabella accepts the Duke's proposal has provoked considerable commentary. However, Shakespeare has embedded in his plot a series of scenes involving Isabella's increasing willingness to be directed by the friar/Duke; see 3.1.151; 3.1.205, 270; 4.1, and 4.3.136.

10 The play's ending has prompted a wide range of arguments. Among those who find the ending unsatisfactory in some way are Wheeler (1981: 12), Watson (1990: 423), and Dawson (1988: 341). A more equivocal reading is Bevington's (1980: 464). Positive readings, which generally depend on taking the Duke as a godlike figure dispensing divine justice, are offered by Gless (1979: 254) and Knight (1949: 95). A particularly illuminating essay on specifics of Calvinist theology and the "dissatisfaction" at the play's end is Diehl (1998).

11 I use "proverb" to cover a wide range of rhetorical forms, including aphorisms, sententia, maxims, and so on. In addition to those attributed to Shakespeare (see, for example, Rushton 1859), proverbs were popular throughout the early modern period as maxims and as a structure for organizing texts and assisting memory. Collections included Nicholas Udall's translations of Erasmus' apophthegms (1542); John Heywood's compilation (1562); John Florio's compilation (1578); Lyly's *Euphues* (1579 and 1580); Camden's *Remaines* (1614); and Francis Bacon's proverbs on common laws (1630).

12 For a range of perspectives on this topic, see, for example, Goldberg (1983); Greenblatt (1988; 1982); Tennenhouse (1986).

13 Goldberg's essay then argues for a different kind of relationship between James I and the play, one based on representation in which James's sovereign power depends on reduplication and on the "power-in-absence" manifested in the Duke and the substitutions in the play (Goldberg 1983: 230–9, 286–7).

REFERENCES AND FURTHER READING

Abbott, L. W. (1973). *Law Reporting In England, 1485–1585*. London: Athlone Press.

Altman, J. B. (1978). *The Tudor Play of Mind: Rhetorical Inquiry and the Development of Elizabethan Drama*. Berkeley: University of California Press.

Bache, W. B. (1969). *"Measure for Measure" as Dialectical Art*. Lafayette, IN: Purdue University Studies.

Bacon, F. (1972). *Essays*, ed. M. J. Hawkins. London: Dent.

Baker, J. H. (1986). The Inns of Court and Legal Doctrine. In T. M. Charles-Edwards, M. E. Owen, and D. B. Walters (eds.) *Lawyers and Laymen*. Cardiff: University of Wales Press, 274–86.

Baker, J. H. and Thorne, S. (eds.) (1990). *Readings and Moots at the Inns of Court in the Fifteenth Century, Vol. 2: Moots and Readers' Cases*. London: Seldon Society.

Battenhouse, R. W. (ed.) (1946). "Measure for Measure" and Christian Doctrine of Atonement. *Publications of the Modern Languages Association*, 61, 1029–59.

Belsey, C. (1985). *The Subject of Tragedy: Identity and Difference in Renaissance Drama*. London: Methuen.

Berman, R. (1967). Shakespeare and the Law. *Shakespeare Quarterly*, 18, 141–50.

Bevington, D. (ed.) (1980). *The Complete Works of Shakespeare*, 3rd edn. Glenview, IL: Scott, Foresman.

Cohen, S. (1999). From Mistress to Master: Political Transition and Formal Conflict in *Measure for Measure*. *Criticism*, 41, 431–64.

Cook, A. J. (1981). *The Privileged Playgoer of Shakespeare's London, 1576–1642*. Princeton, NJ: Princeton University Press.

Dawson, A. (1988). *Measure for Measure*, New Historicism, and Theatrical Power. *Shakespeare Quarterly*, 39, 328–41.

Diehl, H. (1998). "Infinite Space": Representation and Reformation in *Measure for Measure*. *Shakespeare Quarterly*, 49, 393–410.

Dollimore, J. (1985). Transgression and Surveillance in *Measure for Measure*. In J. Dollimore and A. Sinfield (eds.) *Political Shakespeare: New Essays in Cultural Materialism*. Ithaca, NY: Cornell University Press.

Douglas, M. (1966). *Purity and Danger: An Analysis of Concepts of Pollution and Taboo*. New York: Frederick Praeger.

——(1978). *Cultural Bias*. London: Royal Anthropological Institute of Great Britain and Ireland.

Eagleton, T. (1986). *William Shakespeare*. Oxford: Blackwell.

Finkelpearl, P. J. (1969). *John Marston of the Middle Temple*. Cambridge, MA: Harvard University Press.

Gifis, S. H. (1991). *Law Dictionary*, 3rd edn. Hauppauge, NY: Barron's Educational Series.

Gless, D. F. (1979). *Measure for Measure, the Law, and the Convent*. Princeton, NJ: Princeton University Press.

Goldberg, J. (1983). *James I and the Politics of Literature*. Baltimore, MD: Johns Hopkins University Press.

Green, R. F. (1999). *A Crisis of Truth: Literature and Law in Ricardian England*. Philadelphia: University of Pennsylvania Press.

Greenblatt, S. (ed.) (1982). *The Forms of Power and the Power of Forms in the Renaissance*. Norman: University of Oklahoma Press.

——(1988). *Shakespearean Negotiations: The Circulation of Social Energy in Renaissance England*. Berkeley: University of California Press.

Gurr, A. (1987). *Playgoing in Shakespeare's London*. Cambridge: Cambridge University Press.

Harper, C. (1998). *"'Twixt Will and Will Not": The Dilemma of Measure for Measure*. Niwot: University Press of Colorado.

Hawkins, H. (1987). *Measure for Measure*. Twain's New Critical Introduction to Shakespeare. Boston, MA: Twayne.

Hayne, V. (1999). Performing Social Practice: The Example of *Measure for Measure*. In R. P. Wheeter (ed.) *Critical Essays on Shakespeare's Measure for Measure*. New York: G. K. Hall.

Holdsworth, W. (1942). *A History of English Law*, Vol. 3, 5th edn. London: Methuen.

Kantorowicz, E. (1957). *The King's Two Bodies: A Study in Mediaeval Political Theology*. Princeton, NJ: Princeton University Press.

Knight, G. W. (1949). *Measure for Measure* and the Gospels. In *The Wheel of Fire*, 4th revd. edn. London: Methuen, 73–96.

Leggatt, A. (1988). Substitution in *Measure for Measure*. *Shakespeare Quarterly*, 39, 342–59.

Lever, J. W. (ed.) (1965). *Measure for Measure*. Arden Edition. New York: Vintage.

Lupton, J. R. (1996). *Afterlives of Saints: Hagiography, Typology, and Renaissance Literature*. Stanford, CA: Stanford University Press.

Maus, K. E. (1995). *Inwardness and Theater in the English Renaissance*. Chicago, IL: University of Chicago Press.

Rackin, P. (1990). *Stages of History: Shakespeare's English Chronicles*. Ithaca, NY: Cornell University Press.

Rushton, W. L. (1859). *Shakespeare's Legal Maxims*. London: Longman, Green, Longman and Roberts.

Schanzer, E. (1963). *The Problem Plays of Shakespeare*. New York: Schocken Books.

Schleiner, L. (1982). Providential Improvisation in *Measure for Measure*. *Publications of the Modern Languages Association*, 97, 227–36.

Shuger, D. K. (2001). *Political Theologies in Shakespeare's England: The Sacred and the State in "Measure for Measure"*. New York: Palgrave/St. Martin's Press.

Sidney, Sir Philip (1992). An Apology for Poetry. In H. Adams (ed.) *Critical Theory Since Plato*, revd. edn. New York: Harcourt, Brace, Jovanovich. Originally published 1583, 1595.

Smith, P. (1860). *A History of Education for the English Bar*. London: Butterworths.

Tennenhouse. L. (1986). *Power on Display: The Politics of Shakespeare's Genres*. New York: Methuen.

Tilley, M. P. (1926). *Elizabethan Proverb Lore in Lyly's "Euphues" and in Pettie's "Petite Pallace."* New York: Macmillan.

——(1983). *A Dictionary of Proverbs in England in the Sixteenth and Seventeenth Centuries*. New York: AMS Press. Originally published 1950.

Watson, R. N. (1990). False Immortality in *Measure for Measure*: Comic Means, Tragic Ends. *Shakespeare Quarterly*, 41, 411–32.

Wheeler, R. (1981). *Shakespeare's Development and the Problem Comedies: Turn and Counterturn*. Berkeley: University of California Press.

17

"Doctor She": Healing and Sex in *All's Well That Ends Well*

Barbara Howard Traister

Talk of two dead men (the Count of Roussillon and his physician, Gerard de Narbonne), of an incapacitated and dying king, and of a weeping woman opens the comedy *All's Well That Ends Well*. It ends with the King, now healed, presiding over the apparent reconciliation of the woman, now visibly pregnant, and her estranged husband. I read this play as concerned throughout with issues of sickness, healing, and health. When "all is well" – a word emphasized by its double use in the title and in the Clown's verbal play in 2.4 – all is, on one important level, "sound in health."[1]

All's Well is peculiar among Shakespearean comedies, the only one in which a woman selects an unwilling marriage partner, systematically removes the obstacles to the match, and claims her mate against his own will. It is also his only comedy where a single pair of young people moves toward marriage. Because Helen and Bertram's relationship is the only view of marriage which the play offers, nothing blunts the impact of their unorthodox coupling.

The play's rudimentary subplot, Paroles and his braggadocio behavior, rarely diverts attention from Helen's relentless pursuit of Bertram. The King, Bertram's mother, and Diana's mother – the older generation which, in a typical comedy, would block or oppose the young people's marriage – all become Helen's supporters. The woman who is briefly the object of Bertram's desire, Diana, shows no real interest in the war hero who attempts to seduce her, but rather cooperates fully with Helen, turning over to her not only the assignation with Bertram but also Bertram's family ring which Diana has coaxed from him by promising admittance to her bed.

Helen is both physician and wooer, social roles ordinarily reserved for males. But she puts on neither male clothing nor a male persona, props which supported Rosalind, Portia, and Julia, other comic heroines who engage in stereotypical "male" behaviors. Helen shares characteristics with each of these female characters: like Julia, she pursues an unwilling man; like Portia, she acts as a professional in a profession from which women were barred; and like Rosalind, she deals with love as a sickness or malady. Yet Helen approaches all these issues as a woman, never shielding the unorthodoxy of her behavior with male disguise. Critics have identified Helen's plot functions as originating in two folktale motifs, one the healer of the sick king, the other the clever wench who manages the bed trick. Such old folktale antecedents, however, sit cheek by jowl in *All's Well* with precise contemporary medical language and a brief but accurate glance at the range of early modern medical practice.

Helen's role as healer does not end with her cure of the King's fistula.[2] His recovery, from Helen's perspective at least, is merely instrumental to another cure, that of her own "erotic melancholy," or green sickness. Diagnosing her disease, Helen is determined to pursue its cure, and her first medical triumph merely makes possible her larger, personal medical purpose.

In its combination of folkloric materials with details drawn from contemporary London, *All's Well* resembles its near contemporary, *Measure for Measure*. Set in Vienna, *Measure* uses a bed trick for its plot resolution and includes graphic details about sexual profligacy which allude to conditions present in James's London. *All's Well* similarly relies on folkloric elements in a play infused with language about medical practice and the body's ailments which reflects the medical politics and practice of contemporary London. A defining characteristic of these "problem plays" seems to be their engagement with contemporary urban London even as they employ distant settings and folk motifs.

In *All's Well* the King himself introduces the notion of a medical hierarchy:

> [We] may not be so credulous of cure,
> When our most learned doctors leave us, and
> The congregated college have concluded
> That labouring art can never ransom nature
> From her inaidible estate. I say we must not
> So stain our judgment or corrupt our hope,
> To prostitute our past-cure malady
> To empirics. (2.1.114–21)

Despite the play's French setting, the "learned doctors" and the "congregated college" are usually glossed as referring to the College of Physicians of London.[3] Established in 1518 by Henry VIII on the advice of Thomas Linacre for the purpose of overseeing medical practice within London and its environs, the College had the power to grant licenses permitting medical practitioners to work in the London area. Those who practiced without the license of the College were subject to fines and jail terms if they came to the College's attention.

The size of the College was limited by its internal by-laws; it numbered thirty physicians when James came to the throne. Royal physicians were almost automatically admitted to membership, and the other College members were prominent London practitioners, usually educated at Oxford or Cambridge. A committee of College members examined practitioners who applied for licenses. Those granted licenses formed a larger, less elite body of "legitimate" practitioners. All non-licensed medical personnel – by far the largest group of medical practitioners in London – were labeled "empirics" and considered to lack proper medical training (Traister 2001: 81–3).[4]

When Helen is introduced to the King by Lafeu as "Doctor She," someone who may be able to cure his fistula, the King immediately recognizes her as an empiric. Her gender alone would disqualify her from consideration as a licensed physician. Women who practiced medical arts were by definition empirics, and a number of the unlicensed practitioners brought before the London College and accused of illicit practice were women. For example, in the years immediately surrounding the composition of *All's Well*, women such as Katherine Clark ("accused of practising Physick and convicted by the testimony of others and likewise by her own confession"), Cecilie Pople, Mrs. Woodhouse ("a Famous Emperick living at Kingstand"), Anne Dickson, Mrs. Sadler, and Rose Griffin (accused of giving pregnant women violent purgatives), were all examined by the College, and fined or imprisoned or both (Goodall 1684: 349–68).

Marked as an empiric not only by gender but also by her claim to have a single remedy appropriate for a particular disease or condition, in this case the King's fistula, Helen makes no attempt to suggest a range of remedies or to give "advice" gleaned from medical authorities; those were behaviors expected only of licensed physicians. Men and women who set up as medical practitioners in London often relied on one remedy, such as a "strong water" or a medicinal oil, with which they treated either a variety of physical ills or sometimes a single specialized complaint such as eye cataracts or kidney stones. Their focus on a product which would heal, rather than on diagnosis and then advice about which medicine or regimen to choose, differentiated empirics from licensed doctors. Doctors rarely dispensed medicines themselves but sent their patients to apothecaries for the actual remedies which they prescribed. Empirics usually dispensed their own remedies since apothecaries who filled their "bills" could get in trouble with the College of Physicians.[5]

The root of many of the distinctions made between physicians and "empirics" was education. Peter W. G. Wright remarks that "physicians were marked off from all other practitioners by their learning, or apparent learning, certified by the M.D.'s. But that was the sole distinguishing mark of the physician, his only clear claim to medical superiority" (Wright 1979: 56). In *All's Well* this distinction, and Helen's lack of education, make the success of her plan seem doubtful. The Countess, hearing of Helen's scheme to cure the ailing King, worries:

> But think you, Helen,
> If you should tender your supposed aid,
> He would receive it? He and his physicians
> Are of a mind: he, that they cannot help him;
> They, that they cannot help. How shall they credit
> A poor unlearned virgin, when the schools,
> Embowel'd of their doctrine, have left off
> The danger to itself? (1.3.230–7)

Her first concern is that the "unlearned" Helen cannot hope to compete against the learned physicians. The Countess's violent image of the schools "embowel'd of their doctrine," eviscerated and stripped of all their learning in the attempt to find a cure, suggests a thorough canvas of medical knowledge, all of which has proved useless in the King's case. Indeed, once the success of Helen's treatment becomes common knowledge in the court, the courtiers reiterate the wonder of having the physicians' knowledge bested by the unlikely "miracle" that the King's cure represents.[6]

> _Lafeu._ To be relinquish'd of the artists –
> _Paroles._ So I say – both of Galen and Paracelsus.
> _Lafeu._ Of all the learned and authentic Fellows – (2.3.10–12)

The cure must be a miracle because orthodox Galenic physicians recognized no new remedies, only those which had been proved by long testing. Francis Herring, writing in 1602, comments that the physician "shunneth and shutteth out all churlish, malignant, new-found, & suspected medicines, admitting those only in his Practise, which are . . . approved by long Vse, and certaine Experience of the ancient Worthies, and great Maisters in Phisicke" (p. 8). Herring is arguing specifically against those who prescribe the new chemical medicines introduced by Paracelsus and gradually creeping into the pharmacopoeia of English practitioners. Some critics discuss Helen as a Paracelsian healer (Stensgaard 1972; Solomon 1993), although the courtiers quoted above clearly do not identify her with Paracelsus any more than they do with Galen. By offering a new remedy which is successful, Helen, a female empiric of whom nothing was expected, has produced a paradox which the courtiers can construe only as a miracle.

Representation of the cure as miracle begins even before it takes place, and Helen herself starts it. After her pragmatic reason for expecting success – the remedy left her by her physician father – has been rejected by the King, Helen searches for a convincing rhetorical strategy to persuade him to accept her medical services. By systematically devaluing her own contribution to the cure, calling herself "weakest minister" and urging that the King "of heaven, not me, make an experiment," she manages to turn the King's prejudice against her sex into an asset. The King comes to believe in the possibility of a cure, a miraculous healing, specifically because Helen is so unlikely in the role of healer: "Methinks in thee some blessed spirit doth speak / His powerful sound within an organ weak" (2.1.74–5).

When he first considers her merely a female empiric, his language suggests that to submit to her ministrations would be similar to submitting to the attentions of a prostitute. The sexual slur in the series of verbs the King uses when he labels her an empiric – "stain," "corrupt," "prostitute" – is cleverly picked up in Helen's own language when she tells the King what she will submit to if she fails:

> Tax of impudence,
> A strumpet's boldness, a divulged shame
> Traduced by odious ballads; my maiden's name
> Seared otherwise; nay, worse of worst, extended
> With vilest torture let my life be ended. (2.1.170–4)

Helen understands that failure of her medicine will effectively ruin her sexual reputation and prove to the court audience that she is the whore the King first suspected.
Success will make her merely the instrument of a heaven-sent miracle. There seems
little room in this binary for medical competence.

Although Helen is willing to suggest, as a strategy for persuading the King, that
her healing power is a miracle from above, she remains relentlessly pragmatic about
the terms of her compensation: "Not helping, death's my fee. / But if I help, what do
you promise me?" (2.1.189–90). The arrangement they make resembles – in all except
the stakes – medical "fee bargains" of the period. The fee bargain was a negotiation
in which a practitioner agreed to receive his fee if, and only if, the cure was successful. Sometimes he was paid a sum up front, which would be returned if the treatment
failed. The College of Physicians forbade the practice of fee bargaining to its members.
Margaret Pelling suggests a reason for this ban:

> London physicians demanded payment for advice, regardless of outcome . . . It was also
> an attempt to copy the liberal professions by evading the slur of having to earn a liveli-
> hood. Fees were to look like unearned income. Thus, like the clergy, physicians wanted
> to be paid simply for talking and being. (Pelling 1996: 109–10)

Eventually, market demand – patients who were willing to pay only if helped by prac-
titioners – prevailed and, in statutes written early in the seventeenth century, the
College of Physicians reluctantly removed the penalty for fee bargaining (Clark 1964,
I: 180).

In *All's Well* her skeptical patient forces Helen to provide additional surety that
the cure will be successful, and she puts first her good name and then her life on the
table. Her willingness to risk even her life should not come as a great surprise, since
she has earlier announced that she expects to die if she cannot win Bertram. In return,
Helen demands a specific fee to be paid upon successful healing. The contrast with
Shakespeare's source is telling. In Painter's version of Boccaccio's tale, the King himself
proposes giving Giletta a good husband if her cure succeeds; only then does Giletta
ask that the husband should be one of her own choosing. Helen, however, demands
up front "what husband in thy power I will command" (2.1.193). The bargain struck,
the medical treatment goes forward. Like many empirics, Helen bargains for her fee
in advance and expects to be paid only for a cure, not simply for advice. Should she
fail – and here the play goes beyond the fee bargain model – she will not merely be
deprived of her fee, but will pay with her life.

These details about Helen's brief, dangerous moment as the King's physician correspond fairly closely to the conditions unlicensed empirics might expect in London.
Though their lives were not at risk unless they were implicated in the suspicious death
of an important person, complaints to the College from disgruntled patients or too
great success, which might also bring them to the College's attention, could result in
substantial fines and jail terms. The play's few speeches about medical practice resonate deeply. By insisting on its medical, not just its folkloric context, they alert the

audience to the possibility of other medical issues in the play — an important matter for a work that represents a *second* medical problem.

From her first appearance, an audience can view Helen herself as ill and in need of healing. Critics have noted Helen's silence in the opening lines of the play (Styan 1995: 159–60) when she weeps but responds only briefly to the Countess's direct address and offers no response to the perfunctory farewells of Bertram and Lafeu. Her tears, she explains once she has the stage to herself, are tears for Bertram. Her language is revealing: "I am undone. There is no living, none, / If Bertram be away" and "the hind that would be mated by the lion / Must die for love" (1.1.78–9, 86–7). Paroles, always alert to others' weaknesses, apparently guesses something of Helen's condition. Why else his abrupt and impertinent question, "Are you meditating on virginity" (1.1.105)?

The disease from which Helen is suffering is never named in the play, but the early modern period had a number of names which might apply to her condition. Elizabethans, including Shakespeare, refer to a malady they call green sickness (*chlorosis*), which was a kind of anemia. In the course of her study of seventeenth-century Dutch genre painting, Laurinda Dixon (1995) focuses on a variety of uterine disorders, variously named in medical texts dating from the sixteenth century, for which she selects as a general descriptor *furor uterinus*. Jacques Ferrand wrote in the early seventeenth century an encyclopedic treatise entitled *De la maladie d'amour ou melancholie erotique* (1623). Ferrand's book, translated into English in 1640, appeared as *Erotomania*. Robert Burton called one of his principal types of melancholy "love melancholy" and also wrote encyclopedically about it. Despite their somewhat different physical symptoms and explanations of the cause of those symptoms, all these medical conditions arise from unrequited love or from celibacy. Both men and women can suffer from love melancholy or erotomania, but only women — given their distinctive anatomy — suffer *furor uterinus* or green sickness. Green sickness was thought to be particular to young unmarried women, while women of all ages could suffer from uterine misbehavior. Most susceptible, however, were virgins and widows.

Shakespeare's texts mention green sickness four times, always in passing. Twice the term is used to feminize men: Lepidus, because he is weak and loves both Caesar and Antony (*Antony and Cleopatra*, 3.2.6), and Prince John, whom Falstaff indicts for drinking no sack (*2 Henry IV*, 4.2.84), are scornfully said to suffer from green sickness. When Marina refuses sex with the brothel customers in *Pericles*, the pander attributes her refusal to green sickness (scene 19.20), that is, to melancholy and lack of sexual experience. Old Capulet, seeing his daughter's excessive tears and misunderstanding her refusal to wed Paris, diagnoses green sickness and exclaims "Out, you green-sickness carrion. Out, you baggage, / You tallow-face!" (*Romeo and Juliet*, 3.5.156–7). Capulet refers to the very pale or "green" face which was the most distinctive symptom of the disease.

Dixon argues that the Dutch genre painters who created repeated scenes of young women being visited by physicians made this greenish face a feature of their paintings. Other physical signs of female lovesickness include excessive tears, a fixed gaze, and an altered pulse, signs which were represented in the Dutch paintings, where physicians are often pictured as checking the pulse of pale young women who gaze past them, and which could have been represented upon the stage as well. Paroles's abrupt and rude question about virginity may have been cued by the actor's posture or gesture or simply by an unstaunched flow of tears.

After scene 1, Helen does not again refer to her unrequited love for Bertram as life-threatening, but other characters speak of the physical problems associated with unfulfilled desire. Most blunt is the clown Lavatch's explanation of why he will marry: "My poor body, madam, requires it. I am driven on by the flesh" (1.3.25). Snyder (1992) writes that the Clown is "a voice available to say the unsayable, in his sexual aversion speaking for Bertram but in his obsessive, driving desire speaking for Helen . . . Only the Clown has license to talk of the body's compelling needs" (p. 23). Surprisingly sympathetic when she hears of Helen's love for her son, the Countess herself recalls physical passion: "Even so it was with me when I was young. / . . . This thorn / Doth to our rose of youth rightly belong." She claims to discover physical signs of Helen's passion – "Her eye is sick on't. I observe her now" (1.3.113–15, 120) – and continues to notice symptoms of Helen's malady as she interviews her: Helen's pulse changes when the Countess talks of their being mother and daughter and she becomes "pale again" (1.3.153).

To consider the clichéd "lovesickness" as a genuine physical malady is difficult for a twenty-first century audience. Perhaps it was nearly as difficult for Shakespeare's own audience. Certainly although symptoms of lovesickness appear regularly in other Shakespeare comedies, they are as regularly laughed away or mocked. The most obvious examples occur in *As You Like It*, where Touchstone's explanations for why he wants to marry Audrey are just as frank as Lavatch's and where the passion of Orlando and Rosalind provides the textual center of the play. In *As You Like It* Orlando is "sick" for love, and the witty Rosalind, taking up the medical metaphor, declares that no one has ever died for love and promises to cure him through a series of disciplinary measures, changes in regimen. Love in *As You Like It* is "a cage of rushes," a condition from which characters who wish to can easily escape, and an appropriate metaphor for a play whose four sets of couples ring many changes on love and gender. Rosalind can mock Orlando's excesses precisely because she knows his (and her) ultimate cure is at hand, hers to administer when finally Orlando can "live no longer by thinking" (5.2.45). Lovesickness in the Forest of Arden is never more than a metaphor, never a physical disease.

In *All's Well* the case is more serious. Only Helen is afflicted; the play provides no other lover with whom to compare her. Lavatch and Bertram, the only other characters who express sexual desire, are males for whom satisfying physical lust is an altogether more straightforward and transitory affair. Though Bertram protests his passion to Diana, his speech to his fellow soldiers about the sixteen businesses he has dispatched in one evening – businesses which include burying Helen (metaphorically) and mourning her, and seducing Diana (4.3.83–9) – makes clear that his passion involved only lust. Indeed, Bertram hopes he will be able to get out of town (now that Helen is reported dead he could marry Diana; instead he sees Helen's death as an occasion to return to Roussillon) without hearing any more of the business with Diana.

In the play's opening lines Helen seemed prepared to sink into a Petrarchan cliché, sighing and weeping for her unattainable "bright star." But after her frankly physical talk with Paroles about how a woman might lose her burdensome virginity "to her own liking," Helen transforms herself from weeping passivity to action: "Our remedies oft in ourselves do lie / Which we ascribe to heaven" (1.1.199–200).

However much lovesickness may be a cliché to audiences, both in the sixteenth century and now, Shakespeare constructed in Helen a character who feels sick and in need of cure. In representing her condition as an actual, not metaphoric, sickness, Helen is supported by certain medical texts of the period, most especially those derived from Hippocrates, who taught that women were subject to their bodies and to the sexual appetites of those bodies.

Writers who discussed erotic illnesses, whether associating them with melancholy – like Ferrand and Burton – or seeing them as more highly determined by the form of women's bodies and their troublesome wombs, proposed all sorts of cures: alterations in diet, surgery, and aversion therapy. Burton suggests:

> bethink thyself that it is but earth thou lovest, a mere excrement . . . and thy raging soul will be at rest. Suppose sick . . . hoary-headed, hollow-cheeked, old, within she is full of filthy phlegm, stinking, putrid, excremental stuff. (Burton 1932, III: 212)

Occult cures, music, and pharmaceutical preparations were other common remedies. On one treatment, however, all were in agreement: sexual relations, preferably with the object of one's desires, would cure the sufferer. Ferrand quotes Hippocrates: "All young women taken by this disease should be forthwith married," a remedy which Capulet tries to put into effect immediately upon diagnosing his daughter's problem as green sickness. According to Burton "the last refuge and surest remedy when no other means will take effect, is to let them go together, and enjoy one another" (Burton 1932, III: 228). A less formally couched expression of this remedy appears in the often-copied manuscript poem, "A Cure for ye Greene Sicknesse":

> **A** mayden faire of ye greene sicknesse late
> **P**itty to see, perplexed was full sore
> **R**esoluinge how t'amend her bad estate,
> **I**n this distresse Apollo doth implore
> **C**ure for her ill; ye oracle assignes,
> **K**eepe ye first letter of these severall lines.
> (Bodleian MS. Rawlinson poet. 172, f2v)[7]

Ferrand, amidst a welter of other remedies for men and women suffering from erotomania, cautiously remarks: "No physician would refuse to someone suffering from erotic mania or melancholy the enjoyment of the object of desire in marriage in accordance with both divine and human laws" (Ferrand 1990: 334).

Helen, the daughter of a physician, knows that the ultimate cure for her malady is a sexual relationship, preferably with "the object of desire," or, as she says to Paroles: "to lose it [virginity] to her own liking" (1.1.140). Helen also knows that her answer must not be as simple as the anonymous poem's – a prick. She must try, more in tune with Ferrand's decorous wording, to enjoy the object of her desire within the bounds of marriage, or she will indeed become the whore which the King first assumes her to be. Helen spends her time in the play carefully teasing this combination of physical and social satisfaction from the always reluctant Bertram. Her priority is the "prick" but, at first, like Ferrand, she assumes the physical relationship she needs will come automatically with marriage. Bertram foils this expectation, however, withholding from her not his title or his estate but his body, and thus precipitating Helen's second bag-packing spate of travel and plotting.

Support for this reading of Helen's disease and her determination to find its cure comes from the sexualized, usually comic, discourse which permeates the play. Helen's sexuality is at issue from the moment Paroles asks whether she is meditating on virginity until she appears in the play's final scene with swollen belly, undeniable evidence of sexual activity.

Following Paroles's and Helen's frank conversation about virginity and how to lose it, Lafeu's introduction of Helen to the King (2.1) is rife with sexual innuendo (Snyder 1992: 25). As he exits, Lafeu compares himself to Pandarus leaving "two together" (2.1.97). Even the possible location of the King's deadly fistula proves ground for salacious speculation. In Painter's tale the fistula is decorously located on the King's breast, a body part which can be bared for a young woman's inspection. Moreover, the cure is specified as a mixture of herbs which will be applied to the breast over an eight-day period. In Shakespeare's version the location of the fistula is unspecified, as is the nature of Helen's cure. She does tell the King that it will take two days or perhaps only twenty-four hours until he will be well. The best-known kind of fistula was anal (Cosman 1991: 90). A treatise on the subject, originally written in 1376 by a famous English surgeon, John Arderne, had been published in London in 1588 with the title *Treatises on Fistula in Ano*. In *All's Well* the audience is left free to imagine the location of the King's problem in a very intimate part of his body. If Helen conducts an examination of the fistula, she does so offstage and thus in secret. The lack of specificity about the location of the King's fistula and about the nature of the cure Helen applies, leaves space for male characters verbally to characterize the healing as sexual and therefore as particular to the oxymoronic "Doctor She."

After the cure, and despite its reception as a heaven-sent miracle, sexual undertones continue. When the recovered King enters with Helen in 2.3, they dance to the accompaniment of Lafeu's knowing comment: "*Lustig*, as the Dutchman says. I'll like a maid the better whilst I have a tooth in my head" (39). The response Helen elicits from certain male characters – Paroles, Lafeu, and occasionally Lavatch – makes her seem like a sexual time bomb, her needs written on her body for other characters to read, much as Dixon claims the Dutch painters made obvious the love melancholy of their young female subjects.

Helen is aware of the effect her cure of the King and her demand for the husband of her choice must have. Her usurpation of male prerogatives is risky. Burton writes:

> A woman should give unto her parents the choice of her husband, lest she be reputed to be malapert and wanton, if she take upon her to make her own choice; for she should rather seem to be desired by a man than to desire a man herself. (Burton 1932, III: 238)

Just before choosing from among the young men the King has assembled, Helen goes to enormous pains to assert her maidenhood and virginity even as she once again hints at her malady:

> I am a simple maid, and therein wealthiest
> That I protest I simply am a maid. –
>
> . . .
>
> The blushes in my cheeks thus whisper me:
> "We blush that thou shouldst choose; but, be refused,
> Let the white death sit on thy cheek for ever,
> We'll never come there again." (2.3.63–9)

Bertram, in his response to the King's command that he accept Helen because she has "raised" the King from his bed of sickness, plays with the pun in ways which stress his repugnance for the sexual duties involved in the proposed marriage: "But follows it my lord, to bring me down must answer for your raising?" (2.3.108–9).

Helen is interested, first and foremost, in a physical relationship with Bertram. When Bertram sends her back to Roussillon from the court after their wedding, she seeks some gesture of physical intimacy by asking for a kiss; Bertram ignores her request without comment. On receiving Bertram's letter of rejection, Helen focuses on the physical danger to Bertram's beloved body, his "tender limbs" and "forward breast," and declares that her own physical suffering is preferable to physical danger to Bertram: "Better 'twere / I met the ravine lion when he roared / With sharp constraint of hunger; better 'twere / That all the miseries which nature owes / Were mine at once" (3.2.116–20).

The play's final scene focuses on Helen's pregnant body, not on a child in her arms. In Painter's tale, Giletta arrives at the court of Count Beltramo with twin sons "carefully noursed and brought up" who look "very like unto their father" (Painter 1966, I: 178). The emphasis is on the next generation; Giletta's husband welcomes her as the mother of his children. Helen carries her child within, its sex, its appearance, indeed its very survival, as yet undetermined. She cannot "show" Bertram the child begot of his body that his original letter demanded. As critics have noticed (Asp 1986: 55; Parker 1987: 20), the original wording of his letter – "show me a child begotten of thy body that I am father to" (3.2.56–7) – has changed when Helen produces the letter on stage in the final scene. There she reads it as "When from my finger you can get this ring / And are by me with child" (5.3.319–20). All she can show is that their physical passion was mutual, resulting in her pregnancy. Indeed, in brutal fact, her pregnancy does not even show that; for there is no real evidence – lacking the look-like-their-father twins of Giletta – that the child she carries has anything to do with Bertram. The focus in this final scene is on Helen's body, now presumably healthy, and on her character. If Helen is virtuous, and audiences do not doubt that she is, the child is Bertram's. But no child is on stage to steal attention from Helen herself and her second cure.

Helen is consistently successful as a healer within the play. She cures the King, besting his educated physicians into the bargain, and heals herself, first by arranging her own marriage to a member of the nobility, a role ordinarily left to fathers or guardians, and next by insuring its consummation, a function usually in the power of the husband. Thus, she exercises power far out of proportion to her gender and her class. But neither Helen nor anything else can eliminate that unease about the play's ending that is a dominant audience response even though, in plot terms, at the play's end "all's well" both physically and socially. This uneasiness is due in part to the play's lack of closure, to Bertram's stipulation that he will love Helen only *if* she can make him know without doubt that she has fulfilled his demands, a stipulation which he addresses not to Helen but to the King.

Even more, I would argue, this unease arises from the containment and soiling of Helen's triumphs. Her cure of the King is contaminated by the salacious remarks which precede and follow it. Male characters who make sexual jokes about the nature of her revivifying services contain her in the "feminine" position; if the healing is sexual in nature, these remarks imply, no wonder "Doctor She" is successful where male physicians have failed. There is no evidence, of course, that Helen's cure of the King has even the remotest connection to sexual matters, but the remarks and the jokes remain to diminish her accomplishment.

Secrets and absences are one of the hallmarks of *All's Well*. Secrets which are never revealed include the nature of Helen's wonderful remedy, the location of the King's fistula, whether Helen made her announced pilgrimage to Saint Jaques le Grand, and how the rector there came to write a letter certifying her death. Absent women are also a notable feature of this play. Lavatch asks permission of the Countess to marry "Isbel the woman" (1.3.15), a character who never appears on stage and whom Lavatch effectively erases from the play on his return from the Paris court: "I have no mind to Isbel since I was at court . . . I begin to love as an old man loves money: with no stomach" (3.2.12–15). Similarly, Lafeu's daughter Maudlin is introduced in conversation and, provided Bertram sends her "a favour," will "quickly come" to be his bride (5.3). When the favor turns out to be Helen's ring, however, Maudlin too is erased from the play in which she never made an appearance. Despite Helen's worries that at the court Bertram will have "a thousand loves" (1.1.153), no women appear in the court scenes except Helen herself.

Despite Helen's dominance of the action of the play, the scenes which feature her as a physician, actually healing the King and accomplishing her own cure in the bed trick, are withheld from the stage, shielded from audience view by what Susan Snyder (1992) has called "screen scenes" (p. 27), much as the child which apparently lies within Helen is shielded from view at the play's end. In fact, Helen is notably absent from the stage in her most triumphant moments, absences which permit those moments to be "read" by male characters in the screen scenes in slightly tarnished ways. Much as Lafeu speculates about the nature of the King's healing, Second Lord Dumaine imagines that Bertram "fleshes his will in the spoil of her honour" (4.3.16) in the scene which screens the suppressed bed trick. On one level the audience "knows" what Helen accomplishes, but we are not permitted to see her at work, and we must filter our "knowledge" through the misleading comments of male characters.[8]

With regard to Bertram, Helen's success is even more powerfully qualified and contained. The closer she comes to grasping her "bright particular star," the more worthless her goal appears. Never particularly attractive to the audience, Bertram in the play's first half is little more than a boy, packed off to the King's court, forbidden to go to Italy and the war with the rest of the courtiers because he is too young. Bertram shows no interest in women, particularly in Helen, the woman with whom he has been brought up and whom he regards as his mother's servant. Characters like Paroles and his mother still call him "Boy," and he runs away from Helen, from the King, and from his mother like a schoolboy, refusing to explain his decision to them directly and instead sending them petulant letters which arrive after he has departed for Italy.

Though callow, Bertram has reason for distress. He is treated as a commodity, a fee for the King's cure. Young men, like young women, should not be forced to marry against their will. The value which Helen and his mother place on him gives him a certain luster and intimates that he will become what Helen apparently sees when, at her moment of choice, she says "This is the man" (2.3.100).

The first reports of him from Italy augur well for his maturation:

Diana. They say the French Count has done most honourable service.
Widow. It is reported that he has taken their greatest commander, and that with his own hand he slew the Duke's brother. (3.5.4–6)

The boy has become a war hero. Even reports that, through Paroles, he has been soliciting Diana are not greatly disturbing, especially since Paroles is being unmasked and, presumably, Bertram will learn to reject his counsel. The wooing scene with Diana, where Bertram is so entranced by her that he agrees to give her his family ring, may be seen as part of his maturation, the first evidence of his desire for a woman and thus a step toward maturation (despite his marriage). Because the audience is aware of Helen's role in the coming bed trick and Diana herself notes the formulaic nature of his words – "all men / Have the like oaths" (4.2.71–2) – Bertram's desire here poses no threat to his marriage or to Diana's peace of mind.

The play's final scene provides an opportunity to judge the "new" Bertram, shorn of the influence of Paroles, newly returned to Roussillon with success from the foreign wars. The King decides not to hold Bertram's former conduct against him:

> Let him not ask our pardon.
> The nature of his great offence is dead,
> And deeper than oblivion we do bury
> Th' incensing relics of it. Let him approach
> A stranger, no offender. (5.3.22–6)

Bertram acquits himself well until Helen's ring, given to her by the King, is recognized. Truly amazed, he begins the first of an increasingly convoluted web of lies. In the course of his twists and turns to rid himself of blame, Bertram lies and slanders Diana repeatedly. Bertram might have grown up to resemble his father, whom the King earlier praised as a model of honor, humility, and appropriate speech. Instead, Bertram has grown up to be like Paroles, full of lies and slander. The callow boy has become the self-serving man.

In the play's final moments Helen stands on the brink of collecting her full fee for the King's cure. In London a successful empiric might have been dealt with in several ways by the College of Physicians. He could be "contained" by granting him a license to practice from the College, thus enfolding him within the accepted medical hierarchy. He could be pressured by threats of fines and prison terms to cease practicing in London, or (if he resisted such pressure) he could become the object of ongoing surveillance and harassment by the College. For someone as publically successful as Helen, famed for curing the monarch, containment would probably have been the College's choice.[9] If the empiric were female, however, containment by acceptance would not have been an option. No females were licensed to practice in London. As a successful female empiric, Helen would have created great uneasiness: she could not be licensed and yet her achievement could not have been ignored.

Within the play, the problem of Helen is solved, however uneasily, by containing her within the folkloric plot as the clever wench who has won her husband. She no longer needs to worry about how to dispose of her virginity. But her success is qualified by the nature of the prize she has gained, just as her cure of the King was qualified by the salacious atmosphere which surrounded it. As wife to the loutish Bertram, she is contained by that role. There is no suggestion that she will ever practice the healing arts again; the troubling female empiric has been erased and replaced by the "licensed" reproductive wife. She and the King are now "well," restored to good health, but it is difficult to believe, nevertheless, that "all's well."

Notes

1　Shakespeare used "well" in other contexts to mean "healthy." Three of the examples cited by the *Oxford English Dictionary* (1971) for this sense of "well" (sb. 5) are from Shakespearean drama, though none is from *All's Well* itself.

2　A fistula is a long, narrow passage or canal which develops from an untreated or badly treated abscess. It carries infection from the original site to other organs or body parts. Without antibiotics, it is extremely difficult to treat because reaching and cleaning out the infection is complicated (Hoeniger 1992: 293–8).

3   See, for example, G. K. Hunter in the Arden edition, p. 41. Ben Jonson also refers to the College of Physicians in another play set outside England: "They have had, / At extreme fees, the College of physicians / Consulting on him" (*Volpone*, 2.6.26–8).

4   For the standard history of the College of Physicians, see Clark (1964), especially 1: 1–216. More recent and more critical treatment of the College can be found in the work of Harold J. Cook (1986, 1996).

5   Goodall (1684) records a case in which a search of an accused apothecary's shop by the College Censors turned up "divers bills found upon the file written by Empiricks and ignorant Mountebanks" (p. 374). All the apothecary's medicines were subsequently destroyed.

6   Susan Snyder (1992) writes, "It is tempting to see this miracle talk as a way of rationalizing a woman's success in a male province where men had failed" (p. 26).

7   At least ten versions of this anagrammatic poem appear in early modern manuscripts held by the Bodleian Library, Oxford, the British Library, London, and the Folger Shakespeare Library, Washington DC. The text of this version was provided by John O'Neill (Hamilton College).

8   In her Lacanian examination of women writers and their female characters, Margaret Homans (1986) makes an apposite comment: "There is an implicit contradiction between the novel's continuous representation of female experience and the text's seeming suddenly to become aware that the implication of such representation is, from the perspective of the symbolic order, the silence and objectification of women . . . The word that . . . female characters often bear is the word of their own exclusion from linguistic [and in the case of a play text 'dramatic'] practice" (pp. 32–3).

9   Licenses and sometimes even membership in the College, following earlier refusals to license and fines for illicit practice, were granted by the College of Physicians to several practitioners who were employed by Queen Elizabeth and the family of James I (Furdell 2001: 83–134).

REFERENCES AND FURTHER READING

"A Cure for ye Greene Sicknesse." Bodleian MS. Rawlinson poet. 172, fol. 2v.

Asp, C. (1986). Subjectivity, Desire and Female Friendship in *All's Well That Ends Well*. *Literature and Psychology*, 32, 48–63.

Burton, R. (1932) [1651]. *The Anatomy of Melancholy*, 3 vols. New York: Dutton.

Clark, G. (1964). *A History of the Royal College of Physicians of London*, 2 vols. Oxford: Clarendon Press.

Cook, H. J. (1986). *The Decline of the Old Medical Regime in Stuart London*. Ithaca, NY: Cornell University Press.

——(1996). Institutional Structures and Personal Belief in the London College of Physicians. In O. P. Grell and A. Cunningham (eds.) *Religio Medici: Medicine and Religion in Seventeenth-Century England*. Aldershot: Scolar Press, 91–114.

Cosman, B. C. (1991). *All's Well That Ends Well*: Shakespeare's Treatment of Anal Fistula. *The Upstart Crow*, 19, 78–95.

Dixon, L. S. (1995). *Perilous Chastity: Women and Illness in Pre-Enlightenment Art and Medicine*. Ithaca, NY: Cornell University Press.

Ferrand, J. (1990) [1623]. *A Treatise on Lovesickness*, trans. and ed. D. A. Beecher and M. Ciavolella. Syracuse, NY: Syracuse University Press.

Findlay, A. (1999). *A Feminist Perspective on Renaissance Drama*. Oxford: Blackwell.

Furdell, E. J. (2001). *The Royal Doctors 1485–1714: Medical Personnel at the Tudor and Stuart Courts*. Rochester, NY: University of Rochester Press.

Goodall, C. (1684). *The Royal College of Physicians of London . . . And an Historical Account of the College's Proceedings against Empiricks and Unlicensed Practisers*. London.

Herring, F. (1602). "A short discourse, or discovery of certain stratagems, whereby our London-Empericks, have been observed strongly to appugne, and oft time to expugne their poore patients purses." Appended to John Oberndorff, *The Anatomyes of the True Physition and Counterfeit Mountebanks*. London.

Hoeniger, F. D. (1992). *Medicine and Shakespeare in the English Renaissance*. Newark: University of Delaware Press.

Homans, M. (1986). *Bearing the Word: Language and Female Experience in Nineteenth Century Women's Writing*. Chicago, IL: University of Chicago Press.

Painter, W. (1966) [1566]. *The Palace of Pleasure*, 3 vols, ed. J. Jacobs. New York: Dover.

Parker, P. (1987). *Literary Fat Ladies: Rhetoric, Gender, Property*. London: Methuen.

Pelling, M. (1996). Compromised by Gender: The Role of the Male Medical Practitioner in Early Modern England. In H. Marland and M. Pelling (eds.) *The Task of Healing: Medicine, Religion and Gender in England and the Netherlands 1450–1800*. Rotterdam: Erasmus Publishing, 101–33.

Shakespeare, W. (1997). *The Norton Shakespeare*, ed. S. Greenblatt, W. Cohen, J. E. Howard, and K. E. Maus. New York: W. W. Norton,

Snyder, S. (1992). "The King's not here": Displacement and Deferral in *All's Well That Ends Well*. *Shakespeare Quarterly*, 43, 20–32.

Solomon, J. R. (1993). Mortality as Matter of Mind: Toward a Politics of Problems in *All's Well That Ends Well*. *English Literary Renaissance*, 23, 134–69.

Stensgaard, R. K. (1972). *All's Well That Ends Well* and the Galenico-Paracelsian Controversy. *Renaissance Quarterly*, 25, 173–88.

Styan, J. L. (1995). The Opening of *All's Well That Ends Well*: A Performance Approach. In R. F. Willson, Jr. (ed.) *Entering the Maze: Shakespeare's Art of Beginning*. New York: Peter Lang, 155–67.

Traister, B. H. (2001). *The Notorious Astrological Physician of London: Works and Days of Simon Forman*. Chicago, IL: University of Chicago Press.

Wright, P. W. G. (1979). A Study in the Legitimization of Knowledge: The "Success" of Medicine and the "Failure" of Astrology. In R. Wallis (ed.) *On the Margins of Science: The Social Construction of Rejected Knowledge*. Keele: University of Keele Press, 85–101.

18

"You not your child well loving": Text and Family Structure in *Pericles*

Suzanne Gossett

In act 4, scene 3 of *Pericles*, the murderous queen Dionyza is upbraided by her husband Cleon for her apparent murder of Pericles' motherless daughter Marina, who has been raised by the Tarsian couple since infancy. Dionyza's reply unexpectedly paints a picture of family life in the royal household, including competitive evaluation of children, maternal over-investment, and paternal lack of sympathy and warmth:

> She did distain [overshadow] my child, and stood between
> Her and her fortunes. None would look on her,
> But cast their gazes on Marina's face,
> Whilst ours was blurted at and held a malkin
> Not worth the time of day. It pierced me through,
> And though you call my course unnatural,
> You not your child well loving, yet I find
> It greets me as an enterprise of kindness
> Performed to your sole daughter. (4.3.31–9)[1]

In the current state of the text her accusation of indifference remains unsupported, never referred to elsewhere. Like so much that is uncertain in *Pericles*, the elision may arise from damage in the course of the play's transmission from manuscript(s) to stage to print, from aesthetic or structural inadequacies in the original conception, from differences between the authorial collaborators, or from a generic romance treatment that reduces Dionyza and Cleon to fairytale wicked stepparents and ignores psychological and social motivation.

Interpretation of *Pericles* must begin by accepting that *Pericles* is a radically indeterminate text, the only play from the accepted Shakespeare canon of which we have only a "bad Quarto" with no better controlling authority such as the First Folio, from which the play is omitted. Furthermore, multiple methods of analysis – examination of patterns of vocabulary and rhyme schemes; comparisons of the use of infinitives, "function words" (e.g., "by," "but"), and rare forms such as the Latin resumptive (beginning sentences with "which" or "to which"); and stylometrics or statistical computations of such indicators as the first word of every speech, frequently occurring words, and specific pairs of words (collocations) to distinguish between works of different authors – all confirm the subjective impression that the play is the product of two hands and cumulatively demonstrate that the second hand, author of acts one and two, is almost certainly that of the minor playwright George Wilkins (Lake 1969a, b; Jackson 1990, 1993; see Jackson 1990: n. 1 for further references).

Though such collaboration has been treated by bardolators as unlikely or even scandalous, it is not at all surprising for Shakespeare at this point in his personal and professional life. The first performance of *Pericles* can be dated from a convergence of diplomatic and epidemiological events to April–June, 1608; the play was probably written early that year or late in 1607.[2] Shakespeare would have recently completed *King Lear*, *Macbeth*, and *Antony and Cleopatra*.[3] In the summer of 1607 the first of his daughters married; on December 31, 1607, his younger brother, Edmund, died. Both events created unknowable psychological consequences (discussed below), as well as demands on Shakespeare's time. In any case, as chief dramatist for the King's Men he had a professional interest in identifying new writers. A few years earlier he had worked "in friendly collusion and competition" with John Marston (Duncan-Jones 2001: 208); soon after completing *Pericles* he began collaborating with his eventual successor, John Fletcher. It is not surprising, then, that he might have proposed a joint project to George Wilkins, an apparently promising younger writer. Wilkins had recently written *The Miseries of Enforced Marriage* for Shakespeare's company, as well as collaborating on plays for the Children of the Revels and for the Queen's Men.[4] This is the normal portrait of a freelance dramatist, employed by a variety of companies and "making it" by having a play of his own produced by the leading players of London. Though Wilkins later deteriorated, in 1607–8 the King's Men had no reason to think of him as an "unscrupulous petty criminal" (Wells and Taylor 1997: 558).[5] Shakespeare knew Wilkins personally because he frequented the same house in which Shakespeare had lodgings in 1604 "and perhaps for a time before and after" (Schoenbaum 1975: 208). Flatteringly, the aspirant writer's earlier work had been heavily influenced by Shakespeare's own.[6]

The collaboration is easy to imagine. One night Shakespeare chats with Wilkins, whose work suggests a continuing interest in the history of the Mediterranean, about travel tales.[7] Shakespeare had used bits of the familiar story of Apollonius of Tyre as the frame for his *Comedy of Errors*, and the two men sketch out a full play on the Apollonius legend. Indeed, Shakespeare does much of the sketching, because the play he envisions reiterates elements of his earlier writing and, apparently, his recurrent psychological concerns: separation of husband and wife, conflicted attitudes toward paternal power in family and state, shipwreck, the seeming death of women. Echoing *King Lear*, *Macbeth*, and *Coriolanus* – the last possibly written alongside *Pericles* – are the redemptive daughter, the murderous queen, and the famine. The play is to be built around repeated father–daughter relationships and structured in narrative sections separated by choruses; these will be spoken by Gower, whose tomb Shakespeare had recently seen in St. Saviour's (now Southwark Cathedral), where Edmund was buried. Shakespeare sends Wilkins off to begin; precisely why he took over at act 3 we will never know, but Georgio Melchiori proposes a somewhat similar history for *Edward III*, Shakespeare at first participating in "plotting" a collaborative work, and then becoming sole author of one section.[8]

But collaboration by itself will not account for the state of *Pericles* or for its gaps in plot and motivation. Wilkins may have been a hack writer, but as *Miseries* shows, he was competent. The playtext printed in 1609 is instead at many points incoherent. Not only is a substantial amount of the verse printed as prose, but lines and occasionally whole passages make little sense. Emendations are themselves often uncertain and contested. Key issues of interpretation depend on disputable textual interventions. For example, leaving his child with Dionyza and Cleon, Pericles promises that "till she be maried . . . All vnsisterd shall this heyre of mine remayne, / Though I shew will in't" (E4v). Is he promising, as seems confirmed in the final scene when he says "now this ornament makes mee looke dismall, will I clip to forme, and what this fourteene yeeres no razer touch't, to grace thy marridge-day, Ile beautifie" (I3r), that he will leave his hair "unscissored" and show "ill" until Marina marries? Or is he promising, like Leontes in *The Winter's Tale*, that Marina will remain "unsistered," that he will "live without an heir, if that which is lost be not found" (*WT* 3.2.134)? Similarly, in the final chorus summarizing the fate of the characters, Gower recounts that "For wicked *Cleon* and his wife, when Fame / Had spred his cursed deede, the honor'd name / Of *Pericles*, to rage the Cittie turne" (I3v). In early modern law murder was one of the crimes for which a married woman, a *feme covert*, could be held responsible apart from her husband. Is Cleon blamed because silent concealment of his wife's actions constitutes a "deed"? Or is Q4 (1619) correct to emend to "their" deed?

It is easier to deconstruct the proposals that have been made to account for the state of *Pericles* than to support them. These proposals include a text reported, perhaps surreptitiously by one or two actors (Taylor 1986), perhaps openly by a group of King's Men putting together a performance text (Gurr 1999: 72, 85); a shorthand version, either by a scribe taking dictation from a group of actors or by someone who, as happened in Spain, took notes in the playhouse, but in either case with mistaken expansion of the shorthand explaining the errors (Davidson 1992); particularly "foul" papers, that is, a difficult-to-read rough draft sent to the printer (DelVecchio and Hammond 1998). All these theories are open to attack: Laurie Maguire (1996), analyzing the playtexts suspected of memorial reconstruction, classifies *Pericles* as a dubious case, supported only by its "wrecked verse" (pp. 294–5); most textual critics do not believe any system of shorthand available in England could have produced full playtexts; the very concept of foul papers has been dismissed as "essentially metaphysical" (Werstine 1996). In any case the Quarto was printed in two different printing shops by three compositors of varying expertise and competence (Edwards 1952), and apparently one entire signature, B, had to be redone.[9]

It seems entirely plausible that the surviving text of *Pericles*, published by Henry Gosson without registration in 1609, is not the one entered by Edward Blount in the

Stationers' Register on May 20, 1608. Blount, who later participated in the printing of the Folio, never published the play, and may have lost or misplaced his text. Or, on the contrary, the bad text may have been his and he could have ceded it to Gosson without entering the transfer. From July 1608 through January 1610 the theatres were closed by plague: Leeds Barroll (1991) suggests that both Wilkins's novella, *The Painfull Adventures of Pericles Prince of Tyre*, which claims to be "the true History of the Play of *Pericles*, as it was lately presented by the worthy and ancient Poet John Gower" (1608), and eventually the Quarto were published to meet the desires of a public wanting information about "this unseeable and vastly popular drama" (p. 197). If, in the confusion attending a long plague closing, the text had gone missing, a few of the King's Men might well have cobbled together a text, either officially or clandestinely; some sort of report remains the simplest way to account for the peculiarities of the play's confusions and aural errors. Equally uncertain is why Shakespeare permitted this inadequate Quarto, published with his name on the title page, to remain uncorrected and without competition from a better text: it could have been indifference to bad theatrical texts, another period of mourning (his mother died in September 1608), absence from London during the theatre closings, or absorption in other projects.[10] In a related uncertainty, Blount and Jaggard may have eventually omitted *Pericles* from the Folio because they thought the text too bad, too "maimed, and deformed by the frauds and stealthes of injurious impostors" (Heminge and Condell, "To the great Variety of Readers"), or they may have considered it too extensively collaborated to claim as Shakespeare's.

Attempts to clarify the text and the characters' motivations by examining the sources only multiply uncertainties. The *Historia Apollonii*, from which *Pericles* derives, was widely disseminated: Elizabeth Archibald (1991) mentions 114 Latin manuscripts from the ninth to the seventeenth centuries, and vernacular versions all over Europe. The presence of Gower suggests that the play's primary source was that poet's *Confessio Amantis* (1393). There the tale forms the bulk and climax of Book VIII, on "loves lust" or unlawful love. Yet much of the play derives from Laurence Twine's *Pattern of Painefull Adventures*, entered in the Stationers' Register in 1576 but surviving only in editions from circa 1594 and 1607. The latter publication may have been the stimulus for Shakespeare returning to the story. Twine in turn depended for his version on the 153rd story in the Latin *Gesta Romanorum* of the fourteenth century. Further complicating matters is Wilkins's *Painfull Adventures*, with its claim to be not source but report. Wilkins's version varies considerably from the Quarto, sometimes merely by plagiarizing from Twine, at other points, as in the brothel scene between Marina and Lysimachus, providing new speeches and different motivations. The precise intertextual relation of play and novella remains much debated: possibilities include that Wilkins followed a version that was later changed (Muir 1960: 72–4); that Wilkins did not have access to a text and, for the second part of the play which was entirely by Shakespeare, was driven to copy Twine (Wells and Taylor 1997: 557–8); or simply that, free of time and staging constraints, Wilkins modified and expanded as he liked.

Pericles is a sort of limit case for the hermeneutic difficulties and opportunities offered by all of Shakespeare's plays. Jonathan Bate (1998) has argued that "one of the major characteristics of Shakespeare's handling of his sources is a removal of obvious motivation," that his characters, rather than "the fixed entities they tend to be in his sources . . . are the embodiments of the fluidity, the *play*, of emotion" (pp. 146, 151). In a Shakespearean universe whose laws are "aspectuality" and "performativity," Bate suggests that "a vacuum is created in the space which belongs to motive; spectators and readers rush in to fill that vacuum, thus performing their own versions" (p. 332). The vacuum is especially large in *Pericles*. Gower promises to "stand i' th' gaps to teach you / The stages of our story" (4.4.8–9), but these gaps stubbornly remain. Despite Bate's implication that such openness is intentional, for *Pericles*, which is short but not suspiciously so,[11] the gaps have consistently been treated as textual deficiencies requiring intervention and expansion. As early as George Lillo's 1738 *Marina*, plot and motive were rationalized. Lillo adapted only the last three acts and restructured them as a straight female rivalry between Marina and Philoten, Dionyza's "sole daughter," who has become queen after the death of "fond Parents." Lillo sorted out the confusion between unsistered and unscissored and clarified such matters as Pericles' long absence and Thaisa's failure to search for her husband once she is rescued and revived.

Criticism of *Pericles* has followed in Lillo's footsteps, sometimes by looking at what isn't there (Mullaney (1988) builds his interpretation on the occlusion of "mercantile traces" in the source story, part of the play's "radical effort to dissociate the popular stage from its cultural contexts" (pp. 139, 147)); and sometimes at what is (e.g., music and tempests, for G. Wilson Knight (1947) the structuring symbols of Shakespearean romance). Earlier criticism concentrated on the hero and his simultaneous journeys through life and the Mediterranean, or examined the play as preparation for the other three romances (Frye 1965). New historical scholarship has paid attention to the lacunae in the hero's rule or to Pericles' similarities to James I (Jordan 1997; Bergeron 1985; Palfrey 1997). Psychoanalytic criticism has usually focused on Pericles (Kahn 1980; Adelman 1992; Nevo 1987), but some feminist scholarship has looked at Marina (Helms 1997) or at the family unit of Pericles, Thaisa, and Marina (Barber 1969; Neely 1985).

Little notice has been taken of Cleon and his invisible daughter. Yet tracing out relations within the Tarsian family illuminates the play and complicates judgments about its central concerns. For example, the opening incest between Antiochus and his daughter has led interpreters of *Pericles* to see the play as structured against the dangers of excessive sexual love. For C. L. Barber (1969), "where regular comedy deals with freeing sexuality from the ties of family, these late romances deal with freeing family ties from the threat of sexual degradation" (p. 61); for Ruth Nevo (1987), "the progress of the play is the haunting of Pericles by the Antiochus in himself, the incest fear which he must repress and from which he must flee" (p. 42). Richard McCabe (1993) summarizes that "*Pericles* constitutes the most forthright contribution to the drama of father–daughter incest since the medieval *Dux Moraud* . . . the final act is carefully designed as the thematic obverse of the first, and the gradual progress from damnation to redemption is meticulously executed" (p. 180). But Dionyza's murderous favoritism extends the forms of excessive love beyond the sexual. Her feelings may be immediately evident when she replies to Pericles' request to "make me blessed in your care / In bringing up my child." Her reassurance, "I have one myself / Who shall not be more dear to my respect / Than yours, my lord" (3.3.32–5), is untrustworthy, as an awkward pause after "myself" and a pointed glance from Cleon may clarify. The language of preference suggests precisely the possibility that she denies.

More importantly, to justify her actions Dionyza charges her husband not with excess but with failure to love, or to love enough. Although she refers only to Cleon and Philoten, "you not your child well loving" articulates and generalizes the form family failure takes in *Pericles*. Not loving a child, whether foster or natural, is the unforgivable action on which the play is built and to which it repeatedly returns. Incest, important as it is, is a variant, the point at which loving too well is the same as not loving well enough. The issue unites both halves of the play and is handled by both authors, yet another sign that the play was planned collaboratively.

Cleon's deficiency is not isolated. The absent parent is the play's earliest family description, preceding the introduction of Pericles, though foreshadowing his, and his daughter's, later experience – "This king [Antiochus] unto him took a fere / Who died and left a female heir" (1.0.21–2). Images of lethal contest between the generations recur: in famished Tarsus, "Those mothers who, to nuzzle up their babes, / Thought nought too curious, are ready now / To eat those little darlings whom they loved" (1.4.42–4); the riddle posed to suitors identifies Antiochus' incestuous daughter as "an eater of her mother's flesh"; Boult, hawking the captured Marina's charms, describes the eager attention of the "younger sort" who "listened to me as they would have harkened to their father's testament" (4.2.90–2).

Recent research on the family has served as a corrective to Lawrence Stone's contention that a lack of warmth and affect was the accepted early modern norm. Historians such as David Cressy, Linda Pollock, and Ralph Houlbrooke have convincingly demonstrated that "Far from there being a paucity of emotional warmth in these families . . . their emotional lives" were "complex and intense, especially affected by grieving and loving" (Cressy 1999: 10). Anthony Fletcher (1995) finds "plenty of evidence . . . that most mothers and many fathers were deeply involved with and strongly attached to their children"; many men were "far from remote from their children" (pp. 188–9).

Pericles, when we first see him, seems adrift, without family. No mother is mentioned, and throughout the play the hero is in search of a father – one of his earliest claims is that he "would be son to great Antiochus" (1.1.27).[12] Like Hamlet, Pericles remembers his father as splendid and remote. Sitting at Simonides' court he observes:

> Yon king's to me like to my father's picture,
> Which tells me in that glory once he was,
> Had princes sit like stars about his throne,
> And he the sun for them to reverence.

> None that beheld him, but like lesser lights
> Did vail their crowns to his supremacy;
> Where now his son's like a glow-worm in the night,
> The which hath fire in darkness, none in light. (2.3.37–44).

But his first mention of his father, though obscured by a textual crux, instead describes an intimate family scene. Examining the rusty armor pulled in by the fishermen, Pericles calls it

>   mine owne part of my heritage,
> Which my dead Father did bequeath to me,
> With this strict charge euen as he left his life,
> Keepe it my *Perycles*, it hath been a Shield
> Twixt me and death, and poynted to this brayse,
> For that it saued me, keepe it in like necessitie:
> The which the Gods protect thee, Fame may defend thee. (C3v; 2.1.119–25)

The best emendation of the last two lines is: "For that it saved me, keep it; in like necessity, / The which the Gods protect thee from, may't defend thee." Unlike Volumnia, who relishes Coriolanus' wounds, the king of Tyre here remembered hopes to protect his son not abstractly, by fame, but concretely by the family armor, standing metonymically for the sustaining love of the family itself.

The armor comes to Pericles just as he finds the first of his substitute fathers in the first fisherman. Identified by the other fishermen as "Master," this presumably older man is horrified when Pericles, calling himself "a man thronged up with cold," requests, "For that I am a man, pray see me buried." Like a good parent the fisherman immediately offers food, clothing, shelter, and encouragement: "Die, quotha? Now gods forbid't, an I have a gown here! Come, put it on, keep thee warm. Now afore me, a handsome fellow! Come, thou shalt go home, and we'll have flesh for holidays, fish for fasting-days, and moreo'er puddings and flapjacks, and thou shalt be welcome" (2.1.71–81). This fisherman anticipates the Old Shepherd of *The Winter's Tale*, who saves the abandoned babe Perdita after a similar storm and then fathers her; Shakespeare was willing to build on Wilkins's foundations.

Pericles himself is a dubious father. Gower asserts that his daughter is "all his life's delight" (4.4.12), but Pericles' failure to contact or visit Marina surprises not only modern readers, accustomed to easy transport and frequent communication, but, in both Twine and Wilkins, Dionyza, who notes that in fourteen years "we have not received so much as a Letter, to signifie that he remembers her, or any other token, to manifest he hath a desire to acknowledge her, whereby I have reason to conjecture, that he is either surely dead, or not regardes her" (Wilkins, in Bullough 1966: 527). Significantly, Wilkins adds the latter possibility; in Twine, Dionyza concludes only that silence indicates death. The play offers no explanation for Pericles' long absence, yet it is apparently also the only version in which Marina grows up aware of her identity and thus, implicitly, of her real father's silence. It is certainly possible that

Pericles finds it difficult to love or even be with the child whom he may unconsciously blame for his wife's death, or who he fears will remind him of her. In the storm during which Marina is born he is stunned by Lychorida's order to "Take in your arms this piece / Of your dead queen" (3.1.17–18), a nightmare version of a midwife's traditional formula presenting the newborn child, "Father, see there is your child, God give you much joy with it" (Cressy 1999: 62). His first address to his daughter repeatedly conflates loss with happiness:

> Now, mild may be thy life!
> For a more blusterous birth had never babe;
> Quiet and gentle thy conditions, for
> Thou art the rudeliest welcome to this world
> That ever was prince's child. Happy what follows!
> Thou hast as chiding a nativity
> As fire, air, water, earth and heaven can make
> To herald thee from the womb.
> Even at the first thy loss is more than can
> Thy portage quit, with all thou canst find here.
> Now the good gods throw their best eyes upon't! (3.1.27–37)

Stage action may emphasize his ambivalence. Pericles instructs Lychorida to "Lay the babe / Upon the pillow" while he says "A priestly farewell" to his apparently dead wife (3.1.67–9). According to Jacob Rueff's *The Expert Midwife* (1637), "the child being washed and wrapped . . . must be laid by his mother, lying in her bed" (quoted in Cressy 1999: 81). A touching stage picture would be created if the babe were laid on a pillow next to the mother she has presumably lost, yet the image could suggest that on some level she is as dead to Pericles as is his queen. When mother and child both died in the birth they were usually buried together.

Critics divide about whether Pericles' absence or inattention is responsible for Marina's sufferings. Even the new historicists who find analogies of family and state in the romances disagree. Constance Jordan (1997) refers to his "tenuous attachment to Marina" and blames Pericles for leaving her with Cleon, calling it a consequence of "misplaced confidence" comparable to his abandonment of his people in the face of possible invasion (pp. 62, 47). Simon Palfrey (1997), on the other hand, sees his leaving Marina in Tarsus as a symbol of "symbiotically responsive public estates" (p. 70). In a more traditional reading, F. D. Hoeniger (1963) excuses Pericles, an "impeccably good man," from responsibility because the course of his life "is shaped mainly by Providence and only secondarily by his human contacts and his own actions" (lxxx–lxxxi).

Pericles' ambiguous relation to his child is embodied in a symbolic gesture about which the text is, as usual, unclear, and about which the sources, as often, suggest something that may or may not have become part of the play. At the beginning of the great recognition scene (5.1) Pericles is finally aroused from his withdrawn mourning by the unrecognized Marina's greeting, "Haile sir, my Lord lend eare." His reply is almost inarticulate: "Hum, ha" (H3v). Later, however, Pericles acknowledges that the grunts were accompanied by action: "when I did push thee backe, which was when I perceiu'd thee" (H4r). How violent was this "push"? In Gower "hir with his honde / He smote" (ll. 1701–3); in Twine, he "stroke the maiden on the face with his foote, so that shee fell to the ground, and the bloud gushed plentifully out of her cheekes" (Bullough 1966: 466–7). Wilkins omits the blood, but still has Pericles strike Marina on the face (ibid: 543). A violent push, even if not with the foot, even if without blood, will communicate hostility. Marina herself protests, "if you did know my parentage / You would not do me violence" (5.1.95–6).

Parental love is never entirely unmitigated in the play until the final reunion. The weak attachment to his child of which Cleon's wife accuses him parallels his failure to provide for his people. Learning that ships have been sighted, Cleon thinks immediately of himself, assuming "Some neighbouring nation, / . . . Hath stuffed the hollow vessels with their power / To beat us down . . . And make a conquest of unhappy me" (1.4.65–9). Even Simonides, unlike Antiochus and Cleon an apparently "good father," may not be entirely beneficent. The uncertainty is buried in another textual crux. When he receives a letter from his daughter Thaisa announcing "Shee'le wedde the stranger Knight, / Or neuer more to view nor day nor light," Simonides comments, in the Quarto text, "T'is well Mistris, your choyce agrees with mine: / I like that well: nay how absolute she's in't" (D3v). If this is punctuated " 'Tis well, mistress. Your choice agrees with mine. I like that well," it simply means "good, we agree." But if the Quarto is followed more closely and the line is punctuated, " 'Tis well, mistress, your choice agrees with mine. I like that well," that is, "it's a good thing *that* your choice agrees with mine," Simonides becomes more menacing, implicitly suggesting what might have happened had they disagreed. The distinction is important at an historical moment when there was debate about parental control of marital choice and in a play in which three fathers are involved in arrangements for their daughters. Simonides later stages a mock demonstration of what could have happened if Thaisa's choice had not agreed with his (2.5.22–82). Though he is ultimately revealed as testing and teasing, the threat is present.

Marina suffers, it seems, a double failure of love, first from her apparently indifferent father – the phrase with which she finally announces her identity, "I am the daughter to King Pericles, if good King Pericles be" (5.1.174–5), ambiguously queries both her father's existence and his virtue – and then from her foster family. Feminist and new historical critics have noted that the separated families in three of Shakespeare's late romances mirror, in various ways, the early modern outplacement of upper-class children, usually for wetnursing. Marianne Novy (2000) suggests that *Pericles* explores the conflicting claims of nature and nurture in the raising of children and ties the play's popularity to the fact that the occasion for the disastrous loss of the child was such "ordinary behavior" (p. 246).

Yet in the early seventeenth century the outplacement of children was not simply taken for granted, even in the upper classes. Not only were there the first glimmerings of a movement for aristocratic women to nurse their own children (*The Countesse*

of Lincolnes Nurserie, 1622; see Mendelson and Crawford 1998), but there could be disagreement, as there was between Robert Sidney and his wife, about whether to keep
adolescent daughters and sons at home or to send them to other households for further
training. Separation from children was a very public cause of contention between King
James and Queen Anne. She had refused to come to England until she could reclaim
Prince Henry from the Earl of Mar, with whom his father had insisted he be placed
shortly after birth. At the time of *Pericles* Anne was eager to have her surviving
children with her. In 1606 and again in 1607 she had had an infant daughter die. In
1608 her only remaining daughter, Princess Elizabeth, who had been sent away at
three months and once in England had again lived in another family, finally came to
court.

In *Pericles* Marina's experience is neither typical nor paradigmatic. The three other
aristocratic young women – daughters of Antiochus, Cleon, and Simonides – are all
"bred" at home. The justifications offered for placing Marina with the Tarsians are
two: first, once his wife "dies" Pericles orders "make for Tarsus! . . . for the babe /
Cannot hold out to Tyrus. There I'll leave it / At careful nursing" (3.1.77–9). This is
the argument from necessity in an age without artificial baby formula. But a year
later, as he departs alone for Tyre, Pericles makes a different request of his hosts:
"Beseeching you to give her princely training, / That she may be mannered as she is
born" (3.3.16–17). It is this "training" which provides the opportunity for one of the
possible complications of fostering, sibling rivalry or preference.

In concluding that *Pericles* "clearly poses evil foster parents against good biological parents" (p. 239) Novy (2000) says nothing about the neglected biological daughter of Cleon and Dionyza. Philoten is known to the audience only in the constructions
of Gower and her mother; the existing text never calls for the girl's appearance on
stage.[13] But in a striking example of performance as interpretation/appropriation, in
the summer of 1999 at the Ashland, Oregon Shakespeare Festival, the two girls
appeared together while Gower described their relationship:

> This maid
> Hight Philoten, and it is said
> For certain in our story she
> Would ever with Marina be,
> Be't when they weaved the sleided silk
> With fingers long, small, white as milk,
> Or when she would with sharp nee'le wound
> The cambric which she made more sound
> By hurting it, or when to th' lute
> She sung, and made the night bird mute
> That still records with moan, or when
> She would with rich and constant pen
> Vail to her mistress Dian; still
> This Philoten contends in skill
> With absolute Marina. (4.0.17–31)

The Ashland Philoten, rather than contending, mutely demonstrated affectionate desire to "ever with Marina be." Emphasis fell upon the girls' effective sisterhood, as in the description of Helena and Hermia in *A Midsummer Night's Dream* and Emilia and Flavina in *Two Noble Kinsmen*. This feminist interpretation worked against the male voice of authority in Gower and climaxed during 4.3, when Philoten mutely eavesdropped on her mother's account to Cleon of Marina's death. Dionyza stood before a mirror making up her face, symbolizing the narcissistic motivation of her hatred of Marina, whose "excellent complexion . . . did steal / The eyes of young and old" (4.1.39–40). Philoten, listening, became increasingly horrified as she realized that her mother's justification for murder was her own inferiority. The scene ended with her running off, weeping.

It is not unreasonable to fill one of the gaps in *Pericles* by accepting Dionyza's accusation of her husband's preference for the more talented foster child. Gower describes Marina as "by Cleon trained / In music's letters, who hath gained / Of education all the grace / Which makes her both the heart and place / Of general wonder" (4.0.7–11). Music is first in Marina's list of the accomplishments she will use to support herself outside the brothel (4.5.185–6); she demonstrates her skill when she sings to Pericles. Nevertheless she herself reports that "cruel Cleon, with his wicked wife, / Did seek to murder me" (5.1.167–8). A similar change of attitude occurs in *Cymbeline*, where the gentlemen describe the history of Posthumus as a case of aristocratic fostering: his father

> quit being; and his gentle lady,
> Big of this gentleman (our theme) deceas'd
> As he was born. The king he takes the babe
> To his protection, calls him Posthumus Leonatus,
> Breeds him, and makes him of his bed-chamber,
> Puts to him all the learnings that his time
> Could make him the receiver of. (1.1.38–44)

Like Marina, Posthumus has a mother dead in childbirth, is educated in another royal family, and becomes dearly loved by his "sister" – "Sir, / It is your fault that I have lov'd Posthumus: / You bred him as my playfellow" (1.2.74–6). Dionyza sets the pattern for Cymbeline's queen, and Marina, like Posthumus, loses her foster father's protection when she overshadows a "child" with more claim to be a "real" member of the family – Imogen "mightst have had the sole son of my queen!" (1.2.69). The unloving Cleon's "wicked deed" not only endangers Marina but destroys his own innocent daughter – "him and his they in his palace burn" (5.3.99) – as Cymbeline's error endangers Posthumus and Imogen. Not to love a child, foster or natural, is unforgivable and potentially irremediable.

The unloving foster family in Tarsus is parodied by Marina's second outplacement in the brothel. On stage the Bawd and her husband the Pander frequently double Dionyza and Cleon, and before Marina ever arrives we learn the Bawd's history as a foster mother. Reminded by the Pander that there is a "conscience to be used in every trade," the Bawd self-righteously agrees, "Thou sayst true. 'Tis not our bringing up of poor bastards, as I think I have brought up some eleven –" but their man Boult interrupts with a more cynical view of her charity: "Ay, to eleven, and brought them down again –" (4.2.11–15). These "bastards," presumably the children of the brothel's prostitutes, supply the constant need for "fresh ones" in a trade which rapidly consumes its offerings: "We have but poor three, and they can do no more than they can do, and with continual action they are even as good as rotten" (4.2.6–9). To the Bawd, Marina is a "dish of chastity" to be devoured in the "way of womankind" (4.5.152–3). "Bringing down" implies more than sexual initiation; it may mean becoming "pitifully sodden," like the brothel's other "creatures" (4.2.6–18). As Margaret Healy (1999) points out, "For early modern playgoers child prostitution and syphilis were very real and allied diseases" (p. 96). Marina seems unable to escape the world of murderous substitute mothers, women who know, in the emendation of yet another crux, that "to foster is not ever to preserve" (4.3.15; see Gossett forthcoming).

Despite the uncertain lines and the possibly incomplete text, the recognition scene between Pericles and Marina is one of the most moving in all of Shakespeare, a slow reawakening to life and joy. The reunion with Thaisa is, necessarily, sketchy and more rapid. Some have seen these proportions as experimental, or erroneous, especially as they are reversed in *The Winter's Tale*, where the "finding" of Perdita is reported and the climactic reanimation of Hermione is staged. Yet the end of *Pericles* seems calculated to keep the primary focus on appropriate parental love rather than on restored marital happiness. That the purpose is to clarify the psychological trajectory is suggested by Shakespeare and Wilkins's elimination of two characters they found in their sources: the daughter of Athanagoras/Lysimachus and the son that Apollonius/Pericles and his wife have after their reunion.

In Twine the governor Athanagorus allows Tharsia/Marina to preserve her virginity for two reasons: "surely I rue thy case, and I my selfe have also a daughter at home, to whome I doubt that the like chances may befall." This unnamed daughter is repeatedly mentioned, Athanagoras promising to keep secret what Tharsia has told him "unlesse I tell it unto my daughter, that she may take heede when she commeth unto the like yeares, that she fall not into the like mishappe" (Bullough 1966: 457). Even when Tharsia is freed from the brothel, Athanagoras "had evermore a speciall regard in the preservation of her virginitie, none otherwise than if she had been his owne daughter" (ibid: 459). The play's authors must have realized that the insistent equation of the daughter and the young heroine meant that Tharsia/Marina's eventual marriage to the governor would once again elide father and lover; psychologically and symbolically the play would end where it began, in intergenerational incest.[14] Shakespeare avoided a similar danger in *The Winter's Tale* by adding to his source, Robert Greene's *Pandosto*, the return of Hermione and repressing almost, though not completely, the motif of the hero's incestuous attraction to his unrecognized daughter.

A later child of Thaisa and Pericles is most obviously eliminated for structural reasons: both the play and the plot conclude with the double restoration, the finding of that which was lost. In all the late romances the central figure gains a new son through the marriage of his daughter. The motif is clearest in *The Winter's Tale*, which unlike the others includes a really dead child and insists that Florizel becomes for Leontes the replacement for Mamillius, "What might I have been / Might I a son and daughter now have look'd on, / Such goodly things as you!" (5.1.175–7). Generally, as Carol Neely (1985) writes, the "reestablishment of the bond between parent and child and the acknowledgment of the powerful physical connection between them overshadows in the romances the sexual union – or reunion – of husband and wife, who are 'one flesh' only symbolically and by means of their children" (pp. 175–6). Janet Adelman (1992), more radically, sees the absence of more children as the final repression of the threatening female sexual body (pp. 196–8). But in *Pericles* there is an additional motive. The late introduction of a new (male) child would once again displace Marina through sibling competition. She is the child Pericles needs to love well; no other is needed. "Our son and daughter shall in Tyrus reign" (5.3.83).

Recently there has been a renewed acceptance, from diverse theoretical positions, for what Richard Wheeler (2001) calls "giving the life record a place in our under-standing of [Shakespeare's] texts" (p. 131). In Wheeler's hands biographical criticism is concerned not merely with "direct response" to the outward events of life but with the unconscious fantasies those events breed and the textual "inflections that might register such a response" (p. 140). His example is the way Shakespeare's plays in the period after the death of his only son Hamnet work through that experience, overtly in *King John* but most suggestively in *Twelfth Night*, where the quasi-magical power of a young woman to transform herself into a young man may manifest the drama-tist's unconscious desire that his surviving daughter Judith become her lost twin. "In the dream logic of *Twelfth Night*, Viola is the twin who, by making herself identical to her brother, permits the lost brother to return to life . . . What releases the comic action from mourning is that magic moment when, in Janet Adelman's formulation, Viola . . . 'splits . . . into male and female components' . . . The recovery of the male twin meets a need – completes a fantasy driven by that need – that makes it possi-ble for the play's desires to be fulfilled" (p. 149).

Wheeler notes that Shakespeare does not return "to the motif of the lost-and-recovered child . . . until he puts it at the center of the action in *Pericles*, which appears to have been performed some months before Shakespeare's mother died in September 1608" (p. 153). A more likely biographical stimulus for the reappearance of the motif was Susanna Shakespeare Hall's pregnancy through the fall and winter of 1607–8, that is, during the planning and writing of *Pericles*. (Elizabeth Hall was baptized on February 21, 1608.)[15] Here was reason to fear the loss of another child. In all four of the last romances mothers die in, or shortly after, childbirth. The research of Roger Schofield (1986) has corrected excessively high estimates for such deaths:[16] as Cressy (1999) summarizes, "9.3 per 1,000 or just under 1 per cent of mothers died in childbed in Elizabethan England . . . It would be misleading to deduce . . . that childbed mortality was common. In fact the opposite is true. Most women survived childbirth without complications and most mothers quickly recovered. Childbirth . . . emphatically had more to do with life than with death." Yet "one does not need actuarial precision to be frightened" (pp. 30–1). Mendelson and Crawford (1998) claim that "During every pregnancy, each woman feared her own death" (p. 152). While we do not know how long Hamnet was ill before he died or where his father was, whether Shakespeare suffered weeks in anxiety or was shocked with sudden misfortune in 1596, he may well have spent fall and winter 1607–8 fearing a second loss.

That fear would certainly have been compounded when, in the seventh month of Susanna's pregnancy, Shakespeare's younger brother Edmund died. Duncan-Jones (2001) suggests that after the death of little Hamnet Edmund may have become more like "an adopted son than a brother," in whom Shakespeare invested "his deepest hopes for posterity" (p. 199). It is hard not to see the long mourning embodied in Pericles' almost catatonic withdrawal after his second blow, the loss of Marina, as a projection of Shakespeare's own feelings and experiences. Excessive mourning was well recognized as dangerous – Pericles is reduced to an animal-like condition, abstaining from food, cleanliness, and human contact – but "despite the conceit that death entailed release, and despite the powerful hope that the departed had gone ahead to heaven, immediate survivors often experienced convulsions of grief" (Cressy 1999: 393). In Shakespeare's plays those who inveigh against "unprofitable woe," as Dionyza does when Marina mourns Lychorida's death (4.1.24), often merely express their own hard hearts and sinfulness. Dionyza is preceded by Claudius and Gertrude.

Yet unlike Cordelia and Mamillius, both "gone forever," Marina survives. Perhaps the years between *Twelfth Night* and *Pericles*, between the death of Hamnet and the death of Edmund, had brought Shakespeare to a new realization: the new child to long for was not his own but his daughter's, another reason for eliminating Apollonius' late-in-life son. Like the king whose man he was, and whose life his so frequently shadowed, by 1607 Shakespeare must have known that there would be no more children to replace the one who had died. But unlike that king, he seems not to have abandoned his daughters but to have turned back towards them.[17] The conclusion of *Pericles* is not the transformation of the surviving daughter into the lost son but the well loving of the female child at the end of long separation or indifference. The shape of the play demands that we accept the brothel-going Lysimachus' conversion into an acceptable son-in-law and assume that the betrothal will secure generations of rulers for Tyre and Pentapolis.[18] The fantasy of transformation becomes an anticipation of grandchildren. The splitting to which *Pericles* looks forward is that of mother and child.

NOTES

1   All modernized citations of *Pericles* are from the forthcoming Arden three edition, ed. Suzanne Gossett. All other citations from Shakespeare are to the most recent Arden edition.

2   The play was seen by the Venetian ambassador Zorzi Giustinian with the French ambassador La Broderie and his wife, who is first known to have joined him in England in April 1607 (Hoeniger 1963: lxiv, n. 3). The theatres were closed because of plague for all of 1607 except one week in April; they did not reopen until April 1608 and in July 1608 closed again through January

1610 (Barroll 1991: figure 1, p. 173). The play was entered in the Stationer's Register in May 1608.

3   See Wells and Taylor (1997: 128–30) and Barroll (1991: 169–71), for views on the dating of *Macbeth, Antony and Cleopatra*, and *King Lear.*

4   *Miseries*, based on the Calverley murders, was popular enough to receive three printings in 1607, 1611, and 1629. In the years immediately preceding *Pericles* Wilkins had written *Law Tricks* with John Day for the Children of the Revels (published 1608) and *The Travails of Three English Brothers* with Day and Rowley for the Queen's Men (published 1607).

5   Prior (1972: 144) notes that in the compressed period, roughly 1608–10, when Wilkins was writing and publishing, he does not appear in the various court records and there are no indications of his future criminality, though Eccles (1975: 250) shows in 1602 Wilkins was enjoined by the court to keep the peace towards one Richard Story.

6   A major character of *Travails* copies Shylock, and Rudnytsky (1999) claims that *Miseries* is "pervasively indebted to *King Lear* as well as to *Twelfth Night*" (p. 304). If Shakespeare had something to do with *The Yorkshire Tragedy* (or with the four plays of which it formed one part), Wilkins's elaboration of the Calverley story in *Miseries* may indicate his again following the established dramatist's lead.

7   Besides *The Painfull Adventures of Pericles Prince of Tyre* and *Travails*, Wilkins's work includes a largely plagiarized translation of *The history of Iustine* (1606) and *Three Miseries of Barbary* (1606 or 1607).

8   In *Edward III* Shakespeare "contributed in some measure, in conjunction with other more or less experienced script-writers, to the first stages" of outlining and writing, and "took over completely in the last stage." His "hand as collaborator can be detected in many scenes of the play, but his sole authorship of at least Act 2 is undeniable" (Melchiori 1998: 16–17).

9   I discuss the textual complexities and editorial theories more fully in Gossett (forthcoming).

10 Duncan-Jones (2001) suggests that he prepared the sonnets for publication in 1609, hoping to gain a reward similar to that which followed *Venus and Adonis* during an earlier plague closing (p. 214).

11 Maguire (1996) does not consider its length, which she gives as 2,358 overall, 2,271 dialogue, as suspicious (p. 294), but Gurr (1999: 85–6) is less sure. Shakespeare's late plays tend to be long, but while *Cymbeline* is one of the longest, *The Tempest* is shorter than all the others except *The Comedy of Errors.*

12 Nevo (1987), reading Pericles psychoanalytically, sees him as in the grip of "oedipal guilt," fleeing "a powerful potential enemy," a "father-figure," and seeking "a symbolic personage representing the mother, lost and forbidden" (pp. 42–53). Kahn (1980) claims that the recurrent father-figures Pericles encounters "represent his continuing difficulty in resolving his image of the father and his position in relation to him" (p. 231).

13 Philoten was included in the list of "actors' names" appended to the first appearance of *Pericles* in a Shakespeare folio, the second issue of F3 in 1664.

14 Fiedler (1972) claims that the logic of the Apollonius myth demands that in the brothel the heroine be confronted by her father without recognition. "Only in this way can the pattern be fulfilled: the deliberate incest avoided in one generation accomplished unwittingly in the next. Shakespeare, however, characteristically shies away from this, splitting the second-generation father into Pericles and Lysimachus, as he had the first-generation father into Antiochus and Simonides" (p. 219).

15 Richard Wilson (1993) also suggests the relevance of the pregnancy to *Pericles*, but his concern is the way the romances "license maternity" to male doctors. "From the first Shakespearean scene of this text the discursive function of the romances is revealed, then, to be the Harveian project of separating childbirth from those wayward sisters already demonised in tragedy . . . the mother's body is salvaged when it is removed from the perils of the women's room and transferred to the safety of the clinic" (p. 176).

16 Wilson (1993) follows the earlier work of McLaren for his statistic of 25 of 1,000 women dying in childbirth, with mortality higher "in time of plague and famine, the scenario of *Pericles*" (p. 176).

17 Once Princess Elizabeth married, in 1613, and left for the Continent, she never saw her father again.

James was widely criticized for failing to assist her after her husband Frederick was expelled from Bohemia.

18 Adelman (1992) disagrees, arguing that "literal begetting is not part of the celebratory design" and that "the rather hugger-mugger betrothal . . . carries . . . no hint of heirs to rule in Tyre" (p. 198).

REFERENCES AND FURTHER READING

Adelman, J. (1992). *Suffocating Mothers*. New York: Routledge.

Archibald, E. (1991). *Apollonius of Tyre: Medieval and Renaissance Themes and Variations*. Cambridge: D. S. Brewer.

Barber, C. L. (1969). "Thou that beget'st him that did thee beget": Transformation in *Pericles* and *The Winter's Tale*. *Shakespeare Survey*, 22, 59–67.

Barroll, L. (1991). *Politics, Plague, and Shakespeare's Theater: The Stuart Years*. Ithaca, NY: Cornell University Press.

Bate, J. (1998). *The Genius of Shakespeare*. New York: Oxford University Press.

Bergeron, D. (1985). *Shakespeare's Romances and the Royal Family*. Lawrence: University Press of Kansas.

Bullough, G. (1966). *Narrative and Dramatic Sources of Shakespeare*, Vol. 6. London: Routledge and Kegan Paul. Includes Gower Twine, and Wilkins.

Clinton, E. (1622). *The Countesse of Lincolnes Nurserie*.

Cressy, D. (1999). *Birth, Marriage & Death: Ritual, Religion, and the Life-Cycle in Tudor and Stuart England*. Oxford: Oxford University Press.

Davidson, A. (1992). Shakespeare and Stenography Reconsidered. *Analytical and Enumerative Bibliography*, ns 6, 77–100.

DelVecchio, D. and Hammond, A. (eds.) (1998). *Pericles*. Cambridge: Cambridge University Press.

Duncan-Jones, K. (2001). *Ungentle Shakespeare*. London: Arden.

Eccles, M. (1975). George Wilkins. *Notes and Queries*, 220, 250–2.

Edwards, P. (1952). An Approach to the Problem of *Pericles*. *Shakespeare Survey*, 5, 25–49.

Fiedler, L. (1972). *The Stranger in Shakespeare*. New York: Stein and Day.

Fletcher, A. (1995). *Gender, Sex and Subordination in England 1500–1800*. New Haven, CT: Yale University Press.

Frye, N. (1965). *A Natural Perspective: The Development of Shakespearean Comedy and Romance*. New York: Columbia University Press.

Gossett, S. (forthcoming). "To foster is not ever to preserve": Feminist Inflections in Editing *Pericles*. In A. Thompson and G. McMullan (eds.) *Editing Shakespeare: A Festschrift for Richard Proudfoot*. London: Arden.

Gurr, A. (1999). Maximal and Minimal Texts: Shakespeare versus the Globe. *Shakespeare Survey*, 52, 68–87.

Healy, M. (1999). Pericles and the Pox. In J. Richards and J. Knowles (eds.) *Shakespeare's Late Plays: New Readings*. Edinburgh: Edinburgh University Press, 92–107.

Helms, L. (1997). *Seneca by Candlelight and Other Stories of Renaissance Drama*. Philadelphia: University of Pennsylvania Press.

Hoeniger, F. D. (ed.) (1963). *Pericles*. London: Methuen.

Houlbrooke, R. (1984). *The English Family, 1450–1700*. London: Longman.

Jackson, M. P. (1990). *Pericles*, Acts I and II: New Evidence for George Wilkins. *Notes and Queries*, 235, 192–6.

——— (1993). Rhyming in *Pericles*: More Evidence for Dual Authorship. *Studies in Bibliography*, 46, 239–49.

Jordan, C. (1997). *Shakespeare's Monarchies: Ruler and Subject in the Romances*. Ithaca, NY: Cornell University Press.

Kahn, C. (1980). The Providential Tempest and the Shakespearean Family. In M. Schwarz and C. Kahn (eds.) *Representing Shakespeare*. Baltimore, MD: Johns Hopkins University Press, 217–43.

Knight, G. W. (1947). *The Crown of Life: Essays in Interpretation of Shakespeare's Final Plays*. Oxford: Oxford University Press.

Lake, D. (1969a). Rhymes in *Pericles*. *Notes and Queries*, 214, 139–43.

——(1969b). Wilkins and "Pericles" – vocabulary. *Notes and Queries*, 214, 288–91.

McCabe, R. (1993). *Incest, Drama and Nature's Law 1550–1700*. Cambridge: Cambridge University Press.

Maguire, L. E. (1996). *Shakespearean Suspect Texts: The "Bad" Quartos and their Contexts*. Cambridge: Cambridge University Press.

Melchiori, G. (ed.) (1998). *King Edward III*. Cambridge: Cambridge University Press.

Mendelson, S. and Crawford, P. (1998). *Women in Early Modern England*. Oxford: Clarendon Press.

Muir, K. (1960). *Shakespeare as Collaborator*. London: Methuen.

Mullaney, S. (1988). *The Place of the Stage: License, Play, and Power in Renaissance England*. Chicago, IL: University of Chicago Press.

Neely, C. (1985). *Broken Nuptials in Shakespeare's Plays*. New Haven, CT: Yale University Press.

Nevo, R. (1987). *Shakespeare's Other Language*. New York: Methuen.

Novy, M. (2000). Multiple Parenting in *Pericles*. In D. Skeele (ed.) *Pericles: Critical Essays*. New York: Garland, 238–48.

Palfrey, S. (1997). *Late Shakespeare: A New World of Words*. Oxford: Clarendon Press.

Pollock, L. A. (1983). *Forgotten Children: Parent–Child Relations from 1500 to 1900*. Cambridge: Cambridge University Press.

Prior, R. (1972). The Life of George Wilkins. *Shakespeare Survey*, 25, 137–52.

Rudnytsky, P. (1999). "The darke and vicious place": The Dread of the Vagina in *King Lear*. *Modern Philology*, 96, 291–311.

Schoenbaum, S. (1975). *Shakespeare: A Documentary Life*. New York: Oxford University Press.

Schofield, R. (1986). Did the Mothers Really Die? Three Centuries of Maternal Mortality in "The World We Have Lost." In L. Bonfield, R. M. Smith, and K. Wrightson (eds.) *The World We Have Gained: Histories of Population and Social Structure*. Oxford: Blackwell, 231–60.

Taylor, G. (1986). The Transmission *of Pericles*. *Papers of the Bibliographical Society of America*, 80, 193–217.

Wells, S. and Taylor, G. (1997). *William Shakespeare: A Textual Companion*. New York: Norton.

Werstine, P. (1996). Editing After the End of Editing. *Shakespeare Studies*, 24, 47–54.

Wheeler, R. (2001). Deaths in the Family. *Shakespeare Quarterly*, 51, 127–53.

Wilson, R. (1993). *Will Power: Essays on Shakespearean Authority*. Detroit, MI: Wayne State University Press.

19
"Imagine Me, Gentle Spectators": Iconomachy and *The Winter's Tale*
Marion O'Connor

As its title advertises, *The Winter's Tale* is no play for all seasons. Convincingly argued to have been written early in 1611, the play was certainly performed at the Globe on May 15, 1611, when Simon Forman recorded having seen it there, and again at court on November 5, 1611, when the King's Men were paid for performing it before their patron (Barroll 1991: 199–207; Orgel 1996: 233, 80). Perhaps because the fact and the location of at least some of its early performances have been known to scholarship since 1821 (Furness 1964: 313), and probably also because its staging requirements, though few, are so peculiar, studies of *The Winter's Tale* as theatre have long acknowledged its historical specificity, even when they analyzed formal features which were taken to transcend time (Coghill 1958; Ewbank 1964; Wickham 1972; Bergeron 1978; Leech 1978; Batholomeusz 1982; Gurr 1983; Ewbank 1989). And late in the twentieth century, studies of *The Winter's Tale* as drama read the play in relation to a range of cultural phenomena more or less contemporaneous with it: Italian Renaissance sculpture (Barkan 1981); English Renaissance sculpture (Smith 1985); Cartesian skepticism (Cavell 1987: 195–221); Elizabethan attacks on the stage (Lamb 1989); relations among King James I, his second parliament, and Salisbury (Kurland 1991); early modern gynecology and upper-class infant care (Paster 1993: 215–80); Elizabethan folklore, festivals, and almanacs (Bristol 1991); Jacobean political ideology (Morse 1991); Tudor vagrancy narratives and social legislation (Mowat 1994); Continental Renaissance aesthetic theory (Sokol 1994); and Jacobean domesticity (Belsey 1999: 85–127).

Most of these large topoi impinge upon the small, but stormy, discursive space in which this essay is particularly interested and in which it will situate *The Winter's Tale*, particularly its culminating scene – English Reformation iconomachy. This is not to say that this or any other Shakespearean play will, or should, be read for evidence of Shakespeare's opinions on theological questions and ecclesiastical issues, let alone his personal allegiance. Nor is it to construe the play as some dramatic allegory of any version of Christian theological doctrine. It is, however, to say that *The Winter's*

Tale yields evidence of Shakespeare's awareness of the implications (which included dramatic potential) of an argument ongoing throughout his life. That argument finally concerns representation in general, but it was articulated in religious language, and the positions taken on it were inflected by confessional loyalties. As Cavell noted some years before questions of Shakespeare's beliefs grabbed headlines, "Religion is Shakespeare's pervasive, hence invisible, business" (Cavell 1987: 218). And as a later section will make clear, it was also a going concern of other dramatists of his time.

Iconoclasm, construed as the physical defacement or destruction of religious images, particularly three-dimensional ones, crashed through English ecclesiastical buildings in successive waves for more than a century from 1536 (Aston 1988, 1996; Duffy 1992; Phillips 1973). In the sixteenth century, breakage became particularly heavy whenever the crown changed the tune to which all were required to dance: in 1538 after Henry VIII, in the second set of Royal Injunctions which he issued in his self-proclaimed capacity as Head of the Church in England, gave an order which could be construed as commanding the destruction of religious images venerated in churches; in 1547 after Edward VI's first Royal Injunctions extended the iconoclastic hit list to include *all* religious images in churches *and* private households; and in 1559 when iconoclasts undertook preemptive strikes in the months between Mary I's death and Elizabeth I's religious settlement. As a rule, the more hallowed an image had been, the more it was targeted. The verisimilitude which had once made three-dimensional images likely to attract devotional veneration, now rendered them especially vulnerable to iconoclastic attention (Aston 1988: 401). Among some sensational accounts in the 1530s there were reported discoveries of mechanical frauds – anticipating Dorothy's discovery in *The Wizard of Oz* – whereby images had appeared to fix eyes upon the beholder, turn their heads, and lift their limbs. The most notorious contraption of this kind was exposed in 1538. The Cistercian monastery at Boxley in Kent housed a crucifix, made of wood, wire, paste, and paper, on which the figure of Jesus was said to be able to

> bow down and lifte up it selfe, to shake and stirre the handes and feete, to nod the head, to rolle the eies, to wag the chaps, to bende the browes, and finally to represent to the eie, both the proper motion of each member of the body, and also a lively, expresse, and significant shew of a well contented or displeased minde: byting the lippe, and gathering a frowning, froward, and disdainful face, when it would pretend offence: and shewing a most milde, amyable, and smyling cheere and countenance, when it woulde seeme to be well pleased. So that now it needed not Prometheus fire to make it a lively man, but onely the helpe of the covetous Priestes . . . to deifie and make it passe for a verie God. (Lambarde 1596: 228, sig. P7ᵛ)

In the same monastery a stone statue of St. Rumwald tested the condition of pilgrims' souls as they came from confession of sins: only a penitent who could shift the statue was in a state of grace, so immobility was embarrassing. The statue's movement, however, was controlled by the priests through a mechanism concealed at its back:

And therefore, the matter was so handled, that without treble oblation . . . first to the Confessour, then to Sainct Rumwald, and lastly to the Gracious Roode, the poore Pilgrimes could not assure themselves of any good . . . No more than such as goe to Paris-gardein, the Bell Savage, or Theatre, to beholde Beare baiting, Enterludes, or Fence play, can account of any pleasant spectacle, unlesse they first pay one pennie at the gate, another at the entrie of the Scaffolde, and the thirde for a quiet standing. (Ibid: 233, sig. O2^r)[1]

Theatrical analogies were observed elsewhere. A 1623 compendium of anti-Roman anecdotes presents mainly Continental material to its English readers, but a section "Concerning coozening deuices" opens with insular examples:

Are not yet men liuing, that can remember the knauerie of Priests to make the Roodes and Images of the Churches in England in the dayes of Queen Mary, to goggle with their eyes, and shake their hands: yea, with Wiers to bend the whole body, and many times to speake as they doe in Puppet playes, and all to get money, and deceiue the ignorant people? (Goad 1623: sig. B2^v)

In 1537 iconoclasts at the priory of St. Mary in Worcester even uncovered something like theatrical crossdressing among the icons: divested of the rich robes in which late-medieval statues were arrayed, Our Lady of Worcester turned out to be an anonymous bishop. The reporter of the statuesque transvestism at Worcester shrugged it off: "The similitude of this is no worse to pray unto . . . than it was before" (Phillips 1973: 75, citing *Letters and Papers of Henry VIII*, XII.ii, 587).[2] Embedded in this understatement are the hooks from which hung the iconoclasts' principal objections to religious images: (1) worship and (2) similitude.

The primary objection to images was that they were being prayed unto: whoever the Worcester statue was supposed to represent, whether Our Lady or His Grace, to use it thus was to abuse it. To pray to images, kneel to them, kiss them, light candles before them, adorn them in rich garments and jewels, or hang votive offerings on them – all this was worship and thus idolatry. That idolatry was forbidden by the Judaeo-Christian decalogue, the list of commandments which the Old Testament books of Exodus and Deuteronomy present as divine law, was uncontentious. What was contested – within ancient and medieval Christian tradition, by Reformers, and then within Protestantism – was the question of just what the prohibition covered.[3] Much depended on the definition of what constituted worship, and the identification of whom that worship addressed. Conservative doctrine (1) distinguished two levels of honor, one (*dulia* or veneration) proper to saints and one (*latria* or adoration) proper to God; (2) insisted that honor was not addressed to the things but referred to the persons, human or divine, whom they represented (Phillips 1973: 15–7, 43–8) – not to the signifier but to the signified; (3) invoked the educative role of visual signs in the indoctrination of the illiterate and their emotive and/or mnemonic role in the devotions even of the learned. The first point on this list was dismissed as a "lewde distinction" (Stuart 1616: fol. 53^r / sig. Gg7^r). The third was initially conceded as principle, but increasingly condemned as practice (save by monarchs in their own private chapels) for reasons which also exploded the conservatives' second point. Precisely because images were physically attractive and emotionally affective, they were perniciously seductive, diverting attention unto themselves and away from God. The official Elizabethan Homily Against Idolatry urges "this lesson of the experience of ancient antiquity . . . that . . . as a shadowe followeth the body when the sunne shyneth, so Idolatry followeth and cleaveth to the publique havyng of Images in Temples and Churches" (*Certaine Sermons* 1563: fol. 65 / sig. Ii3).[4]

The Reformers' second level of objection to images was more radical than the first. Regardless of use, religious images were deemed idolatrous merely because they were similitudes, representations of that which could not or should not be represented. The initial and least extreme stage in this objection was to protest at any image of God, pure spirit whom no image-maker had ever seen. So much for God the Father as old man with white beard. But other things followed, as in this passage from the third part of the Elizabethan Homily Against Idolatry:

> no image can be made of Christ, but a lying Image . . . For Christ is God and man. Seing therfore, that of the Godhead . . . no Image can be made, it is falsely called the Image of Christ. Wherfore images of Christ be not only defectes but also lyes. Whiche reason serveth also for the Images of Saintes, whose soules . . . can by no images be presented and expressed. Wherfore they be no Images of Saintes, whose soules raigne in joy with God, but of the bodies of Saintes, which as yet lie putrified in the graves. Furthermore, no true Image can be made of Christ's body, for it is unknowen now of what fourme and countenaunce he was . . . Wherefore, assoone as an Image of Christ is made, by and by is a lye made of him, which by god's word is forbidden. Whiche also is true of the Images of any Saintes for antiquity, for that it is unknowen of what fourme and countenaunce they were. Wherefore seying that religion ought to be grounded upon trueth, images whiche can not be without lyes, ought not to be made, or put to any vse of religion, or to be placed in Churches and Temples, places peculierly appoynted to true religion and service of God. (Ibid: sig. A5)

In disallowing that spirit might be figured in matter, and in denying that whatever has not been seen can ever be truly imaged, such reasoning takes two giant steps down the path to rejecting all representation. The Elizabethan homilist, however, tries to draw a line in the shifting argumentative sands by emphasizing that his prohibition pertains only to religious images:

> For we are not so superstitious, or scrupulous, that we do abhorre eyther flowers wrought in carpettes, hangynges, and other arras, either Images of Princes, prynted or stamped in theyr coynes . . . neyther do we condemn the artes of payntying and ymage-making, as wicked of themselves. But we woulde admit and grant . . . that Images used for no religion, or superstition rather, we mean images of none worshipped, nor in danger to be worshipped of any, may be suffered. But Images placed publiquely in Temples can not possibly bee without daunger of worshipping and Idolatry, wherefore they are not publiquely to be had or suffred in Temples and Churches. (Ibid: fol. 47 / sig. Gg1)

In an examplary Anglican compromise, the homilist has here retreated from rejecting images as untrue and returned to rejecting them as abused. Yet he has left the way clear for the Laputan Academicians who, in Part III of Jonathan Swift's *Gulliver's Travels*, propose a scheme whereby they would express themselves with things rather than words. That is, further pursuit of the truth of similitudes risks a rejection of all forms of representation, verbal as well as visual. This implication was picked up by conservatives like Stephen Gardiner, who argued that if graven images could be reviled as sticks and stones, then books could equally be dismissed as "cloutes and pitch" – rags for paper and tar for ink – and that if anything should be rejected as a graven image, it was printers' type (Gardiner 1933: 274, 258). The iconoclasts could not push their case to the point at which it would have undermined its own basis in scripture. Despite ample and recent evidence of uncertainty in the transmission, translation, and transparency of Judaeo-Christian sacred texts, the word of God was privileged on its own authority. Biblical texts displaced most visual images in English churches, and Elizabethan English Christianity became a religion of words centred on the Word. The 1563 homilist records this change within "An Information for them which take offence at certain Places of the Holy Scripture":

> Christes image made in wood, stone, or mettall, some men for the love they beare to Christ, do garnishe and beautifie the same wyth Pearle, Gold, and precious stone. And shold we not . . . much rather embrace and reverence Goddes holye bokes, the sacred Bybble, which do represent Christe unto us more truely than can any Image? The Ymage can but express the form or shape of his body, if it can do so much, but the Scripture doeth in suche sorte sette foorth Christ, that we maye see hym both God and man. (*Certaine Sermons* 1563: fol. 169ʳ / sig Yy1ʳ)

The point is rather more pithily put by Reginald Scot in his 1584 *The Discoverie of Witchcraft*: "Now that the word of GOD hath appeared . . . sights, spirits and mockeries of images are ceased" (Scot 1930: 87).

As Scot's interest suggests, iconoclastic argument, particularly the rejection of images as false worship, connected with ideas about witchcraft. According to English laws passed in 1542 (33 Henry VIII, chapter 8), 1563 (5 Elizabeth I, chapter 16) and 1604 (1 James I, chapter 12), the crime of witchcraft combined (1) *maleficia*, i.e., evil-doings to other people, usually by harming their persons and/or their property, and (2) conjuration, summoning up spirits. The first was anti-social and the second was a(nti-)theistic. The relative emphasis between them changed across the successive statutes, as did the penalties. Both in learned treatises about witchcraft and in popular accounts of particular cases, images were presented as possible paraphernalia for *maleficia*: an image of the witch's human victim might be modeled (usually in wax, which was cheap, malleable, and flammable), stuck with pins or bristles (usually in the anatomical area on which the curse centered), and then buried or burned.[5] Although the aim could be sexual fascination (deemed malevolent because temptation to sin), the intention was more often murderous, and image magic could even be used *against* a witch (Scot 1930: 46–7). However, since figurines were not indispensable equipment for *maleficia*, this link between images and witchcraft was accidental. The essential connection was made via conjuration. To summon spirits was to worship false gods: witchcraft was idolatry. Image worship was also idolatry. Therefore witchcraft was image worship, and image worship was witchcraft. The logical fallacy may be obvious, but a quick slide across an undistributed middle is an important means for manufacturing propaganda.

Prophecy was another plum embedded in the ideological pudding of the Reformers' first and second commandments. Divine prohibition of idolatry obviously extended to pagan oracles, "which," according to Scot, "for the most part were idols of silver, gold, wood, stones, &c." As throughout *The Discoverie of Witchcraft*, this hard-headed jurist proposes rational explanation, without reference to supernatural forces, for the apparent operation of pagan idols and fulfillment of their prophecies. Whoever was behind them, their game was up:

> and whatsoever hath affinitie with such miraculous actions, as witchcraft, conjuration, &c is knocked on the head, and nailed on the crosse with Christ, who hath broken the power of divels, and satisfied Gods justice, who also hath troden them under his feete, & subdued them . . . If anie one remained, I would ride five hundred miles to see it: but in the whole world there is not one to be seene at this houre; popish cousenages excepted. (Scot 1930: 92)

By the time Scot was writing, of course, even papist cousenages were becoming matters of memory in England: "Our Rood of grace, with the help of little *S. Rumball*, was not inferior to the idoll of *Apollo*" (ibid: 78).

The onstage deployment of statues in Elizabethan and Jacobean drama was informed by the Reformation rejection of religious images as objects of false worship, and their association not just with Roman Catholicism, but also – through the elastic concept of idolatry – with witchcraft and with pagan divinities and their oracles. Across the stage directions in the texts of some 500 plays written for the English professional theatre between 1580 and 1642, statues are required for ten plays (Dessen and Thomson 1999: 214, 119). Four of these plays antedate *The Winter's Tale*, and five are rather later (1620–35), as is Francis Bacon's mention of "statuas mouing" among the features of antimasques.[6] Most of the statues are either Roman Catholic religious images or classical pagan ones. As will be seen, Lyly's *The Woman in the Moon* represents a partial exception to this rule, and *The Winter's Tale* represents a complete exception to it. The massed entry direction at the beginning of 5.3 of Shakespeare's play includes "*Hermione (like a Statue)*".[7] Among the ten statuesque plays from 1580 to 1642, Shakespeare's play is also unusual in that the stage direction refers to a "statue," which appears in no other stage direction save a single direction in one of the manuscripts of Middleton's *A Game at Chess* (1624).[8] In the other eight plays stage directions call for "images." Yet in these, too, it is clear that what they require is the particular kind of image on which accusations of false worship were centered – a statue.[9] The eponymous heroes of Anthony Munday's *Fedele and Fortunio* (1584/5) are both suitors to one Victoria, as is a braggart soldier named Crackstone. The lady having transferred her affections from devoted Fedele to unresponsive Fortunio, Victoria's maid Attilia procures the amorous assistance of an enchantress named Medusa. When this spell-binder unpacks her box of aphrodisiacs, Victoria's eye is caught by

> the image of a man, made out in virgin wax,
> Which being pricked or toasted in the flame of burning flax,
> He that you love shall come and throw himself before your feet (398–400)

Attilia agrees: "This is it must do my mistress good: / By images it must be wrought; love is a holy rood" (402–3). The next scene but one is set in a chapel, to which the three women, "*with lighted tapers in their hands*," come at "almost one o'clock, the fittest hour to bind the sprites" (498). Conjuration centers on the waxen image, which must be fairly large since it bears the names of ten spirits. It gets further inscribed with Victoria's and Fortunio's names before being partly melted and applied to Victoria, then cooled and pricked with a needle. The women's necromantic activity has two unseen observers: one is Fedele's erstwhile instructor Pedante, whose asides cap Medusa's very Continental invocations of spirits ("Nettabor, Temptator, Vigilator, Somniator, Astarot, Berliche, / Buffon, Amachon, Suchon, Sustani, Asmodeus": 583–4) with a litany of English bogeymen ("Ottomanus, Sophy, Turk, and the Great Cham: / Robin Goodfellow, Hobgobin, the Devil and his Dam": 585–6). The other scopophiliac at the scene is Crackstone, concealed in a tomb: when the women, with explicitly incendiary intent, throw their candles into the captain's hiding place, he stands up, holding the candles. Frightened, the women drop the image and flee, as does Pedante. Crackstone takes up the image. In the next scene the image serves to disabuse Fedele of his faith in Victoria, whom he threatens with moral opprobrium and physical violence. Ultimately, and via an unsurprisingly intricate route, *Fedele and Fortunio* comes to the usual comic conclusion: multiple marriages. Even Pedante and Medusa are paired off to open a co-educational grammar school. Their pedagogic project is one of the many insular variations which *Fedele and Fortunio* makes upon its Italian original, *Il Fedele* (1576).[10] Around the image, and especially in the conjuring scene where it figures so prominently, the changes emphasize the setting as Roman Catholic and therefore superstitious. Thus in *Il Fedele* the women arrive "dressed as maid-servants" ("*vestite da serve*") and invent a cover story "that we are virtuous women and that we are going about some good deed" ("che fossimo santuccie, & ch'andassimo à far qualche bene": sig. C4ʳ of 1576 edition, reproduced in Munday 1981: 82); but in *Fedele and Fortunio* they are "*disguised as nuns*" and propose that "unto the church we swarm . . . we will make as though we meant to pray" (Munday 1981; stage direction before 495, 504–5). And where in *Il Fedele* the women flee because they mistake a man rising from a tomb and holding candles for a ghost, in *Fedele and Fortunio* they take him – who is required to have a candle in mouth as well as in hand – for the Devil.

The title page of the earliest text of *Fedele and Fortunio*, a 1585 Quarto, advertises the play as having "beene presented before the Queenes moste excellent Maiestie." The same claim to have been "presented before her highnesse," is also made on the title page of the 1597 Quarto imprint of John Lyly's *The Woman in the Moon* (reproduced in Lyly 1902: 239). The principal "image" required by Lyly's stage directions early in the first act is a full-scale human figure, fully clothed: Nature's attendants, Concord and Discord, *"draw the curtains from before Nature's shop, where stands an image clad, and some unclad; they bring forth the cloathed image"* (ibid: 1.1 stage direction before 57). This image, presented by a male actor wearing female costume, is at first genderless: Nature refers to "this lifelesse image" with neuter pronouns. Given movement by the embrace of Concord, he/it comes to life as she, her gender pronounced by Nature. Then, her tongue untied by Discord, the *Image speakes* obeisance to Nature, who in response confers her name: Pandora. Within sixty lines *She playes the vixen with every thing about her* (ibid: 1.1 stage direction after 176). Thus Pandora continues, influenced by successive divinities, until the final scene, when this animated statue achieves stasis in metamorphosis as the permanently changing Woman in the Moon. Pandora's most interesting moment occurs when, in 3.1, she is seized by a fit of palindromic prophecy. Of the two Apollonian oracles which she utters backwards and forwards, in Latin, one sustains a single sense either way; but the other can be construed in two opposed senses, and this semantic ambiguity becomes obvious when predication is reversed. Such are the vagaries of Latin syntax, classical divinities, and pagan prophecies: even unreliability is unreliable.

Thomas Dekker's *The Whore of Babylon* (printed 1607) begins with a dumb show which allegorizes the reign of Mary I, and then the accession of her half-sister Elizabeth I, in terms of the fortunes of Time and his daughter Truth. They present the Bible ("*a Booke*") to Elizabeth (figured as Titania). Truth and Time exit only to "*returne presently, driuing before them . . . Cardinals, Friers &c. . . . with Images, Croziar staues &c.*" (Dekker 1955: 500). In the second act the King of Spain consults a Conjuror for some image magic against the queen. This "slaue well moulded / In profound, learned villany" produces "*Titaniaes* picture right" – his intended victim's effigy:[11]

> *Conjuror.*   This virgin waxe,
> Burie I will in slimie putred ground,
> Where it may peece-meale rot: As this consumes,
> So shall shee pine, and (after languor) die.
> These pinnes shall sticke like daggers to her heart,
> And eating through her breast, turne there to gripings,
> Crampt-like Convulsions, shrinking vp her nerues,
> As into this they eate.
> *3. King.*   Thou art fam'd for euer,
> If these thy holy labours well succeed,
> Statues of molten brasse shall reare thy name . . .
> Where wilt thou burie it?
> *Conjuror.*   On this dunghill.
> (2.2.168–77, 180)

Dirty work is disrupted by the timely arrivals of Truth and Time, plus a trio of Titania's counsellors who are backed up by a Guard. The Conjuror vanishes from the play: nothing more is seen of the waxen image used for *maleficium*, nor is anything further said of brass images promised for memorials. *The Whore of Babylon* is an elaborate allegory of Reformation politics decades before Dekker's play: of the several incidents which are condensed into its sequence of image magic, the best known had occurred in 1578.[12] Yet however backward-looking the play, the aggressively anti-Catholic tones of *The Whore of Babylon* – the clarity and certainty of its caricatures – were well in tune with the time of its publication, when the exposure of the Gunpowder Plot had enlarged the division between Anglican and Roman allegiance.

Mapping Reformation events onto a pagan setting, Beaumont and Fletcher's *Cupid's Revenge* (1607/8) presents iconoclasm as the occasion of a divine revenge tragedy. *Cupid's Revenge* urges the dire consequences of the denial of human sexuality. Its moral allegory of repression is figured in terms of an historical narrative of destruction. Hisdaspes and Leucippus, daughter and son of Leontius Duke of Licia, are convinced that the local cult of Cupid is

> A vaine and fruitlesse Superstition;
> So much more hatefull, that it beares the shew
> Of true Religion, and is nothing else
> But a selfe-pleasing bold lasciviousness
> (Beaumont and Fletcher 1970: 1.1.48–51)

Especially scandalized by statues of Cupid, they urge their father

> That these erected obsceane Images
> May be pluckt downe and burnt: and every man
> That offers to 'em any sacrifice
> May lose his life (1.1.74–8)

Leontius gives orders for the statues to be broken down, and his nephew Ismenus reluctantly complies: "Sir, I will breake downe none my selfe, but I will deliver your command: hand I will have none int, for I like it not" (1.1.93–4). Soon a stage direction requires the entrance of "one with an Image," and the response of a courtier indicates that this statue is on its way to destruction: "There he goes. Lord! This is a sacriledge I have not heard of" (1.1.139). The next scene enacts iconoclasm on a site signaled as sacred by the initial entrance of a "Priest of Cupid, with foure young men and Maydes." Their rites – singing, dancing, kissing, and token-giving – are curtailed by a court official:

> No more of this: here breake your Rights for ever,
> The Duke commands it so; Priest do not stare,
> I must deface your temple, though unwilling,
> And your god *Cupid* here must make a Scarcrow
> For any thing I know, or at the best

Adorne a Chimney-peece . . .
Take downe the Images and away with 'em.
Priest change your coat you had best, all service now
Is given to men (1.2.35–44)

Cupid descends in the next scene to swear the revenge which the title of the play has
promised and which will occupy the rest of *Cupid's Revenge*. Leucippus outlives his
father and sister, but his own death is one of four that occur onstage in the last 100
lines. All four fatalities are wrought by stab wounds, visual statements of Cupid's
revenge. At point of death, Leucippus reverses his father's iconoclastic orders:

. . . Couzen *Ismenus*,
That shall be the Duke, I pray you let
The broken Image of *Cupid* be reedified,
I know all this is done by him.
Last, I beseech you that my Mother-in-Law
May have a buriall according to –
                                        Dyes. (5.4.214–20)

These earlier instances of onstage statues clearly provide a context of meanings for
the culminating scene of *The Winter's Tale*, and that context is strikingly correspon-
dent with some of the principal preoccupations of this Shakespearean play: idolatry,
prophecy, necromancy – forbidden representations all. Although commonly cited as
the "statue scene," the final scene of *The Winter's Tale* is more accurately designated
the "pseudo-statue scene," a qualification which keeps the crucial fiction in sight – as
Shakespeare does. One of the distinctions of the scene is the way in which theatrical
limitations are turned to dramatic advantage. Unfolding the dramatic discovery that
apparent stone is living flesh, Shakespeare exploits the theatrical impossibility of
living flesh appearing as stone. No performer can completely conceal, let alone
suspend, respiration or circulation, and immobility is difficult to sustain for more than
a few minutes. Anticipating audience observation and curiosity, the dialogue of *The
Winter's Tale* 5.3 draws attention to the signs of life which the Hermione actor is bound
to show, willy-nilly, and it suggests a succession of explanations. These dramatic
hypotheses reiterate the discursive slide whereby iconoclasts conflated the veneration
of religious images with witchcraft and prophecy.

By the final scene of *The Winter's Tale* Hermione has been effectively canonized, a
saint in all but name. At the end of the trial scene, after the successive reports of
Mamilius' death (true) and Hermione's (false), the suddenly repentant Leontes had
proposed to give his wife and son a shared tomb which would serve as a shrine for his
own devotional rites:

One grave shall be for both: Vpon them shall
The causes of their death appeare (vnto
Our shame perpetuall) once a day, Ile visit
The Chappell where they lye, and teares shed there

Shall be my recreation. So long as Nature
Will beare vp with this exercise, so long
I dayly vow to vse it. (288A)

The King's sepulchral project is never mentioned again: whether it has been completed, or whether it has been modified, even displaced, by Paulina's own architectural arrangements over the next 15 or 16 years of fictional time, is left open. That Leontes has carried out his penitential program, however, is clear from the opening of the last scene but one in *The Winter's Tale*, when Cleomenes tells Leontes that he has

> ... perform'd
>
> A Saint-like Sorrow: No fault could you make,
> Which you haue not redeem'd; indeed pay'd downe
> More penitence, then done trespas: At the last
> Doe, as the Heauens haue done; forget your euill,
> With them, forgiue your selfe.
> *Leontes.*   Whilest I remember
> Her, and her Vertues, I cannot forget
> My blemishes in them (298A–B)

Indeed, that moral symbiosis will never be forgot as long as Paulina is around to jog the royal memory:

> If one by one, you wedded all the World,
> Or from the All that are, tooke something good,
> To make a perfect Woman; she you kill'd
> Would be unparalll'd (298B)

The ensuing discussion of the possibility of a royal remarriage is conducted more in terms of Leontes' personal virtue than of his political responsibility; and even then, business of state gets sanctified.

The final scene of *The Winter's Tale* firmly designates its fictional space as a chapel (302B), but just as firmly indicates its proximity to a gallery (302A). The gallery is said to house Paulina's private collection of "many singularities," and the chapel is seen to contain a shrine. The courtiers set off "to see the Queenes Picture" (301B) and arrive to worship at the pseudo-statue of St. Hermione. Hermione stands behind a curtain such as served to protect paintings hanging on the walls of private houses, but she occupies a full-height space like a niche in a church or chapel wall.[13] Posed there, her figure would be legible both as the devotional image of a saint and as the monumental portrait of a deceased lady – the second superimposed upon the first. Either way, the figure signified something other, and more enduring, than the stone of a statue or the flesh of a human being. To beholders willing, and able, to follow this referral of meaning, the figure offered access to the transcendent: the image of a saint opens onto a community of belief across space and time, and the portrait of a lady opens onto a continuity of social and cultural elitism.

Thus when, in the final scene, the kings and their courtiers come to Paulina's chapel, they have come to see the similitude of a female saint, a "she [who] liu'd peere-lesse" (302A), with Paulina as priestess-like promoter of Hermione's cult and Leontes as cult devotee. Shakespeare makes Paulina take her time over showing her guests what they seek, and he makes them take even more time about reacting to what she shows them. The dialogue demands a very long pause after the drawing of the curtain ("behold, and say 'tis well. / I like your silence"); and several other lines invite similar punctuation in performance. The neophyte observer of what looks like image worship on stage is thereby given pause in which to wonder at that which Paulina displays and indeed to wonder about it. The dialogue not only guides perceptions – "Comes it not something neere?" – but it also implies explanations. Indeed, the sequence of perceptions and explanations actually follows the trajectory of iconomachic argument, from allowing religious images some value as mnemonic aids, to forbidding them as occasions of idolatry, to condemning them as diabolical inventions. Contemplating what he takes to be the image of his sainted wife, Leontes enacts the devout responses of a believer to a cult statue of a saint. He is instantly impressed by its verisimili-tude. He articulates its likeness, in the first place, to his memory of Hermione, and then, prompted by Paulina, to his projection of what she might now have looked like. (Its resemblance, in other words, is to his own devout imaginations.) At the same time, he also responds to the pseudo-statue as if it were directly addressing himself:

> *Leonies.*   Her naturall Posture.
> Chide me (deare Stone) that I may say indeed
> Thou art *Hermione*; or rather, thou art she,
> In thy not chiding: for she was as tender
> As Infancie, and Grace. But Yet (*Paulina*)
> *Hermione* was not so much wrinckled, nothing
> So aged as this seemes.
> *Polixenes.*   Oh, not by much.
> *Paulina.* So much the more our Caruers excellence
> Which lets goe-by some sixteene yeeres, and makes her
> As she liu'd now.
> *Leontes.*   As now she might have done,
> So much to my good comfort, as it is
> Now piercing to my Soule. (302A)

What Leontes proceeds to derive from this lifelike image is, in the first place, remem-brance of her whom he thinks it represents – the use of images deemed notionally acceptable but actually unsustainable. He takes the pseudo-statue as a reminder of Hermione's merits and thus also of his own failings:

> Oh, thus she stood,
> Euen with such Life of Maiestie (warme Life,
> As now it coldly stands) when first I woo'd her.
> I am asham'd: Do's not the Stone rebuke me,
> For being more Stone then it? (302A)

After this self-castigating question, Leontes' reactions step well beyond the pale of Reformed iconic doctrine: what he next perceives in the statue is beneficent supernatural power. Moreover, in voicing the effect of this grace upon him and Perdita, he uses the language of witchcraft. Instead of a magic in which a human being conjures up spirits to assist him in evil deeds, Leontes speaks of a magic which conjures up memories of the evil deeds already done, by himself, and which takes spirits out of human beings:

> There's Magick in thy Maiestie, which ha's
> My Euils coniur'd to remembrance; and
> From thy admiring Daughter tooke the Spirits,
> Standing like Stone with thee.

Perdita, however, shifts out of her stance of petrified astonishment into the posture and gestures of image worship. She kneels before the pseudo-statue. She speaks to it in prayer, and her terms of address are proper not so much to her own mother as to the Mother of God – "Lady, Dear Queen." She even attempts to venerate this madonna-minus-baby by kissing its hand:

> And give me leaue,
> And doe not say 'tis Superstition that
> I kneele, and then implore her Blessing. Lady,
> Deere Queene, that ended when I but began,
> Giue me that hand of yours, to kisse

Yet all this sanctimoniousness is also, and by the same tokens, somewhat sinister. Leontes hypothesizes reverse necromancy to explain the effect of the pseudo-statue upon himself and Perdita: black magic was commonly constructed as a diabolical parody of true religious worship, so his speech predicates a double negative. Perdita herself, in turn, rejects superstition as the significance of her apparently idolatrous actions. Idolatry being worship of false gods, Perdita too is made to voice a double negative. Through the reactions of Leontes and Perdita alike, Shakespeare pulls off the dramatist's equivalent to the classical rhetorician's trick of "negatio" or "apophasis" – a disclaimer which indicates a possibility by ostentatiously dismissing it. And since Anglican orthodoxy attributed Roman idolatry, like necromantic images, to "the suggestion of Sathan" (Stuart 1616: sig. Cc2), the possibility which is raised by Leontes' reaction to the pseudo-statue intersects with the possibility raised by Perdita's. Prompted by Paulina to perceive movement in that which she presents as inanimate stone, Leontes asks, parenthetically, "What was he that did make it?" The question, which goes unanswered here, is unsettling. Paulina's steward, AKA Gentleman 3, appears to have anticipated it in the immediately preceding scene, when he speaks of

> The Princesse . . . her Mothers Statue (which is in the keeping of *Paulina*) a Peece many yeeres in doing, and now newly perform'd by that rare Italian Master, *Iulio Romano*, who (had he himselfe Eternitie, and could put Breath into his Worke) would beguile Nature of her Custome, so perfectly he is her Ape: He so neere to *Hermione*, hath done *Hermione*, that they say one would speake to her, and stand in hope of answer. (301A)

"Had he himselfe Eternity," were he able to "put Breath into his Worke," then "that rare Italian Master" would be eternal creator: no longer Nature's ape, but God's rival.[14] Thus when Leontes follows his own question about the maker with observations that the image indeed appears to be alive ("Would you not deeme it breath'd? and that those veines / Did verily bear blood?"), and that its eyes appear to be following him ("The very fixure of her Eye ha's motion in't"), diabolical agency grows ever more obviously available as an explanation. Paulina finally spells out this possibility even as she raises the stakes:

>   Either forbeare,
> Quit presently the Chappell, or resolue you
> For more amazement: if you can behold it,
> Ile make the Statue move indeed; descend,
> And take you by the hand: but then you'le thinke
> (Which I protest against) I am assisted
> By wicked Powers.

The ostensible grounds which Paulina here gives for delay are well chosen. Leontes has been heard to lash her with accusations of witchcraft in the same scene (2.3) when he commanded that his wife and newborn daughter be burnt alive – the punishment of heresy and (on the Continent albeit not in England) of witchcraft as a species of heresy. That dispensation may, of course, be distant memory by this point in the play. Yet in a more amicable, and recent, exchange, Leontes and Paulina have each evoked the possibility of Hermione's soul reanimating her corpse. Leontes there, in 5.1, posited that a second wife, inferior to the first but better treated than her,

> . . . would make her Sainted Spirit
> Againe possesse her Corps, and on this Stage
> (Where we Offendors now appeare) Soule-vext,
> And . . . would incense me
> To murther her I marryed.
> *Paulina.*   I should so:
> Were I the Ghost that walk'd, Il'd bid you marke
> Her eye . . . then I'd shriek, that euen your eares

Should rift to heare me, and the words that follow'd
Should be, Remember mine (298B–299A)

The reminder that Paulina can be trusted to remain "a callat of boundless tongue" (285A) under any circumstances – even as someone else's ghost! – ensures that what is jointly imagined in this exchange is not wholly sinister. Moreover, Antigonus' report, back in 3.3, of his dream of Hermione has suggested that the queen needs no help with shrieking. And here in 5.1 the distorted echo of old King Hamlet's ghostly exhortation to his son discourages any simple gloss upon its implications. Yet however qualified, the undertone is threatening: Reformed opinion held that the souls of the dead did not return to life on earth, that such apparitions as were taken to be human ghosts were supernatural spirits, sometimes good but more often evil, and that their works would indicate whether they had come from God or from the devil (Lavater 1596). The Hermione ghost that Leontes and Paulina have imagined could never pass the moral litmus test, incitement to murder being amply sufficient grounds for failure. This nasty piece of imaginative work hovers over the conclusion of this exchange, when Paulina undertakes to find a second wife for Leontes:

> . . . she shall be such
> As (walk'd your first Queenes Ghost) it should take ioy
> To see her in your armes.
> *Leontes.*   My true *Paulina,*
> We shall not marry, till thou bidst vs.
> *Paulina.*   That
> Shall be when your first Queene's againe in breath:
> Neuer till then.
> > *Enter a Seruant* (299A)

The Servant has been brought on to change the topic of conversation by giving notice of the arrival of visitors from Bohemia. The interruption means that the last words on the subject of royal remarriage are Paulina's. Precisely because it is left unanswered and unexplained, Paulina's rejoinder echoes after its utterance. Moreover, what she has spoken is a statement of an apparently impossible condition for future action. As such, it functions as a prophecy. And when, in the next scene but one, the impossibility appears to occur, beholders are teased to wonder how Paulina's prediction has come to pass. It seems that the "first Queene's againe in breath": How comes this? What is that breath? An illusion wrought by the mysterious sculptor, perhaps, but Leontes eliminates that explanation with his rhetorical question, "What fine Chizzell / Could euer yet cut breath?" (302B). Or perhaps – given the longstanding association, both philosophical and iconographical, between breath and the soul – it is Hermione's ghost come back to earth? But since the souls of the dead cannot return, then it must be a spirit that is animating Hermione's image; and from both ideological presumption and the dramatic expectations raised in the last scene but one, such a spirit would be up to no good.

No wonder, then, that Paulina instructs the onstage audience to "awake [their] Faith" – the Reformed protection against all spiritual perils, including damnation – and that she demands the departure of "those that thinke it is vnlawfull Businesse / I am about." Paulina's indirect disavowal of illegitimacy imputes interpretations to her beholders. Like the speech with which Paulina unveiled the figure of Hermione, the speech by which Paulina cues the figure's descent is punctuated by pauses. The very fact that it does not get immediate results guarantees close attention:

> *Paulina.* Musick; awake her: Strike:
> 'Tis time: descend: be Stone no more: approach:
> Strike all that looke vpon with meruaile: Come:
> Ile fill your Graue vp: stirre: nay, come away:
> Bequeath to Death your numnesse: (for from him,
> Deare Life redeemes you) you perceiue she stirres: (302B)

Both Hermione's stasis and Paulina's syntax now start to tease: even as the speaker guides perceptions, she equivocates about explanations. Paulina asserts a direct proportion between legitimacy on her own part and sanctity on the pseudo-statue's: "Start not: her Actions shall be holy, as / You heare my Spell is lawfull" (302B). Alternative interpretations of the figure's animation are thus kept in play until the last possible moment. That moment comes when Leontes touches Hermione – contact which Paulina has earlier prevented by telling him, and Perdita before him, that "the Coulour's / Not dry" (302A) and "You'le marre it" (302B) – and finds that

> Oh, she's warme:
> If this be Magick, let it be an Art
> Lawfull as Eating. (302B–303A)

The conditional sentence hints, once again and for the last time, at the iconomachic argument within Christianity. For ears attuned to Reformation debate, Leontes' comparison carries an echo of that argument's abiding and overriding issue – the nature of the eucharist (Rubin 1991; Aston 1988: 6–9). Viewed anthropologically, the consecration of bread and wine looks like magic. Viewed artistically, the reenactment of Jesus's final meal with his apostles looks like theatre. Construing the eucharist from within the belief structure of Christianity, Roman Catholicism finds in it the Real Presence of Christ and Protestantism finds in it a memorial. But questions of Christian sacramental theology are warded off by Leontes' exclamation, "Oh, she's warme." Once the figure of Hermione is no longer perceived as an image but recognized as a living being, iconomachy loses its main mooring point within the dramatic fiction.

Yet that dramatic fiction has also touched on those radical implications of iconomachy which condemned theatre and challenged the mimetic substance of drama –

a matter of showing as well as telling. The living being who was warm onstage in 1611 was no "she" but an actor (a) posing as a queen and (b) standing still as stone through 100 lines of blank-verse dialogue. This visual double-cross invites consideration of the play with regard to the second level of Reformed objections to images as forbidden and false similitudes. Even within the dramatic fiction of *The Winter's Tale*, visual signification generally seems to be more treacherous than verbal. Leontes misreads the gestures of Hermione and Polixenes; Antigonus doubly misconstrues his dream – a *visio* – as evidence that Hermione has died and had been an adultress; and the Clown fooled by Autolycus' show of rags in 4.1 and in 5.2 hopes that his own new finery will fool others. By contrast, Apollo's oracle is altogether unequivocal, and its predictions, which include the death of Mamilius as well as the discovery of Perdita, all come to pass. Indeed, the wording of the oracle in Shakespeare's play is even less ambiguous and more explicit than it had been in his narrative source, Robert Greene's *Pandosto* ("Pandosto [is] treacherous; the babe is innocent" in *Pandosto* becoming "*Leontes* a iealous Tyrant, his innocent Babe truly begotten" in *The Winter's Tale*); and where Greene's Pandosto repents immediately on hearing the oracle, Shakespeare's deferment of Leontes' change of heart until after the news of Mamilius' death presses home the accuracy of the oracle (and/or the vindictiveness of Apollo). Even the Clown's account of Antigonus' death is trustworthy. His reporting style might never secure him a position with the BBC or CNN, but there is never any hint that the report is inaccurate or incomplete. During the penultimate scene of the play the Clown's story is reiterated in precis, and thereby confirmed, by Gentleman 3: Antigonus, he says,

> was torne to pieces with a Beare: This auouches the Shepheards Sonne; who ha's not onely his Innocence (which seemes much) to iustifie him, but a Hand-kerchief and Rings of his, that *Paulina* knowes (301A)

There too, in 5.2, Gentleman 3 gives a long account of the reunion of Leontes with Polixenes and of the recognition of Perdita. He is prompted to this narrative by Gentleman 1, who had been "present at this relation" for its beginning alone. Having then been evicted from the presence chamber, Gentleman 1 could only see, not hear, further developments:

> but the changes I perceiued in the King, and *Camillo*, were very Notes of admiration: they seem'd almost, with staring on one another, to teare the Cases of their Eyes. There was speech in their dumbnesse, Language in their very gesture: they look'd as they had heard of a World ransom'd, or one destroyed: a notable passion of Wonder appeared in them: but the wisest beholder, that knew no more but seeing, could not say, if th' importance were Ioy, or Sorrow; but in the extremitie of the one, it must needs be. (300B)

Considered as theatre, moreover, *The Winter's Tale* can be seen to play with the fact of visual signification. All of its spectacular junctures repay such consideration, but for sheer preposterousness the twin peaks of bear and baby are irresistible. Theatre historians' preoccupation with precisely what happened on stage at the Globe in May 1611, at the Whitehall Banqueting House in November 1611, and at five subsequent performances before King James's court, has recently been dismissed as critical slumming:

> The problem of the bear has been addressed primarily as a practical and contingent question of theater history, an aspect of the play as spectacle . . . By concentrating on how the bear was actually staged, however, rather than on why there is a bear at all, these discussions ignore the manifold symbolic functions of this device and its specific function as a significant marker of spatiotemporal form. (Bristol 1991: 159)

Yet the question of "how the bear was actually staged" does bear on "why there is a bear at all," and *a fortiori* on "the manifold symbolic functions of this device." *If* a real live bear is used to represent a real live bear, then it is questionable whether this device has any symbolic functions at all: the bear becomes a sign in which the signifier signifies only itself. Insofar as it is so construed, the possibility of any further significance is precluded. However, there is a crucial gap between the signifier (theatrical bear) and the signified (dramatic bear): the theatrical bear must be under control, the dramatic bear must appear to be out of control. Insofar as that difference has any symbolic function, it is to indicate that someone is in control – i.e., the audience will not be eaten, at least not on this occasion. (Any temptation to abstract this indication into overloaded antinomies of, for example, Art and Nature should be resisted.) On the other hand, if the bear was presented by an actor in a bear suit, then the gap between signifier and signified becomes a gulf, unbridgeable without more practice than *The Winter's Tale* 3.3 gives. Either way, the bear looks likely to have been a self-referential joke in 1611 and for however long thereafter that audiences relished *Mucedorus*.[15]

Whether ursine or human, a living being represented the dramatic bear in *The Winter's Tale*. When it and Antigonus make their exits, the one in pursuit of the other, they leave behind baby Perdita, a written statement of who she is, and clothing which confirms her exalted social status. *The Winter's Tale* pins a great deal on the little princess in this scene. On her identity (in the sense of parentage) depend the histories of two royal houses, that of Sicily and that of Bohemia. Making antiphonal drama out of two narrative crises, Shakespeare plotted both the near tragedy of the first half and the muted comedy of the second half around the issue of Perdita, to which the much-analyzed relationship between these dramatic halves draws attention (Schanzer 1964; Siemon 1974; Proudfoot 1976; Riemer 1987). A baby framed with such careful symmetry must be important. Dramatically speaking, the presence of Perdita is indeed everything at this point. Theatrically speaking, however, it is nothing at all. There is no baby. There is nobody on stage. The playing space has been depopulated – emptied of all but a bundle and/or basket. What makes the theatrical thing(s) into a dramatic baby is the word of Antigonus, "Blossom . . . there lye" (289A). A visual metaphor is addressed in verbal metaphor, and the command given to it is a pun which is pretty shameless even by Shakespearean standards.

Such a pun precludes even the notional possibility of *The Winter's Tale* being taken as a validation of Reformed logocentrism. Images may be less reliable than words in *The Winter's Tale*, but the difference is one of degree, not of kind. Verbal signification is not to be trusted either, not in a play which deploys dialogue of disturbing opacity, obscurity, and indeterminacy, and which recurrently mocks narratives as norms of implausibility (Felperin 1985). The caution of Gentleman 1 is one of the play's reminders that both words and images are languages, sign systems. Images may be the more difficult to interpret – particularly when they fall outside the interpreter's experience or expertise. (The Clown miscontrues clothes, but he makes no mistakes about bears. Polixenes appears unfamiliar with the semantics of rural Bohemian flower language, but this king reads the unspoken signs of royal Sicilian snub fluently enough.) Words, however, have no advantage of proximity to, let alone plenitude of, truth: they are part of a coordinated deception, one which people willingly purchase. In the scene of Perdita's abandonment and discovery, what theatrical audiences are shown is an inanimate object, on which dramatic speech confers life as a female infant of high status. In the scene of Hermione's restoration, what Jacobean theatrical audiences were shown was a young boy, costumed and made up as a middle-aged female of high status, whom dramatic speech transformed into an inanimate object, and then slowly, by fits and starts of perception, brought to life. The Protestant privileging of words over images was the Reformation version of the Renaissance *paragone*, or competition among the arts: in *The Winter's Tale*, as throughout Shakespearean drama, the outcome is no contest but, rather, a collaboration.[16]

NOTES

1   In the first edition of *The Perambulation* the entertainment venues had been "Parisgardein, the Bell Savage or some other such common place" (Lambarde 1576: 187, sig. Aa2ʳ).

2   Aston (1988: 173) refers to this report as unverified, presumably forever, as the statue was one of the idolatrous statues which were burned in 1538.

3   The answer depended in part on which bits of biblical text were brought into play. The King James translation of the passage in Exodus chapter 20 is:

> [2] *I am the Lord thy God* . . . [3] *Thou shalt have no other gods but me.* [4] Thou shalt not make unto thee any graven Image or any likeness of any thing that is in heaven above, or that is in the earth beneath, or that is in the water under the earth. [5] Thou shalt not bow down thy self to them, nor serve them: For I the LORD thy God am a jealous God, visiting the iniquitie of the fathers upon the children unto the third and fourth generation of them that hate me: [6] And shewing mercy unto thousands of them that love mee, and keep my Commandements. [7] *Thou shalt not take the name of the Lord thy God in vaine*; for the Lord will not hold him giltlesse that taketh his Name in vaine. (*Bible* 1611–13, sig. Gg4ˡ)

Western medieval Christianity (and then Roman Catholicism) identified a single commandment (the first) in verses 2 and 3 and another (the second) in the first clause of verse 7. Reformers agreed about the first commandment but made verses 4, 5, and 6 into a second commandment against idolatry and thereby amplified the force of their interpretation of the first. Aston's discussion of "The Structure of the Decalogue" (1988: 371–93) is characteristically lucid, comprehensive, and helpful.

4   The homilist elaborates the notion of images as women's sexual seduction of men: "the nature of man is none otherwise bent to worshipping of Images (yf he may have them and see them) than it is bent to whordom and adultery in the company of harlottes. And as unto a man given to the lust of the flesh, seing a wanton harlot, sitting by her & embracing her, it profiteth litle for one to say, Beware of fornication, God will condemn fornicators and adulterers. For neither will he, being overcome with greater enticements of the strompet, give eare, or take hede to such godly admonitions, and when he is lefte afterwardes alone with the harlotte, nothing can follow but wickednes: even so, suffer images to be in syght in the Churches and Temples, ye shall in vayn byd them beware of Images . . . and flee iolatry . . . ye shal in vain preach and teach them against idolatry. For a number wil, notwithstanding fall headlonges unto it, what by the nature of Images, and by the inclination of their own corrupt nature. Wherefore, as for a man geven to lust, to sit down by a strumpet, is to tempt God: So is it likewise to erect an Idol in this proneness of mans nature to Idolatry, nothyng but a temptyng." (*Certaine Sermons*, 1563: fol. 66, sig. Ii4).

5   For learned treatises, see Stuart (1616: 116–18 / sig. K4ᵛ–5ᵛ). For accessible cases, Rosen (1991) 70 (Dorset in 1566), 87 (Windsor in 1579), 308 (Chester in 1595), 324 (Hertford in 1606), and 361 (Lancashire in 1616): all but the penultimate case, which uncovered a two-dimensional colored diagram of a human, involved three-dimensional figures of individuals – portraits or pictures in wax or clay.

6   As was noted nearly forty years ago by Inga-Stina Ewbank (1964: 98): (1) no masque writer prior to *The Winters' Tale* used the device of a statue coming to life; but (2) shortly after Shakespeare's play, the device was used in wedding masques for the Princess Elizabeth by Campion and by Beaumont; and (3) Beaumont's masque, which Bacon had procured, used "statuas moving" in an antimasque.

7   Here and hereafter quotations from *The Winter's Tale* are made from the facsimile edition of the Yale University Elizabethan Club's copy of the First Folio, edited by Helge Kokeritz and Charles Tyler Prouty (New Haven, CT: Yale University Press, 1955), and will be cited by page number and column.

8   Trinity College Cambridge MS O.2.66, in Middleton's hand, calls for *"An altar discovered and statues, with a song"* (Dessen and Thomson 1999: 119). The ensuing song implies at least one further stage direction:

> May from the altar flames aspire
> Those tapers set themselves afire.
> May senseless things our joys approve
> And those brazen statues move

With or without the spontaneous combustion which the first couplet of the song invokes, the second couplet's call for the statues to move is evidently achieved. The dialogue immediately following the song rejoices; "A happy omen waits upon this hour; / All move portentously, the right-hand way." From the song and the dialogue together, then, it is quite clear that the senseless things which *A Game at Chess* has moving so auspiciously – because towards the right – are statues. In two other manuscripts of Middleton's play, however, the stage direction for the discovery of these statues designates them not as statues but in the more usual way: *"An Altar discovered with Tapors on it: and Images about it,"* and this designation is repeated in an explicit stage direction for their movement: *"The Images move in a Dance."* These manuscripts, Bodleian MS Malone 25 & British Library MS Lansdowne 690, are two of the three transcripts which Ralph Crane made of *A Game at Chess*. (See N. W. Bawcutt's diplomatic edition of Malone 25 in *Collections*, XV [Oxford: Oxford University Press for the Malone Society, 1993], 78–9, 109; and T. H. Howard-Hill's Revels Plays edition of *A Game at Chess* [Manchester: Manchester University Press, 1993]). It is now generally accepted that a transcript by Ralph Crane served as the copy from which the First Folio text of *The Winter's Tale* was set.

9   While early seventeenth-century English usage, like that of the twenty-first century, might designate any three-dimensional image as a statue, the anticipated images were likely to be anthropomorphic ones. Thus John Bullokar's *English Expositor*, a Jacobean dictionary of difficult words, defines: "*Statue*. A carued, or cast image, made in proportion like a man" (B[ullokar] 1616: O1ʳ). "Proportion" here bears the no-longer-current sense, no. 7 in the *Oxford English Dictionary* definition of the noun, as "configuration, form, shape": Shakespearean texts always deploy the word in this sense.

10 In the apparatus to his critical edition of *Fedele and Fortunio*, Richard Hosley discusses how Munday changed Pasqualigo's *Il Fedele* and demonstrates that he was working from the second (1579) imprint of the Italian play (Munday 1981: 30–1, 89–93, 237–51). He also summarizes Abraham Fraunce's *Victoria*, a Latin adaptation of *Il Fedele* which survives in a manuscript from Penshurst Place.

11 Dekker here uses the word "picture" in the sense of "portrait." Where both words now commonly designate two-dimensional images, in early modern English usage they were commonly deployed for three-dimensional ones as well. The sculptor Nicholas Stone indiscriminately records a sepulchral or monumental effigy as a "picture," as a "statue," and "statue or picture" and even as "statue or portraighture" (Stone 1919: 50, 52, 61–2, 90–1 ["the fineshen of Doctor doons pictor" – i.e., John Donne's memorial in St. Paul's Cathedral], 120–4). The first Earl of Southampton specified "portraites of white alabaster or such lyke upon the . . . Monumentes" which he requested in his will (Esdaile 1952: 27).

12 Three wax images, 18 inches high, were found in a stable in Islington. One was inscribed with the queen's name, and the others dressed as her councillors. All were stuck full of pig bristles. Nobody was caught (Hoy 1980: 340–1).

13 This spatial arrangement is both necessary, given the demands of the dialogue, and possible, given the features of the performance spaces for which Shakespeare wrote. The former require Hermione to be standing upright and within reach of Paulina's visitors; but they do not require more than one stage door to be used in the course of the scene, into which no one enters after the massed entry of its initial stage direction. The latter include doors in the tiring-house wall at the Globe and in the screens of the Great Halls of the royal palaces at Hampton Court and Greenwich and Whitehall. The first (1607–19) Jacobean Banqueting House at Whitehall does not appear to have had a screen. It did, however, have a two-story colonnade, which would have easily assimilated the "chapel" of the final scene of *The Winter's Tale*. See Astington (1999: 44–64).

14 A notorious puzzle for critics, the citation of "Iulio Romano" may have been equally teasing in 1611. The previous century had produced an Italian artist, Giulio Pippi, styled Romano, (1) whose work includes *trompe-l'oeil* paintings which appear to be sculpted; (2) whose epitaph, as reported by Vasari, celebrated the animated lifelikeness of his representation of human bodies ("Videbat Iuppiter corpora sculpta pictaque spirare . . . Julii virtute Romani" [quoted in Pafford 1963: 150 n.]); (3) and who had had his hands slapped for representing God the Father (in *Symbolic Images*, II (London: Phaidon, 1972)), E. H. Gombrich quotes, in translation, from the artist's 1541 account via Frederick Hartt's 1958 *Giulio Romano*, I (New Haven, CT: Yale University Press, 1958, 149–50). Among recent discussions of Giulio Romano, see Sokol (1994: 85–115) for his subject (sex) and Greenwood (1988: 25–52) for his style (Mannerist). The fact that the sixteenth century had also seen two Roman Pontiffs who styled themselves Julius, the first and second of that name, is perhaps pertinent to the particular interests of the present essay.

15 As revived by the King's Men around 1610, this pantomime-like romance appears to have featured both a live dramatic bear and a dead one. The latter, signified by a bear's head which is carried on by the victorious hero, was a requirement of the play from its earliest extant version, a 1598 Quarto (STC 18230). The former, signified either by an actor in a bearskin or a bear on a lead, was one of the "new additions" proclaimed on the title page of the third edition in 1610 (STC 18232).

16 A recent book which I regret having been unable to consult is Michael O'Connell's *The Idolatrous Eye* (Oxford: Oxford University Press, 2000).

References and Further Reading

Astington, J. H. (1999). *English Court Theatre 1558–1642.* Cambridge: Cambridge University Press.

Aston, M. (1988). *England's Iconoclasts, Vol. 1: Laws Against Images.* Oxford: Clarendon Press.

Barkan, L. (1981). "Living Sculptures": Ovid, Michelangelo, and *The Winter's Tale. English Literary History,* 48, 63–7.

Barroll, L. (1991). *Politics, Plague, and Shakespeare's Theater: The Stuart Years.* Ithaca, NY: Cornell University Press.

Bartholomeusz, D. (1982). *The Winter's Tale in Performance in England and America 1611–1976.* Cambridge: Cambridge University Press.

Beaumont, F. and Fletcher, J. (1970). *Cupid's Revenge* (1607). In F. Bowers (ed.) *The Dramatic Works in the Beaumont and Fletcher Canon,* Vol. 2. Cambridge: Cambridge University Press.

Belsey, C. (1999). *Shakespeare and the Loss of Eden.* London: Macmillan.

Bergeron, D. M. (1978). The Restoration of Hermione in *The Winter's Tale.* In C. M. Kay and H. E. Jacobs (eds.) *Shakespeare's Romances Reconsidered.* Lincoln: University of Nebraska Press, 125–33.

Bible (1611–13). *The Holy Bible . . . Newly Translated . . . by his Maiesties speciall Commandement.* London: Robert Barker (STC 2224).

Bristol, M. (1991). In Search of the Bear: Spatiotemporal Form and the Heterogeneity of Economies in *The Winter's Tale. Shakespeare Quarterly,* 42, 145–67.

B[ullokar], J[ohn] (1616). *An English Expositor: Teaching the Interpretation of the hardest words vsed in our Language.* London: John Legatt (STC 4083). Facsimile Hildesheim: Georg Olms Verlag, 1971.

Cavell, S. (1987). *Disowning Knowledge: In Six Plays of Shakespeare.* Cambridge: Cambridge University Press.

Certaine Sermons (1563). *Certaine Sermons appoynted by the Quenes Maiesty, to be declared and read, by al Parsons, Vicars, & Curates, eueri Sunday and holiday, in their Churches, Vol. II, The Seconde tome of homelyes.* London: Richard Jugge and John Cawood (STC 13665).

Collinson, P. (1988). *The Birthpangs of Protestant England: Religious and Cultural Change in the Sixteenth and Seventeenth Centuries.* London: Macmillan.

Dekker, T. (1955). *The Whore of Babylon* (1607). In F. Bowers (ed.) *The Dramatic Works of Thomas Dekker,* Vol. 2. Cambridge: Cambridge University Press.

Dessen, A. C. and Thomson, L. (1999). *A Dictionary of Stage Directions in English Drama, 1580–1642.* Cambridge: Cambridge University Press.

Duffy, E. (1992). *The Stripping of the Altars: Traditional Religion in England 1400–1580.* New Haven, CT: Yale University Press.

Esdaile, K. (1952). Some Fellow-Citizens of Shakespeare in Southwark. *Essays & Studies,* n.s. vol. 5, 26–31.

Ewbank, I.-S. (1964). The Triumph of Time in *The Winter's Tale. Review of English Literature,* 5, 83–100.

——(1989). From Narrative to Dramatic Language: *The Winter's Tale* and Its Source. In M. Thompson and R. Thompson (eds.) *Shakespeare and the Sense of Performance: Essays in the Tradition of Performance Criticism in Honor of Bernard Beckerman.* Newark: University of Delaware Press, 29–47.

Felperin, H. (1985). "Tongue-tied our queen?": The Deconstruction of Presence in *The Winter's Tale.* In P. Parker and G. Hartman (eds.) *Shakespeare and the Question of Theory.* London: Methuen, 3–18.

Furness, H. H. (1964) [1898]. *A New Variorum Edition of Shakespeare "The Winter's Tale".* New York: Dover Books.

G[oad] T[homas] (1623). *The Friers Chronicle, or the true legend of priests and monkes lives.* London: Robert Milbourne.

Greenwood, J. (1988). *Shifting Perspectives and the Stylish Style: Mannerism in Shakespeare and his Jacobean Contemporaries.* Toronto: University of Toronto Press.

Gurr, A. (1983). The Bear, the Statue, and Hysteria in *The Winter's Tale. Shakespeare Quarterly,* 34, 420–5.

Hoy, C. (1980). *Introductions, Notes and Commentaries to texts in The Dramatic Works of Thomas Dekker, edited by Fredson Bowers*, Vol. 2. Cambridge: Cambridge University Press.

Kurland, S. M. (1991). "We need no more of your advice": Political Realism in *The Winter's Tale. Studies in English Literature 1500–1900*, 31, 365–86.

Lamb, M. E. (1989). Ovid and *The Winter's Tale*: Conflicting Views towards Art. In W. R. Elton and W. B. Long (eds.) *Shakespeare and Dramatic Tradition: Essays in Honor of S. F. Johnson*. Newark: University of Delaware Press, 69–87.

Lambarde, W. (1576). *A Perambulation of Kent . . . Collected and written (for the most part) in the yeare 1570*. London: Ralphe Newbery (STC 15175.5).

——(1596). *A Perambulation of Kent . . . increased and altered.* London: Edmund Bollifant (STC 15176).

Lavater, L. (1596). *Of Ghostes and Spirites, Walking by Night . . . translated into English by R.H.* London: Thomas Creede (STC 15321).

Leech, C. (1978). Masking and Unmasking in the Last Plays. In C. M. Kay and H. E. Jacobs (eds.) *Shakespeare's Romances Reconsidered.* Lincoln: University of Nebraska Press, 40–59.

Lyly, J. (1902). *The Woman in the Moon* (1597). In R. W. Bond (ed.) *The Complete Works of John Lyly*, Vol. 3. Oxford: Clarendon Press.

Morse, W. R. (1991). Metacriticism and Materiality: The Case of Shakespeare's *The Winter's Tale. English Literary History*, 58, 283–304.

Mowat, B. A. (1994). Rogues, Shepherds, and the Counterfeit Distressed: Texts and Infracontexts of *The Winter's Tale* 4.3. *Shakespeare Studies*, 22, 58–76.

Munday, A. (1981). *A Critical Edition of Anthony Munday's Fedele and Fortunio, ed. Richard Hosley.* New York: Garland Press.

Orgel, S. (ed.) (1996). *The Winter's Tale.* Oxford: Oxford University Press.

Pafford, J. H. P. (ed.) (1963). *The Winter's Tale.* London: Methuen.

Paster, G. K. (1993). *The Body Embarrassed: Drama and the Disciplines of Shame in Early Modern England.* Ithaca, NY: Cornell University Press.

Phillips, J. (1973). *The Reformation of Images: Destruction of Art in England, 1535–1660.* Berkeley: University of California Press.

Proudfoot, R. (1976). Verbal Reminiscence and the Two-Part Structure of *The Winter's Tale. Shakespeare Survey*, 29, 67–78.

Riemer, A. P. (1987). Deception in *The Winter's Tale. Sydney Studies in English*, 13, 21–38.

Rosen, B. (ed.) (1991). *Witchcraft in England, 1558–1618.* Amherst: University of Massachusetts Press.

Rubin, M. (1991). *Corpus Christi: The Eucharist in Late Medieval Culture.* Cambridge: Cambridge University Press.

Schanzer, E. (1964). The Structural Pattern of *The Winter's Tale. Review of English Literature*, 5, 72–82.

Scot, R. (1930). *The Discoverie of Witchcraft* (1584), introd. M. Summers. London: John Rodker; reprint New York: Dover Books, 1972.

Shakespeare, W. (1623). *Mr. William Shakespeares Comedies, Histories, & Tragedies*, facsimile edition by Helge Kokeritz and Charles Tyler Prouty. New Haven, CT: Yale University Press, 1955.

Siemon, J. E. (1974). "But It Appears She Lives": Iteration in *The Winter's Tale. Publications of the Modern Languages Association*, 89, 10–16.

Smith, B. R. (1985). Sermons in Stones: Shakespeare and Renaissance Sculpture. *Shakespeare Studies*, 17, 1–23.

Sokol, B. J. (1989). Painted Statues, Ben Jonson and Shakespeare. *Journal of the Warburg and Courtauld Institutes*, 52, 250–3.

——(1994). *Art and Illusion in The Winter's Tale.* Manchester: Manchester University Press.

Stone, N. (1919). *The Note-Book and Account Book of Nicholas Stone, Master Mason to James I and Charles I*, ed. W. L. Speirs. Walpole Society Vol. 7. Oxford: Oxford University Press for the Walpole Society.

Stuart, James I & VI (1616). *A Premonition to All Most Mightie Monarches, Kings, Free Princes, and States of Christendom* (1609); and *Daemonologie* (1597), in *The Workes of the Most High and Mightie Prince, James . . . King of Great Britain, France & Ireland*. London: Robert Barker & John Bill. (STC 14344).

Wickham, G. (1972). Romance and Emblem: A Study in the Dramatic Structure of *The Winter's Tale*. In D. Galloway (ed.) *The Elizabethan Theatre*, Vol. 3: *Papers given . . . at the University of Waterloo . . . 1970*. London: Macmillan, 82–99.

20

Cymbeline: Patriotism and Performance

Valerie Wayne

Much would depend on how the play was staged . . . By interweaving the play's "authorized reading" with a subtle critique of ideas about textual authority, Shakespeare gave the play back to the institution of the theatre, created a potential for multiplicity and diversity in performance that the Stuart *Cymbeline* did not – by definition, could not – have.

(Marcus 1988: 158–9)

Since 1947 when G. Wilson Knight first published *The Crown of Life*, the historical elements of the tragical–comical–historical–pastoral play called *Cymbeline* (or *The Tragedy of Cymbeline* or *Cymbeline, King of Britain*)[1] have received sustained attention from critics. Particularly in the last fifteen years, the most provocative and wide-ranging area of critical work on the play has concerned its historiography, nationalism, its geopolitical spaces and ethnic alignments. From Emrys Jones and Philip Edwards to Leah Marcus, Jodi Mikalachki, and numerous others, including some important forthcoming work by Peter Parolin and Mary Floyd-Wilson, critics have explored the play's evocations of James I's project of union, its appropriation of Roman, British, and Welsh historiography, its manipulation of anachronism and historiographic anglocentrism. Yet this work has proceeded apart from a recognition that *Cymbeline* was staged as a nationalist play 200 years before those subjects were addressed in critical discourse. Most eighteenth-century productions – and there were many – foregrounded and enhanced its nationalism, and in very different ways some twentieth-century productions tested *Cymbeline*'s investments in nation and empire. As I discuss four of these productions from two different centuries, I want to examine the intersections between the theatrical events and the concerns of the play's contemporary historical critics. While suggesting that the traditions of criticism and performance have sometimes worked with similar preoccupations about this play, I will consider how these very different productions have promoted *Cymbeline* as a patriotic text, appropriated it to a postcolonial context, transposed its patriotism into resistance, and subverted it through parody. Appreciating the play's historical invest-ments is especially important at a time when what it means to be British in Great Britain, Europe, and the Commonwealth has come under considerable pressure, for the issues of cultural identity that the play raises relate to current concerns about the problem of Britishness and account in part for the heightened attention to history and nation that has appeared in the critical discourse. Willy Maley contends that "Shakespeare is our contemporary exactly because the British problem has the same currency, indeed, the same urgency, that it possessed when he grappled with it" (Maley 1997: 88).

Eighteenth-Century Nationalism

During the eighteenth century *Cymbeline* became such a popular play that it was fre-quently chosen by actors for their benefit performances, from which they would collect the night's receipts after management expenses were deducted. The plays chosen for this purpose had to be attractive to audiences, and *Cymbeline* fitted the bill for actors and for "multiple members of [the] house company, for charities, and at the request of 'persons of quality'" (Stone 1975: 313). It was performed 193 times during the century in three very different texts: Thomas Durfey's *The Injured Princess, or, The Fatal Wager*, written in 1682 and staged once or twice before 1700,[2] was revived for twenty-two performances from 1702 to 1746; William Hawkins's *Cymbeline* of 1759 was per-formed seven times; and David Garrick's version of the play was staged 163 times from 1761 to 1800 (Stone 1975: 310–11; Pedicord and Bergmann 1981: 413). The total number of performances in the second half of the century "places *Cymbeline* in the top third of Shakespeare's plays in terms of popularity" (Jacobs 1982: 469). Durfey's play adds a subplot by giving Pisanio a daughter named Clarina who is almost raped by Iachimo and Cloten. Pisanio does not believe in Imogen's[3] innocence and instead tries to kill her. In this "sordid" world appropriate to 1682 with its threat of anarchy, Durfey turns romantic faith into distrust and "develops the theatre of vio-lence, replacing Shakespeare's hints with blatant deeds of cruelty" (McVeagh 2000: 42–6). Hawkins's play, highly altered to fit classical standards and enhance its patri-otic appeal, observes the unities of time and place by keeping all of the action in Britain and extensively revising the last two acts: Cymbeline offers no tribute to Rome after Britain has won the war and ends the play not with pardon and peace but by demanding a large ransom for the Roman prisoners (Dobson 1992: 207). Garrick's text, by contrast, restores much of Shakespeare's and even apologizes in its "Adver-tisement" for what he omitted. Garrick rearranged scenes to consolidate locations and minimize the scene changes that were used on eighteenth-century stages. He also cut 610 lines from the play, 524 of them from the last act: the jail scene, Posthumus's dream vision, Jupiter's descent, and the soothsayer were all excised and the battle scenes reduced. After the first night's performance forty-six more lines about the Queen's death were cut (Pedicord and Bergmann 1981: 416, 97, 162–3). These changes were nonetheless so minor in comparison to Durfey's and Hawkins's that G. C. D. Odell pronounced this "the most accurate of Eighteenth-Century acting versions" of *Cymbeline* (quoted in Pedicord and Bergmann 1981: 417). Garrick himself played the role of Posthumus twenty-three times and established it as the most important male role in the play (Stone 1975: 311). It was only with Macready in 1843 that Iachimo's part came to be preferred by actors.[4]

Garrick enhanced the play's nationalist appeal by creating new lines for Posthumus that offer "praise for, or advice to, the newly crowned George III" (Stone 1975: 317):

> and more than that,
> They have a king whose love and justice to them
> May ask and have their treasures and their blood.
> (Garrick 1981: 3.1.28–9)

Cymbeline becomes a more admirable ruler through this and other changes. Like Hawkins, Garrick also eliminates any mention of the Britons paying tribute to the Romans at the end of the play, so the British victory is complete and uncompromised. He makes major cuts in act 3, scene 1 where Cymbeline, the Queen, and Cloten negotiate with Lucius over the question of tribute that prompts the war. Garrick cuts Lucius's reference to the Romans conquering Britain, cuts the entire patriotic speech by the Queen about the "natural bravery" of the isle and its ability to repel a Roman invasion, cuts Cloten's second rejection of tribute, and cuts Cymbeline's reference to spending his youth with and being knighted by Augustus Caesar (Garrick 1981: 3.3.1–38). Taken together, these changes not only minimize the influence of the Romans on British history but disassociate British patriotism from the two villainous Britons of the piece, thereby simplifying the conflicting allegiances that Shakespeare sets up and making it much easier for audiences to support the Britons' cause. Garrick's text went through seven editions and fourteen printings between 1762 and 1795 (Stone 1975: 313): this was a *Cymbeline* that those seeking to confirm their national identity could really get behind.

It was this text of the play that was staged as a subscription performance in 1798 when Britain feared invasion from the troops of Napoleon that were poised at the channel ports. The playbill read: "In Aid of the Voluntary Subscription for the Defence of the Country, This Present Tuesday February 27, 1798, Will be performed an Historical Play, (not acted this Season) call'd CYMBELINE; OR, THE INVASION OF BRITAIN" (see plate 1). The performance was staged in Bath, a town whose fame as a fashionable spa depended on its Roman heritage; it drew many elite visitors, especially during the winter months, and was the first theatre beyond London to receive a royal patent, which was granted in 1768 (Penley 1892: 35). Sarah Siddons had made her reputation at the Bath Theatre Royal in 1778–82, first performed the role of Imogen there on April 15, 1779 (Hogan 1968: 2, 949), and was warmly welcomed when she returned in later years. Her brother, John Philip Kemble, performed there on occasion, always to a full house, and William Macready and Edmund Kean took

Theatre-Royal, Bath.

IN AID OF THE

Voluntary Subscription

FOR THE DEFENCE OF THE COUNTRY.

This Prefent TUESDAY February 27, 1798,
Will be performed an HISTORICAL PLAY, (not acted this Season) call'd

CYMBELINE;

OR,

THE INVASION OF BRITAIN.

Pofthumus Leonatus . . Mr. DIMOND.	Philario . . Mr. SMITH.
Cymbeline . Mr. ROWBOTHAM.	Firft Lord . Mr. ATKINS.
Cloten . . Mr. CUNNINGHAM.	Second Lord Mr. CRUMPTON.
Bellarius . . Mr. BLISSETT.	Jachimo . Mr. ELLISTON.
Guiderius . Mr. GALINDO.	
Arviragus . Mr. SEDLEY.	Queen . . Mrs. CHARLTON.
Caius Lucius Mr. EYRE.	Helen . . Mifs SUMMERS.
Pifanio . . Mr. CHARLTON.	Imogen . . Mifs ALLINGHAM.

In Act Second, A SERENADE,

By Mr. WILLIAMSON, Mr. TAYLOR, Mr. CRUMPTON, and Mr. HILL.

BETWEEN THE PLAY AND FARCE (FOR THAT NIGHT ONLY)

An Interlude,

(Written exprefsly for the Occafion, by the Author of THE CHIMNEY CORNER)

CALLED

Voluntary Contribution.

Englifhman Mr. Harley,	Oftler - - Mr. Cunningham,	Sailor (with a Song) Mr. Biggs,
ift Irifhman Mr. Williamfon,	Mail Guard Mr. Atkins,	
nd Irifhman Mr. Crumpton,	Waiter - Mr. J. Tebay,	And BRITANNIA
Scotfman - Mr. Rowbotham,	Landlord - Mr. Smith.	Mifs Allingham,

TO CONCLUDE WITH

A View of the British Fleet, & Rule Britannia in Full Chorus ;

ON WHICH OCCASION,

THE MISS CANTELOS

Have liberally offered their much admired Performance on the Harp.

To which will be added a Mufical Farce, (altered from Sprigs of Laurel by Mr. O'Keeffe) called

The Rival Soldiers.

Lennox, . . Mr. TAYLOR.	Major Tactic Mr. CHARLTON.
Sinclair, . . Mr. HILL.	Corporal Squib, Mr. ROWBOTHAM.
Capt. Cruizer, Mr. EYRE,	Soldiers, Mefsrs. CRUMPTON, DOYLE, &c.

Nipperkin, (with the Song of " DOLLY the COOK") Mr. BIGGS.

Mary, . . . Mifs GOPELL.

. Tickets at the ufual prices) to be had of the Committee at the Guildhall, at the New-Rooms, Libraries,
and at the Box-Lobby of the Theatre,

MEYLER, PRINTER.

Playbill for the 1798 production of *Cymbeline* in Bath. This item is reproduced by permission of the Huntington Library, San Marino, California.

the Bath stage in 1814–15 (Hopkins-Clarke 1992: 124–5, 130). *Cymbeline* was a popular play in the company's repertoire from 1772 to the closing of the Orchard Street Theatre (the first home of the Bath Theatre Royal) in 1805. It was produced there each year but five in that thirty-three year period for a total of sixty-three performances (Hare 1977).

But this performance of *Cymbeline* was different. Its purpose was to gather contributions towards Britain's resistance to an invasion by the French. Given Napoleon's recent victories on the Continent, the French could maintain their newly acquired territory and claim more either by invading the British Isles or by attacking Britain's overseas interests and damaging their commerce. In the end they chose the second alternative, moved their forces to the Mediterranean and Egypt, and were defeated by Nelson at the Battle of the Nile on August 1, 1798. But from late 1797 through the early months of 1798, invasion was a serious possibility. Napoleon was ordered to command the "Army of England" on October 27, 1797. The French people were then informed "that the best method of obtaining permanent peace was to defeat England by landing on British shores and marching on London." By early 1798 the Army of England assembled 56,400 men at the channel ports, and Britain responded:

> In January Parliament passed a bill to permit ten thousand militiamen to join the regular army. Pitt called for vastly increased taxes, and . . . the House of Commons, frightened at the prospect of pro-French subversive activity, supported a governmental proposal to suspend the Habeas Corpus Act. The army moved seventy-eight hundred men into the London area.

But the French lacked the necessary ships to move their men across the channel, and by mid-February that problem was not solved (Ross 1969: 139–44). On February 15, 1798, the *Bath Chronicle* reported that "Embargoes are laid on all American vessels in French ports: which vessels are to be detained until the attempt be made of invading the British isles, and which, the French papers say, is to be made betwixt this and the month of April."

Britain prepared its civilians for war. The Bath archives include forms to be used throughout the country on which millers were to commit to provide certain quantities of ready-made flour every twenty-four hours; bakers to promise to bake and deliver certain quantities of "good wholesome well-baked Bread"; and the nobility, gentry, and yeomanry to engage to furnish wagons and carts with multiple horses. There was a form for men from 15 to 60 to sign up for military service, to act as pioneers or laborers, as servants with cattle or with teams, or as guides. The papers call for specific information – names and situations of water mills or wind mills, kinds of fuel needed to heat the ovens, numbers of drivers and conductors. On another paper, inhabitants of the parish could commit to marking their cattle before moving them to places of security still to be determined.[5] Reading these documents shifts one's attention from the rhetoric of war to its daily, material consequences for those who work to feed a nation. The French had solicited a subscription to fund their invasion, and Britain also sought nationwide contributions for its defense. On February 13, 1798, the Mayor and Corporation of Bath subscribed £1,000 to the defense effort[6] and invited residents to a town meeting at the Guildhall two days later for the purpose of determining how to raise money "for the DEFENCE of the COUNTRY at this highly important crisis" (*Bath Chronicle*, February 15, 1798).

Theatre was a part of these preparations for war. Like the London theatres, the Bath Theatre Royal had a long tradition of providing benefit nights to "long-serving and leading members" of the repertory company to supplement their regular incomes (Hopkins-Clarke 1992: 130), so they already had in place a means for raising additional money. A subscription performance had been staged at Covent Garden on Friday, February 9 when the manager, "with a laudable spirit of patriotism," had devoted the profits of an evening to the voluntary subscriptions for the defense of the country. The main piece presented on that occasion was "Mr. Watson's Historical Play of *England Preserved*," followed by an interlude that included "loyal and patriotick songs" such as "God *save the King!*" and "*Rule, Britannia!*" and toasts to the King, Lord Bridport, and the British Navy. *The Bath Chronicle* reprinted Mr. Holman's patriotic prologue in reporting on the event (February 22, 1798). From the receipts of £518. 8s., an unusually high amount, £394. 15s., was paid to the Fund for Voluntary Contributions (Hogan 1968, 3: 2042–3). (For Sarah Siddons's benefit performance of *Cymbeline* at Drury Lane on January 29, 1789, with Kemble playing Posthumus, the total receipts came in at £344. 17s. 6d. (Hogan 1968, 2: 949), and Stone (1975) identifies this as perhaps the "high point of a single performance" of that play in the century (p. 311)).

Bath followed London's subscription night with its own. The play's title, *Cymbeline, or the Invasion of Britain*, evoked the very threat that Britons most feared at that moment, yet the subtitle is appropriate to a play that dramatizes a military invasion of the country. William Wyatt Dimond, who played Posthumus, was also the theatre's manager;[7] Caroline Allingham played Imogen. *Cymbeline* "was performed with an energy and feeling inspired by the occasion" and was followed by an interlude called *Voluntary Contributions*, written "expressly for the purpose" (*Bath Chronicle*, March 1, 1798) by W. Porter, whose *The Chimney Corner* had been performed at Drury Lane to great acclaim (*Bath Journal*, February 12, 1798). The interlude's first scene represented "all classes crowding to pay in their mites [small sums], and prove their attachment to their King and Country." This scene, designed to produce the very actions that it represented, met with "unbounded and incessant" applause. In the second scene the children of Britain, equipped with harps and lyres, invoked the aid of Britannia, at which point Miss Allingham descended "in a cloud" and promised her protection in a long speech that recollected the famous victory of 1588:

> Recall to mind those glorious feats of yore,
> When Spain's Armada sought your envied shore!
> Think how your fathers bled in Freedom's name, –
> Be then their sons, and emulate their [aims];
> Be but *resolv'd* – immortal is your cause,
> 'Tis for your King, your Liberties, and Laws!

Then the audience was offered an elaborate scenic tableau of the British Fleet, followed by "Rule Britannia" in full chorus and a musical farce called "The Rival Soldiers." One review of the evening said "the house overflowed at an early hour" (*Bath Chronicle*, March 1, 1798); another described it as "crowded in every part" and attended by "one of the most brilliant audiences that ever assembled" (*Bath Herald and Register*, March 3, 1798). The receipts for this performance were reported at £154 10s. 6d. (*Bath Journal*, March 5, 1798), and the same program was staged again three days later, on March 2, 1798 (Hare 1977: 173). The actors accepted no payment for these shows, Mr. Dimond made no deductions for management, and he volunteered another subscription performance at Bristol, the company's companion playhouse to Bath (*Bath Herald and Register*, March 3, 1798). By March 15 the City of Bath had collected more than £15,000 in voluntary contributions (*Bath Chronicle*, March 15, 1798). This amount was published in the newspapers along with listings of individual contributions and reports of money gathered by other cities beyond London. By the end of the national subscription, more than £2,000,000 had been collected for the defense effort (Ross 1969: 144).

Although the money generated by these productions is small in proportion to the total amount raised, it is nonetheless unusual that *any* profits from theatrical performances would go directly for a country's military defense. Benefit performances were sometimes used to fund other concerns: receipts from some London productions of *King Lear*, *Hamlet*, and *Cymbeline* during the century were collected for those who had to retire from the stage, and other Shakespearean adaptations provided money for persons in particular need (Hogan 1957, 2: 54ff.), but the use of theatre to collect money for military purposes reflects the urgency of the situation in 1798 and the way in which theatre was related to the politics of the nation. France affirmed that connection when the Theatre de la Republique et des Arts planned to stage an opera called *The French in England* but deferred the production after Napoleon suggested it was unwise for the French "to betray the least symptom of braggartism" respecting the current conflict and "to irritate that [British] pride which prevents them from coming to a pacification on reasonable terms" (*Bath Chronicle*, March 15, 1798). Whether staging or postponing these events, the British and French used theatre to produce both economic and cultural forms of capital that were integral to the war effort. Theatre could directly support the state apparatus as well as having a more symbolic importance in the life of the nation. While the struggle between the French and the English earlier in the eighteenth century had been played out as "a contrast between French absolutism and English liberty," after the revolution and Burke's *Reflections on the Revolution in France*, those positions required revision.

Instead, the French (and American) belief that a society could be rationally planned, that a blueprint could be intellectually conceived and then imposed upon recalcitrant human materials, was contrasted with the English belief that a society naturally evolved, organically, by gradations and consolidations, like a tree, like Burke's British royal oak in particular. (Taylor 1989: 148–9)

Cymbeline was well-suited to this post-revolution concept of history since it grounded British identity on the country's Roman past. Garrick had cut the original's prophecy with its reference to the king and his sons as a "stately cedar" and "lopped branches" (5.4.439), but the "gradations and consolidations" of Britain's development over time were still an integral part of the play's approach to national identity.

Yet *Cymbeline* needed pruning beyond that cedar and its branches if it was to serve Garrick's purposes. Even Shakespeare's English history plays include a "rather bewildering complexity of response to England's history" in which "patriotic hysteria, genuine pride in his country, and consciousness of error and evil" all coexist (Edwards 1979: 68). While G. Wilson Knight (1947), writing in the wake of World War II, characterized *Cymbeline* "mainly as an historical play" much as it was described 150 years earlier in the Bath playbill, he too acknowledged that the play's most patriotic characters are "conceived as types which Cymbeline, that is, Britain, must finally reject" (pp. 129, 137). Still Knight connects the patriotism voiced by Posthumus with "precisely the same thoughts expressed even more satisfyingly by the Queen and Cloten" (p. 134), presumably because the latter are more explicit and aggressive. Recent critics have questioned Knight's assertions. "Why does Shakespeare place some of his most patriotic speeches in the mouths of his two villains (3.1)?" For John E. Curran, Jr., who puts the question this way, the answer is historiographic: their patriotism "becomes perverted" because it is "refracted through a Galfridian lens" (Curran 1997: 288–9), a false national history constructed by Geoffrey of Monmouth and repudiated by historians more contemporary to Shakespeare such as William Camden. For James M. Redmond, the reason is intentional incoherence: "they permit the dramatist to give voice to English opposition [to the union with Scotland] even as he makes the obligatory gesture of trying to contain it," because the play has a kind of "ideological incoherence" that "allows for dissident reading" (Redmond 1999: 311). For Mary Floyd-Wilson, the reason is ethnicity: the Queen and Cloten are relatively barbaric Scoto-Britons who misrepresent their past and whose insularity "becomes a mocking indictment of the British Isles' mingled stock," while Posthumus is a more refined, early modern Scot "poised . . . to receive England's embrace in union."[8] For Peter Parolin, the reason is narrational: "Shakespeare deploys anachronism to subvert a straightforward nationalistic narrative," so the play shows the difficulty or impossibility of "constructing 'desirable' forms of national identity purged of unwanted elements," such as an identity based on ancient Rome uncontaminated by its development into Renaissance Italy.[9]

Whatever the reasons – and these all seem to me important alternatives that interpret the play in relation to its historical moment of production – in order to rewrite *Cymbeline*, Garrick was less concerned with what the play meant around 1610 than what it would mean to his own audience in 1761. He distinguished between Posthumus's patriotism and that of the Queen and Cloten, retained all of Posthumus's predictions about a British victory except his reference to tribute, and extended that speech to include praise of George III (Garrick 1981: 3.1.17–28). He also cut nineteen lines – the Queen's entire speech – on Britain as an impregnable island that had twice beaten Julius Caesar from its shores, six lines from Cloten's refusal of tribute, and sixteen lines from Cymbeline's historical account of the two Caesars, Britain's first king Mulmutius, and previous British resistance. He created a leaner, cleaner, less complicated play that did not attempt to engage with early modern historiography or ethnicity, was less open to interpretative incoherence or narrative multiplicity, and was more appropriate to a context of cultural conservatism, nationalism, and imperialism. But the revisions he made identify the very faultlines in that text that recent critics are still coming to terms with.

Garrick solved the problem of tribute by eliminating any reference to it from the last scene. For him it compromised the British victory, as it has for so many others. William Hawkins's 1759 *Cymbeline* had reversed the monetary exchange so that Rome paid ransom to Britain for its prisoners rather than receiving money from them. Garrick's solution was not as "power-hungry and avaricious" (Dobson 1992: 207), but it did mitigate what J. P. Brockbank (1958: 48) saw as an "ethical" endorsement to the "political solution," what Robert Miola (1983: 233) described as "a scene of toleration and forgiveness," what John Curran (1997: 282) sees as a "victorious surrender to Roman power," and James Redmond (1999: 311) characterizes as a "comic reconciliation [that] negates the rewards of winning" the war. For Shakespeare's contemporaries the play's resolution could be read in connection with James I's project of union between England and Scotland, as Leah Marcus has persuasively shown:

> In the new alliance, the "justice" of Roman tribute and the mercy of peace and reconciliation are not opposed to one another but work together for harmony, just as James I envisioned an empire of Great Britain in which tolerance and respect for the "alien" Roman law would cement, not cancel, union. (Marcus 1988: 152)

For Garrick, however, this topical reference was superfluous. He was staging the play after union had finally been achieved in 1707, and any payment of tribute would have undermined the expansion of empire that was James's legacy to later centuries.

Other critics have considered the tribute in relation to imperialism. Building on Knight's observation of the "close reference of the sexual to the national in *Cymbeline*" (Knight 1947: 149) but disputing his assertion that Britain becomes Rome's successor as an imperial power, Philip Edwards says:

> the war was fought to secure a divorce, and when the war was won, the marriage was renegotiated on different terms. So far as I understand it, *Cymbeline* implies a total rejection of the prevalent idea of civilizing Ireland by conquest, and a rejection of the Roman analogy which was used to justify the idea. (Edwards 1979: 93–4)

For Edwards, *Cymbeline* is not an imperialist text because Britain does not take on Rome's mantle of empire at the end. Although Jodi Mikalachki has argued that Britain assumes a "subordinate status in the Roman empire" through its concluding events (Mikalachki 1998: 114), Heather James claims that through its use of the Troy legend and the Augustan Soothsayer's interpretations of the Roman eagle, the play "is deliberately vague about whether the transference is a matter of Rome's expansion or her eclipse by Britain" (James 1997: 153–4). James sees the play as a "mingle-mangle" of Roman histories and legends that does not clearly position Britain as the inheritor of Rome's imperialist destiny. Yet any ambiguity in Britain's status was inappropriate for Garrick's purposes. He eliminates the tribute and Posthumus's jail scene, including the jailor's plea for unity: "I would we were all of one mind, and one mind good" (5.3.295–6);[10] Posthumus's vision of his family and Jupiter's descent; and the soothsayer's rendering of the prophecy that connects Posthumus's identity with Britain's future. Garrick avoided an ending that was "driven not so much by the decisive wills of the characters as by their openness to events as they unfold."[11] The 570 lines that he cut from the last act effectively resituate the play's victory as a consequence of British courage in the face of an outside, invading force that had to be subdued.

For all of these reasons, Garrick's *Cymbeline* was especially appropriate for raising money in the time of a threatened French invasion. The appearance of the actress who played Imogen as the figure of Britannia in the afterpiece in the Bath productions was also entirely in keeping with what critics have seen as that character's historical identity. Following J. P. Brockbank's (1958) initial observation that "Innogen" is the wife of Brute (p. 43), J. C. Maxwell suggested in 1960 that the Folio's "Imogen" was an error for "Innogen" (p. 133), and Emrys Jones "almost wishes" that Maxwell had made the emendation that was eventually made sixteen years later by the *Oxford Shakespeare*, "for something positive is added to *Cymbeline* if we recognise that Shakespeare's heroine shares her name with the legendary first queen of Britain" (Jones 1961: 99). The doubling of Miss Allingham as Imogen and, in the afterpiece, Britannia, the female personification of the nation under its Latin name, emphatically stages that association. Although Garrick's text cut Jupiter's descent on an eagle, the Bath production provides, almost as a surrogate, the descent of Miss Allingham as Britannia in a cloud of glory, speaking lines invoking the Spanish Armada as it had been invoked by Cymbeline's Queen in her patriotic speech that was cut from 3.1. Knight claims that her speech about the island "ribbed and paled in / With oaks[12] unscalable and roaring waters, / With sands, that will not bear your enemies' boats / But suck them up to the topmast" (*Cymbeline* 3.1.19–22) "expressed precisely the sentiments many Elizabethan Englishmen must have felt after the failure of the Spanish Armada" (Knight 1947: 135). The afterpiece transfers the Queen's characterization of an impregnable Britain onto the figure of Britannia associated with the actress who played Britain's first queen, thereby restoring for the Bath audience some semblance of the longest speech of patriotism in Shakespeare's text that had to be cut by Garrick because it was associated with the wrong queen. The afterpiece finally got the nationalism into the right queen's mouth.

That production also used a subtitle to foreground the invasion of Britain that occurs in Shakespeare's text. Coppélia Kahn identifies six references to Julius Caesar's invasion in the play (Kahn 1997: 161 and n.3), which reinforced the threat of the invasion staged in *Cymbeline* and anticipated the threat of 1798. In "Palisading the

Body Politic" Linda Woodbridge explores the "seige mentality" suggested by it and asks, "Is there not a peculiar intensity to the almost paranoid self-palisading of the *English* Renaissance psyche – something akin to what Canadian literati used to call a garrison mentality?" (Woodbridge 1991: 340–1). She notes parallels between the penetration of the country "though a lane whose narrowness is repeatedly emphasized" and the attempted invasions of Imogen's body through seduction, murder, rape, mouth-poisoning, and ear-poisoning (pp. 334–5). The Bath production confirms the connections that Woodbridge makes and speaks to the mentality she describes. It also shows Britain's vulnerability, for in 1798 those fears nearly became a palpable reality. What protected the country in the end was what Cloten refers to as "our salt-water girdle" (Garrick 1981: 3.3.33). The Bath production assured its audience of protection in the person of Britannia, who recites lines in her speech from "Rule Britannia," which was sung after the display of an elaborate tableau of "England, protected by her own fleet" (*Bath Chronicle*, March 1, 1798). But in the event it was not Britannia or England's fleet that offered the most important protection; it was the lack of ships in the French fleet to carry its soldiers across the water. That salt-water girdle did provide the protection that Cloten claimed it would, and his lines in the Bath production probably seemed less obstreperous than optimistic to his audience.

There is of course a risk to inferring anything about a play's politics from what had to be cut in order to make it into a nationalistic text, and I do not wish this reading of the Bath production in relation with contemporary critics to be taken as the only or my only rendering of *Cymbeline*'s politics. But I do think it is important that the issues in the play that have so preoccupied historical critics – the Queen and Cloten, the payment of tribute after Britain has won the war, the relation of Posthumus and Imogen to national identity – are the issues that required revision in the eighteenth century if the play was to serve a patriotic function. Even when the questions raised by contemporary critics are answered by identifying concerns quite specific to early modern culture, ones that usually have not found their way into subsequent productions of any period, the subjects at issue often overlap with the revisions made in the eighteenth-century acting editions. The allegiances set up by the play as Shakespeare wrote it are more nuanced and complex than the affinities elicited by Hawkins or Garrick, but that does not mean that a less fully revised *Cymbeline* was incapable of eliciting a patriotic response. I want now to complicate this reading with a discussion of three twentieth-century productions that will show how the play can elicit widely disparate responses while maintaining its character as an historical text. Patriotism is very much a function of one's temporal and national location, and when Shakespeare's texts were carried around the globe as vehicles of art and imperialism, they were met with enthusiasm, resistance, parody, and a variety of other reactions. Theatre in the twentieth-century could more readily present alternative political interpretations and perform them in unofficial venues than was possible in the eighteenth century. It was also affected directly and indirectly by critical discourse. These more recent productions illustrate how *Cymbeline* was enlisted not only in nationalist but in postcolonial and anti-imperialist enterprises.

Race, Empire, and the Ridiculous

In 1986 Robin Phillips directed a production of *Cymbeline* in Stratford, Ontario that was set in the late 1930s and early 1940s. Because he assumed that Shakespeare's audience "would have been watching an ancient British story that reminded them of the immediately preceding wars that had happened between England and Spain" and he wanted to create a similar response in his own audience, he chose a period "when war meant something in the sense that it could have happened to someone I knew." Cymbeline appeared as George V in naval uniforms and shooting outfits. The Queen was dressed as Queen Mary and as a "bluestocking lady doctor in a white lab coat." Posthumus and Imogen evoked Edward VIII and Mrs. Simpson in reverse (Warren 1989: 87–8). After a battle scene that recalled the horrors of World War II, Posthumus appeared as having been badly shell-shocked and "the Jupiter scene then emerged as the exhausted sleep of someone who had just been through a violent battle" (Warren 1988: 163). The most spectacular event in the play was the descent of Jupiter in a World War II bomber named *Eagle*, with Jupiter himself as the pilot roaring his message into a "radio" in front of him. Roger Warren says "the public military violence of the bomber made perfect sense in terms of Posthumus's dream" and "focused attention on the maturing Posthumus in a way that few productions have done" (Warren 1989: 95–6).

What happened after the play was over was an extension of the performance. Alexander Leggatt provides this account:

> The last scene was set in a field hospital. As the audience filed out of the theatre it found the cast, still in uniform, gathered around the piano in the lobby, drinking beer and singing the old war songs; song sheets were passed out and we all joined in: "Pack up your troubles in your old kit bag," "Bluebirds over the white cliffs of Dover." Many older members of the audience did not need song sheets, and sang out lustily from memory. The production did a lot for them; what did it do for *Cymbeline*? It brought out, more clearly than any other production I have ever seen, the importance of the national feeling that runs through the play, coming to a climax in the war scenes. It did so by evoking for the Canadian audience a time when England's fight was their fight too.[13]

Brian Carney has a similar memory of patriotic songs in the lobby, which he says included "It's a Long Way to Tipperary."[14] Leggatt recalls that the production "resonated strongly with veterans and ex-Brits in the audience . . . What's paradoxically Canadian about it is the appeal to memories of a time when Britain was the Mother Country and Canada helped out." The production's "nationalism was English rather than Canadian, but that works in Canada for a certain audience."[15] To elicit patriotism in this production, the performance returned to a war that had provoked fervent patriotism and huge sacrifices on the part of English Canadians. Those members of the audience identified with the Britons in the play, whom they associated with "the

Mother Country," while the invading Romans were analogous to a generalized continental power. The production evoked nostalgia for a time when loyalties to England
were simpler, stronger, and more urgent.

Emrys Jones's work on *Cymbeline* was useful for Robin Phillips's decision to present
Cymbeline as a Western King who could be seen as a symbolic figure through his
historical equivalent in George V (Warren 1989: 87). Phillips's production can also
be read through Mary Floyd-Wilson's historiographic account of the play:

> *Cymbeline* spins out an English historical fantasy in which the Scots and early Britons
> must submit to Roman rule (thus providing a historical precedent for submitting to
> Anglo-Britain rule in the proposed union), while the English emerge as a superior and
> naturally civilized race, unaffected by Britain's ancient history of mingled genealogies
> and military defeats.[16]

Floyd-Wilson considers the racial implications of discarding Geoffrey of Monmouth's
myth of Britain's Trojan past in favor of William Camden and Richard Verstegan's
line of biological English inheritance from the Anglo-Saxons. Unlike the mingled
stock of the polyandrous early Britons, "the English-Saxons are praised for having
preserved an undiluted genealogy, thus setting them apart from all the other mingled
populations of Britain." In this typological reading, Guiderius and Arviragus represent the Anglo-Saxons "who will resist the cycle of degeneration implicit in the translation of empires" by possessing an innate civility that is untaught, unlearned, hardy,
and gentle. As the play draws on competing constructions of Britain's history from
Scottish, English, and Roman historiographers, it offers anglocentrism as a means
of extricating the English people from a history of "Briton savagery, Roman domination, and Scottish kinship."

Floyd-Wilson's reading is deeply embedded in the competing investments of early
modern culture, but it also shows how the play participates in the construction of
a national identity that developed increasing influence during the eighteenth and
nineteenth centuries when Britain was becoming an imperial power.[17] The Canadian
production of *Cymbeline* rehearses some founding moments of English identity while
creating an emotional connection through war that replicated English Canadians' relation to their own past, much as the play had done for its past. Members of that audience may have particularly identified with Posthumus, the aspiring Briton who was
fighting to prove his patriotism and earn a reunion with his chaste English Queen.
The historiographical contests of this reading and Posthumus's identity as an early
modern Scot have lost their immediacy. Yet the problems of Posthumus's unknown
origin and his position in the British court as an adopted son who would never be an
heir may have resonated with those English Canadians who aspired to be, but could
never become, more entirely English. Phillips's use of international conflict to evoke
these frustrated affinities recreates, like the recollected threat in 1610 and the contemporaneous threat in 1798, the clarifying (and distorting) effects of war's urgency
that had become much more complicated for Canadians by 1986. The production
appropriates a form of anglocentric patriotism to a postcolonial context.

Issues of race were even more clearly foregrounded in a production of *Cymbeline* at the Etcetera Theatre above the Oxford Arms pub on London's Camden High Street, where the Rented Space Theatre Company staged a mixed-race, Anglo-Indian production in 1994. Playing to a nearly full audience for three weeks, this was the most successful play yet produced in that theatre, and although this claim is made even more modest by the small size of the space, in terms of its postcolonial conception of the play this was an important production. It used a cast of ten Indians or part-Indians and three Caucasians, set the play in the time of the British Raj, turned the Romans into Britons and the Britons into Indians. Cymbeline was "the aging king of a princely state under Imperial rule,"[18] Imogen was an Indian princess, and Posthumus was an English orphan raised in their household. Iachimo was a British soldier. The director, Ajay Chowdhury, had grown up in India and found the play especially appropriate to Indian culture for several reasons: the marriage of a princess and a commoner was a frequent theme in Indian mythology; there were many small kingdoms under the Raj that were analogous in some respects to the play's historical time period; and Belarius, Guiderius, and Arviragus reminded him of rural villagers in their relation to urban elites. Chowdhury was especially interested in the political and racial issues that would be raised by his production.[19] Cymbeline's objections to his daughter marrying Posthumus became racially motivated, and Iachimo's near rape of Imogen when he was dressed as a British soldier not only replicated actual historical events but Britain's symbolic rape of Indian culture. As one reviewer put it, the production was effective in "highlighting the cultural differences that really drive the action of the play."[20] Chowdhury's transposition of cultures made those differences and their tensions real again for his audience.

The Queen and Cloten in this production spoke their lines as they had in Shakespeare's text, and they were taken seriously as the only characters in the play standing up for Indian nationalism. They might be seen to support Ania Loomba's emphasis on "an alternative aspect of colonial hybridity – one which highlights the *multiple* relationships to the dominant alien culture that can and do exist within any 'colonised' society" (Loomba 1997: 110). The payment of tribute seemed appropriate in this context for, as the program explained, "The British in ruling India left around 600 petty kingdoms to their own devices . . . These kingdoms often paid tribute to the British and were ultimately answerable to the Empire." The ending cut Posthumus's dream with the Leonati and Jupiter, putting the emphasis instead on the family drama. But there was no complete reunion of Posthumus and Imogen, and no physical contact between them. In an image of hands almost touching that came from Satyajit Ray's film *Charulata*, and a revision of the text that drew upon George Bernard Shaw's *Cymbeline Refinished*, when Posthumus offered Imogen the bracelet and the ring, she turned to glare at him.[21] This unresolved ending anticipates the eventual break between India and Britain in 1947, and in a larger sense the refusal of Shakespeare's resolution anticipates the more recent devolution in Scotland and Wales. What Willy Maley has described as Britain's "problem of internal colonialism" that was "momentarily resolved by the union with Scotland" (Maley 1997: 105) and then became externalized in the colonialism of the ensuing centuries, did not achieve Shakespeare's harmonious conclusion: those uneasy relations are figured in this production as an absence of touch and a resistant glare. The entire production is born from that resistance, because the transposition of colonized into colonizer becomes a way of staging the violence that followed when the translation of empire enabled British dominance. Maley's claim that the British problem has the same currency now as when Shakespeare wrote applies not only to groups within the British isles but to the colonized peoples beyond it, whose "*multiple* relationships" (Loomba 1997: 110) and differing responses even now may range from those who long for a closer connection to the mother country to those whose identity in the present is inflected by resisting what Britain imposed in the past.

Americans resisted the British much earlier, so their more distant relation to British patriotism may in part account for the production of *Cymbeline* staged at Santa Cruz in 2000. But the genesis of this production also rests with its ingenious director, Danny Scheie, whose postmodern vision made the play "a parody of patriotic sentimentality" (Ross 2000: 29).[22] Union Jacks were everywhere in evidence, but never with reverence: they flanked each end of the stage that looked like a vaudeville or pantomime music hall; they were emblazoned on the elaborate costumes of the Queen dressed alternately as Mrs. Thatcher, the Queen of Hearts from *Alice in Wonderland*, Elizabeth I from the Rainbow portrait with Union Jacks on the farthingale of her wing-collared dress, and Elizabeth II. Cloten had a garish shirt and knee socks made out of Union Jacks; Cymbeline had them fluttering from the handles of his wheelchair while dressed in red, white, and blue pajamas and a red bathrobe trimmed in ermine; and a naked Posthumus desperately fighting for Britain had a Union Jack "painted in savage strokes of blue and red" grease paint on his chest (Ross 2000: 30). Scheie's *Cymbeline* made patriotism look hilariously ridiculous. The Queen "was a walking sham of fraudulent nationalism and open narcissistic greed," Cloten was "the epitome of a dangerously vain and cowardly spoiled royal brat" (Ross 2000: 30), and since Cymbeline was being regularly poisoned by the Queen, he was a flagrantly ineffectual ruler. The finale included the "treacly patriotic hymn, 'I Vow to Thee My Country,'" which was Princess Diana's favorite, and at the performance that Stephen Orgel attended, that song "had every expatriate Briton in the audience – a large group in Santa Cruz – singing along" (Orgel 2001: 283). The earnestness of the Canadian sing-a-long was converted to parodic glee.

Yet this was a historical *Cymbeline* situated amidst a welter of actual events. Six television monitors showed clips of "Edward VIII and Mrs. Simpson, scenes from Mrs. Thatcher's Britain, odd bits of The Beatles, Elizabeth Taylor as Cleopatra, *Upstairs Downstairs* upside down" (Orgel 2001: 283), each made more comical by their juxtaposition with the action of the play. The more one knew about history, music, and current events, the more there was to appreciate in this cultural pastiche. In 1988 Margaret Drabble found in *Cymbeline* "bathos heaped on bathos, implausibility upon implausibility, and not concealed, not mitigated, but almost, as it were, flaunted" (Drabble 1993: 132). The play that she calls "postmodernist" shamelessly flaunted its bathos and implausibility at Santa Cruz. According to Orgel, "nobody has ever made *Cymbeline* funny in this way, because nobody has been willing to acknowledge the genuine craziness of Shakespeare's conception, to do the play and remain true to its manic energy" (Orgel 2001: 285). Part of that energy arises from the simultaneous presentation of asynchronous events. Peter Parolin argues that "*Cymbeline* reads historical processes disruptively, deconstructing rather than confirming tenuous Jacobean fantasies" by foregrounding anachronism and the tensions associated with the union project. These strategies "subvert a straightforward nationalistic narrative"[23] in Shakespeare's text. The Scheie production confronts the viewer with repeated anachronism (on six screens) in greater multiplicity and dissonance than would have been possible in Jacobean England. Rather than trying to rewrite it to make patriotic sense of it, Scheie works within the text's own anti-realism, its self-parodies of genres and of Shakespeare's own plays. The gleeful engagement with its anarchic energy might not be replicable in quite this way after 9/11/01, but it offered a brilliant, contemporary, and historical experience of the play.

So when considering *Cymbeline*'s patriotism beyond its original performances, "much would depend on how the play was staged" (Marcus 1988: 158). On whether the Queen and Cloten were admirable or contemptible; whether tribute was paid; whether the resolution of hostilities was conclusive (1798), uneasy (1986), doubtful (1994), or excessively harmonious (2000). It mattered what the invading country was, whether the Romans (1798), the Italians (1986 and 2000), or the Britons themselves (1994). Two productions were emphatically patriotic: the 1798 Bath performances created a hyper-nationalistic extravaganza, and the 1986 production appealed to English-Canadians by evoking nostalgia for times of solidarity with English nationalism. Two productions interrogated patriotism: the Anglo-Indian production created a critique of British imperialism and the Santa Cruz show parodied British patriotism. The descent of Jupiter serves as an ideological index in each instance, since it projects Posthumus's dream of a deity who is in charge of the play's events. In Bath, Jupiter did not descend but Britannia did, as if the nation in its female persona became a protective presence to defend the country from invasion. In Canada, Jupiter appeared as a British bomber pilot broadcasting assurances alongside the promise of suffering: "Whom best I love, I cross, to make my gift / The more delayed, delighted" (5.3.195–6). This literalization of the *deus ex machina* (Warren 1989: 95) situated the fighting man as the object of fear and reverence, a mere mortal ruling the world by violence. There was no Jupiter or surrogate in the Anglo-Indian production: any peace or truce was strictly a matter of human negotiation, and the action was suspended without resolution in a postcolonial stand-off. At Santa Cruz, Jupiter appeared on the video screens as an "animated classical dramatic mask with flaming eyes and a booming voice" descending to the strains of Mozart's Jupiter Symphony. Highly artificial, metatheatrical, in this production God was nothing but a representation, and his voice "was actually the voice of the director, run through a distorting effect" (Ross 2000: 29). Life in this version is all theatre, with a ham behind the scenes. If that makes patriotism look ridiculous, it could also look necessary, and anglocentric, and imperious in productions of this play. Knight was right. *Cymbeline* is sometimes historical to the core.

NOTES

1   The play was included among the tragedies in the First Folio and *The Tragedy of Cymbeline* was its running title. In the catalog of plays in the First Folio it was called *Cymbeline King of Britaine*. Both titles have been used in subsequent editions.

    For help on the 1798 Bath production, I am very grateful to Mac Hopkins-Clarke, Kenneth Hillyard, Ann Meddings of the Bath Theatre Royal, and Mary Blagden, Assistant Archivist in the Guildhall Archives. For information on the Canadian production, I want to thank Alexander Leggatt, Craig Howes, and Brian Carney. I learned about the 1994 Anglo-Indian production from Mark Heberle, who saw it, Ajay Chowdhury, who directed it, and Tom Barnes, who played Posthumus. Thanks also to David Baker, Jean Marsden, the Huntington Library, the Bath Public Library, and the London Theatre Museum.

2   The play was first staged in March 1682 and may have been revived during the 1697–8 season (Van Lennep 1965: 307, 484).

3   In this essay I use "Imogen" rather than "Innogen" because it was the name used in the productions under discussion.

4   Jean Marsden, unpublished theatre history of *Cymbeline*, p. 30.

5   Miscellaneous Papers, Bath Archives.

6   Bath Council Minutes, February 13, 1798, No. 12, Council Book from 1794 to 1801, 278–9.

7   Dimond co-managed the theatre with Keasberry after 1785 and alone from 1795 to 1805 (Penley 1892: 38, 65).

8   *Cymbeline's Angels*, forthcoming.

9   "Anachronistic Italy: Cultural Alliances and National Identity in *Cymbeline*," forthcoming in *Shakespeare Studies*.

10   All citations to Shakespeare's *Cymbeline* are from Warren (1998).

11   Alexander Leggatt, "Canada, Negative Capability, and *Cymbeline*," forthcoming.

12   Knight's quotation uses "rocks," Hanmer's emendation, instead of the Folio's "oaks." *The Oxford Shakespeare* emends to "banks." See notes to 3.1.20, Warren's edition.

13   Alexander Leggatt, "Shakespeare Production in Canada: The Case of Stratford Ontario," paper presented in Sydney, Australia on January 25, 1996.

14   Email from Brian Carney, June 26, 2001.

15   Email from Alexander Leggatt, January 5, 2002.

16   *Cymbeline's Angels*, forthcoming.

17   See MacDougall (1982).

18   Program of *Cymbeline* at the Etcetera Theatre, September 27 to October 16, 1994.

19   Interview with Ajay Chowdhury in London on August 14, 2001.

20   Naomi Conran, review of *Cymbeline* in *What's On*, 1994.

21   Interview with Ajay Chowdhury, and email from Tom Barnes on June 23, 2001.

22   I saw the Santa Cruz production in preview on July 22, 2000.

23   "Anachronistic Italy," forthcoming.

REFERENCES AND FURTHER READING

Adelman, J. (1992). Masculine Authority and the Maternal Body: The Return to Origins in the Romances. *Suffocating Mothers: Fantasies of Maternal Origins in Shakespeare Plays, "Hamlet" to "The Tempest."* London: Routledge.

Bath Archives (1798). Council Minutes of February 13, No. 12 Council Book. Miscellaneous Papers.

Bath Chronicle (1798). February 15, 22; March 1, 15.

Bath Herald and Register (1798). March 3.

Bath Journal (1798). February 12; March 5.

Boling, R. J. (2000). Anglo-Welsh Relations in *Cymbeline. Shakespeare Quarterly*, 51, 33–66.

Brockbank, J. P. (1958). History and Histrionics in *Cymbeline. Shakespeare Survey*, 11, 42–9.

Conran, N. (1994). Review of *Cymbeline. What's On.*

Curran, J. E., Jr. (1997). Royalty Unlearned, Honor Untaught: British Savages and Historiographical Change in *Cymbeline. Comparative Drama*, 31, 277–303.

Dobson, M. (1992). *The Making of the National Poet: Shakespeare, Adaptation, and Authorship.* Oxford: Clarendon Press.

Drabble, M. (1993). Stratford Revisited: A Legacy of the Sixties. In M. Novy (ed.) *Cross-Cultural Performances: Differences in Women's Re-Visions of Shakespeare.* Urbana: University of Illinois Press.

Edwards, P. (1979). *Threshold of a Nation: A Study in English and Irish Drama.* Cambridge: Cambridge University Press.

Floyd-Wilson, M. (2002). Delving to the Root: *Cymbeline*, Scotland and the English Race. In D. Baker and W. Maley (eds.) *British Identities and English Renaissance Literature.* Cambridge: Cambridge University Press, 101–15.

——(forthcoming). *Cymbeline's Angels: English Ethnicity and Race in Early Modern Drama.* Cambridge: Cambridge University Press.

Garrick, D. (1981). *Cymbeline. A Tragedy.* 1762. *The Plays of David Garrick*, Vol. 4, ed. W. Pedicord and F. L. Bergmann. Carbondale: Southern Illinois University Press, 95–169.

Hare, A. (ed.) (1977). *Theatre Royal Bath: A Calendar of Performances at the Orchard Street Theatre 1750–1805.* Bath: Kingsmead Press.

Hogan, C. B. (1957). *Shakespeare in the Theatre 1701–1800: A Record of Performances in London 1751–1800*, Vol. 2. Oxford: Clarendon Press.

——(1968). *The London Stage 1660–1800, Part 5: 1776–1800*, Vols. 2 and 3. Carbondale: Southern Illinois University Press.

Hopkins-Clarke, M. (1992). A Change of Style at the Theatre Royal, 1805–1820. *Bath History*, 4, 124–35.

Jacobs, H. E. (1982). *Cymbeline.* Garland Shakespeare Bibliographies. New York: Garland.

James, H. (1997). *Shakespeare's Troy: Drama, Politics, and the Translation of Empire.* Cambridge: Cambridge University Press.

Jones, E. (1961). Stuart *Cymbeline. Essays in Criticism*, 11, 84–99.

Kahn, C. (1997). *Roman Shakespeare: Warriors, Wounds, and Women.* London: Routledge.

Knight, G. W. (1947). *The Crown of Life: Essays in Interpretation of Shakespeare's Final Plays.* Oxford: Oxford University Press.

Leggatt, A. (forthcoming). Canada, Negative Capability, and *Cymbeline.* In D. Brydon and I. Makaryk (eds.) *Shakespeare in Canada: A World Elsewhere?* Toronto: University of Toronto Press.

——(unpublished). Shakespeare Production in Canada: The Case of Stratford Ontario. Paper presented at a conference on "Shakespeare: Perspectives on Performance," Australia–New Zealand Shakespeare Association, Sydney, Australia on January 25, 1996.

Loomba, A. (1997). Shakespearean Transformations. In J. J. Joughin (ed.) *Shakespeare and National Culture.* Manchester: Manchester University Press.

MacDougall, H. A. (1982). *Racial Myth in English History: Trojans, Teutons, and Anglo-Saxons.* Montreal: Harvest House; Hanover, NH: University Press of New England.

McVeagh, J. (2000). *Thomas Durfey and Restoration Drama: The Work of a Forgotten Writer.* Aldershot: Ashgate.

Maley, W. (1997). "This sceptered isle": Shakespeare and the British Problem. In J. J. Joughin (ed.) *Shakespeare and National Culture.* Manchester: Manchester University Press, 83–108.

Marcus, L. S. (1988). *Cymbeline* and the Unease of Topicality. In H. Dubrow and R. Strier (eds.) *The Historical Renaissance: New Essays on Tudor and Stuart Literature and Culture.* Chicago, IL: University of Chicago Press, 134–68.

Marsden, J. (unpublished). Theatre History of *Cymbeline*.

Maxwell, J. C. (1960). *Cymbeline*. Cambridge: Cambridge University Press.

Mikalachki, J. (1998). *The Legacy of Boadicea: Gender and Nation in Early Modern England*. London: Routledge.

Miola, R. (1983). *Shakespeare's Rome*. Cambridge: Cambridge University Press.

Olsen, T. G. (1999). Iachimo's "Drug-Damn'd Italy" and the Problem of British National Character in *Cymbeline*. In H. Klein and M. Marrapodi (eds.) *Shakespeare and Italy. Shakespeare Yearbook* 10. Lewiston, ME: Edwin Mellon Press, 269–96.

Orgel, S. (2001). *Cymbeline* at Santa Cruz. *Shakespeare Quarterly*, 52, 277–85.

Parker, P. (1989). Romance and Empire: Anachronistic *Cymbeline*. In G. M. Logan and G. Teskey (eds.) *Unfolded Tales: Essays on Renaissance Romance*. Ithaca, NY: Cornell University Press.

Parolin, P. (2002). Anachronistic Italy: Cultural Alliances and National Identity in *Cymbeline*. *Shakespeare Studies*, 30.

Pedicord, H. W. and Bergmann, F. L. (eds.) (1981). Notes to *Cymbeline*. *The Plays of David Garrick*, Vol. 4. Carbondale: Southern Illinois University Press, 412–20.

Penley, B. S. (1892). *The Bath Stage: A History of Dramatic Representations in Bath*. London: William Lewis and Son.

Redmond, M. J. (1999). "My lord, I fear, has forgot Britain": Rome, Italy, and the (Re)construction of British National Identity. In H. Klein and M. Marrapodi (eds.) *Shakespeare and Italy. Shakespeare Yearbook* 10. Lewiston, ME: Edwin Mellon Press, 297–316.

Ross, S. T. (1969). *European Diplomatic History 1789–1815: France Against Europe*. New York: Doubleday.

Ross, V. W. (2000). *Cymbeline. Shakespeare Bulletin*, fall, 29–31.

Skura, M. (1980). Interpreting Posthumus' Dream from Above and Below: Families, Psychoanalysis, and Literary Critics. In M. M. Schwartz and C. Kahn (eds.) *Representing Shakespeare: New Psychoanalytic Essays*. Baltimore, MD: Johns Hopkins University Press.

Stone, G. W., Jr. (1975). A Century of *Cymbeline*; or Garrick's Magic Touch. In *From Chaucer to Gibbon: Essays in Memory of Curt A. Zimansky. Philological Quarterly*, 54, 310–22.

Sullivan, G. A., Jr. (1998). Civilizing Wales: *Cymbeline*, Roads, and the Landscapes of Early Modern Britain. *The Drama of Landscape: Land, Property, and Social Relations on the Early Modern Stage*. Stanford, CA: Stanford University Press.

Taylor, G. (1989). *Reinventing Shakespeare: A Cultural History from the Restoration to the Present*. New York: Oxford University Press.

Van Lennep, W. (1965). *The London Stage 1660–1800, Part 1: 1660–1700*. Carbondale: Southern Illinois University Press.

Warren, R. (1988). Shakespeare's Late Plays at Stratford, Ontario. *Shakespeare Survey*, 40, 155–63.

——(1989). *Cymbeline*. Shakespeare in Performance Series. Manchester: Manchester University Press.

——(ed.) (1998). *Cymbeline*. Oxford: Oxford University Press.

Wayne, V. (forthcoming). The Woman's Parts of *Cymbeline*. In J. G. Harris and N. Korda (eds.) *Staged Properties in Early Modern English Drama*. Cambridge: Cambridge University Press.

Wickham, G. (1980). Riddle and Emblem: A Study in the Dramatic Structure of *Cymbeline*. *English Renaissance Studies: Presented to Dame Helen Gardner in honour of her Seventieth Birthday*. Oxford: Clarendon Press.

Woodbridge, L. (1991). Palisading the Elizabethan Body Politic. *Texas Studies in Literature and Language*, 33, 327–54.

21
"Meaner Ministers": Mastery, Bondage, and Theatrical Labor in *The Tempest*
Daniel Vitkus

Should these fellowes come out of my debt, I should have no rule with them.

Philip Henslowe

The Tempest traditionally has been thought of as a "farewell to the stage," a valedictory work in which Prospero stands in for Shakespeare himself, the refined poet and gifted artist, forced to use the stage to make a living but eager to abjure the "rough magic" of theatre, once he has made his fortune. Prospero "retires" to Milan, just as Shakespeare retired to Stratford, "drowning" his playbooks and heading for home. Correlative to this reading of the play is an extended allegory that associates magic with theatrical illusion, the magician with the playwright, and Ariel and the spirits with players. This allegorization of the play as an autobiography about the magic of theatre has a long genealogy, beginning with the Scottish poet Thomas Campbell, who, in his 1838 edition of Shakespeare's *Dramatic Works*, was the first literary critic to claim that Prospero is really Shakespeare himself.[1] Campbell and subsequent proponents of this autobiographical interpretation return to the same key passages from *The Tempest* as evidence for their interpretations.[2] They focus their attention on three moments in the play: Prospero's speech to Ferdinand and Miranda at 4.1.148–58, his soliloquy at 5.1.33–57, and the "Epilogue," "spoken by Prospero." These critics suggest that at the end of the play Shakespeare speaks through Prospero, telling the audience that his creative "charms are all o'erthrown" and asking them for "release" from his theatrical labors.

Recent scholarship continues to assert a connection between Prospero's "art" and Shakespeare's. David Bevington, for example, concludes his 1999 essay, "Shakespeare the Man" (in Kastan 1999), by arguing, albeit somewhat furtively, for an autobiographical Prospero: "In today's critical stance toward *The Tempest*, Prospero's stock has diminished considerably; yet I cannot but imagine that I see in Prospero the deep conflict between pride and humility in the artist as he considers his creation and reflects on what it will be to lay aside not only art but life itself" (p. 20). Annabel

Patterson, in *Shakespeare and the Popular Voice* (1989), also assumes that Prospero speaks for Shakespeare himself. After citing the play's "Epilogue," she asks, "What can this mean (beyond the conventional actor's appeal for applause) if not that Shakespeare, at the end of his career, found himself in the carceral space of his own intelligence and its limits, partly self-imposed, partly the constraints of time, place, profession and belief" (p. 160)? Bevington and Patterson's reliance upon authorial intention is anomalous, though, because in recent decades leading Shakespearean scholars have tended to avoid reading *The Tempest* as autobiography. Nonetheless, the notion that the play was the Bard's farewell to the stage is certainly as prevalent as ever in our culture at large.

In recent decades, author-centered readings of *The Tempest* have given way to a different interpretation, one in which Prospero is not so much a playwright as a colonizer and master.[3] This shift is clearly symptomatic of the general trend in literary studies away from humanist readings that focus on the intentions of great authors toward more politically sensitive, historicized readings of early modern plays as contingent texts. For a time, writing about *The Tempest* was dominated by colonial and postcolonial readings that focused on the violent exploitation of Caliban by his master, Prospero. But the zealous politicizing of first-wave new historicism perhaps went too far in its forceful anti-colonialist readings of *The Tempest*, or at least that is the charge leveled by those who have recently disputed the claim that colonialism is the dominant discourse through which *The Tempest* communicates its meanings (see Fuchs 1997; Kastan 1999; Skura 1989; Schneider 1995; Willis 1989; Wilson 1997). David Scott Kastan (1999) suggests that in reading the play as an allegory of colonialism, we merely "substitute another allegory" for "the biographical one of Prospero as Shakespeare, or the humanistic one of his magic as art" (pp. 193–4), and Deborah Willis (1989) argues that anti-colonialist interpretations reproduce "an error that has haunted criticism of *The Tempest* – that is, the conflation of Prospero with Shakespeare" (p. 279).

All of this critical controversy just seems to engender further contextualizing treatments of *The Tempest*. An array of topical and local readings has amply demonstrated the multivalent and overdetermined nature of Shakespeare's text. Prospero has been identified, not only with Shakespeare himself, but also with John Dee, Sir Robert Dudley, James I, and Rudolf II. The almost endless capacity of Shakespearean critics to tease out new and more localized signification from *The Tempest* might seem to overload the text with topical meanings that threaten to crush "the play itself." Clearly, the play is not simply a play "about" colonialism; nor is it exclusively a representation of Mediterranean concerns. In this essay, I am interested in showing how the text of *The Tempest* produces various domestic and exotic meanings, and I want to locate these meanings within a broader discursive matrix that deals with power and labor, mastery and bondage. Both the New and Old World contexts are important, I would argue, for understanding the play historically, but here I will discuss the colonial environment only briefly so that I may concentrate on the Old World and its playhouses.

The concept of mastery, which was so basic to early modern order and hierarchy, brings together various readings of *The Tempest* that highlight different discourses or referential patterns. The Old World and New World readings of *The Tempest* come together in the practice of coerced labor and in the concepts of freedom and bondage that define the play's plot and dramatic "timing." In their remarks on *The Tempest*, Francis Barker and Peter Hulme attempt to move beyond topicality and source study, theorizing the play within a multiplicity of "discursive con-texts." Barker and Hulme call for a "politicized intertextuality" and reject "the autotelic text with its single fixed meaning" (Graff and Phelan 2000: 232), but once they set forth their specific textual analysis of the play, they emphasize "English colonialism," which they define as an "ensemble of fictional and lived practices" that comprise "*The Tempest*'s dominant discursive con-texts" (p. 236). At the moment of its origination, and in its early performances, the text of *The Tempest* emerged from and functioned within a "preexisting set of linguistic and discursive possibilities" (Kastan 1999: 39). The plurality of histories and significations with which the text engages can never be completely foreclosed, and they are not limited to any one discourse or context – the New World colonies, Mediterranean politics, theatrical labor, for example. But this does not imply that the text can mean what any Humpty Dumpty-like critic wants it to mean. The playtext activates part of that matrix of semiotic possibilities, but the manifestation of that activation is not a random play of meanings. All readings are biased, but some readings of *The Tempest* are so heavily weighted with the concerns of the interpreter that they fail to pass the test of historical validity. Standing between the opposite poles of relativism and particular historical meaning, what we can do is identify a pattern of signification that emanates from the text's engagements with its historical surroundings. *The Tempest* is a social text that identifies certain fields of discourse as its concerns. One such field of discourse engaged by *The Tempest* is the social practice of mastery and bondage. Once we have identified such a pattern, it may help us to see how various, seemingly conflicting analyses of *The Tempest* are really pieces of the same messy, open-framed puzzle.

At this point, I want to return to the notion of Prospero as a playwright or master of theatrical illusion, as a version of Shakespeare – but with a difference. It may still be possible, I wish to suggest, to sustain a reading of *The Tempest* as a play about theatre, about theatre's power to influence and control minds and about the conditions of labor that made the cultural production of theatre possible – without engaging in the mystifications of Romantic or idealist criticism. Douglas Bruster's fine essay on *The Tempest* and "the work of the early modern playhouse" has already established some connections between the thematic or figurative meaning of theatre in the play and the very real, material conditions of stage labor. According to Bruster, "[The Tempest's] portrait of playhouse labor and experience includes not only Prospero as playwright/director, but Miranda as a figure of idealized spectatorship, and Ariel as a boy actor" (Bruster 1995). While making the case for a "local" reading of *The Tempest*, Bruster wishes to "call into question a thoroughly colonialist interpretation of the play" (p. 258), but this sort of "either-or" approach to historicizing the play is unnecessary if we accept the notion that there are many, simultaneously operable discursive contexts within which the text registers its prolific meanings. In order to claim, as Bruster does, that *The Tempest* is a play about the conditions of labor in the playhouse, we are not required to deny the validity of the "colonialist interpretation." I would maintain that these readings are overlapping and mutually reinforcing, not mutually exclusive. The politics of *The Tempest* function locally, referring to the playhouses and social relations in London, but the play also signifies at the level of the intercultural and the transatlantic.[4] In fact, Bruster's fascinating demonstration of the similarity between early modern playhouses and ships shows how the issues of mastery and servitude were mobile, and could move from London, by sea and through tempest, to Virginia or the Mediterranean.

In an essay titled "Industrious Ariel and Idle Caliban," Andrew Gurr (1996) also points to the question of servitude as it is dramatized in the relationship of Prospero to Ariel, and Prospero to Caliban. According to Gurr, "Both Ariel and Caliban serve through the play in roles somewhere between that of bound apprentice, paid servant and unpaid slave" (p. 202). Gurr, like Bruster, seeks to correct and replace the allegedly reductive "colonial" reading of power in *The Tempest*: "what we now prefer to read as colonialist power is verbalized as a pair of master–servant relationships. Patriarchs colonized their servants" (p. 198). Gurr is surely correct, but the complexity and ambiguity of the Shakespearean text, I would argue, allow for a play that presents power as both masterly and colonial. After all, these two went hand in hand in the practice of New World colonialism.

Surprisingly, Gurr does not connect *The Tempest*'s representations of labor or servitude to the play's concern with the production of theatrical illusion. While Bruster and Gurr have both written in illuminating ways about servitude and labor in *The Tempest*, they have not identified the correspondence between the play's concern with bondage and the specific practice of "bonding" theatrical laborers within a particular theatrical company. Through its representation of theatrical labor, the play comments on how the production of dramatic illusion in the playhouses of Shakespeare's London relied upon the "bondage" of theatrical workers. The power of Prospero over the other characters in the play suggests, not only the power of the colonial governor over his subjects and servants, but it also provides an image of a theatrical impresario controlling and exploiting the players and playwrights whom he has hired to put on plays. The allusions to theatricality in *The Tempest*, and the staging of the false banquet and betrothal masque in act 4, present the character of Prospero as the one who commands and controls all of the dramaturgical effects and performances within the play. The text offers the possibility of seeing Prospero's power and control as analogous to the power exercised by a wealthy playhouse owner and manager over those who serve him. There are no direct, one-to-one correspondences at work here (such as Prospero = Shakespeare, Prospero = playwright, or Ariel = player). Rather, Prospero, Ariel, and Prospero's "meaner ministers" represent a range of different theatrical identities. As Anne Barton (1962) has observed, "Prospero is like a dramatist, contriving a play, but he himself is actor in that drama as well, involved with the illusion on his own level" (p. 201).

Shakespeare was not only a playwright; he was also a sharer in a theatrical company, someone involved in the business of producing theatre, and of employing and managing a group of laborers. Shakespeare was actor, playwright, "housekeeper," and sharer. As a hired actor, early in his career on the London stage, it is quite likely that he was "bound" to a theatrical master.[5] Later, he was freed and became a master over those who were bound to him and his company. Probably as early as 1589, Shakespeare began acting and writing plays, and in 1594 he bought his first share in the company known then as the Lord Chamberlain's Men. By the turn of the century he was making at least £50 annually from the theatre (probably much more), and by 1602 he was able to raise £320 to pay for 107 acres of land in Old Stratford. After 1608, when he became a sharer in the Blackfriars theatre, his income increased even more. With his wealth came power, and his employees in the playhouse were undoubtedly subject to that power.

The scholarship of Andrew Gurr, G. E. Bentley, Harold N. Hillebrand, Michael Shapiro, and others bears ample witness to the abusive and exploitative relationship that existed between playhouse owners or company sharers (like Shakespeare) and the theatrical laborers they employed, including playwrights and players. We know very little about Shakespeare's business practices in London (though in Stratford he hoarded grain and enclosed common lands), and even less about Shakespeare's managerial role in the running of his company; but we can assume that the Lord Chamberlain's Men (and later the King's Men) carried out many of the same business strategies as their competitors. The playhouse owner we know the most about is, of course, Philip Henslowe. If *The Tempest*'s subtext of theatricality refers, as I would argue, not exclusively to Shakespeare and his company, but comments on the material conditions of playing in London in a general way, then we may take the evidence of Henslowe's diary as a useful resource for comparing the business of the early modern theatre to the words and actions of *The Tempest*.

Though Shakespeare's relations with his playhouse underlings may have been more benign, let us consider, nonetheless, the example of Philip Henslowe, who, as he grew wealthier and more powerful, became increasingly distant and exploitative in his relations with the players who worked with and for him.[6] He kept a book, now known as his "diary," in which he entered accounts and memoranda that manifested and documented the economic power he exercised over others. "Prospero's books" may be compared to Henslowe's diary, or to the account books kept by masters, shareholders, or playhouse owners like James Burbage, Langley, Henslowe, Beeston, Heminges, or William Shakespeare. The books kept by Prospero in his cell may suggest, not only magical books of spells and conjuration, full of occult knowledge, but also financial account books that kept track of debts, purchase and sale of commodities, noting goods held as collateral to secure outstanding debts, and theatrical services rendered. What "the book" stood for in early modern England was the power of literacy and of technocratic discourses (legal, ecclesiastical, financial) that were used to maintain mastery over the lower classes. Caliban declares that the key to a successful rebellion against Prospero is "First to possess his books, for without them / He's but a sot, as

I am, nor hath not / One spirit to command" (3.2.92–3). Without his written records and account books, Henslowe (or any other theatrical impresario) would not have been able to maintain the network of economic control required to produce commercial theatre and make a profit from it.

Throughout the period that Shakespeare worked in the theatre, and until his death in January of 1616 (just before Shakespeare's), Henslowe maintained a complex web of financial relations with a series of theatre companies who performed in his play-houses. In 1615 one of these companies, the Lady Elizabeth's Men, drew up a legal document, the "Articles of Grievance and Oppression against Philip Henslowe," that accused Henslowe of a series of unjust and exploitative practices.[7] Even if we take into account that the articles only provide one side of the story, it is still clear from his own records that Henslowe systematically used the practice of the legal "bond" to control and profit from various groups of players. Like Prospero's partnership with Ariel, the contracts made between Henslowe and the companies involve the over-whelming power of the master over his theatrical servants. The case of the Lady Elizabeth's Men was only one among many. They accused Henslowe of various abuses, accomplished primarily through alternating acts of "bonding" (or "bounding") and then "breaking" the company:

> In ffebruarie last 1614 perceav[ing]e the Companie drew out of his debt and called uppon him for his accompts hee brooke the Companie againe; by with drawinge the hired men from them . . .
>
> Hee hath taken all boundes of our hired men in his owne name whose wages though we have truly paid yet att his pleasure hee hath taken them a waye; and turned them over to others to the breaking of our Companie.
>
> . . . Uppon everie breach of the Companie hee takes newe bondes for his stocke; and our securitie for playing with him Soe that he hath in his handes, bondes of ours to the value of £5000 and his stocke to; which hee denies to deliver and threatens to oppresse us with.
>
> . . . The reason of his often breakinge with us; he gave in those words[:] should these fellowes Come out of my debt, I should have no rule with them[.]
>
> Alsoe wee have paid him for plaie bookes £200 or thereaboutes and yet hee denies to give us the Coppies of any of them.
>
> Also with in 3 yeeres hee hath broken and dissmembred five Companies.

Henslowe the playhouse patron sounds like Antonio the politician, who knew "how to grant suits, / How to deny them, who t' advance and who / To trash for over-topping" (1.2.79–81).

It was advantageous to a playhouse owner to break a company and then enter into a new relationship with a new or reconstituted company. This did not happen to Shakespeare's company because they owned their playhouse building and did not need to rent one from a landlord like Henslowe. But *The Tempest*'s representation of theatrical labor is not about the King's Men. It refers to theatrical labor in a much more indirect and general way. Our awareness of the economic practice of breaking companies may help us to see in Prospero's breaking of his staff, drowning of his book, and his final plea, not only a renunciation of magic, or the end of a performance, but at the same time, the end of a contractual relationship with those who serve him.

For Henslowe, it was not only the gallery rents or monies collected from play-goers that enriched and empowered him, but also the usurious profits that he made from his loans to players, playwrights, and the shareholders in theatrical companies. Debt and the threat of more debt were the bonds that kept players and playwrights in thrall. Various letters to Henslowe, preserved in the Dulwich College papers, add further evidence to the picture of Henslowe as a master of theatrical workers who were short on money.[8] These documents reveal that Henslowe combined pawnbroking and moneylending with his theatrical affairs. An interesting example of Henslowe lending to a theatrical laborer is revealed in the extensive correspondence maintained between Henslowe and the playwright Richard Daborne between April 1613 and July 1614. In these letters, which are preserved in the Dulwich College manuscripts, Daborne promises to deliver a series of plays for Henslowe's use and repeatedly begs for and receives cash advances.[9] At about the same time, the actor Nathaniel Field and others wrote to Henslowe asking for £5 as bail to get them out of debtor's prison. Henslowe was the company store, and those who labored in his mines soon found themselves bound to him.

As Gurr informs us, even those who were sharers in a theatre company were committed to their investment through a coercive principle: "It was an essential feature of the share system that it should operate not only as an investment for the sharer but as a commitment binding the owner to play for the company and to keep its interests its own. If a sharer left without his fellows' consent he was not reimbursed for his share" (Gurr 1992: 68). Sharers and actors like Shakespeare were contractually bound in some cases to remain with a company for a period of years, usually three; and they could be fined for failing to attend rehearsals, for being drunk, or for wearing the company's apparel outside of the playhouse.[10]

Playhouse owners like Langley and Henslowe had players agree to a "bond" requiring them to remain with a particular company for several years, and if they left the company before the expiration of that period they could be sued for the amount of their bond (sometimes as much as £100). For example, Henslowe recorded in his diary on October 6, 1597, the following bond: "Thomas dowten came & bownd hime sealfe unto me in xxxx *li* in & a some sett by the Receving of iii *d* of me before wittnes the covenant is this that he shold . . . come ii yeares to playe in my howsse & in no other a bowte London publickeley yf he do with owt my consent to forfet unto me this some of money above written" (cited in Rutter 1984: 58). Although they were subject to such bonds, players serving a specific theatrical master could leave one company and join another, as many members of Langley's Pembroke's Men did in 1597 after the royal authorities shut down Langley's Swan playhouse. When one of those actors, William Bird, was sued for collection of the bond by Langley, Bird's new master, Henslowe, made loans to Bird so that he could reach a financial settlement with his former employer. But these debts then bonded Bird, in turn, to Henslowe. Similarly,

Ariel owes Prospero a debt of gratitude because Prospero freed him from the bondage of Sycorax. Prospero, like Henslowe, saved his servant from imprisonment or set him free from onerous servitude under a competing master. Of course, both Henslowe and Prospero did this only to obtain the services of the grateful laborer, who was then strictly bound to his new master.

The role of Ariel was played by a boy actor, and boys were bought, sold, and "bound" in the theatre (as well as in other trades).[11] In one of his diary entries, Philip Henslowe recorded the following transaction: "Bowght my boye Jeames brystow of william agustin player the 18 of desember 1597 for [£8]" (cited by Rutter 1984: 127). In some cases, boy actors were seized and "impressed" without any payment at all. This was a practice carried out by the theatre managers who ran boy companies like the Chapel Children. Records reveal that when in 1597 Nathaniel Gyles was appointed "Master of her Majesties Chyldren of the Chapell of Saynt George," he received a royal writ that gave him the power to seize schoolchildren and force them to work as actors in his company. Apparently, this power was also enjoyed by his predecessors in that office, Hunnis and Edwards.[12] In 1601 the managers of the Chapel company were accused of abusing the privilege of impressment and engaging in what amounts to kidnapping. They ran into trouble because they made the mistake of abducting Thomas Clifton, a boy whose father, Henry Clifton, brought a suit in Star Chamber against the company directors, claiming that they had systematically kidnapped boys who were "noe way able or fitt for singing, nor by anie the sayd confederates endevoured to be taught to singe, but by them the sayd confederates abusively employed . . . only in playes & enterludes" (cited in Hillebrand 1964: 161–2). Among those impressed by the Chapel Children at this time was Nathaniel Field, who went on to become one of the most renowned players in London at the time that Shakespeare was writing for the King's Men.[13]

Whether they worked for the choirboy companies or the "adult" companies, boy actors were bound to their theatrical masters for a period of three to twelve years. Boy actors received none of the profits and served without the pay that hired actors received.[14] The boys were treated as apprentices, but without the rights that some apprentices enjoyed under the protection of the guild organizations. An established sharer would act as the boy's master during his time with the company, and under these circumstances the boy was subject to the whims of his master, who was not accountable to any guild authorities. Boy actors could expect to work in the theatre for the period that they were bound, and though some of them went on to find employment as adult actors, most would be turned out on the street when they grew too old to play the women's parts. According to G. E. Bentley, only thirty to thirty-five actors are known to have successfully advanced from bondage as a boy actor to become "free" members of adult companies (Bentley 1984: 134).

In *The Tempest* Ariel's desire for freedom is analogous to a boy actor's desire to complete his years of bond-servitude and be freed. Throughout the play, Ariel's labor is associated with the elapsing of carefully regulated, contractual time. The timing of *The Tempest* is clearly linked to the time it takes to put on a play (and the word "tempest" is derived from the Latin *tempestas*, meaning a portion of time). Prospero, while delivering his orders to Ariel, makes it plain that the play will transpire during the time of day that plays were performed in the public playhouses – "The time twixt six" and "two glasses" (1.2.240) – 2–6 p.m. This short-term period also stands for Ariel's many years of bondage under Prospero. As the Arden editors indicate, "Ariel is Prospero's indentured servant, under an oral agreement to work for a fixed period, though . . . Ariel suggests that the magician had offered him a one-year reduction in return for services rendered" (Vaughan and Vaughan 1999: 166). From the moment of his first entrance until the play's final scene, Ariel does Prospero's bidding like an actor who must do whatever is scripted for him. Ariel's actions are keyed as theatrical labors: "Ariel, thy charge / exactly is performed" (1.2.238), says Prospero, referring to the preceding scene, the one that began the play. In the first act, Ariel demands his "liberty" (1.2.245), which he claims is overdue, but he is only threatened and told to continue his labors. The show must go on, and each time that Ariel performs, "there's more work" (1.2.238) assigned by his master. At the beginning of *The Tempest* it is two o'clock and time to begin another performance.

Prospero acts as scriptwriter and prompter, commenting on the play's early progress in an aside, "It goes on, I see, / As my soul prompts it" (1.2.420–1). Here, he needs the "actors" in his play, Ferdinand and Miranda, to fall in love, so that his dynastic scheme can be fulfilled. Prospero prescribes, then watches and guides, the performance enacted by Ariel and the other spirits. The timing of the young lovers' first meeting is gauged to induce mutual attraction. Prospero has to play the role himself of the conventional comic "blocking figure," so that the desires of Ferdinand and Miranda have an obstacle against which they can intensify the pressure of their longing for each other. The audience overhears Prospero's delight at the outcome of the lovers' first encounter, but then sees him move suddenly into the role of the overprotective patriarch, who speaks "ungently" (1.2.445) to Ferdinand and accuses him of spying. Throughout this scene, and in the play as a whole, attentiveness and timing are essential to both the Machiavellian plotter's political success and to the leading actor's facilitation of an effective theatrical performance that combines rehearsed and improvised action.

The play's two conspiracies are both figured as prescribed scenes that the plotters begin to perform but fail to enact completely. They are weak counter-plots to Prospero's well rehearsed play. Antonio tells Sebastian that he has imagined a scene which will conclude with Sebastian's coronation: "My strong imagination sees a crown / Dropping upon thy head" (2.1.208–9), and, when Stephano addresses his co-conspirators, his plan to murder Prospero is explicitly proposed as the synopsis of a play: "Monster, I will kill this man. His daughter and I will be king and queen – save our graces – and Trinculo and thyself shall be viceroys. Dost thou like the plot, Trinculo?" (3.2.106–9). In his edition of *The Tempest*, Frank Kermode (1954) glosses Stephano's use of "plot" as "a skeleton programme giving a synopsis of a masque or entertainment."

Stephano and Trinculo turn their tragic assassination plot into drunken farce, but Prospero orchestrates a more refined and controlled drama (though not without its own improvisational moments). Whenever Ariel appears to carry out Prospero's orders, he is associated with performativity and is often the object of dramatic ironies that remind the audience of the play's status as illusion. His invisibility, which is entirely visible to the spectators, is one such reminder; and whenever he directs the other "spirits," the audience observes him as he labors to produce a dramaturgical deception. The banquet overseen by Prospero and performed by Ariel's spirits is called "A living drollery" (2.3.21) by Sebastian, who does not expect to find a courtly dumb show on a desert island. He and the other courtiers react with wonder, and their deludedness places them at two removes from non-dramatic reality – the spectacles they view are staged by Ariel, who is impersonated by a boy actor. The audience knows that Gonzalo's mistaken interpretation – "for certes, these are people of the island" (3.3.30) – is only a product of Prospero and Ariel's stage trickery. And the wonderment expressed by Alonso – "I cannot too much muse / Such shapes, such gesture and such sound" (3.3.36–7) – is praise for just those elements that make up a skillful theatrical performance. The music used by Ariel to calm Ferdinand in 1.2 is another example: Ferdinand believes that the music is supernatural ("no mortal business": 1.2.407), while the playgoers know it is merely the effect of a theatrical show. Magic, including the powers possessed by Ariel and the other spirits, is made possible by the labor and technology of theatre – along with the audience's suspension of disbelief. Because of Prospero's powers and Ariel's labors, Prospero can charm Ferdinand from moving, Ariel can dry and freshen the sea-soaked clothes of the castaways, induce sudden sleepiness, make a banquet appear and then suddenly disappear, create packs of dogs to pursue the conspirators, present a betrothal masque for Ferdinand and Miranda, and more.

In 1.2 Prospero reminds Ariel of the conditions under which Ariel suffered before he came to serve Prospero. It sounds as if working for Sycorax was like working in another trade altogether, something requiring hard manual labor and close confinement – not the task of performing the wide-ranging repertory of a first-rate theatre company. "It was mine art," boasts Prospero, "that made gape / The pine and let thee out" (1.2.291–3). "Art" here means "skill" in magic, but the general idea is that a master who uses knowledge as power will gain and maintain mastery over the means of production.

The false banquet and the betrothal masque, more than any other scenes in *The Tempest*, present Prospero and Ariel as theatrical creators and performers. These two plays within the play demonstrate clearly that theatre is a collaborative enterprise, and that the labor necessary to carry out plots and create illusions must be undertaken by a group of cooperative and mutually dependent agents (much like the playhouse owner, the sharers, the players, the stage-prompter, the other playhouse employees, and, of course, the spectators, all of whom come together to make drama happen). After staging and performing in the false banquet, Ariel is praised by Prospero for his acting skills: "Bravely the figure of this harpy hast thou / Performed, my Ariel; a grace it had, devouring" (3.3.83–4). He sounds like a playwright who is pleased that the actors have followed his intended script, without leaving out any lines or employing undue improvisation:

Of my instruction hast thou nothing bated
In what thou hadst to say. So, with good life
And observation strange, my meaner ministers
Their several kinds have done. (3.3.85–8)

"I must use you / In such another trick" (4.1.36–7), says Prospero to Ariel, and the
betrothal masque follows immediately, one scene after another, allowing time for
Ariel's "meaner fellows" (4.1.35) to change costumes. What Prospero calls "Some
vanity of mine art" (4.1.41) is the necessary illusion and impersonation required by
the stage-master in order to carry out the profit-making business of theatre. Calling
for extra actors to fill up the troupe, Prospero gives the word for the performance to
begin: "Appear, and pertly. / No tongue, all eyes. Be silent!" (4.1.54–5). Ferdinand
does not remain silent, though. He interrupts in order to praise the quality of
the masque performance. Its verisimilitude is so impressive that he has to ask if the
performers are human or superhuman:

> *Ferdinand.* This is a most majestic vision, and
> Harmonious charmingly. May I be bold
> To think these spirits?
> *Prospero.*   Spirits, which by mine art
> I have from their confines called to enact
> My present fancies. (4.1.118–22)

In a masque, in particular, the audience members were known to merge with the
actors at the end, and they, along with the King himself, left their seats and participated directly in the performance. But this does not occur. Instead, the masque illusion is shattered, interrupted by Prospero's recollection of the "conspiracy / Of the
beast Caliban and his confederates" (4.1.139–40). The famous speech that follows
reminds the audience of the ephemerality and – implicitly – the materiality of the
Globe Theatre and the play that is being staged therein:

> Our revels now are ended. These our actors,
> As I foretold you, were spirits and
> Are melted into air, into thin air;
> And – like the baseless fabric of this vision –
> The cloud-capped towers, the gorgeous palaces,
> The solemn temples, the great globe itself,
> Yea, all which it inherit, shall dissolve,
> And like this insubstantial pageant faded,
> Leave not a rack behind. (4.1.148–56)

Perhaps these words were intended by Shakespeare to be his farewell to the stage. We
will never know his intention, but it is clear that these lines refer to the production
of theatrical illusion. All of the frenetic activity, rehearsal, and the performance itself

– all of the labor and imaginative energy that are materially manifest in a play's action on a stage – are merely an "insubstantial pageant." Like the play itself, Prospero suggests, human life and consciousness are also performative and transitory. But the troubling thoughts that have distempered and angered Prospero are not meditations on the nature of theatre or even of the theatricality of "our little life." What Prospero is still thinking about is mastery, and his plot to regain it.

Prospero's renunciation of magic in act 5 brings an end to playing. The actors will return to their proper identities, just as Prospero will "break" his charms so that the courtiers can "be themselves" once more, no longer distracted with grief or fear, but ready to recover their proper positions under Prospero's rule without the need of magical inducements. Prospero's soliloquy celebrates the power of magic (or the "magic" of theatre) to produce awesome illusions, but the use of Medea's speech from Ovid on witchcraft indicates that there is something dangerous about the use of this "rough magic," something that the magus must "abjure" (5.1.50–1). Theatre could be dangerous, illegitimate, or unreliable. The playhouses might be forced to close because of plague, the opposition of the city authorities, or because of royal displeasure. It was an unstable business, one that could make a lot of money, but disreputable and transgressive. Commercial theatre could make a sharer wealthy, but a less risky, more respectable form of mastery might be more desirable after years of working in the playhouses – to enjoy the privileges of owning land, to buy a coat of arms for one's family, and to settle down in the country with an entailed estate to leave to one's heirs. After writing a play in which theatre is shown to rely upon bondage, Shakespeare retired from the theatre and settled down in Stratford as "Master William Shakespeare, Gentleman."

The first recorded performance of *The Tempest* took place on November 1, 1611, at Whitehall, and after that, as far as we know, Shakespeare stopped writing his own plays. It is true that as late as 1613 he was still contributing portions of plays and is known to have shared with John Fletcher in the authorship of three more (*Cardenio, Two Noble Kinsmen,* and *Henry VIII*), but once the Globe had burned to the ground in June of 1613, during a performance of *Henry VIII*, Shakespeare seems to have severed his professional ties to the London playhouses.[15]

Prospero's relationships with Caliban, Ariel, and Ferdinand represent various forms of mastery known to Shakespeare and his audience, and recent anti-colonialist readings of *The Tempest* also focus tightly on Prospero's power. The play's representations of servitude and slavery were staged within a context of economic expansion that encouraged fantasies about new powers that could be used in new lands, or used in new ways at home. Stephen Greenblatt has argued that the Virginia Company and Shakespeare's theatrical company, the King's Men, are analogous "joint-stock companies" (Greenblatt, in White 1999: 103). Greenblatt compares Shakespeare to Strachey (who was a shareholder and the secretary of the Virginia Company) and proposes "that the relation between the play and its alleged source is a relation between joint-stock companies" (p. 103).

At the time that *The Tempest* was first appearing on the London stage, English "venturers" were accelerating their economic involvement in both the "Old"

Mediterranean world and the "New World" of the Americas. In both contexts, slavery, servitude, and bondage of various kinds were essential practices for maintaining profitable economic systems and for regulating lower-class labor. In the Mediterranean, in Spain and Portugal, and in the New World colonies, slavery and harsh forms of servitude were observed by the English, who began to carry out similar practices once they established their own colonies in the Americas. In the post-1492 New World Order, emergent, globalizing capitalism relied heavily on the use of slave labor and indentured servitude – at home and abroad.

The "bonds" that held theatrical laborers in London operated similarly to the "bonds" that held colonial laborers and "redemptioners" in servitude abroad. Before slaves were brought from Africa to Virginia, English subjects were transported to provide the labor needed to run the struggling new colonies.[16] In the colonial practice of indenture, not uncommonly, landowners treated servants like slaves. Those who did have contracts often found themselves at the mercy of masters who mistreated them, provided the bare minimum in terms of food, clothing, and shelter, and prevented them from obtaining ownership of land. Those who arrived without a preexisting contract could simply be sold by those who had transported them to the New World.

Shakespeare's source text, William Strachey's "True Repertory of the Wracke," describes the plight of a ship that was on its way to Virginia and was carrying laborers to relieve the colony. The crew that shipwrecked at Bermuda was under the command of Sir Thomas Gates, an official who was sent to establish discipline and order in Jamestown and who, once he finally arrived, established martial law there and carried out severe punishments and forced labor. The regulations established by Gates upon his arrival in the beleaguered colony were published in 1612 by Strachey under the title *For the Colony in Virginea Britannia. Lawes Divine, Morall, and Martiall.* Appearing at the beginning of this code of martial law is one of the colony's most basic precepts concerning the enforcement of daily labor:

> Every tradsman in their severall occupation, trade and function, shall duly and daily attend his worke upon his said trade or occupation . . .
>
> All overseers of workemen shall be carefull in seeing that performed, which is given them in charge, upon paine of such punishment as shall be inflicted upon him by a martiall Court.
>
> 28 No souldier or tradesman, but shall be readie, both in the morning, & in the afternoone, upon the beating of the Drum, to goe out unto his worke, nor shall hee returne home, or from his worke, before the Drum beate againe, and the officer appointed for that businesse, bring him of[f], upon perill for the first fault to lie upon the Guard head and heeles together all night, for the second time so faulting to be whipt, and for the third time so offending to be condemned to the Gallies for a yeare. (13–14)

For Ariel and Caliban, there was no place to run from forced labor, but the next prohibition listed in the *Lawes* reminds us that there was a way out for Virginia's colonial laborers: "29 No man or woman, (upon paine of death) shall runne away from the

Colonie, to Powhatan, or any savage Weroance whatsoever" (14). In this sense, at least, the imaginary setting of *The Tempest* is unlike the New World because Prospero's island is so strictly bounded by time and place and by an omnipresent system of mastery.

In the variety of relations between Prospero and others, one thing remains constant: Prospero is a master to whom the others are "bound." All efforts to acquire freedom are contained by Prospero's plot. Throughout the play, the actualization of upper-class mastery is contrasted to lower-class dreams and desires for power. The drunken rebellion of Caliban and the utopian dreams of Gonzalo are two different attempts to replace the usual asymmetries of power with a new order.[17] Both fail. Gonzalo's call for a "commonwealth" (2.1.148) without "occupation" (2.1.155), contracts, or bondage (including marriage) remains a fantasy, and its impracticality is mocked to scorn by Antonio and Sebastian. As for the lower-class challenge to Prospero's rule, it descends rapidly into the mock mastery of Stephano over Trinculo and Caliban, parodying and legitimating by contrast the order and hierarchy upon which Prospero's rule depends. In *The Tempest* all are bound, one to the other, in a vast, inescapable hierarchy of dependencies. The "tribute" and "homage" (1.2.113) paid by the Duke of Milan to the King of Naples is but a magnified version of the service paid by Caliban to Prospero.

Like Ariel, Caliban is bound to Prospero against his will and even Ferdinand must prove himself by submitting to forced labor (though he is later released and rewarded). Prospero cannot carry out his revenge and restoration plot without his "meaner ministers." He needs his servants and slaves, just as any playhouse owner needed the players. He confides in Miranda, referring to Caliban: "But as 'tis / We cannot miss him; he . . . / serves in offices that profit us" (1.2.311–14). Giving up his magic means that Prospero will no longer be able to command Ariel and the other spirits to do his bidding (although perhaps we may assume that in Milan he will no longer need them). The suspense that builds up to Prospero's renunciation, culminating in the "farewell" Epilogue, is directly connected to the termination of Ariel's coerced bondage. And yet there is a strong sense of deferral and delay in all this, tied to the play's sense of timing. Prospero seems curiously unwilling to give up his magic and free Ariel. He makes a series of promises in order to reassure Ariel and motivate him:

. . . after two days / I will discharge thee. (1.2.298–9)

. . . spirit, / I'll free thee / Within two days for this. (1.2.421–2)

Delicate Ariel / I'll set thee free for this. (1.2.442–3)

Thou shalt be as free / As mountain winds, but then exactly do / All points of my command. (1.2.499–501)

Shortly shall all my labors end, and thou Shalt have the air at freedom. For a little, Follow and do me service. (4.1.264–6)

Quickly, spirit, / Thou shalt ere long be free. (5.1.86–7)

I shall miss thee, / But yet thou shalt have freedom. (5.1.95–6)

Prospero doth protest too much.

The last we see of Ariel, he is sent off to perform yet another assigned task, to produce the right weather for the Italians' voyage home:

> My Ariel, chick,
> That is thy charge. Then to the elements
> Be free, and fare thou well! (5.1.317–19)

It seems that this is Ariel's moment of liberation, but the last action that the audience witnesses in the play is Ariel's continued obedience and labor, not his release. That is deferred yet again.

The Tempest, in its conclusion, follows the generic pattern of comedy by forging bonds rather than breaking them. In the end, Prospero chooses not to destroy those who are in his debt, but to forgive them – to show mercy. The power required to destroy one's foes when they are "at one's mercy" is less than the power needed in order to rule over them indefinitely, receiving their continuous homage. In this sense, the ultimate power is the power to be able to forgive one's enemies and know that they will return that forgiveness with constant "love" and submissive service. This is the god-like power that Prospero acquires through his art, and it resembles the power of the Christian deity to "forgive those who have trespassed."

As a master and creditor, Philip Henslowe also exercised the power to forgive the debts of his debtors. Scribbled in the margin of a leaf in Henslowe's book, next to all of his records of debt and bondage, is the following piece of proverbial wisdom: "A man with oute mercye of mersey shall myse & he shall have mersey yt mersey full ys" (Greg 1904, 2: 144). The good master, like any good Christian, must respond with mercy when his servants submit.

The Epilogue's final lines reiterate the concepts of mercy, repayment, and theatrical illusion:

> But release me from my bands,
> With the help of your good hands.
> Gentle breath of yours my sails
> Must fill, or else my project fails,
> Which was to please. Now I want
> Spirits to enforce, art to enchant;
> And my ending is despair,
> Unless I be relieved by prayer,
> Which pierces so that it assaults
> Mercy itself, and frees all faults.
> As you from crimes would pardoned be,
> Let your indulgence set me free. (Epilogue, 11–20)

Here the motif of freedom and bondage takes on an explicitly Christian signification, culminating in a reference to the Lord's Prayer. The development of the mastery theme earlier in the play, however, encourages us to place the "mercy" required to "free all faults" within the context of bond-labor and the business of theatre. The player acting the part of Prospero asks for an end to his labors.

In the Epilogue the speaker gives voice to a dual identity: he speaks as player-servant to the audience, but he also retains his role as the master of the play's performances. In order to gain release from his "bands," the speaker of the Epilogue asks for "prayer" from the audience, but this request is backed by an implicit threat: if you wish to be "pardoned," you must yield to me. Otherwise, the play's final lines imply, you will face damnation at the day of reckoning. (The Latin root of "indulgence," the verb *indulgere*, means "to yield to.") The power of theatre having been renounced, a new power is acquired through a cooperative "indulgence" that will "free all faults." Prospero the playmaster is powerless without applause because applause means money. The alchemical "project" of theatre is to magically convert the insubstantial pageant of theatrical performance into cold, hard cash. That is the "project" that made Shakespeare a rich master and carried him back to his land in Old Stratford. And for that, perhaps he, too, must ask forgiveness.

NOTES

1   Annabel Patterson (1989) points out that the association between Prospero and Shakespeare must have existed at least as early as Dryden's Restoration adaptation of *The Tempest*, which includes these lines:

> But Shakespeare's Magick could not copy'd be,
> Within that Circle none durst walk but he.
> I must confess t'was bold nor would you now
> That liberty to vulgar wits allow
> Which works by Magick supernatural things:
> But Shakespeare's pow'r is sacred as a Kings. (11.19–24; cited in Patterson 1989; 162)

2   Other critics who claim that Shakespeare ventriloquizes through Prospero include the following: Lowell (1870: 200–1); Wilson (1936: 3–6); Knight (1947: 220–3); Masefield (1954: 157–60); Peterson (1973: 244–7).

3   Three studies of *The Tempest* were particularly influential in putting forward this kind of interpretation: Paul Brown's "'This thing of darkness I acknowledge mine': *The Tempest* and the Discourse of Colonialism," Peter Hulme and Francis Barker's "'Nymphs and Reapers Heavily Vanish': The Discursive Contexts of *The Tempest*," and Stephen Greenblatt's comments on *The Tempest* in *Learning to Curse*.

4   Barbara Mowat's (2000) suggestions about "Reading *The Tempest* Intertextually" comprise a useful methodology that can integrate disparate sources and allusive patterns of meaning in the play.

5   Other playwrights were bound in this way. While Thomas Heywood was writing plays for various companies, he was hired by Henslowe as an actor: Henslowe's diary contains the following "memorandum," recorded on March 25, 1598; "Thomas hawoode [Heywood] came & hiered hime seallfe with me as a covenante servante for ij yeares . . . & to beginne at the daye a bove written & not to playe any wher publicke a bowt London not while thes ij yeares be exspired but in my howsse yf he do then he dothe forfett unto me the Receivinge of these ijd fortie powndes" (Greg 1904: f. 231).

6   W. W. Greg (1907), who edited the Henslowe archive, declared "That [Henslowe's] methods of business were harsh and often involved injustice can hardly be disputed" (p. 144). Some scholars have defended Henslowe, claiming that he has been unfairly demonized. For example, Carol C. Rutter (1984) claims that loans extended by Henslowe to the Admiral's Men during the 1590s were not "Henslowe's attempt to achieve an economic stranglehold around a company of players who, lured into debt, were thereafter shackled to his playhouse and enslaved to his management" (p. 101). See also the discussion in Carson (1988: ch. 2).

7   The full text of the document is reproduced in *Henslowe Papers* (Greg 1907: 86–90). See Gurr (1992: 68–72), on how the companies, including Henslowe's, were administered.

8   Greg (1904) summarizes the contents of these letters in *Henslowe's Diary*, vol. 2, pp. 127–44.

9   See Greg (1904, 2: 141–3).

10 Gurr (1992) reproduces a contract stating, among other things, that if one Robert Dawes were to leave the playhouse "with any of their apparell on his or their bodies," he would be liable to pay Henslowe and Jacob Meade a fine of £40 (p. 69).

11 See Burnett (1997: ch. 1), on "Apprenticeship and Society."

12 Impressment of boy choristers is described by Hillebrand (1964: 160).

13 On Field, see Gurr (1992: 58): Field was employed by Henslowe at the time that Shakespeare wrote *The Tempest*, and he seems to have had a close relationship with Henslowe, but as a member of the Lady Elizabeth's Men he was among the signatories to the articles of oppression.

14 See the account of various indentures that held actors in service in Bentley (1984: ch. 5) on "Apprentices." According to Bentley, "The fees paid each week by the company for his services went to the master and not to the boy" (p. 145).

15 In my view, Richard Dutton (1989) is quite right to suggest the "strong possibility . . . that" (after the Globe burned down) "Shakespeare decided at this juncture to withdraw from the venture (and, conceivably, all other theatrical investments), by selling his shares to the other remaining sharers" (p. 156).

16 On colonial bondage and servitude in North America, see Smith (1947).

17 See Dolan (1994: 60–71), for a helpful reading of "The Servant-Monster's Foul Conspiracy" in *The Tempest*.

References and Further Reading

Barton, A. (1962). *Shakespeare and the Idea of the Play.* London: Chatto and Windus.

Bentley, G. E. (1984). *The Profession of Player in Shakespeare's Time.* Princeton, NJ: Princeton University Press.

Bloom, H. (ed.) (1988). *William Shakespeare's "The Tempest." Modern Critical Interpretations.* New York: Chelsea House.

Brotton, J. (1998). "This Tunis, Sir, was Carthage": Contesting Colonialism in *The Tempest*. In A. Loomba and M. Orkin (eds.) *Post-Colonial Shakespeares.* London: Routledge, 23–42.

Brown, P. (1985). "This Thing of Darkness I Acknowledge Mine": *The Tempest* and the Discourse of Colonialism. In *Political Shakespeare: New Essays in Cultural Materialism.* Manchester: Manchester University Press.

Bruster, D. (1995). Local *Tempest*: Shakespeare and the Work of the Early Modern Playhouse. *Journal of Medieval and Renaissance Studies*, 25, 1, 33–53.

Burnett, M. T. (1997). *Masters and Servants in English Renaissance Drama and Culture.* New York: St. Martin's Press.

Campbell, T. (ed.) (1838). *Dramatic Works of William Shakespeare.* London.

Carson, N. (1988). *A Companion to Henslowe's Diary.* Cambridge: Cambridge University Press.

Cartelli, T. (1987). Prospero in Africa: *The Tempest* as Colonialist Text and Pretext. In J. E. Howard and M. F. O'Connor (eds.) *Shakespeare Reproduced*. New York: Methuen.

Cohen, D. (1996). The Culture of Slavery: Caliban and Ariel. *Dalhousie Review*, 76, 2, 153–75.

Dolan, F. E. (1994). *Dangerous Familiars: Representations of Domestic Crime in England, 1550–1700*. Ithaca, NY: Cornell University Press.

Dutton, R. (1989). *William Shakespeare: A Literary Life*. London: Macmillan.

Fuchs, B. (1997). Conquering Islands: Contextualizing *The Tempest*. *Shakespeare Quarterly*, 48, 45–62.

Graff, G. and Phelan, J. (eds.) (2000). *Case Studies in Critical Controversy: William Shakespeare, The Tempest*. Boston, MA and New York: Bedford/St. Martin's Press.

Greenblatt, S. (1988). *Shakespearean Negotiations: The Circulation of Social Energy in Renaissance England*. Berkeley: University of California Press.

——(1990). *Learning to Curse: Essays in Early Modern Culture*. New York: Routledge.

Greg, W. W. (ed.) (1904). *Henslowe's Diary*, 2 vols. London: A. H. Bullen.

——(ed.) (1907). *Henslowe's Papers*. London: A. H. Bullen.

Gurr, A. (1992). *The Shakespearean Stage, 1574–1642*. Cambridge: Cambridge University Press.

——(1996). Industrious Ariel and Idle Caliban. In J.-P. Macquerlot and M. Willems (eds.) *Travel and Drama in Shakespeare's Time*. Cambridge: Cambridge University Press.

Hillebrand, H. N. (1964). *The Child Actors: A Chapter in Elizabethan Stage History*. New York: Russell and Russell.

Hulme, P. and Barker, F. (1985). "Nymphs and Reapers Heavily Vanish": The Discursive Con-Texts of *The Tempest*. In J. Drakakis (ed.) *Alternative Shakespeares*. London: Methuen.

Hulme, P. and Sherman, W. (eds.) (2000). *The Tempest and Its Travels*. Philadelphia: University of Pennsylvania Press.

Kastan, D. S. (1999). *Shakespeare After Theory*. New York: Routledge.

Kermode, F. (ed.) (1954). *The Tempest*. London: Methuen.

Knight, G. W. (1947). *The Crown of Life: Essays in Interpretation of Shakespeare's Final Plays*. Oxford: Oxford University Press.

Lowell, J. R. (1870). Shakespeare Once More. In *Among My Books*. Boston, MA.

Masefield, J. (1954). *William Shakespeare*. London: William Heinemann.

Mowat, B. (2000). "Knowing I loved my books": Reading *The Tempest* Intertextually. In P. Hulme and W. Sherman (eds.) *The Tempest and Its Travels*. Philadelphia: University of Pennsylvania Press.

Murphy, P. M. (ed.) (2000). *The Tempest: Critical Essays*. New York: Routledge.

Patterson, A. (1989). *Shakespeare and the Popular Voice*. Oxford: Blackwell.

Peterson, D. L. (1973). *Time, Tide and Tempest: A Study of Shakespeare's Romances*. San Marino, CA: Huntington Library.

Rutter, C. C. (ed.) (1984). *Documents of the Rose Playhouse*. Manchester: Manchester University Press.

Schneider, B. R., Jr. (1995). "Are We Being Historical Yet?": Colonialist Interpretations of Shakespeare's *Tempest*. *Shakespeare Studies*, 23, 120–45.

Shapiro, M. (1977). *Children of the Revels: The Boy Companies of Shakespeare's Time and Their Plays*. New York: Columbia University Press.

Skura, M. (1989). Discourse and the Individual: The Case of Colonialism in *The Tempest*. *Shakespeare Quarterly*, 40, 42–69.

Smith, A. E. (1947). *Colonists in Bondage: White Servitude and Convict Labor in America, 1607–1776*. Chapel Hill: University of North Carolina Press.

Strachey, W. (1612). *For the Colony in Virginea Britannia. Lawes Divine, Morall, and Martiall*. London.

Taylor, M. (1993). Prospero's Books and Stephano's Bottle: Colonial Experience in *The Tempest*. *CLIO*, 22, 2, 101–13.

Vaughan, V. M. and Vaughan, A. T. (eds.) (1999). *The Tempest*. London: Arden Shakespeare.

White, R. S. (ed.) (1999). *The Tempest, William Shakespeare: Contemporary Critical Essays*. New Casebooks. New York: St. Martin's Press.

Willis, D. (1989). Shakespeare's *Tempest* and the Discourse of Colonialism. *Studies in English Literature 1500–1900*, 29, 2, 277–89.

Wilson, J. D. (1936). *The Meaning of The Tempest*. Newcastle: Literary and Philosophical Society of Newcastle upon Tyne.

Wilson, R. (1997). Voyage to Tunis: New History and the Old World of *The Tempest*. *English Literary History*, 64, 2, 333–57.

22

Queens and the Structure of History in *Henry VIII*

Susan Frye

Henry VIII, originally titled *All Is True*,[1] by William Shakespeare and John Fletcher, presents an unstraightforward account of some sixteen years of Henry's reign. Rather than announce major historical milestones clearly, like Henry's separation and divorce from Katherine of Aragon, his marriage to Anne Bullen (First Folio's spelling of Anne Boleyn), or the birth of Elizabeth I, *Henry VIII* rearranges, foreshortens, and dislocates historical events, creating a fragmented structure noted by two audience members at either end of the seventeenth century. Sir Henry Wotton, newly returned to the court of King James from Venice, provided a famous account of the performance on June 29, 1613, during which the exploding crackers meant to herald the King's entry at Wolsey's banquet ignited the roof of the Globe, on a day when "The King's players had a new play, called *All is true* representing some principal pieces of the reign of Henry VIII" (Wotton 1907, 2: 32). Similarly, the first time that Samuel Pepys saw *Henry VIII*, he found it a play "made up of a great many patches" (Pepys 5.2: January 1, 1664).

For Wotton and Pepys, as for many scholars including myself, this pieced or patched structure[2] highlights the critical issues inherent in what Judith Anderson (1984) has called the play's "displaying of the torn seams of truth" (p. 126). This structure serves Shakespeare and Fletcher well, because, as I argue, assembling moments from the middle years of Henry VIII's reign forms a political play whose fragments permit and even encourage a wide frame of reference. In particular, the events staged in *Henry VIII* function as a version of history connecting the courts of King Henry and Queen Katherine, King James and Anne of Denmark. But *Henry VIII* is not merely a topical play. Instead, the play's structure produces its engagement with the Jacobean political world, at the same time that Jacobean politics, especially because they involved the queen consort, may well have suggested the play's historical timing and structure. For *Henry VIII* returns queens to the history play[3] within a dramatic structure whose fragments summon the sexual politics of James's succession after the death of Elizabeth and the ensuing conflicts between his male favorites and Anne of Denmark.

The play's sequence of scenes coheres around two narratival trajectories even as they fail to cohere to one another. The first of these trajectories, the interconnected fortunes of Katherine and Wolsey, Anne Bullen and Cranmer, examines the differences and similarities between queens and male favorites as they compete for proximity to the king's power. The second trajectory features the sequence of people who must fall and rise in order for Elizabeth to be born and for Cranmer to connect the Tudors to the Stuarts as he prophesies the accession of James and his progeny. Much of the criticism on *Henry VIII* focuses on one or the other trajectory, but the ways in which not only James but also Anne of Denmark provided the play's context have not yet been considered. Stuart Kurland (1987), for example, notes that "the characters' interest in politics is focused on the rivalries at court" (p. 204), but leaves out the conflicts between Katherine and Wolsey because the queen's participation in the political events outside her divorce have not seemed worth noting. And even though a number of studies focus on Katherine – as she relates to Hermione or Vittoria Corombona, to the Virgin Mary, or to the divorce trial of Frances Howard[4] – the points of resemblance with Anne of Denmark are only becoming apparent as scholarship, particularly Leeds Barroll's *Anna of Denmark, Queen of England: A Cultural Biography* (2001), focuses on her. Throughout *Henry VIII* each character's rise and fall is spelled out distinctly, but gains larger importance because the play's piecemeal, loosely organized structure asks readers and audiences to relate characters and political contexts to one another, to interpret historical events in the light of specifically Jacobean anxieties.

Why did Shakespeare and Fletcher choose to situate their "new play" (Wotton 1907: 2.32; Henry Bluett, quoted in Cole 1981: 352) during the reign of Henry VIII? The choice of Henry makes good generic sense, both from a twentieth- or twenty-first century perspective, and, as Leah Marcus argues, from the perspective of a reader of the First Folio, who would find the plays in chronological order (Marcus 1988: 95). Scholars have long argued that the choice of Henry VIII fills out the end of Shakespeare's earlier histories by moving from Henry VII, whose success concludes *Richard III*, to the reign of his son, Henry VIII, the birth of his daughter, Elizabeth, and thence to Cranmer's prophecy foretelling the future monarchies of James and his progeny (Richmond).

But in 1612–13 the choice of Henry VIII made good marketing sense, given the success that Samuel Rowley's play, *When You See Me, You Know Me*, had been enjoying and was continuing to enjoy. Indeed, any discussion of the collaboration of Shakespeare and Fletcher in producing *Henry VIII* should include the interrelations between Rowley's play and their own. As Jo Carney points out, not only are Holinshed and Foxe clear sources, but also Rowley (Carney 1995: 198; cf. McMullan 2000: 79). English playwrights, as Jeffrey Masten defines their collaboration, often "wrote with another playwright, or with several others, or revised or augmented scripts initially produced by others" (Masten 1997a: 358). With or without the knowledge of Rowley, Shakespeare and Fletcher worked to rewrite his popular play, first printed in 1605 and reprinted in 1613, the year of *Henry VIII*, as well as in 1621 and 1632.

When You See Me, You Know Me, or the famous Chronicle Historie of Henry VIII, with the Birth and Virtuous Life of Edward, Prince of Wales, as it was played by the High and

Mightie Prince of Wales his Servants proclaims a straightforward relation between Henry and James as kings who have successfully produced the requisite male heir, by featuring the birth and upbringing of a Prince Edward whose careful training in many ways parallels that of Prince Henry, James's heir. The connections between Prince Henry and Prince Edward are overt, given that Samuel Rowley was not only a member of the company known as Prince Henry's (*DNB* 17: 362; Bergeron 1985: 205) but also that the title page of the 1613 edition lists its playwright as "Samuell Rowley, servant to the Prince." Shakespeare and Fletcher replace Rowley's professional and dramatic orientation toward the Prince of Wales in his play featuring father and son, king and heir, with a contrasting series of trials and spectacles to produce a play that recalls the relations between Henry VIII and James quite differently. In speculating about the reasons for rewriting several aspects of *When You See Me, You Know Me*, it helps to recall that in November of 1612, James's immediate heir, Henry, Prince of Wales, had died in anguish. Although Henry's death left the Stuart second son, Prince Charles, able to succeed to the throne, the evidence testifies to the general mourning for Henry and only a gradual turning to Charles as heir. The year 1613 saw the publication of several verse collections in Henry's memory, including William Drummond's *Mausoleum* and John Taylor's *Great Britain All in Black*. Charles was only created Prince of Wales three years after Henry's death, and even then his mother Anne, who, after Henry's death, had "ceased masquing," found herself unable to attend the ceremony (Barroll 2001: 11, 142–3, 134; see also Waage 1975: 299, 301–2). Although Prince Henry's political leanings had attracted the group of militant Protestants that surrounded him, and he and his mother worked together to oppose James's favorite of the moment, Robert Carr, James shared the assumption of his wife and indeed the entire nation that Henry would succeed him. In 1612–13 Rowley's completely masculine view of the succession, however tempered by the appearance of two intelligent queens beloved by Henry, must have seemed momentarily less appropriate, and a few months after Prince Henry's death *All Is True* appeared as a "new play" with a different point of departure.

When You See Me, You Know Me – a title that like *All Is True* encourages recognizing the past as present – had featured, in addition to Prince Edward, a confident King Henry with two queens for whom he displays open affection: Jane Seymour shortly before her death in childbirth and Katherine Parr. Cast as a witty "Lutheran," Parr debates Bonner, the Bishop of London, who, fearing Katherine's power through the king, attempts to destroy her (Rowley 1913: H2v; H3–I1). Bonner fails not only because Katherine out-debates him, but also because Henry delights in her rhetorical abilities. Henry's sister Mary, whom the play puts at Henry's court, has a shorter but nonetheless important role. To a certain extent, then, *Henry VIII* updates Rowley's play in terms of Prince Henry's death by situating its action earlier in Henry's reign, before the birth of a male heir – replacing the relationship between the king and his son with a celebration of Henry's second daughter, the one Tudor who survived to connect Henry with James and his heirs, who go unnamed in the absence of the Prince of Wales.

Henry VIII retains the earlier play's fragmented structure, its loose ways with historical chronology and genre, and its interest in queens. For example, Rowley's Henry VIII salutes Jane Seymour as "chiefe of thy sex, / Me thinks thou art a Queene superlative" (A4) and Shakespeare and Fletcher's Henry salutes Katherine of Aragon even at the point of their divorce as the type of womanhood and so "The queen of earthly queens" (2.4.138). *Henry VIII* not only sidesteps Edward the male heir by never reaching Jane Seymour, it desentimentalizes Rowley's play by replacing Henry's strongly voiced affection for the two queens to whom he remained married with his affection for the two queens he would divorce on the way to producing a son. Indeed, the king of *Henry VIII*, wary of all around him, is immersed in politics that decide the lives and deaths of queens and courtiers caught in the crosscurrents of various policies designed to reproduce himself. Because this Henry inhabits a more ruthless political world than the Henry of *When You See Me*, a world where an ideal queen can and must be put aside, reviving Elizabeth's father as a king without a male heir produces a less cozy play. And although this particular timing eventually creates an elaborate compliment to James in Cranmer's prophecy of his succession, positioning Henry amid queens and favorites who point to connections with James and Anne, *Henry VIII* raises embarrassing, half-forgotten questions about James's succession.

After a decade in England, in 1613 James and Anne were firmly seated on the English throne and in the manors, castles, and palaces that had once belonged to Henry VIII. But the principal obstacle to James's accession had been Henry VIII's will: produced by the king in parliament, it excluded the Stuart line from the English succession. For about seventy years, as Mortimer Levine explains in his indispensable *Early Elizabethan Succession* (Levine 1966: 120–9, 147–61), pamphleteers for and against the Stuarts had argued this provision, especially when, in the 1560s, Mary Queen of Scots's claim to the English throne heated the debate surrounding the "alien exclusion," as this part of the will was known, and the courts continued to maintain that a Scot was an alien, unable to inherit or own English lands. Had Elizabeth proclaimed James her successor or allowed him to inherit the English lands belonging to his father, Darnley, as he continually pressed her to do, James could have overcome these legalities, but when Elizabeth did not give way on either front, James was forced to spend years initiating various diplomatic initiatives, including contact with the pope, in search of supporters for his claim to England's throne (Willson 1967: 138–40). As it happened, of course, James's claim was not seriously questioned after Elizabeth's death, although her Privy Council met for several hours before proclaiming James her heir (Nichols 1964, 1: 26).

The result of this history was that in 1603–4 no mention was made of Henry VIII, either in the numerous poetic tributes marking the transition from Elizabeth's reign to James's or the dozens of civic entertainments that welcomed James and Anne as they progressed to their coronations. Once the plague that had prevented their triumphant entry into London had passed, they entered the city with pomp, but the entertainments offered James and Anne there also made no mention of Henry VIII. Instead, they referred repeatedly to Elizabeth as the phoenix who gives mythic birth to James, a second phoenix: "One Phenix dead, another doth survive," wrote Thomas Byng (Nichols 1964, 1: 8). Cranmer's prophecy at *Henry VIII*'s conclusion returns to this convenient image from 1603–4, announcing that when the "maiden phoenix" dies "Her ashes new create another heir / As great in admiration as herself" (5.4.40–2). In contrast with the poets who evoked this conveniently parthenogenic figure, Samuel Daniel's "Panegyric Congratulatory at Burley, 1603" raised the problem with James's succession that the phoenix image was meant to erase and transcend. Penned by a writer who, like Shakespeare and Fletcher, had witnessed Elizabeth's final years and the transition to James, Daniel's panegyric announces that James's excellencies are so great

> That hadst thou had no title (as thou hast
> The only right; and none hath else a right).
> We yet must now have been enforc'd t' have cast
> Ourselves into thy arms, to set all right;
> And to avert confusion, bloodshed, waste,
> That otherwise upon us needs must light.
> None but a King, and no King else beside,
> Could now have sav'd this State from being destroy'd. (Nichols 1964, 1: 129)

Daniel makes clear that James's masculinity, together with the fertile femininity of the queen, whom Daniel – future collaborator on the queen's masques and groom of the queen's privy chamber – calls "Chaste mother of our Princes" (p. 131), convinced James's subjects to consider his right to succession.

In spite of the lingering succession issue, James took possession of, inhabited, and altered properties that had once belonged to Henry VIII and, in the case of Hampton Court and York Place (renamed Whitehall), Henry took over Cardinal Thomas Wolsey's finest palaces. *Henry VIII* reminds spectators that the places themselves, especially Hampton Court, Whitehall, the scene of Wolsey's banquet (McMullan 2000: 256n.), and Blackfriars, the scene of Katherine's divorce trial, connect the two kings across time as museums of royal prerogative. At Whitehall, as the accounts of foreign visitors attest, Holbein's full-length portraits of Henry VII and Henry VIII – their poses copied for Prince Henry's portrait by Robert Peake (Strong 1986: 114) – were on display alongside those of Edward VI and several of Queen Elizabeth, as was the large picture featuring Henry's appearance at the Field of the Cloth of Gold, the spectacle whose account opens the play (Ernest 1967: 160–3). Thus Whitehall, so newly renamed in Henry VIII's time that one of the play's gentlemen still refers to it by Wolsey's name (4.1.96–9), and whose origin as Wolsey's estate was remembered at the turn of the seventeenth century by London visitor John Norden (1967: 99), was a site not only of James's court life, court theatricals, and tilting, but also a memorial to James's Tudor predecessors, a standing reminder of the royal right to destroy favorites and take over their property.

The play specifically recalls Henry's acquisition of Wolsey's property by emphasizing Wolsey's inventory, accidentally left – or slipped in – with his compromising

letter to the pope opposing Henry's divorce, an inventory that records such an astonishing range of possessions that its existence equals the treason Wolsey commits by
opposing the king's divorce in correspondence to the pope. The king weighs the
import of this inventory, "The several parcels of his plate, his treasure, / Rich stuffs,
and ornaments of household, which / I find at such proud rate that it outspeaks /
Possession of a subject" (3.2.126–9), and in doing so alerts audiences not just to the
significance of Henry's acquisition but also to how places and other possessions are
material reminders of the interchangeability of kings from one century to the next.
Locating Katherine's divorce trial at Blackfriar's (McMullan 2000: 10) also worked
to remind the play's first audiences of the connections across the decades between
Blackfriars, the site of Katherine's divorce trial in 1529 (Stow 1994: 319–20) and
Blackfriars, in 1613 the winter playhouse of the King's Players. These places function as signifiers for the interchangeability of performed ceremonial from Henry VIII
to James.

Henry VIII makes continual use of this kind of cross-referencing between Tudor
and Jacobean sites and courts, between beheaded queens, and between the names of
royals, including *Henry* VIII and the newly dead Prince *Henry*, *Anne* Bullen and *Anne*
of Denmark, and James and Anne's daughters, Princesses Elizabeth and Mary. The
references made possible by naming Stuart children for Tudors cross easily but complexly into the play, simultaneously one of Shakespeare's last and one of Fletcher's first
(McMullan 2000: 113). The playwrights, like their audiences, inhabited a present
with one foot in the previous century and one in the century that would bring civil
war and the execution of James's second son. Noting that seventeenth-century playwrights faced growing challenges to James's inherited prerogatives, which required
employing "radically discontinuous political strategies for idealising political authority," Leonard Tennenhouse offers an increasingly acceptable way to frame the relation
between James's accession and shifts in dramatic genres (Tennenhouse 1994: 110).
Although Shakespeare's first theatrical successes had occurred a decade earlier than
Fletcher's, even as James's accession approached, Shakespeare's comedies, tragedies,
and histories of the earlier 1590s explored the increasing vulnerability and impending death of Elizabeth. After James's accession, his presence and patronage caused even
generic changes, such as Fletcher's successful development of the "romantic tragicomedy" (McMullan 2000: 114; see also 113, 445–7). Writing *Henry VIII* together
and in response to Rowley called upon their combined skills to recall and transform
the previous decade's history plays – to find "radically discontinuous political
strategies" that would not only respond to but create the Jacobean frame of reference
engendered by the concerns of 1612–13.

However evocative the Tudor–Stuart referencing of place and name, *Henry VIII*
most frequently references the Jacobean court structure within which a queen competed with male favorites for access to the king's presence and thus to his regard and
influence. The play's fragmentation of events during Henry VIII's reign was especially
appropriate in 1613, because not only were the king and queen still mourning the
recently deceased Prince of Wales, but also because even before Henry's death James

had been responding to the deaths of key courtiers by elevating his new favorite, Robert Carr, soon Viscount Rochester, whom the queen opposed. From 1611 to 1614, as Leeds Barroll writes, "the attrition of James's strongest and most experienced advisers proceeded so speedily that by June 1614, George Home, earl of Dunbar, Robert Cecil, earl of Salisbury, and Henry Howard, earl of Northampton, all of them central to James's original attainment of the English crown, were dead" (Barroll 2001: 113). In 1612–13, then, the court was reeling from multiple losses while the accelerated rise of Robert Carr deepened the queen's opposition to James's favorite and to James.

Consequently, Queen Anne's position in 1612–13 resembles Queen Katherine's repeatedly staged opposition to Wolsey in *Henry VIII*, first over Buckingham, then over the taxation of the clothiers, and finally over her divorce and whether she ought to appeal to the pope. Katherine calls Wolsey "that great child of honour" (4.2.6), as if the king, by choosing favorites, can reproduce himself without her help – a kind of same-sex reproduction making court politics treacherous for queens. Like Katherine, Anne was careful for the most part not to express her direct opposition to James's favorites. As John Chamberlain wrote of the appearance of civility between Anne and Carr, "The Queen is perfectly reconciled to him" (Barroll 2001: 133). At her trial, Katherine points out to Henry that she has been cautious about his favorite, Wolsey: "which of your friends / Have I not strove to love, although I knew / He were mine enemy?" (2.4.27–9). Since Katherine earlier had questioned Wolsey's key witness against Buckingham and his taxation of the clothiers, we know that she phrases the truth carefully. When summoned to Blackfriars for her divorce trial, Katherine has lost the conflict with Wolsey over Buckingham but won on the issue of the clothiers – a success that may have implied a compliment to James, who in 1607 had dined with the Company of Clothworkers in the city and registered "in their Book as free Brother of the said Company" (Nichols 1964, 2: 133–4). But at Blackfriars Wolsey triumphs over Katherine in the reproductive interest of his king.

Conflicts similar to those played out between Katherine and Wolsey prevailed between Anne of Denmark and James's favorites even before their arrival in England. In a letter recording part of their quarrel about where and with whom Prince Henry would live, James articulated his wish for Anne to stay out of the power relations he exercised through his male favorites around 1603. Making clear that he alone has the right to determine his son's upbringing at the hands of a favorite, and that Anne has disobeyed him by criticizing the man in question, John Erskine, Earl of Mar, to whom he had entrusted Henry, James's letter lectures her on her need to "cure you of that rooted error," urging her to think of his favorites as "friends that are true servants to me." Reminding her that he carries "that love and respect unto you which, by the law of God and nature, I ought to do to my wife and mother of my children," James also points out that in spite of Anne's "honourable birth and descent," "whether ye were a king's or a cook's daughter, ye must be all alike to me being once my wife." Having told her that her status depends entirely on his honor – which she implicitly sullies by questioning Erskine's care of their son – he asks her to "leave these womanly apprehensions" about his favorite (James 1984: 214–15). Anne's opposition to the king through opposing his favorites registers in the character of Katherine, for the courtly world in which she finds herself records a similar sense of Henry's homosocial and homoerotic interests, especially the extent to which his physical and emotional closeness to male favorites eclipses her own attempts to produce a male heir. Katherine's desire to mobilize the power for queens inherent in heterosexual forms of reproduction have in part been cut off by her inability to produce a son in spite of her physical intimacy with Henry, and in part cut off by Henry's need and desire to create his own "child of honour."

Although the king's players were not his "servants" in the sense of intimate courtiers, the king's players were his liveried servants, "technically members of the royal household" (Orgel 1982: 44). Thus the Shakespeare–Fletcher collaborations, part of what Jeffrey Masten calls "the all-male collaboration of the theatrical enterprise" (Masten 1997b: 57), exist at the homosocial intersection between the king's patronage and the marketable shows that their theatres offered both court and city dwellers. But in selecting the parts of Henry VIII's reign that resulted in Elizabeth's birth and James's subsequent succession, Shakespeare and Fletcher offer a politically aware, less overtly misogynistic strategy for containing the queen's power than James's epistolary attempt to end the queen's competition with his favorite. The play's treatment of Katherine, whom neither Henry nor Wolsey can silence, and whose political staying power ends only with her death, serves as a reminder that James did not always defeat Anne: he had succeeded in keeping Prince Henry with John Erskine, but once they moved to England he conceded Anne's right of access to the heir.

Although the play eventually transforms her political power into a heavenly ascent, Katherine claims center stage. Indeed Katherine's presence, command of rhetoric in public debate, and importance in formulating policy resembles that of Katherine Parr in *When You See Me, You Know Me* – with an important difference. Shakespeare's and Fletcher's Katherine is notably Catholic, although a reformist whose attitude toward Wolsey suggests a distaste for clerical corruption, which Henry comes to share. In her religion as in her conflicts with Henry's favorite, Katherine of Aragon resembles Anne of Denmark. As Leeds Barroll writes, Anne's reputation was as a Catholic; nonetheless, "Anna's Catholicism" did not influence "her political decisions" (Barroll 2001: 170, 172). The longstanding question of why the Catholic queen, Katherine, receives the play's sanction as a chaste and truly royal queen, even though the Protestant Anne Bullen is the baby Elizabeth's mother, may in large part be addressed by the several points of connection between Henry's queen of twenty years and James's queen of twenty-four.

While Katherine is the unquestionable focus of much of *Henry VIII*, the play is not, as Glynne Wickham suggests, so much "a Requiem Mass and an entombment" of Katherine "in the national interest" (Wickham 1984: 165), as it is a staging of a queen shaped in ways that recall Anne of Denmark's lively presence in England's political and cultural affairs. Although Katherine's death necessarily limits the expression of her political power, Anne returns to the play in Cranmer's prophecy concerning James and his progeny, the offspring to whom she gave birth, and possibly in the

Epilogue as well. All the more reason, then, to present Katherine's Catholicism in terms of the religious discourse of the ideal and pious woman. As Lynne Magnusson writes, such a discourse, however much it enshrines "the ideological work of patriarchy by idealizing nonassertive speech," also offered historical women "its characteristic disjunctions between boldness and humility" (Magnusson 1999: 30). The effect of sidestepping Edward's birth in this "new play" by overwriting the forceful Protestantism of Rowley's Katherine Parr with the subdued Catholicism of Katherine of Aragon is that the play soft-pedals the Reformation in order to avoid making the Catholic queen's religion a dramatic issue, and so preserves her virtuous centrality while evoking Anne of Denmark.

Through Katherine, the playwrights' collaboration develops a strong feminine presence that stands in contrast to James's revolving door policy toward his favorites. To the extent that Katherine would have reminded early seventeenth-century audiences of James's queen, the play's glimpses of the queen's court apart from the king's might also have increased a sense of connection. Shakespeare and Fletcher pay Anne of Denmark the compliment of fashioning their most central queen to resemble her, while the crucial point of difference between them, that Katherine proved unable to produce the male heir who would have helped her retain her power and Anne had produced two princes, functions as a compliment to Anne.

In spite of Katherine's importance to *Henry VIII*, the play's fragmented structure allows no single character to dominate its pageants, gossip, or events. Although the play returns to queens and refers them to one another and to Anne of Denmark, they must share the stage with the male favorites with whom Henry enjoys even greater physical intimacy. At several points in particular, the play strives to equate female and male favorites in ways that deny the reproductive capacity of queens and their ability to influence policy because of their birth and social status, their family's international alliances, and their proximity to the king. In singling out the three Tudor queens, Katherine, Anne Bullen, and Elizabeth, who failed to produce a male heir, the play creates a need to consider the alternative forms of reproduction available to a king – even a king like James, with his spare son positioned as heir. Moreover, *Henry VIII* demonstrates that the king's ability to choose queens and create favorites is only part of his power. For if he can reproduce himself through these relations, he can also destroy those whose intimacy proves unnecessary or undesirable. Both heterosexual and homosocial/homoerotic forms of reproduction carry risks: a son may not be born; a son may die young; a son may inherit the throne and be beheaded. Or, alternatively, the male favorite may help to poison a rival, as Carr may have done, or, as in the later case of George Villiers, produce a family toward whom the king shows more affection than to his own but that cannot be substituted for his own when it comes to inheriting the crown.

Because not only life but also death derives from the king, "divorce" in *Henry VIII* is repeatedly associated with images of execution for male favorites and queens alike. As Judith Anderson points out, "Divorce is more than an historical problem in *Henry VIII*. It is a theme in a broader and more conceptual way, involving the disjunction of inner and outer and private and public lives. It is a disjoining of the aspects of reality" (Anderson 1984: 126) – one that allows the king to participate in creating the play's fragmented structure by eliminating those whom he wishes. Addressing a sympathetic crowd just before his execution, Buckingham, the first object of contention between Katherine and Wolsey, asks that "as the long *divorce* of steel falls on me, / Make of your prayers one sweet sacrifice / And lift my soul to heaven" (2.1.77–9; my emphasis). His "divorce" from life (the play's first use of the word) is then juxtaposed with rumors of Katherine's divorce as the two gentlemen who step forward after Buckingham's exit speak immediately "Of an ensuing evil, if it fall, / Greater than this" (2.1.141–2) – "A buzzing of a separation / Between the King and Katherine" (148–9). When speaking to the Old Lady about both Katherine, whom she still serves as lady-in-waiting, and her own prospects, Anne Bullen connects divorce and beheading. It would be better not to have been elevated to pomp, she says: "Yet if that quarrel, fortune, do divorce / It from the bearer, 'tis a sufferance panging / As soul and bodies severing" (2.3.12–16). These words cannot help but recall – in the play's future and the audience's past – not just Katherine's divorce and eventual death, but also Anne Bullen's eventual divorce from the same king and her beheading. Katherine herself, during her trial, says to Wolsey, "Nothing but death / Shall e'er divorce my dignities" (3.1.140–1). Katherine's death quickly follows the divorce she will not acknowledge, paralleling the fall and death of Wolsey.

The disjunction of these scenes invites finding similarities among characters and thinking about the political trajectories they inscribe. Just as Buckingham's execution-as-divorce slips into Katherine's divorce and death and Katherine's into Anne Bullen's anticipated divorce and execution, Bullen's coronation appears spliced between the key spectacles of Katherine's divorces – her trial and death. As the First and Second Gentlemen meet again to view a public spectacle, the first announces that Katherine and Henry are divorced, "the late marriage made of none effect," and that meanwhile Katherine has "removed to Kimbolton, / Where she remains now sick" (4.1.32–5). Hearing the news of Katherine's illness, her physical response to divorce from the king, the Second Gentleman completes the First Gentleman's line with "Alas, good lady!" (35). At that moment they are interrupted by a "Flourish of trumpets within" as the new Queen Anne appears – regal but silent – in pre-coronation dumbshow. And in the following scene, as the old queen dies, she hears from the king not that Anne has been crowned queen, but that he sends her "his princely commendations" (4.2.119). After answering that his comfort "comes too late; / 'Tis like a pardon after execution" (121–2), she prepares for her death, preceded by a masque-like vision of angelic presence.

These similarities of language uniting queens and male courtiers to some extent acknowledge the political import of queens at court regardless – or even because of – their vulnerability. But Henry's male favorites, like James's, enjoy more physical intimacy with the king than do his queens. Henry's initial entrance leaning on Wolsey, as Stuart Kurland notes, replicates James's well-known habit of leaning on his favorite courtiers (Kurland 1987: 205), particularly on Carr. As Thomas Howard, Earl of Suffolk informed John Harington in a 1611 letter delivered by Howard's son, Carr was quickly ingratiating himself, for the king "leaneth on his arm, pinches his cheek, smoothes his ruffled garment" (Nichols 1964: 2: 412–14). First Folio's stage directions, *"Enter King Henry, leaning on the Cardinals shoulder,"* followed by *"the Cardinall places himselfe under the Kings feete on his right side"* (entry at 1.2), connect the physical behaviors of Henry and James toward their favorites. And during Katherine's divorce trial, even before she says she has been forbidden Henry's bed, on her entrance the queen *"takes place some distance from the King"* and later *"kneeles at his feet,"* while Wolsey and the other cardinal, Campeius, *"sit under him as Iudges"* (Folio, 2.4). In a play whose stage directions are unusually precise about placement, these directions are significant.

In accordance with the interactive political worlds that *Henry VIII* stages and recalls, the play's attitude toward its queens' relations with favorites and the king is inconsistent. *Henry VIII* exalts Katherine even as it removes her; it equates male favorites and queens through the language of divorce and execution, but more often features the king's physical intimacy with his male favorites than with his queens. Even as the play separates the two, it also connects them. Remarking on gender inconsistencies in the earlier histories, Jean Howard and Phyllis Rackin write: "Sometimes the gender ideologies deployed in a single play were inconsistent, showing that there was not one true version of masculinity and femininity, but competing versions serving different social interests" (Howard and Rackin 1997: 35). It makes sense to apply their comment to *Henry VIII*'s conflicting versions of royal power relations, versions that at times acknowledge the power of queens, and at others, despite Katherine's centrality and pathos, come down on the side of the powerful male favorite, Cranmer. The play's contradictory representations of the king's unquestionably masculine power and the queens' and courtiers' more feminized power dependent on the king suggest the playwrights' and players' own complex subject-positions as males operating within a dynamic of courtly power that feminized them as well. In presenting no "one true version" of the power of queens and favorites, *Henry VIII* appeals to a range of political positions among its first audiences while exploring the domesticated power of those who collaborated in producing it.

The play's presentation of a variety of contentious power relations is at once evident in the treatments of Queen Katherine and Cardinal Wolsey, whose discords occupy much of the play's first half but whose conflicts dissolve in the second half, as their falls from power cause them to resemble one another. Shortly after having lost royal favor and access to royal presence, both conveniently die within hours of one another, when in fact they died six years apart, Wolsey in 1530 and Katherine in 1536. Although *Henry VIII*'s first half plays and replays their animosity, contrasting the cardinal's machinations with the queen's chaste goodness, in the second half Wolsey's deathbed intrudes on Katherine's, not simply to provide another example of her fair dealing as she offers to rethink her poor opinion of him, but also as a way to emphasize their interconnections as former rivals for the king's ear now fallen in *de casibus* fashion – a figuring that makes sense in a world where fortunes were made and broken by the favor of a king whom the play stages as incontrovertibly royal.

If Wolsey and Katherine fall and die together in spite of their differences as favorite and queen, corrupt and moral versions of the fallen favorite, Anne Bullen and Cranmer rise together on terms that once again emphasize the physical intimacy of favorites over queens – even a new and highly desirable queen. And once again the play demonstrates that royal favoritism means physical intimacy with the king regardless of the favorite's gender. In fact, Cranmer, to whom Henry gives his ring and whom Henry takes by the hand (5.1.116), seems more thoroughly wed to Henry than Anne does, despite her coronation pageant, for the king's ring rescues Cranmer at the moment he appears about to fall from favor. Unlike *The Merchant of Venice*, in which the ring connects Portia's heterosexual interest in Bassanio with Antonio's homoerotic interest in her husband, the ring in *Henry VIII* is male-to-male business. As Henry tells Cranmer when giving him the ring in "private," "If entreaties / Will render you no remedy, [*giving his ring*] this ring / Deliver them, and your appeal to us" (5.1.150–3). Although Cranmer's response – to weep – is one that Katherine, like Hermione, deems unfit for a queen, it proves to Henry that "He's honest, on mine honour. God's blest mother, / I swear he is true-hearted and a soul / None better in my kingdom" (5.1.154–6). As the ring's exchange represents the joining of bodies, the king and Cranmer also exchange emotion that the play deems unseemly for a queen. This scene, interrupted by the Old Lady bringing news of the birth of Anne's "lovely boy" (165) who turns out to be Elizabeth, echoes the announcement of Prince Edward's birth in *When You See Me, You Know Me* (*Henry VIII*, 5.1.163–70; Rowley sig. B4). Heralding an already transgendered Elizabeth with lines transposed from a play about the birth of a male heir is bad news for Henry on stage but eventually good news for James and the Stuarts.

Henry's god-like reference to Cranmer's being the best "soul" in "my kingdom" further increases Cranmer's proximity to Henry. Not only does the king have a new male favorite, of the same religion as Anne and apparently on Anne's political side, but that favorite replaces Anne Bullen even as she gives birth to Elizabeth. If Katherine and Wolsey nearly share a deathbed, at the moment that Anne occupies the childbed, Cranmer and Henry get into bed together. While historically mothers were not present at christenings, Anne's understandable absence from the christening leaves Cranmer center stage. And it is he who foretells Elizabeth's reign, a prophecy that Barbara Hodgdon marks as simultaneously prophecy and Elizabeth's eulogy (Hodgdon 1991: 229). If Anne disappears quickly from the play, it may be because the placement of her coronation between Katherine's trial and death invites spectators to imagine that Anne's future trial and death already have taken place – as indeed, for the play's first audiences, it had. As time in *Henry VIII* doubles back on itself, the present moment of the playwrights, players, and playgoers runs alongside the play's multivalent structures. Similarly, the evocation of Princess Elizabeth also works in two ways. On the one hand, Cranmer uses her birth to remind the audience that the baby will become the virgin queen. On the other, Elizabeth is a reminder that, all fantasies of parthenogensis through favorites aside, there can be no dynasty and no passing of power from one generation to the next without marriage and the production of children. In 1612–13, when the marriage of Princess Elizabeth to the Elector

Palatine demonstrated the dynastic value of girls as well as boys, this point would have been particularly timely.

Still another way that Shakespeare and Fletcher counter their own arguments for the king's power to create himself king despite Queen Elizabeth's help and to re-create himself through male favorites is to provide two crowd scenes featuring female fertility on a large scale. If the dynasty cannot exist without women's fertility, neither can the nation. The women in the crowd who gather at the gates in the hope of seeing the processions of Anne's coronation and Elizabeth's christening possess such rampant fertility that they become as indistinguishable from one another as the queens both within and outside the play. According to the Third Gentleman, who recounts the scene to the First and Second Gentlemen, "Great-bellied women / That had not a half a week to go" "shake the press" (4.1.78–9, 80); among the crowd "No man living / Could say 'This is my wife' there, all were woven / So strangely in one piece" (4.81–3). And again, just before the christening of the baby Princess Elizabeth at the play's close, the porter together with a servant from the larder hold off an unruly crowd, of whom the porter asks:

> Have we some strange Indian with the great tool come to court, the women so besiege us? Bless me, what a fry of fornication is at door! On my Christian conscience, this one christening will beget a thousand. (5.3.31–5)

However, it is not the sight of a male procreative "tool" but that other object of London spectacle from the Indian, the royal female, that produces this carnivalesque reaction: "this one christening" that will "beget a thousand." In these fertile crowds, as even the men become indistinguishable from one another – "Here will be father, godfather, and all together" (5.35–6) – it is as if the spectacles of two females, Anne Bullen and her daughter, Elizabeth, privileged by the favor and fertility of Henry VIII, spread dynastic fertility into the streets in ways that blur familial connection and genealogical record, giving rise to a nation of subjects. In the world of the theatre, of course, that nation of subjects is made up of audience members. The prospect of observing these privileged females is one that results in widespread fertility, because time controlled and slowed by ritual events like the coronation or christening of queens results in procreation and so lies at the heart of dynastic business. The fertile spectators of Anne's coronation and Elizabeth's christening processions not only suggest connections between the spectacles authorized by James and Henry and par-ticipated in by Anne of Denmark and Katherine of Aragon, but also point to the con-nections between the theatre audience – especially the women in that audience – and their female progenitors in the play's crowds. Whether on or offstage, the female spec-tators clamoring for a view also remind us of the permeability of the physical barriers between commoners and royalty, audiences and players, as people gaze beyond them and conceive what they will.

The fear and awe that the crowds of fertile women incite in their onlookers func-tion as unruly versions of the emotions evoked by *Henry VIII*'s queens. For if the play stages a Jacobean fantasy of a queen who offers nothing more than male favorites and may as easily be removed, the play, by making Katherine dominate the play's central scenes, also serves as a reminder of the queen's political importance, an importance to which both Prologue and Epilogue speak. When the Prologue warns that "those that can pity here / May, if they think it well, let fall a tear" (Prologue, 5–6), it foretells Katherine's position as the only character whose downfall occasions strong emotion. Returning to the Prologue's implicit emphasis on the feminine, the Epilogue asserts that "this play at this time is only in / The merciful construction of good women, / For such a one we showed 'em" (Epilogue, 9–11). "Such a one" showed the "good women" of the audience may quite likely refer to the baby Elizabeth,[5] whose christening we have just witnessed (Hodgdon 1991: 229–34). But "such a one" also presents a wonderfully ambiguous "good woman" who seems an amalgam of the women "shewn," of Katherine and Elizabeth in particular. The "good woman" may also suggest a living woman, perhaps even one present at a performance, like the Princess Elizabeth, who may have seen this play as part of the months-long celebration of her marriage to – and England's alliance with – the Elector Palatine. Or perhaps, as I suggest in pushing for the links between the Tudor and Jacobean courts afforded by the play, "such a one" recalls Anne of Denmark as well.

The play's performance history helps to explain why the structural interrelationships between the courts of James and Anne of Denmark and the court of the play have only begun to be discussed. Barbara Hodgdon writes that the play when performed did not conclude with Elizabeth's christening until 1855, and not again until 1938, when the existence of a Windsor Princess Elizabeth provided a reason to play the final scene. Instead, the christening and prophecy were cut in favor of either a triumphant conclusion with Anne Bullen's coronation or a tragic conclusion with Queen Katherine's deathbed vision (Hodgdon 1991: 218–19, 293 n.20). Failing to end the play with Elizabeth's christening stages Tudor history without acknowledging the play's insistence on the Stuart teleology, the connections between Henry and James that culminate in the announcement of James's succession. Without Elizabeth's christening and Cranmer's prophecy, the play's rich references, odd connections, disconnections, and elisions of key historical events make little sense, when in fact its fragmented structure enables its wide frame of Jacobean reference to embrace the conflicts between James, Anne, and their courts, between the heterosexual valuation of motherhood and the production of both male and female heirs and between the homosocial and homoerotic production of court and collaborative theatre.

The play's staging of the difficulty that kings experience in reproducing themselves through either apparently trustworthy favorites or queens steps forth in the current Prince Charles's remark after seeing Greg Doran's 1996 staging of *Henry VIII* at Stratford's Swan Theatre. His divorce behind him and the succession provided for in his own two princes, Harry and William, the twentieth-century Charles, asked for his thoughts, responded, "It makes you realize how little things have changed. When one is born into a certain position you have people advising you all the time, whispering in your ear. It's only when you get to my age that you begin to work out who's telling you the truth" (McMullan 2000: 54n.). Charles's search for "the truth," of whom to trust and whom to divorce, reminds us that the play's alternative title, *All Is True*, may to some extent have been directed at the king. In the way that the elaborate perspective scenery of some court masques could be perfectly viewed only from the monarch's perspective, the play offers views of queens and favorites that may seem "true" or whole to the king or a royal heir, but increasingly pieced or patched the further the audience member stands from the royal presence.

But why end with a masculinist perspective when the play itself ends with an appeal to women audience members to consider "such a one"? From the perspective of Anne of Denmark in 1613, if as seems likely she saw the play, the conflicts between Katherine and Wolsey may well have revealed Jacobean political practice at the moment when she most found herself opposed to Robert Carr, already Viscount Rochester and the future Earl of Somerset. But even as Carr began to take his position for granted, and then fell amid the accusations that surrounded the poisoning of Thomas Overbury, as early as 1614 Anne was navigating her way out of the dynamic of conflict with James's favorites by actively promoting George Villiers, the future Duke of Buckingham. Although the elevation of a male favorite whom she supported could not put an end to courtly infighting, it is notable that on Carr's fall in London she appropriated Somerset House. Although it owed its name not to Carr but to the Lord Protector of Edward VI, Anne's claim to the royal property registers symbolically. Just as Henry had acquired Wolsey's palaces as sumptuous trophies of his own power, so Anne of Denmark took over Somerset House, renaming it Denmark House, "thereby," writes Barroll, "effecting a physical separation from the ambience of James's monarchic court" (Barroll 2001: 39). Unlike the queens in Shakespeare's and Fletcher's play, caught within the structures that lock them in competition with the king's favorites, Anne of Denmark found ways to move beyond the court of the king.

ACKNOWLEDGMENTS

My thanks to Peter Parolin for his valuable comments on many drafts of this essay, and to Barbara Hodgdon, who read and edited this essay with a generous spirit.

NOTES

1   *All Is True* was apparently the play's initial title, but the First Folio's editors chose to place it at the end of the histories, titled *The Life of King Henry the Eight*. See Gary Taylor in the Norton edition (Shakespeare 1997), 3118. Citations are from the Oxford edition, ed. Jay Halio (Shakespeare 1999).

2   I employ Robert Weimann's (1984) definition of *structure* as "the art work's verbal and conceptual modes of organization," with his attendant concern that "the structure of literature is correlated with its function in society" (p. 5). Besides the work of Barbara Hodgdon (1991), Judith Anderson (1984), and Gordon McMullan (2000), all of which help to make sense of *Henry VIII*'s difficult structure, see also Howard Felperin (1966), Lee Bliss (1975), Edward Berry (1979), Anston Bosman (1999), and Ivo Kamps (1966).

3 On the diminishing importance of queens from the first tetralogy to the second, see Howard and Rackin (1997: 24–5, 157–8). As they write, "In the first tetralogy, *King John*, and *Henry VIII*, the playscripts assign over four times as many lines to female characters as they do in the canonical plays" (p. 24).

4 On Katherine's centrality, see Noling (1988), Carney (1995), Micheli (1987), and Magnusson (1999: 27–34), as well as Lapotaire (1998), who discusses playing the role; on relations between Katherine and Hermione, see Kaplan and Eggert (1994), see also Vanita (2000). On Katherine and John Webster characters, see Candido (1980). On Marian imagery, see Vanita (2000). Baillie (1979) discusses the proximity of the Frances Howard divorce trial and the performance of *Henry VIII*.

5 For a nuanced discussion of Elizabeth's centrality to *Henry VIII*, see Hodgdon (1991: 212–34). I focus on Henry VIII's relation to James as mediated by Elizabeth, but rely on Hodgdon's analysis.

References and Further Reading

Akrigg, G. P. V. (1963) *Jacobean Pageant or The Court of King James I*. Cambridge, MA: Harvard University Press.

Anderson, J. (1984). *Biographical Truth: The Representation of Historical Persons in Tudor–Stuart Writing*. New Haven, CT: Yale University Press.

Baillie, W. M. (1979). *Henry VIII*: A Jacobean History. *Shakespeare Studies*, 12, 247–66.

Barroll, L. (2001). *Anna of Denmark, Queen of England: A Cultural Biography*. Philadelphia: University of Pennsylvania Press.

Bergeron, D. (1985). *Shakespeare's Romances and the Royal Family*. Lawrence: University of Kansas Press.

Berry, E. I. (1979). *Henry VIII* and the Dynamics of *Spectacle*. *Shakespeare Studies*, 12, 229–46.

Bliss, L. (1975). The Wheel of Fortune and the Maiden Phoenix of Shakespeare's *King Henry the Eighth*. *English Literary History*, 42, 1, 1–25.

Bosman, A. (1999). Seeing Tears: Truth and Sense in *All is True*. *Shakespeare Quarterly*, 50, 4, 459–76.

Candido, J. (1980). Katherine of Aragon and Female Greatness: Shakespeare's Debt to Dramatic Tradition. *Iowa State Journal of Research*, 54, 4, 491–8.

Carney, J. E. (1995). Queenship in Shakespeare's *Henry VIII*. In C. Levin and P. A. Sullivan (eds.) *Political Rhetoric, Power, and Renaissance Women*. Albany: State University of New York Press, 189–202.

Cole, M. J. (1981). A New Account of the Burning of the Globe. *Shakespeare Newsletter*, 32, 3, 352.

Dictionary of National Biography (DNB) (1973). Ed. L. Stephen and S. Lee. 22 vols. Oxford: Oxford University Press.

Ernest, John (Duke of Saxe-Weimar). Pictures and Other Works of Art in the Royal Palaces. In Rye, 159–73.

Felperin, H. (1966). Shakespeare's *Henry VIII*: History as Myth. *Studies in English Literature*, 6, 2, 225–46.

Heywood, T. (1606). *If You Know Not Me, You Know No Body: Or the Troubles of Queen Elizabeth*. London.

Hilberdink-Sakamoto, K. (1999). "O God's Will, Much Better She Ne'er Had Known Pomp": The Making of Queen Anne in Shakespeare's *Henry VIII*. *Shakespeare Studies*, Shakespeare Society of Japan, 37, 21–44.

Hodgdon, B. (1991). *The End Crowns All: Closure and Contradiction in Shakespeare's History*. Princeton, NJ: Princeton University Press.

Howard, J. and Rackin, P. (1997). *Engendering a Nation: A Feminist Account of Shakespeare's English Histories*. New York: Routledge.

James VI and I (1984) *Letters of King James VI and I*, ed. G. P. V. Akrigg. Berkeley: University of California Press.

Kamps, I. (1966). Possible Pasts: Historiography and Legitimation in *Henry VIII*. *College English*, 58, 2, 192–215.

Kaplan, M. L. and Eggert, K. (1994). "Good queen, my lord, good queen": Sexual Slander in *The Winter's Tale. Renaissance Drama*, n.s. 25, 89–118.

Kurland, S. M. (1987). *Henry VIII* and James I: Shakespeare and Jacobean Politics. *Shakespeare Studies*, 19, 203–18.

Lapotaire, J. (1998). Queen Katherine in *Henry VIII*. In R. Smallwood (ed.) *Players of Shakespeare 4: Further Essays in Shakespearian Performance by Players with the Royal Shakespeare Company.* Cambridge: Cambridge University Press, 132–51.

Levine, M. (1966). *The Early Elizabethan Succession Question 1558–1568.* Stanford, CA: Stanford University Press.

McMullan, G. (2000). Introduction. In G. McMullan (ed.) *King Henry VIII (All Is True).* London: Arden Shakespeare, 1–199.

Magnusson, L. (1999). *Shakespeare and Social Dialogue: Dramatic Language and Elizabethan Letters.* Cambridge: Cambridge University Press.

Marcus, L. (1988). *Puzzling Shakespeare: Local Reading and its Discontents.* Berkeley: University of California Press.

Masten, J. (1997a) Playwriting: Authorship and Collaboration. In J. D. Cox and D. S. Kastan (eds.) *A New History of Early English Drama.* New York: Columbia University Press, 357–82.

——(1997b). *Textual Intercourse: Collaboration, Authorship, and Sexualities in Renaissance Drama.* Cambridge: Cambridge University Press.

Micheli, L. (1987). "Sit By Us": Visual Imagery and the Two Queens in *Henry VIII*. *Shakespeare Quarterly*, 38, 4, 452–66.

Nichols, J. (1964) [1828]. *The Progresses of King James the First*, 4 vols. New York: Burt Franklin.

Noling, K. H. (1988). Grubbing Up the Stock: Dramatizing Queens in *Henry VIII*. *Shakespeare Quarterly*, 39, 3, 291–306.

Norden, J. (1967) [1592]. Notes on London and Westminster. In Rye, 161–7.

Orgel, S. (1982). Making Greatness Familiar. *Genre*, 15, 1, & 2, 41–8.

Patterson, A. (1994). *Reading Holinshed's Chronicles.* Chicago, IL: University of Chicago Press.

——(1996). "All is True": Negotiating the Past in *Henry VIII*. In R. B. Parker and S. P. Zitner (eds.) *Elizabethan Theater: Essays in Honour of S. Schoenbaum.* Newark: University of Delaware Press, 147–66.

Pepys, S. (2000) [1971]. *The Diary of Samuel Pepys*, 11 vols., ed. R. Latham and W. Matthews. Berkeley: University of California Press.

Richmond H. M. (1997). The Resurrection of an Expired Form: *Henry VIII* as Sequel to *Richard III*. In J. W. Velz (ed.) *Shakespeare's English Histories: A Quest for Form and Genre.* Tempe, AZ: Medieval and Renaissance Texts and Studies, 205–28.

Rowley, S. (1913) [1605/13]. *When You See Me You Know Me.* New York: AMS Press.

Rudnytsky, P. L. (1991). *Henry VIII* and the Deconstruction of History. *Shakespeare Survey*, 43, 43–57.

Rye, W. B. (ed.) (1967) [1865]. *England as Seen by Foreigners in the Days of Elizabeth and James the First.* New York: Benjamin Blom.

Shakespeare, W. (1957). *King Henry VIII*, ed. R. A. Foakes. London: Methuen.

——(1995). *The First Folio of Shakespeare 1623*, ed. J. Heminge and H. Condell. New York: Applause Books.

——(1997). *The Norton Shakespeare Based on the Oxford Edition*, ed. S. Greenblatt, W. Cohen, J. E. Howard, and K. E. Maus. New York: W. W. Norton.

——(1999). *King Henry VIII, or All is True*, ed. J. L. Halio. Oxford: Oxford University Press.

Slights, C. W. (1991). The Politics of Conscience in *All Is True* (or *Henry VIII*). *Shakespeare Survey*, 43, 59–68.

Stow, J. (1994). *A Survey of London Written in the Year 1598.* Dover, NH: Alan Sutton Publishing.

Strong, R. (1986). *Henry, Prince of Wales, and England's Last Renaissance.* London: Thames and Hudson.

Tennenhouse, L. (1994). Strategies of State and Political Plays: *A Midsummer Night's Dream, Henry IV, Henry V, Henry VIII*. In *Political Shakespeare: Essays in Cultural Materialism*, ed. J. Dollimore and A. Sinfield. Ithaca, NY: Cornell University Press, 109–28.

Vanita, R. (2000). Mariological Memory in *The Winter's Tale* and *Henry VIII*. *Studies in English Literature*, 40, 2, 311–37.

Waage, F. O., Jr. (1975). *Henry VIII* and the Crisis of the English History Play. *Shakespeare Studies*, 8, 297–309.

Weimann, R. (1984). *Structure and Society in Literary History*. Baltimore, MD: Johns Hopkins University Press.

Wickham, G. (1984). The Dramatic Structure of Shakespeare's *King Henry the Eighth*: An Essay in Rehabilitation. *Proceedings of the British Academy*, 70, 149–66.

Willson, D. H. (1967). *King James VI & I*. New York: Oxford University Press.

Wotton, H. (1907). *The Life and Letters of Sir Henry Wotton*, 2 vols., ed. L. P. Smith. Oxford: Oxford University Press.

Young, M. B. (2000). *James VI and I and the History of Homosexuality*. New York: New York University Press.

23

Mixed Messages: The Aesthetics of *The Two Noble Kinsmen*

Julie Sanders

The Two Noble Kinsmen has always had an uneasy relationship with the Shakespearean canon. Based on Chaucer's *The Knight's Tale* (from *The Canterbury Tales*), it was first published in 1634 and attributed to Shakespeare and John Fletcher, a dramatist better known for his collaborative relationships with Francis Beaumont and Philip Massinger. The Fletcher–Shakespeare pairing has been credited with two further creations, the lost *Cardenio* and *Henry VIII; or, All is True*. All three playtexts are presumed to have been written between 1612 and 1613. Some critics have cast doubt on Shakespearean participation in *The Two Noble Kinsmen*; others have suggested alternative or additional collaborators, such as professional actor and playwright Nathan Field (Hedrick 1989). The inclusion of the play in all standard series of Shakespeare today would suggest that his contribution is now less in doubt, although the critical consensus as to which sections of the play he wrote varies. Collaboration *per se* is only now beginning to receive due attention in literary criticism, due in large part to the pioneering scholarship of Gordon McMullan and Jeffrey Masten (McMullan 1994; Masten 1997). What is certain, however, is that any essay such as this, a contribution to a volume on Shakespeare, must pay due attention to the contributions of Fletcher to the play under discussion. In some cases this contribution can be seen to operate in tension with Shakespeare's, in others to shape and even radicalize the latter. This essay is less concerned with the attribution of specific scenes to either dramatist under discussion than with the wider aesthetics of the play. John Shawcross has noted that "Genre . . . involves structure and form, characteristics, and authorial intent toward the piece of writing" (Shawcross 1987: 17), and it is at this level that this essay will focus the discussion: at the level of genre, structure, and form.

Adding to the critical confusions that surround *The Two Noble Kinsmen*, the play's assigned genre of "tragicomedy" (as attributed by the 1634 edition's title page) has led to differences of interpretation. Its oddly somber ending, with an imposed marriage following hard on a tragic death, strikes a bleak note which for many sits uneasily with the tone of reconciliation and reformation in other Shakespearean late romances.

This response underestimates the mixed messages at the end of those plays – Mamillius, after all, remains lost to Leontes and Hermione at the close of *The Winter's Tale* – as well as the tragicomic aspects of earlier works such as *Measure for Measure* or *All's Well That Ends Well*, but it also ignores the fact that, generically at least, *The Two Noble Kinsmen* is very much a product of its time. As McMullan and Hope (1992) have observed: "Tragicomedy was arguably the single most important dramatic genre of the period 1610–50" (p. 1), and it was certainly Fletcher's preferred dramatic mode. What is important in recognizing Shakespeare's late accommodation with the genre of tragicomedy is to register that it is attended by an interest in many of the central motifs of that genre. McMullan and Hope have stressed, for example, a particular interest in margins: country settings and local, even regionalist, concerns; women's issues, an interest encouraged by increasingly female audiences, and female participation in courtly and aristocratic theatrical practice; and pastoral, even folkloric subjects (largely popular rather than elite forms) (ibid: 9). In its formal structures, too, tragicomedy expresses an interest in margins, staging major events just offstage; this convention, which follows ancient Greek and Roman dramatic tradition, is adhered to with interesting results by *The Two Noble Kinsmen*.

As a product of its time, *The Two Noble Kinsmen* is also a product of contemporary aesthetics: a dominant interest in tragicomedy, influenced by the theories of Italian playwright Giovanni Battista Guarini (Loewenstein 1987), being matched by the increased influence of the parallel genre of the masque. Suzanne Gossett has been instrumental in stressing the significance of the masque form to commercial theatre in the early Stuart period. She argues that Jacobean and Caroline tragicomedy became increasingly masquelike and identifies an aesthetic logic for this: "By its inherently tragicomic nature and its abrupt romanticizing of a situation threatening to become simply tragic or comic, the masque proved a major asset in the search for the difficult balance which creates tragicomedy" (Gossett 1972: 208). The physical setting of the first performance of *The Two Noble Kinsmen* at the Blackfriars indoor theatre also encouraged these aesthetic links between the essentially aristocratic form of masque and the public playhouse. The Blackfriars had a more elite audience and repertoire, but its architectural make-up, not least the provision of space and acoustics for musicians, contributed to the ability to stage more masquelike dramas, or dramas that exploited masquelike elements. This essay will interrogate those aspects of *The Two Noble Kinsmen* which have consistently interested critics and productions – such as the essential debunking of the central narcissistic friendship of the two protagonist cousins and the concomitant expression of sympathy and empathy for the female characters – and offer precise political and practical reasons for their treatment in such a way in such a play in 1613.

The impact of political situations on genre should never be underestimated (Shawcross 1987: 16) and Fletcher has long been identified as a dramatist with a determined political and social purpose: "The Fletcherian form, though it may grow out of generic concerns, grows out of social ones as well" (Williams 1987: 142). Most essays on the play remark upon the topical allusions of *The Two Noble Kinsmen* and this will be no exception. What this essay seeks to do, however, is to draw a series of links between the generic and aesthetic structures of the play that connect it both to the physical playing conditions of its original performance and the political situation of 1613. It will identify in the choice of genre (and even genres: masque and tragicomedy are seen to be virtually inseparable in terms of the play's aesthetics) an artistic logic that can tell us much about the theatrical impact of the play and the mixed messages it conveys.

"Shrunk . . . into / The bound": The Architecture of the Play

The mixed generic structure of *The Two Noble Kinsmen* is aptly reflected in the intricate dramaturgy of the playtext. It may seem obvious to state that this is a five-act play, but those five acts need to be carefully considered as individual entities since, as a 1613 play, written specifically for the Blackfriars playhouse, *The Two Noble Kinsmen* is one of those plays which Gary Taylor has persuasively argued were specifically designed in five sections with four intervals (Taylor and Jowett 1993: 42). The Blackfriars, at some point in its early history a Dominican priory but in its more recent incarnation a children's company playhouse, was acquired by the King's Men as their winter playing space in 1608. It is perhaps not entirely surprising that the company inherited some of the boys' companies' acting traditions along with their indoor playhouse. This included the observation of *entr'acte* intervals. Taylor has argued that this was one of the most fundamental shifts in playwriting and performance between 1610 and 1642. Whereas plays prior to those dates tended towards continuous action, all 245 extant plays for 1616–42 have five acts in both printed and manuscript manifestations, indicating that they were being performed with intervals between the acts by this time (Taylor and Jowett 1993: 4). Several reasons for the propensity to between-the-acts intervals in the so-called "private" playhouses have been advanced, one being that the use of candles to light these indoor spaces necessitated regular intervals for the wicks to be trimmed (ibid: 31). Another is that because these playhouses had improved architectural facilities for musicians, the deployment of music between the acts became a desirable feature of performances. Taylor also suggests that as well as the boys' company traditions, the influence of theatrical practice at the court, the universities, and the Inns of Court (all elite and academic arenas) can be registered, perhaps reflecting the increasingly elite audience composition at the private theatres (ibid). That change was all the more significant in the work of someone like Shakespeare who, unlike Jonson, or even Fletcher, who had written for the boys' companies and the court domain, had little or no past experience of writing within the five-act tradition.

What *The Two Noble Kinsmen* evidences on close interrogation is a quite brilliant mastery of the possibilities of the five-act structure. It is worth pausing to consider exactly how, practically and intellectually, the action divides between those five acts. Act 1 has been identified by the play's most erudite editor, Lois Potter, as highly formal, ritualized, and almost tragic in tone (Potter 1997: 2). The three queens, attired in mourning black, who plead with Theseus to intercede with the tyrannical Theban leader Creon to allow them to bury their late husbands, echo the formal laments of Greek tragedies such as Euripides' *The Suppliants* or *The Phoenician Women*. It has become a commonplace of criticism to observe that the play begins with a wedding and a funeral in the first act (the union of Theseus and Hippolyta and the funerals of the three queens' spouses) and ends with the same inhospitable combination in the fifth (the funeral of Arcite and the wedding of Palamon and Emilia), an extended reworking of *Hamlet*'s theme of "mirth in funeral and . . . dirge in marriage" (*Hamlet*, 1.2.12). But on closer inspection the first act actually performs in microcosm the overall architectonic design of the play: wedding to funeral. Audiences are encouraged to register the contained structure of the opening act by means of the formal rhyming couplet, spoken by one of the mourning queens, that marks its closure: "This world's a city full of straying streets, / And death's the market-place where each one meets" (1.5.15–16).

The interval between the first and second acts allows for a substantial change in pace and tone. Act 2 ushers in the play's subplot of the Jailer and his daughter as well as releasing a more comic, even ironic, element in such scenes as 2.2, which depicts Palamon and Arcite in an Athenian prison, quickly turning from their idealistic declarations of loyalty to each other to childlike squabbling over who loves Emilia more. This rapid collapse of a solemnly sworn edict resembles that of an earlier Shakespearean comedy *Love's Labour's Lost* and, indeed, the second and third acts of *The Two Noble Kinsmen* have been likened to the romantic comedies as a whole by Potter, "with their lovers and hunters escaping into the forest, their rivalry of two men for one woman" (Potter 1997: 15–16). The forest-based events of act 3 echo the setting of romantic comedies such as *The Two Gentlemen of Verona* and *A Midsummer Night's Dream*. Taylor has suggested that the significant stage property of scenes 1, 3, and 6, where the fugitive Palamon (who has escaped his jail with the help of the love-smitten Jailer's Daughter) appears "*out of a bush*," would have remained onstage throughout the entire third act to signify this cohesive locale (Taylor and Jowett 1993: 42). Palamon's sudden appearances out of the bush would also conjure up for alert audiences images of the "wild man" of medieval literature, adding to the multiple generic references of the play. Potter has further demonstrated how the forest-based scenes of the play, along with the theme of disguised competitors in royal sports (Arcite wins the wrestling competition before the Duke in disguise as a poor laborer), are suggestive of the rich folkloric tradition of Robin Hood (Potter 1997: 4). Here again the precise architecture of the individual act rewards close attention. The scenes in which Palamon appears from the hawthorn brake, where the Jailer's Daughter has persuaded him to hide while she brings him food and a file with which to remove his shackles, are punctuated by scenes of her alone in the woods. In *The Knight's Tale* Chaucer made much of the double meaning of "wood" – which also meant "mad" in Middle English. The connection remains only implicit in Shakespeare and Fletcher's rewrite, but is nevertheless embedded in the Daughter's mental isolation in these scenes (3.2 and

3.4). Her emotional solitude is underlined by her use of soliloquy. Act 3, scene 5 might appear on the surface an exception to this rule, with its large onstage gathering of the Schoolmaster and his morris dancers who are preparing a May Day entertainment for Theseus, but the Jailer's Daughter proves alone in this crowd too, as her madness isolates her from the reality of the scene.

The fourth act is significant not least because neither of the two noble kinsmen, the play's joint protagonists, appears onstage. Instead they are present only as they are conjured up in the minds of Emilia and the Jailer's Daughter. Here again soliloquy emphasizes the essential loneliness of the female condition in this play. Emilia's version of the knights is idealized and abstract, the daughter's colored by passion and insanity, but in both respects, the space of act 4 is firmly located in the female imagination. The fourth act and its attendant interval therefore provide a mental breathing space, a time for reassessment before the return to the formal, and essentially tragic, mode of the ritualistic fifth act. In that denouement, as well as witnessing the triple prayers at the altars of Mars, Venus, and Diana (of Arcite, Palamon, and Emilia respectively), we return to the mode of Greek tragic drama where the majority of the physical action occurs unseen and offstage. The battle for supremacy between Palamon and Arcite in act 5, scene 3 (in which the first to touch the pyramid wins Emilia, the loser being resigned to death) occurs just offstage with the audience sharing instead Emilia's auditory experience of the event. This is a skillful dramatic means of engaging empathy for the female situation. In a further deployment of Greek theatrical conventions, in 5.4 a messenger brings onstage the dramatic announcement of Arcite's fatal riding accident. This means that Palamon's onstage execution is halted at the last moment — one of the play's most dramatic twists of fortune.

Gordon McMullan has remarked on Fletcher's highly "particular dramaturgy" (McMullan 1994: x) and, in another context, James Yoch has spoken of the dramatist's "balanced architecture of incidents" (Yoch 1987: 128). These would seem equally apposite terms to apply to *The Two Noble Kinsmen*'s delicate use of contrast, juxtaposition, containment, and symmetry. As well as the juxtaposed weddings and funerals, the topical and political import of which will be explored in the final section of this essay, the play both invokes and subverts binaries at several turns. The two noble kinsmen are paralleled yet demarcated. Critics vary as to how important their differences are, but the essential factor is that while Arcite prays to Mars, god of war, in the fifth act, Palamon prays to Venus, the goddess of love. Their fates are therefore entirely consistent with the actions of the gods, as Theseus observes at the close: Arcite wins the war, but Palamon wins in love. The arbitrary impact of these allegiances to the gods is heightened by the rapidity with which these events occur, which stands in stark contrast to Chaucer's elongated version (which saw Palamon and Emilia mourn for several years before being joined in marriage). As well as love and war, male friendships and female friendships are contrasted in the play, and, according to Laurie J. Shannon (1997), the female versions prove both preferable and more sustainable. *The Two Noble Kinsmen*'s investment in binaries and dualisms also operates at the level of main plot and subplot, requiring all the comparisons and contrasts usually associated with that dramatic strategy. Binaries prove unsustainable even at the level of genre, where the tragic and comic elements of the text prove increasingly difficult to separate by the close.

If symmetries are invoked and pressurized at the level of the text, juxtaposition is a driving force of the play in performance. In act 2, scene 2, Palamon and Arcite swear that their friendship will never die, only for Emilia's immediate entrance onstage to cause them swiftly to discard their pledge:

> *Palamon.* I do not think it possible our friendship
>   Should ever leave us.
> *Arcite.*   Till our deaths it cannot.
>   *Enter* EMILIA *and her* WOMAN. (2.2.114–15)

Juxtaposition functions as an element of signification between scenes and between acts as well as within scenes. In 2.3 Arcite is released from his prison but banished from Athens (a situation he laments because it tears him from Emilia's presence). In the scene immediately following, the Jailer's Daughter soliloquizes on her love for Palamon, a love that will see her banished from all that is familiar in her life, including emotional stability: "To marry him is hopeless; / To be his whore is witless" (2.4.4–5). The subsequent two scenes in some respects repeat the pattern of parallel and juxtaposition: 2.5 sees Arcite winning the royal wrestling competition, in a practical sense enjoying the effects of society, but alone in a crowd since he cannot reveal his true identity, whereas 2.6 sees the Jailer's Daughter alone in her thoughts once more, despite having freed Palamon from his jail.

The plotline of the Jailer's Daughter is one of Shakespeare and Fletcher's important interpolations to their source material and one which contributes to the less-than-idealized reading of Palamon, which Alan Stewart has argued is essential to an understanding of the debunking version of the kinsmen in the play (Stewart 1999: 58). Susan Green has astutely observed how the scenes involving the Daughter (which are often significant in terms of audience reaction to the play in performance)[1] help to skew the conventional assumptions which might otherwise shape responses to the play and its protagonists: "the Jailer's Daughter moves frenetically, slightly off-center, but always . . . a crucial locus of the play's illusioning power" (Green 1989: 121). A further important alteration to the Chaucerian source material that Shakespeare and Fletcher effect is to compress and compact the time-scales in which events occur, as well as to downscale some of the more extravagant descriptions: most famously the one hundred knights who accompany Palamon and Arcite in *The Knight's Tale* are reduced here to just three each (Thompson 1978). It has already been mentioned how the marriage of Emilia and Palamon follows swiftly on from Arcite's death in *The Two Noble Kinsmen*, a strategy which renders the action far more disturbing (and Theseus's insistence on the nuptials far more unsettling) than the union which takes place after several years at the close of Chaucer's narrative poem. The compression of time contributes to the audience unease nurtured by the tragicomedy. Unease of this nature colors the mood at the end of the play; several critics have remarked how precarious the sense of closure is in *The Two Noble Kinsmen*. Unlike the clearly end-stopped rhyming couplet that closes the first act on such a contained note, the play proper ends on a half-line: "Let's go off / And bear us like the time" (5.4.136–7). It is possible that the newly demarcated five-act structure of Blackfriars' plays that *The Two Noble Kinsmen* realizes, and of which it makes such dramatic capital, also contributes to the destabilization of closure. Boys' company plays drew attention to their own artifice and any audience in a state of awareness of artificiality is predisposed to question neat closures or happy endings: Ben Jonson was to make an art of this in his Caroline playtexts. The place in which *The Two Noble Kinsmen* was performed is therefore crucial to a full understanding of its dramaturgy. Relevant too, however, are the multiple specific spaces and places which the play invokes and explores and it is to these that the next section turns.

"This must be done i' th' woods": Space and Place

The motive behind Shakespeare and Fletcher's compression of time-scales and cast-lists from their Chaucerian source is occasionally a simple matter of performability: one hundred knights to accompany each noble kinsmen in the fifth act would be impossible to achieve onstage. Similarly, Palamon's several-year sojourn in prison, or more importantly his extended period of grief following Arcite's demise, would require the kind of artificial dramatic pause provided by Time's speech in the middle of *The Winter's Tale*, when the action leaps geographically from Bohemia to Sicilia but also over the "wide gap" of sixteen years (*The Winter's Tale*, 4.1.7). In terms of dramaturgic placement, this would be virtually impossible to achieve in *The Two Noble Kinsmen* without bifurcating the all-important fifth act.

Chaucer had compacted the spatial aesthetics of his own source, Boccaccio's *Teseida*, reducing the multiple spaces of that text to a salient few where the action appears almost to crowd in on the locations, such as the royal forest where Palamon and Arcite's two combative encounters occur. The forest always provides a resonant locale in early modern literature (Sanders 2001), and *The Two Noble Kinsmen* is no exception. As already noted, the forest contains medieval connotations of both the wild man of the woods and stories and ballads relating to Robin Hood (despite the Prologue's anxiety to dissociate itself from such literature (lines 20–1)). We have also observed how its deployment as the setting for the entire central act of this play draws resonant associations with Shakespearean romantic comedy. This forest is a site of male competition as in *The Two Gentlemen of Verona* and *A Midsummer Night's Dream*, and, as in *Dream*, a site for amateur theatricals to be performed before Duke Theseus – in this instance Gerard the schoolmaster's efforts to rehearse his under-staffed morris dance. In *Dream*, Peter Quince's efforts to stage his heavily revised version of "Pyramus and Thisbe" involves rehearsals in a specific spot in the Athenian forest: "here's a marvellous convenient place for our rehearsal. This green plot shall be our stage, this hawthorn brake our tiring-house, and we will do it in action as we will do it before the Duke" (*Dream*, 3.1.2–5). Quince's theatricals are located in the third act of Shakespeare's moonstruck drama (the "central plateau" of Shakespearean dramaturgy (Holland 1997: 4)), and this centrally located scene of romantic comedy would seem to possess intrinsic connections to the hawthorn brake from which Palamon appears in *The Two Noble Kinsmen*. In both plays, the occasion for the festivities, and the Duke's hunting trip through the lands and rides of the wider forest, is May Day (*Dream*, 1.1.167; 4.1.2; 4.1.129–30; *Two Noble Kinsmen*, 3.1.1–4), rendering relevant to *The Two Noble Kinsmen* the same rich elements of carnival and social ritual that have proved so revealing in application to earlier Shakespearean comedy.

The hunting topos of *The Two Noble Kinsmen*, as with *Dream*, also relates to the Amazonian background of Theseus's bride, Hippolyta, who here, as in *The Knight's Tale*, is given a sister: Emilia. Any spatial connection with the self-sufficient female community of the Amazons raises gender issues, and this is certainly true of *The Two Noble Kinsmen*, where Shannon has argued for the importance of "female proprietary spaces" (Shannon 1997: 661). Emilia is one of Shakespeare and Fletcher's notable expansions rather than compressions of the Chaucerian source-text. In *The Knight's Tale* Emelye speaks only once and that is in the formal context of an address to the temple of Diana. The agency of Emilia in the play provides a striking contrast. It is her choice – or rather her steadfast refusal to make one – which determines the fate of Palamon and Arcite, and her presence which initially fissures their supposedly unbreakable homosocial bond. Fletcher has been linked by a number of critics to a career-long investment in striking female heroines with genuine stage agency, a fact which may help to explain his renewed popularity in the Caroline era when Queen Henrietta Maria forged her own influential brand of feminocentric theatricals at court (McMullan 1994: x), and Potter has noted that *The Two Noble Kinsmen* has an unusually large cast of speaking female parts in the Shakespearean canon (Potter 1997: 64). Nevertheless, it is important to stress that the other central female character of the play, and one who is in structural terms juxtaposed with Emilia throughout (note their interleaved scenes in act 4 – the act in which the kinsmen make no onstage appearance) – the Jailer's Daughter – offers many striking parallels with the earlier Shakespearean canon, most significantly with the figure of Ophelia. It would be wrong in stressing the significance of the Fletcherian contribution to this play (and it is considerable) to devalue its Shakespearean elements. Like Ophelia, the Daughter not only runs mad and finds a discourse for her insanity in bawdy ballads (Bruster 1995), but she is also linked to the natural world throughout.[2] Her experience of the woods is very different to the controlled royal space of hunting and lists that Theseus and the knights prescribe and describe: while Palamon and Arcite invoke the pastoral tradition merely to brag of their sexual exploits ("There was a time / When young men went a-hunting, and a wood, / And a broad beech; and thereby hangs a tale –" (3.3.39–42)), her woodland is a frighteningly real one of wolves and howling. The pun on "wood" that remained ironic for Palamon and Arcite becomes all too real in the Daughter's experience. Similarly, when her suitor, the Wooer, finds her distraught in her madness in the fourth act (an event which, akin to Ophelia's drowning, occurs offstage and only meets with the audience's experience in the form of onstage report: compare *Hamlet*, 4.7.134–54), the spatial context for this event is emphatically "natural," located far away from the ducal palace and its controlled rhetoric (4.1.52–65; 4.1.82–90). In a further Ophelia parallel, the Jailer's Daughter is aligned with the flora and fauna of this environment: the Wooer tells how she sings of the garlands she will bring to her lost love, Palamon:

> I'll bring a bevy,
> A hundred black-eyed maids that love as I do,
> With chaplets on their heads of daffadillies,
> With cherry-lips and cheeks of damask roses,
> And all we'll dance an antic 'fore the Duke
> And beg his pardon. (4.1.71–6)

The traditional association of women and flowers and the enclosed space of the garden is deployed earlier in the play at 2.2 where Emilia's joy in the outside world is juxtaposed with the incarcerated condition of Palamon and Arcite. Shakespeare has elsewhere depicted women in gardens and such scenes are frequently images of enclosure and restriction rather than agency (Mariana in the moated grange in *Measure for Measure*, and the walled garden in which Angelo plans his seduction of Isabella in the same play; Richard II's isolated queen in 3.4 of that historical tragedy, where the garden serves as a synecdoche for England). It is dramatic juxtaposition that enables us to read Emilia's scene in the garden rather differently. She is empowered to cross the stage while Palamon and Arcite, for all their lyrical and poetic claims to make their little prison a substitute for the world ("This is all our world. / We shall know nothing here but one another" (2.2.40–1); "Let's think this prison holy sanctuary, / To keep us from corruption of worse men" (2.2.71–2)), are shackled and held. After the static nature of much of the first act, it seems significant that the two characters that we first associate with movement on the stage are female.

Spatial metaphors of enclosures and bounds are dominant in the play at a linguistic level, as well as in terms of stage settings and movements. If Creon is a "most unbounded tyrant" (1.2.63), then passion threatens to exceed the bounds of sanity and decorum throughout, most obviously in the case of the Jailer's Daughter, but also in the sense that Palamon and Arcite are prepared to risk everything for love of Emilia. The play's two dominant images of water and horses play vividly with these ideas of boundaries and the exceeding of them. Early modern audiences would have been well aware of the story of Hippolytus, the child of Theseus and Hippolyta who, like Emilia, devoted himself to Diana, but found that the passion of his stepmother Phaedra dragged him down, both morally and literally: he dies a horrible death at the hands of the gods amid the crashing of hooves and waves (Potter 1992: 83).[3] Through the metaphors and described spaces of this drama, then, the tragic element invades even those scenes and acts most obviously associated with the generic conventions of romantic comedy. Invaded spaces and interrupted rituals provide a further pattern in the drama, emblematized in the disrupted wedding of the opening scene. The most dramatic moments of the play occur, however, not before the spectators' eyes but just offstage, tantalizingly close in the case of the final combat of Palamon and Arcite. We hear the gathered crowd's cheers but, like Emilia, find ourselves reliant on the messages brought onstage of how the "sport" goes. The offstage spaces of *The Two Noble Kinsmen* extend far beyond these imagined dramatic tableaux, however, and into a wider context of the political and aesthetic world of 1613. To conclude, therefore, this essay will concentrate on the spatial world beyond the play that helps us to define and interpret its aesthetic messages.

"Out of the play": Offstage Events and Contexts

In Ben Jonson's 1614 play *Bartholomew Fair*, the two quarreling suitors of Grace Wellborn, Quarlous and Winwife, adopt self-consciously literary pseudonyms in their erotic competition. Quarlous chooses to be referred to as Argalus, a character from Sir Philip Sidney's prose pastoral, the *Arcadia* (elsewhere posited as a possible source for the subplot of the Jailer's Daughter in *The Two Noble Kinsmen* (Thompson 1979)) and Winwife elects to be Palamon (Jonson actually spells it Palemon) "out of the play" (Jonson 2000: 4.3.67–8). This reference is proof alone that *The Two Noble Kinsmen* must have been a theatrical success in 1613, since Jonson assumes audience knowledge of the subject of his parody. It also guides the audience to expect the eventual outcome: that Winwife as Palamon will get the girl (Dutton 1983: 168). A theatrical in-joke may even have been involved: Nathan Field (a potential third collaborator on the text as we have heard) had most likely played Palamon in the Blackfriars staging and he was certainly Winwife at the Hope theatre in 1614. All this is evidence of the play's significant afterlife. Muriel Bradbrook has suggested a further spatial mapping of Shakespeare and Fletcher's tragicomedy onto Jonson's cynical urban drama in the puppet play of act 5, demonstrating with brilliant visual wit how the puppets leaning out of their booth in Lantern Leatherhead's show would have reminded 1614 theatre audiences of Palamon and Arcite as "prisoners, leaning out of their prison window" (Bradbrook 1976: 241). What all this serves to indicate is that offstage events are significant in reading and interpreting *The Two Noble Kinsmen* in two senses, both in respect that the play itself is structured around significant events that occur offstage, engaging the audience's imagination in a very vivid manner, and in the sense that events outside the strict remit of the play ("out of the play," indeed) inform and affect its meanings and messages.

The deliberately uneasy proximity of weddings and funerals in *The Two Noble Kinsmen* has long been recognized as having topical resonance in 1613.[4] As Julia Briggs has noted: "The incongruous combination of hearses, mourning rites and weddings . . . links . . . with that strange period of 'funerals and hornpipes' that followed the sudden death of Prince Henry in November 1612" (Briggs 1999: 222). The premature demise of the heir to the throne led to the postponement of his sister Princess Elizabeth's scheduled wedding to Frederick, Elector Palatine. James VI and I had initially wished the nuptials to be deferred until May 1613, but they eventually went ahead on St. Valentine's Day. As was traditional on such occasions, numerous theatrical events and specially commissioned masques were performed, including interrelated works by Thomas Campion, Francis Beaumont, and George Chapman. One of these masques, Beaumont's Inns of Court-sponsored *The Masque of the Inner Temple and Gray's Inn*, is directly appropriated in *The Two Noble Kinsmen* in the context of the third act morris.[5] This act of borrowing lends credence to arguments that the events of 1612–13 are relevant to Shakespeare and Fletcher's drama.

In Beaumont's script, Iris and Mercury compete with each other as representatives of Juno and Jupiter respectively as to who will present the best wedding entertainment. Their efforts constitute the two antimasques: Mercury offers a dance of Naiads and Hyades (water-nymphs), but Iris scornfully rejects the single-sex composition of the dancers. Her riposte is a country dance in celebration of May Games (Potter (1997: 350) speculates that Beaumont devised this when the wedding was still scheduled for May). The *dramatis personae* for this antimasque find an almost exact analogue in *The Two Noble Kinsmen*. Beaumont has a May Lord and Lady (that these characters were often portrayed as Robin Hood and Maid Marian effects its own links with the commercial drama where Robin Hood elements have already been identified); a Servingman and a Chambermaid; a Country Clown or Shepherd and a Country Wench; a Host and Hostess (presumably of an inn); a He-baboon and She-baboon; and a He-Fool and a She-Fool. In the Schoolmaster's presentation to Duke Theseus in the central act of *The Two Noble Kinsmen*, we are introduced in turn to a "Lord of May and Lady bright" (3.5.124); a Chambermaid and a Servingman (line 125); a Host and his "fat Spouse" who regularly embezzle their inn guests (lines 126–9); a clown, a fool, and a baboon with a "long tool" (line 131). A performative pragmatism should not be discounted when considering the restaging of this aspect of Beaumont's masque in a public theatre context. The dance had been a success with King James who requested an encore, so the King's Men, who both performed in the masque at court and staged *The Two Noble Kinsmen* at Blackfriars, may simply have recognized a potential money-spinner. It is also possible that, as was common practice, the performers had been allowed to retain the costumes from the court performance, the recycling and reuse of which would have enabled obvious economies. Even the settings of the 1613 masque and the subsequent play (woodlands and temples) would have allowed for the reuse of sets, although Potter has questioned how practical elaborate court machinery would have been in a commercial theatre context (Potter 1997: 353). But Gordon McMullan has suggested that the reasons for the appropriation go deeper than mere theatrical practicality. Observing how the "context of rural buffoonery" serves to burlesque the Beaumont original, he argues that Fletcher (and therefore Shakespeare) was questioning the political optimism of early 1613, when the marriage of Frederick and Elizabeth was perceived by many as cementing a Protestant ascendancy in European politics (in truth, the outcome was the Thirty Years War). He suggests that as "each of Beaumont's dancers . . . receives a downgraded counterpart in the parts played by the morris dancers, carnivalized by the Schoolmaster's appalling half-rhymes . . . Fletcher seems to have mocked his own involvement as well as that of his friends in the political consensus of 1613" (McMullan 1994: 106). Many of the tropes and topoi of *The Two Noble Kinsmen*, not least the chivalric romance context of the whole, would seem to effect a visual and intellectual connection with the chivalric, militaristic, and self-consciously masculine, as well as Protestant, iconography that surrounded the household of the late Prince of Wales (Strong 1977), but if such images are under tension and strain in the play, as we have already suggested, it would seem valid to argue that the political optimism of 1612 (what McMullan refers to as "illusory glories") is undergoing serious revision by late 1613.

The mutual influence of commercial drama and courtly masquing traditions has long been accepted, but there is a specific shift in style in the late Shakespearean canon which is worth registering and which the deployment of masque aesthetics in *The Two Noble Kinsmen* both serves to evidence and confirm. It is not only in Blackfriars plays such as *The Tempest* and *The Winter's Tale* – which in terms of their more elite context and intimate playing conditions might be expected to approximate aspects of court theatricals – that these deployments manifest themselves: masque influence can also be traced in Globe plays in the 1610s, including Shakespeare and Fletcher's other extant collaboration, *Henry VIII: or, All Is True*. A reasonable conclusion might be to argue that Shakespeare's work is being affected by the collaborative process, but the impact upon his work of changing playing conditions (increased female roles, use of music, observation of the five-act structure) is equally relevant. What is clear is that a nuanced notion of the genre (and generic variety) of the early Stuart masque is crucial to a proper understanding of the political as well as dramatic aesthetics of *The Two Noble Kinsmen*. In a related argument about *The Tempest*, James Knowles (1999) has made the stimulating case that we must factor in aristocratic country house masques and entertainments as well as royally sponsored court masques to our notion of Stuart masquing culture. The politics of great households that was such a driving force of early Stuart culture had a clear impact on the content and tone of Fletcher's writing career (McMullan 1994): the two most significant links of his patronage network being to the Earl of Huntingdon's circle, based largely at Ashby-de-la-Zouch in Leicestershire, in the region of the east Midlands, and the Beaumont family who were based at nearby Coleorton and to which Fletcher's playwriting collaborator Francis was related. That literary milieu was closely aligned to country-house entertainments and masques. A brief glance at some of the dramatic entertainments associated with this group in the 1610s can be revealing for a reading of *The Two Noble Kinsmen* and may help to explain some of the more radical (even un-Shakespearean) aspects of the text.

The Beaumont group is perhaps best known for the wedding masque that was staged at Coleorton in 1618 to honor the marriage of Sir William Seymour and Frances Devereux, sister of the Earl of Essex. The text of the occasion, which survives in a manuscript in the Victoria and Albert Museum, is anonymous, but Fletcher has been posited, along with Leicestershire cleric Thomas Pestell, as a possible author, and certainly there appear to be analogies in the themes and topics of the masque with those of his public theatre plays (McMullan 1994: 283 n. 71; Finkelpearl 1990). The exquisite antimasque of Puck and the buttery-spirit Bob is less our concern here than the main masque's radical gender politics, although its mention of the traditional hospitality of "honest Harry of Ashby" (Anon. 1995: lines 68–9) indicates the connections between the Beaumont group and the literary and theatrical circle surrounding Henry Hastings, 5th Earl of Huntingdon (the "Harry" referred to).[6] In the masque proper, a group of six male dancers representing the traditional chivalric values of nobleness, valor, wisdom, justice, temperance, and courtesy are matched step for step by six "Brave Amazonian dames" (line 238) who, despite their surface representation of traditional female virtues of meekness, simplicity, truth-in-love, modesty, silence, and chastity, make bold declarations of the desirability of same-sex communities. McMullan has discussed at length the ways in which this masque functions both as "a glorification of the established country aristocratic households exemplified by the Huntingdons of Ashby and the Beaumonts of Coleorton and an assertion of equality between the sexes that suggests a certain degree of feminocentrism in the households in question" (McMullan 1994: 32). Knowles has further stressed that in expanding our notion of Stuart masquing culture to include these aristocratic entertainments we also allow for a greater feminocentrist emphasis (Knowles 1999: 124). The feminine empathies of *The Two Noble Kinsmen* have already been discussed and the role of Amazons both in the play and the Coleorton masque may encourage us to foster these links in reading the aesthetics of the Blackfriars drama.[7]

The Coleorton Masque, of course, post-dates *The Two Noble Kinsmen*, although it does allow us an insight into the theatrical politics of Fletcher's Huntingdon circle. One entertainment of this kind that comes out of the same moment as the play is *The Caversham Entertainment*, written by Thomas Campion for a staging by Lord Knollys at Caversham House, near Reading, in honor of a visit by Queen Anne of Denmark. Anne went on progress to Bath in April 1613 following her daughter's February wedding and stayed en route at Caversham. In keeping with the tradition of such entertainments, the masque marks her entry into the estate and formal gardens surrounding the house, as well as her departure the following day. As was also traditional on such occasions, a formal gift-giving sequence occurs. What is intriguing in terms of reading the influence of an entertainment of this nature on the aesthetics of a public theatre play such as *The Two Noble Kinsmen* is not just the pastoral setting of *The Caversham Entertainment* but the role of specific characters. Two keepers of the estate appear dressed in green along with "two Robin-Hood-men" (Campion 1995: line 83) advancing themes we have already identified as of note in *The Two Noble Kinsmen*. The appearance of characters out of bushes and bowers in this script, a feature that was common in such progress entertainments, also recurs in Palamon's repeated appearances out of a bush in the third act of the play. That Campion's own masque for the wedding celebrations for Princess Elizabeth in 1613, *The Lord's Masque*, featured a woodland setting with a wild man emerging from a thicket serves to underline the kinships between these contemporary entertainments: *The Lord's Masque* also closes with a wedding tableau which features a bride and groom placed on either side of a silver obelisk (Potter 1992: p. 80).

After a formal speech of welcome and a song, the Queen progresses in *The Caversham Entertainment* through the estate (on a cloth since "some wet had fallen that day in the forenoon": line 146), eventually entering the lower garden where she is greeted by a Gardener and his two assistants. Lois Potter has likened the role of the Gardener, as organizer of the entertainment, to that of the Schoolmaster in *The Two Noble Kinsmen*, as well as to Jonson's "Schoolmaster of Mansfield" in his 1633 *Entertainment at Welbeck*, commissioned by William Cavendish, Earl of Newcastle to mark another royal progress, this time by Charles I (Potter 1997: 354). The Gardener's symbolic presentation of flowers in *The Caversham Entertainment* – "I have flowers for all fancies: thyme for truth, rosemary for remembrance, roses for love, heartsease for joy, and thousands more" (lines 167–9) – is another archetypal sequence in the masque, comparable versions of which can be seen in *The Two Noble Kinsmen* in Emilia's garden scene (2.2) and the Jailer's Daughter's offstage mad scene at 4.1 (itself recalling Ophelia's behavior at 4.5 of *Hamlet*, as well as Perdita's exchange with Polixenes in *The Winter's Tale* (4.4.72–134)). In *The Two Noble Kinsmen* the language of flowers will invite a tragic rereading in the fifth act when Emilia sees the falling rose at Diana's altar.

But it is less precise mappings of particular masques onto the play that serve our purpose here, than a recognition that the aesthetics of masquing culture have a particular influence on the text. As well as the Caversham and Coleorton masques, we might also wish to invoke Jonson's 1604 *Entertainment at Highgate* which was staged to welcome James and Anne on a May Day visit, as well as the pastoral evocations of another Huntingdon circle masque, the 1606 *Entertainment at Ashby*. In addition to the pastoral and chivalric topoi of these entertainments, their often striking feminocentric emphases help to shed light on the investigations and interrogations of masculinity and the radical empathy for women which have frequently been noted in readings and stagings of *The Two Noble Kinsmen* (Erler 1996: 20). Another theatrical tradition from the early Stuart period that may add to our understandings of the performative politics of *The Two Noble Kinsmen* is one hinted at by Lois Potter (1997). In an almost throwaway line in her Arden edition of the play, she remarks of the opening sequence's formal and tragic structure that: "The first act is largely static, almost a closet drama" (p. 2). Closet drama, essentially drama designed to be read aloud, is a form strongly associated in the Elizabethan and Jacobean period with elite women writers such as Mary Sidney, Countess of Pembroke, and Lady Mary Wroth. Fletcher's feminocentric milieu at Ashby, under the guidance of the fifth earl's wife, Elizabeth Stanley, might have encouraged the working of such influences into his commercial drama. What is intriguing about such connections is that they draw Shakespeare more fully into the aesthetic world of his contemporaries such as Jonson and Fletcher, a world from which his work is too often abstracted.

What this widening of the sphere of aesthetic reference in *The Two Noble Kinsmen* helps us do is to provide a detailed context, political and theatrical, for what are often identified as the strangenesses and innovations of the play, at least in the context of the Shakespearean canon. This is a carefully structured play, its tragicomic architecture not a messy result of collaboration by two authors with different dramatic discourses and dramaturgic approaches, but rather the product of a coherent and cohesive attitude to the events of their day by two brilliant and insightful writers.

NOTES

1 The performance history of *The Two Noble Kinsmen* had been fairly limited until the late twentieth century. It seems, however, that the ambiguities and generic hybridity of the text have had genuine appeal for recent directors. In the UK, for example, there have been productions at both the Royal Shakespeare Company (in 1987) and at the Globe Theatre, London (2000). For a detailed account of the play's stage history, see Potter (1997: 78–95).

2 Fletcher frequently depicts insane characters, both male and female. See, for example, plays such as *The Mad Lover* and *The Wild Goose-Chase* (Potter 1997: 49). The representation of the Jailer's Daughter has also been linked to the character of Viola in Fletcher's *The Coxcomb*: she elopes but does not go mad.

3 Peter Holland (1994) has discussed the way in which understandings of the wider implications of Theseus's story impact upon the comic confines of *A Midsummer Night's Dream*.

4 Wickham (1980) goes so far as to suggest that the play operates as an allegory with Emilia representing Princess Elizabeth and Palamon and Arcite the warring qualities of her husband the Elector Palatine and her late brother, Henry, Prince of Wales, respectively. This seems excessive although the connections Wickham draws elsewhere in the article between the topics and contexts of *The Two Noble Kinsmen* and *A Midsummer Night's Dream* are valuable.

5 A full text of Beaumont's masque is provided in Appendix 3 in Potter's (1997) Arden edition of *The Two Noble Kinsmen* (pp. 340–9).

6 Hastings's Leicestershire environs also fostered connections between him and the Robin Hood myths in much of the literature dedicated to him or alluding to his community. See, for example, Jonson's unfinished pastoral tragicomedy *The Sad Shepherd* (1637). For a detailed account of the Hastings family's paternalistic government in Leicestershire, see Cogswell (1998).

7 It may also be significant that Elizabeth Stanley, the 5th Earl of Huntingdon's wife, danced in Jonson's 1609 court masque, *The Masque of Queens*, which included powerful Amazonian representations.

REFERENCES AND FURTHER READING

The edition of *The Two Noble Kinsmen* referred to throughout the essay is that edited by Lois Potter for the Arden 3 series (London: Thomas Nelson, 1997). All references to other Shakespeare plays refer to the Norton edition of the works of Shakespeare (gen. ed. Stephen Greenblatt) (London and New York: Norton, 1997).

Abrams, R. (1985). Gender Confusion and Sexual Politics in *The Two Noble Kinsmen*. In J. B. Redmond (ed.) *Drama, Sex and Politics: Themes in Drama 7*. Cambridge: Cambridge University Press, 69–76.

Anon. (1995) [1618]. *The Coleorton Masque*. In D. Lindley (ed.) *Court Masques*. Oxford: Oxford University Press.

Berggren, P. S. (1984). "For what we lack / We laugh": Incompletion and *The Two Noble Kinsmen*. *Modern Language Studies*, 14, 3–17.

Bertram, P. (1965). *Shakespeare and "The Two Noble Kinsmen"*. New Brunswick, NJ: Rutgers University Press.

Bradbrook, M. (1976). *The Living Monument: Shakespeare and the Theatre of his Time*. Cambridge: Cambridge University Press.

Briggs, J. (1999). Tears at the Wedding: Shakespeare's Last Phase. In J. Richards and J. Knowles (eds.) *Shakespeare's Late Plays: New Readings*. Edinburgh: Edinburgh University Press, 210–27.

Bruster, D. (1995). The Jailer's Daughter and the Politics of Madwomen's Language. *Shakespeare Quarterly*, 46, 277–300.

Campion, T. (1995) [1613]. *The Caversham Entertainment*. In D. Lindley (ed.) *Court Masques*. Oxford: Oxford University Press.

Chaucer, G. (1987). *The Knight's Tale*. In *The Riverside Chaucer*, ed. F. N. Robinson, gen. ed. L. D. Benson. Oxford: Oxford University Press.

Cogswell, T. (1998). *Home Divisions: Aristocracy, the State and Provincial Conflict*. Manchester: Manchester University Press.

De Sousa, G. (1999). *Shakespeare's Cross-Cultural Encounters*. London: Macmillan.

Dutton, R. (1983). *Ben Jonson: To the First Folio*. Cambridge: Cambridge University Press.

Edwards, P. (1964). On the Design of The Two Noble Kinsmen. *A Review of English Literature*, 5, 89–105.

Erler, M. C. (1996). "Chaste Sports, Juste Prayses, and All Soft Delight": Harefield, 1602 and Ashby 1607, Two Female Entertainments. In A. L. Magnusson and C. E. McGee (eds.) *The Elizabethan Theatre 14*. Toronto: Meany, 1–25.

Finkelpearl, P. J. (1990). *Court and Country Politics in the Plays of Beaumont and Fletcher*. Princeton, NJ: Princeton University Press.

——(1996). Two Distincts, Division None: Shakespeare and Fletcher's *The Two Noble Kinsmen*. In R. B. Parker and S. P. Zitner (eds.) *Elizabethan Theater: Essays in Honor of Samuel Schoenbaum*. Newark: University of Delaware Press, 184–99.

Frey, C. H. (ed.) (1989). *Shakespeare, Fletcher and "The Two Noble Kinsmen"*. Columbia: University of Missouri Press.

Gossett, S. (1972). Masque Influence on the Dramaturgy of Beaumont and Fletcher. *Modern Philology*, 69, 199–208.

Green, S. (1989). "A mad woman? We are made, boys!": The Jailer's Daughter in *The Two Noble Kinsmen*. In C. H. Frey (ed.) *Shakespeare, Fletcher and the "The Two Noble Kinsmen"*. Columbia: University of Missouri Press, 121–32.

Guarini, G. B. (1914) [1601/2]. *Compendio della poesia tragicomica e Il Pastor Fido*, ed. G. Brognoligo. Bari: Laterza.

Habicht, W. (1971). Tree Properties and Tree Scenes in Elizabethan Theater. *Renaissance Drama*, 4, 69–92.

Hadorn, P. (1992). *The Two Noble Kinsmen* and the Problem of Chivalry. *Studies in Medievalism*, 4, 45–57.

Hedrick, D. K. (1989). "Be Rough With Me": The Collaborative Arenas of *The Two Noble Kinsmen*. In C. H. Frey (ed.) *Shakespeare, Fletcher and "The Two Noble Kinsmen"*. Columbia University of Missouri Press, 45–77.

Hillman, R. (1991). Shakespeare's Romantic Innocents and the Misappropriation of the Romance Past: The Case of *The Two Noble Kinsmen. Shakespeare Survey*, 43, 69–80.

Holland, P. (1994). Theseus' Shadows in *A Midsummer Night's Dream. Shakespeare Survey*, 47, 139–51.

——(1997). *English Shakespeares*. Cambridge: Cambridge University Press.

Jonson, B. (2000). *Bartholomew Fair*, ed. S. Gossett. Manchester: Manchester University Press.

Knowles, J. (1999). Insubstantial Pageants: *The Tempest* and Masquing Culture. In J. Richards and J. Knowles (eds.) *Shakespeare's Late Plays: New Readings*. Edinburgh: Edinburgh University Press, 108–25.

Loewenstein, J. (1987). Guarini and the Presence of Genre. In N. K. Maguire (ed.) *Renaissance Tragicomedy: Explorations in Genre and Politics*. New York: AMS Press, 33–55.

McMullan, G. (1994). *The Politics of Unease in the Plays of John Fletcher*. Amherst: University of Massachusetts Press.

McMullan, G. and Hope, J. (eds.) (1992). *The Politics of Tragicomedy: Shakespeare and After*. London: Routledge.

Maguire, N. K. (ed.) (1987). *Renaissance Tragicomedy: Explorations in Genre and Politics*. New York: AMS Press.

Masten, J. (1997). *Textual Intercourse: Collaboration, Authorship, and Sexualities in Renaissance Drama*. Cambridge: Cambridge University Press.

Potter, L. (1992). Topicality or Politics? *The Two Noble Kinsmen*, 1613–1634. In G. McMullan and J. Hope (eds.) *The Politics of Tragicomedy: Shakespeare and After*. London: Routledge, 77–91.

——(ed.) (1997). *The Two Noble Kinsmen*. Arden Shakespeare. London: Thomas Nelson.

Sanders, J. (2001). Ecocritical Readings and the Seventeenth-Century Woodland: Milton's *Comus* and the Forest of Dean. *English*, 50, 1–18.

Shannon, L. J. (1997). Emilia's Argument: Friendship and "Human Title" in *The Two Noble Kinsmen*. *English Literary History*, 64, 657–82.

Shawcross, J. T. (1987). Tragicomedy as Genre, Past and Present. In N. K. Maguire (ed.) *Renaissance Tragicomedy: Explorations in Genre and Politics*. New York: AMS Press, 13–32.

Stewart, A. (1999). "Near Akin": The Trials of Friendship in *The Two Noble Kinsmen*. In J. Richards and J. Knowles (eds.) *Shakespeare's Late Plays: New Readings*. Edinburgh: Edinburgh University Press, 57–71.

Strong, R. (1977). *Henry, Prince of Wales and England's Lost Renaissance*. London: Thames and Hudson.

Taylor, G. and Jowett, J. (1993). *Shakespeare Re-Shaped, 1606–1623*. Oxford: Clarendon Press.

Thompson, A. (1978). *Shakespeare's Chaucer: A Study in Literary Origin*. Liverpool: Liverpool University Press.

——(1979). Jailer's Daughters in *The Arcadia* and *The Two Noble Kinsmen*. *Notes and Queries*, 224, 140–1.

Wickham, G. (1980). *The Two Noble Kinsmen* or *A Midsummer Night's Dream*, Part II? In G. R. Hibbard (ed.) *Elizabethan Theatre*, vol. 7. London: Macmillan, 167–96.

Williams, W. P. (1987). *Not* Hornpipes and Funerals: Fletcherian Tragicomedy. In N. K. Maguire (ed.) *Renaissance Tragicomedy: Explorations in Genre and Politics*. New York: AMS Press, 139–54.

Yoch, J. J. (1987). The Renaissance Dramatization of Temperance: The Italian Revival of Tragicomedy and *The Faithful Shepherdess*. In N. K. Maguire (ed.) *Renaissance Tragicomedy: Explorations in Genre and Politics*. New York: AMS Press, 115–38.

Index